INTO THE NIGHT

THE CRISIS OF WESTERN CIVILIZATION

INTO THE NIGHT

THE CRISIS OF WESTERN CIVILIZATION

IVY SCARBOROUGH

Issachar Press
34 Casey Jones Lane
Jackson, Tennessee 38305

INTO THE NIGHT
The Crisis of Western Civilization

Issachar Press
34 Casey Jones Lane
Jackson, Tennessee 38305

ISBN-13: 978-0-578-04661-7
Printed in the United States of America
by Jostens Publishing & Printing in State College, Pennsylvannia

Cover photo (also on pages i and iii) courtesy of NASA
(National Aeronautics and Space Administration);
All instances of same NASA image (including cover, pages i and iii, and pages 1, 19, 25, 33, 43, 59, 81, 89, 113, 153, 173, 185, 195, 213, 227, 247, 259, 295, 307, 355, 401, 405, 441, 467, 487, 501, 517, 525, 537, 549, 579, 583, 595, 611, 623, 633, 649, 673, 691, 711, 743, 765, 801, 827, and 851) have been altered.

In this publication, the following versions of the Bible were used:

KJV–King James Version
NIV–New International Version
ESV–English Standard Version
NKJV–New King James Version
NASB–New American Standard Bible
AMP–Amplified Bible

See Bibliography for more specific information.

Original Cover Design by the Author
Final print files prepared by Jostens Printing and Publishing
Layout by
Martha Nichols/aMuse Productions®
Bellvue, Colorado

To my wife, Ramona,

whose faith, love, wisdom, and encouragement

filled the sails during the voyage.

ACKNOWLEDGMENTS

I owe a great personal and intellectual debt to Drs. Bill and Pat Bouchillon whose generous and caring lessons about human nature have stood me in good stead for more than thirty years. Dr. John Adams and Dr. Herbert Higdon encouraged me in this work at a time when its prospects were daunting. My chief researcher Nick Ellis's research skills, erudition, and selfless efforts were critical to the endeavor; I am confident he will excel in the completion of his doctorate at Oxford. Ruby Schoonover, a special kind of warrior, continually fought the battle of encouragement and the search for wisdom throughout; she is an exceptional friend. Much is due to another exceptional friend, kindred spirit, and inspiring leader, Brigadier General Herb Lloyd, whose four tours of duty in Vietnam, special operations, black ops, and experiences around the world fighting terrorists have been a source of real world insights. Dave Brandt, with implacable loyalty, encouraged and supported the mission. An old and dear friend, Rik Yandell, encouraged and advised. With the realism you would expect from a native of Northern Ireland and former member of the Ulster Defence Regiment, Dr. James Wilson advised and supported. Marine Colonel Chuck Armstrong (ret.) was a much appreciated source of information, counsel and encouragement. One could not ask for a more devoted and conscientious professional than Dan DePriest in marshalling resources and guiding *Into the Night* to publication. His commitment to the cause could not be overstated. Similarly, the phenomenal memory and computer-like attentiveness to detail of Alan Yoshioka in proofing were extraordinary. Author John Perry provided valuable counsel. I thank Jody Russell from the Media Resource Center of NASA's Johnson Space Center for her speed and insight in finding the photograph of Earth we used as part of our cover graphic.

Most of all, I owe my greatest debt to my wife Ramona, who served as editor, sounding board, creative source, advisor and encourager throughout. Her role was central above all others. Finally, I am especially grateful to my late parents, Leon and Edith Scarborough, whose Christian faith and unstinting love allowed me to grow from childhood to manhood untrammeled by any impulse or need to conform. They freed me to think critically, act independently, choose boldly, and defy all convention—subject to no man, subject only to God. I was blessed beyond measure to have been born to them.

Volentem fata ducunt, nolentem trahunt.

The Fates lead the man who is willing,
but drag along the one who is not.

There is the moral of all human tales;
'Tis but the same rehearsal of the past.
First Freedom and then Glory—when that fails,
Wealth, Vice, Corruption [come] at last.
And History, with all her volumes vast,
Hath but one page.

Childe Harold's Pilgrimage;
George Gordon, Lord Byron

TABLE OF CONTENTS

INTRODUCTION

Up to now everyone has been at liberty to hope what he pleased about the future.
Where there are no facts, sentiment rules.
Oswald Spengler[1]

"Dwell on the past and you'll lose an eye," they say.
But the proverb goes on to say: "Forget the past and you'll lose both eyes."
Alexander Solzhenitsyn[2]

He who learns must suffer, and, even in our sleep, pain that cannot forget falls drop by drop upon the heart, and in our own despair, against our will, comes wisdom to us by the awful grace of God.
Aeschylus

The voyage of discovery is not seeking new landscapes but in having new eyes.
Marcel Proust

Western civilization has entered an epic phase of profound crisis. The crisis is not of external enemies, though their role is a factor. Nor is the crisis economic, political, cultural, ecological, demographic, or a product of warfare, though these features of a civilization's existence also have a bearing. Largely unconsciously, we of this age are living through what are likely the final paroxysms of a dying civilization. Western civilization, like others before it, is experiencing the entropy of the everlasting—the final running down of that which most of its members assumed would last forever.

The nature and characteristics of civilizational decline and decay have been critically scrutinized only by a very small group of scholars, most of them writing in the twentieth century. Concerning the fate of our own culture, one of the earliest of these observers, the German philosopher and historian Oswald Spengler, declared, "…[W]e have not chosen this time. We cannot help it if we are born as men of the early winter of full Civilization…. Everything depends on our seeing our own position, our destiny, clearly, on our realizing that though we may lie to ourselves about it we cannot evade it."[3] Later scholars have made similar observations urging realism and honesty, though not all of them share the implacable determinism suggested by "we cannot evade it."

Western man has a choice. He *can* arrest the decline described by these observers. He can alter his fate. But to do so he must honestly see his own position clearly. He cannot continue to lie to himself about it, for to do so is itself a characteristic trait of a civilization in decay. This then is the first intent and purpose of this book: to honestly assess the position, and the trajectory, of Western civilization in our age.

To achieve this, destiny beckons us to scale the highest vantage points of history from where we can gaze, not only upon the near decade, but far across the breadth of the foreboding valley of the coming century. A challenging, daunting pilgrimage, this journey is neither for the faint of heart nor for the eternal optimist who prefers the positive and optimistic to the truth. The objective is to scrutinize the most deeply entrenched and sacrosanct institutions, values, and beliefs of Western civilization, see where they have taken us, and determine what we should and must do henceforth, if we are to save our civilization.

SEEING THE ELEPHANTS

Our journey is in three parts. The first will gather facts, insights, and perspectives from among the great global thinkers of the last century on civilizational decline and decay. The gravity of their observations is admittedly unsettling, as is their breadth and complexity. But the synthesis of their ideas with the major themes of this book will lead us to an understanding not only of our time, but also what is likely to follow just over the horizon of history. We must persist in trudging up the steep heights and be neither discouraged by the effort nor deterred by the desolation that comes into view from these lofty vantage points.

Along the way we will penetrate the obscurantism of our age masquerading in the guises of sophistication, modernity, science and technology, and a materialist worldview. We will see ideas and events from a new and unimagined perspective, the way a soldier who has seen combat comes to understand war in a way a non-combatant never can. Veterans of the American Civil War called it "seeing the elephants." Until you've seen it, you can't imagine it. The gulf between the average citizen and a battle hardened veteran is comparable to the gulf between the understanding and beliefs held close by most citizens of Western civilization today and those few who have come to some recognition of the reality. The soldier has received an education no amount of training or indoctrination could have proffered him. He has learned the difference between long held assumptions, biases, prejudices, and harsh, objective reality. He will glean those lessons and inculcate them, or he will die—and his cause with him.

The soldier recognizes intuitively, if not expressly and analytically, that much he assumed and believed before he "saw the elephants" was not true. Truth, once fully revealed, may violently challenge our most deeply held beliefs about life and reality. The shock of this realization propels the soldier toward embracing the reality he now knows he must come to grips with if he is to survive. *Volentem fata ducunt, nolentem trahunt.* ("The Fates lead the man who is willing, but drag along the one who is not.") From this point on in his life, he will never be able to fully relate to the civilian who has never shared his baptism of fire. Only those who have lived through the experience can fully comprehend what he now understands.

War metaphors will embellish these pages. Entering eight war zones on four continents has contributed immeasurably to my understanding of reality and our age. In 1993, in the battle-scarred port city of Mogadishu, Somalia, just prior to the infamous Blackhawk Down incident that took the lives of eighteen Army Rangers and elite Delta Force troops, I talked with a young soldier who had in his own way "seen the elephants." Blonde, athletic, and looking as if he surely had just fallen off a surfboard near his home in southern California, he was tilted back in a battered chair, an M-16 resting on his lap. His youthful face betrayed a weariness that was not just of the body. "I will never see the world the same again," he declared, as he stared into an unfathomable distance. "Reality is not at all what I thought. No matter how hard I try I cannot get my friends at home to understand."

Reality is not what probably most in the West think. The true condition of Western civilization is something most people have no clue about. We can only learn what we have been exposed to. If our exposure is to a cultural milieu that is limited, propagandistic, self-deluded, and shallow, our understanding will fall equally short.

Self-delusion, tenuous values, and some sense of invulnerability only survive in an insular environment that shields its inhabitants from reality. Probably no culture since the latter days of the Roman Empire has been as insulated from the hard realities of life and history as has ours, despite our vaunted institutions of learning and the traumas of two world wars. This is in part because intellectual cognizance of a historical fact or abstract principle is not the same as insight and understanding. Though the former has value, the latter is the path to true wisdom. The former is cheaply bought with time and money; the latter is expensive, purchased with the currency of sacrifice and suffering.

We must think realistically and courageously about questions, events, and ideas that most people would prefer to avoid, or that, if they ever touch upon them, they transmute into something very different from their reality—something more palatable, less frightening. Man has always been predisposed to self-delusion, but that tendency is a salient trait of our time and civilization.

Related to this tendency is Western man's obsession with the superficial. Perhaps in no other time or place has there been such a pervasive focus on the surface of life. When propagated by the powerful technological forces of modern communication, this shallowness becomes "reality" for millions. The free peoples of democratic, capitalistic Western societies who are convinced of their access to "truth" are thus made slaves of the most persuasive and pervasive fallacies. This is the worst of states: It is a curse to be deceived or kept from the truth and to know this is your lot, but it is the ultimate blindness not to see the truth yet be supremely confident you possess it.

Among our observers, the British historian Arnold Toynbee—whose monumental life work, *A Study of History*, addressed civilizational decline and decay—decried the Western proclivity for focusing on the ultimately meaningless:

> The things that make good headlines attract our attention because they are on the surface of the stream of life, and they distract our attention from the slower, impalpable, imponderable movements that work below the surface and penetrate to the depths. But of course it is really these deeper, slower movements that, in the end, make history, and it is they that stand out huge in retrospect, when the sensational passing events have dwindled, in perspective, to their true proportions.[4]

Everything herein disabuses of self-delusion about our culture; yet it will also simultaneously praise and elevate Western civilization's greatest redeeming virtues. We cannot do one without the other and achieve an honest analysis. As with any living organism, too much of that which might be otherwise necessary or useful can not only be harmful but sometimes fatal, just as the injudicious exposure to forces that are, under appropriate circumstances, benign can also be deleterious. Therefore, with some exceptions, much of what is said critically herein by our observers or this writer does not necessarily reflect a blanket indictment or complete rejection of the value, attitude, institution or behavior being analyzed. More often the critique sheds a light on unwise attitudes, ill-advised behavior, unsound reasoning, and the abuse, or misuse, of that which otherwise might be salutary and sanguine.

RED SKY IN THE MORNING

Implicit throughout this work is a warning of imminent peril. A personal experience will illustrate. In 1997, I wrote a commentary on terrorism and the future of the West for a Nashville, Tennessee newspaper. The commentary was distinctive and unsettling in its prediction that within the foreseeable future there would be a major and potentially catastrophic terrorist attack within the United States; the 1993 bombing of the World Trade Center would, it said, be "a pinprick rehearsal for what will follow."[5]

In a speech before Parliament shortly after the terrorist attacks of September 11, 2001, British Prime Minister Tony Blair observed that anyone predicting such a catastrophe beforehand would have been regarded as an "alarmist." Indeed so. Some viewed my 1996 essay as alarmist. I had made the same observations and predictions in television and radio interviews in the preceding years—and would continue to do so until September 11. Though there were other warning voices, few were admonishing America and the West to take heed. The traumas of history often expose a lack of realism, which was itself an underlying cause of the disaster that befell America and of related disasters of lesser magnitude suffered by other Western nations.

Rejection of the notion that modernity is, by definition, sophisticated and progressive—much less wise—should be central to any thinking person's reasoning. The greatest truths have been with us for millennia, even as man often banished them from the center stage of world history to loiter, unacknowledged, unpraised, backstage. Modern Western man's prideful rejection of them has no valid centrifugal force with which to spin them away from their position at the center of moral gravity of the universe.

THE BAYEUX TAPESTRY OF HISTORY

Compartmentalization of this highly complex subject into many chapters is for the sake of clarity, order, and understanding. But this practice should not be viewed as in any way indicating that these topics are independent of one another or freestanding. To the contrary, one of Western man's most often replicated mistakes was deprecated by one of our observers, Immanuel Wallerstein,

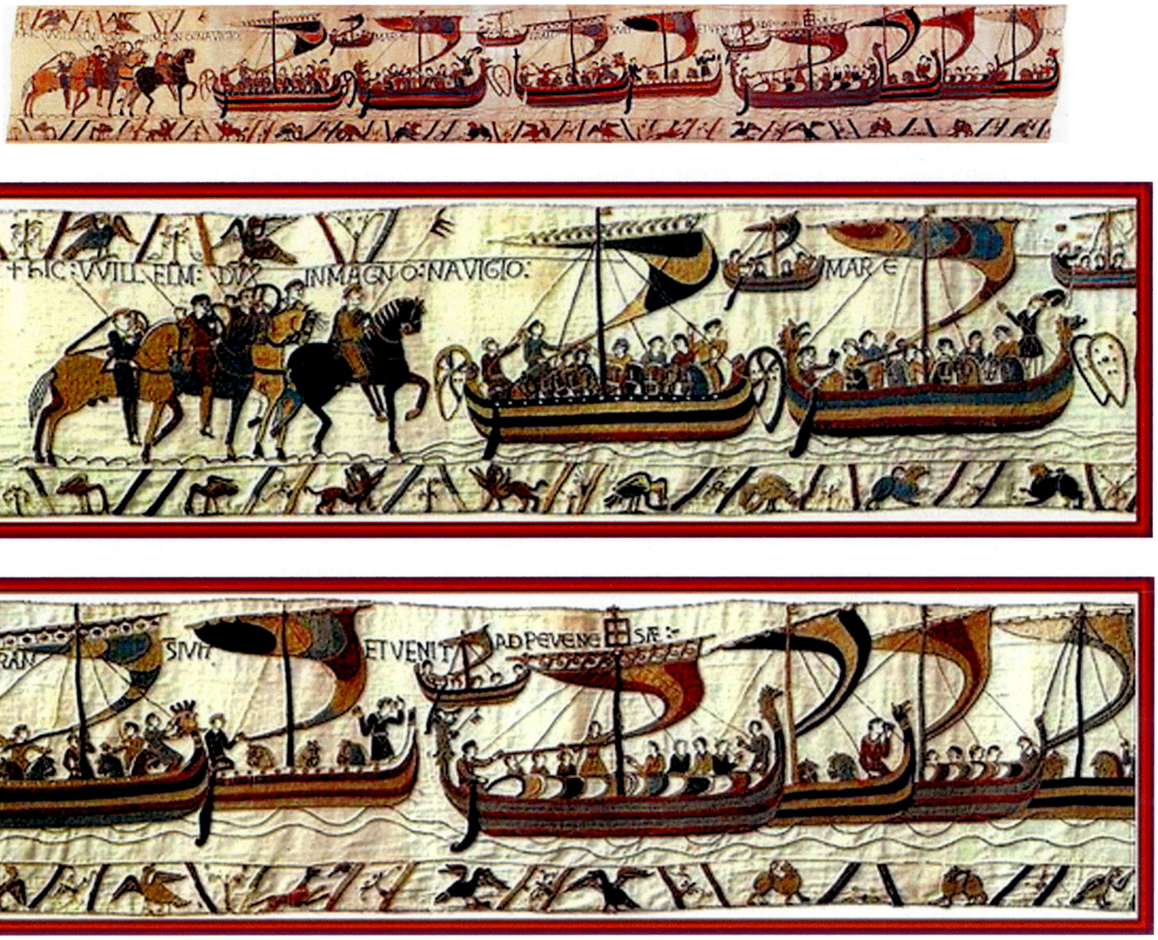

PD-old

Bayeux Tapestry. 1476. *Invasion fleet of Duke William of Normandy.*

with the phrase the "partitioning of reality"[6] the compartmentalization of the examination of life and our world. I go further in my condemnation of this foolish propensity: Western man's passion for compartmentalization and specialization—often to an absurdly particularist degree—is part of the *modus operandi* that prevents him from seeing the greater truths.

Western man compartmentalizes every facet of his life: religion and morality here, politics, government and law there, education and learning in yet another compartment, economics and business in another, and so on *ad infinitum.* But these are false polychotomies. They compound our mistakes and failures by blinkering our view of the connections and relationships among the many threads of our lives as individuals and a culture. Life and history are a great cosmic Bayeux Tapestry. Everything bears upon everything else. Nothing is severable. This foundational truth is central to this book's approach. Remove one thread—or simply pull it out of place—and everything is affected.

Western man, given as he is to this specialization and compartmentalization of his thinking and his life, often fails to see the connections. The discerning reader will begin to perceive the nexuses that knit seemingly disparate topics, ideas, and behaviors into the great tapestry we call history.

TAKING THE FISH OUT OF THE OCEAN

The materialism and competitiveness of Western culture nurtures an environment in which perceiving with any objectivity and insight is frustrated, if not completely impeded. There is a frenzy to "succeed." Such an environment inevitably leads to the dominant pattern we see today in every realm of politics, media and entertainment, business and marketing, sports, education, and even religion, leading to a proclivity for telling people what they want to hear rather than what they need to hear. The truth—and, with it, grave realities—is lost in the cacophony of voices clamoring for our attention and drawing us to this or that ideological position, political, religious, or social cause, or product.

Compounding the danger, the skill and artistry with which each of these competitive voices presents itself can make the appeal compelling and, in some instances, extraordinarily plausible. People come to not only believe what is false, but vigorously defend it as sacrosanct—ultimately to their own detriment. They become, metaphorically speaking, buyers of great bridges that are not for sale.

A fish, it has been said, would never contemplate water unless someone took it out of the ocean. In like manner, Western provincialism is not apparent to its practitioners who swim about in it constantly from birth. Neither I nor our observers can pull you, the reader, completely free of the depths of our Western cultural ocean, but their often meticulous, detached examinations of Western history, thought, and life do the next best thing: they help us see ourselves with a clarity we cannot achieve merely by looking through a purely Western lens or by staring into our own mirrors. And since self-examination is, for the individual as well as a society, the necessary prerequisite to self-improvement, these observers—especially the most relentlessly honest and forthright—do us, intentionally or not, benevolently or not, a service.

The rest of the world is acutely aware that the West sees and touts itself as not only the most advanced and "successful" civilization of history, but also the most virtuous. But the adjective "virtuous" carries a possible duality of meaning not lost on anyone who has spent any significant time surveying our native civilization from the perspective of foreign shores. Historically, we have presumed, we do presume, and we may continue to presume to a moral virtue that the rest of our fellowman on the planet do not always perceive, especially in the benighted shadows of twenty-first century trends.

Though Western history is surfeited with the religious impulse, it is increasingly—and very conspicuously to some, if not to Western man—debased by materialism and the depravity of unbridled, self-centered individualism. Man, for Western man, is his own god. Throughout this book we will return, with the certain rhythms of planetary orbits, to this theme. It is central to understanding the dangers and nemeses of our time.

The stark and often pathetic juxtapositions of the Western civilization that was with the Western civilization that *is* will not be lost on us—as they are not lost on many of our observers. Just as gigantic trees were commonly available to make the immense beams used to build the eighteenth century American edifices of government, education, and faith, such trees can no longer be found in American forests; just so, the immense and stalwart character of the people who built those edifices is elusive in our self-indulgent and shallow culture.

Though "pathetic" is not an adjective most proud Westerners would ever think of applying to their civilization's life, it is the inescapable impression left by some of the stopovers on our journey through the West's history. A few of our latter-day de Tocquevilles look at our art and architecture, our government and law, our business and economics, and our entertainment and see more of the West's soul than many social observers can manage when dissecting that soul in the far more common—but often superficial—surgeries of the social sciences.

Clearly, when taken to mind and heart, many of the declarations herein are painful, but they are never malicious. Typically, they are pointed insights—slender, smooth, and stainless thrusts skewering beliefs and views Westerners hold sacrosanct. This is intellectual acupuncture: not intended to wound but to deflate.

LOCKING EYES WITH REALITY'S UNNERVING STARE

The reader should not presume that the quoting of a given civilizational observer, or even repeated quoting, is necessarily an imprimatur for their viewpoint. My views are unique and will not be in full concert with anyone referenced herein. This would seem self-evident, but many years as a trial lawyer taught me that that which may seem self-evident to one may be wholly obscure to another. Furthermore, there necessarily must be selectivity in the use of quotes. In this respect, I naturally focused on those expressed views that most closely comport with the overriding themes of this work.

Some might interpret apparent inconsistencies or differences in the viewpoints and theories of these historians, sociologists, and anthropologists as proof that there is no model or definitive indicator of civilizational decline, and, therefore, what they have to say does not foretell our civilization's collapse. But that is a speciously optimistic view that ignores the detritus of dead civilizations scattered about the planet. A viewpoint more consistent with the blindness and wishful, even hubristic, thinking of our time, it is itself evidence of civilizational decay. Ideas in conflict with reality are a phenomenon not unknown to the human species in any time and place, but they are particularly prevalent in individuals and cultures plodding the trail of self-delusion to their doom. The wiser and infinitely safer course is to study the civilizational collapses of the past, paying particular attention to the signposts along the way indicating the imminence of their destruction, with the recognition that there certainly will be patterns, indicators, commonalities, etc.

Reality has an unnerving, stern, relentless stare, and we quail at locking eyes with it. But the wise soul, the courageous man and woman—and, especially, the noble, unselfish leader—always does so.

REARRANGING OUR THINKING, NOT OUR PREJUDICES

Communicating this complex and multifaceted message is a challenging task. Serving in a variety of communication roles—trial lawyer, college professor, radio program host, TV, radio, and print commentator, and writer—gives me fair warning that the ways human beings may misunderstand one another are legion. Sometimes this is due to failures in the transmission (e.g., a lack of clarity and thoroughness in the expression of ideas and thoughts) or from failures in the reception (e.g., a lack of attentiveness to what is being said or simply a level of ignorance that impedes understanding). Unfortunately, it is also frequently the result of prejudice and bias: an unwillingness to truly open one's mind and heart to what is being said. William James observed, "A great many people think they are thinking when they are merely rearranging their prejudices."[7] If you read this book in that way—from the perspective of preconceived ideas, and perhaps with the intent of preparing your own internal rebuttal—nothing useful will come of it for you. If you are honestly and courageously looking for answers and understanding, you and I will seek them together.

There will be scant resort herein to statistics, numbers, surveys, charts, or mathematical formulas, sociological, psychological, legal, or otherwise. To describe the present state of Western civilization in this manner would be like a dispassionate observer standing in the midst of a vast ongoing battle and blandly citing casualty figures. Furthermore, it should be superfluous: a reader who does not already recognize the trauma and acknowledge the decay is unlikely to be the venturesome pilgrim who would travel this road in the first place. We begin not with a question about *whether* Western civilization is in decay and decline—which would present a vain opportunity to waste time and indulge in the self-delusion that is a hallmark of our age—but from the conspicuous premise that it is. To the inveterate, blind optimist or the skeptic demanding a "scientific" diagnosis, we will only challenge: Look about you. What do you see?

Into the Night is a collection of facts, interpretations, and observations, not a debate. Years of experience have proven to me that debate in any form is one of the most overrated methods for getting at the truth. Debate is more often an exercise in vanity and egotism focused on that most Western of goals: winning. My objective is not simply to be right. I was right in 1996 in predicting a catastrophic attack by Islamic radicals. But my greater purpose then was to add to the scant few voices daring to give the same warning in the hope of being heeded. I hereby add my voice now to a very small coterie of those who, on the grand scale of a civilization, are proclaiming dire warnings. Though we speak from different perspectives, the fundamental alarm is the same—but far more grave than the warnings antecedent to September 11, 2001.

THREE DESTINIES

Western history will culminate in one of three possible termini. The first, which we will call the moral and intellectual "default" outcome, will feature an accelerating decay and decline with all the attendant miseries and confusion this implies. Such a decline will be retarded at intervals by seemingly rational acts aimed at ameliorating or blocking some of the consequences of man's increasingly selfish and reckless choices. But the magnitude of the problem, coupled with what history teaches us about human nature, suggests impending disaster—though we cannot predict its precise timing. The second possible outcome could be described as "apocalyptic" either in the sense of war and revolution or in the religious sense—a cataclysmic, abrupt end to Western civilization. Of course termini one and two could ultimately prove to be the penultimate and final chapters in the same drama. The third possible outcome would be "redemptive"—a humble coming to grips with the evils of the heart and the defects of thought that afflict Western culture and thence turning in a completely new direction.

Our questions will include, What have the leading thinkers on the subject of civilizational decline and decay had to say about modern Western civilization? What characteristics and indicia of decline and decay recur in their writings and observations? What are the central features—the axes of human thought and action—which are the most determinative of a civilization's health and longevity?

Since the true strength of any nation or civilization is in its soul, what the people believe and hold true determines their destiny. As character is destiny for an individual, so it is for nations and civilizations.

Therefore, a critical question for any civilization or nation is, Are their values of any value? Do their beliefs stand the tests of reality and eternity? Emerson made one of life's most important observations when he noted that "beneath each depth a greater depth lies." We probe the greater depths of these great questions.

Later, we will focus on the key institutions and beliefs that form the superstructure of Western civilization. We will discern what they are and come to grips with their parallel decline and decay. We will see that the West's destiny will be shaped neither by fate, science and technology, nor Western man's intellectual aptitudes, but will lie solely in the province of the human will and character.

We will elevate Western man's character and spiritual state to what should be its proper status: the zenith of man's hopes for change for the better and, by extension, hope for his civilization and his world. We will see what Western man can and must do if he has any prospect of avoiding the abyss history reserves for decaying civilizations.

THE GREAT WHEEL OF HISTORY BEARING DOWN ON US

The traditional metaphor for history is the most apt, of a great wheel rolling inexorably forward through time but with a significant difference: Though the themes and the behavior of its actors relentlessly recur—just as the same point on a rolling wheel contacts the ground over and over with a languorous monotony—these do not reflect cycles of purposeless redundancy. They are manifestations of a sweeping purpose—a forward movement through the mountains, plains, and swamps of millennia of growth, learning, adversity, and suffering to a divine revelation.

Whether ours will soon be just one of many civilizations crushed under this mighty wheel of history will be determined by choices made by Western man. In the fullness of time, the words contained herein will prove either to be a prophetic obituary or the heralding of a great awakening and renewal for Western civilization.

OUR "PILLARS OF WISDOM"

Robert Frost observed, "Half the world is composed of people who have something to say and can't and the other half who have nothing to say and keep on saying it."[8] Central to this book is the winnowing of those who have something to say—something of depth, gravity, substance and lasting meaning—from those who receive a great deal of attention in our Western culture but whose every utterance is an expression of the banal, the conventional, the conforming, the shallow, the superficial, and the narrow. There are a multitude of the latter—may their tribe dwindle—and a small coterie of the former. I have sought out this often unheard group and, even among them, winnowed still further.

None of these has been selected or quoted as a "prophet," but as one of the men and women who expatiated in a realm avoided by most of their peers. Though much has been written by historians, anthropologists, and sociologists about civilizations in the broadest sense, remarkably few have written on the subject of the decline and decay of this, the highest and most complex form of human associations. Fewer still have focused on the decline and decay of Western civilization specifically. Of those, the scholars who have clearly been highly attentive to the topic, as evidenced by their research and writings, are an elite group, a mere handful.

The broader group includes Philip Bagby, Adda Bozeman, Fernand Braudel, Rushton Coulborn, Christopher Dawson, Emile Durkheim, S. N. Eisenstadt, Felipe Fernandez-Armesto, A. L. Kroeber, William H. McNeill, Carroll Quigley, Oswald Spengler, Pitirim Sorokin, Arnold Toynbee, Immanuel Wallerstein, Alfred Weber, and Max Weber. Some of these wrote only in a desultory manner about our subject; thus, though we will cite them, their role in this effort will be supplemental and corroborative.

Scant reference herein will be made to Edward Gibbon, whose best known work, *The Decline and Fall of the Roman Empire*, addressed that solitary topic. Though parallels have often been drawn between the decaying Roman Empire and contemporary Western civilization, our focus will be exclusively on Western civilization.

All of our observers are Europeans or Americans who have studied and written within the twentieth and twenty-first centuries. In all other respects they represent different backgrounds, disciplines, and beliefs. They are historians, sociologists, and anthropologists. They are Catholics, Protestants and agnostics. But they stand out, not in their differences, but in their similarities, especially—and this is very important to our purposes—the common denominators in their views about the condition and destiny of Western civilization.

All, with greater or lesser degrees of gravity, view Western civilization as having entered some form or stage of crisis or decline. Indeed, their analyses conflict profoundly with the professed optimism of our time. I use the term "professed optimism" in part to suggest that much of this is founded on self-delusion. Many in Western civilization are frenziedly attempting to distract themselves from an undercurrent of foreboding.

Startlingly, some of the earlier writers (i.e., early and mid-twentieth century) not only predicted the decline and probable eventual collapse of our civilization but described the course of that decline. When read in light of late twentieth and early twenty-first century events and social trends, their insights are truly prescient. They trace the origins of this incipient catastrophe not in generations but in centuries past, an approach worthy of our endeavors as well.

Christopher Dawson, Oswald Spengler, Pitirim Sorokin, and Arnold Toynbee form the core of thought that receives special attention. Not only did these scholars write broadly on the decline and decay of civilizations, particularly of Western civilization, but they displayed a congruence of key themes and conclusions, a remarkable breadth of command of the social sciences and humanities, and a depth of insight that are exceptional. They descry a future that, as we will see, was prescient to a degree that, had they been heeded in their lifetimes, the world of the West would have been a far better place than the confused, anxious, and uncertain civilization that we of the twenty-first century have inherited. Their many common themes—by virtue of their repetition by such august intellects—should tend to accentuate their significance, if not authenticate their validity. The honesty, candor, and frankness of some will be appealing to anyone who values these qualities and regards convention and such notions as political correctness with contempt. Finally, their views and conclusions are largely consistent with my own instincts and conclusions. They are, therefore, quoted herein more than any other scholars or writers. To their number we add Francis Schaeffer, who wrote from a primarily religious perspective about Western civilization, and Samuel P. Huntington, who has also addressed the decline of Western civilization.

Interestingly, Toynbee, Sorokin and Dawson were all born in 1889. In other respects, their lives were colorfully disparate. Dawson and Sorokin remained, in terms of their recognition, largely inhabitants of the province of academia though widely respected by groups of devoted followers.

Arnold Toynbee (1889–1975) gained a significant degree of fame beyond this relatively cloistered world. Born in London, Toynbee wrote his epic *A Study of History*, which may be the most famous historical work of all time if we exclude Gibbon's *Decline and Fall. A Study of History* reviews world history through the rise and fall of 26 societies, 21 of which Toynbee denotes as "civilizations." Toynbee defined the remainder as "arrested civilizations." The classification of civilizations according to cultural criteria, particularly religion, rather than national or political criteria was central to his work. He argued, "An intelligible field of historical study is not to be found within a national framework"[9]—a line of thought consistent with a major theme of this work. The ten volumes of *A Study of History* were later abridged by D. C. Somervell. When Toynbee died in 1975 he was universally recognized for wide ranging erudition encompassing history, religion, philosophy, and politics. His insights and views are compelling and so concordant with my own views in many respects that he is quoted more than any other observer throughout this work. Much of what he had to say, specifically about the condition of Western civilization, came late in his long life in the book *Civilization On Trial.* Oswald Spengler, who wrote before any of our other observers, noted that reviewing "the whole fact of Man from an extreme distance is to imitate Copernicus in the field of history…."[10] This phrasing would be well suited to Toynbee's achievements. He attempted what might be called a stellar perspective, as of a man who removes himself to a remote star from which he gazes back at the earth through time and space seeking an objectivity and breadth of comprehension not heretofore achieved. To be sure, others have studied and written broadly on world history, but Toynbee displayed an insight that transcends mere facts or a recounting of historical events.

Photograph by James Hansen, 1961 PD-LOC

Arnold Toynbee.

Pitirim Sorokin (1889–1968) lived by far the most dramatic and colorful life of all of the scholars cited herein. Like his fellow Russian, Alexander Solzhenitsyn, who is also quoted, it is clear that Sorokin would have throttled anyone or anything that smacked of political correctness. His contempt for the conventional, the disingenuous, the dissembling, and the dishonest was vesuvian. The antithesis of a sycophant or conformist by any measure, when he confronted opposition to his most deeply held views his adversaries surely must have heard the strains of "El Deguello" as he went on the offensive. His blunt pugnacity could be better understood in the context of his birth into one of the most violent and unstable eras in Russian history. Perhaps of greatest significance in weighing his vociferous critics' charges is the reality that he lived through a greater range of experience than the overwhelming number of Western intellectuals who opposed him.

Harvard University Archives

Pitirim Sorokin.

If experience is the best teacher then Sorokin was among the most highly educated of men. He knew desperate poverty, the regal autocracy of a czarist government, the disorienting whirlwind of violent revolution, the rigid, oppressive utopianism of communism, arrests, threats of execution, banishment, beginning of a new life in an alien land, capitalism, democracy, two world wars, and a cold war—all the while struggling to make his life one of meaning and purpose. Sorokin worked as a factory hand, journalist, personal secretary to Alexander Kerensky, and cabinet minister in the ill-fated government associated with Kerensky's name. Despite his peasant family's poverty, the early death of his mother, and abuse from an alcoholic father, Sorokin's tenacity and brilliance would carry him a long way. His incarceration in Czarist as well as Soviet prisons—he was marked for death by both regimes—says everything about his iconoclasm and uncompromising boldness. These are not credentials that armchair academics can challenge, much less match. For these reasons alone, what he has to say should carry weight. He had something to say that stands above the social science of our time.

Within seven years of immigrating to America in the 1920s he became the founding chairman of the first sociology department at Harvard and soon a preeminent voice in American social science. He was removed, however, in a political battle over his theories and techniques. Indeed, throughout his career Sorokin was often vilified in the most disparaging terms on the one hand and applauded for his penetrating brilliance on the other.

Sorokin was deeply influenced by the Russian Orthodox Church, though the precise extent and dimensions of Sorokin's faith are unclear. There is, however, clarity in his absolute certainty of belief in the Christian God and an immutable moral law—which he viewed as mankind's only hope. Sorokin's words often carry a tone of exasperated bluntness similar to that of Alexander Solzhenitsyn a generation later. Both displayed frustration with what they viewed as the moral and intellectual blindness of the West and a painful awareness of its consequences to humanity.

Christopher Dawson (1889–1970), a Welshman, was educated at Trinity College, Oxford, and later taught at several universities including Harvard (1958–62). He wrote twenty three books on culture, history, and religion. His faith as a devout Roman Catholic was the central feature of his long and diverse life and led to preeminent world status as a Catholic thinker. Like Toynbee, Dawson commanded a prodigious breadth of knowledge. A master not only of his central area of study, history, but also philosophy and theology, he was equally learned in sociology, anthropology,

Christopher Dawson Collection, University of St. Thomas

Christopher Dawson.

politics, and economics. This breadth afforded two particularly salutary benefits: he could readily challenge experts in these fields, and he was able to integrate these areas of study into a masterful whole rather than seeing the world in the typical, and highly flawed, method of study in the West through compartmentalization and specialization. In this respect he had much in common with Sorokin and Toynbee. This broad erudition and gift for synthesis make him especially useful to this book; range of comprehension and synthesis of themes and ideas are central to our effort.

Dawson was contemptuous of secular humanism, which he regarded as a severely malformed mutation of Christian humanism. When Dawson spoke of culture this was not a reference to the products of effete practitioners of the usual connotation of the term. Rather, culture, in his lexicon, broadly encompassed all of the arts and institutions of a civilization with primary emphasis on religion, which he viewed as the central nervous system of this, the greatest of all, social organisms.

As we will see, he not only decried secular humanism and what he regarded as its deleterious impact on Western civilization, he rejected the artificial division of the pursuit of knowledge that was the legacy of first the Renaissance and then the Enlightenment. In this view, once again we will see congruence with Toynbee and Sorokin. For Dawson, religion and science were neither polar opposites nor incompatible; they were complementary methods of seeking truth, most efficacious when pursued together. Dawson viewed religion—or, put more precisely, the need for God and an expectancy of something beyond mere physical existence—as reflective of the most fundamental needs of humanity in every culture throughout history. He was not particularly sympathetic to Protestantism, but he was especially critical of what he viewed as liberal Protestantism's spiritual malfeasance. Also in concert with Toynbee and Sorokin, he viewed Marxism as a misbegotten effort to deploy eviscerated components of Christian thought and teaching to meet those fundamental needs of mankind. Western civilization offered far better and was well worth saving—if, for Dawson, it remained true to its founding essentials.

Oswald Spengler (1880–1936) was born in Germany, where he earned a doctorate while studying first in Munich then Berlin. His writings, including his most famous work, *The Decline of the West*, which brought him international fame, were suppressed by the Nazis and received only reluctantly in the West in the wake of World War II. Spengler held that all cultures experienced life cycles from youth to old age to death. Western civilization, he believed, was in its period of decline, from which there was no escape. Though Spengler supported notions of obedience to the state and German hegemony in Europe, he refused to support Nazi theories of racial superiority. This led to ostracism when Hitler became chancellor in 1933.

German Federal Archive. CC

Oswald Spengler.

The sociologist **Immanuel Wallerstein** was born in New York in 1930. He received a B.A., M.A., and Ph.D. (1959) from Columbia University, eventually becoming a professor of sociology at first McGill University then Binghamton. Wallerstein, a visiting professor at several universities, was widely honored for his work. He served for a period as Directeur d'études associé at the École des Hautes Études en Sciences Sociales in Paris. Early in his career he focused on post-colonial Africa but later broadened to a distinguished career as a historian of capitalism. Perhaps his most famous works are the three-volume *The Modern World-System*, published between 1974 and 1989, and *The End of the World As We Know It*, published in 1999, the year of his retirement.

Alexei Kouprianov. CC

Immanuel Wallerstein.

Max Weber was born in 1864 in Erfurt, Germany. He studied law and legal history at the University of Heidelberg, as well as economics and medieval history, later studying at the University of Berlin. He read widely in theology. Weber served intermittently with the German army. Consistent with Toynbee, Sorokin, Dawson, and the majority of the scholars referenced herein, he rejected the Marxian view that economics was the primary determining factor in social and political action. He held that there were many interdependent causes but particularly emphasized the role of religion. In *Protestant Ethic and the Spirit of Capitalism* (1920, tr. 1930) he described a view of Western history that closely linked Calvinism and the rise of capitalism. He eventually advocated an American form of democratic government for Germany. In 1894 he became a professor of economics, first at Freiburg University and then at Heidelberg in 1897. After assisting in the drafting of the Weimar Constitution, he died in 1920 not witnessing the Republic's collapse and the onset of the Nazi era. His major works include *Roman Agrarian History* (1891); "Roscher and Knies and the Logical Problem of Historical Economics" (1903–5), Schmoller's Jahrbuch; "The Objectivity of the Sociological and Social-Political Knowledge" (1904); *The Protestant Ethic and the Spirit of Capitalism* (1905); *Economy and Society* (1914); "Politics as a Vocation" (1918); *General Economic History* (1923); and *The Methodology of the Social Sciences* (1949).

CC

Max Weber.

Samuel P. Huntington (1927–2008) graduated with honors from Yale at the age of 18. After serving in the army, he earned his doctorate from Harvard where he began teaching at the age of 23, becoming a noted expert on international affairs. His work focused on politics, economics, culture, national security and military strategy. Particularly interested in the relationship between the military and civilian government, he served in security planning in the Carter White House. He co-founded and co-edited the journal *Foreign Policy*. His belief that civilizations rather than nation-states will be the primary actors of the twenty-first century has been a major theme of his work. He authored *The Soldier and the State: The Theory and Politics of Civil–Military Relations* (1957); *The Common Defense: Strategic Programs in National Politics* (1961); *Political Order in Changing Societies* (1968); *American Politics: The Promise of Disharmony* (1981); *The Third Wave: Democratization in the Late Twentieth Century* (1991); *The Clash of Civilizations and Remaking of World Order* (1996); and *Who Are We? The*

Photograph by Peter Lauth. CC

Samuel P. Huntington.

Challenges to America's National Identity (2004). *The Clash of Civilizations and the Remaking of World Order* especially lends itself to an understanding of the dynamics of decline and decay of Western civilization today.

Following, in alphabetical order, are other scholars referenced herein:

- **Philip Bagby**, an American anthropologist of the mid-twentieth century was heavily influenced by A. L. Kroeber. He wrote *Culture and History: Prolegomena to the Comparative Study of Civilizations.*
- **Fernand Braudel**, a Frenchman born in 1902, studied history at the Sorbonne. A prisoner of the Germans during World War II, he survived to become one of the most prominent French historians of the twentieth century. He died in Paris in 1985. He wrote *The Mediterranean and the Mediterranean World in the Age of Philip II, A History of Civilizations, Civilizations and Capitalism*, and *On History.*
- **Adda Bozeman** was born in Latvia in 1908 and studied at the Universities of Berlin and Heidelberg and graduated from the Interpreter's College in Mannheim, Germany. In 1934, she earned a diplomary from Section Diplomatique, Ecole Libre des Sciences Politiques in Paris, Europe's elite school for diplomats. She attended the Academy of International Law at The Hague and was inducted into the Middle Temple Inn of Court in London. Bozeman immigrated to the United States in 1936 and graduated from Southern Methodist University Law School in Dallas with a Doctorate of Law. From 1947 to 1977 she served as a professor of international relations at Sarah Lawrence College. Bozeman published *The Future of Law in a Multicultural World, Strategic Intelligence and Statecraft*, and *Politics and Culture in International History.* She died in 1994.
- **Robert Conquest** was born in England in 1917, with a heritage the reverse of Churchill's: a British mother and American father. Educated in politics, philosophy, economics, and history at Winchester, Oxford, and the University of Grenoble, he served in the British infantry during World War II. Conquest held positions at the London School of Economics, Columbia University, the Woodrow Wilson Center, and Stanford. His books include *Demons Don't, The Great Terror, The Harvest of Sorrow*, and *Reflections On a Ravaged Century.*

Robert Conquest.

- British historian **Felipe Fernandez-Armesto** was born in 1950. A devout Catholic, Fernandez-Armesto authored several popular works of history: *Millennium: A History of Our Last Thousand Years* (1995); *Civilizations* (2000); *Food: A History* (published as *Near a Thousand Tables* in North America) (2001); *The Americas* (2003); and *Ideas That Changed the World* (2003). He is Professor of Global Environmental History at Oxford University.
- **A. L. Kroeber**, one of the most prominent American anthropologists, wrote and taught in mid-twentieth-century America. His book *Roster of Civilizations and Culture*, as its title suggests, serves as a list of civilizations as Kroeber defined them.
- **Carroll Quigley**, a Boston-born Irishman, taught at the Georgetown School of Foreign Service, Princeton, and Harvard in the mid-twentieth century. He is best known perhaps for his theory of disintegration of cultures through the deterioration of social "instruments" into "institutions." He wrote *Tragedy and Hope: A History of the World in Our Time* and *Evolution of Civilizations.*
- **Francis Schaeffer**, an American who wrote and taught in the mid- and late twentieth century, was best known for *How Should We Then Live? The Rise and Decline of Western Thought and Culture.* Establishing a home and school in Switzerland, Schaeffer drew upon a wide ranging knowledge of

art, theology, philosophy, history, and sociology to advance his ideas that were all grounded in a deep Christian faith.

Courtesy of the Schaeffer Foundation

Francis Schaeffer.

- **Alexander Solzhenitsyn**, the Russian dissident writer whose most famous works include *August 1914* and *The Gulag Archipelago*, was imprisoned during the Stalinist years for criticisms of the regime. He gained worldwide fame through simultaneously execrating communism ever more vociferously while writing some of the most serious and best known works of the twentieth century. Perhaps one of the great prophets of our time—not infallible, but insightful in a profound way—like all prophets, he was always at risk of being stoned. Stalin stoned him mercilessly in the gulag. In light of that experience and his powerful and angry rebuke of communism, he was lionized by Western intellectuals for a time—as we are wont to do in the West —a fashionable icon who seemed to affirm the West's viewpoint of life. His powers for skewering communism and the socialistic tendencies of some of the West's elite made him attractive to the capitalistic and democratic-oriented forces.

  Thus, for a brief period, no stones came his way. But that soon changed, particularly after his famous address at Harvard in 1978 where he took the West to task for its excesses and spiritual decay. Once again he became a target, this time of his erstwhile allies in the West. Appropriately, an old Russian proverb admonishes, "If you intend to tell the truth, be sure one foot is in the stirrup." Solzhenitsyn repeatedly and often told the truth with both feet firmly planted on the ground—even the turf of his enemies.

Here I enter a *caveat* and qualification regarding our observers: Each has been criticized, some mercilessly, by other scholars and various social observers. Indeed, consistent with the temperament of the West, each has either been in or out of fashion at various times in the years following his work. Though their writing and theories do not receive a blanket imprimatur as final and irrefragable authority in this book, they should be recognized and commended—especially Spengler, Sorokin, Toynbee, and Dawson—for their courageous and prodigious efforts. Each made monumental efforts to understand, and did so without the cultural sycophancy so common to many "intellectuals" of our time. Carrying a message the culture did not wish to hear, they made themselves and their works targets of abuse, just as quoting them here and offering my own nonconforming views will effectively, in the minds of some, paint a figmental bullseye on the front cover of this volume.

This listing is not exhaustive. Other scholars and writers are quoted throughout. In the chapter "Wars and Rumors of Wars," a completely new set of authors will be referenced in addition to those here. Beginning with Chapter 19, I will again introduce a new cadre of additional observers.

END NOTES
INTRODUCTION

1 Oswald Spengler, *The Decline of the West* (New York: A. A. Knopf, 1932), 30.
2 Alexander Solzhenitsyn, *The Gulag Archipelago 1918–1956* (New York: Harper and Row, 1973), ix.
3 Spengler, *Decline of the West*, 34.
4 Arnold Toynbee, *Civilization on Trial* (New York: Oxford University Press, 1948), 213.
5 Ivy Scarborough, "With Nukes Loose, Pessimism's the Best Policy," *The Nashville Banner* (January 14, 1997).
6 Immanuel Wallerstein, *The End of the World As We Know It: Social Science for the Twenty-First Century* (Minneapolis: University of Minnesota Press, 1999), 123.
7 William James and Robert Andrews, *The Routledge Dictionary of Quotations* (London: Routledge, 1987), 208.
8 Robert Frost, cited in William James and Robert Andrews, *The Routledge Dictionary of Quotations* (London: Routledge, 1987), 156.
9 Toynbee, *Civilization on Trial*, v.
10 Spengler, *The Decline of the West,* 70.

PART I

THE DECLINE AND DECAY OF WESTERN CIVILIZATION

CHAPTERS 1–18

These chapters lay the foundation for all that will follow. They describe the historical processes of decline and decay and analyze their applicability to modern Western civilization. Chapters one through four describe the problems of perception that impede Western man from seeing his situation clearly and objectively. The chapters that follow "disassemble"—and test the strength of—the philosophical and intellectual scaffolding upon which Western citizens rest the entire weight of their perceptions of themselves, their sense of security, and their prospects for the future. This scaffolding includes Western man's belief system, perspective on life and history, personal relationships, education, leadership, ideology, politics, government, science and technology, and military power. Part I further demonstrates how Western man came to his perilous state; describes the unprecedented speed with which history is moving and the decline and decay accelerating; and, finally, offers the likely scenarios for the final act of the drama that is Western civilization.

CHAPTER 1
From the Surface to the Depths, the Particular to the Universal

Western man focuses on the grand and sensational events, economic upheavals, political machinations, shifts of power, ideological ascendancies and declines, wars and conflicts, but these are on the surface of history. The trends and direction of history are determined by often hidden, closely held core beliefs and values of the individual. Compounding his problem of perception, Western man attempts to compartmentalize history and reality into narrow areas of study and discipline—a profound mistake that limits his ability to see the great, intricate tapestry of history.

CHAPTER 2
The West and a Western-centric View of History

Western man sees his civilization as the center of contemporary history and the ultimate expression of human culture and advancement in history. This viewpoint is typical of powerful civilizations but never borne out by the broader retrospectives of history. Serving as a catalyst for ill conceived patterns of thought and behavior, it pushes a civilization ever closer to the abyss of collapse.

CHAPTER 3
The Mirage of Immortality—Entropy of the Everlasting

Western civilization's crisis of decline and decay is exacerbated by an unwillingness of its members to recognize the historical patterns and the inevitable consequences should this be permitted to continue. Perspectives of the historians, anthropologists and sociologists who have studied decline and decay provide preliminary insights into this process of gradual collapse.

CHAPTER 4
Perceptions of Reality and Choices of Values

The capacity of a civilization to grow and creatively respond to the challenges of its time is largely determined by the willingness and ability of its members to accurately perceive, and honestly confront, reality and to choose their core beliefs and values wisely.

CHAPTER 5
Relational Breakdown, Mental Illness, Loneliness—Western Man's Forlorn Quest for Intimacy and Meaning

The health of relationships (e.g., man with God; man with man) is central to the health of a civilization. The marked decay and dysfunction in these relationships among members of Western civilization are both causal and symptomatic of the civilization's decline.

CHAPTER 6
The Triptych on the Altar of Western Culture: Materialism, Capitalism, and Competition

The dominant value of Western civilization is materialism, which is manifested through the institution of capitalism and expressed through competition. Though central to Western civilization's material success, the largely unbridled role of each has proven inimical to its health and well-being.

CHAPTER 7
Man as God: The Worship of the State, Government, Law, and Democracy

Political ideologies—particularly as expressed in veneration for notions of democracy, government, and law—have contributed to Western man's overweening sense of self and have led him to believe that his ideological creations are "the answers" to the problems that beset mankind. "Leviathan-worship,"

Toynbee's term for exalting the state, is especially inimical to human relationships and becomes a danger to mankind.

The Western affinity for seeing the state and legal regimens in increasingly paternalistic terms—and as answers to its needs and problems—is not only ill-founded but dangerous and has led to greater and greater surrenders of individual freedoms and personal sovereignty to the state.

CHAPTER 8
Progress and Optimism

Western man's pride and vanity have led him to embrace untested and conventional assumptions with the zeal of religious belief: Western civilization is a reflection of the inevitability of man's "progress" and grounds for optimism are not only sound but extensive. These views are hindering Western man's perceptions of reality and are unsupported by the historical record.

CHAPTER 9
Man as God: Humanism and Communism

The ideological constructs of humanism and communism, which have swept much of the earth, are products of Western civilization and reflect the hubristic attitudes of Western man and his failures to perceive the greater depths and painful lessons of history.

CHAPTER 10
Education and the Vast Limits of Western Man's Knowledge

Education is venerated in Western civilization but often reflects the skewed values and distorted perceptions of reality that characterize Western thought and belief. Increasingly characterized by conformity and the absence of critical and discriminatory thinking, Western education perpetuates many of the dynamics contributing to the civilization's decline and decay.

CHAPTER 11
Western Man's Expression of His Soul: Art, Music, Literature, and Entertainment

The second phase of indicia of civilizational decay and decline is seen in the realms of art, music, literature and entertainment. The trends in Western civilization in these areas are increasingly sensational, decadent, self-deceptive and even pathological in a fashion consistent with the late stages of previous civilizations.

CHAPTER 12
A House Divided

The "multiculturalism" and "diversity" so assiduously touted in modern Western civilization have never proven to be favorable to the growth, vitality, and future of a civilization. They are, more often instead, harbingers of a collapse of the traditional thought and belief systems that molded and guided the civilization during its creative phases. Tacitus' observation of the late Roman Empire as "the common sink into which everything infamous and abominable flows" is increasingly *apropos* of Western civilization. Seeking common ground and bases for unity, rather than focusing on and nurturing differences, is the only wise course for the West.

CHAPTER 13
Man as God: Science and Technology

Science and technology are the almost solitary arenas in which Western civilization has made "progress," but they have proven to be a Faustian boon. For every gain Western man has made in his control over non-human nature, there has been a concomitant loss—with heightened danger to his well-being and even his survival. Advances in science and technology—without corollary or greater advances in the realms of morality, relationships, and spiritual understanding—have become the potential proximate causes of Western man's suicide. As a consequence of the disproportion of his moral faculties with his scientific and technological capabilities, Western man has created an array of potentially lethal threats, not simply to himself and his civilization but to mankind. Weapons of mass destruction, environmental degradation, technologies that are replicating and advancing in sophistication exponentially and over which man may eventually no longer exercise control, and an ever diminishing capacity for keeping pace with the threatening trends, are all portents of a foreboding future.

CHAPTER 14
Philistines at the Helm

The corruption of the thinking and values of a society's leaders is a central feature of the decay and decline of a civilization. In advanced stages of decline, the leadership displays confusion and a promiscuous chaos of beliefs and values coupled with extreme self-centeredness and declining courage. Western civilization's cultural, economic and political leadership has largely rejected the civilization's foundational beliefs and values and bears the greatest moral responsibility for the decline of the civilization.

CHAPTER 15
The Path to the New Dark Age

Western civilization's decline can be historically traced as it passed critical waypoints representing dramatic turns away from its foundational beliefs and values and toward unrealistic and self-deluding thought and belief. Two of the most critical waypoints were the Renaissance and the Enlightenment, which, though touted as great advancements, were in fact, in key respects, regression rather than purely progression. Both contributed to the rejection of religious belief and notions of immutable moral laws and foolishly exalted the highly circumscribed capacities and vision of man.

CHAPTER 16
Hypervelocity—The Turning of the Wheel of History in Our Age

The decline and decay of civilizations can be traced—and to a considerable extent predicted—by examining the historical precedents. The decline and decay of Western civilization is following a known pattern in all but one critical respect: there is an unprecedented acceleration of events with concomitant forms of "hypervelocity" in scientific and technological development, and, to some extent, in human behavior and thought, producing an ever faster pace of decline; all of which will alter the predictable pattern of civilizational collapse to the negative.

CHAPTER 17
"Wars and Rumors of Wars"
"The World Is As It Used to Be"

The speciousness of Western beliefs about the power of its most closely held conventions, ideologies, values and institutions (e.g., democracy, freedom, capitalism, humanism, science and technology, government, law, etc.) to ensure "progress," peace, affluence, and security will be increasingly exposed through the eruption of more aggressive and sophisticated forms of warfare—including Fourth Generation Warfare, to which the West is extraordinarily vulnerable. The end of the Cold War has not diminished the danger of war but increased it. The nemesis of war will manifest itself in new and more virulent forms.

CHAPTER 18
The Destination of the Wheel of History for the West: Apocalypse, Catastrophe, or Redemption?

There are three possible outcomes to the crisis, each of which can be understood in terms of historical precedents and their relative likelihoods as outcomes for Western civilization.

METHODOLOGY EMPLOYED IN *INTO THE NIGHT*

The reader who is mindful of the Bayeux Tapestry Principle presented in the Introduction will more readily understand why certain themes, quotes, and perspectives are repeated in the text, in epigrams, and in image captions throughout *Into the Night.* Since each of these is typically applicable to myriad aspects of our subject, it is important to not lose sight of their importance as we address each new facet. We are consciously interweaving themes so that, once the weaving is completed, an immense mural-like tapestry will have formed in the reader's mind.

Colored type is used throughout to highlight specific passages, thereby drawing attention to especially significant observations and themes.

CHAPTER

1

FROM THE SURFACE TO THE DEPTHS, THE PARTICULAR TO THE UNIVERSAL

Beneath each depth a greater depth lies.
Ralph Waldo Emerson

The things that make good headlines attract our attention because they are on the surface of the stream of life, and they distract our attention from the slower, impalpable, imponderable movements that work below the surface and penetrate to the depths....
Arnold Toynbee[1]

But, even today, it is only partial shapes of [history] that we know and not the shape of it, which is the mirror-image of our own inner life.
Oswald Spengler[2]

Examinations of history, particularly of Western civilization in modern times, typically focus on what could only be properly called the surface of the civilization. Events and people of lesser consequence are granted undeserved gravity and significance. This predilection is magnified many times over in our time by the media (i.e., all forms of modern communication: television, movies, journalism, publishing, Internet, etc.), which, it is often forgotten, are merely another manifestation of the competitive materialism that is central to Western culture. Even this book's pilgrimage into the hands of you, the reader, was threatened by market considerations; a reality that has made that pilgrimage all the more difficult. The media also reflect and depict the culture, which renders most examinations of that culture by the media neither objective nor insightful.

The result for Western civilization is a highly superficial perception of reality. The more insightful of our observers of history and man's behavior recognize this and decry the distortions of perception that result. In order to accurately comprehend what is happening in Western civilization we must search for the truly important. Arnold Toynbee expressed it this way:

> What will be singled out as the salient event of our time by future historians, centuries hence, looking back...and trying to see its activities and experiences in that just proportion which the time-perspective sometimes reveals? Not, I fancy, any of those sensational or tragic or catastrophic political and economic events which occupy the headlines of our newspapers and the foregrounds of our minds; not wars, revolutions, massacres, deportations, famines, gluts, slumps, or booms, but something of

> which we are only half-conscious, and out of which it would be difficult to make a headline. The things that make good headlines attract our attention because they are on the surface of the stream of life, and they distract our attention from the slower, impalpable, imponderable movements that work below the surface and penetrate to the depths. But of course it is really these deeper, slower movements that, in the end, make history, and it is they that stand out huge in retrospect, when the sensational passing events have dwindled, in perspective, to their true proportions. [3]

These "deeper, slower movements" are the focus of this work; the "sensational passing events" will be at best only given cursory, if any, attention. Toynbee's humble self-observation below, originating as it did from a man of such erudition, is a partial reflection of the attitude that pervades this book: man understands much less than he believes he understands; man's vision is profoundly limited:

> The only personal advantage that he can claim to possess is that he happens also to be a historian, and is therefore at least aware that he himself is a piece of sentient flotsam on the eddying surface of the stream of time. Realizing this, he knows that his fleeting and fragmentary vision of the passing scene is no more than a caricature of the surveyor's chart. God alone knows the true picture.[4]

"God alone knows the true picture" should be engraved in the granite of the loftiest venues and most powerful places in Western civilization under the rubric "Most Essential Truths Known to Man." Yet man's pride and vanity implore him to believe he possesses greater understanding as well as power than the evidence indicates. His greatest and deepest insights come with humility and a focus on the depths of the human mind and soul, not the sensational events and charismatic figures of culture.

In *A Study of History*, Toynbee consistently and wisely treated the mass movements and events of history as inferior in significance to the thinking and spiritual awareness of the individual:

> The social schism which we have been examining…is an experience which is collective and therefore superficial. Its significance lies in its being the outward sign of a spiritual rift which scars the souls of the individuals who "belong" to a disintegrating society. Beyond the social expressions of disintegration lie the personal crises of behaviour and feeling and life which are the true essence and origin of the visible manifestations of social collapse. Individual souls which have lost the opportunity (though not of course the personal capacity) for initiating the creative actions by which the growth of a society is sustained are apt to take refuge in a series of alternative reactions to the pressures of disintegration, and these reactions are as it were pathological inversions of some of the growth processes which we tried to identify earlier in this Study.[5]

Christopher Dawson in *Religion and World History* came to similar conclusions about this failure to see the greater depth. But he then noted a related problem: the false compartmentalization in the West of man's deeper quests and needs, as manifested especially in religion, from the culture. The two—the greater and more meaningful depth and the shallow but conspicuous surface—are, however, indissolubly linked: "No doubt it is very seldom that a society is clearly conscious of what is at stake. The issues are complicated by all kinds of social, economic, and political influences, so that the actual decision usually takes the form of a compromise."[6]

Of course the society is "seldom…conscious of what is at stake"; if its members were, their predicament, their crisis, would not likely have been created in the first instance. But all efforts to remedy the situation—to the extent they perceive it—do in fact take the form of a compromise. This form of problem-solving, most common in a democracy, hence the false assumptions of its wisdom and merit—a pseudo-Solomonic "we will cut the baby in half" solution—is rarely productive of a true and lasting resolution; something that can be sustained over time and through the vagaries of life.

Dawson, the devout Christian, correctly understood the relationship between the all-important greater depth of the human heart and mind and the more readily observable culture, and he roundly criticized the Western false and inept effort to try to separate the two:

> Now the creative activity which is the essence of the Christian life takes place far below the visible surface of culture; and the same thing is true of the spiritual failures and apostasies which are the other side of the picture. But this does not mean that religion and culture are two separate worlds with no relation to each other. The assumption of such a separation has been the great error of the Western mind during the last two centuries.[7]

This is true regardless of the individual's religious beliefs: there can be no valid separation between those deeply held beliefs of the individual and the broader culture; the latter is a manifestation of the former.

PD

Le Jugement de Solomon by Gaetano Gandolfi, 1620. *Societies in peril rarely are conscious of what is at stake. All efforts to remedy the situation—to the extent they perceive it—typically take the form of a compromise. This form of problem-solving, common in a democracy, hence the false assumptions of its wisdom and merit—a pseudo- Solomonic "we will cut the baby in half" solution— is rarely productive of a true and lasting resolution; something that can be sustained over time.*

In *Religion and the Rise of Western Culture*, Dawson returned to the theme of the spiritual plate tectonics of history when describing the impact of Christianity on the seemingly unconquerable Roman Empire:

> When St. Paul, in obedience to the warning of a dream, set sail from Troy in A.D. 49 and came to Philippi in Macedonia he did more to change the course of history than the great battle that had decided the fate of the Roman Empire on the same spot nearly a century earlier, for he brought to Europe the seed of a new life which was ultimately destined to create a new world. All this took place underneath the surface of history, so that it was unrecognized by the leaders of contemporary culture, like Gallio the brother of Seneca, who actually saw it taking place beneath their eyes.[8]

Perhaps to the diminishment of a multitude of cultural, media, and political egos, Adda Bozeman affirmed the principle similarly: "International history rightly documents the thesis that political systems are transient expedients on the surface of civilization, and that the destiny of each linguistically and morally unified community depends ultimately upon the survival of certain primary

PD-art.

St. Paul Preaching in Athens, by Raphael. *Dawson observed, "When St. Paul, in obedience to the warning of a dream, set sail from Troy in* A.D. *49 and came to Philippi in Macedonia, he did more to change the course of history than the great battle that had decided the fate of the Roman Empire [at Philippi] nearly a century earlier."*

PD-art.

The Death of Socrates, by Jacques-Louis David. *If Socrates' "unexamined life" is "not worth living," it is also perilous for our entire, seemingly all-powerful, Western civilization. Western man, to a greater or lesser degree, chooses to perceive only on the surface of life. This is the only reality he may want to see. The effect is to make him attitudinally, philosophically, and spiritually incorrigible—and at risk of destruction.*

structuring ideas around which successive generations have coalesced and which thus symbolize the society's continuity."[9]

Bozeman's concept of "primary structuring ideas" is integral to the understanding of any civilization, as it would be with any individual. This parallel is central to our study and is essential to any sound understanding of individuals or humanity collectively. The ability to see beneath the surface and detect the erosion of those ideas is the essence of studying the decline and decay of a civilization. The sociologist Pitirim Sorokin put the issue even more specifically with a passage we will repeat:

> This means that the main issue of our times is not democracy versus totalitarianism, nor liberty versus despotism; neither is it capitalism versus communism, nor pacifism versus militarism, nor internationalism versus nationalism, nor any of the current popular issues daily proclaimed by statesmen and politicians, professors and ministers, journalists and soapbox orators. All these popular issues are but small side issues—mere by-products of the main issue, namely, the sensate form of culture and way of life versus another, different form.[10]

Shocking, is it not, to consider that what Western media and culture generally treat with such fanfare, such gravity, such omnipotent importance, may in fact be a largely useless dissipation of words, thoughts, energy, print and air time? Thus the importance of avoiding the beguiling but misleading views of the surface is redoubled when examining modern Western civilization, which Sorokin believed is saturated with the shallow and often meaningless.

The focus of most media attention, histories written, and social and cultural commentary is essentially shallow; they do not approach the heart of history.

In a section of *The Crisis of Our Age* entitled "Roots of the Crisis," Sorokin, resorting to the terminology of a sociologist and, speaking directly to the crisis in Western civilization itself rather than abstractly, echoed Toynbee:

> ...How has this tragic crisis come about? What are its roots and reasons? Why has contemporary man —so successful in his scientific and technological achievements—not prevented the disintegration of his sensate culture and of his own degradation and tragedy?
>
> Most of the current answers hardly scratch the surface of the problem.They view it as a mere maladjustment of purely economic, or political, or technological, or biological nature. The maladjustment is regarded as something incidental, not inherent in the nature of modern sensate culture. Accordingly, for the elimination of the evil, they prescribe with perfect confidence either an economic readjustment—in money and banking, in prices and wages, in social security and insurance against unemployment, old age, or disease, even to the elimination of private property; or else a modification of the political machinery.... [11]

This is precisely the orientation of most of the "compromises" Dawson was referring to above; the drapes are laundered, the floor swept, the walls painted, yet all the while the termites eat away at the foundation. Finally, Francis Schaeffer bored beneath even the tectonic plates to the molten, restless magma underneath, by expressing the principle in purely religious terms:

> People are unique in the inner life of the mind—what they are in their thought world determines how they act.
>
> "As a man thinketh, so is he," is really most profound. An individual is not just the product of the forces around him. He has a mind, an inner world. Then, having thought, a person can bring forth actions into the external world and thus influence it. People are apt to look at the outer theater of action, forgetting the actor who "lives in the mind" and who therefore is the true actor in the external world. The inner thought world determines the outward action.[12]

Much of the human race, to a greater or lesser degree, chooses to perceive only on the surface of life. This is the only reality they may want to see. Whether that choice is made unconsciously (by default, so to speak) or deliberately, the effect is to make the individual attitudinally, philosophically and spiritually incorrigible. He cannot learn, he cannot see, because he chooses not to. Erudition and intellectual capacity bear less relationship to this infirmity than might be assumed. True learning is the gaining of insight and understanding—and ultimately, wisdom. If Socrates' "unexamined life" is "not worth living," it is also perilous for individuals—and an entire, seemingly all-powerful, civilization.

END NOTES
CHAPTER 1

1 Arnold Toynbee, *Civilization on Trial* (New York: Oxford University Press, 1948), 213.
2 Oswald Spengler, *The Decline of the West* (New York: A. A. Knopf, 1932), 12.
3 Toynbee, *Civilization on Trial,* 213.
4 Toynbee, *Civilization on Trial,* 16.
5 Arnold Toynbee, *A Study of History* (New York: Weathervane Books, 1972), 241.
6 Christopher Dawson, *Religion and World History: A Selection from the Works of Christopher Dawson* (Garden City, NY: Image Books, 1975), 256.
7 Dawson, *Religion and World History,* 256.
8 Christopher Dawson, *Religion and the Rise of Western Culture* (Garden City, NY: Image Books, 1948–1949), 27.
9 Adda Bozeman, *Politics and Culture in International History* (Princeton, NJ: Princeton University Press, 1960).
10 Pitirim A. Sorokin, *The Crisis of Our Age* (Oneworld Publications Ltd., 1941; this edition Sergei P. Sorokin and Peter P. Sorokin, 1992), 20.
11 Sorokin, *The Crisis of Our Age,* 250–251.
12 Francis A. Schaeffer, *How Should We Then Live? The Rise and Decline of Western Thought and Culture* (Wheaton, IL: Crossway Books, 1976), 19–20.

CHAPTER

2

THE WEST AND A WESTERN-CENTRIC VIEW OF HISTORY

The illusions and prejudices... live on and in the late twentieth century have blossomed forth in the widespread and parochial conceit that the European civilization of the West is now the universal civilization of the world.
Samuel Huntington[1]

The West today is still looking at history from that old parochial self-centred standpoint which the other living societies have by now been compelled to transcend.
Arnold Toynbee[2]

...we have not chosen this time. We cannot help it if we are born as men of the early winter of full Civilization.... Everything depends on our seeing our own position, our destiny, clearly, on our realizing that though we may lie to ourselves about it we cannot evade it.
Oswald Spengler[3]

Acquiring a reasonably objective consciousness of, and insight into, Western culture is difficult precisely because of that form of provincialism and egocentric thinking that tends to characterize all nations and all cultures at any time in history. But it is an affliction that especially incapacitates the reasoning of citizens of "successful" and powerful nations and civilizations. None has been more successful or powerful than Western civilization. As we noted in the introduction, this provincialism is usually not apparent to its practitioners simply because they swim about in it—and the culture that spawned it—constantly from birth.

Samuel Huntington throws a wide net in describing this parochialism: "Every civilization sees itself as the center of the world and writes its history as the central drama of human history. This has been perhaps even more true of the West than of other cultures. Such monocivilizational viewpoints, however, have decreasing relevance and usefulness in a multicivilizational world. Scholars of civilizations have long recognized this truism."[4]

Huntington referred to another of our observers to demonstrate how those who have truly reflected recognize the folly in a parochial view of history: "In 1918 Spengler denounced the myopic view of history prevailing in the West with its neat division into ancient, medieval, and modern phases relevant only to the West. It is necessary, he said, to replace this 'Ptolemaic approach to history' with a Copernican one and to substitute for the 'empty figment of one linear history, the drama of a number of mighty cultures.'"[5]

Similarly, he noted a "few decades later Toynbee castigated the 'parochialism and impertinence' of the West manifested in the 'egocentric illusions' that the world revolved around it, that there was an 'unchanging East', and that 'progress' was inevitable."[6] Huntington was affirming the view shared by Spengler and Toynbee that the assumption of the unity of history, the assumption that there is "only one river of civilization, our own, and that all others are either tributary to it or lost in the desert sands" was false. Huntington concluded, "the illusions and prejudices of which these scholars warned, however, live on and in the late twentieth century have blossomed forth in the widespread and parochial conceit that the European civilization of the West is now the universal civilization of the world." [7]

I share Huntington's, Toynbee's, and Spengler's view on this point but would suggest that there is a superficial adherence to it among some in the West that does not ring true. The "political correctness" in Western culture, coupled with the mindless affinity for the amorphous concept of "diversity," lend themselves to the impression that this broader and deeper perspective is honored; but I believe it is neither truly honored nor truly understood, for this planet-wide, history-long perspective does not suggest that somehow all cultures and civilizations are equal or that they have merits we should value. This is more a reflection of the dissipation of the West's belief in itself than of any broad-mindedness.

In any event, the prideful self-centric view of history distorts our perceptions and robs us of the objectivity so necessary to that most redeeming of character traits: the willingness to honestly search one's soul. In a marvelously insightful, prefatory observation Spengler pointed us to Western man's profound self-centeredness, and, in so doing, sounds much like Toynbee's humble recognition of how little he, as a world historian, truly understood: "No doubt we feel world-history, experience it and believe that it is to be read just as a map is read. But, even today, it is only partial shapes of it that we know and not the shape of it, which is the mirror-image of our own inner life."[8] Spengler continued by resort to a metaphor from astronomy:

> The Western European area is regarded as a fixed pole, a unique patch chosen on the surface of the sphere for no better reason, it seems, than because we live on it—and great histories of millennial duration and mighty faraway Cultures are made to revolve around this pole in all modesty. It is a quaintly conceived system of sun and planets! We select a single bit of ground as the natural centre of the historical system, and make it the central sun.[9]

The irony in this—what I believe is an accurate perception of the West—is a phenomenon unknown to Spengler in his time. Despite this lingering West-centric viewpoint, the West itself is losing confidence in itself, its beliefs, its values, and ventures now into a paradoxical realm of extraordinary ambivalence about who it is. This ambivalence, as we shall see, is another hallmark of a civilization in decline and decay.

Displaying the deterministic civilization-as-living-organism view for which he is known, Spengler observed an unending historical variety, and then uttered a particularly powerful condemnation by juxtaposition:

> Each culture has its own new possibilities of self-expression which arise, ripen, decay and never return. There is not one culture, one painting, one mathematics, one physics, but many, each in its deepest

PD-art

Marriage of Queen Victoria and Prince Albert, by Sir George Hayter (1792–1871). *Toynbee pointed out that though biblical accounts of the earth halting momentarily in the heavens provoked recognition of the miraculous in the biblical age, Victorian England's smugness was so pervasive that even the imaginary miracles of that time were taken for granted as the proper due of that apogee of civilization. Victorian–Edwardian England was no different in many respects from twenty-first-century America and much of Europe, which behave as if they are largely immune to the hazards of history.*

> essence different from the others, each limited in duration and self-contained....These Cultures, sublimated life-essences, grow with the same super aimlessness as the flowers of the field. They belong, like the plants and the animals, to the living nature of Goethe, and not to the dead Nature of Newton.[10]

In this last sentence, Spengler asserted a viewpoint that, in one variation or another, is common to most of our observers: the spiritual perspective is closer to the great truth; the material view of life is by far subordinate—and highly blinkered.

Spengler indicted Western man for having greater reason to understand that his world was not the only one, while failing miserably to do so: "It is *this* that is lacking to the Western thinker, the very thinker in whom we might have expected to find it—insight into the *historically relative* character of his data, which are expressions of one *specific existence and one only.*"[11]

Acknowledging, as all our observers do, that Western civilization encompasses more than Europe or America alone, Wallerstein noted that social science itself is a purely Western concept—

a recognition that permits us to extrapolate more fully how distorted the prism must be through which we observe our world:

> Social science has been Eurocentric throughout its institutional history.... This is not in the least surprising. Social science is a product of the modern world-system, and Eurocentrism is constitutive of the geoculture of the modern world. Furthermore...social science originated largely in Europe. We shall be using "Europe" here more as a cultural than as a cartographical expression...we are referring primarily and jointly to western Europe and North America.[12]

An American colleague of Carroll Quigley noted after Quigley's death that Quigley too shared Spengler's, Toynbee's, and Dawson's perplexity at the West-centric view of life and history: "It always frustrated him that each nation, including our own, regards its own history as unique and the history of other nations as irrelevant to it."[13]

An analogue in the physical world should suggest strongly to Western man that his, his tribe's, his nation's, his civilization's experience provide no basis for self-confident certainties. The remoteness and apparent physical inconsequence of the planet earth in the celestial firmament should be profoundly humbling. But as Toynbee pointed out with unconcealed sarcasm, though biblical accounts of the earth halting momentarily in the heavens provoked recognition of the miraculous in the biblical age, Victorian England's smugness was so pervasive that even the imaginary miracles of that time were taken for granted as the proper due of that apogee of civilization:

> The author of the tenth chapter of the Book of Joshua was at any rate aware that a stand-still of Time was something unusual. "There was no day like that before it or after it, that the Lord hearkened unto the voice of a man." Yet the middle-class English in 1897, who thought of themselves as Wellsian rationalists living in a scientific age, took their imaginary miracle for granted. As they saw it, history, for them, was over. It had come to an end in foreign affairs in 1815, with the Battle of Waterloo; in home affairs in 1832, with the Great Reform Bill; and in imperial affairs in 1859, with the suppression of the Indian Mutiny. And they had every reason to congratulate themselves on the permanent state of felicity which this ending of history had conferred on them. "The lines are fallen unto me in pleasant places; yea, I have a goodly heritage."[14]

Disabused as they eventually were of this "permanent state of felicity" by the bloodletting of World War I, Victorian–Edwardian England was, nonetheless, no different in many respects from America, as Toynbee pointed out, or, as we will point out, from twenty-first-century America and much of Europe, which behave as if they are largely immune to the hazards of history even as each gives lip service to abstract notions of vulnerability:

> Viewed from the historical vantage point of A.D. 1947, this *fin de siècle* middle-class English hallucination seems sheer lunacy, yet it was shared by contemporary Western middle-class people of other nationalities. In the United States, for instance, in the North, history, for the middle class, had come to an end with the winning of the West and the Federal victory in the Civil War; and in Germany, or at any rate in Prussia, for the same class, the same permanent consummation had been reached with the overthrow of France and foundation of the Second Reich in 1871. For these three batches of Western middle-class people fifty years ago God's work of creation was completed, "and behold it was very good."[15]

But of course it was "very good" only for those not adversely affected by its consequences. Yet in a greater sense, taking a longer view, it was not good even for its apparent beneficiaries, who, each

PD

Joshua Commanding the Sun to Stand Still by John Martin. *Toynbee alluded to this biblical account as evidence of recognition of the miraculous. Yet the West has a lengthy history of perceiving its achievements and power as latter day miracles of its own creation. There is no humility and thus no capacity for perceiving one's shortcomings and vices—necessary prerequisites for escaping the end of all prior civilizations.*

in turn, were induced to some degree of hubris that inevitably led to trouble for they themselves: "All over the world, in fact, though at that time still under the surface, there were peoples and classes who were just as discontented as the French or the Southerners were with the latest deal of history's cards, but who were quite unwilling to agree that the game was over. There were all the subject peoples and all the depressed classes, and what millions they amounted to!"[16]

This is another way of saying that in the great competitions (a word dear to the heart of the West) of life, winning for some inevitably means losing for others; the contented become ever more smug and self-centered, the discontented, ever more restive and angry, thus setting up the paradigm of much of history that has made it ever so colorful: a vivid, never-staunched shade of red.

Little has changed since Toynbee's mid-twentieth-century review. If anything, there has been further regression. Twenty-first-century Westerners are often so arrogant in their self-centric view of the world that they are blinded to the perceptions, and sufferings, of others who share space with them on this orb. Cat food commercials on American television and the latest in fashions in glossy European magazines, juxtaposed with the harsh realities endured by much of humanity, bespeaks an egocentric moral blindness and hardness of heart beyond measure.

But an obsessive self-indulgence and insensitivity to others may be the least of the West's concerns. The self-centric, success-oriented viewpoint is a delusional hazard to the West's survival, suggested Samuel Huntington, who, in effect, corroborated Toynbee's point with more recent evidence:

> The moment of euphoria at the end of the Cold War generated an illusion of harmony, which was soon revealed to be exactly that. The world became different in the early 1990s, but not necessarily more peaceful. Change was inevitable; progress was not. Similar illusions of harmony flourished, briefly, at the end of each of the twentieth century's other major conflicts. World War I was the "war to end wars" and to make the world safe for democracy. World War II, as Franklin Roosevelt put it, would "end the system of unilateral action, the exclusive alliances, the balances of power, and all the other expedients that have been tried for centuries—and have always failed." Instead we will have "a universal organization" of "peace-loving Nations" and the beginnings of a "permanent structure of peace."[17]

The appealing, specious, naïve, self-deluding folly in all of this would have been apparent to anyone possessing the dual qualities of a) a deep and broad awareness of history (or, put more pedestrianly, an astute understanding of human nature) and b) a courageous, tough-minded determination to see reality as it is rather than as we wish it to be. A few "missing links" with this rare subspecies of humanity have been located, but typically in humble and unpretentious settings, rarely in positions of power and influence.

The consequence of these especial observers' endangered or extinct status in these environs was, in effect, elucidated by Huntington as he continued:

> World War I, however, generated communism, fascism, and the reversal of a century-old trend toward democracy. World War II produced a Cold War that was truly global. The illusion of harmony at the end of that Cold War was soon dissipated by the multiplication of ethnic conflicts and "ethnic cleansing," the breakdown of law and order, the emergence of new patterns of alliance and conflict among states, the resurgence of neo-communist and neo-fascist movements, intensification of religious fundamentalism, the end of the "diplomacy of smiles" and "policy of yes" in Russia's relations with the West, the inability of the United Nations and the United States to suppress bloody local conflicts, and the increasing assertiveness of a rising China.[18]

Huntington was equally dismissive of those who view scientific and technological advancement in the West as a wave that will sweep humanity toward a common philosophical and spiritual utopia. I not only concur but argue throughout this work that the hazards produced—in a multiplicity of obvious and obscure ways—by these forces will prove ultimately to be greater than any benefits. This is heresy of the first rank to Western cultural "religion," but a heresy I am supremely confident will prove in time to be true:

> Little or no evidence exists, however, to support the assumption that the emergence of pervasive global communications is producing significant convergence in attitudes and beliefs. "Entertainment," as Michael Vlahos has said, "does not equate to cultural conversion." Second, people interpret communications in terms of their own preexisting values and perspectives. "The same visual images transmitted

CHAPTER

3

THE MIRAGE OF IMMORTALITY—ENTROPY OF THE EVERLASTING

The facts stare us in the face, and, by exercising our historical imagination, we can perhaps anticipate the compulsory education that is already on its way to us.
Arnold Toynbee [1]

Contrary to the optimistic diagnosis, the present crisis is not ordinary but extraordinary...it is a crisis involving almost the whole way of life, thought and conduct of Western society. More precisely, it consists in a disintegration of a fundamental form of Western culture and society dominant for the last four centuries.
Pitirim Sorokin [2]

...all this, broad and imposing, is the prelude of a future which is still in store for us and with which the history of West European mankind will be definitely closed.
Oswald Spengler [3]

For even though we may not believe in the imminent end of the world, it is hardly possible to doubt that a world is ending.
Christopher Dawson [4]

Hubristically confident as Western man is of a *mens sana in corpore sano* (a healthy mind in a healthy body) unrivalled in history, he is bereft of prospects for diagnosing his potentially terminal illness. Indeed, the absence of humility and the ubiquitous presence of self-delusion are complementary hallmarks of the diagnostic criteria. Here we begin the process of analyzing those diagnostic criteria: what we can conclude about civilizational decline and decay generally from the study of history, and what we can conclude about the West's decline and decay specifically.

First, we should define what we mean by Western civilization. Our observers seem to all share the view that Western civilization is a nonseverable unity of Europe, North America, and Australia/New Zealand. Universally, they make little distinction, except of the more superficial sort, between these geographic segments. The destiny of one, in historical terms, will likely ultimately be the destiny of all. Samuel Huntington provides for us an especially useful definition of what is perhaps most often meant by the term Western civilization:

> The term "the West" is now universally used to refer to what used to be called Western Christendom. The West is thus the only civilization identified by a compass direction and not by the name of a particular people, religion, or geographical area. This identification lifts the civilization out of its historical, geographical, and cultural context. Historically, Western civilization is European civilization. In the modern era, Western civilization is Euroamerican or North Atlantic civilization.[5]

NO CIVILIZATION IS IMMORTAL

They appear suddenly, swell in splendid lines, flatten again and vanish,
and the face of the waters is once more a sleeping waste.
Oswald Spengler [6]

Though their views differ and the gravity with which they regard the trends of Western civilization varies, it would be an understatement to say that our observers all shared deep concerns about the future of our civilization. There is consensus among them that all civilizations die—or at least all preceding civilizations have died.

To the historically informed it may seem a statement of the self-evident to declare that all civilizations eventually die. But what is self-evident to one may be obscure—or anathema—to another, smitten as men tend to be with afflictions such as ethnocentrism and illusions of the power, merit and immortality of their own culture, race, ethnic group or civilization. Alexander Pushkin's lines are apropos of how most of humanity, certainly Western citizens, view their own civilization:

Gazing at a solitary oak,
I think: this patriarch
Will outlive my forgotten age
As it outlived the age of my fathers.[7]

But these infirmities of reason have afflicted millions for millennia and will likely continue to decimate reason and understanding in millions to come. The sober reality must be faced; no civilization has any prospect of even extending its life if its members cling to a belief in its immortality. To be sure, some will accept, even state, the abstract principle that all civilizations, like all human beings, die. But just as most human beings rarely contemplate their own death, unless compelled to do so by circumstance, even fewer citizens of powerful civilizations really think and behave as if their civilization is mortal, much less *in extremis.*

The historical evidence of the folly in this has been visited and revisited by historians, anthropologists and sociologists. In citing the work of Spengler and Toynbee on the question of whether "there is any regularity in the development of civilizations, in their slow growth and their sometimes rapid decline," Philip Bagby articulated a common theme, specifically in his reference to the West:

> It is a problem which seems to be of particular urgency in our own times, for a cold wind has blown across Europe, an intuition that European civilization is doomed to go the way of Egypt and of Rome, of Nineveh and Tyre. The loss of faith, the stagnation of the arts, the shattering of the Liberal dream, the catastrophic character of recent wars, all these have seemed to betoken an imminent decline.[8]

CC

A joint session of the American Congress. *Carroll Quigley explained the disintegration of civilizations in terms of the transformation of social "instruments" into "institutions." By this he meant that the entities created by a society to carry it forward and to meet its needs eventually become self-serving and thus increasingly ineffectual in serving the society. This is especially true of their governments.*

Samuel Huntington, also citing other of our observers, noted the parallels and common features of modern theories of decline and decay:

> While civilizations endure, they also evolve. They are dynamic; they rise and fall; they merge and divide...they also disappear and are buried in the sands of time. The phases of their evolution may be specified in various ways.... While significant differences exist, all these theories see civilizations evolving through a time of troubles or conflict to a universal state to decay and disintegration.[9]

Citing Toynbee, Huntington explained why the West is neither immune to collapse nor in a position to be optimistic:

> History ends at least once and occasionally more often in the history of every civilization. As the civilization's universal state emerges, its people become blinded by what Toynbee called "the mirage of immortality" and convinced that theirs is the final form of human society. So it was with the Roman Empire, the 'Abbasid Caliphate, the Mughal Empire, and the Ottoman Empire. The citizens of such universal states "in defiance of apparently plain facts...are prone to regard it, not as a night's shelter in the wilderness, but as the Promised Land, the goal of human endeavors." ...For the English middle class in 1897, "as they saw it, history for them, was over...." Societies that assume that their history has ended, however, are usually societies whose history is about to decline.[10]

WESTERN CIVILIZATION—ON THE PATH TO OBLIVION?

We have awakened to the truth (how, one wonders, could we ever have been blind to it?) that Western man and his works are no more invulnerable than the now extinct civilizations of the Aztecs and the Incas, the Sumerians and the Hittites.
Arnold Toynbee[11]

Arnold Toynbee, as early as 1948, spoke in terms of these historical lessons when addressing the future of the West:

> Our present situation is formidable indeed. A survey of the historical landscape in the light of our existing knowledge shows that, up to date, history has repeated itself about twenty times in producing human societies of the species to which our Western society belongs, and it also shows that, with the possible exception of our own, all these representatives of the species of society called civilizations are already dead or moribund. Moreover, when we study the histories of these dead and moribund civilizations in detail, and compare them with one another, we find indications of *what looks like a recurring pattern in the process of their breakdowns, declines, and falls.* We are naturally asking ourselves today whether this particular chapter of history is bound to repeat itself in our case.[12]

Toynbee in part answered that question with a foreboding hint:

> All the civilizations that we know of, including the Greek, have already broken down and gone to pieces with the single possible exception of our own Western civilization—and no child of this civilization who has been born into our generation can easily imagine that our own society is immune from the danger of suffering the common fate.[13]

Toynbee addressed the issue in terms of an oft-revisited question:

> Does history repeat itself? In our Western world in the eighteenth and nineteenth centuries, this question used to be debated as an academic exercise. The spell of well-being which our civilization was enjoying at the time had dazzled our grandfathers into the quaint pharisaical notion that they were "not as other men are"; they had come to believe that our Western society was exempt from the possibility of falling into those mistakes and mishaps that have been the ruin of certain other civilizations whose history, from beginning to end, is an open book..... We have awakened to the truth (how, one wonders, could we ever have been blind to it?) that Western man and his works are no more invulnerable than the now extinct civilizations of the Aztecs and the Incas, the Sumerians and the Hittites.[14]

WHY IS TWENTY-FIRST-CENTURY WESTERN CIVILIZATION'S SITUATION PERILOUSLY UNIQUE?

It is a problem which seems to be of particular urgency in our own times, for a cold wind has blown across Europe, an intuition that European civilization is doomed to go the way of Egypt and of Rome, of Nineveh and Tyre. The loss of faith, the stagnation of the arts, the shattering of the Liberal dream, the catastrophic character of recent wars, all these have seemed to betoken an imminent decline.

Philip Bagby[15]

As we will see throughout this work, the evidence suggests Toynbee's mid-twentieth-century optimism (*Civilization* was published in 1948) that Western man has "awakened to the truth" was misplaced. Born at the apogee of the preternaturally optimistic British Empire, Toynbee was apparently congenitally incapable of admitting expressly, despite his starkly realistic assessments of man and history, the implications of his conclusions. He was committed to salvaging from the detritus of recent history—or at least professing belief in—some vestige of optimism. One is left with the impression that his mind and its copious erudition told him one thing, but his heart insisted on more hopeful prospects. In *Civilization on Trial*, Toynbee's manifesto, we see evidence of this as suggested in the acknowledgement of why Western civilization's predicament is unique in history, and dire:

> Why cannot civilization go on shambling along, from failure to failure, in the painful, degrading, but not utterly suicidal way in which it has kept going for the first few thousand years of its existence? The answer lies in the recent technological inventions of the modern Western middle class. These gadgets for harnessing the physical forces of non-human nature have left human nature unchanged. The institutions of War and Class are social reflexions of the seamy side of human nature—or what the theologians call original sin—in the kind of society that we call civilization. These social effects of individual human sinfulness have not been abolished by the recent portentous advance in our technological "know-how," but they have not been left unaffected by it either. Not having been abolished, they have been enormously keyed up, like the rest of human life, in respect of their physical potency.[16]

Science and technology have changed everything—the world and history—and not necessarily, as so glibly believed, for the better. The indicators pointing to the rapid decline and decay of Western civilization are largely consistent with those that marked the decline and decay of every prior civilization, save this one unique feature of the West: the ubiquitous power and influence of science and technology. Western man is pointing a loaded gun at his head. In any earlier time, he would not have had the means.

Toynbee suggested, reluctantly, almost painfully, his true thinking by acknowledging the inevitability of Western man's coming education:

> The facts stare us in the face, and, by exercising our historical imagination, we can perhaps anticipate the compulsory education that is already on its way to us. The Greek Stoic philosopher Cleanthes prays Zeus and Fate for grace to follow their lead of his own will without flinching; "for if," he adds, "I quail and rebel, I shall have to follow just the same."[17]

This compulsory education is an underlying impetus for this book. Toynbee explicitly and realistically acknowledged what I agree is man's fundamental, inherent weakness. This acknowledgment belies Toynbee's proffered optimism, if not his theoretical basis:

> I have already confessed my own adherence to the traditional Christian view that there is no reason to expect any change in unredeemed human nature while human life on Earth goes on. …There has been no perceptible variation in the average sample of human nature in the past; there is no ground, in the evidence afforded by History, to expect any great variation in the future either for better or for worse.[18]

Interestingly, Christopher Dawson used a very similar metaphor to Toynbee's "river" to declare that the river of Western civilization has become "a destructive cataract":

> The modern world is in a state of violent confusion and change, and it is not the traditional Christian culture of the past but the secularized culture of the present which is being tried and found wanting. The material security and the confidence in the future which have long been characteristic of Western civilization have suddenly disappeared. Nobody knows where the world is going. The course of history has suddenly been changed from a broad, placid river into a destructive cataract.[19]
>
> …
>
> For even though we may not believe in the imminent end of the world, it is hardly possible to doubt that a world is ending.[20]

Immanuel Wallerstein, in *The End of the World As We Know It*, published in 1999, offered his perspective, and in so doing wisely disabused his readers of the notion that the event touted as most guaranteeing security and peace for the West did nothing of the sort:

> …while most persons in the ex-Communist world are immensely relieved that the Communist interlude is behind them, it is not at all sure that they, or the rest of us, have moved into a safer or more hopeful or more livable world.[21]

Cataracts of the Nile. *Toynbee and Dawson both resorted to the metaphor of a river to illustrate the course of history. Dawson observed, "Nobody knows where the world is going. The course of history has suddenly been changed from a broad, placid river into a destructive cataract. For even though we may not believe in the imminent end of the world, it is hardly possible to doubt that a world is ending."*

PD

WESTERN MAN FOCUSES ON THE SURFACE, BUT HISTORY IS DETERMINED IN THE DEPTHS

...[the crisis] is infinitely deeper and more significant than the partisans of the 'ordinary crisis' imagine. A change from a monarchy to a republic or from capitalism to communism is utterly insignificant in comparison with the substitution of one fundamental form of culture and society for another.
Pitirim Sorokin[22]

Pitirim Sorokin, who spoke forcefully about the "crisis" of Western civilization as early as the mid-twentieth century, observed, "Contrary to the optimistic diagnosis, the present crisis is not ordinary but extraordinary...it is a crisis involving almost the whole way of life, thought and conduct of Western society. More precisely, it consists in a disintegration of a fundamental form of Western culture and society dominant for the last four centuries.[23]

Sorokin elaborated:

> We are living and acting at one of the epoch-making turning points of human history, when one fundamental form of culture and society—sensate—is declining and a different form is emerging... it is marked by an extraordinary explosion of wars, revolutions, anarchy and bloodshed; by social, moral, economic, political and intellectual chaos; by a resurgence of revolting cruelty and animality, and a temporary destruction of the great and small values of mankind; by misery and suffering on the part of millions—a convulsion far in excess of the chaos and disorganization of the ordinary crises....[24]

Toynbee spoke of our obsessive attention in Western civilization to events and subjects that are merely on the "surface of the stream of life."[25] We will return to this theme in later chapters—all the while striving not to make the same mistake ourselves.

The depth and breadth of the trauma and change that the West faces should not be minimized or seen in superficial terms. Sorokin explained:

> "Hence the magnitude of the crisis of our time...it...signifies one of the greatest possible revolutions in our culture and social life. As such, it is infinitely deeper and more significant than the partisans of the "ordinary crisis" imagine. A change from a monarchy to a republic or from capitalism to communism is utterly insignificant in comparison with the substitution of one fundamental form of culture and society for another—ideational for sensate, or vice versa."[26]

A SALIENT TRAIT OF CIVILIZATIONAL DISINTEGRATION— THE BREAKDOWN OF MENTAL AND MORAL ORDER

The ultimate result of shielding men from the effects of folly is to fill the world with fools.
Herbert Spencer[27]

The superior man thinks always of virtue; the common man thinks of comfort.
Confucius[28]

The most common thread in the thinking of our observers as to the precursors, the indicia, the symptoms, of civilizational breakdown is the disintegration of the thinking, values, and morals of the culture. What was once considered sacrosanct or reverenced is increasingly undermined and eventually rejected. Sound reasoning that fully engaged the hard realities of life is supplanted by denial and self-delusion.

Toynbee, Dawson, and Sorokin especially emphasized this aspect of cultural disintegration. From this critical first crack in the foundation the disintegration of everything else in the culture will flow. All other theories of cultural decline that focus on economics, military power, or institutional failures are shallow perspectives, as of a man who sees a fissure in the ground and does not comprehend the massive tectonic shift beneath. Sorokin described this process succinctly:

> This disintegration of the systems of meanings and values will be reflected in the mentality of individuals and groups...in a similar disintegration of their mentality. Where before there was a mental and moral order...shortly a mental and moral chaos will arise. The distinction between true and false, right and wrong, beautiful and ugly, positive and negative value will be more and more obliterated. Since no sociocultural norms—universally accepted and recognized—exist any more in the culture itself, no such norms can be present in the mentality of the individuals and groups. Mental and moral atomism will grow and, with it, mental and moral anarchy.[29]

CC

Herbert Spencer*'s observation that "The ultimate result of shielding men from the effects of folly is to fill the world with fools" reflected what has gone before in history and anticipated what is taking place now in Western civilization. But the shielding can only go so far, and the worse the folly, the worse the consequences when the reckoning comes.*

A TIME OF TROUBLES, CONFLICTS, AND WAR

The course of history has suddenly been changed from a broad, placid river into a destructive cataract.
Christopher Dawson[30]

We continue with Sorokin to describe another central characteristic of the decline and decay, a feature we will address in depth later: conflicts and wars. In this respect also, Sorokin and our other observers have much in common:

> Its consequence must be an increase and a sharpening of antagonisms and conflicts....an increase of the rule of rude force: wars, revolutions, crimes and other forms of social struggle stripped of all inhibitions and restraint. These will lead to a further destruction of human lives....and material wealth. Such a destruction will deprive sensate culture of its main charm and fascination, defeating its main value, its raison d'etre, and thereby causing the downfall of its prestige, attraction and captivation. Hence follows the increasing defection of human agents from it and the shift of their allegiance to different systems of values and meanings.[31]

PRIDE AND GREED LEADING TO OVERREACHING

Religious–ascetic fundamentals such as "selfless," "sinless," are without meaning in the economic life....Economic activity is never found in a religion or a philosophy, always only in the political organism of a church or the social organism of a theorizing fellowship; it is ever a compromise with "this world" and an index of the presence of a will-to-power.
Oswald Spengler[32]

Oswald Spengler, the most overtly pessimistic of our observers, believed that the collapse of Western civilization was inevitable. Spengler described another indicator of the civilizational end times—one also perceived by the majority of our observers—which parallels so much of twentieth and twenty-first-century Western history:

> Here, then, I lay it down that Imperialism, of which petrifacts such as the Egyptian empire, the Roman, the Chinese, the Indian, may continue to exist for hundreds or thousands of years—dead bodies, amorphous and dispirited masses of men, scrap-material from a great history—is to be taken as the typical symbol of the end....In this phenomenal form the destiny of the West is now irrevocably set. The energy of culture-man is directed inwards, that of civilization-man outwards....The expansive tendency is a doom, something daemonic and immense, which grips, forces into service, and uses up the late mankind of the world-city stage....[33]

Carroll Quigley, in an observation that seems superficially to be removed from Spengler's insight and references to imperialism, told us something that is in truth closely related: "After centuries of expansion our society is now organized so that it cannot subsist; it must expand or it will collapse."[34]

These perspectives describe manifestations of a hubristic view of life born of "success" in the ever expanding quest of Western man to satiate his greed, his pride, and his quest for power. In this he has fallen prey to impulses and temptations that have brought innumerable individuals, nations, and civilizations to their knees—or their graves.

These insights, and others proffered by our observers, theoretically could provide Western leaders with the rudiments of a strategic plan by which to alter the course of the civilization. But Spengler did not foresee that wisdom. Like Dawson and Toynbee, resorting to the metaphor of history as an ever-flowing river, Spengler pronounced the doom of Western civilization as the inevitable latest of many such catastrophes: "But over this surface, too, the great Cultures accomplish their majestic wave-cycles. They appear suddenly, swell in splendid lines, flatten again and vanish, and the face of the waters is once more a sleeping waste."[35]

Times Square, 14 August 1945.
VJ Day and the Greatest Generation celebrating their greatest accomplishment, victory in WWII. In their zeal to shield and protect their children, parents of that generation often gave their children the things they didn't have but forgot to give them the things they did have—lessons in unselfishness, adversity, and enduring: the rudiments of character, rather than comfort, possessions, security, and self-centeredness.

Photograph by Alfred Eisenstaedt/Time & Life Pictures/Getty Images

INSTITUTIONS AND GOVERNMENTS THAT NO LONGER FUNCTION SELFLESSLY OR EFFECTIVELY

The nature of these organizational stresses and tensions arising from a decrease in the rate of a society's expansion can be seen most clearly in contemporary Western civilization.
Carroll Quigley[36]

Carroll Quigley explained the disintegration of civilizations in terms of the transformation of social "instruments" into "institutions." By this he meant that the entities created by a society to carry it forward and to meet its needs eventually become self-serving and thus increasingly ineffectual in serving the society.

In a descriptive passage every modern American or European should find unsettling, Quigley observed,

> When the instrument of expansion in a civilization becomes an institution, tension increases.... The society as a whole has become adapted to expansion; the mass of the population expect and desire it. A society that has an instrument of expansion expands for generations, even for centuries. People's minds become adjusted to expansion. If they are not "better off" each year than they were the previous year, or if they cannot give their children more than they themselves started with, they became disappointed, restless, and perhaps bitter.... The society itself, after generations of expansion, is organized for expansion and undergoes acute stresses if expansion slows up. The nature of these organizational stresses and tensions...can be seen most clearly in contemporary Western civilization.[37]

This passage should remind any American Baby Boomer of an oft expressed and passionate goal of their father's and grandfathers' generations: their children and grandchildren must not endure what they endured in the Great Depression or a world war; peace and, especially, material comfort must be their lot. As a result, parents of that earlier generation often gave their children much they did not have, but many forgot to give them the intangibles of great worth they did have.

This seemingly noble ambition was, in point of fact, a fundamental failure of the Greatest Generation that often did not recognize—or remember—that it is in adversity and enduring, not comfort and security, that character is born.

IS A COLLAPSE IMMINENT?

As the West's primacy erodes, much of its power will simply evaporate and the rest will be diffused on a regional basis among the several major civilizations and their core states.
Samuel Huntington[38]

We will see that our observers have varying views on the imminence of our Civilization's collapse. Samuel Huntington sees Western decay and decline from an indeterministic perspective and without a necessarily catastrophic reversal, though clearly the dark horse's hoof beats can be heard in his words:

PD

Zulu Wars: Battle of Isandhlwana (1879) by Charles Edwin Fripp. *A confrontation between two tribes—the British and the Zulus—one of history's most common features. Toynbee declared in* A Study of History, *a characterization the West would do well to keep in mind, "The so-called 'civilized' state is simply an imposing, high-powered version of the primitive tribe...."*

> The West is overwhelmingly dominant now and will remain number one in terms of power and influence well into the twenty-first century...the power of the West relative to that of other civilizations will continue to decline. As the West's primacy erodes, much of its power will simply evaporate and the rest will be diffused on a regional basis among the several major civilizations and their core states."[39]

The evidence in support of Huntington's prognosis is all about us and apparent in a more advanced state than even Huntington seemed to anticipate. Affirming the thinking of Carroll Quigley, Huntington observed, "In the mid-1990s the West had many characteristics Quigley identified as those of a mature civilization on the brink of decay."[40]

In sum, all of our observers see the peril of Western civilization with a sense of urgency—an urgency born of historical and sociological insight—and dangerously at variance with the thinking and behavior of much of the dominant minority of Western civilization. These two camps, our erudite observers and the modern elite of Western culture, cannot both be correct.

A LOSS OF INTERNAL HARMONY AND THE POWER OF SELF-DETERMINATION

"Whom the Lord loveth he chasteneth" may prove to be as near the ultimate truth as the dictum attributed to Solon by Herodotus, that "to many people God has given a glimpse of happiness in order to destroy them root and branch."
Arnold Toynbee[41]

Toynbee, in *A Study of History*, described the process of decline and decay by singling out key features of the breakdowns of civilizations, one of which, the notion of "horizontal schisms," is less conspicuous, but more important than the more obvious "vertical schisms" he describes:

> Thus the disintegration of a civilization, like its growth, is a cumulative as well as a continuous process... Does not the disintegration of a civilization run to a defeat which culminates either in extinction, or else in a petrifaction which is no true reprieve since it merely condemns the disintegrating society to the temporary limbo of life-in-death before its ultimate and inevitable dissolution?..."Whom the Lord loveth He chasteneth" may prove to be as near the ultimate truth as the dictum attributed to Solon by Herodotus, that "to many people God has given a glimpse of happiness in order to destroy them root and branch...."
>
> ...we found that the ultimate criterion and fundamental cause of breakdown could be described as a loss of harmony which leads to the forfeiture by a society of its power of self-determination... the loss of harmony between elements which had formerly coexisted in a society as an integral whole leads inevitably to an outbreak of social discord. The broken-down society is rent in two different dimensions simultaneously by the social schisms in which this discord is expressed. There are "vertical" schisms between geographically segregated communities, and "horizontal" schisms between geographically intermingled but socially segregated classes. In the vertical type of schism, the articulation of society into a number of parochial states gives rise to an internecine warfare...This warfare exhausts the energies of the society, before it brings itself to a violent end through a "knock-out blow" in which a single surviving state is left staggering among the corpses of its fellow-combatants...but at the same time we may observe that the vertical schism is perhaps not the most characteristic manifestation of the discord which propels a broken-down civilization into disintegration. The articulation of a society into parochial communities is, after all, a phenomenon which is common to the whole genus "human societies" and is not peculiar to the particular species "civilizations." The so-called "civilized" state is simply an imposing, high-powered version of the primitive tribe; and, while the internecine warfare between states in the bosom of a civilization is vastly more destructive in degree than the clashes of tribes within the bosom of a precivilizational society, this method of social suicide is merely an abuse of a potential instrument of self-destruction which is within reach of any society.[42]

The modern West, with its affinity for viewing anything outside the present tense (i.e., modernity) as hardly relevant, misses the chronologically bigger picture to which Toynbee, and other of our observers, continued making reference.

We conclude this chapter with a parallel often drawn in the twentieth century between ancient Rome, as described by Edward Gibbon, and the modern West, in this case as related by Francis Schaeffer:

Edward Gibbon, 1779. *Gibbon said five attributes marked Rome at its end: first, a mounting love of show and luxury (affluence); second, a widening gap between the very rich and the very poor (could be among countries as well as in a single nation); third, an obsession with sex; fourth, freakishness in the arts, masquerading as originality, and enthusiasms pretending to be creativity; and fifth, an increased desire to live off the state. "We have come a long road," said Francis Schaeffer, "and we are back in Rome."*

PD

> Edward Gibbon (1737–1794) in his *Decline and Fall of the Roman Empire* (1776–1788) said that the following five attributes marked Rome at its end: first, a mounting love of show and luxury (that is, affluence); second, a widening gap between the very rich and the very poor (this could be among countries in the family of nations as well as in a single nation); third, an obsession with sex; fourth, freakishness in the arts, masquerading as originality, and enthusiasms pretending to be creativity; fifth, an increased desire to live off the state. It all sounds so familiar. We have come a long road…and we are back in Rome.[43]

Are we back in Rome? Or are we in a new place in history unparalleled by any previous civilization's experience? I believe Western civilization in the twenty-first century is, in a sense, in both. The analogy to ancient Rome is appropriate because of unchanging human nature; yet the pervasive power of science and technology have utterly changed the world in a fashion unprecedented in world history. Of one thing we can be sure: Shaking off the self-delusion that is pandemic in the West is the critical first step if Western man has any hope of avoiding the graveyard of history.

END NOTES
CHAPTER 3

1 Arnold Toynbee, *Civilization on Trial* (New York: Oxford University Press, 1948), 63.
2 Pitirim A. Sorokin, *The Crisis of Our Age* (Oneworld Publications Ltd., 1941; this edition Sergei P. Sorokin and Peter P. Sorokin, 1992), 16.
3 Oswald Spengler, *The Decline of the West* (A. A. Knopf, University of Virginia, 1932), 29.
4 Christopher Dawson, *The Historic Reality of Christian Culture* (New York: Harper & Brothers, 1960), 23.
5 Samuel P. Huntington, *The Clash of Civilizations and the Remaking of World Order* (New York: Simon & Schuster, 1996), 173.
6 Spengler, *Decline of the West*, 73.
7 Alexander Pushkin and D. M. Thomas, *The Bronze Horseman: Selected Poems of Alexander Pushkin* (Viking Press, 1982), 67.
8 Philip Bagby, *Culture and History: Prolegomena to the Comparative Study of Civilizations* (Berkeley and Los Angeles: University of California Press, 1963), 21–22.
9 Huntington, *Clash of Civilizations*, 44.
10 Huntington, *Clash of Civilizations*, 301.
11 Toynbee, *Civilization on Trial*, 29.
12 Toynbee, *Civilization on Trial*, 38.
13 Toynbee, *Civilization on Trial*, 56.
14 Toynbee, *Civilization on Trial*, 29.
15 Bagby, *Culture and History*, 21–22.
16 Toynbee, *Civilization on Trial*, 24–25.
17 Toynbee, *Civilization on Trial*, 63.
18 Toynbee, *Civilization on Trial*, 248.
19 Dawson, *Historic Reality*, 22–23.
20 Dawson, *Historic Reality*, 23.
21 Immanuel Wallerstein, *The End of the World As We Know It: Social Science for the Twenty-First Century* (University of Minnesota Press, 1999), 16.
22 Sorokin, *Crisis of Our Age*, 21–22.
23 Sorokin, *Crisis of Our Age*, 16.
24 Sorokin, *Crisis of Our Age*, 20.
25 Toynbee, *Civilization on Trial*, 213.
26 Sorokin, *Crisis of Our Age*, 25.
27 Herbert Spencer, *Essays: Scientific, Political, and Speculative, Vol. 3, State Tamperings with Money and Banks* (Covent Garden, London: William & Norgate, 1891), 854.
28 Confucius (551–479 B.C.), cited in Richard Alan Krieger, *Civilization's Quotations: Life's Ideal* (Algora Publishing, 2003), 17.
29 Sorokin, *Crisis of Our Age*, 247.
30 Dawson, *Historic Reality*, 23.
31 Sorokin, *Crisis of Our Age*, 247.
32 Spengler, *Decline of the West*, 401.
33 Spengler, *Decline of the West*, 28.
34 Carroll Quigley, *The Evolution of Civilizations: An Introduction to Historical Analysis* (New York: Macmillan, 1961), 141.
35 Spengler, *Decline of the West*, 73.
36 Quigley, *Evolution of Civilizations*, 139.

37 Quigley, *Evolution of Civilizations*, 139.
38 Huntington, *Clash of Civilizations*, 82.
39 Huntington, *Clash of Civilizations*, 82.
40 Huntington, *Clash of Civilizations*, 82.
41 Toynbee, Arnold, *A Study of History* (London: Oxford University Press, 1961), 223.
42 Toynbee, *A Study of History*, 223.
43 Francis A. Schaeffer, *How Should We Then Live? The Rise and Decline of Western Thought and Culture* (Wheaton, IL: Crossway Books, A Division of Good News Publishers, 1976), 227.

CHAPTER

4

PERCEPTIONS OF REALITY AND CHOICES OF VALUES

The major premise of the sensory nature of the true reality and value is the root from which developed the tree of our sensate culture.…Its first positive fruit is an unprecedented development of the natural sciences and technological inventions. The first poisonous fruit is a fatal narrowing of the realm of true reality and true value.
Pitirim Sorokin[1]

…the loss of the ideology of Western civilization…will rest rather on the overemphasis on materialism and selfish individualism than it will on overemphasis of rationalism or spirituality.
Carroll Quigley[2]

How could proud sensate man fail to foresee his degradation, and why did he not prevent it?…no person and no special factor external to sensate society and culture produced the crisis. It developed within contractual sensate society itself, as a natural consequence of elements within that society.
Pitirim Sorokin[3]

Underlying every decision, trend, and event are individuals' perceptions of reality and their choices of values; one derives in some measure from the other and each influences the other. Sorokin asked in regard to the decline and decay of Western civilization: "The next problem is to find out how this crisis has come about. Why has this great tragedy happened? How could proud sensate man fail to foresee his degradation, and why did he not prevent it?" This is another form of the examination of Western civilization common to our observers. Since values are central to the individual's or the culture's well-being and future, it is essential that we examine Western man's values.

UNDERSTANDING VALUES—A HIGHLY SUBJECTIVE ENDEAVOR

Social scientists no doubt have insisted, for the most part, that they were seeking to be value-free.... But to be value-free in this sense does not at all mean that values, in the sense of decisions about the historical significance of observed phenomena, are absent.
Immanuel Wallerstein[4]

Understanding values with any objectivity can be difficult. Immanuel Wallerstein acknowledged that subjectivity is ever present in the social sciences and that even when we talk about values of a culture our own values influence those perceptions.

> This set of values, however we prefer to designate them—civilized values, secular–humanist values, modern values—permeates social science, as one might expect, since social science is a product of the same historical system that has elevated these values to the pinnacle of a hierarchy. Social scientists have incorporated such values in their definitions of the problems.... Social scientists no doubt have insisted, for the most part, that they were seeking to be value-free, insofar as they claimed they were not intentionally misreading or distorting the data because of their sociopolitical preferences. But to be value-free in this sense does not at all mean that values, in the sense of decisions about the historical significance of observed phenomena, are absent.... They are unable to ignore "values" in the sense of assessing social significance.[5]

Values influence our thinking even as we profess to be objectively studying values at arm's length. Rather than pretend to a pseudo-objectivity, we should acknowledge our subjectivity. As every student pilot learns, there will likely be some declination of their compass heading to true north. But simply being aware of it will permit some correction for its influence. In the years I taught international studies and political science as an adjunct university professor, I took pains to explain to students that there would be no pretense of a purely objective, "value-free" approach to the subject; such an effort is impossible. My duty to the students was to simply be overt and clear on the values that I believed in and that therefore shaped my view of the world. This is not the same as proselytizing for those values—though it might have that effect—but is simply a form of intellectual integrity.

VALUES ON THE SURFACE VERSUS VALUES IN THE DEPTHS

Far more significant than economics and demography are problems of moral decline, cultural suicide, and political disunity in the West.
Samuel Huntington[6]

We should now shift our focus, as we have already noted in other realms, from the surface, the usual cynosure of cultural analyses, to the depths; otherwise we will fail dismally to understand. Samuel Huntington, writing the most recently of all our observers, first referred to Quigley's identification of trends that denote a civilization in crisis. These trends are on the surface and, as Huntington observed, do not reach the greater depth that Huntington then confronts. Once again we descry the critically important theme of a distinction being made between the surface subjects most observers of our culture take into account in politics, economics, military power, immigration, population growth, social causes, etc., and the greater depth. Huntington declared, "Far more significant than economics and demography are problems of moral decline, cultural suicide, and political disunity in the West." Manifestations of this moral decline, he said, include the following:

- Increases in antisocial behavior, such as crime, drug use, and violence generally
- Family decay, including increased rates of divorce, illegitimacy, teen-age pregnancy, and single-parent families
- At least in the United States, a decline in "social capital," that is, membership in voluntary associations and the interpersonal trust associated with such membership
- General weakening of the work ethic and rise of a cult of personal indulgence
- Decreasing commitment to learning and intellectual activity, manifested in the United States in lower levels of scholastic achievement.

> The future health of the West and its influence on other societies depends in considerable measure on its success in coping with those trends, which, of course, give rise to the assertions of moral superiority by Muslims and Asians.[7]

The decay of the traditional Western values and the resultant sense of moral superiority it produces in the West's enemies is a significant psychological and tactical advantage for radical Islam and the terrorists it spawns. The West's moral decline is obvious to its enemies—it serves as a major propaganda resource for them—and encourages the belief that the defeat of the West by Islam or the ideology of a communist China, for example, is not only possible but inevitable.

As our observers' own analyses suggest, this view cannot be dismissed as an entirely irrational self-delusion. The horrendous spectacle of American soldiers using sexual debasement and intimidation against prisoners at Abu Ghraib was neither a completely isolated incident (it was in truth many incidents over an extended period of time) nor the actions of a depraved few, though these defenses and rationalizations were offered by the military and many apologists for the indefensible. To the contrary it was a glimpse into the pit of American culture; an insight into a range of depravities that is—in other simulated or actual forms—on display any night on American television screens or in movie theatres.

Courtesy of Jacob Lundberg. CC

Islamist demonstration outside Danish Embassy in London, February 2006.

Sorokin also understood what much of the West's "dominant minority" do not: that struggles over the forms of government, forms of economic structure, over tyranny, and even wars themselves, are "but small side issues—mere by-products of the main issue." For him that "main issue" is expressed as "the sensate form of culture and way of life versus another, different form."[8] We might wonder how Sorokin would have viewed the West today over a half century after he wrote. News produced in thirty-second sound bites that regards the dissipations of entertainers and sports stars as newsworthy can hardly be given weight by a serious mind. Yet this is a reflection of the values of our age: materialistic, sensate, and effete.

The importance of communicating the significance of the issue of sensate versus ideational or idealistic culture and the relative inconsequence of what may appear to be issues of seeming great pith and moment is ever present in Sorokin's work. "Hence the magnitude of the crisis of our time... it nevertheless signifies one of the greatest possible revolutions in our culture and social life. As such, it is infinitely deeper and more significant than the partisans of the 'ordinary crisis' imagine."[9]

A CHAOS OF BELIEFS AND VALUES

Western culture has ceased to be a selective organism. Instead, it has become a vast cultural dumping place where everything is dumped, without any restriction. It has lost its own physiognomy, its own soul and its discriminative ability.
Pitirim Sorokin[10]

The weakening of the value system that supported the development of a civilization leads ultimately to what Toynbee called "*pammixia*," the incongruous mixing of values, ideas, and ideology that are in fundamental conflict with one another in an intellectual and emotional stew that accelerates the civilization's decline.

Consistent with his focus on the inner life of the individual as the paramount feature of history, Toynbee related the increasing internal amorphousness of Western man's beliefs and sense of direction to the broader cultural confusion—like a painting exposed too long to intense, humid heat resulting in an undirected running together of hues and shapes. That which was once clearly defined and striking in its vividness and order has become increasingly formless and dissipated.

> The personal sense of drift has a social counterpart in the feeling of cultural anomie—a total loss of all sense of particularized form and style which is the inverse of the process of the differentiation of civilizations through growth. The soul surrenders itself to the melting-pot, and a negative sense of cultural promiscuity then comes to pervade every sphere of social activity. In the sphere of social intercourse it results in a blending of incongruous traditions and in a compounding of incompatible values (*pammixia*); in the media of language and literature and visual art it declares itself in the currency of a lingua franca or koine, and of a similarly standardized composite style of literature and painting and sculpture and architecture; in the realm of philosophy and religion it produces ritual and theological syncretisms.[11]

In the West in our time, the touting of diversity as an honored value is, in itself, a manifestation of the historical trend Toynbee described. This breakdown in beliefs and values is most obvious in the culture's leadership, what Toynbee called "the dominant minority."

> Of the three factions into which a disintegrating society is apt to split, it is the dominant minority that succumbs most readily to the sense of promiscuity. The mentally or physically uprooted expatriates who form the internal proletariat tend not only to keep a firm hold upon the remnants of their native heritage, but even manage to impart some of this to their masters; and the external proletariat, insulated from the radiation of a dying civilization by the erection of an impassable military frontier, tends on the whole to sustain its vigorous barbarian culture until the moment at which it finally overruns the ruined civilization.[12]

Of all our observers, perhaps none reflected as deeply as did Sorokin on this tendency of decaying civilizations to interpose conflicting values and beliefs. Here too, the similarities in the thinking of these key observers are striking. "*Pammixia*" is the word favored by Toynbee; "chaotic syncretism" is Sorokin's term. But the connotations are much the same. Like Toynbee, Sorokin's analysis anticipated the exaltation of diversity in present day Western culture. Though this is an overt manifestation in the latest generation of the West of the phenomenon they described, it has, in truth, been present and gaining momentum in the culture for generations.

> An emergence of a chaotic syncretism in a given integrated culture is another general symptom of its disintegration. The classical example is given by the over-ripe sensate culture of Greece and Rome. In that stage it became, in the words of Tacitus, "the common sink into which everything infamous and abominable flows like a torrent from all quarters of the world"..... The reason for such a syncretism as a sign of the disintegration is evident.[13]

The phrasing "only such values as did not contradict its soul" is telling and highly descriptive of a process in the West that has advanced—or degenerated, depending on your own values—markedly since Sorokin wrote these words. His prescience in noting this trend should have the effect of corroborating his credibility generally. He saw in the mid-twentieth century that "Western culture has ceased to be a selective organism. Instead, it has become a vast cultural dumping place where everything is dumped, without any restriction. It has lost its own physiognomy, its own soul and its discriminative ability."[14]

The loss of the "discriminative ability" is the most dangerous of the symptoms of the West's condition. This becomes to the intellect and the soul what the gradual ingestion of bits of carrion or arsenic would be to the body; the effect may not be immediately obvious, but it will eventually prove catastrophic.

PD-art

Tacitus *observed that the sensate culture of late Rome became "the common sink into which everything infamous and abominable flows like a torrent from all quarters of the world." This aptly describes the state of modern Western civilization—a condition Toynbee called "*pammixia*" and Sorokin called "chaotic syncretism."*

THE ESSENTIAL DIFFERENCE: A NARROW MATERIALIST OR A BROAD SPIRITUAL VIEW

The systems of Plato and Aristotle, of Albertus Magnus and Saint Thomas Aquinas, are the supreme examples, attempting to embrace in one organic whole divine as well as sensory and dialectic truth.
Pitirim Sorokin[15]

Sorokin told us that "Any integrated society has ethical ideals and values as the highest manifestation of its ethical consciousness."[16] Sorokin's classification of all cultures as ideational, sensate or idealistic was the beginning point for a distinction among their values. Western culture metamorphosed from ideational to sensate and today, in Sorokin's view, would perhaps be the most sensate of any civilization ever. The distinctions between sensate, ideational, and idealistic cultures refine our understanding of how Sorokin perceived culture and chose his preferences. How this translates into a culture's values, particularly its ethics, is best understood when Sorokin's three forms of culture, as manifested in ethics, are juxtaposed.

The ideational system has key characteristics in common, regardless of where it is found: "Different in form but similar in content are the ethical systems of Hinduism, Buddhism, Taoism, Zoroastrianism, Judaism and any other ideational mentality. They all see the supreme ethical value not in this sensory world but in the supersensory world of God or the Absolute." The consequence of this god-centered viewpoint is "ideational ethics" that aim "not at an increase of the sensory happiness and pleasures of this world but at the union with the Absolute, which is supersensory. The norms of such ethics are regarded as revealed by, or emanating from, the Absolute; therefore as absolute, unconditional, unchangeable and eternal."

This view is "the very opposite of the sensate system." For its "main concern is with God and his kingdom as the true reality. Therefore revealed religion and theology become the queen of genuine wisdom and science, empirical knowledge serving as a mere handmaid. The mentality dominated by the truth of faith is dedicated to the eternal verities, in contra-distinction to the temporal truth of the senses."[17]

> Such a unified system of culture, based upon the principle of a supersensory and super-rational God as the only true reality and value, may be called ideational. A basically similar major premise respecting the super-rational and supersensory reality of God, though differently perceived in its properties, underlay also the integrated culture of Brahmanic India, the Buddhist and Taoist cultures, Greek culture from the eighth to the end of the sixth century B.C., and some other cultures. They have all been predominantly ideational. The decline of medieval culture consisted precisely in the disintegration of this ideational system of culture.[18]

The sensate viewpoint dominating the modern West produces an "ethical system that regards sensory happiness, pleasure, utility and comfort, in their refined or unrefined form, as the supreme value...."[19]

> Their supreme aim is to increase the sum of sensate happiness, pleasure, utility and comfort, because they do not believe in any supersensory value. Their rules are therefore not absolute but relative, expedient and changeable, according to the persons, groups and situations involved. They are

PD-art.

Plato and Aristotle in *The School of Athens*, by Raffaello Sanzio, 1509. *These pre-Christian philosophers, according to Sorokin, believed in "the idealistic system of truth [that] occupies an intermediary position between the sensate and ideational systems, blending in its crucible the three distinct elements of sensory, religious and rationalistic truth." Contrary to modern Western practice, they did not believe the search for truth could be compartmentalized or divided but must be pursued as a unitary whole.*

Albertus Magnus, 1352, fresco by Tommaso da Modena. *Magnus, like Thomas Aquinas and the pre-Christian Plato and Aristotle, believed the search for truth and meaning cannot be compartmentalized into science (i.e., the material world) and religion (i.e., the spiritual world) as has since been attempted in Western civilization. Truth can only be pursued holistically, encompassing both manifestations of reality.*

PD-art

> regarded as man-made rules. If they serve the purpose of happiness, they are acceptable; if they do not, they may be discarded.[20]

Here I believe Sorokin makes an error. A common practice in the modern West is to reinterpret or "amend" transcendent divine laws so as to make the new rules appear to be other-worldly in their origin and thus lend them an authority they would not have as purely man-made. In this sense we see the culture showing some deference, albeit hypocritical, to its earlier beliefs grounded in faith and the conviction that there is a supra-human divine moral law. Though the new rules are in fact man-made, much effort may be expended to characterize them otherwise.

The breakdown of the ideational system in Western civilization began "at the end of the twelfth century, when there emerged the germ of a new—and profoundly different—major principle, namely, that the true reality and value is sensory. Only what we see, hear, smell, touch and otherwise perceive through our sense organs is real and has value. Beyond such a sensory reality either there is nothing, or, if there is something, we cannot sense it; therefore it is equivalent to the non-real and the non-existent."[21] This viewpoint came to dominate every aspect of the modern Western world "in its arts and sciences, philosophy and pseudo-religion, ethics and law; in its social, economic and political organization; in its dominant ways of life and mentality." [22]

For Sorokin, the idealistic culture was the zenith to which man can aspire in cultural forms. "...the idealistic system of truth occupies an intermediary position between the sensate and ideational systems, blending in its crucible the three distinct elements of sensory, religious and rationalistic truth. The systems of Plato and Aristotle, of Albertus Magnus and Saint Thomas Aquinas, are the supreme examples, attempting to embrace in one organic whole divine as well as sensory and dialectic truth." [23]

This is simply another way of asserting the point made by several of our observers: the search for truth and meaning cannot be compartmentalized into science (i.e., the material world) and religion (i.e., the spiritual/philosophical world) as has been attempted in Western civilization. Truth can only be pursued holistically, encompassing both manifestations of reality. In this respect, the Scopes "Monkey Trial," and most related battles between the advocates of evolution and those of creationism, are sometimes struggles between equally narrow and misguided perspectives.

Yorck Project

Thomas Aquinas, by Franciso de Zurbaran, 1631. *Aquinas, one of the great minds in Western philosophy, followed the path of Plato and Aristotle in "attempting to embrace in one organic whole divine as well as sensory and dialectic truth." Aquinas observed the extraordinary "order" in everything "apprehended by man" that could only be explained in terms of a Divine hand.*

The idealistic viewpoint produces "ethical norms" that are a "synthesis of ideational and sensate values. Like ideational ethics, idealist ethics perceives the highest value in God or the supersensory Absolute; but, in contradistinction to ideationalism, it views positively those sensory values that are the noblest and that do not militate against the Absolute."[24]

Scopes Trial, 20 July 1925, showing William Jennings Bryan and Clarence Darrow. *The search for truth and meaning cannot be compartmentalized into science (i.e., the material world) and religion (i.e., the spiritual world) as has been attempted in Western civilization. Truth can only be pursued holistically, encompassing both manifestations of reality. In this respect, the Scopes "Monkey Trial" and most related battles between the advocates of evolution and those of creationism, are sometimes struggles between equally narrow and misguided perspectives.*

Photograph by Watson Davis. PD from Smithsonian Institution Archives.

The distinguishing feature of sensate culture is the rejection of a Supreme Being as the highest value and ultimate arbiter of the universe and man's fate. Though lip service may be given in the decaying culture to the notion of God—or even an abstract belief in God—all truth upon which the culture acts is ultimately sensate: only that which can be perceived and understood by the senses is valid or credible.

In his introduction to Oswald Spengler's work, *The Decline of the West*, Arthur Helps noted Spengler's similar recognition that the conflict between the materialist sensory view of the Western world and belief in a spiritual realm as the supreme, greater reality is the greatest of many "tensions" of our time: "On one point Spengler is very definite. The polarity between the pull of the visible and the invisible worlds is more important than other tensions—for example, that between East and West.... Spengler perceives that the balance will swing and the invisible will regain the hold over the Western world that it is has lost since the Middle Ages."[25]

Sorokin, similarly, tells us that the sensate culture cannot survive because it lacks this immutable and transcendent value in the form of the centrality of belief in God and a higher moral law not subject to amendment by man. This leads inexorably to the central issue and crisis of our time.

THE INEVITABLE REGRESSION: A MATERIALIST, SENSATE VIEWPOINT LEADS TO A RELATIVIST REALITY

From the same system of truth and values follows the doctrine of relativism. Since everything is temporal and subject to incessant change, and since sensory perception differs in the case of different organisms, individuals and groups, nothing absolute exists. Everything becomes relative....
Pitirim Sorokin[26]

The term "sensate culture" is of course itself highly suggestive: it implies domination of thought and behavior by materialism, pleasure-seeking and the exaltation of man and his achievements. "In such a culture, material values naturally become paramount, beginning with omnipotent wealth and ending with all the values that satisfy man's physiological needs and material comfort. Sensory utility and pleasure, as we shall see, become the sole criteria of what is good and bad."[27]

Yet it is important to recognize that many fig leaves are sewn together to conceal these primitive pursuits beneath. Western man strives to rationalize and justify his extravagant acquisitiveness and self-indulgence. This sham and charade are the consequence of his waning awareness of the earlier set of values: the stalwart wife who always stood by him and supported him, whom he has since thrown over for the meretricious charms of his new lover of low repute—and one of supreme fickleness at that. He is striving to convince not just others but himself that this is the "right thing to do," that he will not "be happy" without his new love; that life must be seized in true *carpe diem* fashion before it is too late.

Behind this value system is a perception of reality that sets man adrift from the *terra firma* that characterizes an ideational or idealistic culture. In the absence of belief in an immutable law and a transcendent God, the human mind is, as Sorokin put it, "dominated" by the senses.

> A further consequence of such a system of truth is the development of a temporalistic, relativistic and nihilistic mentality. The sensory world is in a state of incessant flux and becoming. There is nothing unchangeable in it—not even an eternal Supreme Being. Mind dominated by the truth of the senses simply cannot perceive any permanency, but apprehends all values in terms of shift and transformation. Sensate mentality views everything from the standpoint of evolution and progress. This leads to an increasing neglect of the eternal values, which come to be replaced by temporary, or short-time, considerations. Sensate society lives in, and appreciates mainly, the present. Since the past is irretrievable and no longer exists, while the future is not yet here and is uncertain, only the present moment is real and desirable. [28]

The natural consequence of this narrow perspective is an expedient *mutatis mutandis* in ethics and morality. Sexual mores are whatever the culture decides they are; conspicuously perverse or abnormal behavior is characterized as simply a different "orientation" or lifestyle; and the killing of an unborn child is nothing more than a choice. Sorokin explained how the material view of life, his "sensate" culture, undermines everything noble and stable through a non-nuclear chain reaction that ultimately spreads its own toxic radiation through every corner of the culture.

> From the same system of truth and values follows the doctrine of relativism. Since everything is temporal and subject to incessant change, and since sensory perception differs in the case of different organisms, individuals and groups, nothing absolute exists. Everything becomes relative—truth and error, moral and aesthetic considerations, and what not. A thing may be good today and bad tomorrow; in a given set of conditions a proposition may appear to be true and under other conditions false. Sensory observation shows that scientific, philosophical, religious, moral, aesthetic and other values, norms and beliefs vary according to the individual, the group, and the period.... Hence [sensate culture's] negative attitude toward any absolute whatsoever. [29]

We would draw attention to the phrase "the period," Sorokin's reference to the relativistic practice of regarding value and truth as malleable through the passage of time.

One of the more common manifestations of this thinking is the practice—implied, if not stated—of assuming that modernity reflects the latest and best. As the perceptive student of history learns, the

Marx, Engels, Lenin, Stalin, and Mao. *All embraced a relativist view of life; there was, for each, no God and no higher law to which they were accountable. The natural consequence of this narrow perspective is an expedient* mutatis mutandis *in ethics and morality. Undermining everything noble and stable through a non-nuclear chain reaction, it ultimately spreads its own toxic radiation through every corner of the culture. The result is catastrophic for mankind.*

maxim "there is nothing new under the sun" applies to all of human behavior. What we may perceive as "new" may in fact be very old; the sensate, materialist view of life is a classic example.

Soldiers who have experienced the more extreme forms of combat speak of seeing comrades "atomized" by exploding artillery rounds or mines. The integrity of the physical system that produced the marvelous unity of the human body is utterly destroyed by the expedient of separating it violently into incoherent parts. This is an apt metaphor for the effect of relativism on the cultural "body" that once formed a coherent cultural unity. Sorokin continued, "But relativism, once accepted, inevitably becomes more and more uncompromising, until finally all relative truths and values are completely 'relativized' and reduced, so to speak, to atoms. Sooner or later, relativism thus gives place to scepticism, cynicism and nihilism. The very boundary line between the true and the false, between right and wrong, disappears, and society finds itself in a state of veritable mental, moral and cultural anarchy."[30]

Red flags, shrieks of alarm, and sirens should be set off in the minds of thinking persons exposed to relativism. This view of life is a minefield of cynicism, nihilism, fickleness, and mistrust. No one can safely trust anyone or anything in such a culture. Suspicion would be the healthy rather than the paranoid response to this environment. Law becomes whatever the dominant forces in the culture say it is (these forces may not even be a majority; just more powerful). "Morality" becomes the dictate of the forces that most profoundly influence the culture, regardless of their wisdom, altruism, maturity, or personal integrity.

Once "necessary" changes have been made in the different dimensions of the culture to accommodate the sensate viewpoint, truth has been savaged and an ersatz version substituted. The primitivism in this *modus operandi* of life is appalling, yet modern Western culture perceives it as sophisticated and advanced. "Since sensory cognition does not seek anything absolute (including valid truth, independent of sensory peculiarities), and since it views any 'truth' as a mere means of adaptation to the sensory universe, designed to make life pleasanter or less painful, the propositions and theories that prove to be useful, enjoyable and convenient become authentic, whereas those that prove to be useless, inconvenient, or non-economical are regarded as false."[31]

But such a view of life is conspicuously expedient—a cobra that eventually bites anyone who insists on holding it, if only by the tail. A relativistic world is the playground, the hunting grounds, for the manipulator and the tyrant. He who can most effectively contrive, manipulate, and deceive becomes the top of the food chain in this jungle.

TRUTH MUTATES INTO "IDEAS IN CONFLICT WITH REALITY"

But our purpose here is different: to note first that we have here a classic example of an idea in conflict with reality.
Robert Conquest[32]

The natural regression of a sensate/materialist view to the expedients of relativism continues with greater and greater mutations of truth and value into the artificial, the contrived, the superficial, and the dissolution of any accurate grasp of reality itself. This is facilitated by a practice Sorokin, as well as several of our observers, noted: the subordination of metaphysics, philosophy and religion beneath the "practical" disciplines in a trend that has been dominant in Western culture for generations: denying the former's validity while elevating the latter to the status of a secular religion—the only source of truth. Sorokin put it this way:

> Science and philosophy, as we have seen, come to be imbued with utilitarian aims. Only those disciplines which, like physics and chemistry, biology and medicine, geology and geography, technology, politics and economics, are eminently practical and serviceable are intensively cultivated. Hence the aforesaid progress of the natural and technological sciences. Other disciplines, either metaphysics and "nonpragmatic" philosophy, or transcendental religion and absolute ethics, are relatively ignored. In so far as they are cherished, they assume the same utilitarian, sensory and pragmatic, or instrumental, character. Psychology, as a science of the human soul, turns out to be a physiology of the nervous system and its reflexes.[33]

This mutation of truth into an expedient "reality" is not peculiar solely to the secular realms of society. It transmogrifies religion in a similar fashion. Theology mutates into ideology. A common manifestation of this is on abject display all across the West every Sunday morning. Sorokin described it thusly: "Religion, as a revelation of God, degenerates into a second-hand 'social gospel'—a sort of political creed."[34]

With biting contempt Sorokin described this same process in the discipline of philosophy.

> Philosophy, as the cognition of essences and true reality, with presuppositions of knowledge, becomes a vague ideology devoted to either the justification or the castigation of this or that system of sensory values and appearances; or a mere generalization based upon the conclusions of utilitarian natural science...or a demonstration of the non-existence of anything save sensory reality; or, ultimately, a system of negative criticism, agnosticism and scepticism (we cannot know any true reality; even if

> we did, we could not express it; if we did somehow express it, we could not convey this knowledge to others). In short, philosophy turns out to be a second-class sensory utilitarian science...all marked by the same utilitarian and economical traits. And so with other disciplines. *Savoir pour pouvoir* becomes one of the supreme criteria. Anything that does not permit a utilitarian control tends to be neglected; anything that does is elevated to the dignity of a scientific or valid proposition.... The essential character of this logico-sensory fabric of thought is revealed by the fact that the terms "scientific" and "true," "unscientific" and "false," are used as synonymous.[35]

Sorokin seems to be alluding to Auguste Comte's lemma to the effect: *voir pour prevoir, prevoir pour pourvoir* (see in order to foresee, foresee in order to provide). (We will address the problems of, and the methods for, learning the truth in the chapter "Seeking Truth—Through a Glass Darkly.")

Since sensate culture cannot tolerate that which is philosophically contrary to its core beliefs, it must somehow twist and stretch all to fit its peculiar Procrustean bed. Sensate culture's constricted viewpoint denies truth beyond its own narrowly defined boundaries.

> The foregoing characterization of the sensate system of truth, science and culture ...has dominated Western society for the past four centuries. Our principal body of truth is scientific. Our science is primarily a nexus of empirical, sensory knowledge derived from observation of, and experimentation with, sensory facts. Some elements of the logical truth of reason—certain basic concepts, including mathematicological conclusions—it undoubtedly contains. But even such concepts and deductions are valid only in so far as they are corroborated by sensory experience.[36]

The truth in Sorokin's observation that Western culture now equates "scientific" with "true" and anything else as beyond the pale of reason is obvious in the most superficial manifestations of popular culture. Every "authority" or spokesperson for an idea or cause rushes to label their conclusions or views as "scientific" and strives to avoid having them stigmatized as "unscientific." The intellectual conformity is appalling, as is the effect on true understanding.

Auguste Comte. *Sorokin seems to be alluding to Auguste Comte's lemma to the effect* voir pour prevoir, prevoir pour pourvoir *(see in order to foresee, foresee in order to provide) when he writes "Anything that does not permit a utilitarian control tends to be neglected; anything that does is elevated to the dignity of a scientific or valid proposition. The essential character of this logico-sensory fabric of thought is revealed by the fact that the terms 'scientific' and 'true,' 'unscientific,' and 'false' are used as synonymous."*

PD-art.

UNDER WHICH SYSTEM CAN MAN FIND FREEDOM AND FULFILLMENT?

[Sensate culture] leads to an incessant struggle of men and groups for as large a share of sensate values—wealth, love, pleasure, comfort, sensory safety, security—one can get. Since one can get them mainly at the cost of somebody else, their quest accentuates and intensifies the struggle of individuals and groups.
Pitirim Sorokin[37]

Taking his juxtaposition of the three cultural forms further, Sorokin distinguished between the primary methods by which a human being can seek fulfillment and freedom from desire:

> A person can therefore become free in two different ways: either by decreasing his wishes to make them equal to or smaller than the means of their satisfaction, or by expanding his wishes and increasing proportionally the means of their satisfaction. The first is the way of ideational liberty, consisting in a reduction of one's wishes, especially sensory ones. The second is the way of sensate liberty, consisting in an ever-increasing expansion of one's wishes for sensory values, accompanied by an equal or greater expansion of the means of satisfying them.[38]
>
> . . .
>
> . . .Ideational liberty is inner liberty, rooted in the restraint and control of our desires, wishes and lusts. It is the liberty of Job with his imperturbable, "The Lord gave, and the Lord hath taken away; blessed be the name of the Lord." Such a liberty does not multiply sensory wishes; it does not lead to an incessant struggle for an ever-increasing expansion of the means of their satisfaction—wealth, power, fame and what not. It is little interested in political and civil rights, in the external guarantees of such rights, such as constitutions and political declarations. Its 'kingdom is not of this world'. On the other hand, it is inalienable—unconquerable by anybody or anything external.[39]

Sorokin's description of sensate "liberty" reminds us of Carroll Quigley's diagnosis of Western civilization: "After centuries of expansion our society is now organized so that it cannot subsist; it must expand or it will collapse." For not only is "sensate liberty" the opposite of "ideational liberty," it "strives to expand endlessly both wishes and the means of their satisfaction. The more one has the more one wants. There is no limit to the expansion of sensory desires, and, according to the modified Weber–Fechner law, the discrepancy between what one has and what one wants increases progressively in a vicious circle."[40] Thus Quigley reached a conclusion that is founded in Sorokin's characterization of the true dynamics of Western culture. To say Western man has overextended himself is an understatement of grand proportions.

As we warned earlier, the sensate/materialist/relativistic viewpoint should alarm the observant and alert. Contrary to its promise of happiness and contentment, it sets up dynamics that lead in a completely different direction.

> Such a liberty leads to an incessant struggle of men and groups for as large a share of sensate values —wealth, love, pleasure, comfort, sensory safety, security—one can get. Since one can get them mainly at the cost of somebody else, their quest accentuates and intensifies the struggle of individuals and groups. Sensate liberty is thus mainly external. It is vitally interested in the external reconstruction of social, economic, and political conditions in guarantees of freedom of speech, of the press and of thought, and of other "inalienable rights of man." For this reason it leads to political

PD

Job, by Bonnat, 1880. *Sorokin referred to "inner liberty, rooted in the restraint and control of our desires, wishes and lusts. It is the liberty of Job with his imperturbable, 'The Lord gave, and the Lord hath taken away; blessed be the name of the Lord.' Such a liberty does not multiply sensory wishes; it does not lead to an incessant struggle for an ever-increasing expansion of the means of their satisfaction—wealth, power, fame, and what not."*

> and economic struggle: each group or person wants to gain as many rights as possible, either by snatching them from others or by sensibly entering into a contractual compromise guaranteeing a minimum number to all the contracting parties.[41]

Sorokin has brought us across the recurring tracks of another Western "value" that promises much but delivers more than expected: competition. We will discuss this central dynamic to Western civilization in a later chapter; suffice it to note here that competition is the method by which the sensate/materialist/relativistic viewpoint is most often expressed.

When viewed with this deeper insight, the implications of man's choices of which to embrace become striking. Wars, rumors of wars, social unrest—and the collapse of whole civilizations—become not only logical but inevitable under one system and ever so remote and improbable under the other. Sorokin's allusion to the Old Testament account of Job echoes the apostle Paul's declaration in the New Testament: "I am not saying this because I am in need, for I have learned to be content whatever the circumstances." (Philippians 4:11) Nothing, as Sorokin is pointing out, could contrast more completely with the thinking and attitudes of Western man in our age.

ARE MODERN WESTERN VALUES OF ANY VALUE?

...they hardly ever stop to ask whether the culture they stand for is really worth saving—whether, on the contrary, it would not be better for it to perish.
Pitirim Sorokin[42]

Sorokin was relentless and uncompromising in his condemnation of sensate culture, damning any notion of salvaging it. In the following passage, Sorokin seemed, however, to expect a level of insight and understanding that, by definition and diagnosis, would be denied to the advocates and practitioners of sensate culture. Operating on the shallow plane of sensate materialism, their frame of reference is narrowly drawn and deprives them of the broader view and the grander aspirations. At most they will merely sense—perhaps in those moments of lessened activity or during personal crisis or pain—that something is amiss. An inner void is the unacknowledged reality of a purposeless life.

> Moreover, they hardly ever stop to ask whether the culture they stand for is really worth saving—whether, on the contrary, it would not be better for it to perish. As we shall see, many of the values of the contemporary culture they advocate hardly deserve being fought for. A large portion of these are already dead and await only a decent burial. Their disappearance is a benefit to humanity rather than a loss—a liberation from poison rather than an impoverishment of culture...[43]

This of course puts the issue very pointedly—and well it should. But Western man is not even asking the question, much less gaining insight into the honest answer.

Sorokin put his views in a historical context.

> ...the present trouble represents the disintegration of the sensate form of Western culture and society, which emerged at the end of the twelfth century and gradually replaced the declining ideational form

> of medieval culture. For the past four centuries it has been dominant. In the period of its ascendancy and climax it created the most magnificent cultural values in most of the compartments of Western culture. During these centuries it wrote one of the most brilliant pages in human history. However, no finite form, either ideational or sensate, is eternal. Sooner or later it is bound to exhaust its creative abilities. When this moment comes, it begins to disintegrate and decline. So it has happened several times before...so it is happening now with our sensate form....[44]

Use of the phrase "creative abilities" is congruent with Toynbee's emphasis on "creative responses" by the individual and the culture to the challenges of their time—the absence of which signal decline and collapse. Sorokin declaimed against the sensory value system of the West in uncompromising terms: "...a value that is no longer universal becomes a pseudo-value, a plaything of individual fancy and wishes."[45]

REINFORCING THE CONFORMING THINKING AND BEHAVIOR

Without any censorship, in the West fashionable trends of thought and ideas are carefully separated from those which are not fashionable; nothing is forbidden, but what is not fashionable will hardly ever find its way into periodicals or books or be heard in colleges.
Alexander Solzhenitsyn[46]

As with all human behavior, reinforcement nurtures the trait. Sorokin noted that Western man had been reinforced mightily by his apparent "success" in the nineteenth century in the materialist/sensate viewpoint: "The success of the nineteenth century...warranted the general optimism of Western society respecting 'bigger and better' progress; man's capacity to build, without the invocation of any supernatural power, in his own right and by his own efforts, a better, more free, more just and more noble society; his ability to eliminate most social evils—crime, exploitation (including the remnants of slavery and serfdom) and autocracy. All of this seemed to be a 'road' that pointed 'to ever fairer prospects.'"[47]

We see more clearly that the philosophical and spiritual gravitas—if we might even call it that—of Western man lies lightly, as dew on blades of grass. Nor does it gain depth or mass since it is self-reinforcing—and demanding of conformity.

Robert Conquest noted one dimension of this in our sensate culture's predilection for the shallow and frivolous—which gains a hearing at the expense of the deep and meaningful: "It is true that movements as such should not be judged by their more extreme adherents. The trouble is rather that it is precisely the sensationalist views that gain the public ear in best-sellers, articles, television programs, and, often, the status of a constituency."[48]

Conquest's assertions harmonize with those of Alexander Solzhenitsyn in his 1978 Harvard address.

> Without any censorship, in the West fashionable trends of thought and ideas are carefully separated from those which are not fashionable; nothing is forbidden, but what is not fashionable will hardly

> ever find its way into periodicals or books or be heard in colleges. Legally your researchers are free, but they are conditioned by the fashion of the day. There is no open violence such as in the East; however, a selection dictated by fashion and the need to match mass standards frequently prevent independent-minded people from giving their contribution to public life. There is a dangerous tendency to form a herd, shutting off successful development. I have received letters in America from highly intelligent persons, maybe a teacher in a faraway small college who could do much for the renewal and salvation of his country, but his country cannot hear him because the media are not interested in him. This gives birth to strong mass prejudices, blindness, which is most dangerous in our dynamic era.[49]

Truth is not defined by fashion, modernity, the views and choices of cultural arbiters, or even by democratic plebiscite. Yet when a culture's perceptions of truth are determined in any of these, or similar, ways, not only will morality erode, but contact with reality with it.

Initially, primarily the individual pays the price for the deprecation of reason and reality; eventually, an entire civilization will. The gatekeepers and social arbiters who make up this *demimonde* of reasonless and morality-deprived unnatural selection could not even fit within the logic of one of their heroes, Charles Darwin, whose theories were based on the notion of some—oxymoronic though it sounds, and should sound—rational order to nature's random choices.

Sorokin predicted it all. "All this means that sensory truth, when made exclusive, inevitably develops into a kind of illusionism in which it undermines itself. Instead of valid cognition of the true reality and values, it increasingly gives us relative and conditional hints respecting the ever-fleeting shadows of ever-changing sensory impressions, which differ with different individuals, groups and conditions."[50]

Movement away from God is synonymous, congruent, or inevitably follows with, movement away from reality. They are the same.

> With the degradation of truth, man is dragged down from his lofty pedestal as a seeker after truth, as an absolute value, to the level of an animal who tends, by means of various "ideologies," "rationalizations," and "derivations," to exalt his greed, his appetites and his egoism. When he does this unwittingly, he becomes a simpleton; when he deliberately resorts to such rationalizations, appealing to "truth" and other high-sounding names, he becomes a downright hypocrite who employs "truth" as a mere smoke screen in order to justify his "residues" and complexes. In either case the result is disastrous to the dignity of man and to the cause of truth and science.[51]

This powerful and grave insight spotlights a form of hypocrisy that suffuses much of what is touted and advanced in Western culture as important or valuable to the society. But it is a sham devised for ultimately self-serving purposes. Thus the greatest lies may be told with alacrity in pursuit of what man wants. Amidst the delirium of Western man's infatuation with himself, cosseted by materialistic gain and sensual gratification and complacent in his ersatz security, he defines truth and value as he will. But neither God nor the laws of the universe will be mocked.

END NOTES
CHAPTER 4

1 Pitirim A. Sorokin, *The Crisis of Our Age* (Oneworld Publications Ltd., 1941; this edition Sergei P. Sorokin and Peter P. Sorokin, 1992), 252–253.
2 Carroll Quigley, *The Evolution of Civilizations: An Introduction to Historical Analysis* (New York: Macmillan, 1961), 347.
3 Sorokin, *The Crisis of Our Age*, 159–160.
4 Immanuel Wallerstein, *The End of the World As We Know It: Social Science for the Twenty-First Century* (Minneapolis: University of Minnesota Press, 1999), 173.
5 Wallerstein, *The End of the World As We Know It*, 173.
6 Samuel P. Huntington, *The Clash of Civilizations and the Remaking of World Order* (New York: Simon & Schuster, 1996), 304.
7 Huntington, *Clash of Civilizations*, 304.
8 Sorokin, *Crisis of Our Age*, 20.
9 Sorokin, *Crisis of Our Age*, 24–25.
10 Sorokin, *Crisis of Our Age*, 203.
11 Arnold Toynbee, *A Study of History* (New York: Weathervane Books, 1972), 244.
12 Toynbee, *A Study of History*, 244–245.
13 Sorokin, *Crisis of Our Age*, 201–202.
14 Sorokin, *Crisis of Our Age*, 203.
15 Sorokin, *Crisis of Our Age*, 85.
16 Sorokin, *Crisis of Our Age*, 109.
17 Sorokin, *Crisis of Our Age*, 85.
18 Sorokin, *Crisis of Our Age*, 18.
19 Sorokin, *Crisis of Our Age*, 111.
20 Sorokin, *Crisis of Our Age*, 112.
21 Sorokin, *Crisis of Our Age*, 18.
22 Sorokin, *Crisis of Our Age*, 19.
23 Sorokin, *Crisis of Our Age*, 84.
24 Sorokin, *Crisis of Our Age*, 112–113.
25 Oswald Spengler, *The Decline of the West* (New York: A. A. Knopf, 1932), xiii.
26 Sorokin, *Crisis of Our Age*, 81.
27 Sorokin, *Crisis of Our Age*, 80.
28 Sorokin, *Crisis of Our Age*, 80.
29 Sorokin, *Crisis of Our Age*, 81.
30 Sorokin, *Crisis of Our Age*, 81.
31 Sorokin, *Crisis of Our Age*, 83.
32 Robert Conquest, *Reflections on a Ravaged Century* (New York: W. W. Norton, 2000), 200.
33 Sorokin, *Crisis of Our Age*, 83.
34 Sorokin, *Crisis of Our Age*, 83.
35 Sorokin, *Crisis of Our Age*, 83–85.
36 Sorokin, *Crisis of Our Age*, 85.
37 Sorokin, *Crisis of Our Age*, 143–144.

38 Sorokin, *Crisis of Our Age*, 143.
39 Sorokin, *Crisis of Our Age*, 143–144.
40 Sorokin, *Crisis of Our Age*, 143.
41 Sorokin, *Crisis of Our Age*, 143–144.
42 Sorokin, *Crisis of Our Age*, 24–25.
43 Sorokin, *Crisis of Our Age*, 24–25.
44 Sorokin, *Crisis of Our Age*, 24–25.
45 Sorokin, *Crisis of Our Age*, 121.
46 Alexander Solzhenitsyn, Text of Address at Harvard Class Day Afternoon Exercises, Thursday, June 8, 1978.
47 Sorokin, *Crisis of Our Age*, 145.
48 Conquest, *Reflections on a Ravaged Century*, 199.
49 Alexander Solzhenitsyn, Harvard Class Day.
50 Sorokin, *Crisis of Our Age*, 81–82.
51 Sorokin, *Crisis of Our Age*, 101.

CHAPTER

5

RELATIONAL BREAKDOWN, MENTAL ILLNESS, LONELINESS—WESTERN MAN'S FORLORN QUEST FOR INTIMACY AND MEANING

Modern man, in his quest for sensate liberty, has been severing most of his social bonds with his fellows.
Pitirim Sorokin[1]

The individual was, indeed, free, but he found himself in a psycho-social vacuum where he did not know what to do with his freedom.
Pitirim Sorokin[2]

Human beings are born mere biological organisms, devoid of solidary attitudes. Some agency must undertake the indispensable function of socializing them. Until recently the family was such an agency....At present this vital mission is performed less and less by the family.
Pitirim Sorokin[3]

Everything that is truly important in life can be summed up in the word "relationships"—first and foremost, man's relationship with God, secondly, his relationships with his fellowman. Prominent among the central themes in studies of civilizational decline and decay from Gibbon to Wallerstein is the breakdown of personal relationships. In terms of an institutional failure that contributes most directly to the collapse of a civilization, this is critical.

As earlier noted, Samuel Huntington cited these breakdowns as one of the "far more significant" problems of "moral decline" and "cultural suicide" in the West.

First in his list are

- Increases in antisocial behavior, such as crime, drug use, and violence generally
- Family decay, including increased rates of divorce, illegitimacy, teen-age pregnancy, and single-parent families[4]

The practice of law, like law enforcement and the therapeutic professions, brings one in contact with the mangled souls of our culture more frequently than in any others. Those of us in these professions do not just see the emotional trauma and the physical wounds, we have to address the problems created by these dysfunctions of our society. Grappling with them makes the depth and magnitude of the broader causes all the more obvious. The result is the recognition that much that we do in our culture is little more than band-aids and first aid for rampaging cancers—if even that.

Western man's materialism, hedonistic obsession with sex and pleasure, avidity for sports and entertainment, and abuse of alcohol and drugs all serve, to a greater or lesser degree, as anodynes for inner pains that otherwise would force themselves to the forefront of his consciousness. He is determined to hold these pains at bay in the corners of a psyche that grows skilled in dissembling, even to itself.

Pitirim Sorokin wrote more and in greater depth on this than perhaps any of our observers. He noted what should be obvious but is often overlooked, or even rationalized away:

> Human beings are born mere biological organisms, devoid of solidary attitudes. Some agency must undertake the indispensable function of socializing them. Until recently the family was such an agency....At present this vital mission is performed less and less by the family...the young are turned over at a very early age to such agencies as nursery schools and kindergartens...an increasingly unstable family is a poor school for socialization. Instead of inculcating in its offspring a strong sense of moral and social integrity, it teaches them lessons of moral laxity and loose relationships, of antagonism and conflict between parents, of purely sensate egotism and the like. Such a family cannot fail to produce, for the most part, unstable, loose, sensate persons.[5]

THE WESTERN DISEASE OF THE SOUL—LONELINESS

Complete psycho-social loneliness is an unbearable burden...
Pitirim Sorokin[6]

Sorokin took up the critical problem of loneliness; a state of being that is pandemic in Western societies but not often recognized because of the shallowness of the culture and its self-deluding tendencies. Millions do not enjoy true intimacy; they may have never experienced it. The ersatz version of intimacy so often characteristic of modern Western art, literature, and entertainment misleads Western man into believing that he can obtain what he so desperately longs for through a variety of expedients. But he ends up, in the words of a once popular song, "looking for love in all the wrong places." Sorokin went to the heart of the matter:

> The disintegration of social institutions and the increase of psycho-social isolation of the individual have likewise proceeded apace. We have seen how the contractual ties of all our institutions have been steadily weakening. Quantitative and qualitative decline of the family means a corresponding increase of psycho-social isolation. This is further accentuated by a decline of the contractual relations in economic, political and labour and other occupational organizations. Modern man, in his quest for sensate liberty, has been severing most of his social bonds with his fellows.[7]

Expressing, from a sociologist's perspective, themes that would be echoed in the religious sphere by figures like Pope John Paul II and the evangelist Billy Graham, Sorokin described the illusory nature of Western man's relational "satisfactions":

> Like the proverbial butterfly, he flitted from one group to another: he married today only to be divorced tomorrow; he associated himself momentarily now with this, now with that, occupation or with this

Loneliness by Travis Ruse. *The pursuits that Western man touts as his greatest achievements—material wealth, scientific discovery, technological invention—are practical impediments to his prospects for relational depth and meaning. Millions pedal the tricycle of their lives with furious speed through crowded days, never giving serious reflection to their effort or the direction in which they have been traveling. Without realizing it they never know true intimacy, only the shallow ersatz variety extolled by the culture.*

> or that religious, political or business group. But all these associations, as a rule, were conditional, limited, temporary and superficial. They rarely afforded an intimate union for life...they could give only a momentary illusion of intimate and genuine unity—no real and abiding psycho-social attachment. The individual was, indeed, free, but he found himself in a psycho-social vacuum where he did not know what to do with his freedom. Like a hungry millionaire in the desert, he could not buy anything with his freedom which presently turned out to be a burden rather than an asset.[8]

Loneliness has spread through Western civilization like the most contagious bacillus. The miraculous antibiotics of faith and authentic, deep love for a transcendent God and for one's fellowman are available, yet unused. The pursuits that Western man touts as his greatest achievements—economic gain, material wealth, scientific discovery, technological invention—are practical impediments that undermine and block his prospects for relational depth and meaning. Drifting further and further from his fellows, Western man would likely sob uncontrollably if he ever stopped his frenzied activities long enough to deeply contemplate the aching void in his heart.

Some do, and end up terminating their own lives precisely because everything they have been taught and absorbed from the culture prepares them not one whit for meeting their own deepest needs. Deprived of hope—and the belief, if not the evidence, that anyone else cares—these denizens of the Western jungle see no escape save through death itself. Others harden themselves, making the intimacy that affords true love and meaning a practical impossibility. Still others just pedal the tricycle of their lives with furious speed through crowded days, never giving serious reflection to their effort or the direction in which they have been traveling.

This is the level to which Western man has been emotionally educated. The external circumstances of a man's life may be squalid, but there is no squalor like the squalor of the heart and soul. Deep within these chambers there can be an immediate hell: both a source and a repository of suffering and pain.

Equating, as he does, science with truth, Western man is uncomprehending of the dangers hidden in this manner of life—even, ironically, the risks inherent to the continued fulfillment of the materialism he pursues with such avidity. As Sorokin observed, Western man has been incredibly gullible: "This paradise sounded quite scientific, plausible and convincing. Being insensible to underground tremors, society was insensible also to the underground forces that were undermining the very well springs of its material prosperity."[9] Obsession with material gain and sensual indulgence will only go so far in even producing more of its own kind. Ultimately even that will be threatened by man's failure to recognize and embrace a higher order of being.

Referring to "the poisonous fruit" of the "fatal narrowing of the realm of true reality and true value," Sorokin brought us around again to the theme of the competitiveness of Western culture—a direct consequence of its materialistic and sensate nature.

> Relationships of employers and employees, bankers and labour unions, of social classes to one another, of rich and poor, of educated and non-educated, of privileged and underprivileged, of political parties, occupational groups and, finally, of nations, are at the present time in an incessant war, controlled mainly by amount of rude force and trickery which a given group has. He who has greater force triumphs, while the weaker party is pitilessly trampled on and crushed.[10]

Especially noteworthy is Sorokin's characterization of these interactions as "relationships"—which should be an unsettling reminder that it is our fellowman in our own culture we are talking about. This self-centered, ruthless competition—operating with the often express, or at least tacit, imprimatur of the culture—is one of the proximate, though not the ultimate, causes of the loss of intimacy and the erosion of every form of relationship, familial, contractual, or economic, in Western culture.

Western man does not understand: He who "wins" loses.

THE ULTIMATE ALIENATION: THE REJECTION OF GOD AND ITS CONSEQUENCES

Instead of being serene, at peace with God, the world and his fellow men, contemporary man is a boiling pot of desires that are at war with one another, and with those of his fellows.

Pitirim Sorokin[11]

In a chapter focused on "Symptoms and Consequences" of the crisis of Western civilization, Sorokin observed

> If a person has no strong convictions as to what is right and what is wrong, if he does not believe in any God or absolute moral values…, if his hunger for pleasures and sensory values is paramount, what can guide and control his conduct towards other men? Nothing but his desires and lusts. Under these conditions he loses all rational and moral control, even plain common sense. What can deter him from violating the rights, interests and well-being of other men? Nothing but physical force.[12]

In effect, then, if there is no god, there is no law. The stronger the internal controls (i.e., a sense of accountability to a Supreme Being and a moral law), the less crime and social dysfunction and the less need to resort to physical force to control their manifestations. Man is at his noblest when responding humbly to his conscience rather than his fears of institutional punishment or social ostracism.

Sorokin asked, "If a person...does not believe in any God or absolute moral values...if his hunger for pleasures and sensory values is paramount, what can guide and control his conduct towards other men?" Answer: "Nothing but physical force." This is why police in Western societies now use body armor and military weaponry. The stronger the internal controls—a sense of accountability to a Supreme Being and a moral law—the less crime and social dysfunction and the less need to resort to physical force.

THE SPREAD OF MENTAL ILLNESS, EMOTIONAL ALIENATION, AND SUICIDE

We well know that the indispensable prerequisite of a sound and integrated mind is the presence of social stability and unchallenged general norms.... Nervous breakdowns are but another aspect of the collapse of socio-cultural order.
Pitirim Sorokin[13]

Sorokin related this internal deficit of spiritual belief and moral accountability to another phenomenon—noted also by Huntington—the proliferation of which is hardly unknown in the West. "Another consequence of periods of transition is an increase of mental disease and suicide. Social life in an over-ripe sensate culture becomes so complex, the struggle for sensory happiness is so sharp, the quest for pleasure destroys the mental and moral balance to such an extent, that the mind and nervous system of multitudes of persons cannot stand the terrific strain to which they are subjected; hence they tend to become warped or even cracked."[14]

This is precisely the condition of many inhabitants of Western society: stressed far more than they recognize—this is the world they know, the only world they have known—and with no broader frame

On 1 May 1947, just after leaving her fiancé, 23-year-old Evelyn McHale *wrote, "He is much better off without me..." and leapt to her death from the observation deck of the Empire State Building. This was the leading edge of a trend in Western civilization, which Sorokin called "an over-ripe sensate culture...so complex, the struggle for sensory happiness is so sharp, [that] the quest for pleasure destroys the mental and moral balance...the mind cannot stand the terrific strain...."*

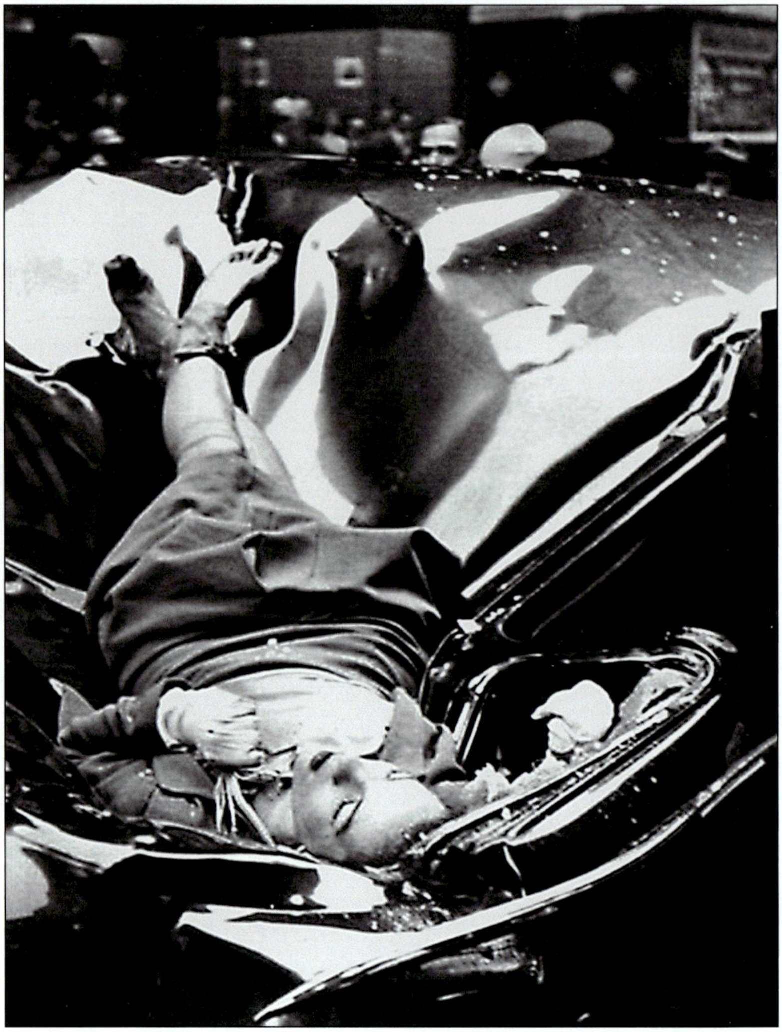

Suicide of Evelyn McHale; Photo by Robert C. Wiles, 1947

vous system of multitudes of persons cannot stand the terrific strain to which they are subjected; hence they tend to become warped or even cracked."[14]

This is precisely the condition of many inhabitants of Western society: stressed far more than they recognize—this is the world they know, the only world they have known—and with no broader frame of reference by which to judge their circumstances or their priorities, most members of this culture press forward, oblivious to that which would give them peace and serenity:

> Deprived of generally accepted norms and values...and surrounded by a chaos of conflicting norms and values, these persons find themselves without any authoritative guide or any super-individual rule. In these conditions they inevitably become erratic, a prey to incidental individual expediencies, momentary fancies and conflicting sensory impulses. Like a rudderless boat in a stormy sea, such a person is tossed hither and thither by the force of circumstances. He has no standard by which to discover how consistent his actions are and whither he is drifting; in brief, he becomes an inconsistent and unintegrated complex of fortuitous ideas, beliefs, emotions and impulses. An increase of disintegration and derangement of personality is an inevitable result...the indispensable prerequisite of a sound and integrated mind is the presence of social stability and unchallenged general norms. When these begin to collapse, an increase of nervous breakdowns ordinarily ensues, and the two trends proceed with equal speed. Nervous breakdowns are but another aspect of the collapse of socio-cultural order.[15]

This complexity is constantly stressing, with ever-escalating tensions, the individual. When the highest good is man's happiness as defined in terms of material gain, social acceptance, and pleasure, man has permitted himself to be placed unwittingly—like a caged hamster on a treadmill—in a posi-

> others must be drawn into the labor supply. The deruralization of the world threatens this essential process and thereby threatens the ability of capitalists to maintain the level of their global profits.[23]

Legal and illegal immigration from primarily Third World countries is an illustration of the process Wallerstein describes. In Europe this has dramatically altered the ancient cultures; in America it has shifted political power and is mutating that culture as well.

In America alone, poor illegal immigrants—eager to meet the capitalists' desires as described by Wallerstein—by the thousands cross the southern border to the point that as of this writing their numbers are only guessed at but are surely in multiple millions. Each of these immigrants has no legal documents and no driver's license. Yet tens of thousands of them are driving on American highways, occasionally drunk, sometimes uninsured. The dishonoring of the nation's laws extends far beyond the obvious illegal crossing but often in multiple ways thereafter. Innocent Americans sometimes pay the price in blood for their government's massive failure to insist on the nation's laws being honored.

Multi-millions of dollars are paid out in liability claims as a result of the actions of illegal immigrants. Attendant medical costs are huge. The American criminal justice system must deal with the legal and budgetary issues created by the related criminal and civil misbehavior. These considerations only refer to direct financial costs, not indirect social and legal consequences and their attendant costs.

The selfish beneficiaries (corporate and individual) of cheap labor are the only true winners in this deceitful and hypocritical game. The rest of the citizenry are subsidizing—in blood, suffering and money—their greed. Thus there is folly and tragedy in triplicate:

- The American people are victimized through crime and their pocketbook;
- The laws of the nation are dishonored—not just by immigrants but by its own citizens—thus undermining the integrity of the legal and social order; and
- Immigrants are exploited for their cheap labor—all achieved surreptitiously.

This is unbridled materialism/capitalism/competition in full gallop.

There can be only two reasons why the American government has permitted this, and they both stem from Wallerstein's initial point: First, a sizable number of businesses and industries have significant financial vested interests in exploiting the labor of these immigrants. Second, these capitalists' political influence (money dominates American politics) coupled with many politicians' timidity about offending what has become a significant voting bloc, has resulted in this spectacle.

Arguments and rationalizations are proffered on the grounds of altruism, but when examined they are clearly hypocritical. There are many ways the American people and government could altruistically aid these immigrants—some of those proposals have been advanced since the mid-80s, without result—but all accomplished and implemented through adherence to the laws of the nation.

Should this continue essentially unabated, or with piecemeal or band-aid remedies, there will likely be several results: First, continued crime at the hands of some immigrants (now illegal but who seek the imprimatur of legality) who were not christened with the notion when they crossed American borders that they must obey all of the nation's laws. Second, the demographic makeup of the nation will shift dramatically (it already has) and with it the social fabric, mores, and values will change fundamentally.

Previous generations of legal immigrants (and that distinction of going about the entry legally is important) sought out America because they were attracted to what the nation stood for, what it believed, its values—not just its wealth and economic opportunity. Thus they embraced America rather than sought to make it over into something of their choosing. The conduct and words of some of the present massive influx of illegal immigrants suggest these are not their motivations or intent. Third, the dangers inherent in permitting entry through uncontrolled borders are obvious to any security analyst or competent military officer and will likely, if not reversed, lead to citizens' paying with their lives.

All of this is the direct legacy of a purely materialistic economic system at work. Where material gain is the dominant value, other human considerations are invariably subordinated—despite any window dressing intended to disguise the reality otherwise.

Wallerstein denotes the second long-term trend as "the ecological crisis." Though the dangerous implications of this go well beyond economic repercussions, Wallerstein describes what those repercussions would be.

> From the point of view of capitalists, this should be called the threat of ending the externalization of costs.…A crucial element in the level of profits has always been that capitalists do not pay the totality of costs of their products. Some costs are "externalized," that is, spread pro rata over the whole of larger populations….. When a river is polluted by a chemical plant, the clean-up (if there is one) is normally assumed by taxpayers. What the ecologists have been noticing is the exhaustion of zones to pollute, of trees to be cut down, and so forth. The world faces the choice of ecological disaster or of forcing the internalization of costs. But forcing the internalization of costs threatens seriously the ability to accumulate capital.[24]

The ecological crisis and other forms of environmental degradation are tied hand and foot to the self-centered materialistic drive. Greed is the primary, though not exclusive, underlying dynamic for all. Wallerstein then proposed a surprising "third negative trend for capitalists," the "democratization of the world," and ends with a shocking statement.

> We have mentioned previously the program of concessions begun in the European zone in the nineteenth century, which we have these days labeled generically the welfare state. These involve expenditures on a social wage: money for children and the aged, education, health facilities. This could work for a long time for two reasons: the recipients had modest demands at first, and only the European workers were receiving this social wage. Today, workers everywhere expect it, and the level of their demands is significantly higher than it was even fifty years ago. Ultimately, these moneys can only come at the cost of accumulating capital. Democratization is not and has never been in the interest of capitalists.[25]

The fourth long-term trend Wallerstein calls the "reversal of the trend in state power." Obviously, for capitalism to function and thrive there must be order in the society. Wallerstein notes that "This has been absolutely crucial for capital despite its anti-state rhetoric. States have guaranteed order, but just as importantly they have guaranteed monopolies, which are the one and only path to serious accumulation of capital." Yet he also insists that "the democratization of the world and the ecological crisis have placed an impossible level of demands on the state structures, which are all suffering a 'fiscal crisis.' But if they reduce expenditures in order to meet the fiscal crises, they also reduce their ability to adjust the system. It is a vicious circle, in which each failure of the state leads to less willingness to entrust it with tasks...."[26]

It would appear that some semblance of this pattern is occurring in Western democracies despite the tendency of the citizenry to repeatedly turn to the state for every need—and despite decreasing evidence of state ability to efficiently and effectively meet those needs.

Wallerstein then suggests the most subtle of his considerations.

> But states are needed most of all not by reformers and not by movements but by capitalists. The capitalist world-system cannot function well without strong states.....But capitalists have never been able to put forward this claim ideologically because their legitimacy derives from economic productivity and expansion of general welfare and not from either order or the guarantee of profits. In the last century, capitalists have relied ever increasingly on the movements to perform on their behalf the function of legitimating the state structures.[27]

Wallerstein further argues that therein lays another major factor propelling the capitalist system into crisis and, ultimately, some new "order."

> Today the movements are no longer able to do this....Thus we see springing forth everywhere nonstate "groups" that are assuming the role of protecting themselves and even of providing for their welfare. This is the path of global disorder down which we have been heading. It is the sign of disintegration of the modern world-system, of capitalism as a civilization.
>
> You can rest assured that those who have privilege will not sit back and watch this privilege go under without trying to rescue it. But you can rest equally assured that they cannot rescue it merely by adjusting the system once again, for all the reasons I have adduced. The world is in transition. Out of chaos will come a new order, different from the one we now know. Different, but not necessarily better.[28]

www.kremlin.ru. CC.

The Russian flag, *on 22 August 1991, acquired the status of a Russian state symbol.* President Boris Yeltsin and the flag *represented the collapse of the U.S.S.R. Immanuel Wallerstein observed, "The relative economic decline of the U.S. has been going on apace since [1973], to the advantage of its economic competitors. The U.S. has been able, up to a point, to contain them politically, primarily by using the menace of the Cold War....This weapon, however, disappeared with the collapse of the Soviet Union."*

Thus we see Wallerstein's predictions for the West. He places his views in a historical context of cycles and focuses on what he calls "hegemony."

> This is the cycle of hegemony that...goes back...to circa 1873, and traces the rise and now the decline of U.S. hegemony in the world-system. It started with a long competition between the United States and Germany to become the successor hegemonic power to Great Britain. This struggle culminated in the Thirty Years War between the two contenders that went on between 1914 and 1945, a war that the United States won. The period of true hegemony followed, from 1945 to 1967–1973. True hegemony, however, cannot last. Its base, which is economic productive superiority, must

> inevitably be undermined by the entry into a strong competitive position of other powers, in this case western Europe and Japan. The relative economic decline of the United States has been going on apace since then, to the advantage of its economic competitors. The United States has been able, up to a point, to contain them politically, primarily by using the menace of the Cold War to keep its allies in line. This weapon, however, disappeared with the collapse of the Soviet Union between 1989 and 1991.[29]

We might challenge some of Wallerstein's reasoning, but it is useful to continue his analysis:

> Every historical system has three moments: the moment of genesis, the moment of normal life or development, and the moment of structural crisis.... There is much reason to believe that the modern world-system, the one in which we all live, has entered into its structural crisis. If this is so, we are unlikely to see the full acting out of another hegemonic cycle.[30]
>
> The sages are right in their critiques of the IMF, but they in turn have little to offer us, because they feel they have to argue that the historical system in which we live is immortal, and thus they must foreswear analyzing its dilemmas. No system, however, is immortal, and certainly not the one that has generated the greatest economic and social polarization in the history of humanity.[31]

On the point that no system is immortal, we can agree. This principle—I have appropriated the term "entropy" to apply to society and its institutions—in one respect or another, underlies the writings of our observers and is fundamental to our analysis. Of course, if Wallerstein is correct in his predictions—and at least some variation of this pessimistic analysis will prove true—this becomes another reason for Western man to question fundamental tenets of his secular religion of life, belief, and action. Though I argue throughout this work that there are other even more compelling reasons for him to do so; the consideration that the house he has inhabited for so long is slowly and irrevocably collapsing is a strong argument for changing one's philosophical and spiritual residence.

THE TRAITS AND CHARACTERISTICS OF MATERIALISM AS EXPRESSED THROUGH CAPITALISM

...the pursuit of wealth, stripped of its religious and ethical meaning, tends to become associated with purely mundane passions, which often actually give it the character of sport.
Max Weber[32]

Wallerstein describes the functioning and priorities of capitalism in terms that amount to voracious materialism. It rewards those who 1) play by its rules, and 2) adapt well to the ruthless competitiveness of the arena in which it functions. "What defines a system, this system, as capitalist? It seems to me that the *differentia specifica* is not the accumulation of capital but the priority given to the endless accumulation of capital.... It is a system whose institutions are geared to rewarding over the middle run all those who give primacy to the accumulation of capital and punish in the middle run all those who attempt to implement other priorities."[33]

PD

PD

(Left) Sid Hatfield (1920), the sheriff in Matewan, West Virginia, *became a national folk hero for miners in the 1920s when he faced down Baldwin–Felts "detectives" sent by mine owners to throw striking miners and their families out of their homes. In a one-minute gun battle, seven detectives were killed. A year later, using legal summons to bring an unarmed Hatfield to a neighboring courthouse, the mine owners arranged for Hatfield to be gunned down.* (Right) The grieving widow of Hatfield, who was present when her husband was murdered, watched with hundreds of miners as his body was buried. *One of the worst examples in American history of the potential for ruthlessness and indifference to others' suffering that can characterize unbridled capitalism, Matewan is a reminder: Never trust an ideology, an institution, or a concentration of power—no matter how venerated.*

Wallerstein has diagnosed one of the great usually unuttered—usually uncontemplated—realities of Western life: It's about money. Anyone who pursues "other priorities" will not be rewarded but at best looked upon as an iconoclast or eccentric.

But this also raises the question, Will such a ruthless, competitive system permit social change to alleviate the damage done to so many who are victimized by its excesses? Wallerstein seems to answer in the affirmative but only to a point: "Can we speak of social change within this system? Yes and no."[34] He then suggests the system's great flaws prepare the ground for its ultimate collapse.

There has, of course, been social change aimed at ameliorating the effects of capitalism's inherent selfishness and ruthlessness; but we would be wise to be ever mindful that capitalism's legacy has extended from the slavery fought for years by William Wilberforce in Britain, through the blood-soaked coal fields of Matewan, West Virginia, to the exploitation of immigrant labor in much of the West today. Though we may continue to choose to ride this tiger, the unwise and insensitive should be advised: you may benefit now, but at any moment it may turn and devour you too.

Wallerstein anticipates capitalism's failures in part because he believes it cannot live up to its promises. "The *raison d'être* of the capitalist world-economy, its motor force, has been the ceaseless accumulation of capital. And the ceaseless accumulation of capital is totally incompatible with these materialist, collectivist promises, because it is based on the appropriation of surplus-value by some from others. Capitalism represents material reward for some, but in order that it be so, it can never be material reward for everyone."[35]

If he is correct in this—and of course capitalism's apologists would deny it—then trouble is surely over the horizon. We already can see for ourselves that capitalism produces disproportionate rewards, with some in the West acquiring unseemly wealth—all carefully justified by the ideology (i.e., "theology" of the Western secular religion) of capitalism—and others struggling to make ends meet.

Yet there is a different but related disproportionality: the West pays huge sums to sports stars, actors, entertainers, and those who amuse its ever-burgeoning lust to be entertained, while the civilizing professions (e.g., teachers, law enforcement officers, social workers, ministers, military professionals, etc.) by comparison may struggle. This of course is clear and compelling evidence of the culture's values.

MEASURING ONE'S "SUCCESS"—THROUGH MONEY

The great fault of modern democracy—a fault that is common to the capitalist and the socialist—is that it accepts economic wealth as the end of society and the standard of personal happiness.
Christopher Dawson[36]

A friend with whom I entered the war zone of Bosnia in 1993 later wrote a book recounting his experiences and identified me as a "successful" lawyer. Though he meant no offense, indeed just the opposite, I was concerned by the use of that term due to my consciousness of its implications. In the West, the adjective "successful" nearly always carries with it the connotation of financial achievement. To an acute observer this can be stigmatic; for "success" on the material and financial plane is often an indicator of failure on higher planes.

At a minimum, when we characterize someone as successful in that way, it is in a sense an unwitting display of primitivism—like one hunter/gatherer/caveman noting another caveman's ability to bring home the slain prey. Purely materialistic—usually with strong overtones of pridefulness—use of the adjective "successful" in the West carries with it no implicit allusion to the integrity, humility, unselfishness, self-sacrifice, or compassion of the subject—all of which are qualities of a high order. This awareness should not be novel: great writers have noted it; Emerson and Thoreau were preeminent in American literature in highlighting it.

In *Religion and World History*, Christopher Dawson correctly tied capitalism with democracy as the handmaid of the latter. There is a highly symbiotic relationship. Acknowledging the damaging emphasis on money in the West in yet another respect, Dawson continued by declaring a great truth that is in conflict with everything the West reputedly stands for, and in so doing touched upon a facet of the West's potential terminal illness: the use of material wealth as the measure of success for an individual or a nation.

> The great fault of modern democracy—a fault that is common to the capitalist and the socialist—is that it accepts economic wealth as the end of society and the standard of personal happiness. We have made the increase of wealth the one criterion of social improvement, and consequently our aristocracy is an aristocracy of money-makers, and our democratic ideal is mainly an ideal of more money for everyone. But the standard of life is really not an economic but a vital thing; it is a question of how you live rather than how much you live on. Just as a man who buys one's house does not buy one's

Adoration of the Golden Calf (1633–1634), by Nicolas Poussin; worship of a golden calf in biblical times. *The West's materialism is a great idol, a golden calf—but now symbolized by the Wall Street Bull—mounted high above us, which the West—even the Christian church—worships, weakening the individual, the church, and the civilization.*

PD

Charging Bull by Arturo DiModica. Bowling Green Park, New York City. Photograph by Katie Sample. Used by permission.

> family and friends and interests—all the things that made up the life that was lived in that house—so two men may possess the same money income and yet have totally different standards of life.[37]

The result of measuring one's life and happiness this way is not only that an entire civilization determines its "success" by essentially primitive standards, but this also leads to an "aristocracy" of money-makers. Those whose primary, if not exclusive, accomplishment is the acquisition of material gain become the role models and leaders of the culture. In this policy, the folly should be self-evident; but there is scant evidence it is recognized. The wealthy and the acquisitively gifted are dominant in their influence on the culture. More exalted gifts and talents—especially those that demonstrate faith, integrity, nobility and unselfishness of spirit—are relegated to a second, third, or fourth tier status, if acknowledged at all. Typically, what is said deferentially about those who practice these exalted attributes is more hypocritical lip service than genuine, deep, and mimetic admiration. Certainly their influence on the culture is slight compared to the materialistically driven among us.

Critical fallout results from this cultural value system. One of the most obvious is its impact on others who do not achieve the same or a similar measure of material success. Dawson attacked the folly of it all.

> The great curse of our modern society is not so much lack of money as the fact that the lack of money condemns a man to a squalid and incomplete existence. But even if he has money, and a great deal of it, he is still in danger of leading an incomplete and cramped life, because our whole

> social order is directed to economic instead of spiritual ends. The economic view of life regards money as equivalent to satisfaction. Get money, and if you get enough of it you will get everything else that is worth having.[38]

Lee J. Cobb as Willy Loman in the original Broadway production of Arthur Miller's *Death of a Salesman. Willy Loman embraced the American materialist dream as his personal gospel; an ersatz religion that he worshipped and obeyed scrupulously. This religion is practiced by millions in the West who often meld it—with the active complicity of the church—with the Christian religion.*

Arthur Miller, through his play *Death of a Salesman,* exposed the misery recumbent behind the façade of this folly. Willy Loman embraced the American dream as his personal gospel; an ersatz religion that he worshipped and obeyed scrupulously. Hard work was in truth its sole ethic and all men were to be judged by their application of this principle in their own lives and their success at achieving the "dream" (i.e., financial gain). Others—who may have questioned the dream's merits—were heretics to be denigrated, if not burned at the stake of materialism's disapprobation. Others' contentment—even that of his own family members—with what they have is an unimaginable lack of fervent belief in the religion to Willy. Living every day for a reality that never proves real and for a success that continually eludes him, Willy eventually disposes of his own meaningless existence.

Millions—especially those who perceive some personal "success" in the practice of this religion—may never reach this depth of disillusionment. But, like Willy, their lives are nonetheless a tragedy—not in their dying but in their never living. This religion is practiced by millions in the West who often meld it—with the active complicity of the church—with the Christian religion; a practice that we will see later is widespread and not recognized as the latter-day Gnosticism it truly is.

Dawson explains there is an alternative view of how life should be lived—and how true happiness can be achieved.

> The Christian view of life, on the other hand, puts economic things in the second place. First seek the kingdom of God, and everything else will be added to you. And this is not so absurd as it sounds, for we have only to think for a moment to realise that the ills of modern society do not spring from poverty; in fact, society today is probably richer in material wealth than any society that has ever existed. What we are suffering from is lack of social adjustment and the failure to subordinate material and economic goods to human and spiritual ones. [39]

This of course is a Western secular heresy. In the capitalistic, materialistic West such a view can only be countenanced as hopelessly idealistic and out of touch with reality. Highly significant to the themes of this present work is that Dawson's point is largely lost on the one institution where it should be most devotedly embraced: the Christian church in the West.

The profound sense of inequity that unbridled capitalism spawns underlies many social ills. This reality gave the motive force to bestial communism. Had this truth been honestly and fully acknowledged in the early to mid-twentieth-century West, communism could have been much more effectively fought and defeated. As it was, the West relied on its own propaganda to defend against communism; and, in the end, communism's own folly and weaknesses brought about its downfall. The West has tended to see this victory as a product of its wisdom and virtue; but that is a misreading: communism was its own worst enemy. Capitalism may make the same mistake.

Dawson gave his definition of richness for a society: "The truly rich society is not the one that goes on piling up economic wealth as an end in itself, but the one that uses its wealth as the foundation on which to build a rich and many-sided culture."[40] This view of course does not, by any measure, reflect Western societies; and therein lie many of the pathologies and infirmities diagnosed by our observers of the decline and decay of Western civilization.

This perspective on the deleterious effects of materialism, capitalism, and competition is not unique to more astute Western observers. Sometimes the critiques of our more felicitous fellows speaking from a very different historical and cultural viewpoint tell us even more—as in this passage from Alexander Solzhenitsyn's address at Harvard in 1978:

> Now at last during past decades technical and social progress has permitted the realization of such aspirations: the welfare state. Every citizen has been granted the desired freedom and material goods in such quantity and of such quality as to guarantee in theory the achievement of happiness, in the morally inferior sense which has come into being during those same decades. In the process, however, one psychological detail has been overlooked: the constant desire to have still more things and a still better life and the struggle to obtain them imprints many Western faces with worry and even depression, though it is customary to conceal such feelings. Active and tense competition permeates all human thoughts without opening a way to free spiritual development.[41]

Solzhenitsyn was correct: it is customary to "conceal such feelings" in the West, and embedded therein is another carcinogen in the declining emotional and spiritual health of Western man. Western man often will not acknowledge his stressors and his despair even to himself; to do so might bring to the surface of awareness the utter futility of the value system he has embraced. Thoreau's man who lives a life of "quiet desperation" is alive and unwell in the West.[42] Succumbing to his pride and swept along in the powerful current of social conformity, Western man denies himself succor and release.

As an enemy of communism and a vociferous critic of capitalism, Solzhenitsyn inhabited a peculiar space. For Solzhenitsyn, the West's materialism is a great idol, a golden calf mounted high above us that the West—even the Christian church—worships. Its effects are weakening the individual: "Even biology knows that habitual extreme safety and well-being are not advantageous for a living organism. Today, well-being in the life of Western society has begun to reveal its pernicious mask."

Solzhenitsyn believed, as Toynbee before him, that man was not placed on the earth to be pampered by material comforts—or, for that matter, to necessarily be happy. His purpose is higher, nobler and spiritual and aimed at a world beyond the pedestrian world of material reality, political struggle, and the pursuit of security.

> If humanism were right in declaring that man is born to be happy, he would not be born to die. Since his body is doomed to die, his task on earth evidently must be of a more spiritual nature. It cannot [be] unrestrained enjoyment of everyday life. It cannot be the search for the best ways to obtain material goods and then cheerfully get the most out of them. It has to be the fulfillment of a permanent, earnest duty so that one's life journey may become an experience of moral growth, so that one may leave life a better human being than one started it. It is imperative to review the table

> of widespread human values. Its present incorrectness is astounding. It is not possible that assessment of the President's performance be reduced to the question of how much money one makes or of unlimited availability of gasoline.[43]

Solzhenitsyn asked some telling questions that only a fool could answer in anything but the negative: "Is it right that man's life and society's activities have to be determined by material expansion in the first place? Is it permissible to promote such expansion to the detriment of our spiritual integrity?"

We are captives to our own materialism. Rather than free—as we believe and insist to ourselves and others—we are enslaved. Western man genuflects before the altar of capitalism and materialism; he stresses himself and his fellows by his devotion to competition as a way of life. This materialistic drive influences every aspect of life, including the issues of security and war.

Were the West, for example, to give the bin Ladens and Islamic jihadists what they want in terms of changed policies, the West would find—as the West's political leadership should understand—that this would mean a sacrifice of much of its way of life, the extravagantly materialistic way of life. The West would substantially relinquish its control over the world's oil upon which it is addictively dependent.

THE CLASH BETWEEN FAITH AND MATERIALISM TO BE THE ETHOS OF WESTERN CIVILIZATION

The personal attitude of Jesus is characterized in classical purity by the typical antique-Oriental plea: "Give us this day our daily bread."
Max Weber[44]

Max Weber observed that the spirit of religious faith that once held sway in the West has not only been displaced by "the spirit of capitalism," but the latter is antithetical to the former.

> The people filled with the spirit of capitalism today tend to be indifferent, if not hostile, to the Church. The thought of the pious boredom of paradise has little attraction for their active natures; religion appears to them as a means of drawing people away from labour in this world. If you ask them what is the meaning of their restless activity, why they are never satisfied with what they have, thus appearing so senseless to any purely worldly view of life, they would perhaps give the answer, if they know any at all: "to provide for my children and grandchildren." But more often and, since that motive is not peculiar to them, but was just as effective for the traditionalist, more correctly, simply: that business with its continuous work has become a necessary part of their lives. That is in fact the only possible motivation, but it at the same time expresses what is, seen from the view-point of personal happiness, so irrational about this sort of life, where a man exists for the sake of his business, instead of the reverse.[45]

Weber erred in assuming that all Western capitalists "tend to be indifferent, if not hostile, to the Church." To the contrary, many are very interested in—and active as a part of—the Western church. But God and mammon cannot be served at the same time or for that matter, the former on Sunday and the latter Monday through Saturday. However, this is the policy and practice of many who claim the title "Christian." They believe they can have both worlds—the world of mammon and the world of God—and the Western church has been complicit in nurturing this belief.

In countless churches and religious institutions the evidence of the dominance of the materialist mindset is everywhere present. Key leadership positions and influence are often reserved for the acquisitively gifted who have also gifted the church or religious institution with their materialist beneficence. That these attitudes, priorities, and practices are belladonna to the spiritual health and vitality of the church is not only unrecognized but would be rejected as a form of heresy—one, however, peculiar only to the doctrines and practices of the Western church.

Weber believed that "...the desire for the power and recognition which the mere fact of wealth brings plays its part. When the imagination of a whole people has once been turned toward purely quantitative bigness, as in the United States, this romanticism of numbers exercises an irresistible appeal to the poets among business men."[46]

"Quantitative bigness" is very important to the Western church, and there is an unquestioned romance with numbers that is anything but spiritual. The truth in this is lost not only on citizens of the culture but members of the church, yet as Weber noted, "...it is just that which seems to the pre-capitalistic man so incomprehensible and mysterious, so unworthy and contemptible. That anyone should be able to make it the sole purpose of his life-work, to sink into the grave weighed down with a great material load of money and goods, seems to him explicable only as the product of a perverse instinct, the *auri sacra fames.*"[47]

The church would deny its culpability in allowing many to "sink into the grave" weighed down by such a system of values and priorities, but its actions—and its own material acquisitions—speak louder than its protestations.

In these passages the German Weber sounds much like the Russian Sorokin (with his condemnation of the West's fixation on "colossalism"), the British Dawson, the Russian Solzhenitsyn, and the American Schaeffer, and, in one respect or another, like most of our observers.

This ruthless acquisitiveness, like a ravenous beast, tugs constantly against any restraints imposed by religion and government—feeble though they may be—now rejecting the former and resisting the latter. The freedom it seeks is the license that comes with the law of the jungle.

> At present under our individualistic political, legal, and economic institutions, with the forms of organization and general structure which are peculiar to our economic order, this spirit of capitalism might be understandable, as has been said, purely as a result of adaptation. The capitalistic system so needs this devotion to the calling of making money, it is an attitude toward material goods which is so well suited to that system, so intimately bound up with the conditions of survival in the economic struggle for existence, that there can today no longer be any question of a necessary connection of that acquisitive manner of life with any single Weltanschauung. In fact, it no longer needs the support of any religious forces, and feels the attempts of religion to influence economic life, in so far as they can still be felt at all, to be as much an unjustified interference as its regulation by the State. [48]

The "capitalistic system" has largely co-opted the Western church, which now has been so thoroughly compromised by materialism, it is no longer a threat to capitalism; it is its ally. The consequence of this unholy alliance—and the capitulation of an entire culture to the dominance of materialism and acquisitiveness as its ethos—is that "men's commercial and social interests...determine their opinions and attitudes. Whoever does not adapt his manner of life to the conditions of capitalistic success must go under, or at least cannot rise. But these are phenomena of a time in which modern capitalism has become dominant and has become emancipated from its old supports."[49]

Weber has shone a light where typically only mold, mildew, and mushrooms would grow—a dark, dank place in which Western man's "opinions and attitudes" are formed. This is close to the primeval and far removed from the cathedral. Predictably, the process of unnatural selection in such a habitat is truly Darwinian: "Thus the capitalism of today, which has come to dominate economic life, educates and selects the economic subjects which it needs through a process of economic survival of the fittest."[50]

The pervasiveness of these primitive rules and attitudes is so complete that few in the West recognize the thickness of the undergrowth entered or the macerations of the human soul that are the consequence. The contrast between, for example, the Christian church of the first century and the modern Western church is suggested by this reminder from Weber: "The personal attitude of Jesus is characterized in classical purity by the typical antique-Oriental plea: 'Give us this day our daily...bread.'"[51] Weber explained further how religious doctrines were appropriated by the capitalist/materialist worldview to strengthen it and gain the subordination of others to its drives and ambitions. He related the "asceticism" of the modern capitalist economy—demanding as it is of its participants—with its origins in religious asceticism; a connection made by other of our observers, most often citing Calvinism or Puritanism.

> The Puritan wanted to work in a calling; we are forced to do so. For when asceticism was carried out of monastic cells into everyday life, and began to dominate worldly morality, it did its part in building the tremendous cosmos of the modern economic order. This order is now bound to the technical, and economic conditions of machine production which today determine the lives of all the individuals who are born into this mechanism, not only those directly concerned with economic acquisition, with irresistible force. Perhaps it will so determine them until the last ton of fossilized coal is burnt.[52]

The truth in Weber's analysis can be partly illustrated by a historical juxtaposition. Question: How would the modern Western church view a man who lived out of doors, far from civilization, surviving off the land, never buying or building a home, wearing clothing made from animal skins, and only having contact with society for the purpose of talking about his religious beliefs? Answer: The church would be first in line to throw a net over him and haul him away to an institution—certainly not invite him into its pulpits. Yet this describes the man Jesus declared to be "the greatest

CC

Max Weber, 1917, at the Lauensteiner Tagung. In background: Ernst Toller. *Weber observed that 'men's commercial and social interests...determine their opinions and attitudes. Whoever does not adapt his manner of life to the conditions of capitalistic success must go under, or at least cannot rise." Quoting Baxter, Weber said what every authentic Christian should know: "...the care for external goods should only lie on the shoulders of the 'saint like a light cloak, which can be thrown aside at any moment'. But fate decreed that the cloak should become an iron cage."*

man ever born," John the Baptist. And of course there are others like him throughout the Bible. It also closely resembles St. Francis et al throughout earlier Catholic Church history.

Quoting Baxter, Weber said what every authentic Christian should know: "...the care for external goods should only lie on the shoulders of the 'saint like a light cloak, which can be thrown aside at any moment.' But fate decreed that the cloak should become an iron cage."[53]

In the script of a possible colloquy with Weber, I would respond, No, Professor Weber, fate did not decree it, Western man chose it. But, as your passage below acknowledged, the fig leaves have been increasingly stripped away—though the church itself has not yet so much as blushed at the sight of the organs and primitive drives thereby exposed.

> Since asceticism undertook to remodel the world and to work out its ideals in the world, material goods have gained an increasing and finally an inexorable power over the lives of men as at no previous period in history. Today the spirit of religious asceticism—whether finally, who knows?—has escaped from the cage. But victorious capitalism...needs its support no longer.
>
> The rosy blush of its laughing heir, the Enlightenment, seems also to be irretrievably fading, and the idea of duty in one's calling prowls about in our lives like the ghost of dead religious beliefs. Where the fulfillment of the calling cannot directly be related to the highest spiritual and cultural values, or when, on the other hand, it need not be felt simply as economic compulsion, the individual

PD

John the Baptist, by El Greco. *Jesus said John—perhaps the most countercultural figure in the Bible save Jesus Himself—was "the greatest man ever born." When one views the world as merely a preliminary stage to a greater, more powerful, more meaningful, eternal world, then one's "investments" (to use a favored Western word) in time, energy, wealth, and resources are shifted dramatically. The true Christian lays up treasures in Heaven and has much less interest in the variety that consumes Western man.*

> generally abandons the attempt to justify it at all. In the field of its highest development, in the United States, the pursuit of wealth, stripped of its religious and ethical meaning, tends to become associated with purely mundane passions, which often actually give it the character of sport.[54]

Many justifications are proffered by the Western players of what Weber calls this "sport," some resorting to at least the pretense of some form of unselfish duty, perhaps to family. But the capitulation to these forces is now so complete that no justification or casuistry seems needed; it is simply what one does in the West. No longer does Western man bestride the world—if he ever truly did—as the idealistic paragon of faith, liberty, and the dignity of the individual, but now largely as the exemplar of the grandest historical "success" at material acquisitiveness.

Weber concluded his study with a declaration that suggests the malformation of mind and heart that has resulted has rendered "modern man" incapable of achieving that which he desperately needs: "The modern man is in general, even with the best will, unable to give religious ideas a significance for culture and national character which they deserve."[55] Indeed, he is frenetically expelling them!

WHAT ARE SYBARITIC WESTERN MAN'S CHOICES?

Only voluntary, inspired self-restraint can raise man above the world stream of materialism.
Alexander Solzhenitsyn[56]

A biblical writer declared, "The love of money is the root of all sorts of evil, and some, by longing for it, have wandered away from the faith and pierced themselves with many griefs."[57] Sorokin elucidated what is essentially congruent with a Christian viewpoint of our world.

> The same root is responsible for present-day society as an enormous number of armed camps, that by direct or indirect application of force and fraud try each to defeat the others. Relationships of employers and employees, bankers and labour unions, of social classes to one another, of rich and poor, of educated and non-educated, of privileged and underprivileged, of political parties, occupational groups and, finally, of nations, are at the present time in an incessant war, controlled mainly by amount of rude force and trickery which a given group has. He who has greater force triumphs, while the weaker party is pitilessly trampled on and crushed.[58]

Christopher Dawson in *Christianity and the New Age* noted the conflict—perceived at least as early as Plato—between a materialistic view and any hope man may have for a life of higher spiritual meaning. The man who seeks the latter will be at a "disadvantage" to the former.

> But though Plato realized as fully as any purely religious teacher the need for bringing social life into contact with spiritual reality and for relating man's rational activity to the higher intuitive knowledge, he failed to show how this could be accomplished by means of a purely intellectual discipline. He saw that it was necessary on the one hand to drag humanity out of the shadow world of appearances and false moral standards into the pure white light of spiritual reality, and, on the other hand, that the contemplative must be forced to leave his mountain of vision and "to descend again to these prisoners and to partake in their toils and honors." But, as he says, the spiritual man is at a disadvantage in the world of politics and business. The eyes that have looked upon the sun can no longer distinguish the shadows of the cave. The man who cares only for eternal things, who seeks to fly hence and to become assimilated to God by holiness and justice and wisdom, is unable to strive for political power with the mean cunning of the ordinary "man of affairs."[59]

In these insights, the pre-Christian Plato anticipated the Christian Augustine who declared in his colloquy with Reason:

> Augustine: "I desire to know God and the Soul."
> Reason: "Nothing more?"
> Augustine: "Absolutely nothing."
> (*Soliloquies* 1.2.7)

In all of these observations we see the intersection of spiritual and cultural values. In the context of the traditional religion of Western civilization, Christianity, the conflict between spiritual and material values was, originally at least, especially conspicuous. Nowhere did Jesus teach—or even give sanction to—competition or materialism. But those values and that way of life are venerated by professing Christians throughout Western civilization.

Evidence of this has run like a black thread through the historical tapestry of the church. Francis Schaeffer struck two bulls-eyes with one brief paragraph. "At certain points the people in the stream of the Reformation were inconsistent with the biblical teaching they claimed to follow. There were many areas where the Bible was not followed as it should have been, but two are outstanding: first, a twisted view of race, and second, a noncompassionate use of accumulated wealth."[60]

If this gulf between shallow, selfish materialism and the higher spiritual values is so expansive, and so dangerous to man's well-being, not to mention Western civilization, why has there been so little effort to close it? Schaeffer explained part of the hidden dynamics.

> And since personal peace and affluence are so often the only values that count with the majority, politicians know that to be elected they must promise these things. Politics has largely become not a matter of ideals—increasingly men and women are not stirred by the values of liberty and truth—but of supplying a constituency with a frosting of personal peace and affluence. They know that voices will not be raised as long as people have these things, or at least an illusion of them.[61]

Yorck Project, PD-art.

St. Augustine, 1472, by Antonello da Messina. *One of the greatest minds in Western thought. Augustine transfigured from a womanizing libertine and prideful materialist as a young man to a wise philosopher who understood where true meaning and value were found. He declared, "I desire to know God and the Soul. Nothing more. Absolutely nothing." Western man—even in the church—has found a way to serve God and mammon—or so he believes. This set of priorities is the source of much of his misery.*

A Russian economist during the Stalinist era, alluded to elsewhere in this book, observed that capitalism only survived because its worst excesses were curbed every generation or so. Stalin dispatched him to the Gulag and death. But this economist perceived something about capitalism that most capitalists do not or will not: that it is fundamentally ruthless and must be restrained; otherwise it breeds injustice leading to either revolution or some form of authoritarianism, or both.

We may delude ourselves that making money is not the focus for each of us individually yet the time records of our thoughts, hours, and energies spent in acquisitiveness tell the real story. The failure to be vigilant and relentlessly honest with ourselves leads us into the kill zone in which the best, the noblest, the most meaningful are mercilessly slaughtered. Eternal vigilance is truly the price of liberty—all forms of liberty. But vigilance focused solely outward is incomplete and dangerous. The greater threats to individuals and cultures are always internal. We may deal with our foreign enemies, at least for now, but the threats concealed within our hearts and minds are at our throats, and we do not see them. We have not met this enemy even though—and because—he is us, in all our ruthless competitiveness and selfish materialism.

END NOTES
CHAPTER 6

1 Oswald Spengler, *The Decline of the West* (A. A. Knopf, University of Virginia, 1932), 399.
2 Christopher Dawson (Introduction by John J. Mulloy), *Christianity and the New Age* (Sophia Institute Press, 1985), 98.
3 Spengler, *Decline of the West,* 396.
4 Immanuel Wallerstein, *The End of the World As We Know It: Social Science for the Twenty-First Century* (Minneapolis: University of Minnesota Press, 1999), 25–26.
5 Spengler, *Decline of the West,* 26.
6 Calvin Coolidge, "The Press Under a Free Government," a speech given before the American Society of Newspaper Editors, Washington, D.C., January 17, 1925.
7 Spengler, *Decline of the West,* 399.
8 Spengler, *Decline of the West,* 400.
9 Spengler, *Decline of the West,* 402.
10 Spengler, *Decline of the West,* 402.
11 Spengler, *Decline of the West,* 402–403.
12 Spengler, *Decline of the West,* 406–407.
13 Wallerstein, *The End of the World As We Know It,* 57–58.
14 Wallerstein, *The End of the World As We Know It,* 57–58.
15 Wallerstein, *The End of the World As We Know It,* 128.
16 Wallerstein, *The End of the World As We Know It,* 182.
17 Wallerstein, *The End of the World As We Know It,* 128–129.
18 Wallerstein, *The End of the World As We Know It,* 128–129.
19 Wallerstein, *The End of the World As We Know It,* 84.
20 Wallerstein, *The End of the World As We Know It,* 129.
21 Wallerstein, *The End of the World As We Know It,* 17–18.
22 Wallerstein, *The End of the World As We Know It,* 30.
23 Wallerstein, *The End of the World As We Know It,* 30–31.
24 Wallerstein, *The End of the World As We Know It,* 31.
25 Wallerstein, *The End of the World As We Know It,* 31–32.
26 Wallerstein, *The End of the World As We Know It,* 32.
27 Wallerstein, *The End of the World As We Know It,* 32–33.
28 Wallerstein, *The End of the World As We Know It,* 33.
29 Wallerstein, *The End of the World As We Know It,* 54.
30 Wallerstein, *The End of the World As We Know It,* 55.
31 Wallerstein, *The End of the World As We Know It,* 56.
32 Max Weber, *The Protestant Ethic and the Spirit of Capitalism* (Courier: Dover Publications, 2003), 182.
33 Wallerstein, *The End of the World As We Know It,* 129.
34 Wallerstein, *The End of the World As We Know It,* 129–130.
35 Wallerstein, *The End of the World As We Know It,* 139.
36 Dawson, *Religion and World History,* 238.
37 Dawson, *Religion and World History,* 238.
38 Dawson, *Religion and World History* 239.
39 Dawson, *Religion and World History,* 239.
40 Dawson, *Religion and World History,* 238.

41 Alexander Solzhenitsyn, Text of Address at Harvard Class Day Afternoon Exercises, Thursday, June 8, 1978.
42 Henry David Thoreau, *Walden; or, Life in the Woods* (Boston: Ticknor and Fields, 1854), 1.a.ix.
43 Solzhenitsyn, Harvard Class Day.
44 Weber, *Protestant Ethic*, 83.
45 Weber, *Protestant Ethic*, 70.
46 Weber, *Protestant Ethic*, 70–71.
47 Weber, *Protestant Ethic*, 71–72.
48 Weber, *Protestant Ethic*, 72.
49 Weber, *Protestant Ethic*, 72.
50 Weber, *Protestant Ethic*, 55.
51 Weber, *Protestant Ethic*, 83.
52 Weber, *Protestant Ethic*, 181.
53 Weber, *Protestant Ethic*, 181.
54 Weber, *Protestant Ethic*, 181–182.
55 Weber, *Protestant Ethic*, 183.
56 Solzhenitsyn, Harvard Class Day.
57 1 Timothy 6:10, *New American Standard Bible*, 1995.
58 Pitirim A. Sorokin, *The Crisis of Our Age* (Oneworld Publications Ltd., 1941; this edition Sergei P. Sorokin and Peter P. Sorokin, 1992), 255.
59 Christopher Dawson, *Christianity and the New Age*, citing 2 Theatetos (Sophia Institute Press, 1985), 52–53.
60 Francis A. Schaeffer, *How Should We Then Live? The Rise and Decline of Western Thought and Culture* (Wheaton, IL: Crossway Books, 1976), 113.
61 Schaeffer, *How Should We Then Live?*, 227.

CHAPTER

7

MAN AS GOD: THE WORSHIP OF THE STATE, GOVERNMENT, LAW, AND DEMOCRACY

The so-called "civilized" state is simply an imposing, high-powered version of the primitive tribe...
Arnold Toynbee[1]

Whenever man has sought to make the state his heaven, he has made it Hell...
Christopher Dawson[2]

Democracy is another leaf from the book of Christianity, which has also, I fear, been torn out and, while perhaps not misread, has certainly been half emptied of meaning by being divorced from its Christian context and secularized...
Arnold Toynbee[3]

It is said that we in the West are nations of laws and not men, but no nation is a nation of laws and not men. Everything in government and law is determined by those who have power. Therefore the character of those in power determines everything in government and law.

The Old Testament describes an appeal by the prophet Samuel to God on behalf of the people of Israel. The Israelites wanted a king. For centuries, they had been ruled by a series of judges, but at this juncture in their history they wished to be ruled—as the nations surrounding them were ruled—by a king. Contrary, the Old Testament tells us, to the divine plan and Samuel's counsel, they persisted until Samuel anointed Saul as king. Tall, physically strong, handsome, and impressive, Saul presented the archetypical image of a great king. Undoubtedly, he would have been the Semitic equivalent from that age of an especially photogenic and charismatic political candidate in the West in our age. Yet he proved to be the source of great misery and disorder for the Israelites.

In many respects, the story of Saul may be an apt analogy for the political dynamics of the West in recent generations. Western man has grown to rely heavily on government as his paternalistic protector and benefactor. Western citizens' expectations of government are nearing the stratospheric as the source of their security and their assurance of material prosperity; and those expectations are ever expanding.

Western man increasingly betrays a line of thought not unlike the ancient Jews: "Government will submit to our will, protect us, grant us security from want and suffering, and ensure ever greater material gain—and our happiness." Yet the reliance on government, even a democracy, for the fulfillment of man's hopes, needs, and aspirations is as misguided in its own way as was the ancient Jews confidence that a strong king would do much the same for them.

THE WORSHIP OF LEVIATHAN

Leviathan-worship is a moral enormity, even at its noblest and mildest...
Arnold Toynbee[4]

There is something more elemental at play in Western man's affinity for his ideologies, governmental structures and legal systems—something fundamentally primitive and dangerous. Toynbee began to ferret out the menacing truth by first declaring that "The so-called 'civilized' state is simply an imposing, high-powered version of the primitive tribe..."[5] This was yet another way of acknowledging that human nature does not change.

Modern Western man—surrounded as he is on all sides by "imposing, high-powered" manifestations of government and legal institutions—is prone to believe that he has achieved a zenith of civilization that distinguishes him from all of his "primitive" forebears. He places virtually the entire weight of his conviction that his nation-state and his systems of law are superior on this belief. This view—like all that are lacking in humility—is self-deluding. The "high-powered version of the primitive tribe" can become far more dangerous to man's welfare, his peace, and his security than the primitive tribe ever could.

Toynbee did not deny the great importance of social relations among men through government even as he warned that "Leviathan-worship is a moral enormity, even at its noblest and mildest..."[6] Man, he observed, "is a social creature" who "cannot achieve the potentialities of his nature except by going outside himself and entering into relations with other spiritual beings. The Christian would say that the most important of the soul's relations is its communion with God, but that it also needs to have relations with its fellow creatures, who are God's other children."[7]

Speaking of individuality in the moral sense of the dignity and worth of the individual, Toynbee cautioned that "worship of Leviathan" debases the individual and substitutes worship of the state—propagating the corollary expectancy that the state will meet all man's needs—for the "personal relation between the soul and God." "Individuality," declared Toynbee, "is a pearl of great moral price, when we observe the moral enormities that occur when this pearl is trampled in the mire."[8]

His illustration of the danger in what he called "Leviathan worship" would be recognizable even to twenty-first-century Western man. Primarily intended to point out the usurpation of the role of religion and faith by government and nationalistic fervor, the illustration exposes Western man's worship of himself in the form of his "high-powered" tribe.

> In religious terms, this treatment of the individual as a mere part of the community is a denial of the personal relation between the soul and God and is a substitution, for the worship of God, of a worship of the human community Leviathan, the abomination of desolation, standing in the place where

it ought not. The German National-Socialist youth leader, Baldur von Schirach, once declared that his task was "to build a great altar to Germany in every German heart."[9]

Even so, modern Western man would probably smugly respond, "Yes, but that was Nazi Germany, not us!" We should rejoin, Yes, it was us (i.e., Western civilization), as were communism and a multitude of forms of human oppression and injustice over the centuries-long life span of Western civilization. Toynbee explained why this form of worship must be wrong—and the only wise and hopeful answer to it.

> It must be wrong to worship a man-made institution which is ephemeral, imperfect, and often utterly evil in its operation…Leviathan-worship was intransigently rejected by early Christianity. If any human community were ever worthy of worship, it would be a universal state, like the Roman Empire, that has brought the blessings of unity and peace to a world long racked by war and revolution. Yet the early Christians challenged the apparently irresistible might of the Roman Imperial Government rather than compromise with a Leviathan-worship that was persuasively commended to them as being nothing more sinister than an amiable formality.[10]

But resist the temptation they did; and that resistance was the precursor to the wariness of power—and deliberate distance from it—inculcated by the Founding Fathers into the American Constitution. The state was not the answer. Rather it was, if not a *bête noire*, a beast with an insatiable appetite for power.

Power accretes power, even in a democracy, and neither the individual nor great principles are ever completely safe in its voracious presence.

ARBITRARY JUDGMENTS OF MEN ARE KING

Whenever man has sought to make the state his heaven, he has made it Hell…
Christopher Dawson[11]

Toynbee's choice of adjectives in describing the institutions of government and law—"man-made," "ephemeral," "imperfect," and "often utterly evil"—should make the ground under Western man's feet veritably tremble. Government and law can be absolutely unreliable in man's pursuit of justice and order. In this respect they need not be overtly oppressive in the fashion of a fascist or communist government; nonetheless, they often confound and impede man's search for an order that is truly just and free. No nation has ever reposed so much faith in law as has the United States, yet Robert Conquest noted one of the great flaws in this system: "…laws are interpreted by judges quite differently from what the legislators who proposed and passed them had explained as their intent. The judiciary is now in effect empowered, in the United States, to interpret general articles of the Constitution…in massive revision, on the one hand, and pettifogging detail on the other… pressing legalism too far ruins legality."[12]

Conquest's observation is related to and reminiscent of Solzhenitsyn's point in his 1978 Harvard address: "A society which is based on the letter of the law and never reaches any higher is taking very scarce advantage of the high level of human possibilities. The letter of the law is too cold and formal to have a beneficial influence on society. Whenever the tissue of life is woven of legalistic relations, there is an atmosphere of moral mediocrity, paralyzing man's noblest impulses."[13]

But we need not plumb those depths—we can loiter on the surface and recognize with Conquest that "...it is hardly any longer even claimed that the Supreme Court merely interprets the law. Its members are openly selected on political grounds, and mostly on political grounds that encroach on social policy. Judges in the circuits of the U.S. Court of Appeals are often far worse examples."[14]

All of this reflects the dominant role of fashionable trends in the culture and the tyranny of the majority that argues—because it is larger or has political power at that moment—that its rules, laws, statutes, etc., are moral and just. There are no truly sacrosanct absolutes even though there may be much pretense to that effect.

The Supreme Court Justice Oliver Wendell Holmes wrote in *The Common Law* (1881) that all law is founded on "experience." Holmes also declaimed, "Truth is the majority vote of that nation that could lick all others." The only "truth" in that statement is solely in the hard realities of power; the abuse thereof by the West, as we will see below, leads to a loss of attraction to Western ideals, ideologies and values. Francis Schaeffer referenced a 1926 letter in which Holmes wrote, "So when it comes to the development of a *corpus juris* the ultimate question is what do the dominant forces of the community want and do they want it hard enough to disregard whatever inhibitions may stand in the way." Schaeffer then pointed out that this attitude is "very different from Samuel Rutherford's biblical base and from Paul Robert's painting in which Justice points to 'The Word of God.'"[15]

Schaeffer continued by quoting Frederick Moore Vinson (1890–1953), a Chief Justice of the United States Supreme Court, "Nothing is more certain in modern society than the principle that there are no absolutes." Schaeffer then added, "All is relative; all is experience. In passing, we should note this curious mark of our age: The only absolute allowed is the absolute insistence that there is no absolute."[16] This of course is the

We the People

Article. 1

The U.S. Constitution, 1787. *A favored aphorism in the West is to declare we are nations of laws and not men. But no nation is a nation of laws and not men. Everything in government and law is determined by those who have power. Therefore the character of those in power determines everything in government and law. The Constitution is only so much aged parchment without men and women of character to honor it.*

PD-Gov

By Jarek Tuszynski (Jarekt). GNU-FDL

U.S. Supreme Court building. *No longer can it honestly be claimed that federal courts merely interpret the law. This regression reflects the dominant role of fashionable trends in the culture and the tyranny of the majority that argues— because it is larger or has political power at that moment —that its rules, laws, statutes, etc., are moral and just. There are no truly sacrosanct absolutes even though there may be much pretense to that effect.*

ironic and illogical reality, comparable to the intolerance of those who declare themselves so vociferously for "tolerance" and "diversity."

Schaeffer predicted the course the stream of modern Western history would take as it left the rock-lined bed of its heritage: "As the Christian consensus dies in countries where it has previously existed, we must expect that it will make a difference not only within the nations themselves but also in their compassion for others. What will be left will be not compassion but only utilitarianism." Furthermore, "open pragmatism" will increasingly supplant "the partial compassion which has existed." Any shortages of necessities in particular will result in an acceptance of the people of "a growing authoritarianism which promises solutions. As insecurity grows, greed—with the goals of personal peace and affluence at any price—grows."[17]

Because the "Christian consensus" is, at best, in extremis, even in America, at worst, already dead—its obituary not explicitly published such that even the most obtuse could read it—many Christians remain in love with an America that no longer is, and to some extent never was. Thus their allegiances are unwittingly divided.

Sadly—and with no hint of irony—true compassion (i.e., that which is founded on sincere caring and transcendent beliefs) will be more and more replaced—already significantly so—by an ersatz altruism that, when the individual or culture is in crisis, will be increasingly shed, like layers of fine dress clothing in tropical heat, until raw human nature in all of its nakedness is fully on display. Another manifestation of the symptoms of the disease of relativism described earlier: only the expedient, the utilitarian, and the self-centered will ultimately be given weight.

Essentially repeating the views of Robert Conquest quoted above, Schaeffer concluded, "Much modern law is not even based on precedent.... Thus...the Constitution of the United States can be made to say what the courts of the present want it to say based on a court's decision as to what the court feels is sociologically helpful...once the door is opened, anything can become law and the arbitrary judgments of men are king. Law is now freewheeling, and the courts not only interpret the laws which legislators have made, but make law. Lex Rex has become Rex Lex."[18]

PD-LOC PD

(Left) 1973 Supreme Court. *The 1973 Supreme Court held in* Roe v. Wade *"that the unborn child is not a person within the meaning and protection of the term 'person' ...[which stripped] all unborn children of all constitutional protection for their lives..." Disingenuously based on an artificial construct, "the right to privacy," which does not appear in the Constitution, it would be more accurately denoted "a doctrine of personal convenience."* (Right) Taney Supreme Court, 1857. *The Roger Taney Supreme Court, when asked in the* Dred Scott *case in 1857 whether a slave was a person, answered "No," thereby condemning tens of thousands to slavery. This decision—made under the influence of moneyed interests at that time and reflecting the status quo of political power—contributed mightily to the outbreak of the most destructive war in American history. In both the* Dred Scott *and* Roe v. Wade *cases, nine middle-aged-to-elderly men in black robes made decisions adversely affecting the lives of millions—and all done under color of law in a republic. Such is the inevitable result of government without moral absolutes.*

That the "arbitrary judgments of men are king" is a damning indictment of any legal system that professes to be just. "Justice" becomes what men say it is—men who have acquired power in the culture. This is all the more dangerous when the people continue to believe that justice in their society is constructed on the rock of immutable principles and values. Profound damage can be done to the fabric of the society, and the structural integrity upon which it was built, while the majority, gullibly and blindly, acquiesce in the results.

WE DECIDE WHO IS A PERSON

We think [Negroes] are not...and were not intended to be included, under the word "citizens" in the Constitution, and can therefore claim none of the rights and privileges which that instrument provides for and secures to citizens of the United States. On the contrary, they were at that time considered as a subordinate and inferior class of beings...
Dred Scott v. *Sandford*, U.S. Supreme Court, 1856

[Roe v. *Wade]...held that the unborn child is not a person within the meaning and protection of the term "person" utilized in the fourteenth amendment [which stripped] all unborn children of all constitutional protection for their lives, liberty, and property.*
Professor Joseph Witherspoon[19]

The moral compass bearing of an entire society can be dramatically shifted by just one or two who wield power. Albeit arbitrary, inconsistent with all moral precedent, and logically groundless,

PD

From the Anti-Slavery Office in New York City, 1837. *This was an effort during the age of slavery to convince others of the personhood of the black man. The callousness that refused to see blacks as "persons" is replicated in our time by the refusal to see the unborn child as a "person," and for related reasons. In the case of slavery, expediency and justification dictated this was necessary in order to sustain a selfish, economic purpose. In the case of abortion, expediency and justification require it in order not to disrupt selfish, personal convenience.*

nonetheless, the decisions by courts and legislative bodies may give lip service to the culture's great decemvirate while pouring the legal and moral equivalent of human wastes on its noble code.

In 1973, the American Supreme Court ruled in *Roe v. Wade* that every American woman had a *right* to an abortion—more precisely, to commit aborticide. Disturbingly, we have been here before. All of this, to a significant degree, is a reprise of one of the most notorious cases in American jurisprudence: the decision by the Supreme Court in the *Dred Scott* case just prior to the Civil War. There the Supreme Court asked, "Can a negro whose ancestors were imported into this country, and sold as slaves, become a member of the political community formed and brought into existence by the Constitution of the United States, and as such become entitled to all the rights and privileges and immunities guaranteed to the citizen?" It took Chief Justice Roger Taney forty-four pages to rationalize and justify the answer: "We think they are not, and that they are not included, and were not intended to be included, under the word 'citizens' in the Constitution, and can therefore claim none of the rights and privileges which that instrument provides for and secures to citizens of the United States. On the contrary, they were at that time considered as a subordinate and inferior class of being...." A slave was "property" and not subject to protection under the Constitution as a "person."

This decision—made under the influence of moneyed interests at that time and reflecting the *status quo* of political power—contributed mightily to the outbreak of the most destructive war in American history.

PD-art

The slave Dred Scott. *The Supreme Court asked, "Can a negro whose ancestors were imported into this country, and sold as slaves, become a member of the political community formed and brought into existence by the Constitution of the United States, and as such become entitled to all the rights and privileges and immunities guaranteed to the citizen?" It took Chief Justice Roger Taney forty-four pages to rationalize and justify the answer: "We think they are not, and that they are not included, and were not intended to be included, under the word "citizens" in the Constitution, and can therefore claim none of the rights and privileges which that instrument provides for and secures to citizens of the United States. On the contrary, they were at that time considered as a subordinate and inferior class of being...." A slave was "property," not a "person."*

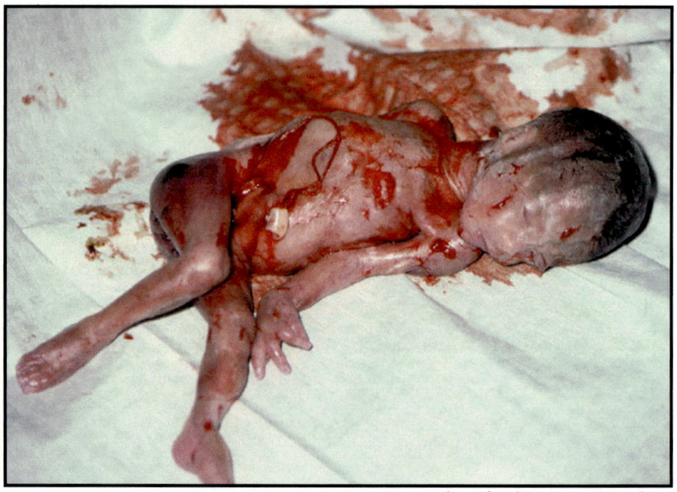

http://frontline-ministries.net/photos

"Am I not a human?" An aborted baby. *The Supreme Court in* Roe v. Wade *made essentially the same determination as the Taney Court in the* Dred Scott *case: "No, this is not a person." All of this is founded on a crass and debauched elitism. Those with power not only presume that their intellects are sufficiently robust that they may discard notions of absolute, transcendent, moral laws, but that, among the members of the culture, they and they alone are capable of making the relativistic judgments about what is best.*

Had the Supreme Court ruled otherwise, the prospects for resolving the issue of slavery less violently would have been enhanced—not to mention what it would have said about the character of American society and the sanctity of the religious principles embodied in the Constitution. Instead, to use Lincoln's words in his Second Inaugural, "all the wealth piled by the bond-men's two hundred and fifty years of unrequited toil" was "sunk," and "every drop of blood drawn with the lash [was] paid by another drawn by the sword." In acknowledgment of the immutable transcendent law of the universe, Lincoln declared, "As was said three thousand years ago, so still it must be said 'the judgments of the Lord, are true and righteous altogether.'"

There is a strong historical relationship between the issue of slavery in the nineteenth century and the issue of aborticide in the twenty-first, though the supporters of the former would surely have righteously denied any connection with the latter, and the modern day supporters of the latter equally righteously deny any association with the former. But each issue addresses the question, Who is to be recognized as a person entitled to the respect of the society and the protection of its laws? On a deeper plane, an unspoken question is being answered: Will the society display magnanimity of thought and compassion of heart to embrace both the slave and the unborn child as, like them, other children of God? On a deeper plane still, will the society honor the teachings of the founder of its traditional religion, Christianity, as irrefragable, transcendent, absolute moral principles? Shamefully, in both times, and with these issues, the American society responded, "No, and Absolutely Not!" respectively. Only the mendicants for the slave's cause managed to turn the first great injustice around—and then only on a torrent of blood.

It remains to be seen whether modern American society will debouch from its cloistered, dark place of callous, self-serving rationalizations into the bright, sunlit uplands of faith and morality. This then, too, may only come when "every drop of blood drawn" with the abortionist's curet is "paid by another drawn by the sword" in a reprise of great national trauma.

There is a deficiency of an emotional and evidentiary stimulus to question aborticide. Slavery presented American citizens of that time with ever-present, tangible human manifestations of the abomination in their midst. In our time, the human manifestations of aborticide are tossed into garbage bags, sewer drains, and incinerators. Thus, the burden of guilt for this great evil is more easily evaded.

But arrogant man will not be denied. As Francis Schaeffer pointed out, the legislative intent behind the fourteenth and the thirteenth amendments was "to prevent any court, and especially the

Supreme Court of the United States, because of its earlier performance in the *Dred Scott* case, or any other institution of government, whether legislative or executive, from ever again defining the concept of person so as to exclude any class of human beings from the protection of the Constitution and the safeguards it established for the fundamental rights of human beings, including slaves, peons, Indians, aliens, women, the poor, the aged, criminals, the mentally ill or retarded, and children, including the unborn from the time of their conception."[20]

If there are no absolutes there can be no absolute or certain justice.

Christians were the one group who took a stand against aborticide when it was commonly practiced in the Roman Empire. If, however, contemporary citizens accept the "arbitrary absolutes of the Supreme Court," why, Schaeffer asked, "wouldn't arbitrary absolutes in regard to such matters as authoritarian limitations on freedom be equally accepted as long as they were thought to be sociologically helpful?"[21] The obvious—but largely ignored—answer is that they likely would. But even if they were not, the practice of the citizenry in accepting prior arbitrary absolutes will ensure that arbitrary absolutes they don't accept will be implemented regardless.

All of this is founded on a crass and debauched elitism. Those with power not only presume that their intellects are sufficiently robust that they may discard notions of absolute, transcendent, moral laws, but that, among the members of the culture, they and they alone are capable of making the relativistic judgments about what is best. The *hoi polloi* are intellectual primitives who require their paternalistic guidance.

Yet it is not at all difficult to eviscerate any "rational" arguments for a relativistic approach to law. They neither stand up to logic nor to the tests of history. Reference to the "legal" actions of Nazi Germany can readily illustrate how everyone is potentially at risk in a culture without moral absolutes. Where there are no moral absolutes, including in democracies, man returns unwittingly to the principle of the jungle: Power is all.

Schaeffer observed that "In...a...Christian culture, a lone individual with the Bible could judge and warn society, regardless of the majority vote, because there was an absolute by which to judge." In the absence of that absolute, law

CC

Civil War dead on Gettysburg Battlefield. *Lincoln suggested that the bloody Civil War might continue until "all the wealth piled by the bond-men's two hundred and fifty years of unrequited toil" was "sunk," and "every drop of blood drawn with the lash [was] paid by another drawn by the sword." Yet, he added, "as was said three thousand years ago, so still it must be said 'the judgments of the Lord, are true and righteous altogether.'" There is a strong historical analogy between the issue of slavery in the nineteenth century and the issue of aborticide in the twenty-first.*

PD

Scene depicting the signing of the Constitution of the United States, painted for the U.S. Capitol Building by Howard Chandler Christy. *American law has shifted from the rock of absolutes to the sands of expediency. Most Americans do not recognize the dangerous extent of the transmogrification. The Founding Fathers would be appalled at the exploitation of their principles to grant legal sanction to behaviors they would regard as unspeakable. Yet they are touted endlessly in support of ideological and legal positions they would reject—undoubtedly with rage at the usurpation of their words to justify what they would never countenance.*

becomes whatever those in power say it is. "...On the basis of the absoluteness of the 51-percent vote," Schaeffer observed, "Hitler was perfectly entitled to do as he wished if he had the popular support."[22]

Sorokin described the *de facto* status of law in Western democracies when speaking of the "sensate" system of law as "man-made—frequently, indeed, as a mere instrument for the subjugation and exploitation of one group by another." "Its norms," he said, "are relative, changeable and conditional; a group of rules expedient under one set of circumstances or for one group becomes useless or even harmful in different situations or for another group. Therefore they are subject to incessant change. Nothing eternal or sacred is implied in such a system of law."[23]

Especially disturbing is the obliviousness of much of Western society to the significance of a system that operates on these principles. Nowhere is the gulf between assumptions, on the one hand, and reality, on the other, more pronounced than in the United States. The shift of American law from the

Perhaps most ironic is the historical significance of the American Second Amendment, which reflects an empowerment of the citizenry and an assurance of freedom that is greater and more extensive than any other law or constitutional provision in Western history. Nothing so bespeaks true freedom as the legal possession of a weapon in the hands of a law-abiding citizen. All other assurances of rights granted constitutionally are highly abstract; this freedom is dramatically concrete and as such does not lend itself to manipulation or abridgement. You either have it or you do not, and no amount of legal or political window-dressing will change that appearance. George Orwell, a man of some sensitivity to the usurpation of power by government, insisted, "That rifle hanging on the wall of the working-class flat or labourer's cottage, is the symbol of democracy. It is our job to see that it stays there."[32] Orwell understood what the more perceptive understand: this is not about weapons purely, but more profoundly it is about freedom and the investiture of power. Orwell did not succeed. Britain is today one of the most restrictive nations in Western civilization regarding the citizenry's ownership, use, or carrying of weapons. Is there a relationship—not causative, but relative—between this and indicia of cultural decline?

WILL THE PEOPLE OR ONLY THE GOVERNMENT BE TRUSTED?

In the end, more than they wanted freedom, they wanted comfort and security.
And in the end, they lost it all—freedom, comfort and security.
Edward Gibbon describing ancient Athens[33]

Ultimately, the central issue of all government is, Will the people be trusted with real and significant power or will this trust only truly be reposed with the organs and agents of government? Historically, power has been reposed in the hands of government not the people. That remains the case in most places in the world today. Even in titular democracies a close scrutiny of the relative and actual powers of the two forces will show that the government is overwhelmingly dominant. Yet late twentieth century and twenty-first-century Westerners find themselves beset by an appeal to permit a kind of governmental theurgy: "We will protect you from harm, and ensure your material well-being and security—if you only repose the power with us."

The speciousness in even the practical application of such a line of reasoning has been clouded by the dual forces of fear and growing dependence by citizenry on government—it is always easier to give in to fear and more lulling to assume others will protect you. Should the shift toward greater and greater governmental power continue—including in America the surrender of large chunks of the granite of the American Second Amendment—Western man will find himself eventually in the position of Sisyphus, striving once again to rid himself of weighty oppression and regain the heights of freedom lost.

With the burgeoning of ever greater and more complex world problems there will not likely be another opportunity like that of the Great American Experiment. Freedom loving man may find himself condemned to roll the stone uphill forevermore in a world grown so dark, so complex, so populous, so technologically and scientifically dangerous, that fear has become the driving force behind every significant act of man. He will come belatedly, poignantly, to realize that he exchanged a boon of inestimable value for the expedient of a mess of pottage.

Some would argue that, even so, Americans still have the other freedoms guaranteed by the Constitution. But few Americans know that throughout the history of the Soviet Union, the Soviet constitution, which was amended many times, always had provisions guaranteeing many freedoms including freedom of speech. As a professor of international studies and political science, I made a practice of reading these "guarantees" to my university international studies' students and asking the question, "What's the difference?" Most Western students, like most Americans, are stymied by anything that appears to be the law or a constitutional "right" that is not honored; it is part of the West's conviction that law is sacrosanct that confuses them. The difference lies in two critical realities: First, we repeat the observation made earlier: there is no such thing as a nation of laws and not men. All government is ultimately of men. And all government is no better than the character and caliber of the men and women who compose it. Second, the power in the Soviet Union was always in the hands of the government, not the people. If the reverse had been true the Soviet people would have truly had freedom of speech.

Freedom is always precarious at best—even in a democracy—and it is forever at threat from those who would kill it. Freedom is not secured purely by a constitution, no matter how noble or wisely drafted. As de Tocqueville saw so clearly, it is only secured by the faith, character, and values of those charged with its care. The wise person will always be wary of those who have power for in power is bred untruth, injustice, tyranny, suffering, and despair.

The consequence of surrendering power to government—of treating government as anything other than a dangerous concentration of power—will be the loss of freedom. Western man has incrementally continued to give up large portions of his birthright of freedom in his quest for a greater sense of security and affluence. But "this same individual," as de Tocqueville stated it, "who has so completely sacrificed his own free will, has no natural propensity to obedience; he cowers, it is true, before the pettiest officer; but he braves the law with the spirit of a conquered foe as soon as its superior force is removed: his oscillations between servitude and license are perpetual."[34]

This is because he has made a self-centered bargain, but in so doing, he is impliedly acknowledging his lack of civic interest and responsibility. This is a crass and cynical negotiation and all who operate thusly come to see the world and others in crass and cynical terms. Americans of an earlier time would have said to an overbearing Washington when it implied that it could do better than they: "If we make mistakes, they're our mistakes, and we want to keep them"—but no longer.

Jean-Jacques Rousseau, by Maurice Quentin de La Tour, 1753. *Jean-Jacques Rousseau, in the words of Christopher Dawson, "...became the founder and prophet of a new faith—the religion of democracy.... [However, it] was not the benevolent abstraction which the disciples of Rousseau had worshipped but a fierce will to power which destroyed every man and institution that stood in its way." Spengler warned that the high-sounding legalism of democracy is not a protection from two instruments of power most resorted to in a democracy: money and rhetoric.*

PD

If de Tocqueville's diagnosis of the progression of the disease that kills freedom was correct, it is self-evident that there has been no change, rather more of the same. As the American Founding Fathers and de Tocqueville insisted, certain character traits and beliefs must be present in the citizens of a democracy; otherwise the term *democracy* will prove to be a euphemism for the tyranny of the majority and/or the end stage of cultural dissipation. It is here that we intersect most completely with the views of our observers of the historical phenomenon of civilizational decline and decay.

THE STATE AS GOD—DEMOCRACY AS RELIGION AND MAN WORSHIPPING HIS CREATIONS

This reinterpretation of liberalism in religious terms was the work of Jean-Jacques Rousseau, who thus became the founder and prophet of a new faith—the religion of democracy.
Christopher Dawson[35]

Sorokin told us what the state and any ideology, including democracy, are not: "Neither capitalism, nor socialism, nor communism, nor totalitarianism; neither private, nor corporate property; neither mechanical individualism nor mechanistic collectivism is an absolute value. Neither monarchy nor republic, neither aristocracy nor democracy, neither national state nor international federation can claim to be absolute values. In certain conditions each of these is the best possible form; under other conditions each of these becomes a mere fetish, empty, hollow, even harmful."[36]

In Sorokin's declaration, a precept is laid down upon which all of our observers appear to stand: No form of government, including democracy, represents an absolute value. Yet in the West, democracy is treated with a reverence once reserved for deeply held religious beliefs. As Christopher Dawson in *Religion and World History* explained, this is precisely because the notion of democracy has in considerable measure supplanted religious conviction as a manifestation of the secular religion of the West. "The situation was ripe for the rise of a new spiritual force which would fill the void created by the temporary breakdown of Catholic action and give an outlet to the religious instincts that found no satisfaction in the rational culture of the Enlightenment, for the Enlightenment had swept and garnished the Western mind without bringing anything to take the place of the religion that it had destroyed."[37]

Since man always worships something—even if only he himself is the pathetic object of his ablutions and genuflections—Enlightenment man needed new doctrines and votaries to sing the praises of the new faith. Who they were and what they devised would be colored by the character of the prophets of the new religion.

> The typical man of the age, like Voltaire or Frederick the Great or Horace Walpole, was the final product of an aristocratic humanist culture. He had all the gifts that a purely intellectual culture could bestow, but the hard-polished surface of his mind reflected light without warmth. If the liberal ideas of the Enlightenment were to penetrate beyond the limited world of the privileged classes and change the thought and the life of the people, they had to make an appeal to psychological forces that lay beneath the surface of rational consciousness. They had to be transformed from a philosophy into a religion,

> to cease to be mere ideas and to become articles of faith. This reinterpretation of liberalism in religious terms was the work of Jean-Jacques Rousseau, who thus became the founder and prophet of a new faith—the religion of democracy.[38]

If we equate "warmth" with love, which we assume Dawson is implying, then he surely was correct. This species of humanism is essentially ruthless; but I do not believe that it "reflected light," except perhaps a tinted fluorescent or incandescent form—but surely not the brilliance of the sun. The Enlightenment brought to fruition in the political realm what was begun in the Renaissance: the exaltation of man and his intellect and the corollary rejection of faith and religion as the ultimate source of truth and moral guidance. This then began the worship in the West of the secular religion of democracy, its economic handmaiden, capitalism, and the philosophical belief, if not in the perfectibility of man, then in man's "innate goodness" that can be appealed to through reason and the intellect. All are doctrinally of the same cloth.

In concept and language consistent with the writings of de Tocqueville and Schaeffer, Dawson noted the corrupting effect of this regression "even in America" where

> the modern democratic state…is something quite different from the form of state envisaged by the men who formed the American Constitution… [T]hey were the enemies of state intervention and aimed at creating a system which would leave the community and the individual free to lead their own lives and frame their own cultural institutions. But the modern democratic state partakes of the nature of the Church. It is the educator and spiritual guide of its citizens and any influence which withdraws the citizen and especially the citizen's children from this universal guidance is felt to be undesirable, if not positively disloyal.[39]

We saw earlier how Arnold Toynbee warned about the worship of the state. He was not narrowly referring to communist, fascist or other authoritarian forms of governance but also to democracy itself.

> In our Western world of today, the worship of Leviathan—the self-worship of the tribe—is a religion to which all of us pay some measure of allegiance; and this tribal religion is, of course, sheer idolatry. Communism, which is another of our latter-day religions, is, I think, a leaf taken from the book of Christianity—a leaf torn out and misread. Democracy is another leaf from the book of Christianity, which has also, I fear, been torn out and, while perhaps not misread, has certainly been half emptied of meaning by being divorced from its Christian context and secularized; and we have obviously, for a number of generations past, been living on spiritual capital, I mean clinging to Christian practice without possessing the Christian belief—and practice unsupported by belief is a wasting asset, as we have suddenly discovered, to our dismay, in this generation….[40]

The accuracy of the latter insight was demonstrated in my presence when the former leader of the Soviet Union, Mikhail Gorbachev, attempted to assert what he believed were the similarities between communism and Christianity and insisted that communism was simply a fulfillment of a Christian doctrine and practice! Were one to see this from the perspective of someone "clinging to Christian practice without possessing the Christian belief," this viewpoint becomes plausible. It is not remotely credible, however, to the true Christian, if for no other reason than the essential truth that Christianity centers on the person of Christ—a concept anathema to communism's atheistic ideology.

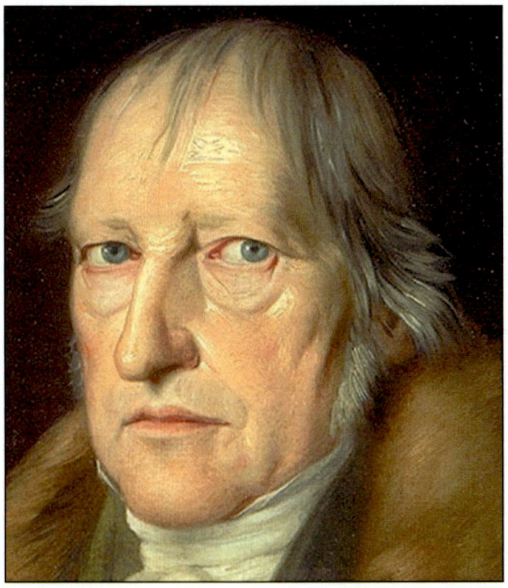
PD

Georg Wilhelm Friedrich Hegel, by Jakob Schlesinger, 1831. *Hegel argued that man must venerate the state as "the Divine upon the earth." Hegelian ideas coupled with Prussian social conformity led to Nazism and the Holocaust.*

Dawson illustrated, through a specific historical experience, how the worship of man through his intellectual achievements or his institutions—conceived first in the mind of misguided philosophers and then spread throughout society—can lead to disaster. The philosopher in this case was Hegel, who viewed the state as more than a "mere political instrument": "As high as mind stands over nature, so high does the state stand over physical life. Man must therefore venerate the state as the Divine upon Earth.... The march of God in the world that is what the state is."[41] The society was Prussian: "For the Prussian people, unlike any other people in Europe, had been made by the State and for the State, by a conscious process of military and political organisation."[42] Calculating the sum of Hegelian philosophy plus the Prussian conformist mindset should be unnecessary. We now know the score without doing the addition. Core ideas, values, and beliefs count for all, as we repeatedly declare. But the math is only obvious to many because of the inescapable horrors of recent history.

The demurrer will surely be, "Yes, but this led to authoritarianism in the form of fascism and Nazism, not to democracy." But this rebuttal betrays a failure to understand the underlying principles Dawson was enunciating.

Such a response reflects, in and of itself, the dangerously reverential notions associated with democracy in the West—another of man's creations and one that is also subject to his abuse in the absence of closely held, absolute, transcendent values and beliefs.

Dawson quoted Hölderlin through the voice of Hyperion addressing his friend Alabanda with a "prophetic criticism of the false path his friend was to follow to the misfortune of Germany and of Europe"[43]—a dramatic warning to anyone who would elevate the state, or any form of government, to a deity status.

> You grant the State yet too much power. It should not demand what it cannot compel. For the gift of Love and of the Spirit cannot be forced. Let it leave them untouched, or let men take its law and nail it to the pillory. By Heaven he knows not how he sins who would make the State a moral schoolmaster. Whenever man has sought to make the State his heaven, he has made it Hell.... The State has no jurisdiction over thee. But if it does not hinder thee, thou wilt yet come, thou wilt come with thine almighty glory and raise us above mortality.[44]

In biblical language, Dawson saw this "descent from these cloudy summits of the romantic Sinai to the worship of the Secular State, that Golden Calf in the desert of materialism, is one of the strangest events in the history of European thought." For Dawson—and for anyone who loves freedom and values the individual—Hegel was a false prophet who "remains as a mighty monument and symbol of this spiritual journey into the wilderness."[45]

But the West assumes that its ideology and its favored form of governance are all above this, and thus it continues deeper into the wilderness. Fascism and Nazism having been so thoroughly discredited by their horrors—and communism equally so by its own horrors, as well as its economic incompetence—Western man now believes he has found the answer in democracy.

DEMOCRACY AND "THE WILL-TO-POWER"

The will-to-power operating under a pure democratic disguise has accomplished its task so well that the object's sense of freedom is actually flattered by the most thorough-going enslavement that has ever existed.
Oswald Spengler[46]

Dawson, in *Religion and World History*, demonstrated how danger was present from the birth of democracy as a Western phenomenon of government. "For as the Revolution advanced, it gradually revealed the naked reality that had been veiled by the antiquated trappings of royalty and tradition—the General Will—and it was not the benevolent abstraction which the disciples of Rousseau had worshipped but a fierce will to power which destroyed every man and institution that stood in its way."[47]

This "naked reality" of the "will to power" has been the subject of many alarms by those whose heads were not turned by vacuous promises and high-flown rhetoric. Perhaps no one was as blunt in warning of the dangers implicit even in democracy as Oswald Spengler, who also used the phrase "will to power" in describing the underlying dynamic of all government. Spengler warned that the high sounding legalism of democracy was not a protection, particularly from two of the instruments of power most commonly resorted to in a democracy: money and rhetoric, or what we might call in today's language propaganda (though it is rarely characterized with such honesty) and media.

The manipulation of others through the resources of money and political or ideological propaganda has been with us since the inception of democracy in the ancient Greco-Roman era. Marcus Licinius Crassus—largely through the currency in his own ample pockets—deftly played the fiddle of the Roman heart to gain and keep greater and greater power. But in the heart of the extravagant wealth and the technological dominance of mass media in the modern West the opportunities to manipulate and control are legion—all the while persuading the objects of the efforts that they are autonomous, free, and self-determining. When in fact, Western "democratic" man is often the object of "an influencing process in the Classical style...by a rhetoric" that works "upon every ear *and eye*; by devices many of which to us would be repellent and almost intolerable, such as rehearsed sob-effects...by shameless flattery of the audience, fantastic lies about opponents; by the employment of brilliant phrases and resounding cadenzas...by games and presents; by threats and blows; but, above all, by money."[48]

For democracy to work as intended, the people must have access to the truth, the wisdom to discern the false and manipulative from the truth, the character to care, and the courage to act upon it. If this statement of principle strikes one as idealistic, that perception is suggestive already of the degree to which cynical manipulation rules the decision-making process in Western democracies.

Though we in the West propagandize ourselves and give frequent lip service to some similar exalted view, the truth is that most Westerners either consciously or, more often, unconsciously sense that this is not the reality. The cynical and self-serving manipulation extends of course beyond the political sphere into the economic, which means it pervades everything in Western culture and, as Spengler put it for his time—which is even more applicable in ours "...politics have created through the press a force-field of world-wide intellectual and financial tensions in which every individual unconsciously takes up the place allotted to him, so that he must think, will and act as a ruling personality somewhere or other in the distance thinks fit."[49]

Admittedly, the precise extent and depth of this control will vary from individual to individual depending upon their diligence in seeking the truth and their powers of discernment. But the salient point that the manipulation exists and has a powerful impact on what citizens of the West think—or think they think—should not be lost. Manipulative plutocracy would perhaps be closer to an accurate appellation for government in the West. Democracy—the best of the worst, perhaps—warrants Burke's eternal vigilance. The forms of power that are recognized as such and accorded any standing in Western civilization are almost exclusively political and economic.

But Spengler and Solzhenitsyn both spoke of manifestations of power that would not necessarily be perceived as such. Political power, as we use the term here, does not mean exclusively that which emanates from government and law, but the ability to influence large numbers of people. Hence media figures, entertainment personalities, and some religious figures have political power. The dynamics of this form of political power can be most clearly discerned by the efforts of politicians to become associated with popular religious, sports, or entertainment figures (e.g., the politician Richard Nixon with the evangelist Billy Graham, etc.) or vice versa.

Spengler suggested a form of stealth tyranny found in a democracy that remains unseen by victims who feel themselves free. "Formerly a man did not dare to think freely. Now he dares, but cannot; his will to think is only a willingness to think to order, and this is what he feels as his liberty."[50] Spengler believed—and I believe the historical evidence at least in part supports him—that this "...is the end of Democracy. If in the world of truths it is proof that decides all, in that of facts it is success. Success means that one being triumphs over the others. Life has won through, and the dreams of the world-improvers have turned out to be but the tools of master-natures."[51]

Mankind has been overrun by "master-natures." History is, in substantial part, the archive of their depredations on humanity. Yet humanity foolishly persists in admiring many of them; Napoleon's pompous, Parisian tomb, a tangible illustration.

Spengler insisted on our looking at a reality of human experience that often remains hidden, or at least unacknowledged: Power attracts—in any society, authoritarian or democratic—and, for those who want it, the ruthless quest for power always means someone's victory, another's defeat. But the harsh reality is never depicted that way; rather it is often luxuriantly dressed in the habiliments of professed unselfishness—even the ersatz nobility of "world improvers." This hidden current of will-to-power in human nature—once it nears its aims—will often shed its finery so that the nakedness of the aggression becomes obvious even to the most obtuse of its victims.

Such was the evolution of communism from an idealistic stratagem to free workers from oppression to the battle plan by which "master-natures" gained and held power over millions. Without the civilizing and ennobling effects of faith and belief, dragons are spawned. The contrast, for example, between the worst of governments in the lifetime of the United States and any government in Russia during the lifetime of communism tells us something, if we are willing to hear. Contrast the cloven hooves in the boots of Stalin, Lenin, and other communist leaders with what we would find in Washington's, Jefferson's, Lincoln's, or Roosevelt's shoes. The machinations and intrigue of most of the communist era read like appalling, heart-stopping soap opera scripts written by Satan himself in the basement of hell. What were the differences? Were the Russians just genetically programmed for deceit, betrayal, cruelty, and evil? Consider perhaps—as Alexander Solzhenitsyn pointed out—the belief system. One acknowledged full accountability to a Supreme Being and a moral code that dictated doing unto others as you would have others do unto you; the other honored no code whatsoever, unless you count the notion that the Party is free to do anything in its quest for power.

Study evil and you will more fully value good—and perhaps learn to recognize its source. The degree of your wisdom can largely be measured by your ability to discern the difference and the nature of the soil in which the latter, and only the latter, will grow. Mankind has spent much time studying evil; and, withal, it is a worthy pursuit. But contrary to popular notion, the question Where does the evil come from? is not the great question. The Great Question is Where does the Good come from?

Christopher Dawson perceived the false premises that have caused democracy to have been so venerated in the West despite the overwhelming historical evidence that no form of government warrants anything other than wariness and perpetual vigilance.

> There are two mistaken views of democracy, both of which have caused infinite misunderstandings … One of these regards democracy as a crude destructive force that cares nothing for the finer values of civilised life, that is indifferent to culture and scientific knowledge, and seeks only to satisfy the vanity and greed of the masses. This is the fallacy of the reactionaries. And, on the other hand, there is the ideal of democracy that is founded on false belief in the perfectibility of human nature. It regards all the evils of society as due to the misdeeds of kings and governments and believes that if once the power

Throughout history, mankind has been overrun by "master-natures." History is, in substantial part, the archive of their depredations on humanity. Yet humanity foolishly persists in admiring many of them; Napoleon's pompous Parisian tomb *is a tangible illustration. Power attracts—in any society, authoritarian or democratic—and, for those who want it, the ruthless quest for power always means someone's victory, another's defeat. But the harsh reality is rarely depicted that way.*

By Javier Cáceres Arroyo. Used by permission.

> is put into the hands of the common people, everything will go well, everyone will be happy, and the world will be transformed into a Utopia.[52]

I agree with Dawson's realistic conclusion: "In reality, democracy is neither the enemy of culture nor a cure for all the ills of humanity. It is simply the culmination of the old European tradition of social and political freedom that has always been one of the essential elements in Western culture."[53]

THE DOMINANCE OF MONEY IN WESTERN DEMOCRACY

...the problem of economic equality is the real crux of democracy. You can give nominal political rights to every citizen without much difficulty, but when you attempt to put into practice the full programme of real democracy—that is to say, to give every citizen equal opportunities of happiness and an equal share in the good things of life—you are faced with a serious dilemma.
Christopher Dawson[54]

Though material wealth is always a power factor in any structure, it is particularly so in a democracy. Spengler referred to it as "that other democratic quantity" that "lost no time in making its appearance and reminding men of the fact that one can make use of constitutional rights only when one has money."[55]

The truth in this observation could be attested to by any candid lawyer in the West. Simply asserting one's rights, much less protecting one's self from heavy-handed and unjust exercise of power by the state, often requires more money—and sometimes years of one's life—than many citizens have at their disposal. Thus democracy often protects the wealthy while merely holding out promises to the less financially fortunate. Spengler's assertion, that in a democracy "one can make use of constitutional rights only when one has money," is effectively affirmed by Dawson.

> ...the problem of economic equality is the real crux of democracy. You can give nominal political rights to every citizen without much difficulty, but when you attempt to put into practice the full programme of real democracy—that is to say, to give every citizen equal opportunities of happiness and an equal share in the good things of life—you are faced with a serious dilemma. Complete economic equality seems attainable only by state socialism, and any thorough-going system of socialism seems to involve, as in Russia, the omnipotence of the state and all the dangers of a return to despotism and the negation of individual rights which that implies.[56]

Dawson's and Spengler's recognition of the great weakness in the democratic system posed by the role of money is central to the arguments of those who oppose democracy as a form of government. Alluded to elsewhere in this book is a debate that I participated in with some of Russia's leading intellectuals in Moscow during the 1980s. Their various thrusts, seeking a joint or weakness in the armor of logic of the democratic system, were parried, until, with belated tactical wisdom, they impaled our case on the assertion of injustice and inequality in democracies stemming from disparate wealth. That their system was, in its way, far worse, did not assuage the wound; it just made a wise and realistic choice easier.

WESTERN MAN'S GRAVE TURN: THE ATROPHY OF FAITH, THE HYPERTROPHY OF THE STATE, AND THE TYRANNY OF THE MAJORITY

The West ended up by truly enforcing human rights, sometimes even excessively, but man's sense of responsibility to God and society grew dimmer and dimmer.... [T]he legalistically selfish aspect of Western approach and thinking has reached its final dimension and the world wound up in a harsh spiritual crisis.... All the glorified technological achievements of Progress, including the conquest of outer space, do not redeem the Twentieth century's moral poverty which no one could imagine even as late as in the Nineteenth Century.
Alexander Solzhenitsyn[57]

The rampant leprosy of modern skepticism treated with the cosmetic surgery of man's vain exaltation of self has led to a disfigured monster that is neither one thing nor the other. Western civilization was once suffused with the conviction that man possessed an immortal soul—one that the state could not touch and that, along with the state, was accountable to transcendent moral laws. This meant that neither the state nor man's laws were the ultimate authority and that the "ultimate authority" was timeless, immutable and inescapable. As Western society became secularized the effects of this belief were not immediately or fully obliterated.

As Dawson noted to the contrary, "...the more men lost their faith in God, the more desperately did they cling to the belief in the liberty and value of human personality which was the fruit of a thousand years of Christian culture."[58] Alluding in another of his works to what the secularization of the West will mean, specifically to the American Christian heritage, Dawson predicted that the situation was "full of dangers for a Christian society."

> So long as an overwhelming majority of members of the American Congress are at least nominal church members, there is little possibility of the State adopting an actively anti-Christian policy. But the prospect for the future is more disquieting. For the more completely secularized public education becomes...the more the Christian element in our culture will diminish and the more complete will be the victory of secularization as the working religion, or rather counter-religion, of the American people....It is only a short step from here to the point at which the Christian way of life is condemned and outlawed as a deviation from the standard patterns of social behavior.[59]

This is further evidence of Dawson's foresight. *Historic Reality* was published in 1961, a year in which the overwhelming majority of Americans would have regarded these insights as improbable, even alarmist. Yet within two generations the trends predicted were undeniably apparent.

Francis Schaeffer, writing a generation or so after Dawson, foresaw the coming clash between the America that had been and the America that would be. In a supreme effort to dismember the ideological propaganda of our time and to illustrate the historical foundations of the American republic, Schaeffer began with some of the philosophical antecedents. Citing the Scotsman Samuel Rutherford (1600–1661)—who wrote *Lex Rex* (Law Is King), which heavily influenced the American Founding Fathers in the drafting of the American Constitution—Schaeffer wrote that Rutherford's book presented "a government of law rather than of the arbitrary decisions of men—because the Bible as the final authority was there as the base."[60]

PD. Photo by Kevin McCoy.

United States Capitol. *Dawson warned, "So long as an overwhelming majority of...Congress are at least nominal church members, there is little possibility of the State adopting an actively anti-Christian policy. But...the more completely secularized public education becomes...the more...complete...the victory of secularization as the working religion...of the American people. [This is] only a short step...to the point the Christian way of life is condemned and outlawed as a deviation...."*

Rutherford's work, Schaeffer said, was "mediated" through John Witherspoon (1723–1794), a Presbyterian educated at Edinburgh University, who was later president of what became Princeton University, and the philosopher John Locke (1632–1704), who, "though secularizing the Presbyterian tradition, nevertheless drew heavily from it. He stressed inalienable rights, government by consent, separation of powers, and the right of revolution. But the biblical base for these is discovered in Rutherford's work."[61] Schaeffer concluded that "without this biblical background, the whole system would be without a foundation." Locke's references to "natural rights" are confounded from multiple values and beliefs but have no foundation other than thin air without an ultimate authority in the form of a god and a higher law. As Schaeffer put it, "He stated the results which come from biblical Christianity without having the base which produced them. That is, he secularized Christian teaching."[62]

Thomas Jefferson and the Christians and deists who largely made up the political and cultural leadership of the time then relied upon the end product to create the democratic structure we know today. The foundation of that edifice—even to the extent it was "secularized"—was "that 51 percent of the vote never becomes the final source of right and wrong in government because the absolutes of the Bible are available to judge a society. The 'little man,' the private citizen, can at any time stand up and, on the basis of biblical teaching, say that the majority is wrong. So, to the extent to which the biblical teaching is practiced, one can control the despotism of the majority vote or the despotism of one person or group."[63]

What Schaeffer did not say here is that the "little man's" only true protection, even in a democracy, is a transcendent belief system that has its authority in something other than what other men say—whether men elected to power or simply a majority of one's fellow citizens. Christianity provided that extraordinary spiritual and moral constitution. Without it, democracy becomes just another

method by which men can impose their will on other men regardless of the merits or the morality of that will. Aborticide and homosexual "marriage" are simply two of the more salient, recent examples in the West.

Contrary to the declarations of secularists, Plato's *Republic* was not the basis of the republican form of government established by the American Founding Fathers. Nothing in *The Republic* is comparable to the unique freedoms granted in the American Constitution. This is because the bases for those freedoms were biblical, and they were consistent with the Founding Fathers' (again, largely a mixture of Christians and deists) oft-stated conviction that there was a God and a higher moral law that transcended all. In their view, without this conviction of a superseding ultimate authority everything rests on man himself—and that is the most uncertain and flimsy of bases. They trusted neither human nature nor human institutions. The notion of "inalienable rights" derives directly from this understanding.

If man is the center and source of all, then rights can be alienated because they are subject to the caprices of man and his culture. For rights to be inalienable there must be a higher authority that is not subject to amendment or abrogation. That higher authority can only be God.

In a passage that should be a reminder of the folly in the vain, modernity-centric notion that the latest is the most sophisticated and the wisest, Schaeffer gave the core of this fundamental recognition upon which American democracy was originally founded: "The Reformers were not romantic about man. With their strong emphasis on the Fall, they understood that since every person is indeed a sinner there is a need for checks and balances, especially on people in power."[64]

Especially apropos for our time was Schaeffer's recognition that democracy and freedom are not abstractions and institutions that possess freestanding authority, nor can they—in the truest and most complete form—be implanted anywhere indiscriminately.

Like a species of imposing and strong oak, a sapling placed in the wrong soil and the wrong climate may never achieve its intended strength and magnificence. The oak of democracy has flourished for so long in the soil of a deeply religious society (and not just any religion, but Christianity) and the climate of conviction that there is a transcendent moral law to which everyone is accountable. These propitious elements cannot be found everywhere, and though it is *en vogue* in our time to tout the development of democracy anywhere and everywhere in the world, Western political and cultural leaders will find that this formula for world peace will go only so far.

But for our purposes, the greater point of this brief historical diversion is to note that when the foundation of such an edifice is piecemeal disassembled and in its place a protean will-of-the-majority substituted, you eventually have freedom—as the American Founding Fathers thought of it—in name only; and the result could be more aptly described by the term "majority license." This is, in fact, what exists today in the West. Though Americans continue to lionize their Founding Fathers, they do so while betraying a fundamental tenet of their ancestors' beliefs and practices.

Not only has this erosion contributed immeasurably to the decline and decay of Western civilization, it has corroded one of the most efficacious forms of social order. Christopher Dawson spoke of the paradoxical effects of "social control" that is externally imposed. Understanding the distinction between freedom and license is important to understanding Dawson's point: "It is the great paradox of civilization that every victory over nature, every increase of social control, also increases the burden of humanity. When man builds a fortress he also builds a prison, and the stronger it is, the greater its cost in human suffering."[65]

This truth is one of the reasons why social control founded on the voluntary acceptance of a transcendent moral order guided by conscience is always superior to unbridled license on the one hand or external forms of social control, such as government and law, on the other. Though the latter are surely necessary, they will never fulfill the functions of both ordering human society and granting man the freedom to pursue his own destiny.

The burdens on government and law to meet social needs are immeasurably greater where there is no internal belief system that is transcendent and that nurtures unselfish choices on the part of the individual. The absolute necessity for compulsion in any form of government, even a democracy, can never approach the freedom proffered through the absence of external compulsion that characterizes the Christian religion.

In respect of the significance of an "internal order" that derived from belief in a god and a transcendent order, Dawson repeated what Toynbee and others also noted, that "...all the great civilizations of the ancient world believed in a transcendent divine order which manifested itself alike in the cosmic order—the law of heaven; in the moral order—the law of justice; and in religious ritual; and it was only in so far as society was coordinated with the divine order by the sacred religious order of ritual and sacrifice that it had the right to exist and to be considered a civilized way of life."[66] This "ancient wisdom" has been forgotten and civilization has "cut adrift from its old moorings." "Custom and tradition and law and authority have lost their old sacredness and moral prestige. They have all become the servants of public opinion and of the will of society." The consequence of this is increasing instability. Then Dawson offered an epidemiological reason why: "As civilization becomes materially richer and more powerful, it becomes spiritually or religiously weaker and poorer."[67] This is a central theme we will revisit: Sorokin et al rejecting the oracularity of the received wisdom of our age.

Dawson explained, in *Religion and the Rise of Western Culture*, the differences between an ideology, such as that of democracy, and a faith—and the confusion of the two common in the West.

> An ideology...is very different from a faith, although it is intended to fulfill the same sociological functions. It is the work of man, an instrument by which the conscious political will attempts to mould the social tradition to its purpose.
>
> But faith looks beyond the world of man and his works; it introduces man to a higher and more universal range of reality than the finite and temporal world to which the

PD

Kemal Ataturk. *The celebrated war hero and later president of Turkey was a conspicuous example of what Toynbee called "Herodianism," the practice of the weaker culture that seeks to learn from and emulate more powerful cultures. Ataturk led Turkey into the twentieth century by emulating the West, first by creating a secular state. Samuel Huntington observed, however, "To become rich and powerful, they would have to become like the West. Now, however, these Kemalist attitudes have disappeared in East Asia."*

> state and the economic order belong. And thereby it introduces into human life an element of spiritual freedom which may have a creative and transforming influence on man's social culture and historical destiny as well as on his inner personal experience....[W]e shall find there is an intimate relation between [a culture's] religious faith and its social achievement. Even a religion which is explicitly other-worldly and appears to deny all the values and standards of human society may, nevertheless, exert a dynamic influence on culture and provide the driving forces in movements of social change. "Religion is the key of history," said Lord Acton, and today, when we realize the tremendous influence of the unconscious on human behaviour and the power of religion to bind and loose these hidden forces, Acton's saying has acquired a wider meaning than he realized.[68]

In this passage Dawson explicitly noted the use of ideology "to fulfill the same sociological functions" of faith—which, of course, it does very poorly. Nor does ideology introduce "man to a higher and more universal range of reality." In Lord Acton's famous observation Dawson is revealing one of the most significant of a handful of elite guiding principles of history. Solzhenitsyn would affirm Acton. Solzhenitsyn also declared that the ideology of democracy is not an answer to man's problems.

> ...in early democracies, as in American democracy at the time of its birth, all individual human rights were granted because man is God's creature. That is, freedom was given to the individual conditionally, in the assumption of his constant religious responsibility....Two hundred or even fifty years ago, it would have seemed quite impossible, in America, that an individual could be granted boundless freedom simply for the satisfaction of his instincts or whims. Subsequently, however, all such limitations were discarded everywhere in the West; a total liberation occurred from the moral heritage of Christian centuries with their great reserves of mercy and sacrifice. State systems were becoming increasingly and totally materialistic. The West ended up by truly enforcing human rights, sometimes even excessively, but man's sense of responsibility to God and society grew dimmer and dimmer. In the past decades, the legalistically selfish aspect of Western approach and thinking has reached its final dimension and the world wound up in a harsh spiritual crisis and a political impasse. All the glorified technological achievements of Progress, including the conquest of outer space, do not redeem the twentieth century's moral poverty which no one could imagine even as late as in the Nineteenth Century. [69]

THE LOSS OF THE WEST'S ATTRACTION: NOBILITY AND PRINCIPLE DISPLACED BY MATERIALISM, RELATIVISM, AND EXPEDIENCY

For several centuries non-Western peoples envied...the success in Western values and institutions, and...attempted to apply it in their own societies. To become rich and powerful, they would have to become like the West. Now, however, these...attitudes have disappeared in East Asia.
Samuel Huntington[70]

The truth in Solzhenitsyn's warnings is affirmed by evidence that notions of a transcendent God and moral law were eroding even in nineteenth-century America. In an insight lost on most Western citizens, who persist in viewing themselves as the apex of history and civilization, Samuel Huntington noted that the very attributes the West values so highly—which Solzhenitsyn condemns—are increasingly rejected by much of the rest of the world.

> Western values and institutions have appealed to people from other cultures because they were seen as the source of Western power and wealth. This process has been going on for centuries. Between 1000 and 1300...Christianity, Roman law, and other elements of Western culture were adopted by Hungarians, Poles, and Lithuanians, and this "acceptance of Western civilization was stimulated by mingled fear and admiration of the military prowess of Western princes." As Western power declines, the ability of the West to impose Western concepts of human rights, liberalism, and democracy on other civilizations also declines and so does the attractiveness of those values to other civilizations. ...For several centuries non-Western peoples envied the economic prosperity, technological sophistication, military power, and political cohesion of Western societies. They sought the secret of this success in Western values and institutions, and when they identified what they thought might be the key they attempted to apply it in their own societies. To become rich and powerful, they would have to become like the West. Now, however, these Kemalist attitudes have disappeared in East Asia.[71]

There will be no more Ataturks—certainly not in the Muslim world nor even in Asia—a consequence of the West's foolishness rather than the rest of the world's indifference. The Herodians, as Toynbee referred to the foreigner from the weaker culture who sought to learn and benefit from more powerful cultures, still covet the wealth and technology of the West, but they no longer see the values and ideology of the West as the route to their acquisition—or at least as a path they wish to take to get them. I differ from Professor Huntington in that I do not believe this is purely a result of the decline of Western power. The evidence suggests that the West's self-centered materialism and dissipations are now the source of revulsion, and even contempt, from large areas of the globe. That there are often elements of hypocrisy in this "righteousness" may also be true, but that changes nothing. Touting democracy—even aggressively promoting democracy in other cultures—will not stem the tide of disrepute for the West.

The West's appeal, such as it is, is now largely materialistic and economic, not moral, idealistic, or ideological. Like the meretricious charms of a woman of low repute, many may seek her favors yet never wish to take her home to meet their parents.

Toynbee, writing *ex cathedra* as one of the world's great historians in *Civilization on Trial* during the height of the Cold War, spoke of world circumstances that have largely changed today. But his implicit insights into human nature give us some idea of why, even in a democracy, freedom may not hold sway despite all the institutions and the declarations created in support of it. Simultaneously, we can see other reasons why the appeal of the West, its ideologies and

PD

Mohammad Mossadegh, *the democratically elected Iranian Prime Minister in 1951, was ousted in a CIA-backed coup in 1953 in a dispute over Western ownership of Iranian oil fields. A foreign policy detached from morality is a prescription for failure and a loss of credibility in the eyes of others. The ruthlessness of* Realpolitik *will gain some "successes"—but only so far. Nations, just as individuals, ultimately pay the price. The U.S. has paid heavily where Iran is concerned and will likely pay yet more.*

its form of governance, has waned so markedly. Neither the "capitalist nor the communist world" is "the earthly paradise that it claims to be." Each revealed "their fears in the measures," which each took "to protect itself" from "the other's radiation." The "iron curtain" spoke "eloquently" of communism's fears, but "on the Capitalist side there" was "a corresponding, though less paralysing, fear of Communist missionary activity" that did not "express itself in governmental bans on personal intercourse" but "very readily" became "inflamed into a panic-stricken hysteria."[72]

This fear led Americans to repeatedly betray their own principles and professed values—especially those of democracy, justice for the individual, and self-determination—in places like Mossadegh's, and later the Shah's Iran, Somoza's Nicaragua, Batista's Cuba, Marcos' Philippines, and, early on, in Diem's Vietnam. But a foreign policy detached from morality—even in the name of survival—is ultimately a prescription for failure and a loss of credibility in the eyes of others. The ruthlessness of *Realpolitik* will surely gain some successes—but only so far. Nations, just as individuals, ultimately pay the price for breaching God's moral laws; and no rationalizations, regardless how high-sounding, will exculpate or parole the perpetrator. Nations, just as individuals who profess and preach one thing yet fail to universally uphold and support it consistently as a value for all others, cannot expect to be believed. Credibility is essential to standing for any great principle—including those values the West assumes are sacrosanct: democracy and capitalism.

PD

PD

(Left) Shah Reza Pahlavi with wife Farah and son. *The Shah gained absolute power in Iran through a CIA backed coup in 1953. He had two credentials that guaranteed Western support: he was devotedly anti-communist and compliant about the West's access to Iranian oil. His secret police, the Savak, tortured and killed to keep him in power. Overthrown in 1979 by the Islamic revolution that brought Ayatollah Khomeini to power, he was an illustration of what one American diplomat referred to as "an SOB, but he is one of our SOBs."* (Right) Fulgencio Batista, president of Cuba in the 1950s, shaking hands with U.S. President Dwight Eisenhower. *Under the profoundly corrupt Batista, Havana became, in the words of one official, a "bordello" as well as a city of casinos controlled by the American mafia. Fear of the spread of communism led Americans to repeatedly betray their own principles and professed values—especially those of democracy, justice for the individual, and self-determination—in places like the Shah's Iran and Batista's Cuba. This played into the hands of the very forces America most feared.*

The task of countering communism having now been largely relegated to, at best, fourth- or fifth-tier status as a national concern, the motives for ruthless, self-centered, and sometimes hypocritical behavior, unfortunately, have not been removed. Now, more than ever—for it was always present in some measure in American foreign policy—the dynamic of materialistic acquisitiveness becomes the hidden agenda behind many diplomatic and military initiatives. That alone, in and of itself, would be expected as part of a nation's initiatives in its own interests; it is the reckless compromise of its stated principles that is the greater problem. The first Gulf War was depicted as a noble crusade against tyranny, invasion, and the violation of international law—and to a considerable extent it served those ends—but this was window dressing that barely concealed the true motive: the preservation of the West's access to oil. Perhaps though we would be hard pressed to find anyone today naïve enough to believe that Kuwait would have been rescued had it been an impoverished Third World state with no oil.

WILL DEMOCRATIZATION BRING PEACE AND ORDER?

Everyone speaks of [democratization], and I believe it is really occurring.
But democratization will not diminish, but add to, the great disorder.
Immanuel Wallerstein[73]

Immanuel Wallerstein, looking at the issue on a very practical plane, expressed scant confidence that "democratization" will resolve many, if any, of the world's most pressing difficulties. Wallerstein has no confidence that democratization will necessarily produce greater order or world stability. Recent elections in heretofore undemocratic countries corroborate this line of thought, albeit not necessarily for the same reasons he anticipates. Just because people freely elect their leaders does not suggest they will 1) choose leaders of vision and wisdom; or 2) forego the aggressive pursuit of their grievances, prejudices, or selfish ambitions.

Democracy alone will not lift man's dragging knuckles from the ground or sever the vines of the jungle that still entangle his ankles.

> Everyone speaks of it, and I believe it is really occurring. But democratization will not diminish, but add to, the great disorder. For, to most people, democratization translates primarily as the demand for three things as equal rights: a reasonable income (a job and later a pension), access to education for one's children, and adequate medical facilities....But having these three, at the level that people are demanding each day, is incredibly expensive, even for the wealthy countries, not to speak of for Russia, China, India. The only way everyone can really have more of these is to have a radically different system of distribution of the world's resources than we have today.[74]

Wallerstein believes that the trend to the welfare state can only be supported at the expense of the capitalists, concluding surprisingly that "Democratization is not and has never been in the interest of capitalists."[75] If he is correct in this analysis, there will inevitably be further clashes among the world's classes. But then, Toynbee warned us about the twin nemeses of mankind—war and class—which, with monotonous regularity, have disrupted the brief interludes of relative tranquility of mankind.

THE FORMS OF FREEDOM AND THE RESPONSIBILITIES THAT GO WITH THEM

When freedom destroys order, the yearning for order will destroy freedom.
Eric Hoffer[76]

What of freedom—that devoutly sought, passionately touted value of the Western world? What is freedom? What does it mean to be free? Sorokin provided some valuable insights utilizing his distinctions between sensate, ideational, and idealistic cultures and, we will recall, concluded that there were two ways in which a person can be free: either

> by decreasing his wishes to make them equal to or smaller than the means of their satisfaction, or by expanding his wishes and increasing proportionally the means of their satisfaction. The first is the way of ideational liberty, consisting in a reduction of one's wishes, especially sensory ones. The second is the way of sensate liberty, consisting in an ever-increasing expansion of one's wishes for sensory values, accompanied by an equal or greater expansion of the means of satisfying them.[77]

But of course, there will not be always "an equal or greater expansion of the means of satisfying them"; as noted earlier, modern, materialistic Western man, like a hamster, is perpetually on a treadmill. But even were this form of material fulfillment possible for everyone, the spiritual and relational void would remain.

As Solzhenitsyn observed about the West, freedom carries moral responsibility; otherwise it becomes mere license. "Destructive and irresponsible freedom has been granted boundless space. Society appears to have little defense against the abyss of human decadence, such as, for example, misuse of liberty for moral violence against young people, motion pictures full of pornography, crime and horror."[78] Then Solzhenitsyn pointed to the flimsy and disingenuous rationalization why this is not stopped: "It is considered to be part of freedom and theoretically counter-balanced by the young people's right not to look or not to accept."[79] Perhaps it is especially ironic that, having been trained as a lawyer, I would agree emphatically with Solzhenitsyn's next conclusion: "Life organized legalistically has thus shown its inability to defend itself against the corrosion of evil... Such a tilt of freedom in the direction of evil has come about gradually but it was evidently born primarily out of a humanistic and benevolent concept according to which there is no evil inherent to human nature; the world belongs to mankind and all the defects of life are caused by wrong social systems which must be corrected."[80]

Years of experience with the legal system, the political and judicial processes, and the mindsets attendant to each, have taught me that the true answers to the most important questions will never be found in any of these arenas. Solzhenitsyn was correct—evil is inherent in human nature and no amount of legal or social engineering will control it, much less remove it. Law and government reflect the corruption of a culture; they do not nullify or expunge it.

The quest for greater "freedom" to do what man wants to do, in the manner alluded to by Solzhenitsyn, is not only morally wrong, it is leading man to ever more depraved forms of slavery. The philosopher Eric Hoffer observed that "The basic test of freedom is perhaps less in what we

The Last of the Mohicans, by Michael Mann, 1992. *Hawkeye, Uncas, and Chingachgook. The screenwriter captured the original, true American attitude with an exchange between a pompous, young British officer seeking volunteers for the King's militia and Hawkeye. British Officer: "You call yourself a patriot, and loyal subject to the Crown?" Hawkeye: "I do not call myself subject to much at all." This independent, self-reliant spirit is all but extinct in twenty-first-century America. De Tocqueville predicted that if Americans moved away from self-reliance and individual freedom—particularly in the context of a society guided by religious principles—they would come to depend on the government more and more; and government, in turn, would expect to control more and more of their lives.*

are free to do than in what we are free not to do."[81] This is true in the moral sphere, as well as the sphere of government and law. Man is readily enslaved by his passions, prejudices, and fears. St. Paul admitted, "For what I do is not the good I want to do; no, the evil I do not want to do—this I keep on doing." (Romans 7:19) This was in truth a confession for all of humanity—at least those portions even making an effort.

The value of freedom—which Western man venerates reputedly above all others—has become the garrote with which his civilization is being strangled since he has no freestanding authority to check the power of his new ultimate god—himself.

Sorokin asserted, "Freedom of speech, of the press and of thought are the greatest boons when they are not dissociated from moral and social responsibilities." But without that sense of moral restraint they "degenerate into irresponsible and unbridled propaganda, the sensationalism of the yellow press, the uncensored production of obscene plays and novels, or the means of discrediting and undermining precious values," and "become a societal and cultural poison infinitely worse than the denial of freedom of thought and expression."[82]

Eric Hoffer reminded us of an inevitable result: "When freedom destroys order, the yearning for order will destroy freedom."[83] I would carry this further. Among the most dangerous human propensities are two that are opposite sides of the same coin: Man craves freedom, which in turn often leads to license—or sin, to use the religious term—which leads to the loss of order. The loss of order, in turn, leads eventually to chaos and to fear, producing a desperate need for order, which results in the loss of freedom. Sorokin declared that sensate culture, therefore, is its own worst enemy because it "releases forces that ultimately destroy the magnificent contractual edifice it proudly builds at the earlier, more sober, and more balanced stages of its development." This destructiveness is not due to any "external forces" though it is the wont of sensate man to assert that someone has "sown tares in his wheat" even though the true "perpetrators" have been the citizens and society of the culture.

There is no hope for the culture "*in extremis*" in this way other than a "reconstruction of absolute moral values and norms, with their 'the law is hard, but it is the law,' obligatory for all, universally binding, not to be brushed aside in the interest of relative, expedient pseudo-values...."[84]

THE FUTURE OF FREEDOM

We promise according to our hopes and perform according to our fears.
La Rochefoucauld[85]

Western man will surely continue his worship of democracy and capitalism as part of his pantheon of most revered idols. Yet, as our observers have noted, democracy can be nothing more than another form of tyranny: the tyranny of the majority—a majority bereft of a transcendent belief and conviction of ultimate accountability. Nothing good can be expected of such—unless you naïvely believe in the "innate goodness of man"—and democracy then is transmogrified into just another form of deception, manipulation, and control of humanity.

We have shown the danger in reposing one's confidence in government, even democracies. Schaeffer's "authoritarian" governments will probably be titular democracies. This concept is neither oxymoronic nor far-fetched. The obsequious deference in the West to the institution of democracy blindly ignores the realities that slavery was at one time a legally protected institution within Western democracies, as have been various manifestations of tyranny of the wealthy and vested financial interests over labor and the poor—a condition closer to plutocracy than democracy, yet concealed behind the Potemkin façade of an ideologically acceptable word. None of these propensities of man will change. Democracy will continue to always be susceptible to serving power and thus be at the beck and call of those who would control—just another form of tyranny by those who have power over those who have less or none. An old Spanish proverb declares, "Laws, like the spider's web, catch the fly and let the hawk go free."

The only hope for democracy as a form of government that will truly provide some semblance of the justice its touted reputation suggests is the hope vested in it by the American Founding Fathers and de Tocqueville: a government peopled by leaders of high moral character and a supporting cast of like-minded citizenry. Just as the Founding Fathers and de Tocqueville believed, such moral character is always the product of belief in God and a transcendent moral law.

In his autobiography, *The Seven Pillars of Wisdom*, T. E. Lawrence described a camel charge he led against the Turks, in the execution of which, to his dismay, Lawrence realized that his much faster camel had put him far out in front of his Arab comrades. He quickly became, or assumed he had become, the target of hundreds of Turkish rifles. Attempting to assuage his fear, Lawrence drew his Webley revolver and began firing back at the Turks.

Moments later, his camel collapsed as if striking an invisible wall. Sailing grandly through the air, Lawrence landed in a stunned heap, expecting to be trampled to death by the herd of camels in his wake. To his astonishment, untrampled and unhurt, he was able to stumble back to his camel to look for evidence of the Turkish bullet that had killed the fleet-footed beast. To his shock, the camel was unmarked except for one strategically placed bullet hole in the back of its head!

In his zeal to protect himself and quell his fears, Western man is in danger of shooting the camel of freedom that has carried him so far. Just as freedom affords personal autonomy, it demands personal responsibility and self-reliance. The forfeiture of either of the latter will inevitably lead to loss of the former. But man cannot and will not display personal responsibility of the highest category without a sense of accountability that transcends him and his institutions. Toynbee made it clear that the Christian religion was the source of the beliefs and commitments—to the worth of the individual, love for one's fellows, and the absolute absence of compulsion to believe or to defer to doctrinal convictions of others—which gave democracy its base and its vitality. Only through a sincere adherence to those values and beliefs could democracy reach its highest expression.

The purpose of this analysis has not of course been to completely debunk the political and legal institutions of Western civilization, but rather to show that none of them is *the answer* to the future of our civilization. At best they are simply tools that we have created—albeit tools man believes to be of a high order—to meet social needs. They will not only manifest the indicia of decay and decline of a civilization but also, as they themselves are corrupted, contribute to that process. Such is the case now in Western civilization. Nationalism, government, the ideologies of democracy and capitalism, and law have all become part of the distracting array of idols that Western man believes harbor his salvation as individuals and as a civilization. This is a source of the gravest danger.

Neither capitalism, nor democracy, nor socialism, nor government, nor humanism, nor science, nor technology, nor education, nor law will save Western man from himself.

END NOTES
CHAPTER 7

1 Arnold Toynbee, *A Study of History* (New York: Weathervane Books, 1972), 223.
2 Hyperion, cited in Christopher Dawson, *Religion and World History: A Selection from the Works of Christopher Dawson* (Garden City, NY: Image Books, a Division of Doubleday & Company, Inc., 1975), 285–286.
3 Arnold Toynbee, *Civilization on Trial* (New York: Oxford University Press, 1948), 236–237.
4 Toynbee, *Civilization on Trial*, 257.
5 Toynbee, *A Study of History*, 223.
6 Toynbee, *Civilization on Trial*, 257.
7 Toynbee, *Civilization on Trial*, 257.
8 Toynbee, *Civilization on Trial*, 255–256.
9 Baldur Von Schirach, cited in Toynbee, *Civilization on Trial*, 256.
10 Toynbee, *Civilization on Trial*, 256–257.
11 Hyperion, cited in Dawson, *Religion and World History*, 286.
12 Robert Conquest, *Reflections on a Ravaged Century* (New York: W. W. Norton & Company, Inc.), 204.
13 Alexander Solzhenitsyn, Text of Address at Harvard Class Day Afternoon Exercises, Thursday, June 8, 1978.
14 Conquest, *Reflections on a Ravaged Century*, 204.
15 Francis A. Schaeffer, *How Should We Then Live? The Rise and Decline of Western Thought and Culture* (Wheaton, IL: Crossway Books, A Division of Good News Publishers, 1976), 217.
16 Schaeffer, *How Should We Then Live?*, 217.
17 Schaeffer, *How Should We Then Live?*, 249.
18 Schaeffer, *How Should We Then Live?*, 218.
19 Professor Joseph Witherspoon, cited in Schaeffer, *How Should We Then Live?*, 219.
20 Schaeffer, *How Should We Then Live?*, 222.
21 Schaeffer, *How Should We Then Live?*, 222.
22 Schaeffer, *How Should We Then Live?*, 223–224.
23 Pitirim A. Sorokin, *The Crisis of Our Age* (Oneworld Publications Ltd., 1941; this edition Sergei P. Sorokin and Peter P. Sorokin, 1992), 126.
24 Abraham Lincoln, *Notes—Lincoln, Abraham—Wisdom and Wit* (White Plains, NY: Peter Pauper Press, Inc., 1965), 40.
25 Conquest, *Reflections on a Ravaged Century*, 205–206.
26 James Bovard, *Lost Rights: The Destruction of American Liberty* (Palgrave Macmillan, 1995), 333.
27 Winston Churchill, cited in Fred R. Shapiro and Joseph Epstein, *The Yale Book of Quotations* (Yale University Press, 2006), 54.
28 Walter Bagehot, *The English Constitution. Second Edition* (Boston: Little, Brown, and Co., 1873), 108.
29 Sorokin, *The Crisis of Our Age*, 258.
30 Alexis de Tocqueville, *Democracy in America*, Vol. 1, translated by Henry Reeve (D. Appleton, 1904), 331.
31 de Tocqueville, *Democracy in America*, 79.
32 Theodorus Johannes Hooning, *George Orwell in zijn tijd* (J. A. Boom, 1968), 120.
33 Edward Gibbon, cited in Eugene C. Gerhart, *Quote It Completely!* (William S. Hein & Co., Inc., 1998), 69.
34 de Tocqueville, *Democracy in America*, Vol. 1, Chap. V, 79–80.
35 Dawson, *Religion and World History*, 220.
36 Sorokin, *The Crisis of Our Age*, 258.
37 Dawson, *Religion and World History*, 220.
38 Dawson, *Religion and World History*, 220.
39 Christopher Dawson, *The Historic Reality of Christian Culture* (New York: Harper & Brothers, 1960), 40.
40 Toynbee, *Civilization on Trial*, 236–237.

41 Dawson, *Religion and World History*, 279.
42 Dawson, *Religion and World History*, 279.
43 Dawson, *Religion and World History*, 285.
44 Dawson, *Religion and World History*, 285–286.
45 Dawson, *Religion and World History*, 285–286.
46 Oswald Spengler, *The Decline of the West* (Allen & Unwin MacMillan, 1922), 394.
47 Dawson, *Religion and World History*, 226–227.
48 Spengler, *Decline of the West*, 392.
49 Spengler, *Decline of the West*, 393–394.
50 Spengler, *Decline of the West*, 395.
51 Spengler, *Decline of the West*, 396.
52 Dawson, *Religion and World History*, 232–233.
53 Dawson, *Religion and World History*, 232–233.
54 Dawson, *Religion and World History*, 235–236.
55 Spengler, *Decline of the West*, 391.
56 Dawson, *Religion and World History*, 235–236.
57 Solzhenitsyn, Harvard Class Day.
58 Dawson, *Religion and World History*, 295.
59 Dawson, *Historic Reality*, 40–41.
60 Schaeffer, *How Should We Then Live?*, 108–109.
61 Schaeffer, *How Should We Then Live?*, 109–110.
62 Schaeffer, *How Should We Then Live?*, 109–110.
63 Schaeffer, *How Should We Then Live?*, 110.
64 Schaeffer, *How Should We Then Live?*, 112.
65 Dawson, *Historic Reality*, 61–62.
66 Dawson, *Historic Reality*, 80.
67 Dawson, *Historic Reality*, 80.
68 Dawson, *Religion and the Rise of Western Culture*, 14–15.
69 Solzhenitsyn, Harvard Class Day.
70 Samuel P. Huntington, *The Clash of Civilizations and the Remaking of World Order* (New York: Samuel P. Huntington, Simon & Schuster, 1996), 92–93.
71 Huntington, *Clash of Civilizations*, 92–93.
72 Toynbee, *Civilization on Trial*, 144.
73 Immanuel Wallerstein, *The End of the World As We Know It: Social Science for the Twenty-First Century* (Minneapolis: University of Minnesota Press, 1999), 18.
74 Wallerstein, *The End of the World As We Know It*, 18.
75 Wallerstein, *The End of the World As We Know It*, 31–32.
76 Eric Hoffer (American philosopher), cited in Schaeffer, *How Should We Then Live?*, 245.
77 Sorokin, *Crisis of Our Age*, 143.
78 Solzhenitsyn, Harvard Class Day.
79 Solzhenitsyn, Harvard Class Day.
80 Solzhenitsyn, Harvard Class Day.
81 Eric Hoffer, *The Passionate State of Mind, and Other Aphorisms* (Harper, 1955; Original from the University of California, digitized June 9, 2008), 107.
82 Sorokin, *Crisis of Our Age*, 162.
83 Eric Hoffer (American philosopher), cited in Schaeffer, *How Should We Then Live?*, 245.
84 Sorokin, *Crisis of Our Age*, 166.
85 François de La Rochefoucauld, *Reflections; Or Sentences and Moral Maxims* (Teddington, Middlesex: The Echo Library, 131 High St., *www.echo-library.com*), 30.

CHAPTER

8

PROGRESS AND OPTIMISM

Thus history—and, not least, current history—shows that Mankind's ignorance and weakness are not temporary symptoms; they are permanent features of human life.
Arnold Toynbee[1]

Brief and powerless is Man's life; on him and all his race the slow, sure doom falls pitiless and dark.
Bertrand Russell[2]

The pessimist complains about the wind, the optimist expects it to change, the realist adjusts the sails.
William Ward[3]

Throughout the twentieth and into the twenty-first century, Western man has been treated to a steady diet of human vanity in the form of relentless assurances of progress and reasons for optimism about man and his future. The gatekeepers of Western culture tend to reject any other serious message—unless it is sensational and therefore highly marketable. Financial gain, recognition, and power only come to those who say what they and their protégés want to hear.

This is worse than its analog in nutrition. The partakers, in the form of most of Western humanity, are not simply malnourished, they are sometimes poisoned. Not only deprived of the truth, Western man is obese from engorgement on falsities. Hence he fails to come to grips with his predicament or to recognize the course of action that would save him.

ARE WE MAKING PROGRESS?

...progress, unlike what the Enlightenment in all its forms preached, is not at all inevitable. ...The world has not morally advanced in the last several thousand years, but it could.
Immanuel Wallerstein[4]

The recent Western view of progress has tended to be a glib compilation of values and beliefs: the merits of technology and science (which ostensibly make life better and easier); greater "understanding" (as manifested in "tolerance" and "diversity"); and confidence in—despite all historical evidence to the contrary—the innate goodness of man. These and other disaffections with reality have become part of the Western materialist culture's stock and trade—they sell extremely well in books, magazines, movies, and television and politics—and are the cynosure of the psychology of a civilization in crisis that refuses to recognize either the nature or the dimensions of that crisis. The recklessness of this mindset has been addressed by several of our observers, as well as some Western philosophers.

Noting the "assumption that cultures inherently tend to progress," A. L. Kroeber added that "this assumption widely dominates the thought of our time, but is, of course, an untested and emotional one."[5] Yet I assert it *has* been thoroughly tested by the vicissitudes of history—and found wanting. It is not that Western man has made no progress, but for every step forward he has taken some cataclysmic steps backward. Throughout his experience on the planet he has pursued the quest for progress primarily in the symbiotic fields of science and technology on the one hand and material gain on the other. Pursuit of higher forms of that which would more appropriately be labeled "progress" has fallen into desuetude; Western man is no longer interested. The low forms that do attract his attention are more often in fact *regression* than anything else.

Immanuel Wallerstein concludes that today's optimistic belief in the reality and inevitability of progress "was a basic theme of the European Enlightenment....it became the consensus viewpoint of nineteenth-century Europe (and indeed remained so for most of the twentieth century as well). Social science, as it was constructed, was deeply imprinted with the theory of progress."[6]

Progress became Western man's stated *raison d'etre* though it fails to stand up under scrutiny either as to its logic or any truly dramatic manifestations of its achievement since the Enlightenment. If there is no God that man can know with scientific certainty as anything more than a vague theistic notion—whether multiple gods, or pathways to god, or a singular god that he must truly obey and pay homage to—then what can Western man resort to as his measure of progress? The search for answers to that question leads up blind alleys and to the necessity of fabricating answers out of whole cloth reminiscent of Nietzsche: man constructing his own plans, purposes, and goals to give life meaning. Western man has developed such systems that often sparkle with high-sounding phrasing and noble themes, but they are artificial constructs that he dare not think beyond lest he find himself in a jungle without end, the thick foliage of meaninglessness enveloping him on all sides.

The reality is that most of what Western man calls progress has been in the non-human, non-relational realms of science, technology, and the propagation of material wealth. But he cannot come out frankly and say as much; he must justify his approach to life with at least a patina of timeless truths and human concern.

Wallerstein sees the achievements of science and technology as the basis for the fallacious Western confidence in progress, and hence, its misplaced optimism. Compelling evidence that Western history does not support these conclusions has been largely ignored:

> As long as the modern world seemed to be one long success story of technological triumph, the necessary political base to maintain a certain equilibrium in the system continued to exist. Amid the success, the world of science was carried from honor to honor within this system, as though it were responsible for the triumph. The social sciences were swept along in the tide. No one was seriously questioning the fundamental premises of knowledge. The many maladies of the system from racism to sexism to colonialism as expressions of the manifestly growing polarization of the world, from fascist movements to socialist gulags to liberal formalisms as alternative modes of suppressing democratization —were all defined as transitory problems...in a world in which the trajectory always returned to the curve of linear upward-moving equilibrium.[7]

> the spirit, and it has been the great tragedy of human life on Earth that this sensational inequality of man's respective achievements in the nonhuman and in the spiritual sphere should, so far at any rate, have been this way round; for the spiritual side of man's life is of vastly greater importance for man's well-being (even for his material well-being, in the last resort) than is his command over non-human nature.[21]

Progress may be defined therefore in two distinct ways: the scientific, technological and materialist achievement of the West, and what I will call "relational progress" that reflects improvement in, and advancement of, man's relationships—first and foremost with his creator, and second, with his fellowman. Only by this latter measure can we determine whether Western history reflects true progress.

TRUE PROGRESS IN WESTERN HISTORY

There is nothing more horrible than the murder of beautiful theory by a brutal gang of facts.
La Rochefoucauld[22]

For he who confesses, shams are over, and realities have begun.
William James[23]

Has true progress—progress in man's relationships—occurred in Western history? The honest answer would be a highly qualified and tentative yes, since Western man seems to make that kind of progress in fits and starts but for every step forward in one dimension or expression of it, he makes two or three to the rear. The problem underlying those regressions is his failure to face up to grave realities and his unwillingness to embrace a different course that would dramatically alter his belief systems and priorities.

PD-old.

Lenin poster. *What Toynbee called* Leviathan *(i.e., government and law) in the modern West is a manifestation of man's conviction that he can progress by dint of his own efforts. This view has been particularly common in modern Western civilization and has found expression in the "communist man" of Marxism, the man of iron will and strength overcoming all adversaries in fascism, in the "innate goodness of man" implied or expressed in contemporary humanism, and even in the democratic man of Western democracies. The Marxist version of this self-delusion, referred to variously as the true "socialist" or "communist" man, found its greatest following in the ideology of the Soviet Union. That there is no historical evidence in support of, and compelling historical evidence that refutes, these views is commonly overlooked or rationalized away.*

In the mid-twentieth century, Sorokin wrote of a distorted nineteenth-century viewpoint that had originated in the Renaissance and found its fullest expression in the Enlightenment, based on man's assumptions derived from his achievements in democracy and some degree of social justice: "The success...warranted the general optimism of Western society respecting 'bigger and better' progress; man's capacity to build, without the invocation of any supernatural power, in his own right and by his own efforts, a better, more free, more just and more noble society....The road of the future destiny of mankind appeared to point to ever fairer prospects."[24]

It was not just man's achievements in science and technology that convinced him of his possibilities, but to some extent his achievements in the realm of social relationships as well. That these were overblown in relation to the magnitude of the problems—including slavery and its progenitor, racism—was another rational lapse. Ironically one of the leaders in these successes, William Wilberforce, who made it his life's work to end the slave trade in the British Empire, would have been the first to disabuse us of the notion that man himself was the champion in this and other similar struggles. Self-congratulatory and optimistic overstatement of the West's case remains a permanent part of our political and social lore.

We have seen that Toynbee warned of worshiping Leviathan—government and the powerful state—as a shepherd that would lead the flock of humanity to the bright sunlit uplands of peace, prosperity, and security. The very fact that Leviathan exists is an argument against such devotion. Leviathan will always have a dominant role in the affairs of men precisely because of every human being's capacity for selfishness and evil. We should see government's place as America's wary Founding Fathers saw it: to corral and control man's worst impulses rather than nurture and guide his supposed innate virtue. Any true virtue comes only through faith in a Supreme Being and belief in a higher moral law to which all mankind is beholden. In biblical terminology, there will always be sin and thus a need for Caesar. Toynbee put it starkly: "...the possibility of evil, as well as of good, will be born into the world afresh with every child and will never be wholly ruled out as long as that child remains alive....so long as original sin remains an element in human nature, Caesar will always have work to do, and there will still be Caesar's things to be rendered to Caesar, as well as God's to God, in this world."[25]

This Leviathan (i.e., man's social arrangements expressed through government and law) in the modern Western world is invariably a manifestation of man's conviction that he can progress by dint of his own efforts, and that those efforts give him every reason to be optimistic. This view has been particularly common in modern Western civilization and has found expression in the "communist man" of Marxism, the man of iron will and strength overcoming all adversaries in fascism, in the "innate goodness of man" implied or expressed in contemporary humanism, and even in the democratic man of Western democracies.

This last is of course a mutated concept. Jefferson, Adams, Hamilton, Franklin, and the other Founders saw government and law primarily as a protective hedge against dangerous impulses—and government the embodiment of another set of dangerous impulses. In this respect they were doubly suspicious. Contemporary Americans looking to government to improve their lot in virtually any arena is a manifestation of the growing self-delusion about man and his perfectibility.

That there is no historical evidence in support of, and compelling historical evidence that refutes, these views is commonly overlooked or rationalized away. The Marxist version of this self-delusion, referred to variously as the true "socialist" or "communist" man, found its greatest following in the

PD

Spirit of the Frontier by John Gast, 1872. *Progress may be defined in two ways: scientific, technological, and materialist achievement; or "relational progress" that reflects improvement in, and advancement of, man's relationships —first and foremost with his creator, and second, with his fellowman. Throughout Western history, progress has been defined primarily in materialist terms. In American history, that included the opening of new territory. But only in relational terms can we determine whether Western history reflects true progress.*

ideology of the Soviet Union. The blind folly of this belief was made especially evident to me when I met with Soviet experts in Moscow who studied the West at the height of the Cold War. Articulate and astute, these Russian intellectuals to some extent and in some respects probably saw the West with greater insight than most Westerners. Inevitably our discussion evolved into a debate pitting communism against capitalism. Their thrusts into the bosom of the West's ideology and inflated self-perception were often quite accurate. But, as is so often the case with human nature, the Russians' capacity for insightful criticism ended when focused inward.

Seeking to demonstrate the weakness in their own version of reality, I asked, "What can you point to in the study of history or human psychology that supports the prospects for development of the true 'communist man'?" The leader of the Russian group, who spoke better English than most American English teachers, claimed that they did not understand the question. A careful rephrasing was met by the same, now tedious, response. A third rephrasing prompted the rejoinder, "We do not understand what you mean by this question and therefore cannot answer it!"

Whereupon they abruptly ended the meeting.

Of course the meaning of the question was clear, as was their awareness that they had no sound answer.

Clinging blindly to an unsupportable version of reality is hardly peculiar to authoritarian ideologies. In one sense, the West's own version of reality is just as misbegotten.

WHY BE OPTIMISTIC?

...the future of the West is not a limitless tending upwards and onwards for all time towards our present ideals, but a single phenomenon of history, strictly limited and defined as to form and duration...
Oswald Spengler[26]

Christopher Dawson corroborated Toynbee's viewpoint by his analysis of notions of American progress and optimism, the locus of the most widespread belief in the inevitability of progress. Here Dawson displayed his gift for finding a nexus between seemingly incompatible ideas or forces. The very faith that should have told Americans to be wary of all notions about man's virtue or innate goodness was also, ironically, the basis for their unregenerate optimism.

Though of course there have been discordant voices like the American poet and pessimist Robinson Jeffers, but

> ...it is just because the American pessimist is so exceptional that he is so extreme. He has to speak violently to make his voice heard. But the great mass of Americans have always had a much stronger faith in the future than any other people, and they owe this faith not to any philosophical theory or ideology like that of Marxism, but to a spiritual tradition or climate of opinion into which they have been born and with which the nation has grown up from the beginning.[27]

The voice of the thoughtful, insightful pessimist in America is as the chirping of a small bird amidst the cacophony of horns, traffic, and frenzied activity of an American city. The possibility of beauty and truth in the song is never considered since manifestations of this kind of music are banished; and when the music cannot be banished, it is drowned out.

Samuel Huntington deflated these nineteenth-century hopes by recounting twentieth-century failures. "The moment of euphoria at the end of the Cold War generated an illusion of harmony, which was soon revealed to be exactly that. The world became different in the early 1990s, but not necessarily more peaceful."[28] This "illusion" has not necessarily been exposed except in the narrowest sense. There is evidence of many illusions—or more accurately, self-delusions—in the twenty-first-century West. Huntington continued by noting: "Similar illusions of harmony flourished, briefly, at the end of each of the twentieth century's other major conflicts." World War I was the "war to end wars" and to make the world safe for democracy. World War II, as Franklin Roosevelt put it, would "end the system of unilateral action, the exclusive alliances, the balances of power, and all the other expedients that have been tried for centuries—and have always failed." Instead we would have "a universal organization" of "peace-loving Nations" and the beginnings of a "permanent structure of peace."

People atop the Berlin Wall near the Brandenburg Gate on 9 November 1989. *Samuel Huntington argued, "The collapse of [communism] in the Soviet Union…does not, however, necessarily mean that these societies will import…Western…liberal democracy." Indeed, even the embrace of democracy does not mean the embrace of Western ideals or the rejection of provincialism, prejudice, and hatred. What does the West do when an erstwhile adversary—perhaps even helped to its feet by the West—accepts democracy and then acts resolutely against Western interests?*

Huntington's observations are critically important not just as lessons of history but as signs of Western man's psychological propensity for believing what is patently without support:

> World War I, however, generated communism, fascism, and the reversal of a century-old trend toward democracy. World War II produced a Cold War that was truly global. The illusion of harmony at the end of that Cold War was soon dissipated by the multiplication of ethnic conflicts and "ethnic cleansing," the breakdown of law and order, the emergence of new patterns of alliance and conflict among states, the resurgence of neo-communist and neo-fascist movements, intensification of religious fundamentalism, the end of the "diplomacy of smiles" and "policy of yes" in Russia's relations with the West, the inability of the United Nations and the United States to suppress bloody local conflicts, and the increasing assertiveness of a rising China.[29]

The self-delusions of more recent vintage are simply reprises of what has gone before. Huntington argued, "The collapse of [communism] in the Soviet Union and its substantial adaptation in China and Vietnam does not, however, necessarily mean that these societies will import the other Western ideology of liberal democracy. Westerners who assume that it does are likely to be surprised by the creativity, resilience, and individuality of non-Western cultures."[30] Let us go a step further: The embrace of democracy does not mean the embrace of Western ideals or the rejection of provincialism, prejudice, and hatred. What does the West do when an erstwhile adversary—perhaps even helped to its feet by the West—accepts democracy and then votes and acts resolutely against Western interests? Do we then acknowledge that life, history, and meaning go much deeper than any ideology? Or do we reject their decisions and revert to an adversarial relationship—this time with a fellow "democracy"?

The resistance of other societies to closely held Western ideological sacred cows will not be simply a matter of differing cultures. Like Toynbee, Sorokin, Dawson, and others, Huntington was contemptuous of the hubris that dominates the West: "The arguments that some sort of universal civilization is emerging rest on one or more...assumptions" that are false: "First...that the collapse of Soviet communism meant the end of history and the universal victory of liberal democracy....This argument...[is] rooted in the Cold War perspective that the only alternative to communism is liberal democracy and that the demise of the first produces the universality of the second." However, Huntington declared, "...there are many forms of authoritarianism, nationalism, corporatism, and market communism (as in China) that are alive and well in today's world."[31]

I would add that it is my belief that liberal democracy will not even prove to be the dominant trend in the twenty-first century. During my travels in the Soviet Union at the height of the Cold War, I was repeatedly struck by the impression that Russians were not broadly attracted to democracy, and were more deeply committed to a paternalistic form of governance. Stalin was still held in high regard by some. The awareness that democracy was a Western concept and a Western ideology made it suspect in the eyes of prideful, provincial, and insecure Russians: "What do we need from the West? Why should we listen to anything they say?" These attitudes can change—they may be changing in the post-Cold War generation—but the point is less that others might come around to the Western viewpoint than that they are under no duty, obligation, impetus, or compulsion to do so.

In one significant and supremely important area of human existence, others are quite likely to not only reject much of the West's vaunted ideology but oppose it, even violently. Religious belief does not often brook compromise; you either are in compliance with the tenets of the faith, or you are not.

PD

Winston Churchill waving to jubilant British upon the defeat of Germany. *Western man's psychological propensity for believing what is patently without historical support was soon demonstrated once again. Franklin Roosevelt had predicted the war would be followed by "a universal organization" of "peace-loving Nations" and the beginnings of a "permanent structure of peace.'" What followed was a worldwide Cold War and the most dangerous period in human history.*

Huntington recognized religion as "a central, perhaps the central, force that motivates and mobilizes people." I go further: Religion is not a central force but surely the central force of all of history, the "key to history" that Lord Acton identified.

But I affirm Huntington fully in his other conclusions, including the observation "It is sheer hubris to think that because Soviet communism has collapsed, the West has won the world for all time and that Muslims, Chinese, Indians, and others are going to rush to embrace Western liberalism as the only alternative. The Cold War division of humanity is over. The more fundamental divisions of humanity in terms of ethnicity, religions, and civilizations remain and spawn new conflicts."[32]

Huntington also dismissed the notion that interaction between peoples, economic or otherwise, will be a panacea for the conflicts and tensions that plague the world with ever-greater intensity. History supports him:

> ...the assumption that increased interaction among peoples—trade, investment, tourism, media, electronic communication generally—is generating a common world culture...[and] reduces the probability of war between nations is, at a minimum, not proven, and much evidence exists to the contrary. International trade expanded significantly in the 1960s and1970s and in the following decade the Cold War came to an end. In 1913, however, international trade was at record highs and in the next few years nations slaughtered each other in unprecedented numbers. If international commerce at that level could not prevent war, when can it? The evidence simply does not support the liberal, internationalist assumption that commerce promotes peace.[33]

All such notions are, once again, on the surface, and hence of dubious validity. Trade and commercial interaction may surely enhance some relationships, but they will neither guarantee a long term bond between cultures and nations nor ensure a mutual dependency such that overt conflict—being in neither party's best interest—would not occur. Many aggressive decisions are made that are not in the best interests of the deciders, and history is replete with examples of nations sallying forth to the battlefield in causes that were clearly never in their best interest. Man has a tendency to act aggressively—even recklessly—out of misbegotten notions of pride or "the principle of the thing."

For every example of trade and interaction bringing cultures together there are other examples of the opposite result. Huntington suggested this: "If states do not expect high levels of interdependence to continue, war is likely to result."[34]

It sounds as if cynical forces are at work, and they are, which suggests once more that high-sounding notions about the peace and harmony to be purchased through trade, commerce, and interaction are more ephemeral than real. Human beings tend to focus on their differences rather than their common ground.

Oswald Spengler reached much the same conclusions as our other observers about the merits of optimism and progress as defined in the West. Spengler did not see "the future of the West" as "a limitless tending upwards and onwards for all time towards our present ideals." In this work, we are striving to offset the phenomenon Spengler decried: "Up to now everyone has been at liberty to hope what he pleased about the future. Where there are no facts, sentiment rules."[35] Sentiment is no more a firm foundation for Western man than is self-delusion.

WHAT THEN OF WESTERN MAN'S PROSPECTS FOR PROGRESS OR HIS GROUNDS FOR OPTIMISM?

...only on the firm foundation of unyielding despair,
can the soul's habitation henceforth be safely built.
Bertrand Russell[36]

Oswald Spengler's answer to the bleak prospects for the West's future is a stoic clenching of the teeth: "I fail to see that it is any disadvantage to discover betimes that some of these hopes must come to nothing. And if the hopes thus doomed should be those most dear, well, a man who is worth anything will not be dismayed."[37]

Optimism founded on anything other than realism is merely a fool's paradise.

In this respect, Spengler serves as our transition to the obvious conclusions of a starkly realistic view of man and history if there is no faith as a final refuge. Below we see, from the pen of the humanist Bertrand Russell, recognition that neither optimism nor progress is supported by the facts. To be sure, the bleakness of his view was universal and timeless, not restricted to the relatively narrow geographic and chronological confines of Western civilization. Though he never accepted the alternative course of faith, Russell, at least here, was not engaging in the self-delusion common to Western man:

> ...even more purposeless, more void of meaning, is the world which Science presents for our belief....That Man is the product of causes which had no prevision of the end they were achieving; that his origin, his growth, his hopes and fears, his loves and his beliefs, are but the outcome of accidental collocations of atoms; that no fire, no heroism, no intensity of thought and feeling, can preserve an individual life beyond the grave; that all the labours of the ages, all the devotion, all the inspiration, all the noonday brightness of human genius, are destined to extinction in the vast death of the solar system, and that the whole temple of Man's achievement must inevitably be buried beneath the debris of a universe in ruins—all these things, if not quite beyond dispute, are yet so

> nearly certain, that no philosophy which rejects them can hope to stand. Only within the scaffolding of these truths, only on the firm foundation of unyielding despair, can the soul's habitation henceforth be safely built.[38]

Perhaps you have known people like Russell: intellectually astute, erudite, possibly even in their own way principled and courageous, but utterly desolate. They have nothing to offer mankind because the ultimate consequence of their worldview is precisely as Russell described here. Ironically, Russell was right in concluding that: "All the noonday brightness of human genius" and the "whole temple of Man's achievement" will be left with not one stone upon another. Russell was also correct: "no philosophy that rejects these conclusions can hope to stand"—but that is precisely the implicit—sometimes now explicit—philosophy of Western man in our age. At least Russell walked this far down the trail of truth; that he went no further is cause for another form of despair. If Western man began this pilgrimage but then chose to loiter here as well, the despair will be multiplied exponentially. But there is an alternative. The trail does not end here.

The historical pattern replicates: for the faithful there is hope, for the agnostic or unbeliever there is only comforting self-delusion followed inevitably by despair. Francis Schaeffer believed this was the reason for Nietzsche's drift into the abyss: "I am convinced that when Nietzsche...went insane, it was not because of venereal disease....Rather, it was because he understood that insanity was the only philosophic answer if the infinite-personal God does not exist."

Schaeffer rationally, candidly, and insightfully wrote, "With no personal God, all is dead." Western man, in the absence of a personal God, will

> ...as Nietzsche [pointed out] make "systems." In today's speech we would call them "game plans." A person can erect some sort of structure, some type of limited frame, in which he lives, shutting himself up in that frame and not looking beyond it. This game plan can...sound high and noble, such as talking in an idealistic way about the greatest good for the greatest number. Or it can be a scientist concentrating on some small point of science so that he does not have to think of any of the big questions, such as why things exist at all. It can be a skier concentrating for years on knocking one-tenth of a second from a downhill run. Or it can as easily be a theological word game within

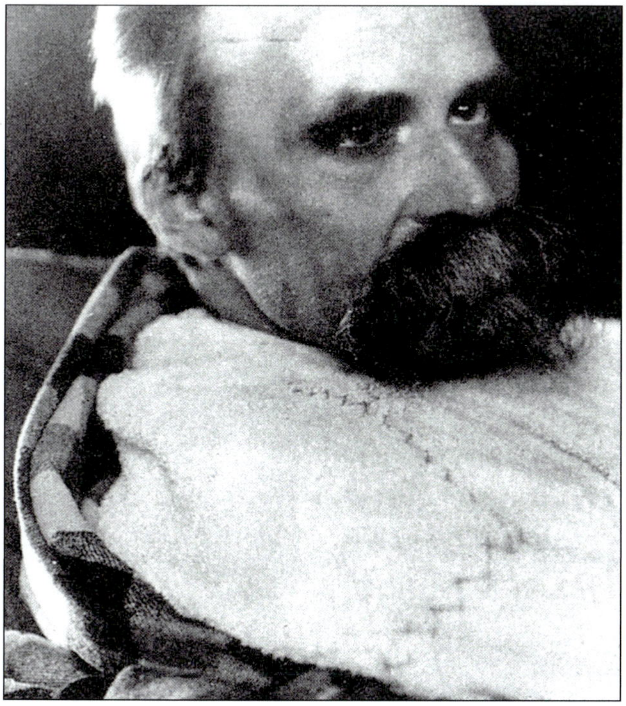

Photograph by Hans Olde. PD

Friedrich Nietzsche. *Devoid of a belief in a personal God, Nietzsche spoke of man devising systems to give his life an ersatz meaning or purpose. Francis Schaeffer believed that Nietzsche did not go insane because of venereal disease but because "...he understood that insanity was the only philosophic answer if the infinite-personal God does not exist."*

> the structure of the existential methodology. That is where modern people, building only on themselves, have come, and that is where they are now.[39]

Schaeffer's description of the Nietzschean "game plans" is stunning and disturbing—all the more so because it should sound so familiar to Western man.

THE ULTIMATE PROGRESS—AND THE ONLY BASIS FOR OPTIMISM

Seeking God is itself a social act.
Arnold Toynbee[40]

What Western man desperately needs is a eurythmic or proportionally balanced and combined relationship among his spiritual, philosophic, social, and material understandings of his world. They must not be compartmentalized. Nor can any be considered less valid because only some can be measured with scientific methods and some cannot. All are valuable and important. In fact, the seemingly most ephemeral is most essential of all. Only faith will meet the most compelling of human needs, and it is through faith alone as the starting point that this harmony—true progress and reasons for genuine optimism—can be achieved.

Huntington, like our other commentators, recognized that religious faith is the most promising answer for other cultures. What then of its prospects as an answer for the West? "...if the traditional religion is unable to adapt to the requirements of modernization, the potential exists for the spread of Western Christianity and Islam...."

In a powerfully significant recognition of what is truly important, Huntington added: "...the most successful protagonists of Western culture are not neo-classical economists or crusading democrats or multinational corporation executives. They are and most likely will continue to be Christian missionaries. Neither Adam Smith nor Thomas Jefferson will meet the psychological, emotional, moral, and social needs of urban migrants and first-generation secondary school graduates. Jesus Christ may not meet them either, but He is likely to have a better chance."[41]

Let us go much further. Toynbee pointed out how "progress" in the improvement of individual man through "seeking God" ultimately produces greater social progress "than could be attained in any other way."

> ...the Christian soul on Earth is a ...citizen of the Kingdom of God, and therefore his paramount and all-embracing aim is to attain the highest degree of communion with, and likeness to, God Himself; his relations with his fellow men are consequences of, and corollaries to, his relations with God; and his way of loving his neighbour as himself will be to try to help his neighbour to win what he is seeking for himself—that is, to come into closer communion with God and to become more godlike....[T]he spiritual progress of individual souls in this life will in fact bring with it much more social progress than could be attained in any other way....[42]

CHAPTER

9

MAN AS GOD: HUMANISM AND COMMUNISM

If humanism were right in declaring that man is born to be happy, he would not be born to die. Since his body is doomed to die, his task on earth evidently must be of a more spiritual nature.
Alexander Solzhenitsyn[1]

...the dreams of the world-improvers have turned out to be but the tools of master-natures.
Oswald Spengler[2]

He is a self-made man and worships his creator.
John Bright[3]

Civilisation is a road by which man travels, not a house for him to dwell in. His true city is elsewhere.
Christopher Dawson[4]

The belief in the certainty of man's progress, and the corollary reasons for human optimism, have formed the philosophical base for belief systems and ideologies that, contrary to their promise, have led Western man further from the bright sunlit uplands of the fulfillment of his hopes and greatest aspirations and deeper into the swamps and jungles infested with self-abasement, selfishness, pride, purposelessness, and war. Fundamentally, this failure has been due to the foundation upon which these belief systems and ideologies have been built: man himself.

Western man clambers like an ant to the top of his anthill, gazes from horizon to horizon—such as he can see them—and then assumes he has taken the rough measure of life and his world. Every day the evidence of this prideful, yet rationally foolish, view of life surrounds us in human words and endeavors. Man-as-the-cynosure-of-the-universe is the dominant viewpoint in Western civilization.

To be sure, some—possessing perhaps a vestigial sense of modesty—conceal its unacknowledged arrogance behind cloaks of religion or specious, idealistic ideologies, but the true humility taught by the book of Job—the most profound work ever to confront man—and dictated by a rigorous realism, can scarce be found.

Sorokin's "poisonous fruit...[the] fatal narrowing of the realm of true reality and true value"[5] is the direct consequence of man's vain, distorted self-perception.

Western man's overweening self-image underlies most of his social pathologies and most dangerous afflictions, be they war, racism, social unrest, and the tendency to construct dangerous and misguided ideologies and belief systems and tout them with the fervency of deeply held religious beliefs.

As some of our observers repeatedly note, these ideologies and belief systems often supplant true religion as ersatz, secular versions.

This elevation of man to the status of his own god results in the construction of ideologies and belief systems that are inimical to true understanding and the peace, purpose, and real meaning Western man seeks. Yet succumbing to his vanity and pride he moves further and further away from the spiritual repositories of those divine, intellectual and spiritual boons.

Typically, egocentric Western man devises his own "salvation," couching these ideas in the most idealistic of terms, then ruthlessly asserts them with an implicit if not overt compulsion to believe, which—he does not recognize—inadvertently serves as compelling evidence of their deficiencies. Were these beliefs that rewarding, why must there be any element of compulsion, whether political, military, economic, or simply through the pressure of the group (e.g., political correctness)?

THE INHUMANITY OF HUMANISM

Man is stripped of his glory and freedom and left as naked human animal shivering in an inhuman universe.
Christopher Dawson[6]

Nowhere have these tendencies been more apparent in recent memory in Western civilization than in humanism and Marxism. The superficial disparities between the two are not as striking as their deeper similarities.

Our observers speak of humanism with two different, but often related, connotations: First, the more historically connected term hearkening back to the Renaissance and the Enlightenment; second, the broader, more contemporary term embodying the nontheistic notion that man is capable of finding fulfillment and a resolution to his greatest problems by dint of his own freestanding reason and efforts.

Sorokin illustrated how man's scientific and technological achievements—narrow though they are—have become a form of intellectual and emotional fertilizer for man's vanity and his belief in his virtuous autonomy. In a segment entitled "The Culture of Man's Glorification and Degradation," Sorokin first implied, and then overtly pointed out, that man's "glorification," of the type cultivated by both forms of humanism, inevitably leads not to his exaltation but his degradation.

> We live, indeed, in an age of the greatest triumph of human genius.[7]
>
> ...
>
> No wonder, therefore, that we are proud of man. It is not strange that our culture has become homo-centric, humanitarian and humanistic par excellence.... Man is its glorious centre. It makes him "the measure of all things." It exalts him as the hero and the greatest value, not by virtue of his creation by God in God's own image, but in his own right, by virtue of man's own marvellous achievements. It substitutes the religion of humanity for the religions of superhuman deities. It professes a firm belief in the possibility of limitless progress based on man's ability to control his own destiny, to eradicate all social and cultural evils, and to create an even better and finer world, free from war and bloody strife, from crime, poverty, insanity, stupidity and vulgarity. In all these respects we live, indeed, in an era of a truly great glorification of man and his culture.[8]

The fallacious nature of this line of thought is often self-evident to the humble, but the dark shadows of pride and the sandstorms of vanity lead man farther into the desert of unreality and away from oases of meaning. "We are so accustomed to such views that we often fail to see the utter depreciation of man and his culture implied in them. Instead of depicting man as a child of God, and a bearer of the highest values in this empirical world, and for this reason sacred, they strip him of anything divine and great and reduce him to a mere inorganic or organic complex."[9]

Fernand Braudel implicitly acknowledged this tendency by reference to Etienne Gilson's definition of Renaissance humanism as "the Middle Ages 'not plus humanity but minus God.' The phrase is unfair and too extreme; but it does indicate the natural inclination, conscious or unconscious, of all humanist thought. Humanism frees and magnifies humanity, diminishing the role of God even if not completely forgetting it."[10]

Francis Schaeffer pointed to the natural consequence of the man-centered view that characterized humanism. "Beginning from man alone, Renaissance humanism—and humanism ever since—has found no way to arrive at universals or absolutes that give meaning to existence and morals."[11]

This "natural inclination" of humanism, as Braudel called it, is its core weakness. Were it not divorced from faith and a humble recognition of man's frailty and dependence on God, humanism could have the most salutary of effects—a beneficent force of the first magnitude. Many of its propensities are overtly Christian. Braudel acknowledged European thought as "inconceivable except in the context of a dialogue with Christianity, even when the dialogue is sharp and the dispute violent. This context is essential to the understanding of humanism, one of the fundamental aspects of Western thought."[12]

Ironically, our observers invariably note humanism's origins in the Christian faith. Christopher Dawson also saw secular humanism as a force deriving much of its dynamic principles from Christianity. When deprived of its roots in faith, humanism, however, becomes man centered and self-defeating.

> ...we have the paradox that at the beginning of the Renaissance, when the conquest of nature and the creation of modern science are still unrealized, man appears in godlike freedom with a sense of unbounded power and greatness; while at the end of the nineteenth century, when nature has been conquered and there seem no limits to the powers of science, man is once more conscious of his misery and weakness as the slave of material circumstance and physical appetite and death. Instead of the heroic exaltation of humanity which was characteristic of the naturalism of the Renaissance, we see the humiliation of humanity....Man is stripped of his glory and freedom and left as naked human animal shivering in an inhuman universe.[13]

Dawson expressed part of his formula for the survival of Western civilization in terms of humanism—but a humanism infused with the Christian faith. In this respect, he is very close to Sorokin's preference for an "idealistic" culture—as contrasted with the West's "sensate" culture. Both Dawson and Sorokin held that faith is central to any civilized culture and will be critical to the survival of Western civilization.

The additional parallel between Sorokin and Dawson is highly significant—their belief that scientific inquiry and faith are not only compatible, but that faith is essential to the highest achievement of which man is capable in science.

Dawson expressed this in terms of his Catholic faith. "...the material organization of the world by science and invention is in no sense to be refused or despised by the Catholic tradition, for to

Photograph by Ivy Scarborough

Lenin's Tomb in Red Square. *Toynbee correctly called Communism "another of our latter-day religions." For generations acolytes of the religion have worshipped at the shrine of the waxy corpse of their messiah. All men are religious; the only distinction is in what they worship.*

the Catholic philosopher no less than to the scientist the progressive *rationalization* of matter by the work of scientific intelligence is the natural vocation of the human mind."[14]

And, as Dawson illustrated, the values of Christianity pervaded this early humanism, giving it a vitality and virtue that Dawson felt was subsequently lost:

> The great men of the Renaissance were spiritual men, even when they were most deeply immersed in the temporal order. It was from the accumulated resources of their Christian past that they acquired the spiritual energy to conquer the material world and to create the new secular culture. It is true that the disparity between the source and the object of their activity tended to produce a sense of strain and spiritual tension, which is perceptible in the work of typical Renaissance geniuses such as Shakespeare and Cervantes, as well as in definitely religious characters like Michelangelo or Campanella. But, at least in Catholic Europe, the two elements had attained to a relatively stable equilibrium by the end of the sixteenth century, and had an equal share in the development of the later Renaissance culture. The spirit of Christian humanism dominated the whole of the seventeenth century and manifested itself alike in the Baroque art of Spain and Italy and Central Europe, in the Jacobean and Caroline literature of England and in the classical culture of France. This religious current which runs through seventeenth-century culture cannot be set aside as a reactionary or negative phenomenon, for it lies at the heart of the higher civilization, of the time and is responsible for some

> of its greatest achievements. Indeed, when in the eighteenth century this equilibrium was destroyed by the final victory of the naturalistic and rationalist tendencies, it involved the fall of the Renaissance culture itself. The new humanism of the Enlightenment was lacking in the vitality and spiritual depth of the earlier type. The one-sided rationalism of the Encyclopedists provoked the one-sided subjective emotionalism of Rousseau and the Romantics. And though both rationalism and romanticism were in a sense the heirs of the Renaissance tradition, neither of them was the true representative of the earlier humanism. Rationalism had lost its spiritual inspiration and romanticism lacked its intellectual order and its sense of form. Thus the disappearance of the Christian element in humanism has involved the loss of its vital quality.[15]

In a passage consistent with Sorokin and Toynbee, Dawson condemned the fatal mistake that led to the present crisis of Western civilization. "But the disease of modern civilization lies neither in science nor in machinery, but in the false philosophy with which they have been associated. At the very moment that man was at last acquiring control over his material environment, he was abandoning the ideal of spiritual order and leaving the new economic forces to develop uncontrolled without any higher social direction."[16]

Resorting to a notion approximately synonymous to Toynbee's favored concept of the "creative response," Dawson argued that the man-centered and materialistic interpretation of reality alone would not have made possible even man's scientific achievements:

> For the creative element in human culture is spiritual, and it triumphs only by mortifying and conquering the natural conservatism of man's animal instincts. This is true above all of science, for the path of the scientist leads him further from the animal than the rest of men. He lives not in the concrete reality of sensible experience, like the animal or the savage, but in a rarefied atmosphere of mathematical abstraction in which the ordinary man cannot breathe. If the materialist interpretation of history were true, the scientific intellectualization of nature could no more have arisen than could the meta-physical intuition of reality, and without science there could be no machine order.[17]

Dawson declared that the materialistic view, which is a fundamental tenet of contemporary humanism, cannot save man. "Material organization alone is incapable of saving civilization. Left to itself it may easily become a destructive force which is hostile alike to spiritual values and to human freedom. True civilization is essentially a spiritual order, and its criterion is not material wealth, but spiritual vision."[18]

In words that defy the man centeredness of humanism, Dawson offered what he believed was the only hope.

> In Christianity the idea of spiritual order...transcends all states and cultures and is the final goal of humanity. For as a modern Thomist has written, "The human personality is not entirely contained in political society; it belongs above all by its innermost and truest being, by its spiritual element, to another and more perfect society, to the universality of being, the World-Whole which includes the living Infinite, God Himself, as its Universal Good and Sovereign Head; and political society, however wide and numerous it may be, is but a minute section of this immense and innumerable Republic," this city of God of which St. Augustine and St. Thomas speak. This society exists in the nature of things as "the republic of all men under the law of God," although the actual disorder of human nature prevented its effective realization by man. It has therefore been reconstituted on a higher plane by the Incarnation, through which mankind is united in a direct and personal relation

> with the Divine Word. And this new unity is something more than a society; it is an organism, a living body whose head is Christ the Word and whose vital principle is the Divine Spirit.[19]

Dawson correctly perceived the damage being done by the mutation of Renaissance humanism into contemporary secular humanism. Though Dawson, like other of our observers, saw secular humanism as an illegitimate form of the earlier Christian humanism; unlike others, he did not just condemn this secular humanism, but argued that a humanism informed and structurally supported by the Christian faith would be of great benefit to Western man. But, should the modern mutation of humanism continue to roam the Western portions of the planet, Schaeffer declared that it will prove self-destructive.

> There is a death wish inherent in humanism—the impulsive drive to beat to death the base which made our freedoms and our culture possible.
>
> In ancient Israel, when the nation had turned from God and from his truth and commands as given in Scripture, the prophet Jeremiah cried out that there was death in the city. He was speaking not only of physical death in Jerusalem but also a wider death. Because Jewish society of that day had turned away from what God had given them in the Scripture, there was death in the polis, that is, death in the total culture and the total society.[20]

MARXISM—THE DEVIL IN FINE CLOTHES

...wherever Marxist–Leninism has had power, it has at no place in history shown where it has not brought forth oppression.
Francis Schaeffer[21]

Dawson's recognition of humanism's origins in Christianity anticipated what for some will be a startling revelation, expressed most succinctly by Toynbee and noted earlier: Marxism too is a mutation of Christian thought and belief. "Communism, which is another of our latter-day religions, is, I think, a leaf taken from the book of Christianity—a leaf torn out and misread."[22]

Francis Schaeffer perceived what was so often missed by Westerners during the Cold War: the implicit idealism in Marxism—an idealism covertly founded on Christian values.

> Materialism, the philosophic base for Marxist–Leninism, gives no basis for the dignity or rights of man. Where Marxist–Leninism is not in power it attracts and converts by talking much of dignity and rights, but its materialistic base gives no basis for the dignity or rights of man. Yet it attracts by its constant talk of idealism. To understand this phenomenon we must understand that Marx reached over to that for which Christianity *does* give a base—the dignity of man—and took the words as words of his own. The only understanding of idealistic sounding Marxist–Leninism is that it is (in this sense) a Christian heresy. Not having the Christian base, until it comes to power it uses the words for which Christianity does give a base. But wherever Marxist–Leninism has had power, it has at no place in history shown where it has not brought forth oppression. As soon as they have had the power, the desire of the majority has become a concept without meaning.[23]

Photograph by Ivy Scarborough

Monument to workers, Kiev, Ukraine. *Another example of what Sorokin called "colossalism," the monument glories in man. Communism, like Western humanism, makes man the center of the universe. Toynbee observed, "Communism, which is another of our latter-day religions, is, I think, a leaf taken from the book of Christianity—a leaf torn out and misread." Man always worships a god, even if that god is only himself.*

From its inception to today, communism's idealistic appeal could not be grasped by most Western minds. It was not grasped primarily because of the West's self-absorption and extraordinary affluence: "Why would we want this? Why would anyone want this? We are making a lot of money!!!" But this blindness to its idealistic appeal betrayed a hardness of heart. The West could not see the appeal because it often did not have sensitivity to the suffering of millions. That lack of sensitivity, coupled with intellectual obtuseness, granted communism great room to maneuver. The West, in turn, feeling threatened—with considerable justification—resorted to the most simplistic and primitive responses: bolstering despots who would oppose communism and using military might to overtly fight it when the West could not suppress it by other means.

When on patrol with Salvadoran Commandos in El Salvador in the mid 1980s during the communist guerrilla wars in Central America, I was struck by the juxtaposition of the rampant poverty on the one hand and the glowing idealistic propaganda of the FMLN (the Communist guerrilla insurgents) on the other. It was easy to see how a poor *campesino* and his family—with the boot of an oppressive government, and an even more oppressive poverty, on his neck—might see their options. In doing so, they would be neither evil nor, necessarily, blind—just desperate.

Photograph by Ivy Scarborough

Salvadoran Commandos on patrol during the communist guerrilla war talk with a poor Salvadoran family. 1988. *Rampant poverty and the idealistic propaganda of the Communist FMLN could easily lead a poor* campesino*—with the boot of an oppressive government and an even more oppressive poverty on his neck—to make the wrong choice. He would be neither evil nor necessarily blind, just desperate. The West, particularly the U.S., long had opportunity to address these circumstances but never did.*

The West, particularly the United States, had long had opportunity to address these circumstances; but that would have called for either munificence and generosity untainted by self-interest, or the foresight to recognize what was clearly in one's self-interest. Neither was present. The United States' self-interest was tied up in the issue, but its short-sightedness had frustrated any prospect for the expensive and long term altruism necessary to displace the influence of communist propaganda. Even after the bloody defeat of the communist movements in Central America, the United States has continued to pay a price for this failure—in part through massive illegal immigration across its southern border.

Ultimately, more than anything else, the invalidity of communism as a viable form of government and economic system brought about its collapse. In a real sense—though forceful resistance to the contagion was sometimes necessary—communism wasn't defeated, it disproved itself. We must be mindful, however, that not everyone learned the lesson. Discredited though it may appear in the West, communism remains the hope and the battle plan for millions.

Dawson referred to the "Messianic Character and Radical Insufficiency of Marxism" in *Christianity and the New Age*, by which he meant its origins in religion yet its utter failure as an explanation for man's history. He perceptively observed that Marxism was a reflection of the mind and

Photograph by Ivy Scarborough

Worshipping the man-god, Lenin. *Schaeffer said of Marxism, "Marx reached over to that for which Christianity does give a base—the dignity of man—and took the words as words of his own. The only understanding of idealistic sounding Marxist–Leninism is that it is (in this sense) a Christian heresy....But wherever Marxist–Leninism has had power, it has... brought forth oppression. As soon as they have had the power, the desire of the majority has become a concept without meaning."*

idiosyncrasies of Marx himself rather than any immutable laws of economics or history. It was said of him, "Dawson indicates the motives which lead men to accept Marxism and the needs which Marxism attempts to satisfy. But he also illustrates the radical insufficiency of Marxism as an explanation either of history, economics, or society, showing that its widespread appeal is based not on Marxism's own worldview, but upon Messianic elements which it has borrowed from the Jewish Prophetic tradition. These elements are in striking contradiction to the basic premises of the Marxist materialist interpretation of history."[24]

Marx, and those who followed him, asserted that their dialectic revealed immutable laws of history and human behavior. This assertion gave evidence of the same man-centered hubristic thinking that has characterized much of Western civilization since the Enlightenment. That the deficiencies in their belief system are now obvious is not nearly as significant as the effect this should have in disabusing Western man of this foundational flaw in his reasoning.

Huntington correctly observed that the failures of Marxism will not necessarily lead to its displacement by liberal democracy, however. The tendency to believe this is another manifestation of the same flaw in thinking that produced Marxism in the first place.

> Marxism was a product of European civilization, but it neither took root nor succeeded there. Instead modernizing and revolutionary elites imported it into non-Western societies; Lenin, Mao, and Ho adapted it to their purposes and used it to challenge Western power, to mobilize their people, and to assert the national identity and autonomy of their countries against the West. The collapse of this ideology in the Soviet Union and its substantial adaptation in China and Vietnam does not, however, necessarily mean that these societies will import the other Western ideology of liberal democracy. Westerners who assume that it does are likely to be surprised by the creativity, resilience, and individuality of non-Western cultures.[25]

We close with Wallerstein, who asks one of the most momentous questions of our age: What belief system will Western man now turn to?

> There were always very many people in all these countries who in no sense shared the original Bolshevik objectives. What made the whole system collapse in the end, however, was that large numbers of those who did share these objectives became as hostile to the regimes as the others—perhaps even more hostile. The spectre that haunted the world from 1917 to 1991 had become transformed into a monstrous caricature of the spectre that had haunted Europe from 1848 to 1917. The old spectre exuded optimism, justice, morality, which were its strengths. The second spectre came to exude stagnation, betrayal, and ugly oppression. Is there a third spectre on the horizon?[26]

END NOTES
CHAPTER 9

1 Alexander Solzhenitsyn, Text of Address at Harvard Class Day Afternoon Exercises, Thursday, June 8, 1978.
2 Oswald Spengler, *The Decline of the West* (New York: A. A. Knopf, 1932), 396.
3 John Bright, in *The Yale Book of Quotations*, eds. Fred R. Shapiro and Joseph Epstein (Printed by R. R. Donnelley and Sons, 2006), 104.
4 Christopher Dawson, *Religion and the Modern State* (New York: Sheed & Ward, 1935), xv.
5 Pitirim A. Sorokin, *The Crisis of Our Age* (Oneworld Publications Ltd., 1941; this edition Sergei P. Sorokin and Peter P. Sorokin, 1992), 253.
6 Christopher Dawson, *Christianity and the New Age* (New York: Sheed & Ward, 1931), 8.
7 Sorokin, *The Crisis of Our Age*, 197.
8 Sorokin, *The Crisis of Our Age*, 198.
9 Sorokin, *The Crisis of Our Age*, 199.
10 Fernand Braudel, *A History of Civilizations* (New York: Penguin Group, 1995), 340.
11 Francis A. Schaeffer, *How Should We Then Live? The Rise and Decline of Western Thought and Culture* (Wheaton, IL: Crossway, 1976), 55.
12 Braudel, *History of Civilizations*, 339.
13 Dawson, *Christianity and the New Age*, 9–10.
14 Dawson, *Christianity and the New Age*, 94–95.
15 Dawson, *Christianity and the New Age*, 89–90.
16 Dawson, *Christianity and the New Age*, 95.
17 Dawson, *Christianity and the New Age*, 97–98.
18 Dawson, *Christianity and the New Age*, 98.
19 Dawson, *Christianity and the New Age*, 99.
20 Schaeffer, *How Should We Then Live?*, 226.
21 Schaeffer, *How Should We Then Live?*, 215.
22 Arnold Toynbee, *Civilization on Trial* (New York: Oxford University Press, 1948), 236.
23 Schaeffer, *How Should We Then Live?*, 215.
24 Dawson, *Christianity and the New Age*, xiii.
25 Samuel P. Huntington, *The Clash of Civilizations and the Remaking of World Order* (New York: Simon & Schuster, 1996), 52–53.
26 Immanuel Wallerstein, *The End of the World As We Know It: Social Science for the Twenty-First Century* (Minneapolis: University of Minnesota Press, 1999), 15.

CHAPTER

10

EDUCATION AND THE VAST LIMITS OF WESTERN MAN'S KNOWLEDGE

Education: that which reveals to the wise, and conceals from the stupid, the vast limits of their knowledge.
Mark Twain[1]

This does not sound like much of what passes for teaching these days, which often implicitly discourages critical thought and explicitly conspires to inculcate the uncritical fashions of the moment.
Robert Conquest[2]

Modern Western man would surely agree that education is a preeminent value of our civilization. Western man's affinity for seeing education as the answer to a multitude of social or economic deficiencies is another manifestation of his overweening sense of self-importance and personal sovereignty. What he would not agree on is the nature of that education, who is to control it, and the priorities to be given to different fields of study. In these differences, much can be discerned about the state of our civilization.

WHAT IS EDUCATION?

Only three people knew the answer and one of them is dead, another went mad, and I am the third, but I forget.
Lord Palmerston[3]

In his book, *Reflections on a Ravaged Century*, and in a chapter titled "The Answer Is Education," Robert Conquest, a veteran of the British army in World War II, debunks the first and foundational premise, particularly as expressed in America. "It has often been said that the 'answer' to most problems is 'education.' But it is obvious that a high level of education in a general sense has often failed to protect twentieth-century minds from homicidal, or suicidal, aberrations. As we have seen, these have often been generated by men of high educational standing. And it has often been in colleges and universities that the bad seeds first bore fruit."[4]

Conquest believes that "all teaching should actively encourage the critical treatment of all historical, social, literary and other doctrine in the humanities." He strikes the bull's-eye when he adds that this does not describe "much of what passes for teaching these days, which often implicitly discourages critical thought and explicitly conspires to inculcate the uncritical fashions of the moment."[5] Indeed, the conformity, shallowness, and even political correctness of teaching in the West generally are consistent with the self-deluding nature of thought. Evidence of a rigorous, tough-minded, probing realism is elusive.

Conquest sounds like Solzhenitsyn, Sorokin, Schaeffer, and other of our observers, each of whom in his own way noted the disparity between the stated abstract principle and professed value on the one hand and the actuality on the other.

Conformity in the society as a whole, including in formal education, is the norm. In America at least, true critical thinking has become as rare as the rugged self-reliance and individual love of freedom that prompted a few hardy souls to cross the Alleghenies.

Why is this the case? The answer lies mainly in Toynbee's "*pammixia*," Sorokin's "chaotic syncretism," and similar concepts of our observers that all outline the relativistic mindset of a culture in decay. The inevitable confusions and self-contradictions afford no bases, no benchmarks, and no reference points for true critical thinking. Like a disoriented deep-sea diver, Western man has great difficulty discerning which way is up. That orientation then becomes what he chooses to say it is. Thus, even were the trait and practice of true critical thinking somehow restored in Western educational systems, there is no immutable standard, no guide, by which critical insight might envelope, weigh, and measure the ideas and beliefs of our age.

Yet there is a deeper level: the moral relativism that this breeds grants man no incentive to be courageous, much less bold, in challenging any norm of the culture that is widely accepted. Thus conflicts of ideas are largely, in truth, ignited by pride, ideological and partisan perspectives, and the drives for power and material gain—hence, the often-touted virtues of "debate." Though a diaphanous loincloth of reputedly noble motives may be draped over the primitive underlying lusts, this too is part of the game.

The absence of true critical thinking has led to universities of banality; banal because the highly secular and humanistic views rigidly taught and adhered to are neither original nor new. Eminently predictable and stultifyingly conforming, they reflect ideas and attitudes that have been with man for centuries—and which, by now, should have been thoroughly discredited by the historical evidence. Yet each new generation, in its prideful way, perceives its thinking as modern and sophisticated and therefore advanced and progressive. Thus we have the triumph of vanity over humility and the ascendancy of human folly over eternal verities.

Would that these gatekeepers of education came to understand that the truth in humorist Josh Billings' famous, rough-hewn remark would apply even to them: "The trouble with most people is not ignorance, but knowing a lot that ain't so." Symbolically perhaps, the bad grammar is eclipsed by the wisdom, and the wisdom is corroborated by Mark Twain in his famous 1898 observation, "Education consists mainly in what we have unlearned."

Favorably citing a viewpoint of Thomas Jefferson, Conquest suggests that this deficit of broad historical understanding underlies many of Western civilization's failures and, to a considerable extent,

Samuel Clemens (1906) by Albert Bigelow Paine. Courtesy of *www.berkeley.edu.*

Mark Twain *corroborated a major theme of this book, the need for humility, when he declared education to be "that which reveals to the wise, and conceals from the stupid, the vast limits of their knowledge." But humility is rare in the West, and conformity in the society as a whole, including in education, is the norm. True independent, critical thinking has become as rare as the rugged self-reliance and individual love of freedom that prompted a few hardy souls to cross the Alleghenies.*

its worsening myopia, not only about the broader world and the irrefragable lessons of history, but about itself. We have, it seems, produced scientific, mathematical, and technological sophisticates whose knuckles drag the ground through the archives of history. "The century's disasters have been due in a major way to ignorance of, or distortion of, history. Thomas Jefferson held that the basic education of the citizens of a democracy should be 'chiefly historical.' His reasoning was that history, 'by apprising them of the past, will enable them to judge of the future; it will avail them of the experience of other times and other nations; it will qualify them as judges of the actions and designs of men.'"[6]

Yet erudite students of history could have been readily found in the upper echelons of the German Nazi and Russian Communist parties, illustrating again that it is not simply knowledge we must seek but understanding, insight and, most of all, wisdom. None of the latter can be achieved in an environment where learning and knowing are proscribed by the scientific method and a purely materialist worldview. The rigidity and narrowness of the Nazi, communist, and materialist worldviews forbid exploration beyond the permissible confines—at least exploration that will be granted any merit or validity. In this milieu heresy and apostasy are not purely theological terms.

Here too, another deficiency we earlier condemned of Western thought and practice impedes understanding: the tendency to narrow specialization and compartmentalization. This blinkered practice is critiqued throughout this book as one of the greatest procedural obstacles to true understanding in the West. Even in the realm of history the foci are often absurdly narrow; great effort may be expended on study, dissertations and books of the most tedious and particularist sort. Therefore, even were the West to repent of its relative indifference to history, it would have to also begin to extol the broad and deep perspective on history and surrender its intellectually indolent attentiveness to the minutiae.

IS WESTERN EDUCATION THE ANSWER?

Information is not knowledge.
Albert Einstein[7]

In a passage that powerfully rebukes the adherents of the view that education and notions like the scientific method are "the answers," Conquest illustrates the tragic human consequences of what is fundamentally a hubristic and prideful attitude rather than insight gleaned from true learning.

> An outstanding example of the failure of academic and theoretical expertise was to be found in Robert McNamara's conduct of the Vietnam War. In his recent apologia, he says that he failed to understand nationalism. No, what he failed to understand was Communism (though he no doubt misunderstood nationalism, too). He had no real idea of the motivations of the leadership on the "other side of the hill," that traditional essential to sound strategy.... But McNamara's central error, which he still does not seem to understand, was that he undertook a responsibility involving the lives of scores of thousands of Americans and many more Vietnamese for which he was totally unqualified. This was true in the political sense adumbrated above, and in the military sense...we find...a complete apparatus of pseudoscientific lore. The whole approach of "signals and responses" was politically illiterate. And the military side had been penetrated by the then fashionable variant of inapplicable "scientific" approaches—"systems analysis."[8]

No, Professor Conquest, it is more than, worse than, and more basic than, that. Secretary McNamara's fundamental mistake was arrogance, which leads to foolish rational judgments as surely as it will to flawed moral judgments. This implacable plague, which has infected the human species since Eden, is ravaging the Western world. Its virulence and contagion grows proportionally to the weakening of the spiritual and intellectual immune system. The antibody humility, produced in the bone marrow of faith, is its only cure. A near-illiterate soldier named Alvin York, whose spiritual and moral immune system were first rate, could potentially have reached judgments about war that were assuredly more sound, and infinitely less dangerous for millions of lives, than the erudite McNamara. This does not suggest York was qualified for such a job, for he surely was not, but is said rather to illustrate the traits of character that are necessary antecedents to the wise use of gifts of intellect.

Education therefore, if it is to be of real merit, must offer insight, understanding, and the rudiments for moral orientation, not simply facts, information, systems, and knowledge. This of course leads away from the altars of man and toward the altar of God. None of this is in the offing in Western civilization. The category of foolish choice illustrated by McNamara is being replicated every day throughout the West in ways whose repercussions will only be felt in generations, not simply years. Blithely oblivious to this rotting albatross suspended around the Western neck, only another superseding civilization may be able to discern with clarity what really happened. Decisions of whether to go to war or how to conduct war are just the more conspicuous species of choices adversely affected by Western man's propensity to see himself, his science, his scientific method, and his technology in vaunted terms.

TRUE REALITY OR A SELF-DELUDING COUNTERFEIT?

It must be clear that the whole mentality of human society—what is regarded as true or false, knowledge or ignorance; the nature of education and the curricula of the schools—all this differs according to the dominant system of truth accepted by a given culture or society.
Pitirim Sorokin[9]

We saw earlier that Samuel Huntington made a connection between understanding and morality on the one hand and education on the other when he listed the five most often cited categories of moral decay observed in the West: increases in crime, drug use, and violence; increased rates of divorce, illegitimacy, teen-age pregnancy, and single-parent families; a decline in membership in voluntary associations and interpersonal trust; weakening of the "work ethic" and rise of personal indulgence; and decreasing commitment to learning and intellectual activity.[10]

Not only should these features of Western civilization be linked, they are facets of the same phenomenon; and—consistent with our central metaphor of the great Bayeux Tapestry of life—they invariably interlock. We cannot compartmentalize them, though the West surely tries, and that is a part of the reason the West is failing to comprehend timeless verities and its own perilous predicament.

Sorokin made the extraordinarily important point that education in a society is a reflection of the society's perception of reality. "It must be clear that the whole mentality of human society—what is regarded as true or false, knowledge or ignorance; the nature of education and the curricula of the schools—all this differs according to the dominant system of truth accepted by a given culture or society."[11]

In a passage that is even truer today than when it was written, Sorokin elucidated what this means in American society in particular.

> Of like character is the educational system, which is first and foremost a training school devoted to "useful knowledge" and the crafts. Its chief business is to prepare successful businessmen, craftsmen, engineers and technicians, politicians, lawyers, doctors, teachers, preachers and so on. Mastery is sought in such arts as amassing a fortune, farming, home cooking, barbering, the invention of machines, research work, teaching and preaching. Elementary, high-school and college education—all are oriented principally in the same direction, paying scant attention, if any, to the forgotten purpose of real knowledge and wisdom: the nature of true reality and true values. Since this is deemed devoid of any immediate, short-term sensory utility, it is given merely lip service, playing little part in the actual curriculum of the schools of sensate society.[12]

Sorokin's insight is so accurate that even when contemporary Western education seems to be addressing "the nature of true reality and true values," such as in the study of theology or religion, we can discern that it is in fact the cloning of man's faith in himself rather than the natural reproduction of the higher principles of faith in a Supreme Being. We have substituted in our universities—even many religious schools and seminaries—the study of religion for faith itself and feel somehow we have done the right thing according to the values of our time. Consistent with the particularism and compartmentalization excoriated herein, there has been a proliferation of courses of study about religion. But the two are poles apart, for the study of religion implicitly worships man (i.e., the intellect) whereas the latter worships God. The former offers no hope for man's future, just knowledge—sometimes, dubious knowledge at that—while the latter offers authentic hope.

WESTERN EDUCATION—HELPING US UP OR LOWERING US DOWN?

If you help me up, I will make my own way back down.
Sir Thomas More to his executioner as he
mounted the scaffold to be beheaded

Christopher Dawson focused a great deal of time and attention on the role of education in Western civilization. He rightly perceived that education's role was not simply an innocuous method of inculcating knowledge, but an instrument of indoctrination and social control:

> The whole tendency of modern life is toward scientific planning and organization, central control, standardization and specialization. If this tendency was left to work itself out to its extreme conclusion, one might expect to see the state transformed into an immense social machine, all the individual components of which are strictly limited to the performance of a definite and specialized function, where there could be no freedom because the machine could only work smoothly so long as every wheel and cog performed its task with unvarying regularity. Now the nearer modern society comes to this state of total organization, the more difficult it is to find any place for spiritual freedom and personal responsibility. Education itself becomes an essential part of the machine, for the mind has to be as completely measured and controlled by the techniques of the scientific expert as the task which it is being trained to perform.[13]

This is another reason for the absence of critical thinking cited in Professor Conquest's indictment and for the presence of such sweeping social conformity.

Education, at least public education, has subtly become "an essential part of the machine." Lest some conclude that this sounds suspiciously conspiratorial, we might add that conspiracy, in the usual connotation of that word, is not required to produce a misbegotten end or loss of freedom. History demonstrates it can happen through a weakening in the character, will, and insight of the individual and a society. Power has a gravitational pull; it always seeks to accrete more power—no conspiracy necessary. And sedition need not be a legally defined crime, but an act of implied or overt social defiance for which some penalty will be exacted.

Dawson displayed similar and special concern for educational trends in America. However, government's seigniorage over education is now a hard reality throughout the Western world. The prescience of Dawson and other of our observers is once again on display as we realize that what follows was written in the mid-twentieth century:

> ...the modern democratic state even in America is something quite different from the form of state envisaged by the men who formed the American Constitution....they were the enemies of state intervention and aimed at creating a system which would leave the community and the individual free to lead their own lives and frame their own cultural institutions. But the modern democratic state partakes of the nature of the Church. It is the educator and spiritual guide of its citizens and any influence which withdraws the citizen and especially the citizen's children from this universal guidance is felt to be undesirable, if not positively disloyal.[14]

Dawson asserted that "the more completely secularized public education becomes, and the more the State acquires an educational monopoly...the more complete will be the victory of secularization as

Courtesy of The Albert Schweitzer Fellowship (ASF), *www.schweitzerfellowship.org*

Dr. Albert Schweitzer *observed, "As we acquire more knowledge, things do not become more comprehensible, but more mysterious." Reflecting a humility that is as rare in Western academia as is truly discriminating thought, such a viewpoint takes Man, with a capital "M," off his pedestal and puts him on his knees.*

the working religion, or rather counter-religion ...."[15] This of course is suggestive of the dangers of conformity of thought and confining perceptions of reality. Though in one sense what Professor Dawson said here should be self-evident to anyone, it nonetheless seems to have been lost on the majority of Americans, religious and agnostic.

Even the agnostic should take heed; for what is being described is not freedom from religion but increasing compulsion to conform to a secular religion. There will be one or the other. The questions solely are which will the American people choose, and will they choose consciously or by default? The question is being answered, has been answered, and—disturbingly—probably will continue to be answered, in favor of the secular religion.

But the point of all truly meaningful learning is not just to "know" more, but to "do" better and, more than that, to "be" better. Ultimately it is who we are in our hearts that most determines our destiny—and our influence on our time. When we properly address that "being" (i.e., who we are in our hearts and minds), "knowing" is already in action and "doing" will naturally follow. These cannot be separated one from another any more than one might attempt to fill one half of a bucket with water vertically rather than horizontally, leaving the remainder to be filled with other things. The human mind and heart are much the same. This is why any form of propaganda is most effective when communicated not directly, but appurtenant to some other form of communication—especially education. Only with age, experience, and wisdom can we hope to distinguish between incoming pristine water and sewage.

Secularists would argue that this is an argument for keeping religion or moral training out of the educational process, so as to give students the opportunity to choose for themselves. Years of standing before university students lecturing and questioning have made it clear to me that there is no such thing as values-free, objectively-neutral teaching. I taught on the premise that I owed my students complete candor and honesty on the one hand about my perspectives and beliefs, and freedom from manipulation of their thinking as their professor on the other. Pretending that teaching can be purely objective and values-free is another form of either self-delusion or hypocrisy.

A teacher should not beat his students about their heads and shoulders with his beliefs and views, but neither should he deny or conceal them. The questions then become, What values and views do you hold in highest esteem? Will you openly acknowledge them?

Dawson clearly preferred a dynamic and central role for the church (in his case, the Catholic Church) in education. He saw this as central to the prospects for the society as a whole. "For in claiming the right to maintain separate schools and to teach its own principles to its own people, the Church is the champion of freedom in the most vital matter, and even the liberal democratic state is becoming totalitarian when it asserts the principle of the single school and claims a universal monopoly of teaching."[16]

Of course the state, in America at least, did for generations claim a monopoly on teaching. This was first broadly undercut, ironically, by racists who wished to remove their children from integrated schools in the mid-twentieth century through the expedient of establishing private schools. The stigma of that initial motive did not aid the movement away from a state monopoly, but that monopoly was, nonetheless, eroded much further by the movement (provoked by the poverty of intellectual stimulation and moral discipline in government-run schools) to religious schools and home schooling. Both were resisted and criticized mightily by the advocates of state education. The religious schools and home schoolers successfully overwhelmed their critics not simply through perseverance but, more importantly, through the exceptional performance of their graduates. Many state-run schools have repeatedly proven to be deficient, not superior, in comparison in terms of educating their charges—not to mention in maintaining a civil and orderly environment in which students can be educated.

Dawson argued vigorously for religious schools simply on the bases of breaking out of the intellectual conformity imposed by state schools and the abysmal, often depraved, moral atmosphere.

> ...today, when the whole population of every civilized country is subjected to an intensive process of schooling during the most impressionable years of their lives, it is the school and not the church that

English cemetery. *A great threat for children and young people is the day-in, day-out, potent, omnipresent exposure to the narrow secular viewpoint and the debased sense of moral values that pervades so much of the Western school system—if not purely in instruction, then in loss of discipline and incontinence of human dissipations. Innocence, a pearl of great price, is ground into the mire of Western culture—and withal great poets, writers, and political and spiritual leaders shall lie unnoted in a latter-day version of Thomas Grey's "country churchyard," lost not to penury or neglectful obscurity, but killed by the selfish, hard-hearted depravity of a prideful age.*

CC

Photograph by Oren Jack Turner. PD-LOC. 1947

Einstein *observed that "information is not knowledge." We could go further and assert that knowledge is not insight, understanding, or wisdom, all of which are of a much higher order than mere information or even knowledge. The latter three are not acquired in a highly compartmentalized regimen of study—indeed, they are diminished—nor in a milieu characterized by Sorokin's "sensate values."*

forms men's minds, and if the school finds no place for religion, there will be no room left for religion elsewhere. It is no accident that the introduction of universal compulsory state education has coincided in time and place with the secularization of modern culture."[17]

I differ with Dawson on but one point: If "the school finds no place for religion, there will be no room left for religion elsewhere" would only be true if the church and individual Christian families failed in their duties. That the church in the West could be successfully court-martialed many times over for dereliction of duty is a subject addressed later.

Even so, the greater threat is the day-in, day-out, potent, omnipresent exposure to the narrow secular viewpoint and the debased sense of moral values that pervades so much of the Western school system—if not purely in instruction, then in loss of discipline and incontinence of human dissipations. To assume that impressionable young people will not be influenced by this makes belief in the "innate goodness of man" seem a plausible notion.

An extraordinarily heavy counterweight of exemplary private or familial education in moral virtue, intellectual range, and spiritual insight would be required to reform and offset the damage done to the plasticity of young minds and hearts. It is probable that we have reached the point that the intellectual, spiritual, and moral damage from such an environment cannot be entirely offset or mended. Jadedness has displaced innocence in the soul of much of the West's youth.

Innocence—a pejorative term in the modern West's lexicon implying a naïve failure to seize whatever life offers despite dubious merit—is a condition that once lost can never be regained. Through volitional choice virtue may return, and through faith the incubus of a lifetime of abasement and transgressions may be lifted. But innocence alone supplies a scintillatingly clear lens through which life and the world can be seen. Its bequests are sensitivity, the power of intense positive emotion, an eloquence of spirit and voice, and most of all, the ability to perceive truths and realities accessible only by mounting the highest mountain peaks of thought, virtue, and unselfishness. A pearl of great price, it is ground into the mire of Western culture—and withal great poets, writers, political and spiritual leaders shall lie unnoted in a latter-day version of Thomas Grey's "country churchyard," lost not to penury or neglectful obscurity, but killed by the selfish, hard-hearted depravity of a prideful age.

END NOTES
CHAPTER 10

1 Mark Twain, cited in Ambrose Bierce, *The Devil's Dictionary* (USA, Plain Label Books, 1925), 74.
2 Robert Conquest, *Reflections on a Ravaged Century* (New York: W. W. Norton, 2001), 215.
3 Lord Palmerston, cited in Lytton Strachey, *Queen Victoria* (New York: Harcourt, Brace and Co., 1921), 308: "Only three people have ever really understood the Schleswig–Holstein business—the Prince Consort, who is dead—a German professor, who has gone mad—and I, who have forgotten all about it."
4 Conquest, *Reflections*, 215.
5 Conquest, *Reflections*, 215.
6 Conquest, *Reflections*, 217.
7 Attributed to Albert Einstein in Caleb Carr, *Killing Time* (New York: Random House, 2000), 5.
8 Conquest, *Reflections*, 234.
9 Pitirim A. Sorokin, *The Crisis of Our Age* (Oneworld Publications Ltd., 1941; this edition Sergei P. Sorokin and Peter P. Sorokin, 1992), 70–71.
10 Samuel P. Huntington, *The Clash of Civilizations and the Remaking of World Order* (New York: Simon & Schuster, 1996), 304.
11 Sorokin, *Crisis of Our Age,* 70–71.
12 Sorokin, *Crisis of Our Age,* 84.
13 Christopher Dawson, *The Historic Reality of Christian Culture* (New York: Harper & Brothers, 1960), 26–27.
14 Dawson, *Historic Reality*, 34.
15 Dawson, *Historic Reality*, 40–41.
16 Dawson, *Historic Reality*, 87.
17 Dawson, *Historic Reality*, 87–88.

CHAPTER

11

WESTERN MAN'S EXPRESSION OF HIS SOUL: ART, MUSIC, LITERATURE, AND ENTERTAINMENT

In great art the technique fits the world view being presented....
Francis Schaeffer[1]

The answer is: the whole thing is demonstratively, and unanswerably, a deception, or self-deception.
Robert Conquest[2]

Art opens even the chilled, darkened heart to high spiritual experience. Through the instrumentality of art we are sometimes sent—vaguely, briefly—insights which logical processes of thought cannot attain.
Alexander Solzhenitsyn[3]

When the ship is going down, the scum rises to the top, or so the old seafaring expression tells us in what could be a metaphor for much that occurs in a declining civilization. Nowhere perhaps is this as evident as early as in the visual arts, literature, music, cinema, and entertainment. All provide insights into the soul of a culture just as they offer glimpses of the inner workings of the minds and hearts of their creators. Attentiveness to these forms of social expression can tell us a lot.

The course that the arts and entertainment have taken in Western civilization is encapsulated in the West's experience with its most ubiquitous medium, television. In the mid-twentieth century the new technology was touted—where have we heard this before?—as a great advancement for mankind, not simply in the realm of technology itself, but as a basis for "education" and the advancement of knowledge. Though Uncle Miltie, as entertainment goes, was as tame by today's standards as anything found in a nunnery, we should have suspected that his presence betokened a future for television that was far more frivolous than profound.

But even the most insightful social observer could not have guessed that within the span of two generations television would become the effluent end of a giant sewer system where all manner of human pathologies and debased behavior would be treated not as cautionary spectacle to educate, frighten, and repel, but as entertainment.

Western man was indeed "uplifted" and "educated" by television, but the lift was on a sea of effluvium and the education has been an advanced study in human depravity and how-to-become-jaded-by-as-early-as-mid-adolescence—if not sooner. Innocence in experience and nobility in aspirations—the

PD-LOC

Milton Berle as Cleopatra. *In the mid-twentieth-century, television was touted as a great advancement for "education" and knowledge. Though Uncle Miltie (Milton Berle), as entertainment goes, was as tame by today's standards as anything found in a nunnery, we should have suspected that his presence betokened a future for television that was more frivolous than profound. Within two generations television became the effluent end of a giant sewer system where human pathologies and debased behavior would be treated as entertainment.*

virtues and values of an exalted life—were supplanted by sordid experience and self-centered lusts.

Of course, in the realm of entertainment, movies were the progenitors of most of it: Feeling a certain freedom (i.e., license) to market whatever they liked in pursuit of the dollar, the pound, the franc, the deutschmark, and now the euro, producers, writers, and directors did not, and do not, typically treat their audiences to painful lessons in the consequences and the shame of self-centered and debased behavior, but, in so many ways and so many attractive guises, either depict such behavior for entertainment—à la Colosseum—or even uplift it as patterns by which to model one's life and priorities—all without fear of antipathy and with confidence in the audience's approbation, and, most especially, its revenues.

The debasement of art and entertainment as moral teachers was evident to more astute observers as early as the beginning of the twentieth century. But even leaders of the dominant religion of the West in the Christian church did not perceive the extent or true nature of it. Josef von Sternberg's 1929 German film, *The Blue Angel*, dwelt on the theme of individual sexual obsession but was a harbinger of a coming cinematic—and eventually cultural—obsession as well. In America the infection could be readily found in the cinema of the 30s and 40s, a time of reputed innocence. In the 1939 movie *Gone With the Wind*, the character Rhett Butler's infamous "damn" was roundly and nearly universally damned by churches in America. Countless words were spilled in print and preaching inveighing against this singular profanity. Yet scarcely anyone noted that the two deliberately and contrivedly attractive central characters were, variously or congruently, adulterous, ruthless, implacably self-centered, utterly materialistic, and devoid of any evidence of regard for a higher moral authority. Their "love," such as it was, ostensibly elevated them above the common herd. Their personas reflected more of their creators' thoughts and values—and the damage being done to the national psyche and character—than one four-letter word ever could. The insidious seeds were already there—even in the earliest days of the cinema, before Rhett could be heard to utter a word—but they were glossed over with the false chimera and meretricious charms that come so easily to the filmmaker's "art."

Photograph by Hulton Archive/Getty Images

The 1929 German film The Blue Angel, *which made Marlene Dietrich a star, dwelt on the theme of sexual obsession but was a harbinger of a coming cinematic and cultural obsession as well. In America, the infection could be readily found in the cinema of the 30s and 40s, a time of reputed innocence. Western cinema has only rarely led man to see his own depravity and weaknesses, much less to surmount them, but rather often to nurture them and treat them even as valuable and attractive assets and experiences.*

If we define art as a creative form of expression that uplifts man and grants him greater insight into his true condition, with a corollary encouragement to rise above it—a definition far closer to my own—then much of recent Western art and entertainment has been an abysmal failure. Worse still, it has done just the opposite: led man to not see his own depravity and weaknesses, much less to surmount them, but rather often to nurture them and treat them even as valuable and attractive assets and experiences.

SEX AND THE SINGLE CIVILIZATION

The more decadent it becomes, the more imitative it grows and the swifter becomes the tempo of the successive phases of the process.
Pitirim Sorokin[4]

Francis Schaeffer focused heavily on the arts when writing of contemporary Western culture. Referring to Edward Gibbon (1737–1794) and the *Decline and Fall of the Roman Empire* (1776–1788), Schaeffer cited Gibbon's often-quoted five key indicators of the dissipated state of the Romans. Among them were "an obsession with sex" and "freakishness in the arts, masquerading as originality, and enthusiasms pretending to be creativity...."[5] "As the Empire ground down, the decadent Romans were given to a thirst for violence and a gratification of the senses. This is especially evident in their rampant sexuality."[6]

That Gibbon's observation of "an obsession with sex" as a characteristic of a culture in advanced decay should be mentioned in a chapter on art and entertainment in the Western world, should not come as a surprise.

The dominance of sex as a theme of Western art, literature, entertainment, and even music, is obvious to all but the most obtuse. However, that dominance and pervasiveness have now been so

PD (still from uncopyrighted trailer)

In the 1939 movie Gone with the Wind, *Rhett Butler's infamous "damn" was roundly damned by churches in America. Countless more words were spilled in print and preaching inveighing against this singular profanity. Yet scarcely anyone noted that the two deliberately and contrivedly attractive central characters were, variously or congruently, adulterous, ruthless, implacably self-centered, materialistic, and devoid of any evidence of regard for a higher moral authority.*

complete for so long that millions of inhabitants of Western civilization would not understand the point being made here—their frame of reference being so truncated and narrowed by the relentless, ubiquitous, percussive effects of the culture itself.

Nor can "an obsession with sex" and "freakishness in the arts, masquerading as originality" be divorced from what Philip Bagby called "the stagnation of the arts" in the West, which he cited as one of several indicia that "have seemed to betoken an imminent decline."[7] The creative impulse cited so frequently by Toynbee and Sorokin as an indicator of a civilization's moral health and intellectual vitality is the antithesis of Bagby's "stagnation" and Gibbon's "freakishness." Any implied, if not stated, assumption that Western art is creative is also suggestive of what Gibbon called "masquerading as originality" and "enthusiasms pretending to be creativity." Carroll Quigley, when noting the irrationality that began to appear in the West in the twentieth century, observed traits that were identical to those described two centuries ago by Gibbon about Rome: "All…characteristics of an age of irrationality began to appear on all sides—increased gambling, increased smoking, the growing use of alcohol and narcotics, a growing obsession with sex and with perversions of sex, an increasing mania for speed, for nervous tension, and for noise; above all, perhaps, a growing tendency to regard violence as a solution for all problems…."[8]

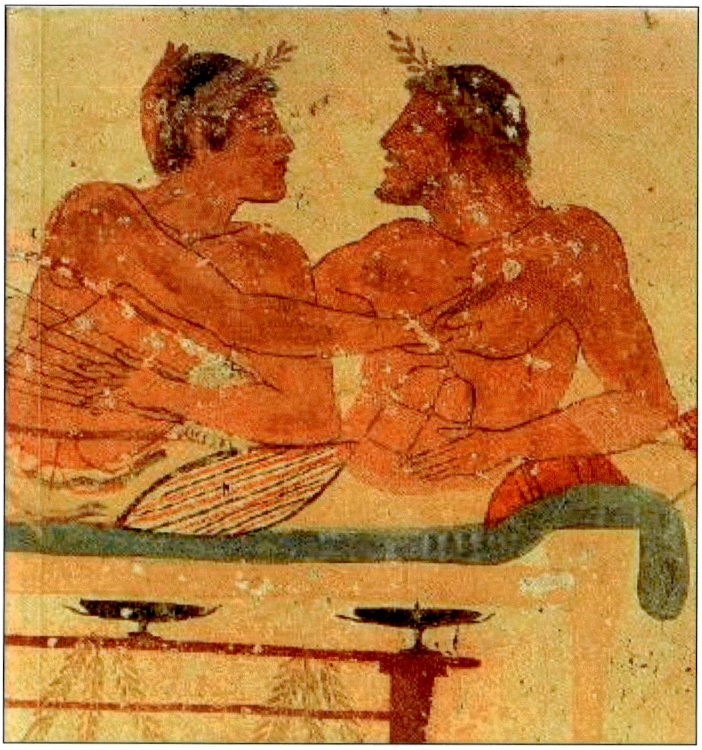

PD

An older man attempting to seduce a younger. *Among Gibbon's often-quoted indicators of the dissipated state of the Romans were "an obsession with sex" and "freakishness in the arts, masquerading as originality, and enthusiasms pretending to be creativity." The dominance of sex, including perversions, as a theme of Western art, literature, entertainment, and even music, is obvious to all but the most obtuse. But millions in Western civilization would not understand the point being made.*

The parallels with the manifestations of Western culture in art, cinema, literature, and music are striking. Two of those themes, sex and violence, have been the subjects of endless debate within Western societies. Yet reliance on these behaviors as an artistic expression or entertainment not only continues but accelerates. All manner of sexual behavior is increasingly regarded simply as a choice of which Western man should be tolerant; perversions of sex are redefined through the deployment of execrably dishonest euphemisms such as "alternate lifestyles"; violence is reputedly opposed by many cultural leaders; yet nothing changes, and one suspects that their opposition is more one of fear of, and aversion to, pain than any truly lofty moral concern; and what can we say about speed, noise, gambling, and the use of addictive substances other than What would you expect in so sordid an environment?

The elevation of a biological function—not dissimilar to eating or urinating in its physiological significance, and decidedly mundane in its actual mechanics—to the very center of the cultural stage of Western civilization says everything about the culture's retrogression to a primordial state.

Love as defined readily and often in Western culture, produces, for the sensitive and intellectually astute, the question from the poet Robert Bridges' *Eros*:

Why hast thou nothing in thy face?
Thou idol of the human race,
Thou tyrant of the human heart...

Rampaging through the art, entertainment, hearts, minds and pocketbooks of Western man, this version of "love" has largely displaced—in words, film footage, and discourse—the authentic article expressed by Yeats in his paean to that which is truly meaningful.

How many loved your moments of glad grace,
And loved your beauty with love false or true,
But one man loved the pilgrim Soul in you,
And loved the sorrows of your changing face...

—*When You Are Old*

PATHOLOGY AS ART AND ENTERTAINMENT

...contemporary art is primarily a museum of social and cultural pathology. It centres in the police morgue, the criminal's hide-out, and the sex organs, operating mainly on the level of the social sewers.
Pitirim Sorokin[9]

No analysis of art and entertainment in the West would be of any consequence if it did not point out what Immanuel Wallerstein called the "commodification" of everything in Western culture. This brings us back to the theme—though truly we have never left it—of the West's profound and obsessive materialism. Sorokin described Western art in graphic and often pejorative terms: "As we move nearer and nearer to contemporary art, we are well-nigh shocked by the contrast that we encounter. Art becomes increasingly a commodity manufactured primarily for the market...; and aimed almost exclusively at utility, relaxation, diversion and amusement, the stimulation of jaded nerves or sexual excitation."[10] The effect of this "commodification" should be anticipatable: it corrupts, demeans, and contravenes the original and noble values of Western art.

Because it panders to the marketplace it is forever searching for new and more sensational means to make itself attractive to the buying public. This is a roadmap to the swamps and quicksand below, not the high mountain passes. It sinks, Sorokin said, "to the level of the common herd." But among the strongest words Sorokin deployed against the depravity and shallowness of Western art is found a description of the pervasive corrosion of the culture: "Since it has to entertain, thrill or relax, how can it avoid becoming progressively more sensational, 'stunning,' exotic and pathological? It has to disregard virtually all religious and moral values, because these are rarely 'amusing' and 'entertaining'....Hence it comes to be more and more divorced from truly cultural values and turns into an empty art known euphemistically as 'art for art's sake,' at once amoral, non-religious and non-social, and often antimoral, antireligious, and antisocial...."[11]

Sorokin may in part have missed the mark—or perhaps a mark. Some of the "common herd" live and think on a higher plane than the purveyors of the art and entertainment of our age, but the "common herd," being neither the creators nor the propagators, are victims—sometimes knowingly, other times unwittingly—of the debasement. Worse still, modern Western art and entertainment plumb depths of depravity that would never occur to most of "the common herd."

Feeling so strongly, Sorokin redeployed this powerful characterization in several ways.

> Like contemporary science and philosophy in their debasing aspects contemporary art mortalizes the immortals, stripping them of everything divine and noble.... [I]t ignores almost all that is divine and noble in man... sadistically concentrating on the mediocre, and especially on the negative, the pathological, the sub-social and sub-human.....[I]t chooses as its 'heroes' either the ordinary, prosaic types of human beings or the negative and pathological. The same is true also of the events with which it deals.[12]

The truth in these observations is on display any night on television sets and movie screens throughout the Western world. Crime, violence, murder, deceit and betrayal, and all forms of sexual behavior, are the stock in trade of these forms of "art" and entertainment. Excise them from the television and movie scripts and the respective industries would collapse overnight.

Toynbee told us in his analyses of a civilization's disintegration that its members are "apt to take refuge in a series of alternative reactions to the pressures of disintegration, and these reactions are as it were pathological inversions of some of the growth processes...."[13]

The individual member of the civilization, benighted in his view of life and the world by a culture that provides him with little or no substance upon which to hang his hat for meaning and lasting purpose, is in crisis without often being conscious of it. Perhaps sensing a deep longing to pursue truly meaningful courses of creative action, he understands not what is available to him. Thus he pursues the specious values and priorities of the broader culture in a desperate—and pathetic—attempt to quench the burgeoning unrest.

Toynbee's point that the "dominant minority" of the civilization bears the greater moral culpability for its decay is illustrated by this tragedy, which is replicated millions of times over every day in Western civilization.

WHAT IS MODERN WESTERN ART AND CULTURE?

... the whole thing is demonstratively, and unanswerably, a deception, or self-deception.
Robert Conquest[14]

Robert Conquest decried the condition of modern Western art by citing the views of the critic Arthur Danto who "argues that on a modern approach anything can be art....[T]he concept 'art' has lost any meaning....[I]n practice [it is] anything an 'artist' produces for which he or she secures a gallery—or poetry page or whatever. Meanwhile, its proponents make a dual, and self-contradictory, claim—that anything is art, and also that anything they produce is 'Art' in the same sense as a painting by Velázquez."[15]

Conquest's answer to the question of whether this is "art" is right out of the central theses of this book: "...the whole thing is demonstratively, and unanswerably, a deception, or self-deception."[16] The ludicrousness of modern Western characterizations of this or that as art would be obvious to an insightful observer from another time or place but is lost on members of a culture that lurches into darker and darker shadows without so much as a candle of perspective to show them where they are going.

The vagaries are supported by copious efforts to contrive theories of "art," or schools of "art," or ideologies of "art," all intended to support and affirm the nonsensical as valid, even enlightened. Gibbon first noted the historical pattern: "A cloud of critics, of compilers, of commentators, darkened the face of learning, and the decline of genius was followed by the corruption of taste."[17]

In the contemporary West to say this is a case of the emperor with no clothes is understating the matter. A legion of stark naked presumptive elites of one stripe or another is fawned over and marveled at by an even larger crowd of jaded—and in a similar state of dishabille—media, politicians, art, literary, cinema, music and television critics, and other social commentators. The distinction between nobility of purpose and means in the political and cultural realms is confused with cultural sophistication. Awareness and knowledge of art and culture are no indicators of morality or civilization, because as Conquest pointed out, "Political culture does not run *pari passu* with

PD-LOC

PD

(Left) Abraham Lincoln. (Right) Nicholas Romanov II and family (1895). *Abraham Lincoln's youthful* tabula rasa *was not contaminated by modern Western art or cinema but rather was stimulated by the arduous realities of the American frontier and a value system that could not only ensure survival but nurture compassion and justice of a high order; whereas the Romanovs, amidst the splendor of material wealth and cultural surfeit, could produce only suffering, injustice, and revolution.*

'culture' in the aesthetic sense. Abraham Lincoln was incomparably more advanced in political civilization than any Romanov or Hapsburg, in spite of all the ballet and opera of St. Petersburg and Vienna....And it was Nero, was it not, rather than Vespasian, who was so keen on the arts?"

Abraham Lincoln's youthful *tabula rasa* was not contaminated by modern Western art or cinema but rather was stimulated by the arduous realities of the American frontier and a value system that could not only ensure survival but nurture compassion and justice of the highest order. The Romanovs, amidst the splendor of material wealth and cultural surfeit, could produce only suffering, injustice, and revolution. The gravitas of such a historical and personal lesson drops ponderously to the bottom of the badly polluted stream of Western art and entertainment with hardly a ripple. The "dominant minority" of Western culture does not want to see this; its acknowledgment would expose the utter meaninglessness and shallowness of their leadership.

Conquest's contempt for the notion that culture, in and of itself, assures us of anything worthy and meaningful is complete. In this he is in concert with Sorokin, whom we shall see shortly, was equally dismissive of *ars gratia artis*. "...A curious little volume might be made of the poems of Stalin, Castro, Mao, and Ho Chi Minh, with illustrations by A. Hitler; and this last name should remind us that the much-touted slogan 'When I hear the word '*culture*,' I reach for my revolver' was uttered by a fictional member of the SA....Hitlerism proper (like Kaiserism) swarmed over Europe to the accompaniment of vast claptrap about *Kultur*...."[18]

Cultural claptrap did not die in a Berlin bunker in April 1945; it survives in a mutated form that is even more resistant to the antibiotics of reason and insight. Such "needle to the pole" honesty and insight as Conquest's are badly needed in massive doses.

Even so, knowing what the truth isn't is not the same as knowing what it is.

By returning to Sorokin's classifications of civilizations as ideational, sensate and idealistic, and applying, as he did, those terms to art, we understand better not only what Sorokin was thinking, and what he believed was unquestionably superior, but how art can be perceived and understood. "Ideational Art…articulates the major premise of ideational culture that the true reality-value is God.…Its 'heroes' are God and other deities, angels, saints, and sinners, and the soul, as well as the mysteries of Creation, Incarnation, Redemption, Crucifixion, and Salvation, and other transcendental events."[19]… "Its objective is not to amuse, entertain or give pleasure, but to bring the believer into a closer union with God."[20]

In contrast to the nobility and exalted nature of ideational art, Sorokin described modern sensate art and in the process referred to *ars gratia artis*—appropriately, the motto of a major American motion picture studio—with contempt:

> The aim of Sensate Art is to afford a refined sensual enjoyment: relaxation, excitation of tired nerves, amusement, pleasure, entertainment.…[I]t must be sensational, passionate, pathetic, sensual and incessantly new…by voluptuous nudity and concupiscence…divorced from religion, morals and other values, and styles itself "art for art's sake."…It has to be eternally changing, presenting a constant succession of fads and fashions, because otherwise it will be boring, uninteresting, unenjoyable.…Since it does not symbolize any supersensory value, it stands and falls by its external appearance.[21]

Conquest illustrated his criticisms by pointing also to the "raw" nature of much that is labeled *art* in the modern West, which is losing the "shock effect in their raw materials, but also to those materials *remaining* largely raw. There is no execution unless at a very low and mechanical level. And this is even praised as 'conceptual.'" With appropriate logic and satisfying sarcasm, Conquest declares "…there is no 'artistry' that a bricklayer—or a butcher and a glazier—could not do, assuming they could spare time from their more useful occupations."[22]

The contrast between these two artistic forms is illustrated in part by the juxtaposition of the movie *The Passion of the Christ* with virtually everything else in recent Western cinema. We will note parenthetically that inherent in the Western world's reaction to this film is a glimmer of light for the civilization. Millions were drawn to the film despite its rejection and ostracism by many cultural elites, particularly in the film industry. Despite their condescension, it became perhaps the most talked about film of its time, and prompted a few of the centers of the cinematic industry to attempt to emulate its success. That they could not successfully do so was due to their lack of insight into its greater meaning and values—neither of which they comprehend. Thus their imitations are ersatz expressions of a spiritual reality that is beyond them.

Christopher Dawson in *Religion and World History* acknowledged the expansive gulf between contemporary Western sensate art and the ideational art described by Sorokin and, in so doing, observed that it "seems almost absurd to expect people to bring the spirit of Galilee and Assisi into the environment of Hollywood…" He added that no one "can deny that it is possible. But it involves something more than pious platitudes and ethical idealism. It calls for a heroic effort.…"[23]

Ideational art was founded on noble and exalted absolutes, be they the ideal of beauty or God himself. This elevated foundation elevated man. Greek art, according to Sorokin, prior to the third century B.C., and the art of the Middle Ages, never suffered from debasement as a "a mere means for sensual entertainment or utility.…[It]was regarded as the incarnation either of Plato's ideal of absolute beauty or of the absolute value of God…indissolubly bound up with all their fundamental values—with God, truth, goodness and the majesty of absolute beauty itself. As such, it was never the empty shell of an 'art for art's sake.'"[24] Of course, we must remind ourselves of the unsettling truth that modern Western art is also indissolubly bound up with [the West's] fundamental values. The sublimity of ideational art could not be found for the most part in modern Western art, which substitutes the vacuous and vulgar for the idealistic and inspiring.

Sorokin described a third, and his preferred, form of artistic expression.

> Idealistic art is an intermediary between the ideational and sensate forms of art. Its world is partly supersensory and partly sensory, but only in the sublimest and noblest aspects of sensory reality. Its heroes are partly gods and other transcendental creatures; partly the empirical man, but in his noblest aspects only. It is an art intentionally blind to everything debasing, vulgar, ugly, and negative.… [I]t represents a marvellous synthesis of the ideational and the noblest forms of sensate art.[25]

That this could describe the art of Western civilization had it taken a more lofty course should be a profound disappointment; but it could also become an aspiration.

Human vanity and pride—we have noted the proliferation of both in Western civilization—prompt a culture to presume that the art of one's time and place is, without question, superior. Yet, for the West this modernist cultural-centrism is an unwitting revelation not of superiority but of primitivism. Western critics and social observers would tend to see ideational art as primitive and unsophisticated, but Sorokin maintained that "the later and more developed stage of culture produced ideational art, rather than the sensate art which had preceded it."[26]

The form of art of a culture is a direct reflection of the dominant values and way of thinking of that culture. Were the validity—and the appalling significance—of that declaration readily acknowledged in the West, millions would be in shock—recognizing, as they must, the debased and depraved nature of much that passes for art and entertainment in their culture. But there is a disconnect, a tendency on the part of citizens of

The 1941 biographical war drama Sergeant York *starred* Gary Cooper as Alvin York*, the deeply religious Tennessee farmer who was called the "greatest civilian soldier" of World War I. The film received 11 Oscar nominations. Christopher Dawson observed it "seems almost absurd to expect people to bring the spirit of Galilee and Assisi into the environment of Hollywood..." but* Sergeant York *appealed to nobler virtues and spiritual values; it not only entertained but inspired millions.*

Western civilization to compartmentalize these manifestations of their culture as products of relatively narrow groups such as groin-clutching Hollywood or the producers in New York of crucifixes submerged in urine. This is self-deluding; the former can only succeed because millions buy their products, and the latter are sometimes funded directly or indirectly by government grants and accorded status as "art" by those whose minds are submerged in the intellectual equivalent of urine.

Sorokin's attentiveness to the historical waxing and waning of the forms of artistic expression led to detailed analyses of the art from different periods of Western history.

> The figures show that medieval painting and sculpture were overwhelmingly religious. This religious factor began to decline after the thirteenth century, becoming quite insignificant in the nineteenth and twentieth centuries, whereas the percentage of secular pictures and sculptures—which were virtually absent in the Middle Ages—has risen since the thirteenth century to approximately 90–96 per cent of all the known pictures and sculptures of the countries in question. A similar situation has prevailed in music, literature, and architecture.[27]

Of particular significance in distinguishing the sensate from the ideational art forms is the motive of the artist. Theophilus illustrated the nobility and selflessness inherent in the ideational artists work: "...neither for the love of men's praise, nor for the desire of temporal reward...but for the greater honour and glory of the name of God."[28] Perhaps one road to hell is paved with good intentions, but the road to heaven—and an exalted life for man on earth—is surely not paved with self-centered and debased intentions. The unselfishness of these artists and creators of cathedrals was such that even today many of their identities remain a mystery.

Francis Schaeffer noted the corruption of ideational art even within the church and the relationship between that art and the church's leadership in a given age: "A parallel can be drawn between the 'living' quality of this early Christian art and the living Christianity of the early church. Leaders like Ambrose of Milan (339–397) and Augustine (354–430) strongly emphasized a true biblical Christianity. Later, in the church, there was an increasing distortion away from the biblical teaching, and there also came a change in art. The naturalism and realism which characterized the art of the 4th and 5th centuries was displaced for 'the fantastic and unreal.'"[29]

Who we are and what we believe manifests itself in everything we do and say. Such is certainly the case with art and entertainment. Schaeffer noted the stark differences between the Reformation art of Rembrandt who "neither idealized nature nor demeaned it" and that of later ages: "Man was great, but man was also cruel and broken, for he had revolted against God. Rembrandt's painting was thus lofty, yet down to earth."[30] By contrast, Schaeffer referred to an early-twentieth-century Western school of art whose very method for choosing its name—"by opening a French dictionary at random and putting a finger down on a chance word"—suggested the internal disorder and drift that characterized its members and their output: *dada*, the French word for rocking horse.[31]

The chance—though, in its own way, deliberately contrived—encounter with the word that became its name symbolized the view that everything is nothing more than chance plus time, leading one to conclude that all is absurd. The most noted proponent of this view of life, Marcel Duchamp (1887–1968), in the words of Schaeffer, "realized that the absurdity of all things includes the absurdity of art itself."[32] Conquest said of him, "Marcel Duchamp, before World War I, was claiming that 'intellectual expression' in the artist's mind was more important than the resulting object. This has now become ideologized."[33]

PD-art

PD-art

(Left) *Nude Descending a Staircase* (1912), by Marcel Duchamp (1887–1968). *The Dada school viewed everything as nothing more than chance plus time, leading one to conclude that all is absurd. Duchamp, in the words of Schaeffer, "realized that the absurdity of all things includes the absurdity of art itself." Conquest said of him, "Marcel Duchamp, before World War I, was claiming that 'intellectual expression' in the artist's mind was more important than the resulting object. This has now become ideologized."* (Right) Rembrandt's *Christ in the Storm on the Sea of Galilee,* 1633. *Francis Schaeffer noted the stark differences between the Reformation art of Rembrandt who "neither idealized nature nor demeaned it" and that of later ages: "Man was great, but man was also cruel and broken, for he had revolted against God. Rembrandt's painting was thus lofty, yet down to earth."*

The logical consequence of such thought and belief —if they are ever truly pondered—is to get in line behind Bertrand Russell to board the boat of despair and sail to Nietzsche's island of solitary insanity.

T. S. Eliot's poem *The Waste Land,* published in 1922 before Eliot became a Christian, was a prime example of these trends as manifested in literature. Reinforcing Schaeffer's point, Eliot's writings, however, changed thematically when he chose the path of religious faith.[34]

Thus, in all forms of art, Schaeffer noted the unfailing pattern: Man's thinking, in a given age, as expressed by the philosophers of that era, ultimately manifests itself in artistic expression. Spread to graphic arts, music, literature and entertainment, this worldview then is carried to "masses of people which the bare philosophic writings never would have touched."[35]

This is a critically important point. Man often assumes that ideas, morals, values, etc., are conveyed intentionally, directly, primarily, or exclusively by words; thus the words are regarded with particular emphasis in assessing their impact on human thought, attitudes, and actions. But dimensions of human experience are influenced by other forms of communication beyond "bare philosophic writings," and the broadest mass of any culture—especially one within striking range of the technology of the twenty-first-century West—will be more fully influenced by other forms of culture, particularly music, television, movies, the Internet, and electronic games.

Here evil often outflanks good and the inattentive citizen, parent, spouse or church leader is made a fool. Partly as a consequence, Western society today is largely a Potemkin village in moral terms. The façade is left standing—though even that is in massive disrepair—while the superstructure (i.e., a core belief in God and an immutable higher law) has long since been largely dismantled.

Self-deception and denial are hallmarks of personal and civilizational decay. Art and entertainment—being as they are, wholly susceptible to the designs of their creators—lend themselves well to ersatz versions of "truth" and "reality."

As a consequence, "modern people are in trouble indeed. These things are not shut up within the art museums, the concert halls and rock festivals, the stage and movies, or the theological seminaries. People function on the basis of their world view. Therefore, society has changed radically.…As a man thinketh, so is he."[36]

According to Schaeffer, this has left modern Western man in an unenviable position, thinking "of the death of man in his own mind, but he cannot live with it, for it does not describe what he is."[37] This bleak assessment of the sterility of contemporary Western man leads us to Sorokin's even earlier, yet strikingly similar, views of the rapidly receding horizon of the past and the oncoming horizon of the future. Sorokin described the disintegration of sensate art in its major phases, "in its quest for sensory and sensational 'hits,' for stimulation and excitement as the necessary conditions for sensory enjoyment, it is increasingly and fatally deflected from positive to negative phenomena…to those which are pathological, from the fresh air of normal socio-cultural reality to the social sewers…."[38]

Were Sorokin describing the symptoms of a fatal disease, any lucid, reasonably objective Western citizen could make the diagnosis based merely on their personal experience. It would not require a professional. What he failed to note is that this also stimulates the emergence of more and worse pathologies. A self-propagating cycle of debasement and evil is in motion.

Sorokin then told us the deeper reason for his revulsion to Western art and in so doing reminded us of the gravity and the sense of personal responsibility that should buttress everything we do as human beings vis-à-vis one another.

> Since man and his values are sacred, the relationship of man to man should be guided by sublime love, as the categoric imperative.…The same principle applies to art. When it turns into a mere means for sensual pleasure and declares itself free from any moral and cognitive obligations, it degrades itself to mere entertainment and becomes a pseudo-value.…[T]hey all are one and all serve one purpose: the unfolding of the Absolute in the relative empirical world, to the greater nobility of Man and to the greater glory of God.[39]

But this noble viewpoint runs counter to virtually every major dynamic in Western societies, from materialism and competition, to the insatiable quest for pleasure and self-indulgence.

SEEKING THE LOWEST LEVEL

In great art the technique fits the world view being presented...
Francis Schaeffer[40]

This all raises a critically important, and usually overlooked, question: Exactly what is in the artist's, writer's, composer's, or director's mind and heart? *Who are we heeding? Are they worthy of our attention?* Conquest in part—but only in part—answers our questions: much of it is "po-faced," a term that he says "refers to a facial expression like an old-fashioned chamber pot, used of people who talk nonsense with great solemnity."[41]

The debased always seek the lower levels—and desire to pull everything and everyone down with them. The higher, the nobler, the exalted, the faithful, the morally upright are an ever present affront to their pride and an indictment of their conduct. The debased human being will display an affinity for demeaning that which is lofty or noble—ridicule and contempt are therefore two oft-deployed tactics. Books are written and movies made that depict both God or Satan in some tactile human form thus degrading the significance of either, the anti-hero is the hero of the age, and the significance of death, heaven, hell, and eternity are rarely treated at all, except with the depth of reasoning of an adolescent and the weight of dew. A movie that addresses *The Meaning of Life* is *prima facie* evidence of human arrogance and insensitivity to the most profound issues mankind must face. Sorokin was correct: "If we are forced to accept it as a faithful representation of human society, then man and his culture must certainly forfeit our respect and admiration."[42]

Ironically, this seeking of the lowest level is manifested in that which nearly everyone would assume is the antithesis of the term "lowest level"—through "colossalism." In the absence of quality, Sorokin noted

Imre Solt. CC

The Burj Dubai—the world's tallest building. *Influenced by the West, the Arabic world reflects what Sorokin called "the disease of colossality, typical of the decadent sensate phase of Graeco–Roman and present-day art. We construct the tallest buildings, and boast that they are the best precisely because they are the biggest...." Magnitude becomes an ersatz merit because its creators have no capacity to do anything better. Creating the biggest and the highest they unwittingly attain the lowest and the smallest.*

possible to "bind up the nation's wounds." Without them only raw power asserted by the North could have held the nation together, and then only for so long. Ironically, the much less violent, and, ostensibly, less traumatic, riven state of the American nation today has much less prospect of recovery; the very beliefs that brought Americans, North and South, back together in the mid- and late nineteenth century have become key points of conflict and national trauma today. There is another form of civil war afoot that cannot be defined by geographic boundaries. The outcome will prove to be foreboding and pyrrhic.

Loss of political and ideological cohesion is, in Huntington's eyes, a more "immediate and dangerous" threat. Echoing Dawson's views as described above, Huntington quoted Arthur M. Schlesinger, Jr., to describe the degree to which internal forces within the U.S. undermine the national identity in the name of multiculturalism.

> Historically American national identity has been defined culturally by the heritage of Western civilization and politically by the principles of the American Creed on which Americans overwhelmingly agree: liberty, democracy, individualism, equality before the law, constitutionalism, private property. In the late twentieth century both components of American identity have come under concentrated and sustained onslaught from a small but influential number of intellectuals and publicists. In the name of multiculturalism they have attacked the identification of the United States with Western civilization, denied the existence of a common American culture, and promoted racial, ethnic, and other subnational cultural identities and groupings. They have denounced, in the words of one of their reports, the "systematic bias toward European culture and its derivatives" in education and "the dominance of the European-American monocultural perspective." The multiculturalists are, as Arthur M. Schlesinger, Jr., said, "very often ethnocentric separatists who see little in the Western heritage other than Western crimes." Their "mood is one of divesting Americans of the sinful European inheritance and seeking redemptive infusions from non-Western cultures."[15]

The institutionalization of these views through legislation and judicial decree reflects the advanced degree to which they have taken hold—all largely achieved with an attitude of sanctity toward multiculturalism once reserved solely for key beliefs upon which the American constitution was founded. "The multicultural trend was also manifested in a variety of legislation that followed the civil rights acts of the 1960s, and in the 1990s the Clinton administration made the encouragement of diversity one of its major goals. The contrast with the past is striking."[16]

This trend in part is a manifestation of the Western, especially American, penchant to be slaves to fads and popular opinion. Civil rights, after a bloody and exhausting battle to become the focus of the attention of American society, eventually succeeded in becoming the *cause celebre* of first the left, from whence it was embraced more broadly by the culture at large. Having gained such status many perceived multiculturalism as a natural extension of the civil rights movement and embraced it opportunistically as evidence of their commitment to the *en vogue* cause of the age. This pandering was less about any merits of multiculturalism—which our observers wisely point out are virtually nonexistent—than about wanting to be on the bandwagon of social trends and acceptance.

Huntington went to the heart of the matter by citing the historical wisdom and pragmatism of the American Founding Fathers, and contrasted that with the "wisdom" of contemporary American leadership.

> The Founding Fathers saw diversity as a reality and as a problem: hence the national motto, *E Pluribus Unum*, chosen by a committee of the Continental Congress consisting of Benjamin Franklin, Thomas

Gunnar Myrdal *referred to the American Creed as "the cement in the structure of this great and disparate nation." But the multiculturalists touting "diversity" erode that traditionally strong cohesion that held a nation together through a civil war, Great Depression, two world wars, and massive unrest over segregation. "A multicivilizational United States will not be the United States; it will be the United Nations," declared Samuel Huntington.*

CC

Jefferson, and John Adams. Later political leaders who also were fearful of the dangers of racial, sectional, ethnic, economic, and cultural diversity (which, indeed, produced the largest war of the century between 1815 and 1914), responded to the call of "bring us together," and made the promotion of national unity their central responsibility. "The one absolutely certain way of bringing this nation to ruin, of preventing all possibility of its continuing as a nation at all," warned Theodore Roosevelt, "would be to permit it to become a tangle of squabbling nationalities." In the 1990s, however, the leaders of the United States…not only permitted that but assiduously promoted the diversity rather than the unity of the people they govern.[17]

Huntington told us what Americans can expect from this disavowal of their cultural legacy:

> The leaders of other countries have, as we have seen, at times attempted to disavow their cultural heritage and shift the identity of their country from one civilization to another. In no case to date have they succeeded and they have instead created schizophrenic torn countries. The American multiculturalists similarly reject their country's cultural heritage. Instead of attempting to identify the United States with another civilization, however, they wish to create a country of many civilizations, which is to say a country not belonging to any civilization and lacking a cultural core. History shows that no country so constituted can long endure as a coherent society. A multicivilizational United States will not be the United States; it will be the United Nations. The multiculturalists also challenged a central element of the American Creed, by substituting for the rights of individuals the rights of groups, defined largely in terms of race, ethnicity, sex, and sexual preference. The Creed, Gunnar Myrdal said in the 1940s, reinforcing the comments of foreign observers dating from Hector St. John de Crèvecoeur and Alexis de Tocqueville, has been "the cement in the structure of this great and disparate nation." "It has been our fate as a nation," Richard Hofstadter agreed, "not to have ideologies but to be one."[18]

Huntington then asked the question, "What happens then to the United States if that ideology is disavowed by a significant portion of its citizens?"

> The fate of the Soviet Union, the other major country whose unity, even more than that of the United States, was defined in ideological terms is a sobering example for Americans. "[T]he total failure of Marxism…and the dramatic breakup of the Soviet Union," the Japanese philosopher Takeshi Umehara has suggested, "are only the precursors to the collapse of Western liberalism, the main current of modernity. Far from being the alternative to Marxism and the reigning ideology at the end of history, liberalism will be the next domino to fall." In an era in which peoples everywhere define themselves in cultural terms what place is there for a society without a cultural core and

> defined only by a political creed? Political principles are a fickle base on which to build a lasting community. In a multicivilizational world where culture counts, the United States could be simply the last anomalous holdover from a fading Western world where ideology counted.[19]

Nowhere in the geography of history has there been a nation more completely defined by ideas rather than topographical boundaries as the United States. The boundaries may remain in place even as the nation itself fragments and dissolves.

Parenthetically, we note findings and conclusions of the British sociologist Steve Bruce, who studied the consequences, positive and negative, of shared belief or loss of a common religious vision:

> The point is obvious and can be seen very clearly in comparing the resistance to communism of the three Baltic states. Lithuania, which was overwhelmingly Catholic, was better able to maintain its sense of identity vis-à-vis Russian communism than was Estonia and Latvia, which were religiously diverse. Religion can serve as a major component in cultural defence only if the people share the same religion. As there is no sign of major religious revivals reuniting religiously diverse populations, we can reasonably see the historical change as being one way.[20]

How much more will cultural cohesion and vitality erode when the broader foundation of Christianity—Catholic, Orthodox, and Protestant—is itself eroded?

Huntington linked the ongoing, gradual rejection of those ideas (i.e., the Creed, etc.) with not simply the end of the United States but the end of Western civilization.

> Rejection of the [American] Creed and of Western civilization means the end of the United States of America as we have known it. It also means effectively the end of Western civilization. If the United States is de-Westernized, the West is reduced to Europe and a few lightly populated overseas European settler countries. Without the United States the West becomes a minuscule and declining part of the world's population on a small and inconsequential peninsula at the extremity of the Eurasian land mass.[21]

Huntington identified this conflict between multiculturalism and Western civilization as central to and undergirding all ideological, political, and social issues in contemporary America.

> The clash between the multiculturalists and the defenders of Western civilization and the American Creed is, in James Kurth's phrase, "the real clash" within the American segment

PD

"The one absolutely certain way of bringing [the United States] to ruin, of preventing all possibility of its continuing as a nation at all," warned Theodore Roosevelt, *"would be to permit it to become a tangle of squabbling nationalities."*

> of Western civilization. Americans cannot avoid the issue: Are we a Western people or are we something else? The futures of the United States and of the West depend upon Americans reaffirming their commitment to Western civilization. Domestically this means rejecting the divisive siren calls of multiculturalism. Internationally it means rejecting the elusive and illusory calls to identify the United States with Asia. Whatever economic connections may exist between them, the fundamental cultural gap between Asian and American societies precludes their joining together in a common home. Americans are culturally part of the Western family; multiculturalists may damage and even destroy that relationship but they cannot replace it. When Americans look for their cultural roots, they find them in Europe.
>
> . . .
>
> Some Americans have promoted multiculturalism at home; some have promoted universalism abroad; and some have done both. Multiculturalism at home threatens the United States and the West; universalism abroad threatens the West and the world. Both deny the uniqueness of Western culture. The global monoculturalists want to make the world like America. The domestic multiculturalists want to make America like the world. A multicultural America is impossible because a non-Western America is not American. A multicultural world is unavoidable because global empire is impossible. The preservation of the United States and the West requires the renewal of Western identity. The security of the world requires acceptance of global multiculturality.[22]

THE ONLY PLACE TO STAND—ON COMMON GROUND

...the third rule for peace in a multicivilizational world is the commonalities rule: peoples in all civilizations should search for and attempt to expand the values, institutions, and practices they have in common with peoples of other civilizations.

Samuel Huntington[23]

In a passage reflecting the personal theme with which I began this chapter, Huntington called for the rejection of multiculturalism and the beginning of a world wide search for common ground:

> ...whatever the degree to which they divided humankind, the world's major religions—Western Christianity, Orthodoxy, Hinduism, Buddhism, Islam, Confucianism, Taoism, Judaism—also share key values in common. If humans are ever to develop a universal civilization, it will emerge gradually through the exploration and expansion of these commonalities. Thus, in addition to the abstention rule and the joint mediation rule, the third rule for peace in a multicivilizational world is the commonalities rule: peoples in all civilizations should search for and attempt to expand the values, institutions, and practices they have in common with peoples of other civilizations.[24]

Dawson pointed out that for much of Western civilization's history there had been a great overarching commonality that gave unity and integrity to the broader culture:

> Without spiritual order the cosmopolitanism of modern culture does not make for peace; it merely increases the opportunities of strife. It destroys all that is best and most distinctive in the local and national cultures, while leaving the instincts of national and racial hostility to develop unchecked. It

> unites mankind in the common enjoyment of the cinema and the Ford car and the machine gun without creating any spiritual unity. The recovery of the Christian idea of order would give a spiritual expression to the universality of modern culture. Its material unification would become subservient to the ideal of the spiritual unity of mankind in justice and charity, an ideal that has a very real attraction for the modern mind, but which secular idealism is powerless to achieve.[25]

Appropriately, we close with Huntington's focus on the common values of the great religions by noting the centrality of the loss of religious faith as the primary indicator of our civilization's decline and decay as described by our other observers. Probing this greater depth, we can see that underlying virtually every dimension of this civilizational drift is the loss by many in the Western world of the core values and the beliefs of Christianity. Religion can serve as a major component in cultural defense only if the people share the same religion. For Western civilization to survive, impliedly therefore, there must be an affirming of that which secured its philosophical and social integrity, and its relational cohesion.

END NOTES
CHAPTER 12

1 Pitirim A. Sorokin, *The Crisis of Our Age* (Oneworld Publications Ltd., 1941; this edition Sergei P. Sorokin and Peter P. Sorokin, 1992), 203.
2 Samuel P. Huntington, *The Clash of Civilizations and the Remaking of World Order* (New York: Simon & Schuster, 1996), 318.
3 Cornelius Tacitus, *The Works of Cornelius Tacitus; with an Essay on His Life and Genius (The Annals of Tacitus: Book XV)*, translated by Arthur Murphy (Washington: David & Forge, 1822), 288.
4 Huntington, *Clash of Civilizations*, 306–307.
5 Christopher Dawson, *The Historic Reality of Christian Culture* (New York: Harper & Brothers, 1960), 101–102.
6 Dawson, *Historic Reality*, 103.
7 Christopher Dawson, *Christianity and the New Age* (Manchester, NH: Sophia Institute Press, 1985), 101–102.
8 Sorokin, *The Crisis of Our Age*, 202–203.
9 Arnold Toynbee, *A Study of History* (New York: Weathervane Books, 1972), 244–245.
10 Huntington, *Clash of Civilizations*, 305–306.
11 Huntington, *Clash of Civilizations*, 305.
12 Huntington, *Clash of Civilizations*, 304–305.
13 Huntington, *Clash of Civilizations*, 67.
14 Huntington, *Clash of Civilizations*, 305.
15 Huntington, *Clash of Civilizations*, 305.
16 Huntington, *Clash of Civilizations*, 305.
17 Huntington, *Clash of Civilizations*, 305–306.
18 Huntington, *Clash of Civilizations*, 306.
19 Huntington, *Clash of Civilizations*, 306.
20 Steve Bruce, *God Is Dead* (Oxford: Wiley-Blackwell, 2002), 33–34.
21 Huntington, *Clash of Civilizations*, 21.
22 Huntington, *Clash of Civilizations*, 307 and 318.
23 Huntington, *Clash of Civilizations*, 320.
24 Huntington, *Clash of Civilizations*, 320.
25 Dawson, *Christianity and the New Age*, 101–102.

CHAPTER

13

MAN AS GOD: SCIENCE AND TECHNOLOGY

But for all of them, too, there was the truly Faustian danger of the Devil's having a hand in the game, the risk that he was leading them in spirit to that mountain on which he promises all the power of the earth. Again and again they succumbed to this ambition; they forced this secret out of God in order themselves to be God. They listened for the laws of the cosmic pulse in order to overpower it. And so they created the idea of the machine as a small cosmos obeying the will of man alone.

Oswald Spengler[1]

Never save here has a microcosm felt itself superior to its macrocosm, but here the little life-units have by the sheer force of their intellect mastered inert matter. It is a triumph, so far as we can see, unparalleled. Only this our Culture has achieved it, and perhaps only for a few centuries. But for that very reason Faustian man has become the slave of his creation. The machine has forcibly increased his numbers and changed his habits in a direction from which there is no return.

Oswald Spengler[2]

Science and technology—the very phrase has become a mantra of modern Western man. Our twenty-first-century advancements, such as they are, can be found almost exclusively in the material realms of science and technology. We tout them as the great achievements of our time, latter day great pyramids that affirm our power and nobility.

From those achievements—real, albeit not nearly so advanced as he believes—Western man has extrapolated that humankind is progressing, or at least the Western subspecies is progressing. Yet, as we have seen, progress is a highly subjective concept infused with value judgments, insights, and religious perceptions, most of which are ignored or overlooked when the term is appropriated to characterize this or that in our civilization.

We noted previously that the term "success" in Western parlance nearly always carries with it the notion of material gain, financial achievement, or, at least, the approbation of one's fellows in the context of economic gain. Yet the significance of that connotation—especially to the exclusion of all others—says something profound and sweeping about the way Western man thinks. Similarly, the narrow conventional connotation of "progress"—focused as it is primarily on some material, scientific, or technological achievement—is also a commentary on Western man, his values, and his perceptions of reality.

Western man's vanity usually has the best of him and with it comes the distortions of reality that the clear prism of humility would resolve. Neither as competent nor as advanced as he has convinced himself, Western man's self-deception threatens his very existence. Science and technology are, at once, a manifestation of Western man's bleak soul-life and the instruments by which he may self-destruct. But the method of self-destruction is unimportant relative to the soul-life and values that will produce it.

Pitirim Sorokin, in *The Crisis of Our Age*, acknowledged man's scientific and technological accomplishments as a prelude to demonstrating the danger to lives and a culture with that focus: "Never before has man displayed such a genius for scientific discoveries and technological inventions. No previous period can rival the power of contemporary man in the modification of cosmic and biological conditions to suit his needs. At no time before has man been the molder of his own destiny to such an extent as he is now."[3]

SCIENCE AND TECHNOLOGY'S OTHER LEGACY: THE COCKED GUNS AT MAN'S HEAD

If we continue to develop our technology without wisdom or prudence, our servant may prove to be our executioner.
General Omar N. Bradley[4]

If we are to fully understand the crisis of Western civilization we must consider all threats, all significant problems—some of which are not localized to the West, and some of which are not within the powers of man to influence. Since the overwhelming majority of us citizens of Western civilization are not scientists (or at least not scientists in the arenas of study alluded to below), we are at the mercy of the "experts." We cannot know of our own direct knowledge and reasoning whether certain conditions or prospective events are realistic, or, if genuine, we cannot know with certainty the degree of the threat. Therefore what follows in this chapter should not be read as an absolute imprimatur of approval for any given viewpoint. It does reflect, however, what appears to be the weight of the evidence and scientific opinion.

Throughout this work our ultimate focus is on the internal—man's closely held beliefs, values and convictions—but how those choices of the heart and mind bear upon man's broader social

U.S. Army portrait. PD-Gov

General Omar Nelson Bradley. *Declaring that mankind had become a technological giant while remaining a moral midget, Bradley warned, "If we continue to develop our technology without wisdom or prudence, our servant may prove to be our executioner."*

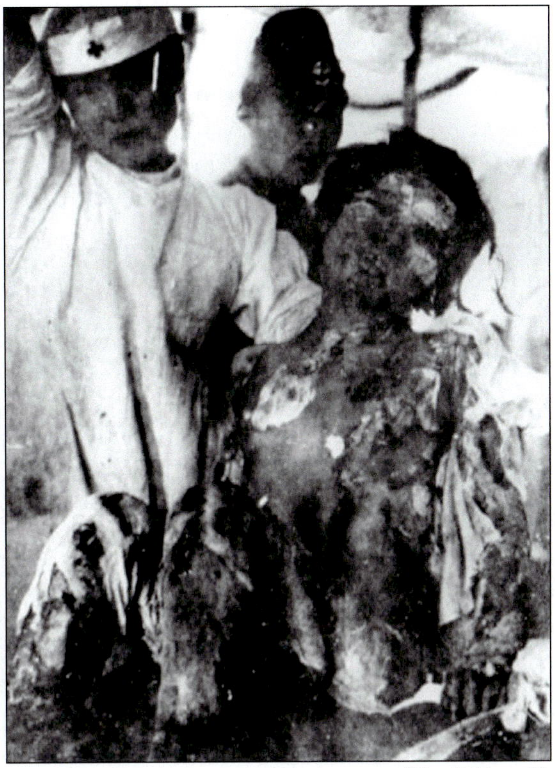

Photo courtesy of U.S. DOE/NNSA. Shiotsuki, Masao. PD

(Left) Operation Castle, ROMEO Event, 1954. *The U.S. and Russia have thousands of warheads with destructive force 80,000 times that of the Hiroshima bomb. This does not include nuclear devices held by European nations, China, India, Israel, Pakistan, or North Korea. Man wonders whether he can control what he has created. The historical record of man's folly does not bode well. But efforts to eliminate nuclear weapons should be undertaken, though with the realistic view that this will likely only mitigate; it will not eliminate. Prospects for a nuclear explosion are very high.* (Right) A 14-year-old student, victim of the atomic bomb explosion over Nagasaki—*one of millions of victims of the unholy marriage between man's arrogance, his rejection of God and an absolute moral law, and his passion for his idols, science and technology. There will be millions more.*

and physical environment are obviously not to be overlooked. There are physical threats to Western civilization—indeed, to all of humanity—that have either their origin in man's choices or are propagated or exacerbated by man's choices.

We should briefly address these—there are four areas of greatest concern—since each, with varying degrees of applicability, may have a bearing upon the future of Western civilization. Here, the secularist and the religious find common ground. So on this topic even hubristic Western man is sometimes compelled to acknowledge his limitations—a practice that would be salutary for him across the board of human experience.

MAN AS "DESTROYER OF WORLDS"

Now I am become death, destroyer of worlds.
Robert Oppenheimer, quoting from the *Bhaghavad Gita*

The British physicist Stephen Hawking uttered what should be a statement of the self-evident when he declared that mankind was at much greater risk from human action than the forces of the universe. Among the man-conceived/man-controlled threats that first come to mind are nuclear weapons. Man wonders whether he can control what he has created. The historical record of man's folly does not bode well.

President John Kennedy's early 1960s address before the UN during which he referred to the nuclear "sword of Damocles" suspended over mankind's head was perhaps the best known of many alarms regarding the dangers of nuclear power. There are at least three models of possible nuclear disaster: First, the deployment of a nuclear weapon by a terrorist group; second, a limited nuclear exchange between two warring nations such as Pakistan and India; third, a full scale nuclear exchange between major powers, such as the U.S. and Russia.

Experts believe the probabilities should be ranked as these possibilities are listed here with a terrorist use the most likely, and a full nuclear exchange between major powers the least. But some experts say the real threat remains with the U.S. and Russia. Russia and the U.S. have thousands of warheads with equivalent destructive force 80,000 times the Hiroshima bomb. Perhaps the single most powerful nuclear warhead ever built was the Ivan Bomb, or the Tzar Bomba, with a total explosive capacity of 100 megatons. By comparison, the Little Boy bomb dropped on Hiroshima was equivalent to only 13 kilotons of TNT.

This unmitigated array of power is particularly dangerous because a simple accident or misinterpretation could trigger a nuclear Armageddon. With only fifteen minutes or so for each side to respond to evidence of a missile launched by the other, the prospects for stopping a cataclysm are poor. Even if counterattacks stopped after an exchange of a dozen or more missiles, Earth would be irrevocably transformed. The effect would be similar, but worse, than the disaster wrought by an asteroid or supervolcano. In sum, man can destroy the planet and himself with bombs in a matter of minutes. Let us look at three other ways such absolute destruction might take place.

Plague. Modern technology empowers man to make microbes that could decimate the human race. Nature may—as it has on many occasions in history—deploy its own. Here too, experts believe that it is just a matter of time before disaster occurs, whether man-made or natural. The 1918 flu pandemic is believed to have killed 40 million worldwide. But avian flu is many times more deadly. We are, says Dr. Michael Osterholm, "overdue for a pandemic."[5]

Yet man should be most frightened by his own man-made microbes. Dr. Sergei Popov, former head of the USSR bioweapons program and now residing and working in the West, believes that the disease man thought he had defeated, smallpox, could be the ultimate weapon. Thirty percent of smallpox victims typically die, but with a man-conceived more virulent strain one hundred percent lethality could be achieved.

To some, creating such a monstrosity would be incomprehensible, but to others this merely reflects shrewd tactical advantage. The zeal with which these weapons are pursued is suggested in a passage from the book *Killer Germs: Microbes and Diseases that Threaten Humanity* by Barry E. Zimmerman and David J. Zimmerman.

> Vector had sent an expedition to Siberian villages to dig up long-frozen bodies of smallpox victims from the turn of the century, in hopes of retrieving viable samples of the virus. Moscow also sent scientists to Africa to collect the viruses Ebola and Marburg—diseases with extremely high mortality that literally liquefy the internal organs, causing horrendous bleed-outs. The expectation was that Vector researchers could develop a smallpox/Marburg hybrid. Marburg was not very contagious, but was extremely deadly, and no vaccine or cure existed. Smallpox was more infectious, but there was a vaccine. First, there would be smallpox symptoms, and then Marburg would hit.[6]

With such a weapon, or others such as the Ebola virus, one or a very small group of individuals could decimate masses of humanity. One infected victim would trigger a series of infections that would be virtually impossible to prevent. With a typical incubation period of three days to three weeks, thousands could come in contact with a disease before the first indicators were apparent. With air travel, the infections could spread around the globe in weeks if not days. Mass panic would ensue as hospitals were overwhelmed with the dead and dying. Any prospects for a vaccine would require months to implement—far too long to prevent millions of deaths.

Artificial intelligence. The 1968 Stanley Kubrick movie, *2001: A Space Odyssey*, was prescient in anticipating a concern that at the time was viewed by most as improbable if not purely fictional. Today it is taken quite seriously. Stephen Hawking is among the scientists warning that computers are likely to overtake humans in intelligence. Dr. Hugo de Garis is far more emphatic. Machines, he believes, could wipe out humanity. The capacity of a machine to become a "trillion" times more intelligent than humans is not so far-fetched when one considers that the power of a microchip is doubling every year.[7]

The American military is developing war making machines that would operate without human control. This, de Garis believes, could result in wars fought and controlled by machines. Lending additional credence to de Garis's fears is the realization that a machine might travel in space and even colonize moons or planets with a freedom and facility that man, the ever vulnerable biological species, could never match. The historical evidence has repeatedly shown that individual men or groups of men will pursue the power and wealth that science and technology promise regardless of any reservations or ethical proscriptions of the larger masses of mankind. It seems probable that de Garis is correct, at least in so far as predicting that our zeal for scientific and technical accomplishment is leading us over a precipice.

Ecological and Environmental Degradation. Man's self-centeredness is in play all across the planet and is especially conspicuous in his treatment of his native—and only—home. The ecological and environmental degradation of his planet is now so multifaceted and so ubiquitous in its effects that only the worst species of foolishness would attempt to rationalize any of it away. None of this should be unexpected; all such effects are manifestations of man's true nature—even the psychological tendency to deny. Many of these issues become ideological and political footballs, further evidence of the decay and decline of a civilization. Only the decadent human species can or would respond to a threat to its survival by turning it into a pretext for communities' going at one another's throats.

But if human choices have any significant bearing on these degradations—and human choice surely does on most—then failing to act upon the problems becomes not only an omission of great

Toynbee warned, "...the impressiveness of the evidence for progress in [science and technology] is matched by the obviousness of the fact that man is relatively good at dealing with non-human nature. What he is bad at is his dealing with human nature in himself and in his fellow human beings. A fortiori, *he has proven to be very bad indeed at getting into the right relation with God....[i]t has been the great tragedy of human life on Earth that this sensational inequality of man's respective achievements in the non-human and in the spiritual sphere should... have been this way round; for the spiritual side of man's life is of vastly greater importance for man's well-being...than is his command over non-human nature."*

By NASA. PD

folly but one of supreme social irresponsibility, even callousness. The arguments against dramatic and decisive action are always couched ultimately in economic terms, and this fits precisely with the view asserted in this book: Western civilization is on its knees before its materialism. Powerful economic interests see their positions of power and wealth at risk from any broad recognition of some of these threats. This should not surprise the perceptive and attentive. The greed in our culture is so great that many human lives have been—and are—sacrificed to its lusts.

Immanuel Wallerstein, speaking broadly of all forms of ecological and environmental degradation, expressed the issue this way: "The entrepreneurs have argued essentially that the issue is one of jobs versus romanticism, or humans versus nature."[8] Wallerstein asserts that the underlying dilemma is a fundamental reason why Western civilization cannot continue as structured:

> We are thus forced back to fundamentals. It is a matter of political economy first of all, and consequently a matter of moral and political choice.
>
> ...
>
> It is precisely Prometheus unbound that has been the problem.
>
> But Prometheus unbound is not inherent in human society. The unbounding, of which the defenders of the present system boast, was itself a difficult achievement, whose middle-term advantages are now being overwhelmed by its long-term disadvantages.
>
> The political economy of the current situation is that historical capitalism is in fact in crisis precisely because it cannot find reasonable solutions to its current dilemmas, of which the inability to contain ecological destruction is a major one, if not the only one.[9]

Previously, Wallerstein had identified what he referred to as the "second long-term trend" that will shake Western civilization to its foundations—"the ecological crisis."

> A crucial element in the level of profits has always been that capitalists do not pay the totality of costs of their products. Some costs are "externalized," that is, spread *pro rata* over the whole of larger populations, eventually over the whole of the world population. When a river is polluted by a chemical plant, the clean-up (if there is one) is normally assumed by taxpayers. What the ecologists have been noticing is the exhaustion of zones to pollute, of trees to be cut down, and so forth. The world faces the choice of ecological disaster or of forcing the internalization of costs. But forcing the internalization of costs threatens seriously the ability to accumulate capital.[10]

Wallerstein's analysis of the intractability of this dilemma, if correct, is a forewarning of massive upheaval.

> There are two different kinds of operations in preserving the environment. The first is the cleaning up of the negative effects of a production exercise (for example, combating chemical toxins that are a by-product of production or removing nonbiodegradable waste). The second is investment in the renewal of the natural resources that have been used (for example, replanting trees). Once again, the ecology movements have put forward a long series of specific proposals that would address these issues. In general, these proposals meet with considerable resistance on the part of the enterprises that would be affected by such proposals, on the grounds that these measures are far too costly....
>
> The truth is that the enterprises are essentially right....These measures are indeed too costly, by and large, if we define the issue in terms of maintaining the present average worldwide rate of profit. They are too costly by far. Given the deruralization of the world and its already serious effect upon the accumulation of capital, the implementation of significant ecological measures, seriously carried out, could well serve as the coup de grace to the viability of the capitalist world-economy. Therefore, whatever the public relations stance of individual enterprises on these questions, we can expect unremitting foot-dragging on the part of capitalists in general.[11]

This leads then, in Wallerstein's view, to three alternatives:

> One, governments can insist that all enterprises internalize all costs, and we would be faced with an immediate acute profits squeeze. Or, two, governments can pay the bill for ecological measures (clean-up and restoration plus prevention) and use taxes to pay for this. But if one increases taxes, one either increases the taxes on the enterprises, which would lead to the same profits squeeze, or raises taxes on everyone else, which would probably lead to an acute tax revolt. Or, three, we can do virtually nothing, which will lead to the various ecological catastrophes of which the ecology movements warn. So far, the third alternative has been carrying the day. In any case, this is why I say that there is "no exit," meaning by that that there is no exit within the framework of the existing historical system.[12]

Wallerstein concludes that not only has Western civilization entered a "time of troubles" the outcome of which is "uncertain," but we "cannot be sure what kind of historical system will replace the one in which we find ourselves. What we can know with certainty is that the very peculiar system in which we live, and in which the states have played a crucial role in supporting the processes of the endless accumulation of capital, can no longer continue to function."[13] This is, Wallerstein declares, a "terminal crisis." "The issue before us is what will replace" our present system. "This will be the central political debate of the next twenty-five to fifty years. The issue of ecological degradation, but not of course only this issue, is a central locus of this debate."[14]

SCIENCE AND TECHNOLOGY DIVORCED FROM MORALITY AND SPIRITUALITY

If science and technology remain morally and socially indifferent, serving with the same equanimity the God of Creation and the Mammon of Destruction, they will be ruined eventually: no successful continuation of scientific and technological work is possible under such conditions. If they cease to be morally and socially indifferent, they will have to stop being what they are; they will be obliged to recognize some universal—and in this sense absolute—norms and values.
Pitirim Sorokin[15]

Science and technology driven primarily by materialism without the constraints of the strong sense of morality and social responsibility inherent in religious faith are as loaded guns fondled by children.

Some of the scientists quoted in this chapter recognize, at least in part, the problem but foolishly perceive the resolution in the human intellect. But is this a question of intellect or morality? I stand with General Bradley; the answer is, obviously, the latter. Man's intellect devoid of a strong sense of morality and social responsibility is precisely what got us into this predicament. The risks increase dramatically with all new scientific or technological progress. Each year that passes without aggressively addressing these issues threatens to add another cartridge into the cylinder of the revolver mankind has pressed against his temple. The generation now alive, particularly in Western civilization, controls the destiny of the planet—and the species.

With a reasoning expressed in a quasi-biblical tone, Arnold Toynbee in *Civilization on Trial* pointed to the delusional quality in Western man's pride in his science and technology and offered a warning from history of the dangerous unintended consequences of his achievements in this arena.

> Yet the fact that our adversary threatens us by showing up our defects, rather than by forcibly suppressing our virtues, is proof that the challenge he presents to us comes ultimately not from him, but from ourselves. It comes, in fact, from that recent huge increase in Western man's technological command

Oxford, bastion of secularism. *Dawson declared, "When Western civilisation lost the faith that formerly inspired it…the more it clung to its material achievement and the more fiercely did it concentrate its energies on the conquest of power…thus it has come about that the immense progress of our civilisation in material resources and…scientific control of nature and human life has become a blind movement to destruction …for dynamism without spiritual purpose or guidance must inevitably be destructive."*

All Souls College by Kamyar Adl, CC

Demonstrating again what our observers each independently note—that the philosophical base, the worldview is everything in determining man's perception of truth and reality—Schaeffer described the regression of "modern modern science."

> As we have seen, modern modern science put aside the epistemological base of early science—this early base being that, because the world was created by a reasonable God, man can find out about the universe by reason. Then, when this Christian base was abandoned, scientists tried to make the philosophy of positivism their philosophic base for knowing. Positivism had been worked out in the first half of the nineteenth century by the French philosopher Auguste Comte (1798–1857) and was developed as the base for science by Herbert Spencer (1820–1903). Related to John Locke's (1632–1704) empiricism, positivism is a naive philosophy which basically says that you look at an object and there it is. The data which reaches you through your senses enables you to know the object in a straightforward and uncomplicated way.
>
> But some years ago people began to realize that science did not really look at an object with total objectivity. In the *Journal of the Franklin Institute* (1936) Albert Einstein pointed out that man makes choices out of the multitude of sense data which comes to him. In other words, there is a subjective element involved in the scientific process....Michael Polanyi (1891–1976), who retired from Manchester University in 1958 and since that time had taught in many universities, in his book *Personal Knowledge: Towards a Post-Critical Philosophy* (1958) destroyed the naive view of positivism. Polanyi pointed out that the observer is always there and always makes the conclusions, and he is never entirely neutral.
>
> And with this, positivism is no longer a viable base for knowing. In science a man arranges the experiment; he has a grid in his thinking into which he fits his observations and makes the conclusions. The positivism I knew when I was younger, which was so very, very strong in the universities of Europe and America, is now dead. No longer are those holding this view so sure of the relationship between themselves and the object they are observing.[28]

Schaeffer observed the oft-made connection between the different connotations of the term relativity, both philosophically and scientifically.

> It is often said that relativity as a philosophy, as a world view, is supported by Albert Einstein's (1879–1955) theory of relativity. But this is mistaken because Einstein's theory of relativity assumes that everywhere in the universe light travels at a constant speed in a vacuum. In other words, we must say with the utmost force that nothing is less relative philosophically than the theory of relativity. Einstein himself stood implacably against any such application of his concepts. We can think of his often quoted words from the *London Observer* of April 5, 1964: "I cannot believe that God plays dice with the cosmos."[29]

Illustrating how an earlier generation of scientists—no less brilliant, no less astute, perhaps in some respects more so—perceived the universe and their role as scientists, Schaeffer suggested an alternative course that lies open to Western man.

> To quote Bacon again, "To conclude, therefore, let no man out of weak conceit of sobriety, or in ill applied moderation, think or maintain, that a man can search too far or be too well studied in the book of God's word, or in the book of God's works." "The book of God's word" is the Bible; "the book of God's works" is the world which God has made. So, for Bacon and other scientists working on the Christian base, there was no separation or final conflict between what the Bible teaches and science.[30]

Schaeffer continued.

> What was the view of these modern scientists on a Christian base? They held to the concept of the uniformity of natural causes in an open system, or, as it may also be expressed, the uniformity of natural causes in a limited time span. God has made a cause-and-effect universe; therefore we can find out something about the causes from the effects. *But* (and the *but* is very important) it is an *open* universe because God and man are *outside* of the uniformity of natural causes. In other words, all that exists is not one big cosmic machine which includes everything.... Things go on in a cause-and-effect sequence, but at a point of time the direction may be changed by God or by people. Consequently, there is a place for God, but there is also a proper place for man. This carries with it something profound—that the machine, whether the cosmic machine or the machines which people make, is neither a master nor a threat—because the machine does not include everything. There is something which is "outside" of the cosmic machine, and there is a place for man to be man.[31]

As we will discover more fully, vestiges of the Baconian perspective carried over into the twentieth century and many scientists and philosophers noted the Christian base for modern science. Modern science does not, Schaeffer declared, "conflict with what the Bible teaches. The belief that there was a god and immutable laws contributed immeasurably to the foundation and growth of science, for without that recognition the early scientists would have concluded that their efforts were hopeless—since they could not be founded on reason or the expectation that everything is governed by immutable laws."[32]

FAITH AND SCIENCE IN THE WEST: ANTAGONISTS OR COLLABORATORS FOR ALL MANKIND?

But the disease of modern civilization lies neither in science nor in machinery, but in the false philosophy with which they have been associated. At the very moment that man was at last acquiring control over his material environment, he was abandoning the ideal of spiritual order and leaving the new economic forces to develop uncontrolled without any higher social direction.
Christopher Dawson[33]

In *Religion and World History*, Dawson explained the progression of science and technology in relation to man's spiritual regression. Western man sought all the more assiduously to fill the void produced by the latter with the products and achievements of the former.

> ...[W]hen Western civilisation lost the faith that formerly inspired it, it did not lose the dynamic character that it had acquired in these centuries of struggle and achievement. Indeed, the more it lost its spiritual aim, the more it clung to its material achievement and the more fiercely did it concentrate its energies on the conquest of power. And thus it has come about that the immense progress of our civilisation in material resources and in the scientific control of nature and human life has become a blind movement to destruction, which finds its embodiment in the Frankenstein monster of the totalitarian state; for dynamism without spiritual purpose or guidance must inevitably be destructive.[34]

Dawson and Schaeffer were leading us somewhere. They wanted us to recognize that faith and science are not in conflict, unless one or the other rigidly insists it is the only form of truth.

Faith and science in concert are the supreme efficacy in man's search for truth—all kinds of truth.

Schaeffer admonished the exclusionary adherents of the respective sides—believers and agnostics and atheists—that "...the Bible tells us true things about people and about nature. It does not give men and women *exhaustive* truth about the world and the cosmos, but it does give truth about them. So one can know many true things about nature, especially *why* things exist and why they have the form they have." Each has "a job to do" because "the Bible does not give exhaustive truth about history and the cosmos"; therefore, scientists and historians are needed. Furthermore, man can know about God because he has "revealed himself and has given man the key to understanding God's world."[35]

Napoleon reputedly asserted, though the quote may be apocryphal, there were only two forces in the world, the sword and the spirit, and that ultimately the spirit would prevail. If truly spoken by Napoleon, this was a clear acknowledgment by a man who venerated worldly power that it is subordinate to the spiritual. Schaeffer gave us one of the reasons why faith, when melded with science in the search for truth, is the only hope to prevent man from pulling the trigger on the pistol of science and technology that he has pointed at his temple: "The ironic fact here is that humanism, which began with Man's being central, eventually had no real meaning for people. On the other hand, if one begins with the Bible's position that a person is created by God and created in the image of God, there is a basis for that person's dignity."[36]

Schaeffer's views were a reflection and affirmation of a virtually identical perspective articulated years earlier by Christopher Dawson in *Christianity and the New Age.* Dawson, as he was wont to do, reconciled what he called Christian humanism and scientific investigation. In Dawson's view, "...the material organization of the world by science and invention is in no sense to be refused or despised by the Catholic tradition, for to the Catholic philosopher no less than to the scientist the progressive *rationalization* of matter by the work of scientific intelligence is the natural vocation of the human mind."[37]

Here we have in part an expression of a principle that squares fully with the understanding of the truly thinking person: There is no valid compartmentalization, contradiction, or conflict between sound science, beauty, moral law, and the recognition of a transcendent reality beyond that which can be discerned by the senses.

CC

Albert Einstein, *in a moment of reflection, may have been thinking of his response to fellow scientists: "I cannot believe that God plays dice with the cosmos." Francis Schaeffer, noting that some claimed "relativity as a philosophy, as a world view, is supported by Einstein's theory of relativity," observed, "This is mistaken because Einstein's theory assumes that everywhere in the universe light travels at a constant speed in a vacuum....Nothing is less relative philosophically than the theory of relativity."*

Roger Bacon, the most brilliant scientist of his time. *Francis Schaeffer quoted Bacon, "'To conclude, therefore, let no man out of weak conceit of sobriety, or in ill applied moderation, think or maintain, that a man can search too far or be too well studied in the book of God's word, or in the book of God's works.' The 'book of God's word' is the Bible; 'the book of God's works' is the world that God has made. So, for Bacon...there was no separation or final conflict between what the Bible teaches and science."*

Oxford University Museum of Natural History. Photograph taken by Michael Reeve. CC

Dawson, like Schaeffer and other of our observers, clearly saw the parental relationship between the values of the Christian faith and the evolution of science in Western civilization.

That science became a prodigal son and wandered to the far country of unbelief and alienation from the Father does not suggest it must remain an exile. For Dawson, Schaeffer, Sorokin, and Toynbee, the prospect of continued alienation was foreboding—not for faith, which will surely survive, but for all humanity, for whom survival is not at all assured.

Toynbee eloquently expressed it thusly:

> ...the impressiveness of the evidence for progress in [science and technology] is matched by the obviousness of the fact that man is relatively good at dealing with non-human nature. What he is bad at is his dealing with human nature in himself and in his fellow human beings. *A fortiori*, he has proved to be very bad indeed at getting into the right relation with God. Man has been a dazzling success in the field of intellect and "know-how" and a dismal failure in the things of the spirit, and it has been the great tragedy of human life on Earth that this sensational inequality of man's respective achievements in the non-human and in the spiritual sphere should, so far at any rate, have been this way round; for the spiritual side of man's life is of vastly greater importance for man's well-being (even for his material well-being, in the last resort) than is his command over non-human nature.[38]

What is to become of Western man then, if he continues to insist on science minus faith, the material minus the spiritual? As we saw previously, Bertrand Russell described with stark, merciless honesty the logical consequence of such a position in psychic terms only—not even considering the cataclysmic practical consequences: "...[E]ven more purposeless, more void of meaning, is the world which Science presents for our belief...."[39]

Thus Western man is faced, in the words of Oswald Spengler, with "a last spiritual crisis that will involve all Europe and America" manifested by its "most distinct expression" in "the cult of exact sciences."[40] Said Spengler over a century ago:

> Never save here has a microcosm felt itself superior to its macrocosm, but here the little life-units have by the sheer force of their intellect mastered inert matter. It is a triumph, so far as we can see, unparalleled. Only this our Culture has achieved it, and perhaps only for a few centuries. But for that very reason Faustian man has become the slave of his creation. The machine has forcibly increased his numbers and changed his habits in a direction from which there is no return.[41]

The alternative to becoming the "slave" of the culture we have created, as Spengler described, or falling into the despair of Russell, was proposed by Dawson in *Christianity and the New Age.*

> ...the restoration of man to his true position as the master of nature and the organizer of the material world, which is the function of science, corresponds in the natural order to the spiritual restoration of human nature in itself, which is the work of Christianity in the supernatural order.
>
> In a Christian civilization the scientific order would no longer offer, as it does at present, the tragic spectacle of vast resources of power and intelligence devoted to producing unsightly and unnecessary objects, and to endowing mankind with new means of self-destruction; it would become an instrument for the realization of man's true destiny as the orderer of material things to spiritual ends....[M]aterial unification would become subservient to the ideal of the spiritual unity of mankind in justice and charity, an ideal that has a very real attraction for the modern mind, but which secular idealism is powerless to achieve.
>
> We must make our choice between the material organization of the world—based either on economic exploitation or on an economic absolutism, which absorbs the whole of life and leaves no room for human values—and the Christian ideal of a spiritual order based on spiritual faith and animated by charity, which is the spiritual will. The triumph of such an ideal in a world that seems governed only by material forces and distracted by hatred and greed may seem, a fantastic dream, but is it any more hopeless than the enterprise of that handful of unknown and uneducated men from a remote Oriental province who set out to conquer the imperial power of Rome and the intellectual culture of Hellenism? In history it is often the incredible that happens—*credo quia impossibile* has been justified again and again. Sooner or later it is inevitable that men's minds should turn once more in search of spiritual reality, and when once the tide begins to flow all the sandcastles that we have built during the ebb disappear.[42]

Dawson shared these aspirations with Sorokin, Toynbee, and Schaeffer. However, in a subsequent passage he referred to the need for minds "not enervated by custom or prejudice" in order for this lofty and exalted revolution to occur.

CC

Bertrand Russell. Sweden, 1950. *Russell observed, "...[E]ven more purposeless, more void of meaning, is the world which Science presents for our belief....Man's achievement must inevitably be buried beneath the debris of a universe in ruins—all these things, if not quite beyond dispute, are yet so nearly certain, that no philosophy that rejects them can hope to stand. Only within the scaffolding of these truths, only on the firm foundation of unyielding despair, can the soul's habitation henceforth be safely built."*

Herein lies the immediate problem: minds so accustomed to generations of sterility masquerading as meaning that they will not open to the light.

St. Paul expressed this thusly: "But a natural man does not accept the things of the Spirit of God; for they are foolishness to him, and he cannot understand them, because they are spiritually appraised." (1 Corinthians 2:14 NASB)

Lincoln once observed of a contemporary, "He can compress the most words into the smallest ideas of any man I ever met."[43] Western civilization, especially in the arena of science and technology, has become like the man Lincoln referred to: prolix to the point of profligacy in words committed to ideas that tell man nothing about that which he most needs to know. Emerson's "greater depth" is never plumbed. There is in this realm an avidity for knowledge—a *facta factorum causae*—spiritually arid and largely devoid of true insight and understanding. We are living not in a time of sophistication but in a profoundly primitive and benighted time, yet Western man's vanity and the shallowness of his soul obscure this reality from his eyes.

Scientific advancement is not the villain but rather the narrow secularist view it both reflects and nurtures in our age. In Dawson's words, "...the disease of modern civilization lies neither in science nor in machinery, but in the false philosophy with which they have been associated."[44] Man is not well served by this blinkered view. The twenty-first century will tell whether he will tear the blinkers from his eyes or advance with ever quickening pace to his destruction, a destruction that in whole or in part will likely be brought about by the very creations for which he is so blindly proud.

END NOTES
CHAPTER 13

1 Oswald Spengler, *The Decline of the West* (New York: A. A. Knopf, 1926), 411.
2 Spengler, *Decline of the West*, 412.
3 Pitirim A. Sorokin, *The Crisis of Our Age* (Oneworld Publications Ltd., 1941; this edition Sergei P. Sorokin and Peter P. Sorokin, 1992), 197.
4 General Omar N. Bradley, cited in Laurence J. Peter, ed., *Peter's Quotations: Ideas for Our Time* (New York: Bantam, 1979), 33.
5 Michael Osterholm, "Preparing for the Next Pandemic" *Foreign Affairs 84.* no. 4 (July/August 2005): 24–37.
6 Barry E. Zimmerman and David J. Zimmerman, *Killer Germs: Microbes and Diseases that Threaten Humanity* (New York: McGraw–Hill, 2002), 214.
7 Hugo De Garis, *The Artilect War: Cosmists vs. Terrans: A Bitter Controversy Concerning Whether Humanity Should Build Godlike Massively Intelligent Machines* (ETC Publications, 2005).
8 Immanuel Wallerstein, *The End of the World As We Know It: Social Science for the Twenty-First Century* (Minneapolis: University of Minnesota Press, 1999), 83.
9 Wallerstein, *The End of the World As We Know It,* 82–83.
10 Wallerstein, *The End of the World As We Know It,* 31.
11 Wallerstein, *The End of the World As We Know It,* 81.
12 Wallerstein, *The End of the World As We Know It,* 81.
13 Wallerstein, *The End of the World As We Know It,* 75.
14 Wallerstein, *The End of the World As We Know It,* 85.
15 Sorokin, *Crisis of Our Age*, 218–219.
16 Arnold J. Toynbee, *Civilization on Trial* (New York: Oxford University Press, 1948), 23–24.
17 Toynbee, *Civilization on Trial*, 24–25.
18 Qiao Liang and Wang Xiangsui, *Unrestricted Warfare* (Beijing: PLA Literature and Arts Publishing House, 1999), 16–17.
19 Toynbee, *Civilization on Trial*, 26.
20 Wallerstein, *The End of the World As We Know It,* 140.
21 Wallerstein, *The End of the World As We Know It,* 140.
22 Wallerstein, *The End of the World As We Know It,* 140–141.
23 Carroll Quigley, *The Evolution of Civilizations: An Introduction to Historical Analysis* (New York: Macmillan Publishing Co., 1961), 422.
24 Quigley, *Evolution of Civilizations*, 422.
25 Wallerstein, *The End of the World As We Know It,* 155.
26 Francis A. Schaeffer, *How Should We Then Live? The Rise and Decline of Western Thought and Culture* (Wheaton, IL: Crossway Books, 1976), 146–147.
27 Spengler, *Decline of the West*, 190.
28 Schaeffer, *How Should We Then Live?*, 198–199.
29 Schaeffer, *How Should We Then Live?*, 138.
30 Schaeffer, *How Should We Then Live?*, 142.
31 Schaeffer, *How Should We Then Live?*, 142–143.
32 Schaeffer, *How Should We Then Live?*, 132–133.
33 Christopher Dawson, *Christianity and the New Age* (Sophia Institute Press, 1985), 95.
34 Christopher Dawson, *Religion and World History: A Selection from the Works of Christopher Dawson* (Garden City, NY: Image Books, 1975), 299.

35 Schaeffer, *How Should We Then Live?*, 86.
36 Schaeffer, *How Should We Then Live?*, 86.
37 Dawson, *Christianity and the New Age*, 94–95.
38 Toynbee, *Civilization on Trial*, 262.
39 Bertrand Russell, *A Free Man's Worship* (Portland, ME: T. B. Mosher, 1923), 265.
40 Spengler, *Decline of the West*, 220–221.
41 Spengler, *Decline of the West*, 412.
42 Dawson, *Christianity and the New Age*, 101–103.
43 Abraham Lincoln (edited by Louise Batchelder), *Wisdom and Wit* (Peter Pauper Press, Inc., 1997).
44 Dawson, *Christianity and the New Age*, 95.

CHAPTER

14

PHILISTINES AT THE HELM

The soul surrenders itself to the melting-pot, and a negative sense of cultural promiscuity then comes to pervade every sphere...it results in a blending of incongruous traditions and in a compounding of incompatible values (pammixia)....*Of the three factions into which a disintegrating society is apt to split, it is the dominant minority that succumbs most readily to the sense of promiscuity....*
Arnold Toynbee[1]

The denial of God by the intelligentsia was the turning point in Western civilisation. From that point the road has led without a turning to the concentration camps and slaughter houses of the totalitarian state.
Christopher Dawson[2]

A decline in courage...may be the most striking feature which an outside observer notices in the West in our days...Such a decline in courage is particularly noticeable among the ruling groups and the intellectual elite, causing an impression of loss of courage by the entire society. Of course there are many courageous individuals, but they have no determining influence on public life.
Alexander Solzhenitsyn[3]

Arnold Toynbee placed primary blame for the decay and decline of a civilization on the elite: "In times of stress the mask of civilization is torn away from the primitive countenance of raw humanity in the rank-and-file; but the moral responsibility for the breakdowns of civilizations lies upon the heads of the leaders."[4] The only truly civilizing force that may be brought to bear with any efficacy on this beast is religion. But if the leadership of the culture is adrift with no clear compass headings of its own, then all decisions will likewise have no sense of consistent direction.

Within the span of lives in being we shall see "times of stress" in Western civilization that rip away "the mask of civilization."

When those "times of stress" come upon us, much of the leadership—which often flounders in periods of relative quiescence—will not know what to do. This is because it is among the "dominant minority" that the first symptoms of the disease that will ultimately kill the culture manifest themselves. As we have seen previously, Toynbee asserted that the soul "surrenders itself" to a cultural "melting pot," which "results in a blending of incongruous traditions and in a compounding of incompatible values *(pammixia).*" He adds that as the society disintegrates, "it is the dominant minority that succumbs most readily to the sense of promiscuity."[5]

Significantly, Toynbee used the term "dominant minority" to describe the culture's leaders rather than another term that would seem more likely, the "elite" or "dominant elite." This was probably an implicit recognition by Toynbee of a principle we affirm: positions of power or influence held do not equate to wisdom, superior capability, or virtue—sometimes just the opposite. This is all the more true of the leadership of a culture in decay.

As the putrefaction of thought and morality advances, the wise and noble abstain from seeking positions of power and influence and are more and more segregated by those who hold power and influence into ghettoized subcultures.

Toynbee's description should strike a chord with any astute observer of Western civilization. Not only is *pammixia* present in every facet of Western life, it is perhaps the salient attribute of the "dominant minority" of our time. As we discussed in the chapter "A House Divided," the touting of multiculturalism and diversity in Western civilization is congruent with this dissonance of values and beliefs that characterize a declining society.

That this phenomenon is not exclusive of the church is clear from Toynbee's reference to religion that "produces ritual and theological syncretisms" as other manifestations of *pammixia.* Ritual, sometimes extravagant in its display, and syncretism, are apparent throughout the historically dominant and traditional religion of the West, Christianity. Doctrinal beliefs and moral absolutes once firmly held are now diluted—if not *de facto* abrogated entirely—by contemporary notions of "tolerance," "diversity," and even "forgiveness" in an overweening conformity to trends in the broader culture. The path of least resistance—a course heretofore reserved to the dissolute—becomes well trodden by religious leaders in positions traditionally held by those who sought the narrow way of nonconformity to the world, conformity to God's Law.

Anyone swimming upstream against this current will inevitably become the victim of some form of propagandistic labeling, perhaps that of "reactionary," "radical," "zealot," or some other appellation intended to disqualify the iconoclast from serious consideration, much less acceptance. The tolerance and diversity so vociferously touted are revealed to be, in fact, narrowly drawn parameters designed to confine to islands of relative obscurity those who would challenge the accepted wisdom of the cultural dominant minority. The message: Remain in your cloistered subculture and you may say what you like; venture into our realm of broad cultural or political power and your voice must be consonant with ours, or you will pay the price.

As noted previously, the individuals most likely to be victimized by this heavy-handed ruthlessness are the "mentally or physically uprooted expatriates who form the internal proletariat" precisely because they "tend…to keep a firm hold upon the remnants of their native heritage…." The third major player in this drama is the "external proletariat" that is largely "insulated from the radiation of [the] dying civilization by the erection of an impassable military frontier." This group "tends on the whole to sustain its vigorous barbarian culture until the moment at which it finally overruns the ruined civilization."[6]

In our age, the "internal proletariat" parallels most closely some of the conservative elements of Western civilization—especially the religious components—which are struggling even now to "keep a firm hold upon the remnants of their native heritage." They are, however, despised by the dominant minority, who regard them as primitive, moralizing reactionaries intent on taking the culture backward in time and restricting the dominant minority's license or power.

The thought that there are immutable, sacrosanct principles of human thought, belief, and behavior that transcend modernity—as the internal proletariat believes—is contemptible to the dominant minority, persuaded as they are not only of man's power to dominate and control but also the proud bearers of a supercilious confidence in their intellectual capacities.

The "external proletariat" parallels perhaps most closely with Islam and Far Eastern cultures, both of which are at once secured and sometimes frustrated by the "impassable military frontier" that the Western powers can still partially maintain. Each for its own distinct reasons would like to see that frontier breached, but for now—whether they recognize it or not—the frontier also serves to insulate their cultures from many of the soul- and reason-consuming viruses eating away at the West.

Sorokin predicted that in the final stages of decay of our "sensate" civilization even the hollow values and leaders of the sensate culture will be supplanted by—can it be possible?—that which is even more specious and meaningless, with a proliferation of "counterfeit criteria," "qualified ignoramuses of the daily press, of radio, of various forums, by writers of bestsellers and of other varieties of cultural chewing gum," of "politicians" who replace statesmen, and "hoary tyrants with a mania for grandeur" who replace "rulers careful about the well-being of the citizens." "Quite imperceptibly," Sorokin warned, "the standards will change so radically that, at the late stages of sensate culture, its 'machinery of selection' will be picking up mainly pseudo-values and neglecting real values."[7]

Sorokin's prediction that this shift will occur "quite imperceptibly" suggests an alarming state of inattentiveness in the citizenry brought on by insensitivity, chronic self-centeredness, and callousness bred from, on the one hand, the repeated denial of real values and, on the other, the practice of contriving rationalized revisions of reality—an unfounded "optimism" among them. The gatekeepers of Western culture already reflect in varying measures this narrowness and superficiality—as do the citizenry themselves.

Francis Schaeffer gave an almost identical warning in different language. Sorokin's "hoary tyrants" and "politicians" are manifestations of Schaeffer's "elite" who "will offer us arbitrary absolutes." Schaeffer declared a generation ago, "The marks of ancient Rome scar us: degeneracy, decadence, depravity, a love of violence for violence's sake. The situation is plain. If we look, we see it." But of equal or greater concern is what Schaeffer called the "second result of modern man's loss of meaning and values.... The elite will exist. Society cannot stand chaos. Some group or some person will fill the vacuum. An elite will offer us arbitrary absolutes, and who will stand in its way?"[8]

The craving for the heretofore perennially available material comforts, freedom from self-sacrifice and risk, and the absence of intrusions on their personal peace (as contrasted with that of others) will have liquefied the spines of many. They will readily surrender large chunks of their personal sovereignty to those who promise to preserve—if not enhance—these perquisites. The birthright of freedom and self-reliance will have been surrendered for a mess of pottage.

Sorokin predicted a sloughing off of this sterile mode of life when he compared it with the last desperate aspirating of the Graeco–Roman culture: "...the aridity of thought and sterility of creativeness will increasingly pervade the whole sensate supersystem until Western society awakens to all the hollowness.... Confronted with this dead shell...it will have but one exit from the situation: to leave the hollow corpse for something that lives and creates, for an ideational or idealistic or integral form of culture."[9] I am not confident of this result and share more common ground with

Toynbee, who pointedly noted not a choice to "exit from the situation," but the overwhelming of the last vestiges of the dying culture by the barbarian hordes.

This rejection of real values for the artificial and contrived values conceived from the "negative sense of cultural promiscuity" on the bed of this confused melting-pot is apparent throughout Western civilization, but perhaps most conspicuous in America due to the stark contrast between the America that was and the America that increasingly is. Secularists and agnostics are in effect tearing down and rebuilding the great magnificent house designed by the American Founding Fathers and constructed through the labors and sacrifices of millions of Americans in each generation since. The blood of those generations provided the vivid color in the tapestries and curtains, their tears mixed with the mortar to hold together the brick and stone, their sweat gave the sheen to the rugged, rough-hewn floors. Yet these modern Americans are not content to live in the house that millions who preceded them sacrificed and died to build. They disingenuously and pridefully argue that this deconstruction is not what it conspicuously is; rather, they claim—all history and evidence to the contrary notwithstanding—that it is simply the making of what those Founding Fathers and preceding generations intended, or—even more incredibly—that the revelations of modernity invalidate the lessons of history. The effrontery of these claims is possible only because of the complacency of masses of Americans who in their hearts may know better, or, in their ignorance of their own nation's history and their professed faith's tenets, they know not. Yet, there is also undoubtedly another reason for this servility and deference to these forces: cowardice.

THE DECLINE IN COURAGE

The person who has nothing for which he is willing to fight, nothing which is more important than his own personal safety, is a miserable creature and has no chance of being free unless made and kept so by the exertions of better men than himself.
John Stuart Mill[10]

In his 1978 address at Harvard, Alexander Solzhenitsyn dwelt on a related theme to Sorokin's "statesmen replaced by politicians" by speaking of a decline in courage in the West, which he believed

> ...may be the most striking feature which an outside observer notices in the West in our days. The Western world has lost its civil courage, both as a whole and separately, in each country, each government, each political party and of course in the United Nations. Such a decline in courage is particularly noticeable among the ruling groups and the intellectual elite, causing an impression of loss of courage by the entire society. Of course there are many courageous individuals but they have no determining influence on public life....Political and intellectual bureaucrats show depression, passivity and perplexity in their actions and in their statements and even more so in theoretical reflections to explain how realistic, reasonable as well as intellectually and even morally warranted it is to base state policies on weakness and cowardice. And decline in courage is ironically emphasized by occasional explosions of anger and inflexibility on the part of the same bureaucrats when dealing with weak governments and weak countries, not supported by anyone, or with currents which cannot offer any resistance. But they get tongue-tied and paralyzed when they deal with powerful governments and threatening forces, with aggressors and international terrorists. Should one point out that from ancient times decline in courage has been considered the beginning of the end?[11]

Whether Solzhenitsyn was fair or fully objective is open to discussion, but surely an honest review of the history of the West since World War II in particular—Chamberlain and Munich beforehand not to be overlooked—would provide much support for his characterization. A "decline in courage"—it would appear this is actually a euphemistic way of expressing the reality—pervades Western culture: citizens who claim religious faith largely confine any expression of it to their churches, cathedrals and synagogues; the Judeo–Christian morality, more or less still given lip service by many, is rarely given forceful public voice due to the pusillanimity of those who may boldly and repeatedly breach it in practice; political correctness not only enforces conformity of expression but strives to do so with thought as well; the most debased in art, literature and entertainment is shielded by specious applications of the notion of "freedom of speech and expression" and thus are never exposed for the scatology they truly are; illicit or irresponsible behavior by certain interest groups, racial, ethnic, or sexual, is handled with the gentility usually reserved for unexploded ordnance; illegal immigration—complete with multitudinous examples of the flouting of the host nations' laws—rarely provokes a disparaging word by the dominant minority directed at the ethnic groups and the nations behind the invasions; enemies of the civilization are fought in a war on terror, the very appellation of which suggests a cowardly unwillingness to admit the identity and character of the enemy; truly powerful nations are never confronted but a third-rate power can be overwhelmed in a sweeping war that is then touted as a great victory for Western military prowess; and all of the above is casuistry and excused rather than exposed for what it truly is.

There is abroad in Western civilization a pervasive fear cloaked on all sides by denial. Most evident in the West's attitudes and behavior toward Islam, this fear is psychologically a second cousin to the Stockholm syndrome and is symptomatic of an ever steeper slide into moral weakness that then demands that the decline must not be acknowledged but hidden behind a series of fabrications, rationalizations and tendentious euphemisms. Enemies—both concrete and abstract—must be somehow made to seem "friends," or innocuous, or at least appeased. These "crocodiles" (to use a Churchillian term) may be consuming others but surely they will not consume us.

PD

John Stuart Mill *anticipated the state of our time in Western culture by declaring a great truth for all time: "The person who has nothing for which he is willing to fight, nothing which is more important than his own personal safety, is a miserable creature and has no chance of being free unless made and kept so by the exertions of better men than himself." Today a selfless minority in the military are ensuring the freedoms of a dissipated and selfish majority. But it cannot and will not last. The reckoning is coming.*

THE DENIAL OF GOD

In the end there are only two kinds of people: Those who say to God, "Thy Will Be Done" and those to whom God says, "thy will be done." All who are in hell choose it.
C. S. Lewis, *The Great Divorce*[12]

In logic highly reminiscent of Soren Kierkegaard, we note once more how Christopher Dawson incised the central cause of this state of affairs—and the result: "The denial of God by the intelligentsia was the turning point in Western civilisation. From that point the road has led without a turning to the concentration camps and slaughter houses of the totalitarian state."[13]

In every major arena of Western civilization—even often in the church itself—the tide of man's worship of self has been sweeping away the humble and the faithful from positions of leadership and influence. Those leaders who give lip service to a God and faith betray their true allegiance to mammon by their pride, love of position and power, self-indulgence, and ready willingness to scratch the multitudinous itching ears of Western man. Even were they not afflicted with these moral infirmities—and some show great diligence and earnestness in condemning one or more of them in others—their failures are obvious to those willing to see.

Dawson decried the shift in the cultural leadership of the West as the inevitable result of the passivity of the members of the dominant religion of the West in the Christian church, spawned by its conformity to the culture at large. "Our civilization has become secularized largely because the Christian element has adopted a passive attitude and allowed the leadership of culture to pass to the non-Christian minority. And this cultural passivity...has...been due to...a tendency toward social conformity and too ready an acceptance of the values of a secularized society."[14]

The inevitable consequence of generations of accelerating secularism and humanism has been the ascendancy of individuals to positions of power and leadership in every sphere of Western life who hold no authentic deep-seated, all-encompassing commitment to God or transcendent beliefs. Commensurate with the vestigial remains of Christianity described elsewhere in this book that pervade all of Western civilization, however, many of these leaders still give nominal assent to faith and religiously based moral principles. They wear the mantle of religion, loosely, even as they "deny the power thereof" (2 Timothy 3:5 KJV) by their actions.

But as Christ declared, "By their works ye shall know them." (Matthew 7:16 KJV) The critical elements of self-sacrifice and bold advocacy for a God-centric view and an absolute moral law are rarely to be found. Indeed, they would not be expected for the dual reasons that such attitudes and conduct would be self-defeating in any ambitious climb for position, power, or wealth in Western culture, and congruently because the citizenry would not expect them—faith and conviction having been so thoroughly diluted that any expression of absolute, uncompromising duty to the Christian God would be regarded as radical and untenable, even by many who profess to believe. Hence it is fashionable in our time among many to exploit the political or social value of professed faith without endangering one's ambitions or comforts. This is most often accomplished by declaring, "Faith is a private matter!"—Christ's example and commands notwithstanding.

But we must acknowledge that in the midst of all these rejections of faith and traditional morality there can exist a humanitarianism in the thinking and conduct of this dominant minority.

Photograph by Ivy Scarborough

Dome of the Rock, Jerusalem. *Ground Zero for one of the worst conflicts in world history. There is a pervasive fear in the West cloaked by denial. Most evident in the West's attitudes and behavior toward Islam, this fear is psychologically a second cousin to the Stockholm syndrome and is symptomatic of an ever steeper slide into moral weakness that demands that the decline not be acknowledged but hidden behind rationalizations. Enemies must be made to seem "friends," or innocuous, or at least appeased.*

Though it is, in Dawson's words, sometimes "based on deep and sincere convictions, with something of the nature of a religious faith," it lacks the transcendent underpinnings of religious conviction. Therefore, this same humanitarianism can, on the one hand, fund a war on poverty, attack racism, and campaign against human immunodeficiency virus (HIV)—all in league with organized religion—and yet, on the other hand, embrace the killing of the unborn. An expedient form of altruism, it can readily be exploited to give ersatz credibility to its practitioners' leadership and specious "validity" to their ideas and policies. Dawson first surprised his readers by the declaration—common in one form or another to Toynbee, Sorokin and Schaeffer—that this form of humanitarianism, in itself, is another of the indicia of decline. Like the hollow belief system that spawned it, this form of benevolence "belongs to the age of transition between Christian and secular culture, and…[when] left to its own resources in a purely secular environment, it tends to wither away like political idealism."[15] There are no deep roots, only a passing need to assuage the conscience, lend credibility to its acolytes, and pacify fears.

Toynbee probed the psyche of the cultural leaders in a civilization *in extremis* in a discussion in *A Study of History* of *peripeteia,* the reversal of roles, or the ascendancy of the weak over the strong,

American Medal of Honor. *Solzhenitsyn spoke of a loss of courage as perhaps "...the most striking feature which an outside observer notices in the West in our days. The Western world has lost its civil courage, both as a whole and separately, in each country, each government, each political party and of course in the United Nations. Such a decline in courage is particularly noticeable among the ruling groups and the intellectual elite, causing an impression of loss of courage by the entire society. Of course, there are many courageous individuals but they have no determining influence on public life...." Indeed, the military may be the last bastion of the selfless courage represented by this award.*

PD-gov.

the humble over the proud. "If one sins against the laws of proportion and gives something too big to something too small to carry it—too big sails to too small a ship, too big meals to too small a body, too big powers to too small a soul—the result is bound to be a complete upset. In an outburst of *hybris* the overfed body will rush into sickness, while the jack-in-office will rush into the unrighteousness that *hybris* always breeds."[16]

Why though the seeming boldness, if we may call it that, of Toynbee's "jack-in-office" when he rushes "into the unrighteousness that *hybris* always breeds?" Does this not conflict with Solzhenitsyn's *j'accuse* the leadership of the West of a "decline in courage"? To the contrary, the two observations are complementary and highly descriptive of the same character type. Toynbee's cultural leader will rush into "the unrighteousness" precisely because he holds no transcendent standards as sacred and no sincere belief in a god to whom he will ultimately be accountable. Thus he sees himself "free" to exercise whatever prerogatives he wishes; especially those that gratify his lusts for power, pleasure, wealth, fame, or simply personal convenience—all inebriants abundantly brewed in Western culture. But his apparent boldness is founded upon his fundamental belief that he will not truly be accountable to a god or a higher moral law.

Yet this same failure of belief deprives him of both a core and a foundation upon which to stand. He is a hollow man. There is nothing transcendent to which he subscribes, no immutable moral law to which he is obeisant, and thus there is often nothing he would readily die for beyond himself. This leaves him cowering before a threat he will acknowledge—a danger that his materialistic view of life and purely empirical approach recognizes. God, for him, is not real, but the "powerful governments and threatening forces" alluded to by Solzhenitsyn are. To boldly confront them is to risk one's position, or possibly one's life; and if one's earthly life is all there is, everything could be lost.

In the 1970s, a popular song addressed the question what must man do with his life if that's "...All There Is?" The lyrics, inspired by a story by Thomas Mann on human disillusionment, gave the answer, "keep on dancing," "break out the booze," and "have a ball." This, in one form of expression or another, is the choice of man when all there is is himself. This distemper will be most evident in the "dominant minority."

> The Christian version of the plot thus presents a double peripeteia, a reversal of a reversal; but the literal historical sequence depicted in the New Testament has at the same time a deeper significance

PD

Arlington National Cemetery. *Secularists and agnostics are in effect tearing down the great magnificent house designed by the American Founding Fathers and constructed through the sacrifices of millions of Americans in each generation since. The blood of those generations provided the vivid color in the tapestries and curtains; their tears mixed with the mortar to hold together the brick and stone; their sweat gave the sheen to the rugged, rough-hewn floors. Yet these modern Americans are not content to live in the house that millions who preceded them sacrificed and died to build. They imply that the revelations of modernity invalidate the lessons of history. The effrontery of these claims is possible only because of the complacency of Americans who in their hearts may know better, or, in their ignorance of their own nation's history and their professed faith's tenets, they know not. There is also another reason for this servility to these forces: cowardice.*

> as an allegory of a mystery which is illustrated in the course of history because it lies at the heart of life. On this plane the operation of the principle of peripeteia is proclaimed in the New Testament in terms that transcend the historical limits of a particular time and place: "If any man desire to be first, the same shall be last of all and servant of all. He that is least among you, the same shall be great."[17]

But this humble understanding of true leadership is completely alien to Sorokin's sensate culture, Toynbee's decadent "dominant minority," Dawson's secular/agnostic/atheistic "intelligentsia," and Schaeffer's supremely self-absorbed Roman Empire.

Thomas Mann, 1900. Mann's writing on human disillusionment inspired the lyrics to a 1970s popular song that addressed the question, What must one do with his life if that's "...All There Is?" The answer: "Keep on dancing," "break out the booze," and "have a ball." This, in one form of expression or another, is the choice of man when all there is is himself. This distemper will be most evident in the "dominant minority"—those we call "Philistines at the Helm."

CC

We can anticipate leadership that increasingly reflects not only an inability to address the true and deep problems of the culture and the world, but whose very ascendancy to power places them in positions that will further frustrate all prospects for hope for the civilization.

All of these features parallel Quigley's concept of institutionalization: the deterioration of social "instruments," which initially served society's needs, into "institutions" that serve themselves. Eventually, this leads to alienation of the leaders from the led, a schism with a psychological parallel within the people themselves of "this unhappy age."

> ...[I]f the process of disintegration is allowed to continue...it seems to follow a common pattern....The masses become estranged from their leaders, who then try to cling to their position by using force as a substitute for their lost power of attraction....I also find a corresponding psychological schism in the souls of people who happen to have been born into this unhappy age. Discordant psychic tendencies which are perhaps always latent in human nature now find free play. People lose their bearings, and rush down blind alleys,

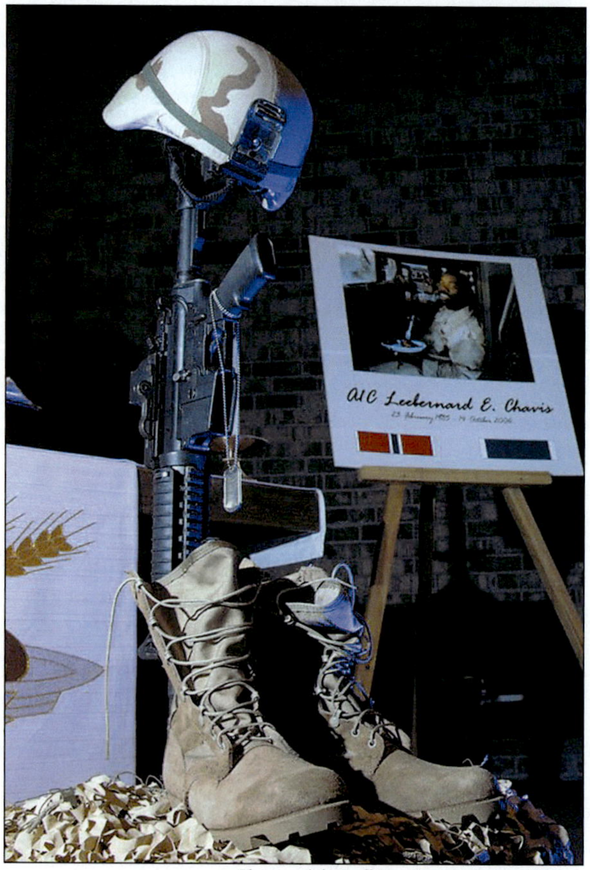

A "fallen soldier" memorial from the chapel at Moody Air Force Base. *Some of the noblest hearts beat beneath a battle dress uniform. Though the decadence and dissipations of a culture in decay will be found everywhere, most prominently in the "dominant minority," the military in the West is one of the last bastions of the selflessness, courage and belief that characterize strength as contrasted with the selfishness, cowardice, and faithlessness of the weak but powerfully positioned dominant minority.*

Photograph by Staff Sgt. Manuel Martinez. PD-gov

> seeking escape. Greater souls detach themselves from life; still greater souls try to transfigure life into something higher than mere life as we know it on Earth, and sow the seeds of a fresh spiritual advance.[18]

As Western culture has sharpened the angle of its dive into decay, the shift in cultural leadership has been commensurate. More and more, leadership is characterized by the drift of relativism and a disdain for the divine and absolutes. Sorokin's "sensate" thinking prevails. The West's cultural leaders display the blissful arrogance of erudite ignorance. Thus the term "Philistines"—this is not only anti-faith; it is the embodiment of primitiveness. One dimension of Western man's only hope will be to embrace as leaders Toynbee's "greater souls" who "try to transfigure life into something higher than mere life as we know it on Earth, and sow the seeds of a fresh spiritual advance."

For now the sensitive souls, the spirits of courage, the bearers of faith have only a plaintive plea like unto that of the wounded supplicant in Edwin Markham's *The Man with the Hoe*:

> Cries protest to the Powers that made the world,
> A protest that is also prophecy.
> O masters, lords and rulers in all lands,
> Is this the handiwork you give to God,
> This monstrous thing distorted and soul-quencht?
> How will you ever straighten up this shape;
> Touch it again with immortality;
> Give back the upward looking and the light;
> Rebuild in it the music and the dream;
> Make right the immemorial infamies,
> Perfidious wrongs,
> Immedicable woes?

END NOTES
CHAPTER 14

1 Arnold Toynbee, *A Study of History* (New York: Weathervane Books, 1972), 244.
2 Christopher Dawson, *Religion and World History: A Selection from the Works of Christopher Dawson* (Garden City, NY: Image Books, 1975), 296.
3 Alexander Solzhenitsyn, Text of Address at Harvard Class Day Afternoon Exercises, Thursday, June 8, 1978.
4 Toynbee, *A Study of History*, 166.
5 Toynbee, *A Study of History*, 244–245.
6 Toynbee, *A Study of History*, 244–245.
7 Pitirim A. Sorokin, *The Crisis of Our Age* (Oneworld Publications Ltd., 1941; this edition Sergei P. Sorokin and Peter P. Sorokin, 1992), 246.
8 Francis A. Schaeffer, *How Should We Then Live? The Rise and Decline of Western Thought and Culture* (Wheaton, IL: Crossway Books, 1976), 226–227.
9 Sorokin, *The Crisis of Our Age*, 246.
10 John Stuart Mill, *Fraser's Magazine for Town and Country*, Vol. LXV (London: Parker, Son & Bourn, 1862).
11 Solzhenitsyn, Harvard Class Day.
12 C. S. Lewis, *The Great Divorce* (New York: HarperCollins, 2001), 75.
13 Dawson, *Religion and World History*, 296.
14 Christopher Dawson, *Historic Reality* (New York: Harper & Brothers, 1960), 46.
15 Dawson, *Religion and World History*, 297.
16 Toynbee, *A Study of History*, 169.
17 Toynbee, *A Study of History*, 167.
18 Toynbee, *A Study of History*, 211.

CHAPTER

15

THE PATH TO THE NEW DARK AGE

Beginning from man alone, Renaissance humanism—and humanism ever since—has found no way to arrive at universals or absolutes which give meaning to existence and morals.
Francis Schaeffer[1]

This means that the mistake must be at the root, at the very basis of human thinking in the past centuries. I refer to the prevailing Western view of the world which was first born during the Renaissance and found its political expression from the period of the Enlightenment. It became the basis for government and social science and could be defined as rationalistic humanism or humanistic autonomy: the proclaimed and enforced autonomy of man from any higher force above him. It could also be called anthropocentricity, with man seen as the center of everything that exists.
Alexander Solzhenitsyn[2]

Instead of the heroic exaltation of humanity which was characteristic of the naturalism of the Renaissance, we see the humiliation of humanity....Man is stripped of his glory and freedom and left as a naked human animal shivering in an inhuman universe.
Christopher Dawson[3]

It does not matter how small the sins are, provided that their cumulative effect is to edge the man away from the Light and out into the Nothing. Indeed the safest road to hell is the gradual one—the gentle slope, soft underfoot, without sudden turnings, without milestones, without signposts.
C. S. Lewis, *The Screwtape Letters*[4]

Just as a pilgrimage across the topography of the earth—whether a deliberate quest or the wanderings of the lost—requires traversing some course, plotted or random, passing waypoints in order to reach a destination, man always must change his position culturally by passing some waypoints philosophically in terms of what he chooses to validate as true and valuable. A civilization does not reach a state of decay and decline by means of external forces working upon it, but through a shift, a movement, in the way the members of that civilization perceive, reason, and believe. Just as archaeologists can trace the route of Napoleon's Grand Army on its disastrous trek of defeat, first into, then out of, Russia, we can find the waypoints that Western man has passed to bring him to his present state.

Having now some comprehension of Western civilization's crisis, decline, decay, and the possible imminence with which "the history of West European mankind will be definitely closed," the sensitive and astute cannot help but wonder: How did the West arrive here? What choices did Western man make—flushed as he was with blessings and opportunities—that brought him to this point?

PD-gov

Reactor team from University of Chicago. Back row, from left: Norman Hilberry, Samuel Allison, Thomas Brill, Robert Nobles, Warren Nyer, and Marvin Wilkening. Middle row: Harold Agnew, William Sturm, Harold Lichtenberger, Leona Woods and Leo Szilard. Front row: Enrico Fermi, Walter Zinn, Albert Wattenber and Herbert Anderson. *Szilard and Einstein, who first urged Franklin Roosevelt to begin nuclear research, later came to regret their decision. What, we might ponder, would the world have been like had Einstein's and Leo Szilard's belated recognition come earlier and Western man had never developed nuclear weapons? We cannot know, but everything we do know should lead us to understand that the world would likely be a far better place. Though perhaps not a triumph of evil, this was surely another example of man's scientific prowess juxtaposed with his moral primitiveness—the disproportion of the two producing a menace that may prove to be the proximate method of mankind's suicide.*

Such questions are among the most important that can be asked of history. Like the soul-searching of an individual trying to discern the source of his failures and the cause of his misery, this is the only way man has any hope of altering his course, changing for the better, and elevating his destiny.

History is not a continual "tending upward and onward." Nor is it a succession of peaks and valleys with the inevitable result of progress. Rather, it is the story of man's individual choices collectively producing what we call history. More often, the choices are made without full consciousness of their implications and without a sense of full responsibility. When the consequences of those choices are adverse, man blames other men, institutions, or God. Mindfulness of the broad and complex consequences—and typically lingering repercussions—of one's choices is rare, as is the moral and intellectual maturity such awareness suggests.

What, we might ponder, would the world have been like had the Kerensky government survived? What would have been the course of world events if von Stauffenberg had been a successful assassin? What would be the state of world affairs had Einstein's and Leo Szilard's belated recognition come earlier and Western man had never developed nuclear weapons? We cannot know, but everything we do know should lead us to understand that the world would be a far better place today if any, or all, had been different. Two represented triumphs of evil; the third, if not a triumph of evil, then an example of man's scientific prowess juxtaposed with his moral primitiveness—the disproportion of the two producing a menace that may prove to be the proximate method, though not the ultimate cause, of mankind's suicide. With each came further destruction and suffering for mankind.

None of this was inevitable, though man is often wont to attempt to absolve himself of his responsibility by taking some variation of either a deterministic view or shifting the blame. The Creator has given man the power of choice, and that in part is what makes him higher than the beasts of the field and only a little "lower than the angels." For man to exercise that power wisely he must recognize his limitations, accept that there is a transcendent God who created him, and acknowledge an immutable law to which he is accountable. In a word, he must be humble.

But Western man is not humble. His arrogance would at least parallel that of the most hubristic civilizations to ever exercise power over any portion of the planet. He has made choices that, had he chosen otherwise, would not have led him "without a turning to the concentration camps and slaughter houses of the totalitarian state."[5] Churchill's implicit—and perhaps unintended—acknowledgment of the actual and direct consequences of the Renaissance/Enlightenment view of man and his universe can be found in one of Western history's most famous passages: "But if we fail, then the whole world, including the United States, including all that we have known and cared for, will sink into the abyss of a new Dark Age made more sinister, and perhaps more protracted, by the lights of perverted science." (Churchill in the House of Commons, 18 June 1940) But these are only the more conspicuous of the miseries Western man has created by his choices. Countless individual lives and souls have been mangled, debased, or destroyed by his foolishness—and the suffering, self-delusion, and hopelessness continue unabated—indeed, are accelerating.

In asking the question how Western man arrived here, we should not be surprised if the answer defies Western man's own long held views of himself and his greatest achievements. An understanding of the spiritual and psychological deficits of Western man's character would lead the insightful observer to immediately recognize—if not anticipate—that the answer so thoroughly reflects pride and self-will that Western man would see the path he has taken not as a perilous excursion into dangerous and desolate places, but as a triumph of his intellect. These are dimensions of the same spiritual and psychological deficits that have led Western man to his ethnocentric, self-centric—Solzhenitsyn called them *anthropocentric*—views of his world. But that form of historical and geographic provincialism is nowhere near as dangerous for him as the distorted view of reality we will examine here.

Two of the primary waypoints (i.e., historical turning points) on Western civilization's pilgrimage to its present condition are the Renaissance and the Enlightenment—terms that today in the West are endeared to every person who regards himself as educated or learned. But the perceptive should challenge and debunk the notions that the former fundamentally represented the rebirth claimed for it, or that the latter was as "enlightening" as is presumed. Though each achieved something of merit, the case for those merits has been overstated with a corollary absence of an objective consideration of the demerits.

The materialistic rationalism that has been the legacy of the Enlightenment and the Renaissance is—contrary to the vainglorious way they are seen and depicted, especially as manifested in the sciences and technology—actually quite primitive. By clinging to the narrow perception that the material world is all there is—or at least the only reality that should be given real credence—it debases and lowers man to the meanest level of human understanding.

The end result of this form of modernity is a confining, highly truncated perspective on reality. Man and his understanding of the universe are profoundly limited in any event—the evidence of this is in part supplied by the massive expanse of time and space we neither know nor understand. The possibility of a greater, transcendent reality is not only not seriously considered, but often vigorously opposed by the blinkered practitioners of this late Western historical view.

Though the medieval period has been conventionally labeled the Dark Ages, the age beginning with the Renaissance has been shadowed by another form of darkness made even more opaque by the Enlightenment. In concert they have produced a New Dark Age—different from the Middle Ages only in the nature of the blindness, but benighted just the same.

In historical retrospect, the New Dark Age is likely to prove more benighted in its way than the earlier—and infinitely more dangerous to mankind.

THE REJECTION OF GOD

We have become accustomed to taking the secular character of modern civilization for granted. We have most of us never known anything else and consequently we are apt to think that this is a natural and normal state of things, so that whatever our own beliefs may be, we do not expect modern civilization to pay much attention to religion, still less to be based upon a religious conception of existence.
Christopher Dawson[6]

Consider the Enlightenment. What was the sermon? It seems to me the essential message was anticlerical: humans were capable of rational judgment and hence had the ability to arrive at both truth and goodness directly, through their own best efforts. The Enlightenment represented the definitive rejection of religious authorities as judges of either truth or goodness.
Immanuel Wallerstein[7]

The Renaissance and Enlightenment were the waypoints in Western history where Western man eschewed the steep, narrow paths that led toward a Supreme Being and a more complex and exalted reality and instead took the easier, declining slopes that exalt man. Arnold Toynbee referred to the era of the Enlightenment in *Civilization on Trial* as "one of the epoch-making events" in modern Western history, but contrary to what might be assumed about the reasons for that appellation, Toynbee shared an insight into a rarely heard, discreditable dimension of the West's history.

> ...about the turn of the seventeenth and eighteenth centuries of our Western Christian era, something happened which, I venture to prophesy, is going to loom out in retrospect as one of the epoch-making events of our modern Western history....This portent was a double event, in which the Jesuits' failure was accentuated by the Royal Society's simultaneous success. The Jesuits failed to convert the Hindus and Chinese to the Roman Catholic form of Western Christianity. They failed, though they had discovered the psychological "know-how," because, when it came to the point, neither the Pope nor the Son of Heaven nor the Brahmans would have it. In the same generation, these tragically frustrated Jesuit missionaries' fellow-Western Catholics and Protestants at home came to the hazardous conclusion that a religion in whose now divided and contentious name they had been fighting an inconclusive fratricidal hundred years' war was an inopportune element in their cultural heritage.[8]

Here we must interrupt the narrative to point out that the "Christianity" behind these events was Christianity in name only: they were not—any of them—Christ-like, and the distinction is critical, one we have made repeatedly in this work and a distinction to which we will return. Had the conduct of the professing Christians of that era been of the latter species rather than the former, there would have been no reason for anyone to consider the question that came next: "Why not tacitly agree to cut out the wars of religion by cutting out religion itself and concentrate on the application of physical science to practical affairs—a pursuit that aroused no controversy and that promised to be lucrative?"

PD-art.

Peter the Great by Paul Delaroche (1797–1856). *Toynbee observed regarding the choice to turn from religion and to science and technology: "This seventeenth-century turning in the road of Western progress was big with consequences; for the Western civilization that has since run like wildfire round the world has not been the whole of the seamless web; it has been a flare of cotton-waste: a technological selvage with the religious centre-piece torn out." This was the "utility" pattern of Western civilization, which was "comparatively easy to take" as illustrated by the choice of Peter the Great, who instantly pounced "on it as soon as it was displayed in the West's shop window."*

Toynbee pointed us to motives that prompted Western man to take a course that he pursues even more assiduously to this day—for much the same motives. This observation is perfectly congruent with Francis Schaeffer's later declaration that Western Christians have focused on personal peace and affluence to the virtual exclusion of bold advocacy for their professed religion.

There was, however, a terrible and momentous price to be paid for this earlier choice: "This seventeenth-century turning in the road of Western progress was big with consequences; for the Western civilization that has since run like wildfire round the world has not been the whole of the seamless web; it has been a flare of cotton-waste: a technological selvage with the religious centre-piece torn out."[9] Having turned from complete commitment to his spiritual convictions and the pursuit of higher truths, Western man settled for the material, not recognizing that though it would prove to be "lucrative," it would not prove to "arouse no controversy," nor protect him from war. To the contrary it would produce weaponry of such lethality that he could obliterate himself from the planet, all the while bereft of any higher beliefs that might deflect him from this disastrous course.

Two responses became discernible in the way the rest of the planet reacted to this choice. One was to embrace assiduously what Toynbee called the "utility" pattern of Western civilization, which was "comparatively easy to take" as illustrated by the choice of Peter the Great, who instantly pounced "on it as soon as it was displayed in the West's shop window." The other, illustrated one hundred years later, by "the subtler and more spiritual Al-Gabarti showed a nicer discrimination." For Al-Gabarti, Toynbee observed, "the touchstone of Western civilization, as of his own, was not technology but justice." We describe elsewhere how the modern West has lost the respect of much of the rest of the world precisely because it has chosen affluence and technology over justice and transcendent principle.

Al-Gabarti "had apprehended the heart of the matter, the issue that the West has still to fight out within itself. 'And though I…understand all mysteries and all knowledge…and have not charity, I am nothing'—'Or what man is there of you whom, if his son ask bread, will he give him a stone? Or, if he ask a fish, will he give him a serpent?'"[10]

The West has been fighting out this issue "within itself," and so far the impetus to morality, justice, and the spiritual has continued to lose ground to the material, the scientific, the technological, the debased, and mammon.

Toynbee felt so strongly about this divergence from the high road of earlier Western history that he spoke of it forcefully in his masterwork, *A Study of History*:

> What the sceptics have denied is that religion is ineradicable. They have claimed that they have eradicated religion in their own case; that what has been accomplished by them can be accomplished by other people too; and that religion ought to be eradicated. The modern opponents of religion have challenged the thesis of the founders of the higher religions; they have not agreed that religion is a built-in faculty of the human psyche. They have maintained that religion is merely one of a number of expressions of human sociality, and that it is an immature expression.[11]

What Toynbee did not say here was that pseudo religion with pseudo religious values and practices were substituted. In inadvertent affirmation of Toynbee's central point—believing in something is a "built-in faculty [i.e., need] of the human psyche"—these ersatz religions and beliefs can be found all about Western man.

Toynbee continued, "...they expect, unwarrantably, to see religion discarded progressively, pari passu with a civilization's advance in sophistication and in potency. They hold that the recession of religion is an index of this advance. Mankind may have needed religion as a prop while it was in its infancy; it can and should discard this prop now that it is coming of age." "These theses," Toynbee states, "are specious" and "...open to challenge in their turn." If Pitirim Sorokin is correct, not only are they specious, the very opposite will be true: As mankind "advances" in "sophistication and in potency"—as defined by these materialists—the corrupt and decaying sensate culture that is created will eventually be abandoned for either an ideational or idealistic culture founded on religious faith. What that religious faith will be for the West is another—and extremely critical—question.

Significantly, Toynbee gave credence to only one aspect of the skeptics' thinking: that they had "diagnosed correctly...man's consciousness of his ignorance and weakness," an observation that would comport with numerous biblical declarations. This is central to most religious belief: man is profoundly limited in mind, body, and soul; he must seek understanding, truth, and morality by reaching beyond himself in faith. Had the compelling need for humility, which is implicit in that recognition, been embraced, a very different and much happier course would have been taken by Western civilization. But the skeptics of that era—as is the wont of the skeptics today—would have none of humility. Exultant in the "power" of man they forged other rationales in support of their "certainties," all founded on a philosophical base that Toynbee insightfully indicted as "not sophisticated" and "naively obtuse."

Their "second thesis" "that Mankind's ignorance and weakness are symptoms of a temporary immaturity, and that these symptoms abate as civilization advances in sophistication and in potency" has never been achieved except in a very limited way in "Mankind's relations with non-human Nature; and to equate non-human Nature with the whole of Nature is not sophisticated; it is naively obtuse." Toynbee pointed out that "nature" should include "human nature," which "is the most intractable and formidable part of Nature that Man has to deal with."[12] This of course is not only true but a foundational belief of many religions.

Western man has stumbled badly in a way that redoubles the danger to him and his: Maximizing his belief in himself, minimizing the possibility of his incompetence in dealing with his own nature, maximizing his conviction that science and technology are great boons, and minimizing the dangers of both, he has posited too much, too long, and too far in the wrong place. Like the oblivious cowboy B-52 pilot in the film *Dr. Strangelove or: How I Learned to Stop Worrying and Love the Bomb*, he may have to ride his technology and his science to his doom.

Why, a thinking person might ask, is there such assiduous diligence in constructing a philosophical superstructure so clearly missing sound underpinnings? The answer lies not only in man's vanity and pride, but more subtly in his desire to be "free." This is not the freedom of noble connotation, but man granting himself the authority of both moral licenser and moral licensee. Licentiousness is the deeply hidden psychological goal, but he knows he must not let it be characterized that way—the immoral must be made amoral or, better yet, redefined entirely by man through the expedient of relativism as moral. Thus man amends or abrogates the highest moral law. To achieve this he must be rid of the Lawgiver–God, and at most only tolerate "god" or "gods."

This rejection of religious faith—at least authentic, deep, intense, all-encompassing faith—out of a misguided notion that this will civilize humanity is with us today. Secularists of every subspecies voice it often, usually as if it is a sophisticated, modern concept. Yet this notion is as old as it is discredited. Despite its age and what should be its obviously simpering "attraction," this truly is the great "issue which the West has still to fight out within itself."

THE EXALTATION OF MAN

In the humanism of the High Renaissance, flowing on to maturity through the Enlightenment, man was determined to make himself autonomous. This flow continues, and by the time we come to modern modern science man himself is devoured: Man as man is dead. Life is pointless, devoid of meaning.
Francis Schaeffer[13]

Western man had placed his feet upon a destructive path, first with the Renaissance, then with the Enlightenment. But with the rejection of God—and not to be unexpected—came pari passu the exaltation of man, a formulation that produced not the best but the worst of both worlds. Dawson referred to the humanism of the Renaissance as a "kind of hubris" that led to the destruction of its practitioners in much of fifteenth-century Italy. Humanism's very successes, Dawson believed, "undermined the foundations of its own vitality."[14]

Man's self-exaltation was at the opposite end of a continuum from where the emphasis had been placed earlier—on the exploration and knowing of the supernatural. In the medieval period, God was the object to be sought and elevated; in the Renaissance, He was supplanted by man. Yet though he may ignore or disavow them, man's obvious limitations do not suit him for the role; he makes momentous and terrible mistakes in assuming it. His incompetence is so great that he unwittingly undermines his own philosophic position in the new order he has created.

Dawson described it thusly: "The Renaissance has its beginning in the self-discovery, the self-realization and the self-exaltation of Man.... The self-affirmation of man gradually led to the denial of the spiritual foundations of his freedom and knowledge. This tendency shows itself in every department of modern thought....This again was followed by a second revolt—the assertion of the rights of man against secular authority that culminated in the French Revolution. But this second revolt also led to disillusion."[15]

The English writer and journalist Malcolm Muggeridge resorted to the writings of the French scientist Pascal and the English poet William Blake to affirm the end consequences of these choices.

> Pascal, one of the most brilliant scientific minds of his time, came to realize that, as a pursuit, science is a cul-de-sac, and results in the dethronement of God and the elevation of men, to the point that they come to see themselves as lords of creation—a role that makes them either go quite mad, or sink into mere animality. Blake, too, in his own bizarre way, saw that the so-called Enlightenment was in truth a darkening of the spirit, and scrawled across his copy of *Bacon's Essays*—a forerunner of Huxley's—"Good Advice for Satan's Kingdom."[16]

Blake also expressed his contempt for the Enlightenment viewpoint through his poetry:

Mock on, Mock on Voltaire, Rousseau:
Mock on, Mock on: 'tis all in vain!
You throw the sand against the wind,
And the wind blows it back again.
—William Blake[17]

Yet preceding the self-inflated anthropocentrism of Rousseau and Voltaire, we should not forget that one of the archetypes of the Renaissance man was Machiavelli—a vaunted product of Western civilization—who, in *The Prince*, became the world's best-known exponent of the merits and methods of the ruthless pursuit of power. Espousing a faith in man unalloyed by a faith in God, Machiavelli embodied not the best but the worst that Western civilization had to offer in thought and belief—or, more precisely, unbelief. Machiavelli, to use Dawson's words, was a classic manifestation of men who "rejected their dependence on the supernatural, and vindicated their independence and supremacy in the temporal order." Turning their backs

PD-art

Blaise Pascal (1623–1662), anonymous portrait. *Malcolm Muggeridge said of him, "Pascal, one of the most brilliant scientific minds of his time, came to realize that, as a pursuit, science is a cul-de-sac, and results in the dethronement of God and the elevation of men, to the point that they come to see themselves as lords of creation —a role that makes them either go quite mad, or sink into mere animality."*

that one's life journey may become an experience of moral growth, so that one may leave life a better human being than one started it."

Another way of distinguishing between these different cultural approaches can be found in Sorokin's classifications of the ideational, idealistic, and sensate systems. Sorokin explained, "Any integrated society has ethical ideals and values as the highest manifestation of its ethical consciousness."[24] The West prior to the Renaissance was characterized by the ideational that, in their "sublimest" form, "are summed up in the Sermon on the Mount."[25]

As the thirteenth century dawned, the Renaissance began a process of transition from the ideational to the sensate that reached its full philosophical expression in the Enlightenment and continues to metastasize in Western civilization to this day.

Like Toynbee and Dawson, Sorokin perceptively traced not only the timing of this history-shaking shift, but the more subtle manifestations of its effects on everyday life: "The hedonism, sensuality and paganism of the ethics of the Renaissance are well known.…Money-making was declared the sign of God's grace; it was elevated to the rank of a primary duty."[26] It is no wonder then that, even more so today, in the Western church, Protestant and Catholic, the Logos often seems less the Word and more the mammon.

THE CHRONOLOGICAL AND PHILOSOPHICAL HINGE OF WESTERN HISTORY

Man stands on the lowest steps of this divine ladder, poised dizzily between heaven and the abyss… the mediator between the two worlds of spirit and matter…whose mission it is to bring spiritual life and light into the sensible world.…The visible world is a shadow, and the importance of man is not to be found in this shadow existence, but in the place that he occupies on the ladder of being.…

Christopher Dawson[27]

The thirteenth century can be seen as the chronological and philosophical hinge of Western history. What preceded it largely centered on religion and a spiritual view of the universe; what followed largely rejected religion and embraced instead a harsh materialist view of the world. Dawson selected it as the apex of what Sorokin would have called an idealistic system. With a passionate vividness, Dawson attempted to explain to the modern Western mind a completely different view of the world—a view with grandeur and scope far surpassing the narrow vagaries of the modern Western intellect.

Dawson's description, completely consonant with Sorokin's ideal of an ideational civilization, should suggest to us that perhaps the apex of Western civilization has not been in our time but in this much earlier age. The beauty of its symmetry, the depth and breadth of its view, the gentleness of its aspirations, all bespeak an extraordinary world, not seen before, certainly not seen since. In the realm of knowledge, there was "a universal synthesis…which was the greatest achievement of the thirteenth century," possessing "an extraordinary unity that is to be seen in its art and architecture and social institutions, no less than in its theology and philosophy." Its success in the realms of theology and philosophy is evident in the authority the writings of "the greatest of the thirteenth-

PD

Signing of the Magna Carta (at Runnymede in 1215) by Albert Herter. *The thirteenth century can be seen as the philosophical hinge of Western history. What preceded it largely centered on religion and a spiritual view of the universe; what followed largely rejected religion and embraced instead a harsh materialist view of the world. Toward the end of the thirteenth century came more and greater corruption of the Catholic Church, the erosion of the moral authority of which could only have the effect of eroding the spirituality and more noble aspirations of the broader culture. This would prove to be a precedent, an historical analogue to the Catholic and Protestant churches in our age, which likewise have failed and become corrupted by the secular and worldly, thereby facilitating the decline and decay of an entire civilization. With the exception of the wise and attentive, the men of the age that followed did not realize what was upon them—an analogue also to the state of affairs within the church and the culture in our age. The loss of the extraordinary zeal and spirit of self-sacrifice that had characterized the time was expressed most poignantly in a message from Ruteboeuf to the French nobleman and knight who had devoted his life to the defense of the Holy Land, Geoffrey of Sergines, "Master Geoffrey de Sergines, I no longer see any sign that they will send you succour. Let the men of Aire make a great cemetery: That is what they will need. The path is overgrown with weeds, which men once trod gladly to offer their 'souls as though they were burning tapers.'"*

century systemizers," such as St. Thomas Aquinas, have retained to this day, primarily within the "Catholic conception of reality." In an observation that reminds us of Toynbee's description of central tenets of modern Western thought and belief as "obtuse," Dawson explained how difficult it is "for us at the present day to understand the mediaeval view of reality...without the help of some work of creative imagination like Dante's great poem." Man in that age saw himself as the subordinate creation of an omniscient and omnipotent Creator in a world that was "theocentric." Every aspect of life was explained in terms of its relationship to God, and all art and science were devoted to the service of this being, and, by extension, to His creation, man. The universe, Dawson, explained, was seen as "nothing but a reflection or image of the glory of God." In poetic language that is at once humbling and uplifting, Dawson described the view of that age: "Man stands on the lowest steps of this divine ladder, poised dizzily between heaven and the abyss...the mediator between the two worlds of spirit and matter...whose mission it is to bring spiritual life and light into the sensible world....The visible world is a shadow, and the importance of man is not to be found in this shadow existence, but in the place that he occupies on the ladder of being...."[28] Strikingly, this last sentence comports so closely with Toynbee's observation about man's focus on that which is "on the surface of life." This suggests *the greater depth, the greater reality.*

Dawson leaves us with a message that might be expressed in terms of probing questions: In its essentials was this worldview not superior and the materialistic worldview of the coming Renaissance and Enlightenment a path away from the higher truth? Has Western man not focused on what Dawson called the "shadow" of this "visible world" and, in the process, lost his own importance in "the place that he occupies on the ladder of being"? The accessibility of the ultimate form of self-actualization—which is available to man through the Christian faith—was very evident in that time but largely lost in ours, supplanted by an ersatz version artificially constructed by the disciplines of psychology and sociology from the whole cloth of man's thought.

Lest this description of that age sound too idealized, too exalted, we would hasten to add—consistent with our oft-stated diagnoses of the human species—that the afflictions of human nature were present and ever striving to bring man down from the lofty position assigned to him by the beliefs of the time. Thirteenth-century man was corrupt—let us not idealize him—but he enjoyed "a vision of spiritual perfection" to which he might aspire that has been lost in our age. In that time and place "all sorts of people in all sorts of ways" could aspire to a more noble character and life: "...a man might be a contemplative monk, like St. Bernard, or a tough fighting man, like a Knight Templar; he might be a philosopher, like St. Bonaventure and St. Thomas, or a politician, like Simon de Montfort the Younger. He might be a beggar, like St. Francis, or a king, like St. Louis; a poet, like Wolfram von Eschenbach, or a scientist, like Roger Bacon."[29] In any and every realm from peasant to king, there was "a common faith and a common purpose, and each had his own personal goal of spiritual perfection." This had the effect of exalting the individual who chose to pursue it. Despite his many shortcomings, the individual might aspire to—and to a considerable extent achieve—a life of nobility, honor, selflessness and purpose incomprehensible in our age, surfeited as it is with notions of selfish ambition and material acquisitiveness.

In an intriguing observation, Dawson pointed to the death of Gregory X in 1276 as the end of "the union between the papacy and the reformers that had created the dynamic unity of mediaeval religion and culture." The Christendom of the past was "gradually replaced by the rivalry of conflicting states and nationalities, which left no room for the supernational institutions and ideals of the earlier period." Withal came more and greater corruption of the Catholic Church, the erosion of the moral authority of which could only have the effect of eroding the spirituality and more noble aspirations of the broader culture. Here we see again a manifestation of Toynbee's point that the moral responsibility for the decline and decay of a culture always lies most heavily on the leaders. Had the Church not succumbed, the moral leadership would have been present to carry forward the ideals and noble aspirations of that great age. This would prove to be a precedent, an historical analogue to the Catholic and Protestant churches in our age, which, as we will demonstrate later, likewise have failed and become corrupted by the secular and worldly, thereby facilitating the decline and decay of an entire civilization. With the exception of the wise and attentive, the men of the age that followed did not realize what was upon them—an analogue also to the state of affairs within the church and the culture in our age. Appeals for reform came primarily from the laity, as will surely be the case in our age. The loss of the extraordinary zeal and spirit of self-sacrifice that had characterized the time was expressed most poignantly in a message from Ruteboeuf to Geoffrey of Sergines, the knight responsible for the defense of the Holy Land: "Master Geoffrey de Sergines, I no longer see any sign that they will send you succour. Let the men of Aire make a great cemetery: That is what they will need. The path is overgrown with weeds, which men once trod gladly to offer their 'souls as though they were burning tapers.'"[30]

Now we see from the retrospective of our time what was happening, and the beginning of that path, no longer simply overgrown with weeds, can scarcely be found today—even in the church, Catholic, Orthodox, or Protestant. The great cemetery begun for such devoted men and women of faith was crowded with generations of self-sacrificing supplicants, though the number from modern Western civilization seeking entry has dwindled to a relative few. Western man had placed his feet upon a very different path, one of descent rather than ascent: a path to a New Dark Age.

The thirteenth-century chronological hinge of history closed the age of belief and opened the age of skepticism. Never again would Western man collectively look to heaven and the spiritual for truth and meaning. The group Toynbee called the "dominant minority," with the "moral responsibility" for the civilization on its shoulders, reveled in man's newly found "powers." For the ensuing centuries, the signposts on the trail were ignored and, with the Enlightenment, Western man no longer walked, but ran pell-mell downhill.

Yet even they sensed something was missing. Unwittingly—without recognizing it for what it was—they sensed Augustine's hearts, which were "restless" until they found "their rest in" God,[31] and Pascal's "infinite abyss," which "can be filled only with an infinite and immutable object; in other words by God himself."[32]

FROM THE EXALTED TO THE MUNDANE

The utopian dream of the Enlightenment can be summed up by five words: reason, nature, happiness, progress, and liberty. It was thoroughly secular in its thinking. The humanistic elements which had risen during the Renaissance came to flood tide in the Enlightenment. Here was man starting from himself absolutely.
Francis Schaeffer[33]

Nagging doubts notwithstanding, Enlightenment man and his progeny forged ahead with the development of a new secular religion that would transform "from a philosophy into a religion" the new ideas so that they became "articles of faith."[34] The worship of democracy and capitalism remain manifestations of this secular religion of the West. From average citizens to presidents, both are touted as answers to the world's problems. And, as with any religion, there must be iconic figures or examples to cite as affirmation of the religion's merits. For the French intellectuals of the Enlightenment, that icon was America. But this was another display of that all too human affinity for seeing what you want and ignoring all else. In the first instance, the America of that age was profoundly religious; but, more significantly, the French intellectuals overlooked the fact that the literal or metaphorical Monticello or Mt. Vernon rested on decaying black bodies underneath.[35]

Unlike Christianity, which speaks often and in depth about man's weaknesses, frailties, ignorance and self-centeredness, this new religion must, of necessity, be heavily reliant on depicting man differently—with "innate goodness" and wisdom—otherwise it becomes logically untenable. That history is neither the archive of man's goodness nor of his wisdom is either lost on, or ignored by, the devotees of this faith. The penalty for such ignorance—or such timorous unwillingness to face reality—is supremely painful.

A quote from Segur about the apostles of the Enlightenment is apropos of our time: "They trod lightly on a carpet of flowers towards the abyss."[36] Dawson observed,

> They did not see that they were on the edge of a precipice...they were a doomed generation, fated to perish at first by ones and twos, and then by scores and hundreds and thousands, on the scaffold, in the streets, and on the battlefield. For as the Revolution advanced, it gradually revealed the naked reality that had been veiled by the antiquated trappings of royalty and tradition—the General Will —and it was not the benevolent abstraction which the disciples of Rousseau had worshipped but a fierce will to power which destroyed every man and institution that stood in its way.[37]

This is the same will-to-power of which Spengler spoke so eloquently and insightfully—the same *bête noire* that roams unrecognized through the ideological, political, and financial halls of power in the modern West.

The "will to power" lay thinly veiled behind the contrived "benevolent abstraction," and the men of that time—as in ours—chose to believe in the appealing ephemera rather than acknowledge the ghastly reality. Dawson referred to it—in terms apropos of themes of this work—as a "time of illusion" and of "boundless optimism" that showed no "regard for the facts of history" that were regarded, as were the "truths of religion," as "unreal," hence to be not only ignored, but actively and ferociously opposed.[38] Modern Western man, in one form or another, has followed their lead by treading on a luxuriant bed of wealth, scientific and technological achievements and hubristic humanism towards his own abyss.

Of course the attractive features of the liberal ideals that sprang from the Enlightenment would appeal to most anyone, yet, ironically, it was one of the most unrealistic theorists of all, Karl Marx, who saw through and debunked those ideals as features of man's thought and behavior that could not be expected to endure. Marx saw the materialism of Western civilization as its dominant feature and the idealism of liberalism as unsustainable. The moral values of Christianity without the spiritual foundation, this liberalism was nothing more than a quasi-religious substitute for true religion.[39]

This is the nexus between the Christian faith and the modern Western world: not the undergirding of the latter by the former in terms of true belief, but the usurpation by the latter of many of the principles and values of the former while "denying its power." (2 Timothy 3:5 NIV) One of the unanticipated—and often ignored—consequences of this state of affairs is the dilution of the credibility of Christianity and the concomitant dilution of the credibility of Western civilization in the eyes of much of the world. Another consequence is the profoundly enervating effect for the modern Western church of its *de facto concordat* with the materialistic culture that surrounds it.

Out of this debilitation arose the challenge to the West from Islam that has reached a frenzy in our time. The ancient West was threatened by orientalism; the modern West is threatened by radical Islam's fundamentalism, which stems largely from its contempt for the West's materialism, rampant self-indulgence, and denial of a higher spiritual order. Like Rome, the modern West has "conquered and organised the world and lost its own soul in the process."[40]

Beneath and guiding all are individual choices—there is that word again, that critical, essential word, heavy with responsibility—within the hearts and minds of men. Made in the vacuum of faithlessness—or a false faith—they are supported by nothing more stable than the shifting sands of human opinion, fashion, prejudice and emotion.

The philosophers of the Enlightenment believed only in science and history as valid sources of truth and knowledge. In time, materialistic science supplanted history as their ultimate "authority." Neither disposed to acknowledge any merit in the West's traditional religion, Christianity, nor, for that matter, religion generally, they believed that all religion was the product of primitive quests and now no longer needed by man.

IF THERE IS NO GOD, THERE IS NO LAW

The Existentialist…finds it extremely embarrassing that God does not exist, for there disappears with Him all possibility of finding values in an intelligible heaven. There can no longer be any good a priori, *since there is no infinite and perfect consciousness to think it. It is nowhere written that "the good" exists, that one must be honest or must not lie, since we are now on a plane where there are only men.*

Jean-Paul Sartre[41]

Dawson attempted to explain—especially for those with no religious understanding—how and why man must bridge the gulf between the material and spiritual worlds. The meaninglessness of life without spiritual insight and purpose, Dawson declared, is sensed by most of humanity and brings with it a profound longing. Even "the life of the animal is also" religious. "Only man is capable of separating himself alike from God and from Nature, of making himself his last end and living a purely self-regarding and irreligious existence." But a man who

PD

Jean Paul Sartre in Cuba, 1960, with Ernesto "Che" Guevara and Simone de Beauvoir. *Sartre admitted the meaninglessness and valuelessness of a world in which God is not acknowledged, "The Existentialist… finds it extremely embarrassing that God does not exist, for there disappears with Him all possibility of finding values in an intelligible heaven. There can no longer be any good a* priori, *since there is no infinite and perfect consciousness to think it. It is nowhere written that 'the good' exists, that one must be honest or must not lie, since we are now on a plane where there are only men."*

finds complete satisfaction in this "self-assertion" and "sensual enjoyment" is rare. The "normal man" will have at least a vague if amorphous sense that there is a greater spiritual reality.[42] His slavery to sensuality and self-centeredness will trouble him, if only at a deep and unacknowledged level.

Even this creature—the most primitive of beings despite his self-proclaimed "sophistication"—reluctantly senses that there is a connection between his self-centeredness and materialist self-aggrandizement and evil itself. They are manifestations of the same sinister force: a dangerous electricity that he has permitted to run through his being, constructed, as he has deliberately made it, from hard conductive materials rather than the soft insulation of spiritual sensitivity and humble consciousness of man's depravity.

His only escape from the prison he has constructed would be through the very thing he has denied even exists. For, as Dawson put it, "...the modern mind no longer admits the possibility or the objective value of spiritual knowledge. The whole tendency of Western thought since the Renaissance, and still more since the eighteenth century, has been to deny the existence of any real knowledge except that of rational demonstration founded upon sensible experience."[43] Yet the greater truths transcend this narrow and shallow view; they are by definition above and beyond it. When that which can be neither touched, nor seen, nor heard, nor otherwise observed is disregarded, man has in effect denied a greater and vaster reality, not unlike insisting that there is no such thing as the universe beyond our solar system.

"Religious knowledge," declared Dawson, "is the highest kind of knowledge, the end and coronation of the whole process of man's intellectual development." But when it is regarded as irrational emotion, as by modern Western thinkers, religion is "reduced to subjective feeling and moral activity." This kind of religion "can have no intellectual authority, and in consequence it also loses its social authority and even its moral influence." Man "cannot live by reason alone. His spiritual life, and even his physical instincts, are starved in the narrow and arid territory of purely rational consciousness. He is driven to take refuge in the non-rational, whether it be the irrational blend of spirituality and emotionalism that is termed romanticism, or, as is increasingly the case today, in the frankly sub-rational sphere of pure sensationalism and sexual impulse."[44]

Nor can man successfully contrive his own religion. "The religious attitude is only possible in the presence of the eternal and the transcendent. Any object that falls short of this fails to inspire the sense of awe and self-surrender that is essential to true religion. Man cannot worship himself, nor can he adore a Time God which is the creation of his own mind. As soon as he recognises its fictitious character, such an idea loses its religious power."[45]

If there is no god, there is no law. In *Christianity and the New Age*, Dawson explained that which should be self-evident: "...social life is impossible without order, it is necessary to resort to some external principle of compulsion, whether political or economic." In ancient Rome this principle was military compulsion, but "in the modern world we have the even more complete and far-reaching organization of the economic machine."[46] There is an implied warning in Dawson's observation of the "external principle," which produces social order. The "even more complete and far-reaching organization of the economic machine" of the modern West is the direct descendant of the Renaissance/Enlightenment view of man and his universe. Like Solzhenitsyn and Václav Havel, Dawson pointed us toward a threat that much of the West sees purely as the source of its blessings, rather than a variation of "666" that may eventually be branded on its foreheads.

Schaeffer declared essentially what Dawson before him had said in his observation that the scientific/materialist view of life devoid of a strong religious base inevitably led "without a turning to the concentration camps and slaughter houses of the totalitarian state." "...these ideas helped produce an even more far-reaching yet logical conclusion: the Nazi movement in Germany. Heinrich Himmler (1900–1945), leader of the Gestapo, *stated that the law of nature must take its course in the survival of the fittest. The result was the gas chambers. Hitler stated numerous times that Christianity and its notion of charity should be 'replaced by the ethic of strength over weakness.'"*

Photograph by German government SS issue

> ...[F]or centuries Christianity has been progressively losing its hold on Western culture, and both its doctrines and its moral ideals have fallen into discredit. The causes of this state of things lie deep in that process of the humanization and rationalizing of Western culture.... Ever since the Renaissance the centrifugal tendencies in our civilization have destroyed its spiritual unity and divided its spiritual forces. The Western mind has turned away from the contemplation of the absolute and the eternal to the knowledge of the particular and the contingent. It has made man the measure of all things and has sought to emancipate human life from its dependence on the supernatural....[W]e see politics, economics, science and art organizing themselves as autonomous kingdoms which owe no allegiance to any higher power....Religion came to be regarded as one among a number of competing interests—a limited department of life, which had no jurisdiction over the rest. And as it lost its universal authority, it lost its universal vision...[47]

Schaeffer ever more forcefully declared what humanity can expect from a system like this. "When people began to think in this way, there was no place for God or for man as man. When psychology and social science were made a part of a closed cause-and-effect system, along with physics, astronomy and chemistry, it was not only God who died. Man died."[48] But sadly, something else died; something critical to man's experience if he has any hope of peace and fulfillment. "And within this framework love died. There is no place for love in a totally closed cause-and-effect system. There is no place for morals in a totally closed cause-and-effect system. There is no place for the freedom of people in a totally closed cause-and-effect system. Man becomes a zero. People and all they do become only a part of the machinery."[49]

This debasement of man continues, and "by the time we come to modern modern science man himself is devoured: Man as man is dead. Life is pointless, devoid of meaning."[50] This inescapable conclusion, nonetheless, is evaded by modern Western man, who devises systems and methods by which to exalt himself even as the logical basis for that exaltation no longer exists in his philosophy.

Confronting the foolishness of this view head-on, Schaeffer pointed to one obvious gaping void in its logic—and then demonstrated the utter futility and meaningless of "values" and "meaning" devised by man from his own thought.

> Most importantly, no one has yet shown how man could have been brought forth from non-man solely by time plus chance. The humanist thinkers...either come to the conclusion that there are no values and meaning or suddenly try to produce values and meaning out of rhetoric. Thus, there are problems of both the how and the why. The concept of an unbroken line from molecule to man, on the basis of only time plus chance, leaves these crucial questions of how and why unanswered. There was no

> necessity to extend biological evolution to "social Darwinism." But it was natural for these men to do this because of their desire to find a unifying principle that would enable autonomous man to explain everything through naturalistic science....[51]

The real logical consequences of insisting on this view of life manifested themselves most clearly in the twentieth century. Schaeffer said essentially what Dawson before him had said in his observation that this led "without a turning to the concentration camps and slaughter houses of the totalitarian state."[52]

> ...these ideas helped produce an even more far-reaching yet logical conclusion: the Nazi movement in Germany. Heinrich Himmler (1900–1945), leader of the Gestapo, stated that the law of nature must take its course in the survival of the fittest. The result was the gas chambers. Hitler stated numerous times that Christianity and its notion of charity should be "replaced by the ethic of strength over weakness."[53]

There were other factors that produced National Socialism, but they all derived from the same worldview. "...[T]he Christian consensus had largely been lost by the undermining from a rationalistic philosophy and a romantic pantheism on the secular side, and a liberal theology (which was an adoption of rationalism in theological terminology) in the universities and many of the churches. Thus biblical Christianity was no longer giving the consensus for German society." In this environment "the theory of the survival of the fittest sanctioned what occurred."[54]

The ruthlessness and cruelty of Darwinism, when applied to human thought and behavior, has been ever before us throughout the twentieth and into the twenty-first century. Schaeffer's observations about how it came to be so overtly accepted in Germany should be heeded for our age. This same ruthlessness is not unknown in the West in our time; it is simply disguised as something acceptable, even admirable. We see it perhaps most conspicuously in the competitiveness of capitalism.

The evisceration of the Christian church from the inside is another critically important point. What appears to be Christianity is often Christianity in name only. But by carrying the name, millions are deluded into believing that this truly is what Christ stood for; and the perpetrators of great sins may even act out their unholiness under the cloak of religion.

CLEAVING THE INFANT OF TRUTH IN HALF

When the rupture between science and philosophy became definitive at the end of the eighteenth and beginning of the nineteenth centuries, social science proclaimed itself science and not philosophy. The justification of this deplorable split of knowledge into two hostile camps was that science was deemed to be empirical in its search for truth whereas philosophy was metaphysical, that is, speculative. This was an absurd distinction....

Immanuel Wallerstein[55]

A third disastrous waypoint on Western man's pilgrimage from one form of primitivism to another can be found in his foolish attempts to construct a wall separating the search for truth into two realms. The foundation was dug in the Renaissance, the wall erected fully during the Enlightenment. Sadly, Western man has continued to lay brick on it ever since with ever-escalating zeal.

A Russian Orthodox priest once declared, "The walls that divide us do not reach all the way to heaven." This wall is an attempt. Rejecting God and exalting himself, Western man took his version of a Solomonic decision and cut the infant of truth in half. Immanuel Wallerstein referred to this momentous and disastrous choice as the "deplorable split of knowledge." Wallerstein directs us to the most critical juncture in this severance—the Enlightenment. Decrying the severance of philosophy (and all forms of abstract, non-material understanding) from science, Wallerstein also debunks the foolishness and artificiality of this false dichotomy—a separation that has cost Western man a great deal and will surely cost him much more.

> When the rupture between science and philosophy became definitive at the end of the eighteenth and beginning of the nineteenth centuries, social science proclaimed itself science and not philosophy.... This was an absurd distinction, since all empirical knowledge has metaphysical foundations that are inescapable, and no metaphysics is worth considering unless it can be demonstrated to speak to this-worldly realities, which means that it must have empirical markers. In the effort to jump out of the frying pan of imposed, revealed truth, the intellectual class jumped into the fire of the mysticism of formal rationality.[56]

That the "intellectual class," as Wallerstein calls it, does not recognize this leap "into the fire of the mysticism of formal rationality" is an indication that something more is at work here than just obtuseness—a dynamic that has less to do with reason, albeit misguided, than with vanity, pride, and self-will. Wallerstein's analysis of how this deplorable state of affairs evolved begins with his question, "What was the sermon of the Enlightenment? It seems to me the essential message was anticlerical: humans were capable of rational judgment and hence had the ability to arrive at both truth and goodness directly, through their own best efforts. The Enlightenment represented the definitive rejection of religious authorities as judges of either truth or goodness." "But who," he queries, "became their substitutes?" "I suppose one has to say the philosophers." Yet these new arbiters had their own limitations, for "in the process of secularizing knowledge, the philosophers enshrined doubt, and this proved to be their own subsequent undoing." A perceptive modern Westerner could anticipate what happened next: "...along came the scientists to proclaim that the philosophers were merely disguised theologians. The scientists began to challenge the right of philosophers as well as of theologians to proclaim truth, asserting stridently that scientists were not philosophers." With the blind arrogance that always results from the hypertrophy of human vanity when stimulated by the steroids of prestige, praise, power, and the obsequious deference of others, the scientists "asserted that they [and they alone] possessed a firm basis for truth, that of empirical investigation leading to testable and tested hypotheses, to those provisional universals called scientific theorems." Though there is perhaps some basis for disputing him on this point, Wallerstein observed, "The scientists...wanted nothing to do with moral laws. They laid claim therefore to only one-half of the task the philosophers had inherited from the theologians. Scientists would search only for truth." Pompously and with an incredible obtuseness that belied their reputedly "inquiring minds," the scientists "suggested that [goodness] was 'uninteresting'" and "incapable of being an object of knowledge as science was defining knowledge." By the early nineteenth century, the "claims of the scientists that science represented the unique path to locate truth" had become enshrined as a secular gospel. Wallerstein further eviscerated the credibility of these claims by noting that simultaneously, "there was a small happening called the French Revolution" in which the Enlightenment-born and -bred "protagonists claimed they were acting in the furtherance of goodness." That this "furtherance of goodness" produced thousands of headless corpses says a great deal. Wallerstein then asserted that "As a result, we have spent the last two hundred years trying to reunite the search for truth and the search for goodness." But I assert that this is what should be, not what has been, or is. "Social science" proclaimed Wallerstein, "offered itself as the ground on which they could be reconciled." However, "social science has not been very successful in its quest since, rather than reunifying them, it has itself been torn apart by the dissonance between the two searches."[57]

Acutely aware that the infant of truth—real truth—cannot survive, much less grow, when cleft asunder, I advance its reunification as one of the key objectives of this book. Truth is in its infancy, despite Western man's depiction of it as a vigorous, mature product of science and technology; indeed, science and technology remain in a primitive state. Borrowing from Keats, we might express it this way: man must understand that not only is "beauty, truth," but beauty, truth, and goodness are all within the providence of God and any search for one cannot be severed from the search for the others—or the search for God. That is not "all ye know on earth, and all ye need to know," but it is a foundational principle.[58]

Wallerstein, in his unique way, explains the natural consequences of the false division. In a fusillade of contempt for *les grande illusions*, Wallerstein authoritatively declares that the search for truth should be singular, for we are all—in all our dimensions—part of the great whole of life and our universe.

> As long as the modern world seemed to be one long success story of technological triumph, the necessary political base to maintain a certain equilibrium in the system continued to exist.…Amid the success, the world of science was carried from honor to honor within this system, as though it were responsible for the triumph. The social sciences were swept along in the tide. No one was seriously questioning the fundamental premises of knowledge. The many maladies of the system from racism to sexism to colonialism as expressions of the manifestly growing polarization of the world, from fascist movements to socialist gulags to liberal formalisms as alternative modes of suppressing democratization—were all defined as transitory problems because they were all thought to be capable of being brought under control eventually, as so many turbulent deviations from the norm, in a world in which the trajectory always returned to the curve of linear upward-moving equilibrium.…The political persons on all sides promised that goodness was coming at the end of the horizon, a prospect presumably guaranteed by the continual progress in the search for truth.
>
> This was an illusion, the illusion bred by the separation and reification of the two cultures. Indeed the separation of the two cultures was one of the main factors pushing the trajectories far from equilibrium. Knowledge is in fact a singular enterprise, and there are no fundamental contradictions between how we may pursue it in the natural and in the human world, for they are both integral parts of a singular universe. Nor is knowledge separate from creativity or adventure or the search for the good society. To be sure, knowledge will always remain a pursuit, never a point of arrival.[59]

This "separation of the two cultures" as one of the "main factors pushing the trajectories far from equilibrium" is fundamental to our understanding of the disorder, chaos, and greater crisis of Western civilization. History, as Wallerstein adds his voice in pointing out, does not follow "the curve of linear upward-moving equilibrium." Yet this view remains sacrosanct among much of the intellectual elite of the West, who, in their determination to continue asserting it, must step ever so carefully over millions of corpses strewn in their path. But disregarding the odor of decaying flesh, the sound of human

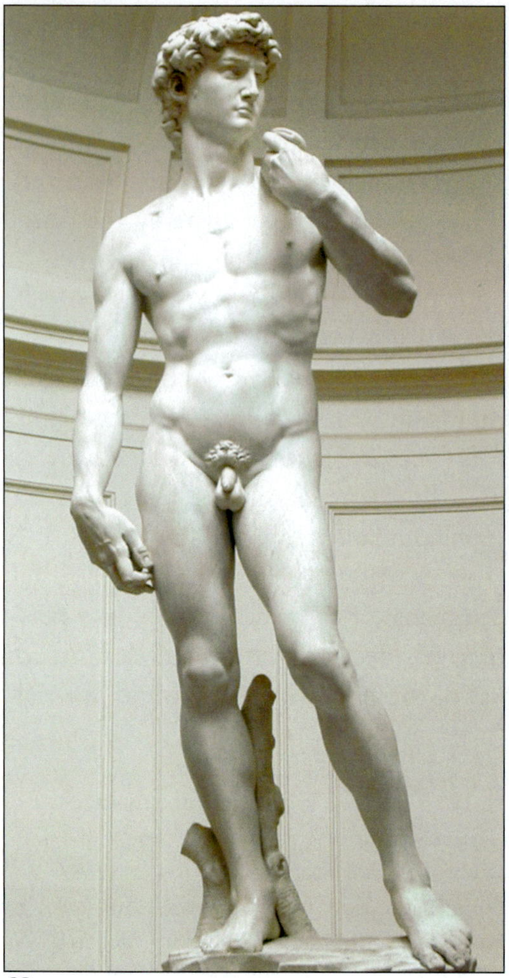

(Left) *David* by Michelangelo. *Francis Schaeffer referred to one of the most famous art works in history to reveal the new and exalted view of man that originated in the Renaissance. "The* David *was the statement of what the humanistic man saw himself as being tomorrow! In this statue we have man waiting with confidence in his own strength for the future. Even the disproportionate size of the hands says that man is powerful. This statue is idealistic and romantic. There was and is no man like the* David." (Right) Michelangelo's *Pietà*, 1499. *The romantic viewpoint of man reflected in the statute of David could not be sustained by Michelangelo in the face of reality. "There are signs," said Schaeffer, "that by the end of his life Michelangelo saw that humanism was not enough....Many of his early works show his humanism....In contrast, stand his later Pietàs (statues of Mary holding the dead Christ in her arms)...in Florence and...Milan..." "...in both of these Pietàs humanistic pride seems lessened, if not absent."*

screams, and a sea of tears must be done—or successfully rationalized away—if they are to retain their dominance in the culture. These are the Philistines "at the helm." They, with their political collaborators, have promised that there is reason for optimism if their values and world views continue to be embraced. Were the lie ever to become fully apparent, their demise as cultural leaders would be immediate. They are saved from exposure primarily by the itching ears of millions who are more than ready to live in the false security of delusion and denial. But their culpability warrants a penalty greater than removal from office as cultural or political leaders. The "separation of the two cultures" is their handiwork—and a bloody handiwork it has proven to be.

Christopher Dawson began tracing this scarlet thread in the Renaissance. We in the West "have become accustomed to taking the secular character of modern civilization for granted" with all of its narrow provincialism. We do so because "most of us [have] never known anything else and consequently we are apt to think that this is a natural and normal state of things." Even the religious have come to "not expect modern civilization to pay much attention to religion, still less to be based upon a religious conception of existence." Contrary to our assumptions, this is not a normal state but may be historically "unique." In all other cultures, in all other times, man's social existence has been seen as "dependent on another more permanent world, so that all human institutions were firmly anchored by faith and law to the realities of this higher world."[60]

That Dawson would use the adjective "abnormal" to describe the state of affairs in the West is an indicator of the alarm with which he viewed the West's predicament. Alarm is even more evident in the following passage: "…the very success of our civilization in terms of material wealth and technical achievement has led modern culture further and further from its spiritual center and has destroyed our sense of spiritual community. This divorce of culture from its spiritual foundations is the malady of our age and it may well be fatal to the society which gives way to it completely."[61]

Referring to a reality of human nature—and a concern that is at the very heart of our purposes here—Dawson helped us to see how Western man wanders into the wilderness that will spell his misery and his doom. "No doubt," Dawson declared, "it is very seldom that a society is clearly conscious of what is at stake. The issues are complicated by all kinds of social, economic, and political influences, so that the actual decision usually takes the form of a compromise." This is precisely the state of affairs in the West today: oblivious to the cancer eating away at the heart of the civilization, there is a relentless competition of ideas that serve at best to only palliate the symptoms, at worst to aggravate the disease. But by deluding himself into thinking these palliatives are the answer, Western man is led further from the cure. The greater depth is never acknowledged, but it is at this greater depth that "the creative activity which is the essence of the Christian life takes place" that is "far below the visible surface of culture"; and "the same thing is true of the spiritual failures and apostasies which are the other side of the picture." This of course is true across the board of human experience—religious or agnostic.

By this point in his pilgrimage it would seem that Western man would have become aware that something was wrong. Had he paused to humbly ponder he would likely have perceived a "cleavage" not unlike that described by an insightful American poet.

I felt a cleavage in my mind
As if my brain had split;
I tried to match it, seam by seam,
But could not make them fit.

The thought behind I strove to join
Unto the thought before,
But sequence raveled out of reach
Like balls upon a floor.

"I Felt a Cleavage in My Mind" by Emily Dickinson

If it is possible, Francis Schaeffer was even more relentless than Dawson, Solzhenitsyn, Wallerstein, or Toynbee in his attacks on the Renaissance/Enlightenment view of reality: "Beginning from man alone, Renaissance humanism—and humanism ever since—has found no way to arrive at universals or absolutes that give meaning to existence and morals."[62] Resorting to his formidable mastery of the history of art to illustrate his points, Schaeffer told us in this unique way what our other observers have told us in their distinctive philosophical dialects. Schaeffer referred to perhaps the greatest figure of Renaissance art, and one of the most famous art works in history, to reveal the new and exalted view of man. "The *David* was the statement of what the humanistic man saw himself as being tomorrow! In this statue we have man waiting with confidence in his own strength for the future. Even the disproportionate size of the hands says that man is powerful. This statue is idealistic and romantic. There was and is no man like the *David*." That romantic viewpoint could not be sustained by Michelangelo in the face of reality. Consequently, "there are signs that by the end of his life Michelangelo saw that humanism was not enough.…Many of his early works show his humanism, as does his *David*. In contrast stand his later Pietàs (statues of Mary holding the dead Christ in her arms) in the cathedral in Florence and in the castle in Milan, which was probably his last." Significantly, "In the Pietà in the cathedral in Florence, Michelangelo put his own face on Nicodemus (or Joseph of Arimathea—whichever the man is), and in both of these *Pietàs* humanistic pride seems lessened, if not absent."[63]

PD-art

Jan Hus in Council of Constance by Václav Broˇzík (1883). *Schaeffer observed, "In contrast to the humanistic elements which had come into the church—and which led to the authority of the church being accepted as equal to, or greater than, the authority of the Bible and which emphasized human work as a basis for meriting the merit of Christ—Hus returned to the teachings of the Bible and of the early church and stressed that the Bible is the only source of final authority and that salvation comes only through Christ and his work." Thus the Renaissance gave one answer to the problem of life, the Reformation another entirely. That the former panders to man's vanity and self-centered nature and the latter insists on human humility are undoubtedly reasons for their relative success and failure in Western civilization. The Catholic Church had been compromised by the influence of humanism in seeing itself as the ultimate spiritual authority—which was simply another, albeit more subtle, method of elevating individual men to the throne of life and the universe. Hus was burned at the stake.*

Nor could Renaissance thinkers make Christianity compatible with the view of man they chose to advance. "The early men of the Renaissance had tried to syncretize Christianity and Aristotelian thought, but had failed. Thereafter, men of the Renaissance tried to syncretize Christianity and Platonism—and likewise failed."[64]

With predictable monotony, we watch through Schaeffer's eyes the same pattern we have witnessed through the eyes of other historians, sociologists, and thinkers—with the same bleak result: "The humanists had been sure that man starting from himself could solve every problem. There was a complete faith in man.…But Leonardo, in his brilliance, saw at the end of his life humanism's coming defeat." Not only had he become conscious of this greater reality, "as an old man, Leonardo was in despondency. *As a man thinketh so is he*—and humanism had already begun to show that pessimism was its natural conclusion."[65]

We have noted earlier that four hundred years later Bertrand Russell would articulate a similar "natural conclusion" with the words, "only on the firm foundation of unyielding despair, can the soul's habitation henceforth be safely built." But even in the midst of the hubristic Renaissance ascendancy of man with a capital "M," other voices were offering another account of reality and man's purpose. "While the men of the Renaissance wrestled with the problem of what could give unity to life…the Reformation, was emerging in the north of Europe.…The High Renaissance in the south and the Reformation in the north must always be considered side by side. They dealt with the same basic problems, but they gave completely opposite answers and brought forth completely opposite results." Reformation thinkers did not accept the "split of knowledge" but saw the quest for truth as singular. Furthermore, "In contrast to the humanistic elements that had come into the church—and which led to the authority of the church being accepted as equal to, or greater than, the authority of the Bible and which emphasized human work as a basis for meriting the merit of Christ—Hus returned to the teachings of the Bible and of the early church and stressed that the Bible is the only source of final authority and that salvation comes only through Christ and his work."[66]

Thus the Renaissance gave one answer to the problem of life, the Reformation another entirely. That the former panders to man's vanity and self-centered nature and the latter insists on human humility are undoubtedly reasons for their relative success and failure in Western civilization.

The Catholic Church had been compromised by the influence of humanism in seeing itself as the ultimate spiritual authority—which was simply another, albeit more subtle, method of elevating individual men to the throne of life and the universe. The Reformers "came to see that the church founded by Christ had since been marred by distortions." In like manner, the church, Catholic and Protestant, has become, in myriad ways, similarly compromised in Western civilization today. Prudently, humbly, the Reformers "in contrast to the Renaissance humanists…refused to accept the autonomy of human reason, which acts as though the human mind is infinite, with all knowledge within its realm."[67] For them, "authority was not divided between the Bible and the church. The church was under the teaching of the Bible—not above it and not equal to it. It was *Sola Scriptura*, the Scriptures only. This stood in contrast to the humanism that had infiltrated the church after the first centuries of Christianity. At its core, therefore, the Reformation was the removing of the humanistic distortions which had entered the church." Schaeffer acknowledged specific failures of the Reformation movement even as he affirmed its ineffably important achievements. "The Reformation…far from perfect, and in many ways it did not act consistently with the Bible's teaching, although the Reformers were trying to make the Bible their standard not only in religion but in all of life." Schaeffer specified "such overwhelming mistakes…as Luther's unbalanced position in regard to the peasant wars, and the Reformers showed little zeal for reaching people in other parts of the world…."[68]

Perhaps, it might be speculated, the ease with which Luther and the Reformers slid into worldly transgressions—especially when the nature of those transgressions is noted—was itself a consequence of the preceding generations of the church leadership wandering from the fold of Christ's teaching and the model of the first-century church. Rather than benefiting from an unbroken line of sound spiritual DNA, the Reformers suffered infirmities brought on by the mutations of the church—even as, with alarm, they began to recognize and reject many of those mutations. Can we not anticipate similar errors in our time—assuming, that is, that reform ever comes to the Western church?

"Because the Reformers did not mix humanism with their position…they had no problem of meaning…." Whereas "the Renaissance centered in autonomous man…the Reformation centered in the infinite-personal God…." Thus, "the problem of meaning…did not exist."[69]

Schaeffer's flat declaration of the true foundation of the Renaissance and the Enlightenment—a conclusion reached by several of our observers—would define the pathetic were it not to become the calculus of chaos and suffering. "The utopian dream of the Enlightenment can be summed up by five words: reason, nature, happiness, progress, and liberty. It was thoroughly secular in its thinking. The humanistic elements that had risen during the Renaissance came to flood tide in the Enlightenment. Here was man starting from himself absolutely."[70]

Once again, we have an example of the consequences of this choice—yet the lesson was not learned in the late eighteenth century and was to be repeated elsewhere over a century later in near identical form: "The men of the French Enlightenment had no base but their own finiteness. They...tried to build without the Christian base, and ended with a massacre and Napoleon as authoritarian ruler."[71] "As in the later Russian Revolution the revolutionaries on their humanist base had only two options —anarchy or repression."[72]

In an analysis Solzhenitsyn would have applauded, Schaeffer explained the turbulence that this line of thought brings in its wake. "Today not only in philosophy but in politics, government, and individual morality, our generation sees solutions in terms of synthesis and not absolutes. When this happens, truth, as people had always thought of truth, has died." But reason without God leads inevitably to complete pessimism, and "one must try to find optimistic answers in regard to meaning and values on an 'upper level' outside of reason." With an ironic but entirely appropriate choice of words, this requires a "leap of faith" in order "to find meaning without reason."[73]

Determinism is a logical terminus to the humanistic thought trail. Yet, determinism nullifies man.

It "affirms that there is only the cosmic machine, which encompasses everything, including people."[74] The absurdity of this was illustrated by Schaeffer through reference to the West's most famous literary figure: "Four hundred years ago there was a collection of molecules named Shakespeare which produced *Hamlet.*"[75]

In one of the more significant observations that undermine this foolishness, Schaeffer asked, "What was the beginning of everything?"

> Ultimately, there are not many possible answers to this question. First, we could say that everything came from nothing—that is, from *really* nothing, what I call *nothing-nothing.* This means that once there was no mass, no energy, no motion, and no personality. This is theoretically a possibility, but I have never heard anyone hold this view, for it seems to be unthinkable. It follows that if we do not hold that everything has come of nothing-nothing, then something has always existed.[76]

This leads to an obvious question—one that is never satisfactorily answered by the modern proponents of the Renaissance and Enlightenment view of reality.

> This equation of the impersonal plus time plus chance producing the total configuration of the universe and all that is in it, modern people hold by faith. And if one does in faith accept this, with what final value is he left? In his lecture at Acapulco, George Wald finished with only one final value. It was the same one with which English philosopher Bertrand Russell (1872–1970) was left. For Wald and Russell and for many other modern thinkers, the final value is the biological continuity of the human race. If this is the only final value, one is left wondering why this then has importance.[77]

Why would this be important? Who authoritatively declares it important? Does man? But who is man to make such a self-serving declaration? From his four score years juxtaposed with the life of the universe how does he reach such a conclusion? He neither created the universe nor controls it. What gargantuan hubris gives him the right to reach such a conclusion? The answer to all of this is as pathetic as the belief system is vacuous. It rests on two features of human nature: first, man's pridefulness and vanity; and, second, his need to believe in something. Thus he strives to satisfy the latter without relinquishing the former. Since the former (i.e., he, himself) is of ultimate importance to him, the "biological continuity of the human race" is all that is left. With this logic man destroys everything:

love, faith, hope, understanding, and meaning. Yet man craves these things—indeed, he deeply needs them—so he attempts to create them through his own contrivance that becomes the great unacknowledged absurdity of his existence.

Somewhat ironically, Schaeffer told us that the great minds of the Renaissance would not have gone so far as this—such was a descending branch on the path to be taken by others during the Enlightenment. Renaissance thinkers would have considered it "intellectual suicide to separate meaning and values from reason in this way.…Such a solution is intellectual suicide, and one may question the intellectual integrity of those who accept such a position.…"[78]

THE LAST—PERHAPS THE FINAL—SIGNPOST

At the very moment that man was at last acquiring control over his material environment, he was abandoning the ideal of spiritual order and leaving the new economic forces to develop uncontrolled without any higher social direction.
Christopher Dawson[79]

Having passed these abysmal waypoints on his pilgrimage, Western man must then confront the challenges and the appalling horrors of the twentieth century. With the continuation of the descent into what Schaeffer called "non-reason," Western man was now desperate for meaning. This desperation was manifest in a particular way at the time of Schaeffer's writing in the mid-1970s. It loiters around the periphery of Western civilization still. "The next accepted version in the West of life in the area of non-reason was the religious experience of Hinduism and Buddhism." This arrived "floodlike into the West with Huxley and the emphasis on drugs, for it followed naturally in the line of what people had been putting into the area of non-reason in the hope of finding meaning and values. Young people (and older ones) tried the drug trip and then turned to the Eastern religious trip. Both seek truth inside one's own head and both negate reason."[80]

Like an epidemiologist tracking the rise of HIV from equatorial jungles, we can see how the viruses of the Renaissance and Enlightenment spread throughout the West. Schaeffer asserted there were three methods by which carriers spread the contagion: "*Geographically,* it spread from the European mainland to England, after a time jumping the Atlantic to the United States. *Culturally,* it spread in the various disciplines from philosophy to art, to music, to general culture (the novel, poetry, drama, films), and to theology. *Socially,* it spread from the intellectuals to the educated and then through the mass media to everyone."[81]

This remains an accurate depiction of the state of the West: a people acting out a lifestyle forged largely through habit and tradition, yet devoid of any deep, abiding spiritual conviction. Like Pavlov's dog, Western man responds in predictable ways to certain stimuli without really knowing why.

In a passage reminiscent of Solzhenitsyn, Schaeffer described the practical end result of this sterile evolution: "…the majority of people adopted two impoverished values: personal peace and affluence."

> Personal peace means just to be let alone, not to be troubled by the troubles of other people, whether across the world or across the city—to live one's life with minimal possibilities of being personally

Photograph by Ivy Scarborough

The Kremlin, Moscow. *Strikingly prominent in this bastion of atheism are the numerous crosses on spires. Communism collapsed and Christianity is experiencing renewal in Russia. Toynbee observed, "...if our secular Western civilization perishes, Christianity may be expected not only to endure but to grow in wisdom and stature as the result of a fresh experience of secular catastrophe."*

> disturbed....Personal peace means wanting to have my personal life pattern undisturbed in my lifetime, regardless of what the result will be in the lifetimes of my children and grandchildren. Affluence means an overwhelming and ever-increasing prosperity—a life made up of things, things, and more things—a success judged by an ever-higher level of material abundance.[82]

The appalling self-centeredness implicit in Schaeffer's description can be metaphorically described as porcine myopia. A pig is perhaps the only one of the few social animals that will ignore his fellows—even their screams of pain—as long as he is unmolested and his trough is full. "Why be educated?" Schaeffer quoted the mid- to late-twentieth-century young person as asking. The answer, explicit or implicit: "Because statistically an educated man makes so much more money a year." Should the inquirer wonder why this was important: "Why make more money?" The answer was, "So that you can send *your* children to the university." Schaeffer noted that "according to this kind of spoken or implied answer, there was no meaning for man, and no meaning for education."[83] The work ethic, without its original spiritual basis, means there is "no reason to work and no values to determine what to do with the products of one's work."[84]

Though Schaeffer did not say it, without that basis every other possible motive becomes, in one way or another, a self-centered pursuit of nothingness, whether it is status, prestige or achievement in one's

PD

Coronation of Napoleon, by Jacques-Louis David. *Like Napoleon placing the crown on his own head, Western man has effectively made himself emperor and the center of his world. Like Napoleon, if he does not choose to humbly accept his true status, his fall will be complete and his tragedy unprecedented in world history.*

field for "the good of humanity." The dissipations spawned by this meaninglessness were, initially at least, concealed behind a diaphanous screen of philosophical/ideological purpose. But in time, even that charade largely ended—it exists today though in a highly diluted form—and dissipation became simply distraction. Thus drugs, for example, went from a philosophical "statement" back to the artificial escape drugs and alcohol have always afforded the individual without real meaning.

Schaeffer expressed his dismay and grief that the younger generation did not continue the search for meaning that their parents had never seriously pursued. The generation of the men in the "gray flannel suits" was, in the natural course of time, supplanted by seekers, but *seekers without stamina and without courage.* "The young people had been right in their analysis, though wrong in their solutions. How much worse when many gave up hope and simply accepted the same values as their parents—personal peace and affluence." Drugs remained, "but only in parallel to the older generation's alcohol." "Promiscuous sex and bisexuality remain, but only in parallel to the older generation's adultery." This pilgrimage went nowhere good: "as the young people revolted against their parents, they came around in a big circle—and often ended an inch lower—with only the same two impoverished values: their own kind of personal peace and their own kind of affluence."[85]

Having capitulated, they not only never found the way out of the swamp created by the Renaissance/ Enlightenment abasement of man, they "ended an inch lower" in the quicksand than their parents.

Swimming upstream was not for them; there was no recourse now but to be swept along with the current of pursuit of personal peace, pleasure, status, and materialism. What else would suffice to stoke their denial and self-delusion?

Some of this generation, as had some of their parents, found "answers" in Marxism–Leninism. Communism might even be perceived as almost an inevitable result of the humanism spawned by the Renaissance/Enlightenment view of reality. Its beckoning promise ended, however, in the harsh reality—one that the Christian religion predicted—that "wherever Marxist–Leninism has had power, it has at no place in history shown where it has not brought forth oppression. As soon as they have had the power, the desire of the majority has become a concept without meaning."[86]

We have been diligent in pointing out that even the desire of the majority will prove a tyranny when divorced from transcendent meaning and moral laws. Yet the pursuit of the moonbeams continues as a means by which to light the way of Western man.

Dawson made it clear that "at the very moment that man was at last acquiring control over his material environment, he was abandoning the ideal of spiritual order and leaving the new economic forces to develop uncontrolled without any higher social direction."[87] The "creative element in human culture is spiritual," he declared. Furthermore, if "the materialist interpretation of history were true, the scientific intellectualization of nature could no more have arisen than could the metaphysical intuition of reality, and without science there could be no machine order."[88]

In these observations, Dawson was congruent with Wallerstein and Spengler. For all of them, the material order is impossible without a higher spiritual order. "For the machine is a proof not of the subordination of mind to matter, but of the subordination of matter to mind....it is itself a vindication of spiritual order, since it frees man from his age-long animal condition of dependence on nature and material circumstance. But if the scientific order is to realize this ideal, it must be related to spiritual ends and must form part of a wider spiritual order."[89] Authoritatively, Dawson declared, "Material organization alone is incapable of saving civilization. Left to itself it may easily become a destructive force which is hostile alike to spiritual values and to human freedom. True civilization is essentially a spiritual order, and its criterion is not material wealth, but spiritual vision."[90]

As we approach our own time in tracing the legacy of the Renaissance and Enlightenment, Sorokin explained why, though the decay is advanced, the edifice has not yet come tumbling down: "...if the ethical system of Christianity had not continued to linger during these sensate centuries, the disastrous results of our sensate ethics would probably have occurred much earlier than they occurred in fact, and their destructive effect would probably have been more terrible than it has been up to the present day."[91] Suffice it to say—with great irony—that "the stone the builders rejected"[92] is holding up what remains. Toynbee viewed this issue as so critical that he ended his manifesto, *Civilization on Trial*, with these words:

> ...[F]or the spiritual side of man's life is of vastly greater importance for man's well-being (even for his material well-being, in the last resort) than is his command over non-human nature. On such a view, this world would not be a spiritual exercise ground beyond the pale of the Kingdom of God; it would be a province of the Kingdom—one province only, and not the most important one, yet one which had the same absolute value as the rest, and therefore one in which spiritual action could, and

> would, be fully significant and worth while; the one thing of manifest and abiding value in a world in which all other things are vanity.[93]

That this great historian—steeped as he was in not simply the facts but the painful, hemorrhaging lessons of world history—should reach such a conclusion and offer it as a warning, clashes starkly with the bleak philosophical aridity and spiritual sterility of modern Western civilization.

If the Renaissance granted to man a standing in the universe that was not his due, the Enlightenment apotheosized him. Like Napoleon placing the crown on his own head, Western man declared himself emperor of the world. Like Napoleon, if he does not choose to remove it and humbly accept his true status, his fall will be complete and his tragedy unprecedented in world history.

All that we know about this path Western man has taken to a New Dark Age suggests not a purely intellectual problem or knowledge deficit, but a blindness born of some other cause—something related to Western man's character, his heart. He will not see because he chooses to not see. Thus his culpability for his predicament is all the greater.

Such "thinking" is beneath the honest seeker's contempt. The sincere seeker of truth will not reach such a cul-de-sac without acknowledging it, turning about face, and taking another course. Those who persist in this state of blind self-congratulation are demonstrating not simply their own intellectual obtuseness but, to use a biblical term, "the hardness of their hearts." Truly "The fool hath said in his heart 'There is no God.'" (Psalms 14:1 KJV) We might add by inference a corollary that could be penned specifically for modern Western man: The fool hath said in his heart that man is the sum of all.

Because of his foolish choices on this 700-year pilgrimage, Western man is behind. The vaunted sophistication and advancement that he believes characterize his accomplishments are in fact narrow in their application and dangerous in their consequences precisely because his growth, such as it is, has been grossly disproportionate. He is, as we previously observed, in General Omar Bradley's famous indictment, a technological giant and a moral midget. A humble willingness to recognize this is an absolutely essential precursor to changing it. Western man's destiny hinges on his willingness to leave the Renaissance/Enlightenment path he has taken to the New Dark Age and take another path entirely: the path of humility.

END NOTES
CHAPTER 15

1 Francis A. Schaeffer, *How Should We Then Live? The Rise and Decline of Western Thought and Culture* (Wheaton, IL: Crossway Books, 1976), 55.
2 Alexander Solzhenitsyn, Text of Address at Harvard Class Day Afternoon Exercises, Thursday, June 8, 1978.
3 Christopher Dawson, *Christianity and the New Age* (Sophia Institute Press 1985), 10.
4 C. S. Lewis, *The Screwtape Letters* (New York: Macmillan, 1964), 60–61.
5 Christopher Dawson, *Religion and World History* (Garden City, NY: A Division of Doubleday & Company, Inc., 1975), 296.
6 Christopher Dawson, *The Historic Reality of Christian Culture* (New York: Harper & Brothers, 1960), 79.
7 Immanuel Wallerstein, *The End of the World As We Know It: Social Science for the Twenty-First Century* (Minneapolis: University of Minnesota Press, 1999), 205.
8 Arnold Toynbee, *Civilization on Trial* (New York: Oxford University Press, 1948), 85.
9 Toynbee, *Civilization on Trial*, 85–86.
10 Toynbee, *Civilization on Trial*, 85–86.
11 Arnold Toynbee, *A Study of History* (New York: Weathervane Books, 1972), 348.
12 Toynbee, *A Study of History*, 348.
13 Schaeffer, *How Should We Then Live?*, 148.
14 Dawson, *Christianity and the New Age*, 7.
15 Dawson, *Christianity and the New Age*, 7–9.
16 William Blake, cited in Malcolm Muggeridge, *Confessions of a Twentieth Century Pilgrim* (New York: HarperCollins, 1988), 43.
17 William Blake, cited in Muggeridge, *Confessions*, 45.
18 Dawson, *Religion and World History*, 296.
19 Dawson, *Christianity and the New Age*, 9–10.
20 Solzhenitsyn, Harvard Class Day.
21 Solzhenitsyn, Harvard Class Day.
22 Solzhenitsyn, Harvard Class Day.
23 Robert Conquest, *Reflections on a Ravaged Century* (New York: W. W. Norton, 2001), 212.
24 Pitirim A. Sorokin, *The Crisis of Our Age* (Oneworld Publications Ltd., 1941; this edition Sergei P. Sorokin and Peter P. Sorokin, 1992), 109.
25 Sorokin, *Crisis of Our Age*, 114.
26 Sorokin, *Crisis of Our Age*, 115.
27 Dawson, *Religion and World History*, 192.
28 Dawson, *Religion and World History*, 192.
29 Dawson, *Religion and World History*, 200–201.
30 Dawson, *Religion and World History*, 200–201.
31 St. Augustine, *Confessions*. Translated by Edward Bouverie Pusey (Oxford: Clark, 1876), 1.1.1.
32 Blaise Pascal, *Pensees #425*. Translated by Hugh Fraser Stewart (London, Routledge and Kegan Paul, 1950).
33 Schaeffer, *How Should We Then Live?*, 121.
34 Dawson, *Religion and World History*, 220.
35 Dawson, *Religion and World History*, 224.
36 Dawson, *Religion and World History*, 226.
37 Dawson, *Religion and World History*, 226–227.
38 Dawson, *Religion and World History*, 229.

39 Dawson, *Religion and World History*, 243–244.
40 Dawson, *Religion and World History*, 249.
41 Jean-Paul Sartre, *Existentialism Is a Humanism*. Translated by Carol Macomber (Yale University Press, 2007), 28.
42 Dawson, *Religion and World History*, 312–313.
43 Dawson, *Religion and World History*, 318.
44 Dawson, *Religion and World History*, 318.
45 Dawson, *Religion and World History*, 319–320.
46 Dawson, *Christianity and the New Age*, 58.
47 Dawson, *Christianity and the New Age*, 58–60.
48 Schaeffer, *How Should We Then Live?*, 147.
49 Schaeffer, *How Should We Then Live?*, 147–148.
50 Schaeffer, *How Should We Then Live?*, 148.
51 Schaeffer, *How Should We Then Live?*, 150.
52 Dawson, *Religion and World History*, 296.
53 Schaeffer, *How Should We Then Live?*, 151.
54 Schaeffer, *How Should We Then Live?*, 151.
55 Wallerstein, *The End of the World As We Know It*, 155.
56 Wallerstein, *The End of the World As We Know It*, 155.
57 Wallerstein, *The End of the World As We Know It*, 205–206.
58 John Keats, *Ode on a Grecian Urn* (Houghton Mifflin Co., 1901), 14.
59 Wallerstein, *The End of the World As We Know It*, 212.
60 Christopher Dawson, *The Historic Reality of Christian Culture* (New York: Harper & Brothers, 1960), 79.
61 Dawson, *Historic Reality*, 94.
62 Schaeffer, *How Should We Then Live?*, 55.
63 Schaeffer, *How Should We Then Live?*, 72.
64 Schaeffer, *How Should We Then Live?*, 74 and 78.
65 Schaeffer, *How Should We Then Live?*, 78.
66 Schaeffer, *How Should We Then Live?*, 79–80.
67 Schaeffer, *How Should We Then Live?*, 81.
68 Schaeffer, *How Should We Then Live?*, 82.
69 Schaeffer, *How Should We Then Live?*, 84.
70 Schaeffer, *How Should We Then Live?*, 121.
71 Schaeffer, *How Should We Then Live?*, 122.
72 Schaeffer, *How Should We Then Live?*, 124.
73 Schaeffer, *How Should We Then Live?*, 163.
74 Schaeffer, *How Should We Then Live?*, 164.
75 Schaeffer, *How Should We Then Live?*, 164.
76 Schaeffer, *How Should We Then Live?*, 164–165.
77 Schaeffer, *How Should We Then Live?*, 165–166.
78 Schaeffer, *How Should We Then Live?*, 166.
79 Dawson, *Christianity and the New Age*, 95.
80 Schaeffer, *How Should We Then Live?*, 170–171.
81 Schaeffer, *How Should We Then Live?*, 182.
82 Schaeffer, *How Should We Then Live?*, 205.
83 Schaeffer, *How Should We Then Live?*, 205–206.
84 Schaeffer, *How Should We Then Live?*, 206.
85 Schaeffer, *How Should We Then Live?*, 210.
86 Schaeffer, *How Should We Then Live?*, 215.

87 Dawson, *Christianity and the New Age*, 95.
88 Dawson, *Christianity and the New Age*, 97–98.
89 Dawson, *Christianity and the New Age*, 98.
90 Dawson, *Christianity and the New Age*, 98.
91 Sorokin, *Crisis of Our Age*, 212.
92 Jesus said to them, "Have you never read in the Scriptures: 'The stone the builders rejected has become the capstone; the Lord has done this, and it is marvelous in our eyes'?" (Matthew 21:42 NIV)
93 Toynbee, *Civilization on Trial*, 263.

CHAPTER

16

HYPERVELOCITY—THE TURNING OF THE WHEEL OF HISTORY IN OUR AGE

There is no doubt that the world is on the move again and that the pace is faster and more furious than anything that man has known before.
Christopher Dawson[1]

The more decadent it becomes, the more imitative it grows and the swifter becomes the tempo of the successive phases of the process.
Pitirim Sorokin[2]

The wicked war-god rages everywhere.
The pace is quickening like the chariots' pace
When they burst out to speed along the course.
No use, poor charioteer, to draw thy reins.
Thy chariot's masters are thy racing steeds.
Virgil, *Georgics*[3]

Toynbee referred to the wheel as the "original simile and permanent symbol of the cyclic philosophy" of history. That there are repetitions and redundancy—"there is nothing new under the sun"—in history suggests two especially important principles: that human nature—as we have observed—does not change, and that we truly can learn from man's past experience since we can expect man to tend to repeat his choices. All prior studies of civilizations' declines depict a movement that was gradual and incremental with occasional desultory dramatic leaps. Decline and decay has always been tracked in terms of centuries and generations, not decades or years.

There is, however, a difference in our age: The speed with which the wheel of history is turning has never been faster. This will dramatically affect the outcome of trends and events in an unprecedented fashion.

Prediction will be more difficult. Whereas human behavior is highly predictable when seen in the context of history and the study of social sciences such as psychology and sociology, this new factor—or hypervelocity as I shall call it to denote its excess—to some extent confounds the process of anticipating what may happen next, or, especially, the probable timing of what may happen next.

Every dimension of human experience has been affected by this acceleration—usually to the negative. The acceleration has diminished the individual's ability simply to cope. Circumstances are changing and events are moving—in relation to the individual's ability to think lucidly and reflectively, react prudently, and sustain his attentiveness and endurance—at hypervelocity. Intellectual, physical, and moral resources are at risk of being overwhelmed. Some will be inherently better equipped to deal with the pace, but most risk being winded by the race emotionally, physically, and intellectually, as long as they persist in trying to keep up with the momentum of Western culture. Even those who have greater reserves of energy and remarkably efficient neurons and synapses will not be able to sustain the pace indefinitely or in all respects, especially if the acceleration is unrelenting—as it will likely prove to be.

This makes every problem Western man faces more intractable, not necessarily in and of itself, but simply because needles cannot be threaded on the backs of racing steeds, and the moral and philosophic imperative of reflection and contemplation cannot be achieved in a cacophony of sound and a blur of images.

The reticulated python of an increasingly complex culture is gradually enveloping Western man in its coils. Minds already reeling from sensory overload and a surfeit of complex circumstances cannot adequately address any of it. Resort to science and technology to cope—ironically, the primary perpetrators of the offence—will only go so far. Each new scientific and technological development that offers promise of relief in one area will only exacerbate the dilemma in other areas. Man will eventually no longer fully control his creation.

The phenomenon of hypervelocity afflicts Western man in three related ways: First, in his state of mind—a psychically induced condition produced by Western man's loss of meaning and purpose in his highly materialistic and sensate culture. This internal restlessness impels him to more strenuous efforts in pursuit of his unfulfilling goals, be they wealth, pleasure, prestige, social acceptance or power. Western man is obsessed with materialism; he always wants more in one way or another. But his resulting choices produce an ever-increasing complexity that exacerbates the problem. In order to cope with the growing complexity and achieve his goals Western man is impelled to ever more frenzied efforts and greater exertions. This manifests itself in a cyclical and relentlessly self-perpetuating greater and greater complexity of the society and economies, which leads invariably to impulses toward more governmental and legal regulation to deal with the complexity. Each generation experiences this escalation.

Second, technologically induced speed is the self-evident product of science and technology. This contributes exponentially to the ever-increasing complexity and demands of the individual a concomitant striving to keep up. Third, the historical, ever-quickening pace of events is largely a product of the interaction of the preceding two.

ACCELERATING THE PACE—THE RESTLESS WESTERN PSYCHE

When we are unable to find tranquility within ourselves, it is useless to seek it elsewhere.
La Rochefoucauld[4]

As we have seen, Carroll Quigley in *Evolution of Civilizations* noted one manifestation of the first form of hypervelocity in his description of one of the late stages of a decaying civilization, "All the characteristics of an age of irrationality [begin] to appear on all sides—increased gambling, increased smoking, the growing use of alcohol and narcotics, a growing obsession with sex and with perversions of sex, an increasing mania for speed, for nervous tension, and for noise...."[5]

The emphasis on speed and activity are, in large part, the external behavioral explication of the psychic unrest. Symptomatic rather than causative, these characteristics exacerbate the underlying cause of today's obsession with speed and activity. Unconsciously fearing the black horse of meaninglessness and despair bearing down on him, Western man must move faster and faster in an unrelenting quest for distraction.

These phenomena also have a bearing on the pace of decay. Historically, that pace would typically be that of a slow growing cancer. However, Toynbee was referring to the example of the disintegration of ancient Egypt, when he noted that the pace of decay may vary: "...disintegration, like growth, is not a single act but a process in time, and, as such, susceptible to changes in tempo."[6]

Sorokin related the acceleration of disintegration to his concept of sensate culture. The individual and the culture that sees their world in sensate terms will inevitably be focused on short-term gain. "Hence the sensate *carpe diem*, 'seize the day'...because only present values can be grasped. As the tempo of change accelerates, this 'present' grows ever shorter and more transitory. To the same source is attributable the stupendous role of time in the life and activities of such a society....[T]ime flies, time changes and we change with it—and...time consumes all things—become the mottoes...."[7]

Sorokin also made reference to decadence in the arts producing an ever-faster momentum: "The more decadent it becomes, the more imitative it grows and the swifter becomes the tempo of the successive phases of the process."[8] The individual focused on eternal values has less need of intense consciousness of the passage of time. His pace will tend to reflect patience and endurance rather than anxiety and haste. I have been struck many times in different cultures with their relative indifference to time and the absence of any sense of urgency. Western man reacts to these attitudes and behaviors as if they are an anomaly without stopping to consider that perhaps his own attitudes and behaviors are of dubious merit or psychic healthfulness.

When the measures of "success," "achievement," and meaning become moral, spiritual, and characterological rather than material and sensate, then speed, anxiety, and urgency diminish to near irrelevance.

ACCELERATING THE PACE THROUGH SCIENCE AND TECHNOLOGY

Thus it is no accident that the period that has seen the culmination of the modern development of scientific and economic power should have brought Western civilisation to the brink of ruin. For it is our power that is our destruction, and the world is drunk and poisoned with power, as primitive peoples have been poisoned by the gin and germs and gunpowder of a more advanced civilisation.
Christopher Dawson[9]

The increased speed of events coupled with what Christopher Dawson called the "breathless advance in population, wealth, and knowledge" inevitably exacerbates many of mankind's problems and creates new ones, even as much of it is intended—and always touted—as ameliorative. Lest one

PD

The Chariot Race, by Alexander von Wagner, Munich, about 1882.

The wicked war-god rages everywhere.
The pace is quickening like the chariots' pace
When they burst out to speed along the course.
No use, poor charioteer, to draw thy reins.
Thy chariot's masters are thy racing steeds.

Virgil's poem reflects the state of our world. We can see from historical precedents that decay and decline accelerate as they advance; and that no era in world history has brought a faster pace than our own.The significance of this, to those who would be willing to recognize the path that Western civilization has taken, is that time is of the essence. The window of opportunity to avert the worst of consequences is small and growing smaller each day. Time—like the evils that exploit it—is not on our side.

see the advance in knowledge, science and technology as the solution, Dawson's final comment in the passage above, "…it is our power that is our destruction," should dispose of the notion. The science and technology that man relies upon to address so many of his problems is in fact the progenitor, directly or indirectly, of many of those problems—and some new ones.

But perhaps nowhere is this more apparent than in twenty-first-century weaponry and war fighting. Though the threat of modern weaponry of mass destruction—nuclear, biological, and chemical—is often discussed, there is a rarely observed phenomenon now menacing modern Western military commanders: the speed and power of weaponry coupled with prodigious amounts of information and intelligence that push command and control and prudent decision making beyond human capacities. Marine Colonel Thomas X. Hammes wrote of this trend in his book *The Sling and the Stone*, "Although change is constant, the rate of change is not. It has been accelerating almost exponentially. We can see that acceleration in the rate of development and adoption of new thoughts, processes, and technologies in all areas of human endeavor."[10]

In the most explicit illustration of machines accelerating the pace to a point that is unmanageable—if even understandable—by the slow-thinking and reacting human being, Dr. Thomas K. Adams, a strategist and retired U.S. Army colonel, wrote for the U.S. Army War College, "In short, the military systems (including weapons) now on the horizon will be too fast, too small, too numerous, and will create an environment too complex for humans to direct. Furthermore, the proliferation of information-based systems will produce a data overload that will make it difficult or impossible for humans to directly intervene in decisionmaking. This is not a consideration for the remote science-fiction future."

Man will not necessarily be in charge of his own weapons and, even if he nominally is, his inability to keep up will produce a form of perilous incompetence: "Humans may retain symbolic authority, but automated systems move too fast and the factors involved are too complex for real human comprehension. When computers are designed and programmed by other computers, the situation will be even further from anything humans can reasonably expect to understand, much less intervene in successfully."[11]

Genetically related to this dangerous and daunting problem are the environmental concerns that plague the planet. Man's science and technology are believed to be the proximate cause of global warming, the proliferation of pollutants in every dimension of the environment, and the profligacy with which nature's resources are exploited. None of this could occur—at least to the extent seen in the twenty-first century—without the much touted advances in science and technology upon which Western man so heavily relies for his power, his wealth, and the satisfaction of his ego needs. The underlying original causes of these dangerous phenomena are the oft-uncited, oft-unobserved psychological and spiritual states from which they spring.

ACCELERATING THE PACE—THE SPREAD OF THE PATHOLOGICAL AND DEBASED IN THOUGHT AND BELIEF

Modern pessimism and modern fragmentation, have spread... Geographically... Culturally... Socially... from the intellectuals to the educated and then through the mass media to everyone.
Francis Schaeffer[12]

As unsettling as these revelations are, we should be most concerned with the underlying psychological and spiritual phenomena: the values, beliefs, and world views that are also mutating at an increasingly rapid pace. For it is within the mind of man that our most daunting problems and dismal failures originate.

Francis Schaeffer, who focused on tracing the decline of Western values culturally, made reference to a key factor in the scope and rapidity of the decline. In discussing the spread of modern pessimism (i.e., the loss of a rational belief in God and moral absolutes that necessitate resort to the ersatz forms of "optimism" so in vogue in the modern West) Schaeffer alluded to a major, if not primary, accelerant: the mass media.

> Modern pessimism and modern fragmentation, have spread in three different ways to people of our own culture and to people across the world. Geographically, it spread from the European mainland to England, after a time jumping the Atlantic to the United States. Culturally, it spread in the various disciplines from philosophy to art, to music, to general culture (the novel, poetry, drama, films), and to theology. Socially, it spread from the intellectuals to the educated and then through the mass media to everyone.[13]

Frank E. Webner. PD

CC

Pony Express Rider, circa 1861. Morse Telegraph Key, 1880. *Ideas, beliefs, values, images, and concepts that may be deleterious to the social health of our culture are now far more dangerous precisely because of the vast scope and technological speed of communication now available, especially via the mass media. Were this a Pony Express and telegraph world, the impact of the communications on the culture at large would be minimal. In the twenty-first century, the impact is exponentially multiplied. This will only worsen.*

It would be impossible to overstate the role of the mass media in communicating contemporary values and worldview. Schaeffer's observations are completely consistent with the "sensate" culture of Sorokin's descriptions and the *pammixia* of Toynbee's. As part of the "dominant minority" in Western culture, media executives, commentators, entertainers, and artists reflect their worldview in their decisions, their behavior, and their products.

Lest we seem to stray from our theme, the point of the discussion is the speed at which this promulgation takes place—precisely because of the vast scope and technological speed of communication now available, especially via the mass media. Were this a Pony Express and telegraph world, the impact of the communications on the culture at large would be minimal. In the twenty-first century the impact is exponentially multiplied. This will only replicate and multiply.

There is in medicine an analogue to Western man's predicament in this regard. Blessed as he is by the technology of fast and distant air travel, his contemplation of the negative consequences or threats from this boon is typically limited to the obvious—airplane crashes. However, epidemiologists traced what is believed to be the course of HIV from the jungles of Africa and into the mainstream of Western civilization via air travel. This remarkable development is noteworthy not simply because scientists believe HIV had languished in those jungles for millennia, but for the speed at which it has been transmitted since escaping its primitive redoubt—requiring, as it does, specific human behaviors before it can spread.

Similarly, the debased and culturally unhealthful can spread in the Information Age like the concussive wave from an exploding bomb. Western man's very success in the material realm of the scientific and technological has made the proliferation of the worst in human thought and behavior all the more complete and rapid. The themes and depictions of violence, sexual obsessions and perversions, pornography, greed and obsessive materialism are spreading with the lethal alacrity of the most aggressive virus, fevering the minds and eventually taking down the hearts of millions. Meanwhile, the purveyors and facilitators dissemble: news media, television and movie producers and executives, publishers, and virtually every manner of Western communicator declaim against and demonize those who would challenge their "freedom of speech" (read "license") and their "noble" purpose of enlightening (read "satiation of greed, pride, and ideological self-interest").

THE FASTER AND FASTER REVOLUTIONS OF THE WHEEL OF HISTORY

It is as though the stream of time had been transformed from a slow-flowing river to a roaring cataract.
Christopher Dawson[14]

Writing in the mid-twentieth century, Christopher Dawson noted the accelerating pace of events in the modern era.

> ....the last hundred years have changed human life more completely than any period in the history of the world. It is as though the stream of time had been transformed from a slow-flowing river to a roaring cataract. A hundred years ago the greater part of the human race was still living as it had always lived....
>
> ...the evils which the nineteenth century thought that it had banished forever—proscription and persecution, torture and slavery, and the fear of sudden death—have returned, and with them new terrors which the past did not know....[E]vil too is a progressive force and...the modern world provides unlimited prospects for its development.[15]

Evil exploits every art, artifice, and attribute of our technological era for its own purposes. Awareness of this should impel Western man to more reflection and discretion about the choices he makes; but so far the evidence suggests he is smugly indifferent to the threat.

The role of ever-escalating speed in the process of cultural decline was manifest in a unique fashion in the aftermath of September 11, 2001. In the wake of that catastrophe, Western man—or at least the American branch of the family—hesitated on the path he had not simply been treading, but jogging, for some decades. Briefly, one could sense an intimation of mortality and the haunting reminders that perhaps there is a higher law and absolutes to which all men are accountable. For a semi-serene moment, life was not as much about material gain and a quest for power and pleasure. Political and ideological opponents spoke mercifully rather than ruthlessly of one another. The tensions of an overwrought, hyper-extended, and increasingly polarized society abated.

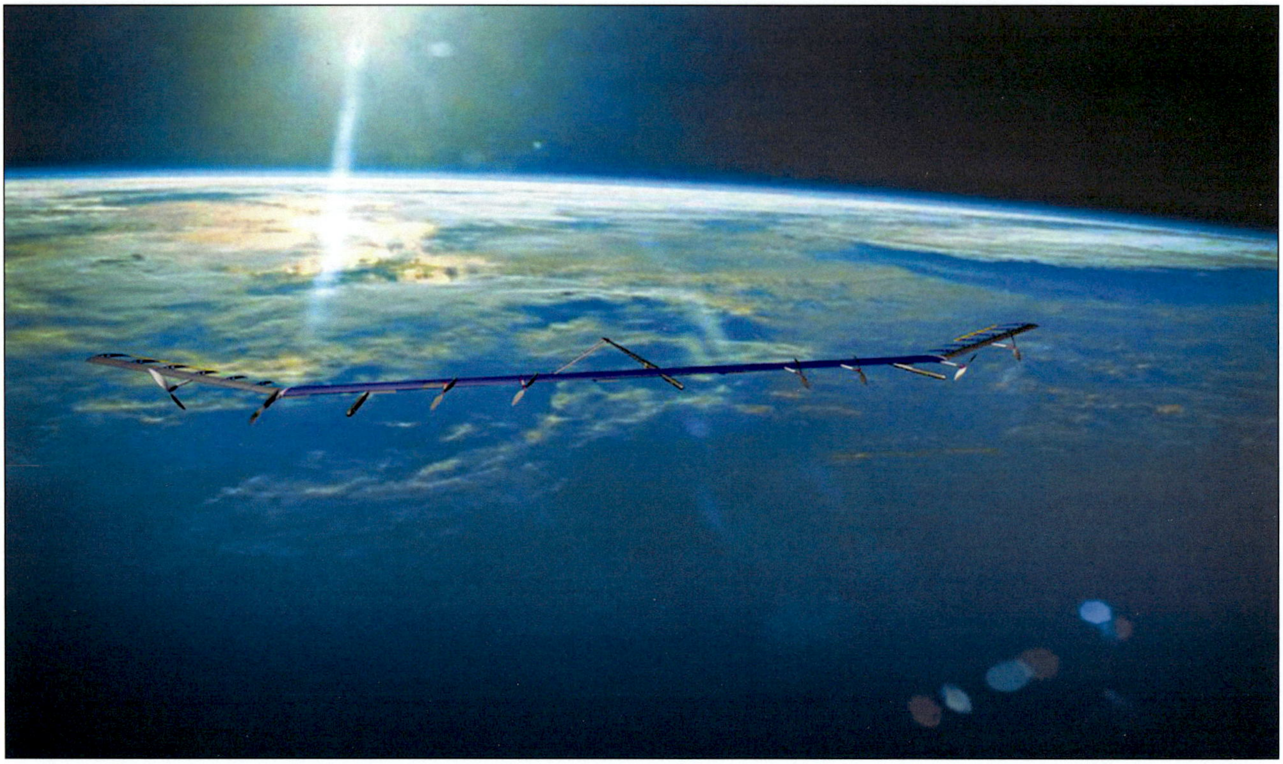

PD-Gov

Vulture solar craft. *Technology has made it possible for the debased and culturally unhealthful to spread in the Information Age like the concussive wave from an exploding bomb. Western man's very success in the material realm of the scientific and technological has made the proliferation of the worst in human thought and behavior all the more rapid. The themes and depictions of violence, sexual obsessions and perversions, pornography, and obsessive materialism are spreading with the lethal alacrity of the most aggressive virus, fevering the minds and eventually taking down the hearts of millions.*

But it did not last. Ironically and perplexingly, Western man returned to his self-obsessed path with renewed vigor. No longer jogging, he seems now to be running; and the movement away from his civilizational heritage in faith and moral absolutes has perceptibly accelerated. It is virtually a certainty that the speed of this decline is unprecedented in world history.

We can see from historical precedents that decay and decline accelerate as they advance; and that no era in world history has brought a faster pace than our own. The significance of this to those who would be willing to recognize the path that Western civilization has taken—and who would alter the course—is that time is of the essence. The window of opportunity to avert the worst of consequences is small and growing smaller each day. We do not have time. Time—like the evils that exploit it—is not on our side.

All images on this page are PD-Gov

September 11, 2001. *No human being should ever have to face the choice between a fiery death and leaping to their demise hundreds of feet below. The horror and significance, culturally and historically, of 9-11 have not been fully grasped by the American people or the West generally. This one event is a reflection of many of the major themes in this work and the viewpoint advocated here—everything is tied to and associated with everything else.*

PD-Gov

In the wake of September 11*, the cultural decline seemed momentarily abated. For a semi-serene moment, life was not as much about material gain and a quest for power and pleasure. Americans hesitated on the trail they had been jogging, seemingly now more conscious of their own mortality and the prospects of a higher moral law to which they would be accountable. But it did not last. Western man's movement away from his civilizational heritage in faith and moral absolutes has perceptibly accelerated. It is virtually a certainty that the speed of this decline is unprecedented in world history.*

END NOTES
CHAPTER 16

1 Christopher Dawson, *Religion and World History: A Selection from the Works of Christopher Dawson* (Garden City, NY: Image Books, 1975), 266.
2 Pitirim A. Sorokin, *The Crisis of Our Age* (Oneworld Publications Ltd., 1941; this edition Sergei P. Sorokin and Peter P. Sorokin, 1992), 57.
3 Virgil, *Georgics*, cited in Arnold Toynbee, *A Study of History* (New York: Weathervane Books, 1972), 158.
4 François de La Rochefoucauld, *Moral Maxims* (University of Delaware Press, 2003), 77.
5 Carroll Quigley, *The Evolution of Civilizations* (New York: Macmillan, 1961), 404–405.
6 Toynbee, *A Study of History*, 222.
7 Sorokin, *Crisis of Our Age*, 81.
8 Sorokin, *Crisis of Our Age*, 57.
9 Dawson, *Religion and World History*, 322.
10 Thomas X. Hammes, *The Sling and the Stone* (St. Paul, MN: Zenith Imprint, 2006), 273.
11 Thomas K. Adams, "Future Warfare and the Decline of Human Decision Making, U.S. Army War College Parameters," *Royal United Services Institute for Defence Studies* 6, no. 2–3 (Sovereign Publications, 2003), 57–71. Internet version at *http://www.carlisle.army.mil/usawc/Parameters/01winter/adams.htm*; accessed June 5, 2009.
12 Francis A. Schaeffer, *How Should We Then Live? The Rise and Decline of Western Thought and Culture* (Wheaton, IL: Crossway Books, 1976), 182.
13 Schaeffer, *How Should We Then Live?*, 182.
14 Dawson, *Religion and World History*, 321.
15 Dawson, *Religion and World History*, 321–322.

CHAPTER

17

"WARS AND RUMORS OF WARS" "THE WORLD IS AS IT USED TO BE"

The world has achieved brilliance without wisdom, power without conscience. Ours is a world of nuclear giants and ethical midgets.
General Omar Bradley[1]

It was so blind and deaf that it still beguiled itself with the fatuous notion of an irresistible and uninterrupted historic trend towards the elimination of war from the course of human history.... Verily, whom the gods would destroy they first make mad! Such blindness is in itself a symptom of derangement and disintegration.
Pitirim Sorokin[2]

Any nation that assumes it is inherently superior to another is setting itself up for disaster.
Colonel Thomas X. Hammes, U.S.M.C.[3]

Perhaps nowhere are the consequences of the dangerous formulation of modern Western history (i.e., *science and technology minus absolute moral values = incipient catastrophe*) more apparent than in twenty-first-century weaponry and war fighting. War—one of the two abiding nemeses of mankind identified by Toynbee—is predictably central to the process of civilizational decline and decay. Toynbee identified it aptly as "a method of social suicide": "...while the internecine warfare between states in the bosom of a civilization is vastly more destructive in degree than the clashes of tribes within the bosom of a precivilizational society, this method of social suicide is merely an abuse of a potential instrument of self-destruction which is within reach of any society."

In the benighted shadows of the twenty-first century, this disquieting truth is now merely the foundation for an entire scaffolding of direct and tangential realities, upon which not merely Western man but mankind generally may hang.

There are four primary areas of greatest threat for Western civilization in regard to war and weaponry as contributing factors in its decay, decline and demise: First, and most conspicuous, the development of increasingly lethal weapons of mass destruction (WMD) and their proliferation; second, the overwhelming of the command and control and decision-making processes of Western militaries by the hypervelocity acquisition of copious information; third, the development of Fourth Generation Warfare (4GW); and fourth, the issue of the will of the majority of citizens of the West to fight and die.

Ironically, all four have their origins in choices made within Western civilization, not within the civilizations that the West has traditionally regarded as enemies or views as potential enemies. Nuclear, biological, and chemical weapons all were developed and deployed initially within the West itself. In that sense they are the analogue in the physical realm of communism and Nazism in the philosophical/ideological—two world nemeses that gestated in the West's philosophical womb after the depraved coupling of Western secularism with innate human pride. But of course, regardless of their parentage, the West's traditional or incipient enemies have adopted and deployed these weapons assiduously. Others are straining at the bit of world opinion and scientific limitations to acquire them.

The deluge of information that threatens to choke the minds and resources of military and political leadership in times of conflict is of course the result also of decades of technological rainmaking. Reminding us of General Bradley's observation about "nuclear giants and ethical midgets," it reflects man's assumption that technology is not only manageable but an ally, when in fact it demonstrates once more man's disproportionality in wisdom to scientific/technological capabilities.

Fourth Generation Warfare is the malevolent product of Western civilization's passion for science and technology that it then deploys against its enemies, who then creatively seek ways to resist and destroy without being destroyed—sometimes by turning the West's own sword against it.

The preceding trends all relate to science, technology, the world economy, and their interaction, as impacting future war. There is considerable recognition of these among military thinkers in the West that has led to some forward thinking atypical of that historically found in the military realm. Just as Billy Mitchell could not convince his peers that planes and bombs were the great killers of the future, and British officers diligently sharpened their swords before leaving for the Great War in France, military leadership historically has proven to be the most hidebound of all a nation's advance guards; not necessarily the least vigilant, just the least forward thinking. There is some evidence to suggest that the American military may have, to a considerable extent, escaped this genetic legacy.

The greater probability is a continuation of the pattern of feverish pursuit of new, more complex, and more lethal technology without due consideration given to its effects on strategy and tactics and, worse yet, mankind.

Finally, the loss of the will within the West—to the extent this will has eroded—to fight and die, is the direct consequence of the loss of faith and belief symbiotically related to the increasingly self-centered dissipations of a materialistic culture that has made man and his indulgence the cynosure of everything. Of the issues relating to war that bear most heavily upon decay and decline, this, our observers will tell us, is the most critical.

But first, before we address each in turn, we consider the future battlefield.

THE BATTLEFIELD IS EVERYWHERE

...the battlefield is omnipresent....If that young lad setting out with his orders should ask today: "Where is the battlefield?" The answer should be: "Everywhere."
Colonels Qiao Liang and Wang Xiangsui[4]

We begin with Toynbee who, when describing the final stages of civilizational decline and decay in *A Study of History*, concluded, "...and the external proletariat, insulated from the radiation of a dying civilization by the erection of an impassable military frontier, tends on the whole to sustain its vigorous barbarian culture until the moment at which it finally overruns the ruined civilization."[5]

When Toynbee wrote those words in the mid-twentieth century the notion of "an impassable military frontier" had been a common historical feature. In the presence of the twenty-first century's weapons of mass destruction and Fourth Generation Warfare (4GW) it has effectively become an anachronism.

No one today is fully secure behind any frontier no matter how seemingly impervious to hostile intent. Henceforth, ultimate physical security for mankind—as, in truth, in one sense, it always was—will be in man's heart and head, not simply his sword or his fortresses.

Two Chinese colonels, Qiao Liang and Wang Xiangsui, in their book quoted earlier, *Unrestricted Warfare*—deemed by strategic thinkers as the rudimentary outline of a strategy for defeating the West, particularly the United States—declare that all is fair in war and that no one will be able to avoid the next serious, widespread conflagration.

> While no military thinker has yet put forth an extremely wide-ranging concept of the battlefield, technology is doing its utmost to extend the contemporary battlefield to a degree that is virtually infinite: there are satellites in space, there are submarines under the water, there are ballistic missiles that can reach any place on the globe, and electronic countermeasures are even now being carried out in the invisible electromagnetic spectrum space. Even the last refuge of the human race—the inner world of the heart—cannot avoid the attacks of psychological warfare. There are nets above and snares below, so that a person has no place to flee. All of the prevailing concepts about the breadth, depth and height of the operational space already appear to be old-fashioned and obsolete. In the wake of the expansion of mankind's imaginative powers and his ability to master technology, the battlespace is being stretched to its limits.
>
> Mankind is endowing virtually every space with battlefield significance. All that is needed is the ability to launch an attack in a certain place, using certain means, in order to achieve a certain goal. Thus, the battlefield is omnipresent. Just think, if it's even possible to start a war in a computer room or a stock exchange that will send an enemy country to its doom, then is there non-battlespace anywhere?[6]

In that vein, we do well to continue to return to a central theme of this book: human nature is neither inherently good nor rational. Immanuel Wallerstein cautioned against "the Enlightenment view of human rationality: all persons will act in their own rational interest, provided they have the chance and the education to perceive it correctly."[7] If history teaches anything, particularly twentieth-century history, man will often act quite irrationally, albeit perversely "rational" by the twisted and delusional reasoning of a Kaiser, Hitler, Tojo, Stalin, Saddam, or inchoate megalomaniacs yet unknown. But the derangement cannot be isolated to the few; millions have followed them and millions will follow others like them. In conjunction with these realities, Wallerstein adds an incommodious set of predictions for the West's immediate future.

> The world has moved decisively on. And while most persons in the ex-Communist world are immensely relieved that the Communist interlude is behind them, it is not at all sure that they, or the rest of us, have moved into a safer or more hopeful or more livable world.
>
> For one thing, the world of the next fifty years promises to be a far more violent one than the Cold War world out of which we have come. The Cold War was highly choreographed, highly constrained by the concern of both the United States and the Soviet Union that there be no nuclear war between them, and just as important by the fact that the two countries had between them the necessary power to ensure that such a war would not break out. But this situation has changed radically.[8]

The change has not necessarily been exclusively salutary. Whereas the prospects for a massive nuclear exchange—for the moment—seemed to have diminished, other forms of violent antagonism are proliferating.

> The results are already clear. It is extremely difficult to contain escalating local violence (Bosnia, Rwanda, Burundi, and so on). It will be virtually impossible over the next twenty-five years to contain weapons proliferation, and we should anticipate a significant increase in the number of states that have nuclear weapons at their disposition, as well as biological and chemical weapons. Furthermore, given, on the one hand, the relative weakening of U.S. power and the emergence of a triadic division among the strongest states and, on the other hand, a continuing economic North–South polarization in the world-system, we should expect the likelihood that there will be more deliberate South–North military provocations (of the Saddam Hussein variety). Such provocations will be increasingly difficult to handle politically, and if several occur simultaneously, it is doubtful that the North will be able to stem the tide. The U.S. military has already moved into a mode of preparing to handle two such situations at the same time. But if there are three? [9]

Parenthetically, we add that the "continuing economic North–South polarization" Wallerstein refers to will likely manifest itself more and more in internal violence within Western nations that, on the one hand, have left their back doors unlocked and open to the South's disaffected and impoverished immigrants, yet, on the other, done little to ameliorate the economic conditions that triggered their pilgrimage. The absence of foresight and a compassionate munificence that could readily have anticipated and headed off this desperate movement has led not only to tectonic population shifts but will lead to massive political and cultural dislocations. The United States—primarily because of vested financial interests' quest for cheap (and unaccountable to the law) labor—has permitted a flood of immigrants who were not even christened as they crossed the border with the notion that all the host nation's laws should be obeyed. The social and political repercussions from this exploitive and irresponsible laxity will be serious. The specious arguments that insistence on immigration control and adherence to the law are a form of racial or ethnic prejudice are another illustration of a decadent logic in conflict with hard reality. Racism's existence is a conspicuous given; but only the obtuse, or the prejudiced, will assume that all resistance to the willful and irresponsible behavior of non-whites is color born.

I
WEAPONS OF MASS DESTRUCTION

It will be virtually impossible...to contain weapons proliferation, and we should anticipate a significant increase in the number of states that have nuclear weapons at their disposition, as well as biological and chemical weapons.
Immanuel Wallerstein[10]

WMD has a longer history than most would assume and some unexpected origins. In centuries past, catapults were used to launch diseased bodies into fortified cities in perhaps the earliest form of biological warfare. Jonathan Tucker in *War of Nerves* noted a particularly ironic origin for chemical warfare.

> Seeking to break the deadlock and regain the offensive, the Germans began to consider the use of toxic chemicals delivered by artillery shells to force the enemy out of his trenches. The idea was not entirely new: in 1862, during the American Civil War, a New York City schoolteacher named John W. Doughty had written to the Secretary of War suggesting the use of poison gas shells against the Confederate forces. He had designed a 10-inch projectile in which one compartment was filled with a few quarts of liquid chlorine and the second with explosives; when the shell burst, the explosion would convert the chlorine into an asphyxiating gas.[11]

Yet, by 1914, international treaty had outlawed such deployments with the supreme confidence of Western man that he, perhaps alone in the species, could and would prevent the bestial.

> At the 1899 International Peace Conference in The Hague, representatives of twenty-six countries, including Germany, signed the first Hague Convention Respecting the Laws and Customs of War on Land. Article 23(a) of this treaty prohibited "poison or poisoned weapons," including the deliberate tainting of arms, bullets, food, or wells. The contracting states also signed a separate document, the Hague Declaration Concerning Asphyxiating Gases, which specifically outlawed "the use of projectiles, the sole object of which is the diffusion of asphyxiating or deleterious gases." This treaty effectively banned the use of chemical shells even before they had been developed.
>
> In late 1914, however, amid the futile slaughter of trench warfare, the traditional legal and moral restraints on the use of poison gas began to erode under the pressure of military necessity.[12]

So much for Western man's deference to another of his vaunted achievements: the rule of law. The rule of power is the only force that man can be counted on to honor. That reality does not suggest that legal regimens are fruitless; to the contrary they are desperately needed. But ultimately only force or the threat of force will alter actual behavior. The only truly effectual alternative—and only a partial one at that—is a force that is applied at the wellsprings of man's aggressive impulses—his conscience. But that implies recognition of a higher authority than man himself—a recognition that Western man rejects more and more completely with each dawn. We can anticipate therefore that power and force will be resorted to more and more—not simply because of the spiritual and moral vacuum, but also due to the proliferation of human problems brought on by burgeoning population, science, technology, and the ever intensifying competition for resources and power.

Furthermore, "military necessity" is of course a label American leadership would have applied to the use of the atomic bomb in 1945. An expedient and highly elastic concept, it has been deployed in a multiplicity of languages since 1914. However, what is "necessary" might best be restricted only to those actions that ensure the survival of the acting state. Such was not the case in 1914 or 1945. The escalation in each instance led—in the moral and historical blindness of the moment—to much worse escalations, the repercussions from which the entire world labors under today.

The caliber, character, and wisdom of the leaders have always been among the most important factors in the great formulations of history. Disturbingly often in the West, the caliber has been small bore, the character weak, and the wisdom parochial—the West's penchant for charm and scratching the itching ears taking priority in the democratic forms of natural selection and survival of the fittest. But the imperative to ignore image, charm and an ingratiating manner, in deference to attributes with gravitas—preferably in a Cincinnatus at the plow with an extraordinarily well-formed sense of responsibility—has never carried more force, as suggested by the British war historian John Keegan:

> An inactive leader, one who does nothing, sets no striking example, says nothing stirring, rewards no more than he punishes, insists above all in being different from the mass in his modesty, prudence

and rationality, may sound no leader at all. But such, none the less, is the sort of leader the nuclear world needs, even if it does not know that it wants him. "Post-heroic" is the title he might take for himself. For all is changed, utterly changed. Passing brave it may once have been to ride in triumph through Persepolis. Today the best must find conviction to play the hero no more.[13]

All images on this page PD-Gov

When Toynbee wrote in the mid-twentieth century of "an impassable military frontier" the concept was a common historical feature. In the presence of the twenty-first century's weapons of mass destruction and Fourth Generation Warfare (4GW) it has become an anachronism. No one today is fully secure behind any frontier, no matter how seemingly impervious to hostile intent.

PD-art

Cincinnatus Leaving the Plow for Rome. *The caliber, character, and wisdom of leaders have always been among the most important factors in the great formulations of history. Often in the West, the caliber has been small bore, the character weak, and the wisdom parochial—the West's penchant for charm and scratching the itching ears taking priority. But the imperative to ignore image, charm and an ingratiating manner, in deference to attributes like those of Cincinnatus, has never carried more force.*

II
INFORMATION OVERLOAD: A SURFEIT OF INFORMATION—A DEFICIT OF UNDERSTANDING

This is not to suggest that there will ever be an overriding decision to exclude humans from decision making. Instead, we will continue to pretend to be in complete control while leading ourselves gradually and incrementally toward systems whose logic demands that human control become more abstract with less and less direct participation.

Dr. Thomas K. Adams[14]

Western man's technological and scientific prowess has put him as the cowboy on the back of an olive drab/desert camouflaged bronc that is becoming too strong, too fast, and too unruly, for anyone to fully control.

We have already scrutinized the multidimensional phenomena of accelerating speed and as part of so doing quoted Marine Colonel Thomas X. Hammes's thought—its pertinence is even more apparent here. "A further challenge is the accelerating rate of change. Although change is constant, the rate of change is not. It has been accelerating almost exponentially. We can see that acceleration in the rate of development and adoption of new thoughts, processes, and technologies in all areas of human endeavor."[15]

Elsewhere in his book he restates the point, "What is less obvious is that the rate of change has been accelerating—and not just over the last sixty years but over recorded history."[16] Colonel Hammes then reveals the obvious, but often overlooked, result.

> At the tactical level, the quantity of information our systems provide has grown exponentially. Unfortunately, although vastly improved in raw amount of data, our ability to turn that information into coherent intelligence products for our commanders has not kept pace. These systems provide so much information that they virtually force the commander to focus his intelligence staff on simply sorting the flow rather than on analysis or developing his own local sources and solutions.[17]

As observed in a preceding chapter, the American military is increasingly attentive to this concern as indicated by the following passage penned for the *U.S. Army War College* by Dr. Thomas K. Adams and quoted in the chapter "Hypervelocity—The Turning of the Wheel of History in Our Age."

> In short, the military systems (including weapons) now on the horizon will be too fast, too small, too numerous, and will create an environment too complex for humans to direct. Furthermore, the proliferation of information-based systems will produce a data overload that will make it difficult or impossible for humans to directly intervene in decisionmaking. This is not a consideration for the remote science-fiction future. Weapons...will function...increasingly without meaningful human intervention. [18]

Adams, a strategist and retired Army lieutenant colonel, observes that weapons and other military systems have reached a point of complexity such that human intervention may disrupt the system—or even become impossible.

> We are faced with the prospect of equipment that not only does not require soldiers to operate it, but may be defeated if humans do attempt to exert control in any direct way. It is easy to see a steadily decreasing role for humans in direct combat as the 21st century progresses....
>
> The fundamental development underlying the loss of human control is that of automated information systems. Furthermore, the impressive current capabilities of such systems may only hint at their future capacity.
>
> ...James Heath, [a] UCLA professor...suggested that a molecular computer with the processing power of 100 conventional personal computers would be about the size of a grain of salt. The implications are almost unimaginable—cheap, ubiquitous supercomputing, and unlimited memory capacity in devices so small that they are on the scale of insects.[19]

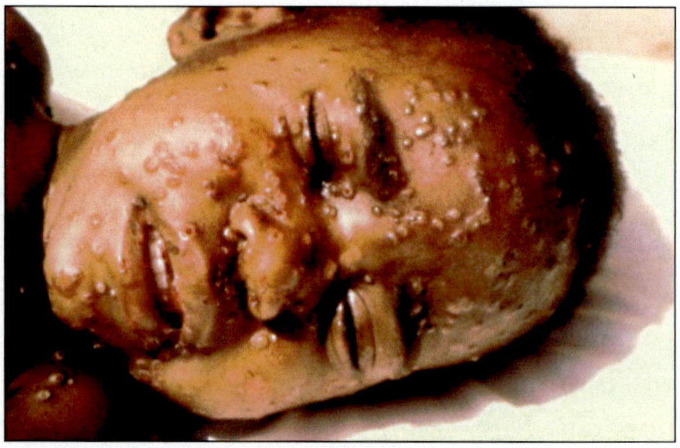

Smallpox victim. *Ostensibly eradicated in the West, smallpox still exists in some biological weapons arsenals in more lethal and resistant strains. Still regarded by some biological weapons experts as one of the optimum weapons, the world faces the prospect of scenes like this replicated on a massive scale.*

PD-gov.

In line with the trite admonition "be careful what you ask for, you may get it," these "successes" will prove to be a two-edged sword. Dr. Adams, in the passage below, uses a verbal phrasing, "continue to pretend to be in complete control," which should be disquieting in the present, not just the future tense.

> This is not to suggest that there will ever be an overriding decision to exclude humans from decision making. Instead, we will continue to pretend to be in complete control while leading ourselves gradually and incrementally toward systems whose logic demands that human control become more abstract with less and less direct participation.
>
> But victory does not always go [to] the commander with the best observation. It goes to the one that can best process observation into data, data into information, information into orders, and then orders into action.[20]

Whereas Alexander, Wellington, and Zhukov might struggle with too little information, the modern commander may have so much that he ignores much of it.

> Unfortunately, the explosion of available information inevitably results in information overload and flawed decisionmaking. Human beings commonly deal with this by ignoring much of the inflow, thus negating the purpose of the information systems in the first place. Recent exercises reveal an alarming number of unread messages because of information overload. As the quantity of data rises, the difficulty of preparing and interpreting it for decisionmaking grows. Furthermore, more information, flowing more efficiently, can easily give the commander conflicting perspectives of the battlespace. Soon it becomes obvious that the slowest element in the process is the human decisionmaker. By reducing the human role, the entire system is enhanced.[21]

If the trajectory of Dr. Adams' reasoning is headed where it appears, then to say there is a need for humility and extreme wariness in modern man's approach to technology, particularly military technology, is an understatement of great magnitude.

> Automated systems can certainly reduce the pressure of information saturation and eliminate conflicts, but at a price. Essentially, they do so by creating a series of information "filters" that establish priorities and eliminate marginal data, reconcile the remaining information conflicts, and present a consensus picture of the situation...This means that the commander is receiving a picture of the battlefield that is designed to emphasize certain things while de-emphasizing others. Still other factors are omitted entirely.
>
> ...Inevitably, some adversary will decide that eliminating humans from the military decision cycle at the tactical level will confer a significant advantage, forcing others to follow suit. The logic leading to fully autonomous systems seems inescapable.
>
> Clearly, the armed forces will want a "person in the loop" no matter how capable the automated system may become. However, if this person has a meaningful role in the operation of the system (for example, a tank, fighting ship, or warplane), then he or she will obviously be the most critical (and probably the most vulnerable) component of the system as well as the most difficult to replace. The obvious course for an adversary attacking the tank, ship, or plane is to concentrate on attacking the human component....This provides a strong incentive not to include humans in the systems at all.[22]

We would add to Dr. Adams' analysis the factor of the West's strong aversion to casualties, which we believe will militate in favor of Dr. Adams' apparent conclusion: increasingly machines, not humans, will control modern warfare.

> Humans may retain symbolic authority, but automated systems move too fast and the factors involved are too complex for real human comprehension. When computers are designed and programmed by other computers, the situation will be even further from anything humans can reasonably expect to understand, much less intervene in successfully....At the same time, loud denials can be expected from some quarters, angrily claiming that humans are as much, if not more, in charge than ever. In a sense this will be true—the new systems will enable people to accomplish far more in war and peace than was even conceivable before their development, or, rather, is even conceivable now. But the simple fact remains, the farther we extend our reach outside "human space," the more we require the assistance of machines.
>
> Future generations may come to regard tactical warfare as properly the business of machines and not appropriate for people at all....Humans may retain control at the highest levels, making strategic decisions about where and when to strike and, most important, the overall objectives of a conflict. But even these will increasingly be informed by automated information systems. Direct human participation in warfare is likely to be rare. Instead, the human role will take other forms—strategic direction perhaps, or at the very extreme, perhaps no more than the policy decision whether to enter hostilities or not. Nevertheless, wars are a human phenomenon, arising from human needs for human purposes. This makes intimate human participation at some level critical, or the entire exercise becomes pointless.[23]

III
FOURTH GENERATION WARFARE (4GW)

We believe that some morning people will awake to discover with surprise that quite a few gentle and kind things have begun to have offensive and lethal characteristics.
Chinese Colonels Qiao and Wang[24]

In the course of his analysis, Dr. Adams cites electronic conflict among computer systems as the premier example of warfare that has already escaped "human space."

> Perhaps the extreme example of warfare outside "human space" is that of "netwar"—electronic conflict within and among computer systems attacking the full spectrum of opposing military and civilian information systems (including computer-controlled networks such as communications, logistics, and transportation). By its nature, the speed of such conflict is limited only by the speed of the electronic circuits in which it occurs....This is another example of conflict that will quickly escalate out of human control due to its complexity and rapidity. Netwar attacks may be too pervasive and rapid for human intervention, adapting instantly to responses. Both attack and defense will be completely automated, because humans are far too slow to participate.[25]

This offers a useful segue into the newest and, in one sense, most formidable type of war—now referred to as Fourth Generation Warfare. The development of this form of human conflict has been the consequence of political and military decisions made in the West that prompted the West's enemies to grope for a new form of sling with which to defeat the Goliath. They have done so with such creativity that Goliath has begun to realize his shield is not large enough and his spear is at once too heavy and too short. Colonel Hammes cites Western man's perennial achievement cum nemesis, his success—predictably in high technology—as the prime motivator behind Western decision making.

Conflicts around the world seemed to confirm that warfare is indeed evolving. Unfortunately, despite the fact that some of these conflicts involved direct attacks on the United States, our defense establishment chose to ignore them. We preferred to focus on our tactical success in the wars with Iraq and the amazing high-technology weapons we were developing. We did not want to deal with the manpower intensive, low-technology conflicts that were actually taking place around the world. It was much more comfortable to theorize about future high-technology conflicts with "near peer competitors."[26]

Colonel Hammes describes rather than defines 4GW for us.

Fourth-generation warfare (4GW) uses all available networks—political, economic, social, and military—to convince the enemy's political decision makers that their strategic goals are either unachievable or too costly for the perceived benefit. It is an evolved form of insurgency. Still rooted in the fundamental precept that superior political will, when properly employed, can defeat greater economic and military power, 4GW makes use of society's networks to carry on its fight. Unlike previous generations of warfare, it does not attempt to win by defeating the enemy's military forces. Instead, via the networks, it directly attacks the minds of enemy decision makers to destroy the enemy's political will. Fourth-generation wars are lengthy—measured in decades rather than months or years.[27]

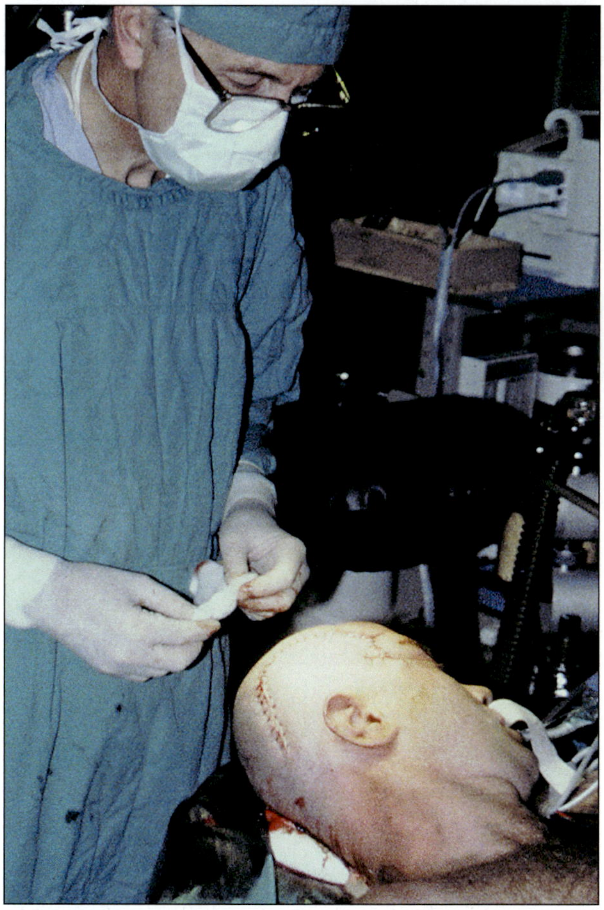

Photograph by Ivy Scarborough

Dr. Mel Cheatham, professor of neurosurgery at UCLA Medical School, on a mission with Samaritan's Purse to war-torn Bosnia, finishes brain surgery on a wounded Bosnian soldier.

The "progression" of warfare reflects the growth of military power as it is braided with man's ruthlessness in war to create a rope of unimaginable strength that now binds humanity.

> Finally, we can see the logical progression of the three generations. First-generation war focused on the direct destruction of the enemy's close force. Second-generation war relied on firepower but still focused on the destruction of the enemy fighting forces.... Both were restricted by the warfighting capabilities of the societies from which they sprang. As society progressed and was able to project power over much longer ranges, third-generation war took advantage of those changes to focus on destruction of the enemy's command and control logistics as the fastest way to destroy his will to fight.[28]

In a sense, 4GW warfare is not only technologically and tactically the most sophisticated form of warfare ever devised, it is also the most sophisticated psychologically. Rather than needlessly expend human and material resources trying to achieve the total destruction of the enemy's forces (e.g., Britain, Prussia, Russia and Austria vs. Napoleon), the capture of his capital (e.g., Napoleon vs. Russia; Nazi Germany vs. Russia) or unconditional surrender (e.g., the Allies vs. Germany and Japan), 4GW aims first simply at Sun Tzu's "supreme excellence": "Supreme excellence consists in breaking the enemy's resistance without fighting." If fighting is necessary, then the objective is "breaking the enemy's resistance" without necessarily defeating him in the field. Thus, in any event, it obviates attempting to go toe to toe with an enemy who is larger and more powerful.

4GW is a particularly promising strategy when contending with an enemy—massive and wealthy though he may be—who already displays marked symptoms of cultural and moral decay.

A capable and relentless aggressor who resorts to 4GW against the West is likely to achieve a victory if, for no other reason, than that the West already bridles at the thought of sacrifice even on a limited scale. It will not abide sacrifice on a grand scale. The "copperheads" of the American Civil War, the peace movement of the Vietnam War, and their correlatives in the second Iraq War and the Afghan War now have proliferated through their genetic progeny throughout the West to the point that they would likely form a majority when a very hard push came to self-sacrificing shove.

Colonel Hammes declares that recent history shows "…only unconventional war works against established powers. Not only does recent history show us that the trend is toward unconventional war, it even shows the strategic, operational, and tactical characteristics future war will take."[29]

America, loath to ever admit losing at much of anything, now must face a hard reality. "Not only is 4GW the only kind of war America has ever lost, we have done so three times: Vietnam, Lebanon, and Somalia. This form of warfare has also defeated the French in Vietnam and Algeria and the USSR in Afghanistan. It continues to bleed Russia in Chechnya and the United States in Iraq, Afghanistan, and in other countries against the Al-Qaeda network."[30]

Colonel Hammes notes that 4GW has been "successful" even when its practitioners lost.

> In sharp contrast, unconventional wars—the Communist revolution in China, the first and second Indochinese Wars, the Algerian War of Independence, the Sandinista struggle in Nicaragua, the Iranian revolution, the Afghan–Soviet War of the 1980's, the first Intifada, and even Chechnya—display a different pattern. Each ended with major changes in the political, economic, and social structure of the territories involved. Although the changes may not have been for the better, they were distinct changes. Even unconventional wars where the insurgents lost (Malaysia, Aden, El Salvador) led to significant changes.[31]

The dangerous flexibility and resourcefulness of 4GW is described by Colonel Hammes in a passage that could be out of bin Laden's playbook.

> The knowledge of how to conduct an attack is developed in one country, then that knowledge is combined with the raw materials, personnel, and training available in other countries, which can include the target country, to create a weapon in the target country. Both the 9/11 and Madrid attacks were conducted using this approach. Further, "ownership" of the action may belong to contributors who are distributed around the world but provide funding to the terror networks planning the attack.[32]

Colonel Hammes has scant confidence in the strategic supremacy of technology since "…the insurgents have proven largely immune to our technology."[33] He perceives that "True believers in technology see warfare as being reduced to a one-sided contest where the technologically superior side dictates all action."[34] This view is fostered by the successes of the past that lead men—as we have demonstrated—to pursue replication of those successes even when the circumstances have radically changed.

> In short, we have an entire culture and industry built around second- and third-generation warfare. As a result, we have convinced ourselves that applying our technology to these older generations of war gives us a unique and virtually unassailable lead, through our ability to conduct precision attacks that surgically remove an enemy's ability to fight.[35]
>
> ...
>
> Unfortunately, DOD publications never address how our precision weapons can attack a target that blends into civilian society.[36]

Thus, the new form of warfare permits enemies of the West to dispense with burdens historically imposed on a warring force. "It relieves him of the strategic necessity of defending core production assets, leaving him free to focus on offense rather than defense. It also relieves him of the logistics burden of moving supplies long distances."[37]

One of the very institutions that the West sees as its greatest strength proves to be—in tactical terms at least—a great vulnerability.

> In our brief case studies, we saw how the Vietnamese and Sandinistas targeted their efforts to neutralize U.S. military power through Congressional action to remove funding for their opponents. A prudent planner will assume the parliaments and congresses of democratic nations will be natural targets in a 4GW struggle.[38]

Photograph by Ivy Scarborough

With the Salvadoran Commandos and Marine Lt. Col. Chuck Armstrong (center) on patrol in 1988, *I noticed an ironic result to the guerrilla campaign: The FMLN was losing the war and yet, in many respects, winning the propaganda campaign. The outcome—an eventually democratic government in power—reflected significant changes in the country despite the fact that the insurgents lost.*

> Each event was tactically separated by time and space, but each tied together operationally to attack America's strategic position in the country. The campaign continues, with each attack designed to prevent a stable, democratic government from emerging.[39]

Obviously, if the people's will to fight has eroded, that erosion will manifest itself in the actions of a democratically elected government. Notions of strategic wisdom—even for the long term security of the nation—will likely be ignored or rationalized away. This great vulnerability among democratic states will be one of many a 4GW enemy will exploit. "At the operational level, a 4GW opponent will examine our entire society to find vulnerabilities. He will then attempt to attack those vulnerabilities to defeat our will."[40]

Though Hammes is referring to America in the following passage, Western impatience generally will prove another vulnerability.

> The United States wants to fight short, well-defined wars. We went into Vietnam, Bosnia, Kosovo, Afghanistan, and Iraq convinced we would "clean it up" quickly.... In each conflict, our leaders told the people we would be out in a year or so. They felt this was important to convince the American people to go to war. For the United States, a long war is five years. That, in fact, is how long we had a major involvement in Vietnam—from 1966 to 1971.... We came in when the war was already being fought and left before it was over. Even then, the U.S. public thought we had been at war too long. In other words, Americans want short wars.
>
> Unfortunately, 4GW wars are long. The Chinese Communists fought for twenty-eight years (1921–1949). The Vietnamese Communists fought for thirty years (1945–75). The Sandinistas fought for eighteen years (1961–79). The Palestinians have been resisting Israeli occupation for twenty-nine years so far (1975–2004). The Chechens have been fighting for more than ten years—this time. Al-Qaeda has been fighting for their vision of the world for twenty years, since the founding of MAK in 1984.... Numerous other insurgencies in the world have lasted decades. Accordingly, when getting involved in a 4GW fight, we should be planning for a decades-long commitment. From an American point of view, this may well be the single most important characteristic of 4GW.[41]

Ho Chi Minh and Vo Nguyen Giap understood that patient perseverance was their most powerful weapon against first France, then America. This recognition is now a central tenet of strategic opposition to the West generally. It plays to the strengths of the West's enemies and against the West's weakness. As Colonel Hammes observes, "The greatest strength of any insurgent is the fact that he doesn't have to win. He simply has to stay in the fight until the coalition gives up and goes home. As long as the insurgents can stay in the fight, it is not over."[42] Thus the West must decide here also whether it will have the will to fight for the very long term.

> They know that time is on their side. Westerners in general, and Americans in particular, are not... known for their patience. We are not a people who think in terms of struggles lasting decades. Fourth-generation-warfare enemies will not seek immediate objectives but a long-term shift in the political will of their enemies. They will accept numerous tactical and operational setbacks in pursuit of that goal.
>
> Colonel Harry Summers noted in his book *On Strategy: A Critical Analysis of the Vietnam War* that after the war he told a North Vietnamese colonel that the United States had never been beaten on the battlefield. The North Vietnamese replied, "That is true. It is also irrelevant." It is essential to understand that 4GW opponents...do not focus on swift battlefield victories. They focus on a long-term strategic approach. They focus on winning wars, not battles.[43]

Photograph by Ivy Scarborough

Kosovo 1999; 82nd Airborne troops conducting a search for weapons. *Colonel Thomas X. Hammes cautioned, "The United States wants to fight short, well-defined wars. We went into Vietnam, Bosnia, Kosovo, Afghanistan, and Iraq convinced we would 'clean it up' quickly.... Unfortunately, 4GW wars are long.... When getting involved in a 4GW fight, we should be planning for a decades-long commitment."*

The Geneva Convention, and its legalistic progeny, will become so much historical wallpaper as 4GW proponents develop their tactical capabilities. "Fourth-generation-warfare enemies do not see international boundaries as an impediment, nor do they see war as primarily a military function."[44]

B. H. Liddell Hart observed that "an army and a state succumb quickest to paralysis of the brain."[45] We might repeat the reminder that this phenomenon is also compounded by prior successes that are not received humbly. Relentlessly searching for and acknowledging one's limitations and failures is an undertaking usually approached reluctantly, especially when the practice has fallen into desuetude.

> Although we can be highly effective against a 4GW enemy, it will require a shift in mindset throughout the government. All changes in a large bureaucracy are hard. Major cultural change is even harder. Cultural change across multiple bureaucratic departments is the hardest of all.[46]

Thus, even if the West does not learn and change, its enemies surely will.

> ...[I]t is clear that our enemies have learned that only 4GW has a chance of succeeding against the massive conventional superiority of the United States.... Anyone who has watched modern conflict on CNN can see that the United States easily dominates high-technology war. Although Americans may applaud the standoff range and videotapes of weapons shown in the news coverage of these conflicts, our enemies around the world see the futility of presenting any kind of target to American forces. They know it will be destroyed. In contrast, the daily video of our soldiers struggling to bring order to Iraq, the difficulty they have with unconventional forces and attacks, and the problems in understanding and establishing a government provide a living example of how to fight the United States.[47]

The pervasive materialism in the West underlies another factor cited by Colonel Hammes in the failure of the United States military/industrial complex to come to grips with the wars the West must now fight: "Therefore, although major constituencies in the United States have an interest in perfecting high-technology war, none of our most dangerous enemies sees it as a viable way to compete against the Unites States. We simply have too great a lead, and the weapons cost too much. We have to give up our cyberwar fantasy and understand that our most dangerous enemies are those who are preparing to fight a 4GW conflict."[48] But the dynamics of a highly materialistic, capitalist society militate against this objective view. As Colonel Hammes puts it, "In a 4GW fight…massive firepower is largely irrelevant."[49] But massive and sophisticated firepower is precisely what this system wants to produce.

Eisenhower's famous warning about the dangers of a military/industrial complex was the first broadly promulgated revelation of a state of affairs that plays into the hands of America's enemies in two respects: First, this aggregation of inordinate political and economic power now powerfully influences the most significant strategic and political decisions of the nation in ways that may be inimical to the future of the nation; second, the drain on the nation's resources required to continue to create these weapons coupled with the delusion that through this means the American people can escape human sacrifice, weakens the nation economically and morally and undermines a sound grasp of hard reality.

None of this analysis is intended to suggest that America should forego seeking a technological edge. Rather, Colonel Hammes seems to be urging a far more realistic and objective assessment of strategic decision-making untainted by self-centered motives.

The self-centered motives are at the heart of the decay and decline warned of in this book. Here we see further evidence that even that which seems far removed from the philosophical/spiritual/psychological state of the citizenry is in fact profoundly influenced by those abstract considerations.

With historical irony, 4GW was initially the brainchild of Mao Tse-Tung, and it has spread almost in lockstep with American strategic military initiatives around the world, now coming full circle—in a much more advanced and refined form—back to the Chinese, who may yet deploy it full bore against the West.

> China can use a number of 4GW avenues to attack the United States—or, more likely, to neutralize our power in what they consider their sphere of influence by threatening such attacks. At the same time, they can limit our ability to concentrate power by ensuring that our enemies throughout the world obtain more advanced weapons that require us to maintain forces in those regions. This is a more sophisticated approach than the Soviet Union's use of proxies. The Soviets attempted to control the proxies. The Chinese simply provide them resources to use for whatever goals the proxies devise. China is engaging her allies in a fashion more resembling that of a venture capitalist than the vertical, bureaucratic approach the Soviet Union used.[50]

Courtesy of Nautilus Institute for Security and Sustainability, San Francisco

North Koreans celebrating their status as a nuclear power. *"China is clearly our most dangerous opponent in this arena," Col. Thomas X. Hammes writes. "It has shown a remarkable, consistent, long-range strategy of making allies of our enemies. It has provided assistance to Iran, Iraq, and North Korea." Indeed, its shrewdness at "investing" in American enemies as well as American assets and property is exceeded only by American foolishness in permitting both to happen largely unhampered. Once again, Western materialism cuts into the West's own throat.*

"China is clearly our most dangerous opponent in this arena," Colonel Hammes writes. "It has shown a remarkable, consistent, long-range strategy of making allies of our enemies. It has provided assistance to Iran, Iraq, and North Korea."[51]

That Colonel Hammes is likely accurate in his analysis has been corroborated by the two Chinese colonels, Qiao Liang and Wang Xiangsui, in their book, *Unrestricted Warfare.* As a game plan by which China could fight the United States through a wide range of means, both traditional military and nonmilitary, it expresses confidence in their expectancy of victory. Americans, they claim, "are slaves to technology in their thinking" and therefore "halt their thinking at the boundary where technology has not yet reached." The Chinese then consider the possibility of ecologically based weapons of mass destruction using man-made earthquakes, control of polar ice caps, or other fantastic yet imaginable means. The revelations of their thinking should unsettle any Westerner, not simply for their inchoate ruthlessness, but even more so for their insights into the Western character and what they regard as the West's eminently predictable behavior.

> When people begin to lean toward and rejoice in the reduced use of military force to resolve conflicts, war will be reborn in another form and in another arena, becoming an instrument of enormous power in the hands of all those who harbor intentions of controlling other countries or regions.[52]
>
> . . .
>
> But whatever you call them, they cannot make us more optimistic than in the past. We have no reason for optimism. This is because the reduction of the functions of warfare in a pure sense does not mean at all that war has ended. Even in the so-called post-modern, post-industrial age, warfare will not be totally dismantled. It has only re-invaded human society in a more complex, more extensive, more concealed and more subtle manner. It is as Byron said in his poem mourning Shelley, "Nothing has happened, he has only undergone a sea change."
>
> Technology today...proves that mankind is now planning to take the place of God the Creator. The fearsome Russian-built SU-27 fighter has not been put to use on any battlefield, and already the SU-35 has emerged to strike a pose, but whether or not, once it has exhausted its time in the limelight, the SU-35 will be able to retire having rendered meritorious service is still a matter of considerable doubt.
>
> Technology is like "magic shoes" on the feet of mankind, and after the spring has been wound tightly by commercial interests, people can only dance along with the shoes, whirling rapidly in time to the beat that they set.[53]

The declarations in the foregoing passage are striking inasmuch as they reflect insights that are major themes of this book: the absence of any sound bases for optimism, man presumptively intent on displacing God, and the obsession with technology creating an irresistible dynamic in the West along an ill advised course. This is a classic example of how human beings (e.g., Western man) can overestimate themselves and underestimate their actual or inchoate adversaries (e.g., China). Sometimes the enemy sees about you what you cannot or will not. That is truly a dangerous state of affairs.

In passages seething with lingering resentment and wounded pride, the colonels give some insight into their own psychology.

> Therefore, new-concept weapons have emerged to fill the bill. However, what seems unfair to people is that it is again the Americans who are in the lead in this trend. As early as the Vietnam War, the silver iodide powder released over the "Ho Chi Minh Trail" that resulted in torrential rains and the defoliants scattered over the subtropical forests put the "American devils" in the sole lead with regard to both the methods and ruthlessness of new-concept weapons. Thirty years later, with the dual advantages of money and technology, others are unable to hold a candle to them in this area.

> However, the Americans are not necessarily in the sole lead in everything. The new concepts of weapons, which came after the weapons of new concepts and which cover a wider area, were a natural extension of this. However, the Americans have not been able to get their acts together in this area. This is because proposing a new concept of weapons does not require relying on the springboard of new technology, it just demands lucid and decisive thinking. However, this is not a strong point of the Americans who are slaves to technology in their thinking. The Americans invariably halt their thinking at the boundary where technology has not yet reached.[54]

All of the foregoing is skinning out one's adversary and examining every vessel, muscle and nerve. If done well and objectively, this dissection grants a strategic advantage, one that can prove to be of more value than massive technological resources.

As if man's carelessness and depredations on his environment were not enough to challenge his abilities to survive, the Chinese colonels hold out the prospect that even ecological forces may be turned against him.

> Ecological war refers to a new type of non-military warfare in which modern technology is employed to influence the natural state of rivers, oceans, the crust of the earth, the polar ice sheets, the air circulating in the atmosphere, and the ozone layer. By methods such as causing earthquakes and altering precipitation patterns, the atmospheric temperature, the composition of the atmosphere, sea level height, and sunshine patterns, the earth's physical environment is damaged or an alternate local ecology is created. Perhaps before very long, a man-made El Niño or La Niña effect will become yet another kind of superweapon in the hands of certain nations and/or non-state organizations. It is more likely that a non-state organization will become the prime initiator of ecological war, because of its terrorist nature, because it feels it has no responsibility to the people or to the society at large, and because non-state organizations have consistently demonstrated that they are unwilling to play by the rules of the game. Moreover, since the global ecological environment will frequently be on the borderline of catastrophe as nations strive for the most rapid development possible, there is a real danger that the slightest increase or decrease in any variable would be enough to touch off an ecological holocaust.[55]

Only a fool would be dismissive of these possibilities. Manipulation of the weather and natural forces is already possible in limited ways. With the continued degradation of the earth's environment through global warming, pollution, and unmitigated exploitation of resources, the prospects for further manipulation with grave consequences are enhanced.

Other fields of struggle and potential weapons have already been considered and/or used, but by and large, the creativity of this approach to warfare knows no bounds.

> Some means and methods include psychological warfare (spreading rumors to intimidate the enemy and break down his will); smuggling warfare (throwing markets into confusion and attacking economic order); media warfare (manipulating what people see and hear in order to lead public opinion along); drug warfare (obtaining sudden and huge illicit profits by spreading disaster in other countries); network warfare (venturing out in secret and concealing one's identity in a type of warfare that is virtually impossible to guard against); technological warfare (creating monopolies by setting standards independently); fabrication warfare (presenting a counterfeit appearance of real strength before the eyes of the enemy); resources warfare (grabbing riches by plundering stores of resources); economic aid warfare (bestowing favor in the open and contriving to control matters in secret); cultural warfare (leading cultural trends along in order to assimilate those with different views); and international law warfare (seizing the earliest opportunity to set up regulations), etc., etc.…In this age, when the plethora of new technologies can in turn give rise to a plethora of new means and methods of

> fighting war (not to mention the cross-combining and creative use of these means and methods), it would simply be senseless and a waste of effort to list all of the means and methods one by one.[56]

These considerations are even of greater significance as special vulnerabilities in a people of wavering spiritual and moral commitment. The paranoia of conspiracy theorists aside, there is reason to believe that enemies of the West are already ramming their swords through some of these chinks in the West's armor.

Interlocking precisely with points made by Colonel Hammes, the passages below by Qiao Liang and Wang Xiangsui reveal how the West's enemies or potential enemies view the West—especially America. The weaknesses are not hidden. The evidence strongly suggests that the West's weaknesses are more obvious to others than they are to the West itself.

> What you must know is that this is a nationality that has never been willing to pay the price of life and, moreover, has always vied for victory at all costs. The appearance of high-technology weaponry can now satisfy these extravagant hopes of the American people.[57]
>
> ...
>
> This inclination makes them rigidly infatuated with and therefore have blind faith in technology and weapons, always thinking the road to getting the upper hand with war can be found with technology and weapons. This inclination also makes them anxious at any given time that their own leading position in the realm of weaponry is wavering, and they continually alleviate these concerns by manufacturing more, newer, and more complex weapons. As a result of this attitude, when the weapons systems which are daily becoming heavier and more complicated come into conflict with the terse principles required of actual combat, they always stand on the side of the weapons. *They would rather treat war as the opponent in the marathon race of military technology and are not willing to look at it more as a test of morale and courage, wisdom and strategy* [emphasis added]. They believe that as long as the Edisons of today do not sink into a sleep, the gate to victory will always be open to Americans. Self-confidence such as this has made them forget one simple fact—it is not so much that war follows the fixed race course of rivalry of technology and weaponry as it is a game field with continually changing direction and many irregular factors.[58]

The foregoing brings us around to an observation whose source we will learn further on: "For in war the chief incalculable is the human will...." Yet this is not simply the "chief incalculable," it is the cornerstone of all.

In a passage that sounds hubristically optimistic—but in today's world, one we should never discount—the Chinese colonels propose an unholy aggregation of forces and tactics to bring the West to its knees:

> Lastly, but certainly not the least important, is whether or not one has thought of combining the battlefield and non-battlefield, warfare and non-warfare, military and non-military which is more specifically combining stealth aircraft and cruise missiles with network killers, combining nuclear deterrence, financial wars and terrorists attacks, or simply combining Schwarzkopf + Soros + Xiaomolisi + [transliteration 1420 5459 6849 2448] + bin Laden.[59]

Earlier in their analysis, the colonels made a point that, contrary to their assessment, seems obscure to the American people and their leadership but that is dangerously true: being top dog does not ensure security; indeed, it draws fire. "Even the United States, which is the only superpower which has survived after the Cold War, has also realized that the strongest nation is often the one with the most enemies and the one threatened the most."[60]

Photograph by James Gordon, 2008. CC

A Kurdish PKK guerilla on the northern frontier of the most volatile and potentially dangerous part of the world—the Middle East and southwestern Asia. *None of this part of the world would be of any significant interest for the West—Israel a lesser exception—were it not for oil. But that oil addiction—which countless American presidents have decried and then done nothing about—has produced a panoply of intractable problems and implacable enemies for the West. Thus the West's obsessive materialism is directly connected to its now lethally dangerous predicament in the world. Having surrendered to its greed and materialism, the West is increasingly paying the price, but the principal on the debt is yet to be paid, and it will be huge.*

The status of the United States as the only world superpower has effectively painted a luminescent bull's-eye on the nation's forehead. Although historically the aggressive among the weaker always wish—if not plot—to bring the stronger down, this is an unprecedented era in history.

Part of the consequence of this, as Colonel Hammes puts it, is that "It is almost inevitable that a terrorist will use a weapon of mass destruction on U.S. soil."[61] The Chinese colonels also perceive the greater risk from terrorist, rather than state, action:

> The reason is that this is a group of maniacs which does not act according to the rules. A terrorist organization which possesses nuclear weapons is definitely much more dangerous than a nation with the same nuclear weapons. The creed of bin Laden is "If I die, then I will also not let others live," and therefore, he would then stop at nothing, so that in order to kill over ten Americans he would also drench several thousand innocent people in a pool of blood.[62]

This of course is the reason why the proliferation of WMD into the hands of terrorists with "no return address" is a critical issue for the West. Those WMDs, or their components, must come from somewhere—the terrorists' prospects for creating them from whole cloth being usually slim to none—and something identifiable as a state or state sponsored group.

This makes eventual confrontation with another nation not simply a possibility but a necessity, if the West has any prospect of avoiding the worst—and it is, as Colonel Hammes suggested, improbable that it will avoid it all.

In that respect the West must be realistic about what it faces philosophically and morally. Here the colonels also provide insight into how the West's enemies will likely reason. Revealing to a degree nothing else has been, the following passage tells us the moral parameters—no simulacrum or shroud is even proffered—that these inceptive opponents of the West would honor in any future conflict. Rejecting even their own countrymen as confining and primitive in his theories, they embrace the Westerner Machiavelli as the zenith in devising strategies and tactics of conflict.

> Before this, even Sun Zi and Claus[e]witz locked themselves in the barrier of the military domain, and only Machiavelli approached the realm of this thought. For a long period of time, owing to the fact that the thought of the Prince and its author were both way ahead of their time, they were held in contempt by the knights or rulers. They would naturally not be able to understand that going beyond all limits and boundaries was an ideological revolution, which included the premise of a revolution of military thought. In the same way, to date, those who only understand an imposing array of troops on the battlefield and who think that war is just killing people and methods of operation are just methods to kill people and that there is nothing worth giving attention to other than this, have been unable to understand this point.[63]
>
> ...
>
> If we want to have victory in future wars, we must be fully prepared intellectually for this scenario, that is, to be ready to carry out a war that, affecting all areas of life of the countries involved, may be conducted in a sphere not dominated by military actions. It is now still unknown what weapons, means, and personnel such wars will use and in what direction and sphere such wars will be conducted.[64]

There is almost an impulse to thank the colonels for their candor—most ruthlessness is carefully hidden behind Potemkin façades and the skills of dissimulation and deceit:

> The [necessary new] method is to create a complete military Machiavelli.
>
> Achieve objectives by fair means or foul, that is the most important spiritual legacy of this Italian political thinker of the Renaissance. In the Middle Ages, this represented a breakthrough against romantic chivalry and the declining tradition of knighthood. It meant using means, some possible comprehensive, without restraint to achieve an objective; this holds for warfare also. Even though Machiavelli was not the earliest source of "an ideology of going beyond limits" (China's Han Feizi preceded him), he was its clearest exponent.
>
> The existence of boundaries is a prerequisite for differentiating objects from one another. In a world where all things are interdependent, the significance of boundaries is merely relative....
>
> Speaking in terms of war, this could mean the boundary between the battlefield and what is not the battlefield, between what is a weapon and what is not, between soldier and noncombatant, between state and non-state or supra-state. Possibly it might also include technical, scientific, theoretical, psychological, ethical, traditional, customary, and other sorts of boundaries.[65]

If this were not enough to disorder the modern West's preconceptions about reality, we offer a quote from the West's side of the fence, the British strategist and war historian B. H. Liddell Hart. "Violence takes much deeper root in irregular warfare than it does in regular warfare. In the latter it is counteracted by obedience to constituted authority, whereas the former makes a virtue of defying

Photograph by Ivy Scarborough

The author (third from left) with Salvadoran Commandos during the communist guerrilla wars. *Any one of these men could go farther and longer under adverse circumstances and with less food than would typically even be expected of an American soldier. Poverty and hardship were the norm for most of them throughout their lives.*

authority and violating rules. It becomes very difficult to rebuild a country, and a stable state, on a foundation undermined by such experience."[66]

4GW—THE SWORD OF RADICAL ISLAM

...the "Zealot's" behaviour is essentially irrational and instinctive—he says in his heart that he will go thus far and no farther; that, having adopted just enough of the Westerner's military technique to keep any aggressive Western power at arm's length, he will consecrate the liberty thus preserved to the "keeping of the law" in every other respect and will thereby continue to win God's blessing for himself and for his offspring.

Arnold Toynbee[67]

Digressing for a moment from our analysis of the four factors that bear upon Western survival in a modern war, we complete a circuit back to Afghanistan, Iraq, and the hostility of militant Islam to the West. The West—with its propensity for ignoring unpleasant and contrary realities where it can and reframing them in different terminology where it cannot—insisted on calling the confrontation a "war on terror." Yet terror is a tactic—an ancient tactic. The Zealots used it against the Romans. Anarchists and communists used it against the czars. Westerners would today regard our fathers and grandfathers as odd had they persisted in saying they were "fighting a war against

Photo by USN Special Operations Forces in Afghanistan. PD-gov

Colonel Thomas X. Hammes believes that "It is almost inevitable that a terrorist will use a weapon of mass destruction on U.S. soil." Those WMDs, or their components, must come from somewhere and something identifiable as a state or state sponsored group. This makes eventual confrontation with another nation not simply a prospect but a necessity, if the West has any prospect of avoiding the worst—and it is, as Colonel Hammes suggested, improbable that it will avoid it all. During a Sensitive Site Exploitation (SSE) mission in the Zhawar Kili area of Eastern Afghanistan members of a U.S. Navy (USN) SEAL Team found valuable intelligence information, including this Osama bin Laden propaganda poster.

blitzkrieg." But if we were to dismissively refer to an adversary by virtue of his tactics—an unprecedented practice historically—we should then properly characterize this conflict as a "war on 4GW," for that is what radical Islam has seized on as its modern sword of the Prophet to defeat the "infidels." Terrorism has been with mankind for centuries; 4GW is the modern way to slaughter and wreak havoc. Terrorism is antiquated and confining tactically; 4GW grants free rein to the most creatively diabolical man can conceive.

Displaying less strategic competence and pragmatism than the Chinese colonels likely would, radical Islamists strive to some degree to make up for the difference through the pathological nature of their tactics. Though pathological, in a sense, is an apropos term for all modern warfare, here we mean it in respect of actions that vault over self-sacrifice and into the abyss of irrational behavior—even as measured by the standards of one's self-interest. Radical Islam not only wants to achieve practical strategic goals: it seeks the suffering and death of its enemies, even if its own must suffer and die equally or more in the process. This is perverse in the extreme.

In 1947, in *Civilization on Trial*, Arnold Toynbee cautioned the Western world about what it could expect from the Islamic world if the West's intrusions persisted.

> Pan-Islamism is dormant—yet we have to reckon with the possibility that the sleeper may awake if ever the cosmopolitan proletariat of a "Westernized" world revolts against Western domination and cries out for anti-Western leadership....That call might have incalculable psychological effects in evoking the militant spirit of Islam...because it might awaken echoes of a heroic age. On two historic occasions in the past, Islam has been the sign in which an Oriental society has risen up victoriously against an Occidental intruder. Under the first successors of the Prophet, Islam liberated Syria and Egypt from a Hellenic domination which had weighed on them for nearly a thousand years.
>
> Under Zangī and N¯u-ad-Dīn and Saladin and the Mamlūks, Islam held the fort against the assaults of Crusaders and Mongols. If the present situation of mankind were to precipitate a "race war," Islam might be moved to play her historic role once again. *Absit omen.*[68]

That bin Laden would likely agree, not simply with the assessment but the "race war" prospect, is an indicator of how accurate these words were and are. In additional words startlingly similar conceptually to those of bin Laden and his comrades, Toynbee seemed to perceive as the Islamists perceive.

> This concentric attack of the modern West upon the Islamic world has inaugurated the present encounter between the two civilizations. It will be seen that this is part of a still larger and more ambitious movement, in which the Western civilization is aiming at nothing less than the incorporation of all mankind in a single great society, and the control of everything in the earth, air, and sea which mankind can turn to account by means of modern Western technique. What the West is doing now to Islam, it is doing simultaneously to the other surviving civilizations....Thus the contemporary encounter between Islam and the West is not only more active and intimate than any phase of their contact in the past; it is also distinctive in being an incident in an attempt by Western man to "Westernize" the world—an enterprise which will possibly rank as the most momentous, and almost certainly as the most interesting, feature in the history even of a generation that has lived through two world wars.[69]

What then is a Muslim to do? His religion does not permit assimilation in the usual sense of that word. Toynbee explained that there are two courses open to him.

> Thus Islam is once more facing the West with her back to the wall; but this time the odds are more heavily against her than they were even at the most critical moment of the Crusades, for the modern West is superior to her not only in arms but also in the technique of economic life, on which military science ultimately depends, and above all in spiritual culture—the inward force which alone creates and sustains the outward manifestations of what is called civilization. Whenever one civilized society finds itself in this dangerous situation vis-à-vis another, there are two alternative ways open to it of responding to the challenge...[become] "Zealots" [or] "Herodians."
>
> The "Zealot" is the man who takes refuge from the unknown in the familiar; and when he joins battle with a stranger who practises superior tactics and employs formidable newfangled weapons, and finds himself getting the worst of the encounter, he responds by practising his own traditional art of war with abnormally scrupulous exactitude...."Zealotism," in fact, may be described as archaism evoked by foreign pressure; and its most conspicuous representatives in the contemporary Islamic world are "puritans" like the North African Sanūsīs and the Central Arabian Wahhābīs.[70]

In an insight that I saw in practice while with the mujahadeen in Afghanistan during their war with the Soviet army, Toynbee noted that the Muslim violates his own code in the use of the infidels' weapons, but rationalizes it as a necessary act. American Stinger missiles in 1986 and following did

Iran's Presidency Office, PD-gov

Mahmoud Ahmadinejad at the Natanz nuclear plant in central Iran, March 2007. *The reckless, unprincipled selfishness that led the West to overthrow a democratically elected government in Iran in the 1950s in order to secure—once again—its access to Middle Eastern oil, led, almost inevitably, to the Iranian revolution of 1979 and eventually to power in the hands of a radical fool like Ahmadinejad. The West, including Israel, now faces the daunting reality of nuclear weapons in the hands of its most implacable enemies.*

Courtesy of Andy Graham, HoboTraveler.com

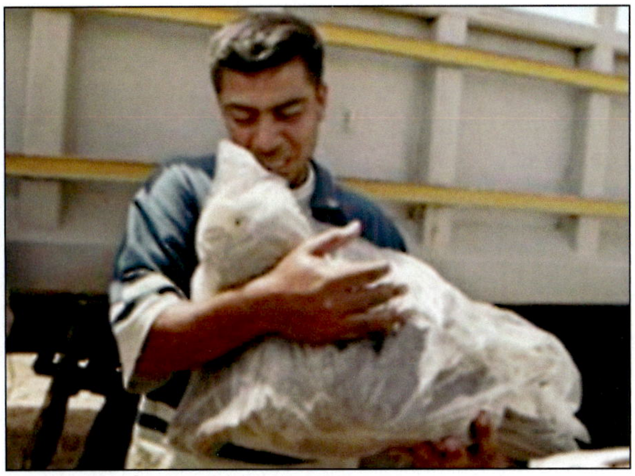

Courtesy of Andy Graham, HoboTraveler.com

Courtesy of Andy Graham, HoboTraveler.com

(Above left) Iraqi mass grave; North of Babylon, Iraq. Approximately 2,000 bodies from a mass grave where Iraqis who opposed Saddam were slaughtered. Grieving parents whose loved ones' bodies were found. *Colonel Thomas X. Hammes aimed part of the condemnation where it belonged: "In 1991, [the Shias] too, answered the elder President Bush's call to revolt following the liberation of Iraq. They, too, were abandoned by the United States and paid a heavy price: perhaps as many as fifty thousand Shias were killed in Saddam's suppression of their revolt." In truth, however, Colonel Hammes was partially mistaken: Iraq was not liberated, Kuwait— or, more precisely, Kuwaiti oil—was liberated. While American leaders made no effort to search for their misplaced sense of loyalty and moral responsibility, the Kurds and Shias continue to search, with mixed results, for the mass graves of their loved ones.* (Above right *and* bottom left) Victims of Saddam's regime.

realm of the modern West, a powerful figure can survive the former, yet be fatally wounded by the latter; and we emphasize "appearing" incompetent—concealing one's incompetence behind a screen of platitudes and shallow banalities has risen to a high art form among Western politicians.

Yet incompetent is the only valid characterization for such decisions if for no other reason than just watching the results. The U.S., having failed to learn from its earlier bad choice in Afghanistan, repeated it merely a decade later, ironically under the leadership of a president who had more than the usual opportunity to learn from the earlier president's mistake. "With the threat of the Taliban apparently gone, the U.S. government shifted its focus elsewhere. We perceived that the bulk of the fighting was over. In keeping with the president's oft-stated policy that the United States doesn't 'do' nation building, we essentially left the Afghans to rebuild their own country."[84]

Colonel Hammes is speaking of course about the vacuum created in late 2001 and 2002 by the decimation of the forces of the Taliban and the exit of America. If the good will of the Afghans—which was literally purchased in the 1980s—has not yet been frittered away, the world need only wait and watch. American politicians are supremely deft in the handling and manipulation of political investments, but display little such aptitude with human investments internationally.

PD

Hamid Gul, former chief of the ISI, the Pakistani intelligence agency. *Gul, sympathetic to the radical Islamists, characterized the U.S.'s abandonment of the Afghans in 1989 as a "classic betrayal." Gul, during the time I was in Afghanistan, was making certain the radical resistance groups received the lion's share of American aid and weaponry. The American acquiescence in this arrangement led to the dominance of the radical Islamist groups after the war ended. Gul's characterization cannot be fully refuted. The Afghans had successfully fought a proxy war for the U.S. aginst the Soviet Union that did more than anything else to bring down the communist empire. The power vacuum in Afghanistan brought about by the U.S.'s abandonment resulted in radical Islamic forces assuming power and providing a haven for the West's most implacable foes. September 11 might not have occurred had the U.S. stayed and aided the Afghans.*

Similar indifference to the discardable ally could be found earlier, again farther east, though perhaps not as egregiously, with the Hmong of Laos and the Montagnards of the Central Highlands of Vietnam. At least departing Special Forces and other American soldiers tried to aid their Asian comrades, albeit in the latter case with no significant help from the American government.

Modern American politicians' anatomies are in striking contrast to Theodore Roosevelt's as suggested by his famous ultimatum—which he fully intended to keep—"Perdicaris alive or Raisuli dead." Apparently, modern Western politicians generally—especially the "successful" ones—are examples of some form of advanced evolution: since hearts and spines are not needed in light of their philosophical and moral framework, they have been bred out of the species entirely.

American political leaders have, certainly in recent decades, demonstrated repeatedly their belief in a diplo-morality: you may profess one principle, yet actually practice another and remain, in your own eyes at least, "upright." The practical message sent: "We want you to fight with us; but if it comes to it, you must die in defeat—alone. You are expendable."

These practices have disfigured the American image abroad. Others may be powerless, but they are not blind. The disfigurement is not simply to the attractiveness of the Western way of life but to credibility, and the assurance that Americans in particular have the will—and can be counted on—to fight and die for their professed principles and their friends, not just their pocketbooks, oil, and their self-interest.

PD-gov.

Siu Beng and Siu Be, Montagnard Christians sentenced to 6+ and 3+ years respectively for fleeing repression in Vietnam's central highlands. *The Montgnards were loyal allies of the U.S. during the Vietnam War. Yet when the U.S. abandoned the field, they became yet another of several discardable allies—including Kurds and Shias in Iraq, and the Afghans—the U.S. has left to their own devices. American political leaders have demonstrated repeatedly their belief in a diplo-morality: you may profess one principle, yet actually practice another and remain, in your own eyes at least, "upright." The practical message sent: "We want you to fight with us; but if it comes to it, you must die in defeat—alone. You are expendable."*

This issue has been at the forefront of the thinking of many nations' leaders, friends and foes of the West, ever since the Vietnam War. "With the success of the Vietnamese, insurgents worldwide took heart. If a small Third World nation like Vietnam could defeat the United States, anything was possible. This led to increased efforts by insurgents in widely separated areas of the world."[85]

Whether one views the Vietnam mission as prudent or as tragically misbegotten does not obviate the question. The issues are different despite their relationship. As Colonel Hammes points out, America's enemies already have made their strategic assessment. "They talk about U.S. aversion to casualties, as proven by Vietnam, Lebanon, and Somalia. They fully expect that when a sufficient number of body bags go home, the United States will withdraw."[86]

They are likely to be proven correct—if we honestly review recent history. In light of recent historical evidence, the only remaining question probably still in the minds of the U.S.'s enemies is Will Americans only die in mass numbers when in the desperate final throes of a struggle for their national survival?

If the West refuses to see the world and its relationships with other peoples in moral terms, it would do well to at least consider them more realistically in terms of its own self-interest. As Liddell Hart observed—with tone and content not unlike a verse from Old Testament Proverbs—moral nobility of purpose is itself a formidable weapon: "A good cause is a sword as well as armour. Likewise, chivalry in war can be a most effective weapon in weakening the opponent's will to resist, as well as augmenting moral strength."[87]

The willingness to courageously face the realities of human nature, history, and the difficult issues that will confront any people in any time is the first step in martial readiness. The second relates to it: the willingness then of political and military leaders to face the reality of the threats peculiar to *their* time—and none will be more intractable than those facing the West in *our* time.

This means in part an acceptance of the notion that how the enemy chooses to fight will not likely pander to one's strengths—more often not—and one must prepare for that reality, not the illusory one that would be preferred.

Military historian Bevin Alexander noted, "Great generals do not repeat what has failed before. They do not send troops directly into a battle for which the enemy is prepared and waiting." In a sentence seemingly aimed precisely at the brain of the West, he then added, "The tremendous advances in military technology since the Korean War have not changed this fundamental truth."[88] Those advances notwithstanding, Alexander also observed the leading edge

Professor Naim Majruh by Ivy Scarborough

Professor Naim Majruh, Peshawar, Pakistan, 1985. *Intelligent and erudite, Majruh became an established source about the plight of his people, the Afghans. Urging that the West recognize the need to rebuild Afghanistan once the war was ended and warning repeatedly that their policies were strengthening the Islamic radicals, he was proven correct by subsequent events. His courage in speaking out against the radical Islamists resulted in his assassination shortly after I visited him.*

of 4GW: "But there is a significant countertrend that portends warfare depending less on overwhelming firepower and more on movements of small bodies of unobtrusive individuals who achieve their goals by surprise, ambushes, and unanticipated movements."[89]

The American military in particular sometimes leaves the track of the elephant when it might do better to leave the track of the wolf. Reliance on mass and technology deprive it of the stealth—its technology by that name notwithstanding—the versatility, flexibility, and the endurance that characterizes many of its potential adversaries. One to one on an even playing field—and war often presents that arrangement at best, sometimes much worse—it may not be able to compete. Hannibal began his thrust toward Rome with a massive "technological" advantage but had lost it—precisely because of its nature—by the time of his first major confrontation with the Roman army.

The ponderously powerful elephant is also more likely to injure friend as well as foe; hence the disturbing numbers of "friendly fire" casualties and "collateral damage" that must sometimes be tallied when the American military is deployed. Euphemisms do not alter reality nor palliate suffering. These casualties will account for more than grief before the hearths of Western homes and synchronic sobs in foreign lands; they will also make casualties of "good will" and assumptions about Western "moral righteousness" and "noble purposes." Thus, in yet another arena, Western man's two-edged sword of science and technology will sever arteries—relational and spiritual.

A noncom in one of America's most elite units once confidently proclaimed his trainees' superior capabilities by describing them as "racehorses." But the appellation was revealing in an unintended respect. Napoleon observed that the salient attribute of a good soldier was not martial skills, physical strength, nor physical courage, but the will to persevere and endure over long periods under the most adverse of circumstances. Napoleon's "warhorse" will be in the fight when the "racehorse" has had to be fed, watered, curried and perhaps taken back to the stable. Napoleon's "warhorse" is the horse that American and Western armies may find themselves up against more and more in the

American and Vietnamese civilians escaping South Vietnam as Saigon falls. *As fighting raged, Marines desperately loaded Vietnamese civilians onto helicopters that would transport them to waiting aircraft carriers. Having abandoned Vietnam to its fate, American political leaders displayed astounding callousness in leaving loyal Vietnamese to the wrath of the NVA. The callousness was exceeded perhaps only by the incompetence and unpreparedness of American officials in the face of what was obviously in the offing. Many Vietnamese who could not escape were executed or sent to "re-education" camps.*

Photo by Hugh Van Es.

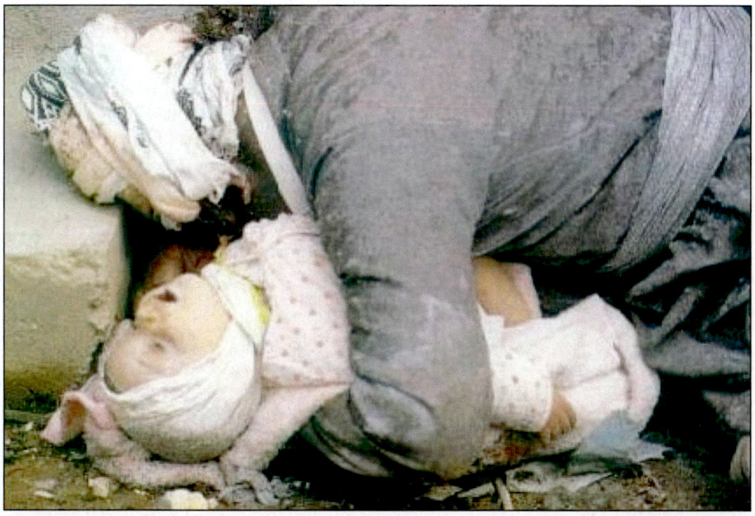
CC

CC

CC

future—and one who is committed to the notion that his death is a necessary sacrifice to boot. Lest it be assumed that this "warhorse's" endurance is primarily physical—and thus subject to being overwhelmed by Western military technology—the term also carries the connotation of psychic and spiritual stamina. I have seen some of these "warhorses" in action; and they are all the more impressive precisely because of their relative primitivism. Colonel Hammes observed, "Any nation that assumes it is inherently superior to another is setting itself up for disaster."[90]

As one of the premier military historians and strategists of the West, Liddell Hart warned of a danger that comes ironically with victory, rather than defeat: "As has happened so often in history, victory had bred a complacency and fostered an orthodoxy which led to

Halabja in Kurdish northern Iraq. *On 16 March 1988, Iraqi planes dropped gas canisters on the town. It was at this point the West should have gone straight for Saddam Hussein's throat. But it took no action until Saddam—now convinced of the West's weakness and passivity—invaded Kuwait two years later. The threat to their oil supplies motivated and mobilized the West in a way that the merciless killings of men, women, and children could not. Then throwing Saddam out of Kuwait—the West's intravenous injections of its most popular addictive substance having been assured—it left another of Satan's progeny free to roam that corner of the Middle East. This was of secondary importance—as long as others (i.e., non-Westerners) paid the price. The Shias and Kurds paid it with extravagant interest.*

U.S. Marine Corps photo by Cpl. Jason W. Fudge (Released)

A CH-46 Sea Knight over Al Taqqadum, Iraq, February 2008. *As Colonel Hammes observes, "True believers in technology see warfare as being reduced to a one-sided contest where the technologically superior side dictates all action." Past successes lead men to pursue replication of those successes even when the circumstances have radically changed. The American military—due to reliance on mass and technology—sometimes leaves the track of the elephant when it should leave the track of the wolf.*

defeat in the next war."[91] Relative to this same line of thought, and as we have seen elsewhere in this book, sociologist Carroll Quigley based much of his theory of civilizational decline and decay on what he called the "institutionalization" of "instruments." Though the evidence is strong that the American military is the most competent and least dysfunctional of that nation's multitudinous organs and bureaucracies, it too is susceptible to this form of social cancer, as suggested by Colonel Hammes. "Yet the DOD is a hierarchal, bureaucratic monopoly—essentially the world's largest since the fall of the Soviet Union. Almost by definition, bureaucracies strive to preserve the status quo. The larger the bureaucracy, the more effective it is at derailing change—particularly change that threatens its power."[92]

This decay, Quigley declared, finds "numerous examples" in military history

> ...of the institutionalization of instruments. The Roman army, which had conquered most of the known world by means of the legion, was unable, and probably unwilling, to transform itself into a

PD-Gov

U.S. Navy Sea-Air-Land (SEAL) members emerge from the water during tactical warfare training. *A noncom in one of America's elite units once confidently proclaimed his trainees superior capabilities by describing them as "racehorses." Increasingly, Western armies may find themselves up against "war horses" with the ability to fight without massive logistics and technology—and committed to death as a necessary sacrifice. Colonel Thomas X. Hammes observed, "Any nation that assumes it is inherently superior to another is setting itself up for disaster."*

force of heavily armed cavalry when this became necessary in the late fourth century of our era. As a result, the Roman army, and the civilization it was supposed to defend, were wiped from the earth by the charging horsemen of Germanic barbarians, beginning with the dreadful defeat at Adrianople in 378. The inability of fighting men to reorganize their ideas and their forces from infantry to cavalry was one of the vital factors in the replacement of pagan Classical civilization by Christian Western civilization.[93]

...

As a consequence of the institutionalization of military tactics by devotion to the bayonet, the saber, and the straight front, the early years of World War I saw the largest casualties in history, suffered, in most cases, to advance over a few miles of devastated terrain. In the early months of 1916 almost a million casualties were suffered by both sides in a single battle (Verdun), while later in the same year another battle (Somme) cost 1,200,000 casualties, mostly by bayonet charges against machine-gun fire.[94]

These latter bloodlettings were perpetrated by revered leaders of their respective states. That supposedly well educated and modern societies (by the standards of the time) would follow these fools until rivers of blood finally washed away at least a portion of their credibility is an important lesson for our time. The difference, tragically, will be that due to modern technology future prodigious bloodlettings will likely take place suddenly, even unexpectedly, and the opportunities for applying coagulants of wisdom may not exist.

From experiences such as these, the French premier, Georges Clemenceau, drew the conclusion that "war is far too important to ever be entrusted to soldiers."

Clemenceau might well have broadened his remark to say that everything is too important ever to be entrusted to professional experts, because every organization...becomes a vested-interest institution more concerned with its efforts to maintain itself or advance its own interests than to achieve the purpose that society expects it to achieve. As a consequence, old established armies and navies have frequently been defeated by new forces that have not yet become institutionalized. Thus the Greeks defeated the Persians; the new Roman navy defeated the Carthaginian fleet; the English defeated the French chivalry in the Hundred Years' War; the English navy, barely seventy-five years old, defeated the

PD-gov

Verdun, 1916. *In 1916 nearly a million casualties were suffered by both sides at Verdun and 1,200,000 at the Somme. Well educated and modern societies followed foolish military leaders until rivers of blood finally washed away their credibility —an important lesson for our time. The difference, tragically, will be that due to modern technology future prodigious bloodlettings will likely take place suddenly, even unexpectedly, and the opportunities for applying coagulants of wisdom may not exist.*

Photograph by Ivy Scarborough

The author (center) with a unit of the 82nd Airborne awaiting a Blackhawk to begin a night patrol during the war in Kosovo. *Despite the American military's incomparable technology some missions can only be achieved the old fashioned way, soldier to soldier, stamina to stamina, nerve to nerve, will to will.*

> Spanish Armada; Braddock was defeated; the Colonists won the American Revolution...the new French armies of Napoleon defeated the old, bedecorated forces of Austria and Prussia; the new Prussian army of Emil von Roon and Helmuth von Moltke defeated Austria and France in 1866 and 1870; the Boers held off the English for years; and Japan defeated Russia in 1905. Such defeats can be avoided only by constant reform that seeks to reorganize an institutionalized force so that its aim—to defeat the enemy—remains always paramount.[95]

Quigley described how a principle theme of this work—that everything in human experience is connected to everything else—applies to war:

> The ability of a society to defend itself on the military level is dependent on its ability to provide domestic order on the political level, wealth on the economic level, companionship on the social level, understanding on the intellectual level, and psychic certainty on the religious level. At the same time the ability of the society to defend itself affects its ability to achieve these five other goals. Thus each level is closely connected with all the others.[96]

In describing the "Stage of Decay," Quigley noted, among many indicia, the feature that would present the unguarded flank, the chink in the corroded armor, through which a civilization's enemies

Photograph by Ivy Scarborough

The author (on right) with Major General Pete Taylor, Commander of the National Training Center, Ft. Irwin, California, in the Mojave Desert. *The laconic and highly disciplined Taylor was an archetypical example of an unsettling reality: the American military may well be the last institution of American society—perhaps in Western civilization generally —that not only retains the capacity and the will to perceive reality as it is but also the capacity and the will to confront it. Certainly the American government—increasingly an archetype of dysfunctionality—is riven with evidence of Toynbee's "*pammixia*" and Sorokin's "chaotic syncretism." Should the decline and decay of American culture continue unabated, the military is likely to be the last cohesive institution around which the vestigial survivors of the waves of decline rally.*

would ram their spear: "There is a growing reluctance to fight for the society or even to support it by paying taxes. This period of decay may last for a long time, but eventually the civilization can no longer defend itself, as Mesopotamia could not after 400 B.C., as Egypt could not about the same time, as Crete could not after 1400 B.C., as Rome could not after A.D. 350, as the Incas and Aztecs could not after 1500, as India could not after 1700, as China could not after 1830, and as Islam could not after 1850."[97]

Returning to our foundational point above regarding the critical nature of a people's will, Quigley explained that the society's demise is brought about ultimately not by inability but the unwillingness that was the inevitable product of the people's spiritual and physical dissipations. "Stage 7 is the Stage of Invasion, when the civilization, no longer *able* to defend itself because it is no longer *willing* to defend itself, lies wide open to 'barbarian invaders.' These invaders are 'barbarians' only in the sense that they are 'outsiders.' Frequently these outsiders are another, younger, and more powerful civilization."[98]

Evidence, of at least an inchoate nature, can already be seen in the West of a massive moral shift of responsibility when it comes to suffering and dying in a battle dress uniform. The premier paladin of Western civilization, America, now relies exclusively on a professional, volunteer military for which financial incentives are a significant recruiting tool—analogous in some ways already to the late stage Roman Empire with its heavy reliance on mercenaries.

Ironically, the evidence is compelling that perhaps the last significant bastion of the values of personal honor and self-sacrifice can be found in Western military organizations. The stalwart souls who would offer their lives on the altar of faith, honor and selfless service are attracted to the one place where those words are more than platitudes: the military. An American Marine captain, later killed in

All images on this page PD-Gov

Iraq, was quoted by his father as having exclaimed while on a brief leave in the States, "Don't these people [his fellow Americans] know there is a war on?! Don't they know people are dying?!"

No, they don't, or at least, they don't want to be reminded, much less share broadly in the suffering and sacrifice. Therein lies the Achilles' heel of American foreign policy and Western security: if it cannot be done by high-tech strikes or quick, small, spec ops actions, it is unlikely it will be done at all; at least not with the long term, sustained commitment of the majority of the people. What it would take to trigger that latter response—if it could now be triggered at all—is surely a matter of strategic contemplation by the West's foes.

At another point in *Evolution of Civilizations*, Quigley briefly alluded—in harmony again with Toynbee, Sorokin, Dawson, Schaeffer, et al—to the greater depth behind civilizational decline and death. "Indeed, there might be good grounds for arguing that the root of our problem was our success in making life an end rather than a means to something higher."[99]

Samuel Huntington, after quoting some of these same passages from Quigley—and displaying the indeterministic viewpoint that we commend—brings us back around to a central issue of this book and of our age.

> The overriding lesson of the history of civilizations, however, is that many things are probable but nothing is inevitable. Civilizations can and have reformed and renewed themselves. The central issue for the West is whether, quite apart from any external challenges, it is capable of stopping and reversing the internal processes of decay. Can the West renew itself or will sustained internal rot simply accelerate its end and/or subordination to other economically and demographically more dynamic civilizations?[100]

Having, however, acknowledged once again the indeterministic view of human history I share with Professor Huntington, I am confident the choices mankind generally will continue to make will be reflected in the poetry of an earlier—once supremely optimistic—generation of the West:

That night your great guns, unawares,
Shook all our coffins as we lay,
And broke the chancel window-squares,
We thought it was the Judgement-day

And sat upright. While drearisome
Arose the howl of wakened hounds:
The mouse let fall the altar-crumb,
The worms drew back into their mounds,

Opposite: Clockwise from bottom left: Korea, Vietnam, first Gulf War, Bosnia (Bosnian man pleading for help just before being shot by Serbs), Kosovo, Somalia, Afghanistan. *Americans don't want to be reminded, much less share in the suffering and sacrifice of war. Therein lies an Achilles' heel of American foreign policy and security: if it cannot be done by high-tech strikes or quick, spec ops actions, it is unlikely it will be done at all; at least not with the long-term, sustained commitment of the people. What it would take to trigger that commitment—if it could now be triggered at all—is surely a matter of strategic contemplation by the West's foes.*

The glebe-cow drooled. Till God called, 'No;
It's gunnery practice out at sea
Just as before you went below;
The world is as it used to be:

'All nations striving strong to make
Red war yet redder. Mad as hatters
They do no more for Christés sake
Than you that are helpless in such matters.
'That this is not the judgement-hour
For some of them's a blessed thing,
For if it were they'd have to scour
Hell's floor for so much threatening...

'Ha, ha. It will be warmer when
I blow the trumpet (if indeed
I ever do; for you are men,
And rest eternal sorely need).'...

So down we lay again. 'I wonder,
Will the world ever saner be,'
Said one, 'than when He sent us under
In our indifferent century!'

And many a skeleton shook his head.
'Instead of preaching forty year,'
My neighbour Parson Thirdly said,
'I wish I had stuck to pipes and beer.'...

Again the guns disturbed the hour,
Roaring their readiness to avenge,
As far inland as Stourton Tower,
And Camelot, and starlit Stonehenge.

"Channel Firing" by Thomas Hardy

END NOTES
CHAPTER 17

1 General Omar Bradley, Speech on Armistice Day, 1948. *Collected Writings,* Vol. 1 (Washington, D.C.: GPO, 1967), 178.
2 Pitirim A. Sorokin, *The Crisis of Our Age* (Oneworld Publications Ltd., 1941; this edition Sergei P. Sorokin and Peter P. Sorokin, 1992), 178.
3 Thomas X. Hammes, *The Sling and the Stone: On War in the 21st Century* (St. Paul, MN: Zenith Press, 2006), ix.
4 Colonel Qiao Liang and Colonel Wang Xiangsui, *Unrestricted Warfare: China's Master Plan to Destroy America* (Panama City, Panama: Pan American Publishing, 2002), 30–32.
5 Arnold Toynbee, *A Study of History* (New York: Oxford Press, 1946), 245.
6 Qiao and Wang, *Unrestricted Warfare,* 32.
7 Immanuel Wallerstein, *The End of the World As We Know It* (Minneapolis: University of Minnesota, 1999), 10.
8 Wallerstein, *The End of the World As We Know It,* 16.
9 Wallerstein, *The End of the World As We Know It,* 16–17.
10 Wallerstein, *The End of the World As We Know It,* 16.
11 Jonathan Tucker, *War of Nerves: Chemical Warfare from World War I to Al-Qaeda* (New York: Pantheon Books, 2006), 9–10.
12 Tucker, *War of Nerves,* 9–10.
13 John Keegan, *The Mask of Command* (London: Penguin, 1988), 351.
14 Thomas K. Adams, "Future Warfare and the Decline of Human Decision Making," *Parameters 31* (2001), 57–71.
15 Hammes, *Sling and the Stone,* 273.
16 Hammes, *Sling and the Stone,* 42.
17 Hammes, *Sling and the Stone,* 194–195.
18 Adams, "Future Warfare," 57.
19 Adams, "Future Warfare," 20.
20 Adams, "Future Warfare," 24–25.
21 Adams, "Future Warfare," 57–71.
22 Adams, "Future Warfare," 57–71.
23 Adams, "Future Warfare," 57–71.
24 Qiao and Wang, *Unrestricted Warfare,* 16–17.
25 Adams, "Future Warfare," 51.
26 Hammes, *Sling and the Stone,* xii.
27 Hammes, *Sling and the Stone,* 2.
28 Hammes, *Sling and the Stone,* 31.
29 Hammes, *Sling and the Stone,* 4.
30 Hammes, *Sling and the Stone,* 3.
31 Hammes, *Sling and the Stone,* 4.
32 Hammes, *Sling and the Stone,* 38.
33 Hammes, *Sling and the Stone,* 189.
34 Hammes, *Sling and the Stone,* 191.
35 Hammes, *Sling and the Stone,* 201.
36 Hammes, *Sling and the Stone,* 202.
37 Hammes, *Sling and the Stone,* 209.
38 Hammes, *Sling and the Stone,* 213.

39 Hammes, *Sling and the Stone*, 216.
40 Hammes, *Sling and the Stone*, 216.
41 Hammes, *Sling and the Stone*, 221.
42 Hammes, *Sling and the Stone*, 183.
43 Hammes, *Sling and the Stone*, 222.
44 Hammes, *Sling and the Stone*, 224.
45 Basil Henry Liddell Hart, *The Decisive Wars of History: A Study in Strategy* (London: G. Bell & Sons, Ltd., 1929), 16.
46 Hammes, *Sling and the Stone*, 224.
47 Hammes, *Sling and the Stone*, 227.
48 Hammes, *Sling and the Stone*, 227.
49 Hammes, *Sling and the Stone*, 262.
50 Hammes, *Sling and the Stone*, 259.
51 Hammes, *Sling and the Stone*, 257.
52 Qiao and Wang, *Unrestricted Warfare*, xxi.
53 Qiao and Wang, *Unrestricted Warfare*, 1–2.
54 Qiao and Wang, *Unrestricted Warfare*, 15.
55 Qiao and Wang, *Unrestricted Warfare*, 42–43.
56 Qiao and Wang, *Unrestricted Warfare*, 42–43.
57 Qiao and Wang, *Unrestricted Warfare*, 75.
58 Qiao and Wang, *Unrestricted Warfare*, 77.
59 Qiao and Wang, *Unrestricted Warfare*, 120.
60 Qiao and Wang, *Unrestricted Warfare*, 96.
61 Hammes, *Sling and the Stone*, 269.
62 Qiao and Wang, *Unrestricted Warfare*, 113–114.
63 Qiao and Wang, *Unrestricted Warfare*, 120–121.
64 Qiao and Wang, *Unrestricted Warfare*, 144–145.
65 Qiao and Wang, *Unrestricted Warfare*, 154.
66 Hart, *Decisive Wars*, 369.
67 Arnold Toynbee, *Civilization on Trial* (New York: Oxford University Press, 1948), 189–190.
68 Toynbee, *Civilization on Trial*, 212.
69 Toynbee, *Civilization on Trial*, 186–187.
70 Toynbee, *Civilization on Trial*, 187–189.
71 Toynbee, *Civilization on Trial*, 189–190.
72 Toynbee, *Civilization on Trial*, 194–196.
73 Toynbee, *Civilization on Trial*, 198–199.
74 Toynbee, *Civilization on Trial*, 199.
75 Toynbee, *Civilization on Trial*, 201.
76 Michael Scheuer, *Through Our Enemies' Eyes* (Dulles, VA: Quicksilver Books, 2006).
77 Carroll Quigley, *The Evolution of Civilizations: An Introduction to Historical Analysis* (New York: Macmillan, 1961), 160.
78 Hart, *Decisive Wars*, 323.
79 Bevin Alexander, *How Great Generals Win: A Military Historian Appraises the World's Greatest Commanders, from Hannibal to MacArthur* (New York: W. W. Norton, 2002), 41.
80 Sorokin, *The Crisis of Our Age*, 177–178.
81 Francis Schaeffer, *How Should We Then Live?* (Wheaton, IL: Crossway, 1983), 251.
82 Hammes, *Sling and the Stone*, 181–182.
83 Hammes, *Sling and the Stone*, 182.

84 Hammes, *Sling and the Stone*, 154.
85 Hammes, *Sling and the Stone*, 76.
86 Hammes, *Sling and the Stone*, 177.
87 Hart, *Decisive Wars*, 322.
88 Alexander, *Great Generals*, 21.
89 Alexander, *Great Generals*, 21–22.
90 Hammes, *Sling and the Stone*, ix.
91 Hart, *Decisive Wars*, 232.
92 Hammes, *Sling and the Stone*, 242.
93 Quigley, *Evolution of Civilizations*, 103.
94 Quigley, *Evolution of Civilizations*, 108.
95 Quigley, *Evolution of Civilizations*, 109–110.
96 Quigley, *Evolution of Civilizations*, 119–120.
97 Quigley, *Evolution of Civilizations*, 159–160.
98 Quigley, *Evolution of Civilizations*, 160.
99 Quigley, *Evolution of Civilizations*, 406.
100 Samuel P. Huntington, *The Clash of Civilizations and the Remaking of World Order* (New York: Simon & Schuster, 1996), 303.

CHAPTER

18

THE DESTINATION OF THE WHEEL OF HISTORY FOR THE WEST: APOCALYPSE, CATASTROPHE, OR REDEMPTION?

At last, in the grey dawn of Civilization, the fire in the soul dies down. The dwindling powers rise to one more, half-successful, effort of creation, and produce the Classicism that is common to all dying Cultures. The soul thinks once again, and in Romanticism looks back piteously to its childhood; then finally, weary, reluctant, cold, it loses its desire to be, and, as in Imperial Rome, wishes itself out of the overlong daylight and back in the darkness of proto-mysticism, in the womb of the mother, in the grave.

Oswald Spengler[1]

...hence the inevitability of a fiery ordeal as the only available means of teaching the otherwise unteachable.

Pitirim Sorokin[2]

The third premise is that the modern world-system, as a historical system, has entered into a terminal crisis and is unlikely to exist in fifty years.... The period of transition will be a terrible time of troubles, since the stakes of the transition are so high, the outcome so uncertain, and the ability of small inputs to affect the outcome so great.

Immanuel Wallenstein[3]

The wheel of history has come a long way in less than a century from its contact with members of Western civilization during the Christmas Truce in the trenches on the Western Front to twenty-first-century members of the same civilization at Abu Ghraib. For the wise and the sensitive, copious volumes of history, sociology, anthropology and psychology are not needed to understand the significance of those two points on that epic and grave passage.

Nonetheless, we have traveled a long way since our introductory chapter, circumnavigating as it were a globe of ideas, theories, and principles of civilizational decline and decay generally and Western decline and decay specifically. We have examined the writings of most of the very short roster of historians, anthropologists, and sociologists who have written on the decline and decay of Western civilization. From this examination we have seen evidence that each has reached some conclusions, if not made predictions, about where this will likely lead. We will, in this chapter, scrutinize those conclusions, taking each author in turn.

But first, we should focus on the wheel of history Toynbee alluded to and consider how this relates to the hypervelocity of our age and the ultimate destiny of our civilization.

HISTORY—THE ARCHIVE OF THE "VAIN REPETITIONS" OF MAN

If I am out of my mind, it's all right with me.
from *Herzog* by Saul Bellow[4]

The speaker from *Herzog* could be expressing the unstated—and uncontemplated—attitude of much of the human race through most of history. Though he sometimes speaks of his foolish choices and dangerous folly, man persists in both. The consequences have led him to speculate whether his plight is self-inflicted or an inescapable curse. Toynbee confronted the problem of the apparent repetitions of history with an understandable dismay and perplexity at the thought that all shall recur regardless of man's choices. "Are these 'vain repetitions' of the Gentiles," he asked, "really the law of the Universe and, therefore, incidentally the law of the histories of civilizations?" If that is true, then we "can hardly escape the conclusion that we are the perpetual victims of an everlasting cosmic practical joke, which condemns us to endure our sufferings and to overcome our difficulties and to purify ourselves of our sins—only to know in advance that the automatic and inevitable lapse of a certain meaningless measure of time cannot fail to stultify all our human exertions by reproducing the same situation again and again *ad infinitum*, just as if we had never exerted ourselves at all."[5]

Toynbee considered that if humanity's future is truly dictated in this way whether man could tolerate his fate.

> This conclusion may be tolerable to an unusually robust intellect in an unusually sanguine mood. A modern Western philosopher has even succeeded in making the "law of eternal recurrence" a matter for rejoicing:
>
>> Sing and bubble over, O Zarathustra, heal your soul with new songs, so that you may bear your great destiny, that was never yet the destiny of any man! For your animals well know, O Zarathustra, who you are and must become: behold, you are the teacher of eternal recurrence, that is now your destiny!...Behold, we know what you teach: that all things recur eternally, and we ourselves with them, and that we have already existed an infinite number of times before, and all things with us....[6]

I would point out, however, Nietzsche went insane—an end not suggestive of a "robust intellect" in a "sanguine mood."

We should see beyond this declaration for what it is: a sham, a self-deluding intellectual affectation born of a desperate need to embolden a fearful soul confronting the ominous blackness of meaninglessness; it is philosophical whistling in the dark—useless for support or succor because it denies reality. Man has futilely attempted to reconcile himself to the monotonous meaninglessness of such a fate throughout history.

We sense in Toynbee's description of these efforts a reasonable skepticism about the professed serenity with which some confront this prospect.

PD-art

Baptism of Constantine. *It would be assumed perhaps that the fifth century—with the utter collapse of the pagan Roman Empire before advancing barbarian hordes—would have produced a hopeful, forward-looking attitude among Christians. But this would fail to take into account two seemingly paradoxical characteristics of the age: the first was the embrace of the Christian faith by Constantine, making it the religion of the Empire, which provided Christians with a political and legal defilade never before available to them. The second was the continuing moral debasement of the Roman citizenry—who had already plumbed depths of depravity seemingly unfathomable, except to the most perverse minds. Christians assumed that the biblical Apocalypse must be nigh. The parallels in our time with the apocalyptic end of history anticipated by Christians in the fifth century suggest that it is possible that modern Western Christians may be making the same erroneous assumptions.*

> Aristotle, too, shows no signs of distress…by making the casual observation…that in human history the recurrence of identical scientific views does not happen just once or twice or a small number of times; it happens *ad infinitum.*
>
> …He contemplates with a dispassionate calm the proposition that "human life is a vicious circle" of repetitive genesis and decay, and feels no pang. Virgil, too…dismisses the recurrent Trojan War as a slight and momentary recrudescence of the Old Adam.…Yet, when the poet returns from his day-dream of an earthly paradise regained to resume the spiritual burden of his own tormented generation, he confesses that the heroic warfare of the Achaeans in the pre-Hellenic interregnum has led on, through a continuous chain of karma, to the internecine warfare of the Roman war-lords.[7]

Toynbee found this deterministic view of history intolerable; and, of course, his rejection of it is completely consistent with the original Western embrace of indeterminism as explicated most fundamentally in the teachings of Christ: Man does have a choice—he can control his own destiny. So, I lay it down here: history is fundamentally indeterministic; man sets his own course; he determines his own destiny.

But this declaration does not satisfy our efforts to understand—it does not explain—why man persists in repeating the same foolish choices and folly with monotonous regularity throughout history. Pitirim Sorokin offered a description of the thought and behavior—if not the deeper reasons why.

> "*Homo sapiens*" seems to be rather purblind so far as the lessons of historical, socio-cultural experience are concerned. He applies and profits by the experience of other persons in matters concerning his physical health. When he is sick, he gives up various pleasures; makes other necessary sacrifices, such as going to bed and taking the prescribed medicine; and behaves in general in a rational manner.... He thus frequently avoids much direr consequences, including possibly death itself. In such matters he does not question the existence of causal relationships and causal consequences. Hence he displays neither recklessness nor stupidity, nor does he expect the impossible.
>
> But from the lessons of history concerning life and death, the blossoming and sickness of society, man learns hardly anything. He behaves either as if past history were non-existent, or as if the past presented no situation essentially comparable to that in which his own society finds itself; as if there were no causal relationships and consequences; as if there were no such thing as socio-cultural sickness, and hence no need to sacrifice momentary pleasures and other sensate utilities and values in order to avoid an infinitely greater catastrophe. In this field of experience he remains virtually unteachable.[8]

To say that "*Homo sapiens*" is "purblind" does not do justice to the blood and misery that are the result of mankind tripping over and bumping into the ponderously heavy furniture of reality or his perennial falling into the deepest ditches of war and self-destructive behavior. The truth of Sorokin's psychoanalysis of the human species is precisely the reason all pessimistic prognoses are likely to have more merit than the popular optimistic ones.

Man could change the course of his life, his nation, and his civilization, but will he? Thus we are faced with a seeming paradox: an indeterministic capacity in the abstract, a seemingly deterministic reality.

Why man is so "purblind" is a compelling question. It may simply be because he does not want to give up the license, dissipations, and materialism central to what Sorokin called the *sensate culture.* It is certainly true that a primary feature of humility is teachability. That man is "virtually unteachable" in this realm is another way of saying he lacks humility. Once again the "virtues" of man touted in the Renaissance and Enlightenment are exposed as vices.

Though man has the power to make the wise choice, more often his chosen course is that of folly. Thus, prediction of the course of history becomes less a matter of preferred possibilities than dangerous probabilities.

We will, however, see a pattern among our observers: Most declare an indeterministic view and, with it, sometimes a form of professed optimism, albeit typically slight or guarded. But their professed optimism belies what are clearly pessimistic analyses of their own making.

Perhaps they—products of Western civilization or acculturated to Western values—were, and are, subject to a culturally mandated optimism not native to objective reality—indeed, often in conflict with it. This is one of those thoughts, beliefs, propensities, etc., that lie at the core of Western man's character, one that, in this case, is inimical to Western man's best interests.

We must defy all cultural conventions and reject it outright—insisting on a tough-minded, relentless realism.

THREE POSSIBLE DESTINIES: APOCALYPSE, CATASTROPHE, OR REDEMPTION?

Memento mori.
(Remember that you must die.)

As outlined in the Introduction, it would appear there are three possible outcomes to the crisis of Western civilization. These outcomes are my own conclusions though, as we will see, they comport in many respects with some of the speculations of our observers.

- **Default:** A gradual, incremental, but ultimately catastrophic end; no profound and sweeping change in the core beliefs and values of Western man; a more or less persistent clinging to the unhealthful values, beliefs, and behaviors that brought him to this crisis; with the inevitable result of complete moral and intellectual collapse, dramatic and continuing erosion of economic and military power, ever deepening internal and external conflicts, leading to the gradual expunging of Western civilization as a viable system of thought and belief, or as an economic or military entity of consequence.
- **Apocalyptic:** Complete and rapid destruction of Western civilization; either of the sort characterized as a biblical apocalypse or a catastrophic death potentially caused by either external powers (the more historically conventional demise) or the sudden manifestation of cataclysmic consequences from the degradation of the environment (a result of the uniquely dangerous state of the modern world as produced by science and technology), leading to an abrupt expunging of Western civilization as a viable system of thought and belief, or as an economic or military entity of consequence.
- **Redemptive:** A timely, sweeping, and unadulterated awakening to the crisis of our age, with a concomitant expurgating of the deleterious ideas, values, beliefs, and behaviors that precipitated the crisis; their supplanting with tested traditional ideas, values, and beliefs; complemented by new corollaries as required by the unique historical status of the modern world, leading to spiritual, moral, and intellectual revitalization of creativity and the resurgence of Western civilization in a new, more vigorous, and spiritually and intellectually powerful form.

As noted in the Introduction, some versions of the Default outcome and the Apocalyptic outcome could conceivably prove to be the penultimate and final chapters in the history of Western civilization.

Furthermore, a Redemptive course is available to any individual citizen of Western civilization—and some will surely take it—but it cannot, by definition, be a successor to the other two, for it presupposes a dramatic and timely shift in course before some unseen "it-is-too-late" threshold is crossed. This is itself another great issue of our time: Has that historical/psychological/spiritual threshold already been crossed?

A BIBLICAL APOCALYPSE?

But in the days when the seventh angel is about to sound his trumpet,
the mystery of God will be accomplished, just as he announced to his servants the prophets.
Revelation 10:7

Before we perambulate the individual conclusions of our observers, we should first examine the possible religious prognosis anticipated by millions of Christians, members of the dominant religious belief system behind and supporting Western civilization. This prospect—the possible imminence of the biblical Apocalypse—would affect not only the West but all life on the planet. This expectancy carries great weight with many Christians. The biblical indicia would appear, in large part, to be present. Should this be the imminent fate of mankind it will not be daunting for the sincere Christian for whom it has long been sought and much to be welcomed.

Since it has been long sought by many of the Christian faithful, there has been a tendency of the modern conservative branches of the Christian church in particular to assume its imminence not simply because of the evidence of modern history when juxtaposed with biblical teaching. There is yet another reason: the despoliation of the Christian heritage of Western civilization—as we have seen, once itself known as Christendom—by secularist and materialist forces has left many Christians feeling desolate.

The bleakness of a world given more and more to self-indulgence, materialism, depravity, and the rejection of spiritual values for the man-centered "Invictus" is its own precursor of hell for the true Christian—as it will prove to be for all of humanity if taken to its ultimate conclusion. Thus the Christian may long for an end to the darkness and eagerly await the final revelation of the Light. But his longing may distort his perceptions and blind him to a greater divine purpose.

A colt waiting on a narrow street in Old Jerusalem, not unlike one that awaited Jesus to ride triumphantly through the streets at Passover two millennia ago. *Symbolic of one of the most momentous events in history and the hopes of millions of Christians, it is also a reminder that, whatever the end of Western civilization, Jerusalem will play a central role in world history right up to the time that history is no more.*

Photograph by Ivy Scarborough

There is nothing new under the sun in this respect as well. Christians have been here before—during the last pathetic act of the drama of the Roman Empire. It would be assumed perhaps that the fifth century—with the utter collapse of the pagan Roman Empire before advancing barbarian hordes—would have produced a hopeful, forward-looking attitude among Christians. But this would fail to take into account two seemingly paradoxical characteristics of the age: the first was the embrace of the Christian faith by Constantine making it the religion of the Empire—if you cannot beat them, join them, or at least exploit them for your own purposes—which provided Christians with a political and legal defilade never before available to them. The second was the continuing moral debasement of the Roman citizenry—who had already plumbed depths of depravity seemingly unfathomable, except to the most perverse minds.

The former, when coupled with the intellectual blight of the "this-is-the-world-we-know-and-all-we-know" syndrome common to most of humanity's thinking (and prominent in the West today) produced dismay and despair even among Christians. When juxtaposed with the latter, Christians assumed that the biblical Apocalypse must be nigh. That their good faith assumption was misbegotten is now apparent, but it is well worth examining how they came to it. Christopher Dawson helped us to understand this and placed it in the broader context of history as well as our time.

> …the ancient world was faced with a crisis that threatened civilisation with destruction almost at the moment when the Church had won the victory over paganism. For one thousand years the Mediterranean world had lived securely in the light of Hellenic culture. Now its sun had set, and the darkness

PD-art

Four Horsemen of the Apocalypse by Viktor Vasnetsov. 1887. *Christians of the fifth century were convinced that the biblical Apocalypse was nigh—all the biblical indicators seemed to be present. Many Christians of the twenty-first-century West may be making a similar mistake, for much the same reasons—thereby failing to come to grips with their responsibility for what is upon us. Contemplating rescue is far easier than facing arduous duty and dire suffering. This nurtures a tendency to passivity and resignation.*

> and cold of the barbarous North descended on the world. The East German warrior peoples driven from South Russia and the Danube, by the advance of the Mongol hordes from beyond the Volga, broke through the defences of the Empire and wrecked the imposing fabric of Roman order. Yet St. Augustine…regarded these things as temporary and accidental. He lived not by the light of Athens and Alexandria, but by a new light that had suddenly dawned on the world from the East only a few centuries earlier. Imperial Rome was, after all, the daughter of Babylon, the incarnation of human pride and material wealth, the persecutor of the saints, and the oppressor of the poor. Man's true destinies were realised elsewhere, in Jerusalem, the City of God, which was being built up through all the ruin and destruction of human kingdoms and empires by the irresistible momentum of a divine purpose.[9]

The parallels in our time with the apocalyptic end of history described in the Bible and anticipated by Christians in the fifth century suggest that it is possible that modern Western Christians may be making the same erroneous assumptions.

In *Religion and the Rise of Western Culture*, Dawson carried this historical account further, first by noting the response of Christians to the events of the fifth century, then recounting a later crisis of the church, likewise lost to the memory of the church in our time. "These things, St. Columban wrote a few years later in his letter to Pope Boniface, were signs of the end. The world was visibly falling to pieces and the Shepherd of Shepherds was about to come for the last time. And therefore it was natural that Christians should turn their eyes to the other world—to the Eternal City, of which they were already citizens by adoption and which was steadily extending its frontiers against the transitory and fading visible world."[10]

It is sobering to consider, inasmuch as I subscribe to the view that history not only does repeat itself but is in the process of doing so in our time, what Dawson related occurred in that era. "It is of these dark years that the chronicler of St. Vedast writes, 'The Northmen cease not to slay and carry into captivity the Christian people, to destroy the churches and to burn the towns. Everywhere there is nothing but dead bodies—clergy and laymen, nobles and common people, women and children. There is no road or

CC

St. Columban's Blessing (from a fresco at the Cathedral Brugnato, Liguria, Italy). *Dawson described St. Columban's reaction to catastrophes of the fifth century through "a letter to Pope Boniface [that these] were signs of the end. The world was visibly falling to pieces and the Shepherd of Shepherds was about to come for the last time. And therefore it was natural that Christians should turn their eyes to the other world—to the Eternal City, of which they were already citizens by adoption and which was steadily extending its frontiers against the transitory and fading visible world."*

place where the ground is not covered with corpses. We live in distress and anguish before this spectacle of the destruction of the Christian people.'"[11]

Who might be the analogues in the collapse of modern Western civilization to the barbarians of the fifth through the ninth centuries is an intriguing, if perverse, matter of speculation. By the ninth century "the climax of the storm had passed and the survival of Christendom was secured." In Dawson's view, "There has never been a war which so directly threatened the existence of Western Christendom as a whole...." Yet the trial of fire had its benefits: "It subjected the inchoate order of Western Christendom to a terrible test which burnt away anything that was weak and superfluous and left only the hardest and most resistant elements which were inured to insecurity and violence." But it also "destroyed the hope of a pacific development of culture that had inspired the leaders of the Church and the missionary movement and reasserted the warlike character of Western society that it had inherited from its barbarian past. Henceforward the warrior ethos, the practice of private war and the blood feud were as prevalent in Christian society as among its pagan neighbours."[12]

We can now see that in its two millennia, the Christian church has truly been here before. Human nature being what it is, we are wont to react similarly to the dangers and disillusionments of our time as did those who preceded us. We may anticipate, either with foreboding or great hope, a similar imminent fate.

Finally, the Christian should be ever mindful of the words of Christ himself: "only the Father" knows when the end will be.[13] If only the Father knows, then who is any man to speculate or hypothesize? That is the height of presumptuousness. Though there have surely been many over the centuries who have presumed, we certainly will not.

Man cannot think God's thoughts for Him. The Christian's duty is to obey; anything that distracts from that duty is of man, not of God.

OUR WISE MEN'S CONCLUSIONS

In the end, more than they wanted freedom, they wanted comfort and security. And in the end, they lost it all—freedom, comfort and security.
Edward Gibbon describing ancient Athens[14]

Regardless of one's beliefs about the prospects for a chronologically proximate biblical Apocalypse, we should turn our attention to other possible penultimate and final chapters in the history of Western man. We should consider what may be over the next rise—whether a prelude to the terminus of history or a new era, either of foreboding or promise. Here we survey the conclusions of our wise men individually.

PHILIP BAGBY

Writing in the mid-twentieth century, Bagby cautioned against drawing too many parallels with the final stages and fate of the Roman Empire. The "relevant factors" have not yet been "isolated," though we "can find confirmation in our observations...for a number of beliefs about the future of our civilization which are already widely held." "...[I]t is probable that the nations whose culture is primarily Western European will eventually achieve some form of political unity, as the Classical world did under the Roman Empire...." We might also conclude that "a simplified form of the common culture suitable for mass consumption (such as we now identify as American) is likely to become predominant in our civilization as it did in the Classical civilization under the Roman Empire." Furthermore, "the rationalism in our civilization has on the whole run its course and...we can look forward to a partial return to religion, a search for a stable balance between faith and reason in the next centuries, something similar to the revival of religion in the ancient world under the Caesars."[15]

Bagby concluded, however, that "we may come to one fairly definite negative conclusion. There is nothing to indicate that the disappearance of Western–European civilization is imminent, as Toynbee seems to think. Classical civilization continued for at least five centuries after 200 B.C...."[16]

This challenge to Toynbee's analysis does not ring true. Bagby seemed incognizant of realities that Toynbee heeded. Does Toynbee's seeming inchoate religious faith perhaps account for his pessimism? Is it the result of the objective awareness of a man steeped in the values of the Christian religion through the British culture that a moral and intellectual decline of the first rank had been sweeping the Western world? Could it be that Toynbee recognized this rejection of faith as the major distinguishing feature of modern Western civilization?

There are other considerations. We might respond to Bagby's flat analogy by first calling into question the dates he selected and then noting, Yes, but even were we to accept your dating, classical civilization survived another 500 years in a time when human activities and change moved—when measured by today's standards—at a glacial pace. In that era, technology did not play the dynamic, dominant role it does in our time. Toynbee, at least in part, acknowledged this difference through his repeated warnings about the effects of science and technology on the world, the West in particular.

As we have already seen in the chapters "Man as God: Science and Technology" and "Hypervelocity—The Turning of the Wheel of History in Our Age," the distinguishing feature of our age that sets it apart from all others is the critical central role of science and technology. As a consequence, our civilization is aging faster than any other in world history. The decomposition processes of decay and decline follow fairly predictable patterns; but those processes can accelerate—and certainly have in our time. Furthermore, certain historically discernible factors or stages might "outrun" others precisely because of the effects of science and technology.

We see in the following passage another example of Bagby's error in the potentially arbitrary selection of dates and time phases: "[T]he whole process of development from the beginnings of a civilization to the formation of a 'Universal State' takes between a thousand and fifteen hundred years."[17] Once again there is no evidence that Bagby took into account the accelerating effects of science and technology.

OSWALD SPENGLER

... all this, broad and imposing, is the prelude of a future which is still in store for us and with which the history of West European mankind will be definitely closed.[18]

Likewise, we might challenge another of Bagby's interpretations, this time of the meaning and intent of Spengler: "Spengler's thought on this point...has usually been misinterpreted or misunderstood; the title of his work, *The Decline of the West,* is certainly rather misleading. He uses the terms 'decline' and 'death' to mean not the end of a civilization, but the end of its youthful, creative phase."[19]

Juxtaposing Bagby's interpretation with Spengler's own words from *The Decline of the West* suggests a different understanding.

> At last, in the grey dawn of Civilization, the fire in the soul dies down. The dwindling powers rise to one more, half-successful effort of creation, and produce the Classicism that is common to all dying Cultures. The soul thinks once again, and in Romanticism looks back piteously to its childhood; then finally, weary, reluctant, cold, it loses its desire to be, and, as in Imperial Rome, wishes itself out of the overlong daylight and back in the darkness of proto-mysticism, in the womb of the mother, in the grave.[20]

Of all our observers, Spengler is the most unequivocally pessimistic. Whether history proves or disproves his views, Spengler, more than any other scholar of decline and decay, had the courage to look beneath the surface and neither bridle at what he saw nor shrink from acknowledging its bleak implications.

Spengler, incidentally, made one very specific prediction—astonishingly from the early twentieth century—that seems unquestionably evident in the twenty-first: "A 'United States of Europe,' actualized through Napoleon as founder of a romantic and popular military monarchy, is the analogue of the Realm of the Diadochi; when actualized as a twenty-first-century economic organism by a matter-of-fact Caesar, it will be the counterpart of the *imperium Romanum.*"[21]

In an especially intriguing passage, Spengler asserted two themes: First, he saw the West's future in terms of a "spiritual crisis." Also like most of our observers, he viewed the modern exact sciences in clearly negative terms—examples of benightedness rather than true or ultimate enlightenment.

> It remains now to sketch the last stage of Western science. From our standpoint of today, the gently sloping route of decline is clearly visible.
>
> The Classical died, as we shall die, but it died unknowing.…But we know our history. Before us there stands a last spiritual crisis that will involve all Europe and America. What its course will be,

CC

The European Union Parliament's hemicycle in Strasbourg. *Spengler wrote, "A 'United States of Europe,' actualized through Napoleon as founder of a romantic and popular military monarchy, is the analogue of the Realm of the Diadochi; when actualized as a twenty-first-century economic organism by a matter-of-fact Caesar, it will be the counterpart of the* imperium Romanum.*"*

> Late Hellenism tells us. The tyranny of the Reason —of which we are not conscious, for we are ourselves its apex—is in every Culture an epoch between man and old-man, and no more. Its most distinct expression is the cult of exact sciences, of dialectic, of demonstration, of causality.[22]

Indeed, "we are not conscious" of much greater realities; our culture is subsumed to a mass of noisy, obstreperous adherents to values and beliefs that have power, not by virtue of merit, but by dint of social, cultural, and economic vociferousness. Anyone daring to reproach them, or their acolytes and advocates, will be damned as a cultural reprobate. Discriminating thought is all but moribund.

Hearkening back in his classic, *The Decline of the West,* to the earliest known civilizations, Spengler's conclusions about the future of the West lead to history's morgue: "...all this, broad and imposing, is the prelude of a future which is still in store for us and with which the history of West European mankind will be definitely closed...."[23] "Let it be realized, then: That the nineteenth and twentieth centuries, hitherto looked on as the highest point of an ascending straight line of world-history, are in reality a stage of life which may be observed in every Culture that has ripened to its limit...."[24]

A. L. KROEBER

...the course of a large multinational civilization may be more complex than a smooth rise-culmination-and-decline; that it may come in successive surges or pulses—what we have called phases.[25]

At the other end of the spectrum, A. L. Kroeber quavered at the prospect of making predictions: "For my part, I refrain from long-range prophecy. It is tempting but usually unprofitable, practically as well as intellectually: its emotional repercussions tend to be high, its probability values low."[26] Yet Kroeber cited the warnings of others, including Spengler and Toynbee, of an imminent end to Western civilization and gave his imprimatur to certain conclusions of fellow scholars whose warnings have been even more dire, particularly Spengler. Then he finally offered a third option: "successive surges or pulses—what we have called phases."

> ...the course of a large multinational civilization may be more complex than a smooth rise-culmination-and-decline; that it may come in successive surges or pulses—what we have called phases...the intervals between the pulses may be, at least over most of the area of the civilization, periods of pattern dissolution, preparatory to pattern reconstruction. Consequently, even if the mid-twentieth century is suffering from a breakdown of its cultural patterns—as is so often alleged and perhaps with most force and reason as regards the arts—the question still remains open whether such a breakdown is part of the final death of our civilization, as is sometimes feared or asserted; or on the contrary is merely symptomatic of an interpulse reconstruction. In the former case, Spengler's prophecies and Toynbee's fears would be right; in the latter, the present time would be only a sort of counterpart of what Transalpine Europe—most of Europe—was undergoing during the Italian Renaissance.[27]

Kroeber is not very helpful to us. He seeks to evade "boldly going where no man has gone before." Though we can respect his desire to be accurate, the perils of this age for Western civilization warrant some venturing. Precisely because Western civilization is in a predicament unprecedented in some aspects in world history, subjective speculation will be necessary. Kroeber did not discount the trauma and upheaval that even an "interpulse" interpretation of modern historical events and trends would imply. The analogy to the period of the Italian Renaissance, however, does not hold up when viewed in the light of modern science and technology and the hypervelocity of events that they largely precipitate.

IMMANUEL WALLERSTEIN

The present historical system is in fact in terminal crisis. The issue before us is what will replace it.[28]

Immanuel Wallerstein believes the "modern world-system" is in "terminal crisis." But his views are expressed in less ethereal or philosophical terms. He anticipates—again, we hear a theme common to all our observers—more conflict, not less, with the wealthier nations, such as the U.S., increasingly and directly affected.

> The first half of the twenty-first century will, I believe, be far more difficult, more unsettling, and yet more open than anything we have known in the twentieth century.
>
> The third premise is that the modern world-system, as a historical system, has entered into a terminal crisis and is unlikely to exist in fifty years. However, since its outcome is uncertain, we do not know whether the resulting system (or systems) will be better or worse than the one in which we are living, but we do know that the period of transition will be a terrible time of troubles, since the stakes of the transition are so high, the outcome so uncertain, and the ability of small inputs to affect the outcome so great.[29]

This latter observation suggests that Wallerstein retains an indeterministic view: Even "small inputs" can greatly affect the outcome.

The greatest perceived achievement of the modern West, outside the realms of science and technology, is, for Wallerstein, a harbinger of more troubles to come rather than—as it has so commonly been touted—the dawning of a new era of freedom.

> It is widely thought that the collapse of the Communisms in 1989 marks a great triumph of liberalism. I see it rather as marking the definitive collapse of liberalism as the defining geoculture of our world-system. Liberalism essentially promised that gradual reform would ameliorate the inequalities of the world-system and reduce the acute polarization. The illusion that this was possible within the framework of the modern world-system has in fact been a great stabilizing element, in that it legitimated the states in the eyes of their populations and promised them a heaven on earth in the foreseeable future. The collapse of the Communisms, along with the collapse of the national liberation movements in the Third World, and the collapse of faith in the Keynesian model in the Western world were all simultaneous reflections of popular disillusionment in the validity and reality of the reformist programs each propagated....I therefore expect considerable turmoil of the kind we have already been seeing in the 1990s, spreading from the Bosnias and Rwandas of this world to the wealthier (and assertedly more stable) regions of the world (such as the United States).[30]

Wallerstein attacked two of the fundamental premises of the modern West and, in so doing, gave voice to two themes of this book.

> The first conclusion [from my premises] is that progress, unlike what the Enlightenment in all its forms preached, is not at all inevitable. But I do not accept that it is therefore impossible. The world has not morally advanced in the last several thousand years, but it could. We can move in the direction of what Max Weber called "substantive rationality," that is, rational values and rational ends, arrived at collectively and intelligently.

> The second conclusion is that the belief in certainties, a fundamental premise of modernity, is blinding and crippling. Modern science, that is, Cartesian–Newtonian science, has been based on the certainty of certainty. The basic assumption is that there exist objective universal laws governing all natural phenomena, that these laws can be ascertained by scientific inquiry, and that once such laws are known, we can, starting from any set of initial conditions, predict perfectly the future and the past.[31]

In a subsequent passage, Wallerstein very explicitly articulates the two notions that he—and, I believe it fair to say, all our other observers—reject as inconsistent with human nature and the lessons of history. It is an indication of the delusional thinking of our age in the West that Wallerstein even need make this point, the evidence against these views being weighty and massive. "One was the Enlightenment view of human rationality: all persons will act in their own rational interest, provided they have the chance and the education to perceive it correctly. The second was that progress was inevitable, and that therefore history was on the side of the socialist cause."[32]

Wallerstein anticipates more regional wars, proliferation of weapons of mass destruction, and greater polarization between the northern and southern hemispheres. I would add that all of this will be exacerbated greatly by the even more dangerous polarization between the secular West and the Islamic world.

> ...the world of the next fifty years promises to be a far more violent one than the Cold War world out of which we have come. The Cold War was highly choreographed, highly constrained by the concern of both the United States and the Soviet Union that there be no nuclear war between them....But this situation has changed radically.[33]

> It is extremely difficult to contain escalating local violence (Bosnia, Rwanda, Burundi, and so on). It will be virtually impossible over the next twenty-five years to contain weapons proliferation, and we should anticipate a significant increase in the number of states that have nuclear weapons at their disposition, as well as biological and chemical weapons. Furthermore, given, on the one hand, the relative weakening of U.S. power and the emergence of a triadic division among the strongest states and, on the other hand, a continuing economic North–South polarization in the world-system, we should expect the likelihood that there will be more deliberate South–North military provocations (of the Saddam Hussein variety). Such provocations will be increasingly difficult to handle politically, and if several occur simultaneously, it is doubtful that the North will be able to stem the tide.[34]

Wallerstein predicts that the present economic system cannot be sustained.

> The democratization of the world and the ecological crisis have placed an impossible level of demands on the state structures, which are all suffering a "fiscal crisis." But if they reduce expenditures in order to meet the fiscal crises, they also reduce their ability to adjust the system. It is a vicious circle, in which each failure of the state leads to less willingness to entrust it with tasks, and therefore to a generic tax revolt. But as the state becomes less solvent, it can perform existing tasks even less well.
>
> But states are needed most of all not by reformers and not by movements but by capitalists. The capitalist world-system cannot function well without strong states (of course, always some stronger than others) within the framework of a strong interstate system.[35]

Sounding like a refugee from the early and mid-twentieth century, Wallerstein anticipates violent conflict between the capitalist "haves" and the "have nots." Once more we are reminded by the following passage of the Russian economist of the Stalinist era alluded to earlier who declared that capitalism survived because it managed to correct its excesses every generation or so. If Wallerstein is correct, capitalism will not be able to continue to do so. We are also reminded of Toynbee's point that the two recurring nemeses of man are war and class. Wallerstein warns that we "can rest assured that those who have privilege will not sit back and watch this privilege go under.... But you can rest equally assured that they cannot rescue it merely by adjusting the system once again, for all the reasons I have adduced. The world is in transition. Out of chaos will come a new order, different from the one we now know. Different, but not necessarily better."[36]

In effect enunciating a principle—nothing man-made lasts forever—Wallerstein anticipates the demise of the world capitalist system. "The modern world-system, like all systems, is finite in duration and will come to an end...via a period of [chaotic] transition the system will come to be replaced by one or several other systems."[37] But when and how would this occur? Despite the certainties of his message to this point, Wallerstein is uncertain on these questions. "What does this portend for the future? Nothing is less sure. There are basically two possible scenarios. The world-system can continue more or less as before and enter into another set of cyclical changes. Or the world-system has reached a point of crisis and therefore will see drastic structural change, an explosion or an implosion, that will end with the constitution of some new kind of historical system."[38]

Subsequently, Wallerstein declares that there "has been an unfortunate tendency to make science the enemy and technology the enemy, whereas it is in fact capitalism that is the generic root of the problem." The West's plight can be traced to capitalism's manipulation that has "utilized the splendors of unending technological advance as one of its justifications. And [argued that] all negative effects of economic expansion would eventually be countered by inevitable scientific progress." "This version of science is today under fundamental challenge from within the community of natural scientists themselves...."[39]

Though we acknowledge the merits in some components of Wallerstein's views, we must conclude they leave much unexplained. Like Marx, who saw the world primarily in economic terms of competition for limited resources and capital (e.g., who possessed the means of production and who did the labor) or Freud, who saw life in terms of sexual impulses, Wallerstein's perspective seems to lack the depth of other of our observers.

Many vaunted theories eventually ricochet away into the ether of history because they fail to strike the heart of human thought and behavior. As Toynbee, Sorokin, and Dawson suggested repeatedly, and Lord Acton famously pointed out, the central dynamics of history are the deeply held values and beliefs of the individual, which are religious or partake of religious significance. Any other focus is bound to lead to error and failure of understanding. Every other aspect of human experience is, to a greater or lesser extent, peripheral, even though it may be accorded great weight and carried forward on a torrent of words.

However, Professor Wallerstein's views may still be of benefit to our understanding of the destiny of the West. His assertion that "the present historical system is in fact in terminal crisis"; and that "The issue before us is what will replace it" rings true even if we believe he has not X-rayed the patient before making his diagnosis.[40]

Sounding the title of Sartre's existentialist play as a question, Wallerstein then answers his question with a concept closely related to the materialism versus faith options presented by other of our observers. As with our other wise men, he decries the divorce of philosophy and science, or what we might also term the search for truth in the spiritual and abstract realm as well as the material realm.

> No exit? No exit within the framework of the existing historical system? But we are in the process of exit from this system. The real question before us is where we shall be going as a result. It is here and now that we must raise the banner of substantive rationality....It involves not only a new social system, but new structures of knowledge, in which philosophy and sciences will no longer be divorced, and we shall return to the singular epistemology within which knowledge was pursued everywhere prior to the creation of the capitalist world-economy.[41]

Wallerstein displays considerable confidence in his timeline by giving the "present world system" fifty more years at most. But he is noncommittal on what precisely will come next.[42] Following a pattern common to many of our observers, Wallerstein, on the one hand, acknowledges that the lessons of history, especially of Western civilization, are not promising, as will be seen in the following passage. Yet he will not relinquish the notion that there is some reason for, as he labels it, "moderate" optimism.

> My own reading of the past five hundred years leads me to doubt that our modern world-system is an instance of substantial moral progress and to believe that it is more probably an instance of moral regression. That does not render me innately pessimistic about the future, just sober.
>
> We are faced today...with historic choices in which our individual and collective inputs will make a real difference in terms of the outcome. Today's moment of choice is, however, in one way different....It is the first one in which the entire globe is implicated....Historic choices are moral choices, but they can be illuminated by the rational analyses of social scientists....I am moderately optimistic that we shall rise to the challenge.[43]

Finally, in a passage that sagely acknowledges that "science is at its very earliest moments," Wallerstein observes that "all knowledge is social knowledge" and suggests an imminent foreboding future while predicting "exciting" years in the world of knowledge: "Much as I think that the next twenty-five to fifty years will be terrible ones in terms of human social relations—the period of disintegration of our existing historical social system and of transition toward an uncertain alternative—I also think that the next twenty-five to fifty years will be exceptionally exciting ones in the world of knowledge. The systemic crisis will force social reflection."[44] Yes, Professor Wallerstein, this book is an effort at that "social reflection."

CARROLL QUIGLEY

After centuries of expansion our society is now organized so that it cannot subsist; it must expand or it will collapse.[45]

Though a sociologist, Quigley often presented his views on the decline of civilizations, the West in particular, similarly to Wallerstein, with an economic orientation. We noted earlier his view that in the latter stages of a civilization the "society as a whole has become adapted to expansion; the mass of the population expect and desire it." The society may have enjoyed expansion for centuries—as is surely the case for the West—and "people's minds become adjusted to expansion." The society "undergoes acute stresses if expansion slows up."[46] This pattern, he wrote in the mid-twentieth century, "can be seen most clearly in contemporary Western civilization."[47]

This psychological phenomenon—we must always have more and better—becomes a prescription for individual frustration as well as, eventually, civilizational decline. Forebodingly he added, "After centuries of expansion [Western] society is now organized so that it cannot subsist; it must expand or it will collapse."[48]

Inevitably, the instrument of expansion becomes an institution unable to provide what the addicted society now expects. The ensuing crisis results in "conflicts between the vested-interest groups ...[which] are sufficiently satisfied with the existing social organization to desire no change and the great mass of the population who are discontented at the dwindling prospects of expansion."[49]

According to Quigley, there are only three possible outcomes: "(1) reform, (2) circumvention, or (3) reaction." Reform means the society reorganizes its expansion so that institutions once again become effective instruments. Circumvention suggests that "the vested-interest groups are left with much of their privileges intact" and "a new instrument of expansion...grows up alongside the older institution and takes over the latter's expansive functions." Finally reaction is the response when the privileged groups prevent reform and circumvention and expansion continues its decline. Reform and circumvention present the prospect of continuing expansion and a revitalization of the society; reaction causes the decline to become "chronic."[50]

Quigley divided the successive stages in a civilization's decline and fall into seven phases, which he acknowledged was an "arbitrary and subjective" classification that could be made in any number of stages. He referred to them as

1. Mixture
2. Gestation
3. Expansion
4. Age of Conflict
5. Universal Empire
6. Decay
7. Invasion[51]

Displaying the reluctance to make predictions that characterized Kroeber, Quigley ventured no definitive answers even after providing a largely pessimistic analytical basis for his views. It was not clear, he opined, "if the society will be destroyed as a consequence of this or if it will be able to straighten itself on a new course of expansion."[52] But of special importance for our purposes, he noted that the "important point is why a society responds or fails to respond, how we can judge the likelihood of either beforehand, and what is the consequence of either alternative."[53]

SAMUEL HUNTINGTON

On a worldwide basis Civilization seems in many respects to be yielding to barbarism, generating the image of an unprecedented phenomenon, a global Dark Ages, possibly descending on humanity.[54]

Huntington, like Wallerstein, writing on the cusp of the new millennium, struck themes that were congruent in many ways with Toynbee, Dawson, Sorokin, Schaeffer, and Solzhenitsyn. "As the world moves out of its Western phase, the ideologies that typified late Western civilization decline, and their place is taken by religions and other culturally based forms of identity and commitment. The Westphalian separation of religion and international politics, an idiosyncratic product of

Western civilization, is coming to an end, and religion, as Edward Mortimer suggests, is 'increasingly likely to intrude into international affairs.'"[55]

Significantly, Huntington observed that the "intracivilizational clash of political ideas" that was "spawned by the West" (as noted earlier, all of these ideologies were the product of the West) is being supplanted by an intercivilizational clash of culture and religion.[56]

As we have seen, the West has been moving further and further away from religion—at least the religion that formed its core and foundation—while much of the rest of the world is gravitating toward religious faith. In a real sense this is the ultimate rebuke of the West. Internally, the West will continue pursuit of its "idiosyncratic" separation of religion and politics and, in so doing, will increasingly punish and persecute those of its traditional religious faith.

Then Huntington presented us with another picture of the West. He descries the downward trajectory of the West's influence—a direct consequence of the manipulations of the "superior heads" in the West unrestrained by a powerful spiritual influence emanating internally from their own convictions, or externally, from the church.

> The second picture of the West is very different. It is of a civilization in decline, its share of world political, economic, and military power going down relative to that of other civilizations. The West's victory in the Cold War has produced not triumph but exhaustion. The West is increasingly concerned with its internal problems and needs, as it confronts slow economic growth, stagnating populations, unemployment, huge government deficits, a declining work ethic, low savings rates, and in many countries including the United States social disintegration, drugs, and crime. Economic power is rapidly shifting to East Asia, and military power and political influence are starting to follow.[57]

Huntington added, "India is on the verge of economic takeoff and the Islamic world is increasingly hostile toward the West. The willingness of other societies to accept the West's dictates or abide its sermons is rapidly evaporating, and so are the West's self-confidence and will to dominate."[58]

They will not "abide" the West's "sermons" largely because of the hypocrisy implicit in nearly every phrase, every gap between profession and action. To be sure, the West continues to zealously preach—primarily of the virtues of its ideologies: democracy, capitalism, and the merits of science and technology.

In its smugness and hubris, the West does not recognize that this was never the ultimate source of its power, or its attraction on the deepest level, to the rest of the world. The virtue and nobility of a faith that valued the individual, sought justice, and embraced an immutable and transcendent moral law was the solar center of this "Big Bang" universe, not the ideologies and political institutions that it influenced. They were the progeny, not the progenitors. For the latter without the former are but cold orbiting forms in a dark void. Ultimately, without their original light they become nothing more than alternative means to exploit and manipulate—a process sometimes apparent to the rest of the world, if not to the West itself.

> [I]n many important respects, [the United States'] relative power will decline at an accelerating pace. In terms of its raw economic capabilities, the position of the United States in relation to Japan and eventually China is likely to erode still further. In the military realm, the balance of effective capabilities between the United States and a number of growing regional powers (including, perhaps, Iran, India, and China) will shift from the center toward the periphery. Some of America's structural power

> will flow to other nations; some (and some of its soft power as well) will find its way into the hands of nonstate actors like multinational corporations.[59]

We note his use of the modifiers "rapidly" (in the first passage) and "accelerating" (in the second) and hearken back to our notion of "hypervelocity." His prediction regarding the flow of power into the hands of nonstate "actors" is already manifested in the growing power of multinationals and the tendency of Western governments to delegate many of its prerogatives to the private sector.

> The West is overwhelmingly dominant now and will remain number one in terms of power and influence well into the twenty-first century. Gradual, inexorable, and fundamental changes, however, are also occurring in the balances of power among civilizations, and the power of the West relative to that of other civilizations will continue to decline. As the West's primacy erodes, much of its power will simply evaporate and the rest will be diffused on a regional basis among the several major civilizations and their core states. The most significant increases in power are accruing and will accrue to Asian civilizations, with China gradually emerging as the society most likely to challenge the West for global influence. These shifts in power among civilizations are leading and will lead to the revival and increased cultural assertiveness of non-Western societies and to their increasing rejection of Western culture.[60]

As to the last point, Western culture, so vaunted and dominant today, will rapidly become passé and viewed as the dissipated remnants of a discredited belief system and life style. Huntington continued his analysis by pointing to three "major characteristics" of the West's decline, the second of which is of special importance. "First, it is a slow process. The rise of Western power took four hundred years. Its recession could take as long. . . .Spengler's first volume appeared in 1918 and the 'decline of the West' has been a central theme in twentieth-century history. The process itself has stretched out through most of the century. Conceivably, however, it could accelerate."[61]

DoD photo by Dennis Rogers, U.S. Air Force. (Released)

Newly commissioned U.S. Air Force second lieutenants toss their hats into the air while F-16s fly over the Air Force Academy graduation. *Despite the enthusiasm born of America's historical power, Samuel Huntington observed that the true picture of the West is very different. "It is of a civilization in decline, its share of world political, economic, and military power going down relative to that of other civilizations. The West's victory in the Cold War has produced not triumph but exhaustion. The West is increasingly concerned with its internal problems and needs, as it confronts slow economic growth, stagnating populations, unemployment, huge government deficits, a declining work ethic, low savings rates, and in many countries including the United States social disintegration, drugs, and crime. Economic power is rapidly shifting to East Asia, and military power and political influence are starting to follow."*

Huntington then added, "The decline of the West is still in the slow first phase, but at some point it might speed up dramatically." Of course I argue that it not only can accelerate, it has, and will even more so.

When scrutinized from the longer perspective of history, we can acknowledge that this is a protracted process—most of our observers explicitly or implicitly acknowledge this—but in these last stages the process is accelerating in a historically unprecedented fashion. If we propose 1900 as the approximate "apogee" of Western civilization, I am persuaded that Western man need not wait longer than 2100 to know unequivocally that his civilization is in process of total collapse; and I do not believe it will likely take that long for this conclusion to be inescapable to many. Some already perceive it. Events are moving too quickly, the deterioration in thought and belief too rapid and pervasive for Western man to have to wait long to know his fate.

> Second, decline does not proceed in a straight line. It is highly irregular with pauses, reversals, and reassertions of Western power following manifestations of Western weakness.
>
> Third, power is the ability of one person or group to change the behavior of another person or group. Behavior may be changed through inducement, coercion, or exhortation, which require the power-wielder to have economic, military, institutional, demographic, political, technological, social, or other resources.... The West's share of most, but not all, of the important power resources peaked early in the twentieth century and then began to decline relative to those of other civilizations.[62]

Like all our observers, Huntington foresees a time of ever-greater troubles and, in describing what he anticipates, resorts to a term that we have favored in this book as part of yet another chapter title: *Dark Ages.*

> Modernization has generally enhanced the material level of Civilization throughout the world. But has it also enhanced the moral and cultural dimensions of Civilization? In some respects this appears to be the case. Slavery, torture, vicious abuse of individuals, have become less and less acceptable in the contemporary world. Is this, however, simply the result of the impact of Western civilization on other cultures and hence will a moral reversion occur as Western power declines? Much evidence exists in the 1990s for the relevance of the "sheer chaos" paradigm of world affairs: a global breakdown of law and order, failed states and increasing anarchy in many parts of the world...a global crime wave, transnational mafias and drug cartels, increasing drug addiction in many societies, a general weakening of the family, a decline in trust and social solidarity in many countries, ethnic, religious, and civilizational violence and rule by the gun prevalent in much of the world. In city after city—Moscow, Rio de Janeiro, Bangkok, Shanghai, London, Rome, Warsaw, Tokyo, Johannesburg, Delhi, Karachi, Cairo, Bogota, Washington—crime seems to be soaring and basic elements of Civilization fading away. People speak of a global crisis in governance.... On a worldwide basis Civilization seems in many respects to be yielding to barbarism, generating the image of an unprecedented phenomenon, a global Dark Ages, possibly descending on humanity.[63]

That Professor Huntington referred to a "global Dark Ages" is of course in part consistent with my thinking as described in the chapter of similar name. However, his meaning is surely different in many respects albeit sharing some common denominators with mine. Huntington seemed to feel—and I believe the evidence does not support it—that there may be salvation in yet more human constructs, this time "an international order based on civilizations." He added ominously, that

PD-Yorck.

Justice by Raphael, 1502. *Justice: An intangible in short supply in our world, it cannot be achieved in the absence of a recognition of a transcendent God and immutable moral law. "Justice" as devised by man from his own thoughts and beliefs in his capacities and virtue will prove false. The failure thereby produced will be a key antecedent to—and contributing cause of—the collapse of Western civilization. True justice is in the providence of God. Man can only create "reasonable facsimiles thereof" by strict adherence to God's declared immutable law.*

man's own needs and ambitions." For Christians, Dawson maintained, "the shock and the disillusionment" of the coming civilizational collapse "should be less severe than to those who have put their faith in the nineteenth-century gospel of secular progress." Christianity "never minimised the reality of the forces of evil in history and society, as well as in the life of the individual, and it has prepared men's minds to face the extreme consequences of the external triumph of evil and the apparent defeat of good." It is, however, "no defeatist philosophy" but "a triumphant affirmation of life—of eternal life victorious over death, of the kingdom of God prevailing over the rulers of this world of darkness."[85]

Dawson spoke with a courageous realism and eloquent insight that eludes other observers. This is "the truth," unvarnished, untainted by any form of conformity or convention and unskewed by a craven longing to make the future somehow "optimistic."

> For the civilisation which has been undermined, and is now threatened by total subversion, is a Christian civilisation, built on the spiritual values and religious ideals of St. Augustine and his like; and its adversary is not the simple barbarism of alien peoples who stand on a lower cultural level, but new powers armed with all the resources of modern scientific technique, which are inspired by a ruthless will to power that recognises no law save that of their own strength. This is almost a reversal of the situation envisaged by St. Augustine. In his day the world was falling, and the gates of the Church stood open as a city of refuge for a defeated humanity.
>
> Today the world is strong, and it has no pity for weakness and suffering. It has no use for Christianity, which it despises as the most dangerous form of escapism and defeatism. It has its own religion—a religion which reverses the Christian moral values, which says, "Blessed are the strong, for they shall possess the earth," but which, no less than Christianity, demands unlimited sacrifices and an undivided allegiance of the whole man.
>
> Thus the situation that Christians have to face today has more in common with that described by the author of the Apocalypse than with the age of St. Augustine. The world is strong, and it has evil masters. But these masters are not vicious autocrats like Nero or Domitian. They are the engineers of the mechanism of world power, a mechanism that is more formidable than anything the ancient world knew, because it is not confined to external means, like the despotisms of the past, but uses all the resources of modern psychology to make the human soul the motor of its dynamic purpose.[86]

We will address later the extraordinary challenge presented to the modern Christian in light of Dawson's last point. In this analysis, Dawson was much like Toynbee in *Civilization on Trial*: Western man does not realize the extent to which he, even in the free and democratic West, is controlled and manipulated by such forces. In *Historic Reality*, Dawson warned—like Toynbee and using the same term Toynbee preferred, "Leviathan"—that the West has only two choices:

> Therefore the whole society has to move together as a single unit. Either it may be a Christian unit which is governed by spiritual standards and directed toward spiritual ends, or it is wholly secular—a power machine, or a machine for the production of wealth or population.
>
> ...[T]he modern world is moving steadily in this direction, and the margin between the old forms of liberal or social democracy and this new Leviathan is growing narrower every year.... [W]hen ultimately a conflict takes place between the new state and the Christian church, it will be far more severe in character than anything that has been known before.[87]

Anticipating the evolution of greater and greater governmental control, Dawson was again prescient. The religious subculture maintained by Western Christians in the twentieth century is increasingly narrowed and undermined as Western man advances into the twenty-first. This, Dawson declared, will worsen—all guarantees of religious freedom notwithstanding.

The assertion of religious values in politics, government, education, and the culture at large will not only become more difficult, but will eventually be fully opposed.

> ...in the highly organized life of the modern secular state it is becoming increasingly difficult for such separate groups to exist and to maintain their own way of life in a sort of religious underworld or subculture. For the modern state, whether it is democratic as in the United States, or communistic as in the [former] U.S.S.R., or Fascist as in pre-war Italy and Germany, or nationalistic as in the new states of Asia and Africa, is no longer content to confine itself to certain limited functions like the liberal state of the nineteenth century. In fact all modern states are totalitarian in so far as they seek to embrace the spheres of economics and culture, as well as politics in the strict sense of the word. They are concerned not merely with the maintenance of public order and the defense of the people against its

PD

St. Augustine, by Sandro Botticelli. 1480. *St. Augustine was one of the greatest minds of Western civilization. But his values and ideals have been rejected. As Dawson put it, "The world is strong, and it has evil masters.... They are the engineers of the mechanism of world power, a mechanism that is more formidable than anything the ancient world knew, because it is not confined to external means, like the despotisms of the past, but uses all the resources of modern psychology to make the human soul the motor of its dynamic purpose."*

> external enemies. They have taken on responsibility for all the different forms of communal activity which were formerly left to the individual or to independent social organizations such as the churches, and they watch over the welfare of their citizens from the cradle to the grave.[88]

Dawson's use of the term "highly organized" to describe all modern states is especially important in distinguishing the declining Western civilization of the twenty-first century and all those that preceded it. Science and technology have made—and increasingly are making—it more and more possible to control every aspect of human existence. Consistent with our principle that "power accretes power" we can expect this to not only continue but gain momentum.

Governments, even democratic governments, will eventually hold in their grasp a *passe-partout* for every human life within their charge. Diligent efforts to arrest this trend will at best only retard it.

In an extraordinarily significant observation, Dawson called us to recognize manifestations of power that prove to be ultimately inconsequential, and usually more completely indicative of the loss of power—true power. Once again, Dawson displayed his intellectual power and courage to get at the truth, a truth that the world of the modern West does not want to countenance.

Pyramids of Giza. *Reminding us of the folly of much of man's pilgrimage through history, Dawson observed, "When we look back at the civilizations of the past, we cannot fail to be impressed by their achievements. The Egyptian pyramids still stand today after nearly five thousand years as monuments of human power. But while we marvel we are appalled at the suffering and the waste of human labor that they represent. For at the heart of the pyramid there is nothing but the corpse of a despot."*

> When we look back at the civilizations of the past, we cannot fail to be impressed by their achievements. The Egyptian pyramids still stand today after nearly five thousand years as monuments of human power. But while we marvel we are appalled at the suffering and the waste of human labor that they represent. For at the heart of the pyramid there is nothing but the corpse of a despot.
>
> So too in Mesopotamia, it was from the spectacle of those vast artificial mountains or ziggurats which towered over the cities of Babylonia that the inspired writer drew his image of the nemesis of human power and pride—the curse of Babel. For whenever a culture reaches its culmination of power and social control, as in the age of the pyramids or the Empires of Babylon and Rome, it breaks down under its own weight which has become too heavy for human nature to endure, and so the whole process has to begin again until a new Babylon has been built.[89]

Smitten as man is with notions of power and glory he foolishly revels in the "achievements" that reflect both. The suffering and human degradation that are the price of these imposing vanities are rarely considered. Not only is the "corpse" at their heart a despot, the corpse is just that—a moldering and now meaningless vestige of a human life not well lived. Will it matter a century hence that the corpses in Arlington and Westminster Abbey are not those of despots but the remains of people of a faith that could no longer be found in those environs?

PD-art

The Tower of Babel by Pieter Brueghel the Elder, 1563. *Christopher Dawson explained, "So too in Mesopotamia, it was from the spectacle of those vast artificial mountains or ziggurats which towered over the cities of Babylonia that the inspired writer drew his image of the nemesis of human power and pride—the curse of Babel. For whenever a culture reaches its culmination of power and social control, as in the age of the pyramids or the Empires of Babylon and Rome, it breaks down under its own weight which has become too heavy for human nature to endure, and so the whole process has to begin again until a new Babylon has been built."*

ARNOLD TOYNBEE

The breakdowns and disintegrations of civilizations might be stepping-stones to higher things on the religious plane. After all, one of the deepest spiritual laws that we know is the law that is proclaimed by Aeschylus.... "it is through suffering that learning comes"....[90]

Toynbee, in *Civilization on Trial*, described the "process of disintegration" as, in part, "a schism of the disintegrating society into a recalcitrant proletariat and a less and less effectively dominant minority." The disintegration does "not proceed evenly; it jolts along in alternating spasms of rout, rally, and rout." The dominant minority might succeed in briefly delaying the pace of this decay through the imposition of a "universal state" but this is only the penultimate to the last act. The "universal church" created by the proletariat of the dying civilization "may live on to become the chrysalis from which a new civilization eventually emerges." The best known historical antecedents are the "Graeco–Roman examples of the *Pax Romana* and the Christian Church." "The establishment of the *Pax Romana* by Augustus seemed, at the time, to have put the Graeco–Roman world back upon firm foundations after it had been battered for several centuries by perpetual war, misgovernment, and revolution." But this was "no more than a respite." Following were two crises, the first in the third century, the final and fatal crisis in the fifth and sixth.[91]

In this historical epic the "true beneficiary of the temporary Roman Peace was the Christian Church. The Church seized this opportunity to strike root and spread; it was stimulated by persecution until the Empire, having failed to crush it, decided, instead, to take it into partnership." Eventually, the church "took over the Empire's heritage." "The same relation between a declining civilization and a rising religion can be observed in a dozen other cases. In the Far East, for instance, the Ts'in and Han Empire plays the Roman Empire's part, while the rôle of the Christian Church is assumed by the Mahayana school of Buddhism."[92]

Yes, the juxtaposition of the experience of the Greco–Roman world to our own suggests at least one salient distinction: The church of the first century was dynamic, bold, and therefore influential—and growing in that influence, not receding. The church in the modern West reflects the opposite—diminishing influence and spiritual atrophy.

Will history therefore witness the supplanting of the Christian church in the West by another, perhaps more vigorous religion, such as Islam?

In one of his most powerful and weighty passages—reminiscent of Sorokin's concern about man's "unteachability"—Toynbee explained what we can expect, and what is truly important:

In the vision seen by the Prophets of Israel, Judah, and Iran, history is not a cyclic and not a mechanical process. It is the masterful and progressive execution, on the narrow stage of this world, of a divine plan which is revealed to us in this fragmentary glimpse, but which transcends our human powers of vision and understanding in every dimension. Moreover, the Prophets, through their own experience, anticipated Aeschylus' discovery that learning comes through suffering—a discovery which we, in our time and circumstances, have been making too.

While civilizations rise and fall and, in falling, give rise to others, some purposeful enterprise, higher than theirs, may all the time be making headway, and, in a divine plan, the learning that comes through the suffering caused by the failures of civilizations may be the sovereign means of progress. Abraham was an émigré from a civilization in extremis; the Prophets were children of another civilization in disintegration; Christianity was born of the sufferings of a disintegrating Graeco–Roman world. Will some comparable spiritual enlightenment be kindled in the "displaced persons" who are the counterparts, in our world, of those Jewish exiles to whom so much was revealed in their painful exile by the waters of Babylon? The answer to this question, whatever the answer may be, is of greater moment than the still inscrutable destiny of our world-encompassing Western civilization.[93]

Becoming more personal in his cautions about human nature, Toynbee warned against a typical human impulse when "up against it":

> ...the test is particularly severe when the adversity comes suddenly at the noon of a halcyon day which one has fatuously expected to endure to eternity. In straits like these, the wrestler with destiny is tempted to look for bugbears and scapegoats to carry the burden of his own inadequacy. Yet to "pass the buck" in adversity is still more dangerous than to persuade oneself that prosperity is everlasting.

> ...Whenever things go awry in circumstances that seem ever more intractable, we tend to accuse the enemy of having sown tares in our field and thereby implicitly excuse ourselves for the faults in our own husbandry. This is, of course, an old story.[94]

Sorokin, Solzhenitsyn, and Schaeffer would certainly have shared Toynbee's contempt for fatuous expectations that Western civilization would "endure to eternity," and, like him, they would warn the insouciant West that the reckoning is much closer than even the more objective might expect. Toynbee offered his hope—consistent with theirs. He was not "a determinist in his reading of the riddle of human life" but believed "that where there is life there is hope, and that, with God's help, man is master of his own destiny, at least to some extent in some respects."[95] In answer to one of the key questions posed early in this book, Toynbee believed that Western civilization's fate was not a "doom from which no civilization can escape."[96]

Yet, the prescription for renewal of Western civilization is daunting and must be ambitious and sweeping in its application. Central to that prescription is the restoration of a spiritual basis for even the culture's most secular institutions and activities.

> There is nothing to prevent our Western civilization from following historical precedent, if it chooses, by committing social suicide. But we are not doomed to make history repeat itself; it is open to us, through our own efforts, to give history, in our case, some new and unprecedented turn. As human beings, we are endowed with this freedom of choice, and we cannot shuffle off our responsibility upon the shoulders of God or nature. We must shoulder it ourselves. It is up to us.
>
> What shall we do to be saved? In politics, establish a constitutional co-operative system of world government. In economics, find working compromises (varying according to the practical requirements of different places and times) between free enterprise and socialism. In the life of the spirit, put the secular super-structure back onto religious foundations....[T]hese are, all of them, ambitious undertakings, and it will call for the hardest work and the highest courage to make any progress at all towards carrying any one of them through to achievement.[97]

However, we should remember, Toynbee wrote these words in 1947. The deterioration and decay that he warned about have progressed much further; and his hopes were contingent: the rescue of the West will not occur without Western man making different choices—choices that he has continued to reject ever more forcefully since 1947. Once again, we search in vain for the evidence that an optimistic viewpoint can be supported. Why, we are inclined then to ask, is man so "unteachable" as Sorokin declared? Toynbee answered this question with an unexpected but plausible reason—man's success. "I then have to account for the failure of creativity, and I ascribe it to the spiritual demoralization to which we human beings seem to be prone on the morrow of great achievements—a demoralization to which we are not bound to succumb, and for which we ourselves therefore bear the responsibility. Success seems to make us lazy or self-satisfied or conceited."[98]

The triumphs of massive economic achievement in the face of the Great Depression of the early twentieth century, the victory in a world war that made even the defeated Germany an ironic success, the opening of space to man's vehicles, indeed, everything in science and technology themselves, have all contributed beyond measure to a hubristic attitude in the West. With supreme irony, the seeming vanquishing of the Soviet Union and its ideology will prove in time to be the locus of these ever burgeoning cancers of the Western soul. Deft and skilled in so many ultimately pedestrian but beguiling endeavors Western man is *maladroit* in the one respect that might save him.

CC

Aeschylus. Toynbee speculated, "The breakdowns and disintegrations of civilizations might be stepping-stones to higher things on the religious plane. After all, one of the deepest spiritual laws that we know is the law that is proclaimed by Aeschylus...'it is through suffering that learning comes'—and in the New Testament in the verse 'Whom the Lord loveth, He chasteneth; and scourgeth every son whom He receiveth.'"

Subsequently, in a passage that would only be cause for hope to a person of faith, Toynbee ascended to greater heights in pondering the meaning and course of history.

> The breakdowns and disintegrations of civilizations might be stepping-stones to higher things on the religious plane. After all, one of the deepest spiritual laws that we know is the law that is proclaimed by Aeschylus—"it is through suffering that learning comes"—and in the New Testament in the verse "whom the Lord loveth, He chasteneth; and scourgeth every son whom He receiveth." If you apply that to the rise of the higher religions which has culminated in the flowering of Christianity, you might say that in the mythical passions of Tammuz and Adonis and Attis and Osiris, the Passion of Christ was foreshadowed, and that the Passion of Christ was the culminating and crowning experience of the sufferings of human souls in successive failures in the enterprise of secular civilization.[99]

Here Western civilization can hang its hat, for it is here, and only here, that there is evidence of any cause for optimism. But of course, for self-indulgent Western man, finding "stepping stones to higher things on the religious plane" through the guide and teacher of "suffering" is hardly an attractive prospect. It presupposes a demanding direction (upward) and a willingness to assume a burden (suffering) that Western man is rejecting more and more completely with every year.

STARING INTO THE FUTURE

There is the moral of all human tales;
'Tis but the same rehearsal of the past.
First Freedom and then Glory—when that fails,
Wealth, Vice, Corruption [come] at last.
And History, with all her volumes vast,
Hath but one page.
George Gordon, Lord Byron, *Childe Harold's Pilgrimage*[100]

Now, like Toynbee, it is appropriate for me to put my cards on the table. Like Toynbee, I have already declared my view of life and history as indeterministic—to be precise, a qualified indeterminism—man has the power to alter his course. As predicted at the outset of this work, it should now be apparent that the views of our wise men have much in common. Some congruent themes and parallels are obvious, others less so. Even where they are not in apparent synchrony, often the differences are manifestations of the unique perspective of the observer or the depth to which he perceived, but not true and complete disagreement.

Parenthetically, before addressing the deeper issues and the overarching themes, I will interject my views on the ascendancy of the next global power, probably in Central or East Asia.

India possesses formidable human resources—millions of hard working, superbly intelligent young people are her greatest asset. Looking at this resource alone, considerable weight would have to be given to the notion of India as possibly the next dominant world power. However, consistent with a key theme of this work, this is unlikely due to the cultural belief systems. Hinduism, for example, will never be the foundation for dynamic achievement in the modern world. Its tenets are out of touch with reality. Should this belief system, however, shift dramatically in a positive direction, the prospects for India's progress will be heightened immensely.

The rise of East Asia has been predicted by many observers but often without insight into the most critical component: the psychology, the mind-set, of the people. When psycho-social strength is merged with rich resources in land and people, the formula for the development of great power is present. This should have occurred with the Russians in the era following World War II, but it did not for two primary and closely related reasons: First and foremost, the Soviet Union was hobbled by its belief system, an ideology that was not only confining of the human spirit but seriously out of touch with reality in many of its fundamental tenets. Secondly, the Russians were insecure, self-doubting, and, to a considerable degree, paranoid. Thus they made policy decisions that were informed by the desire to disprove to the world that they were weak, vulnerable, or ineffectual. This approach by a nation, as with an individual, produces volatility, instability, and potentially dangerous behavior. It is not conducive to great achievement.

The Russians were and are blessed with perhaps as great a combined potential of human and natural resources as any other nation—all of which could theoretically lead to tremendous success and achievement. But the belief system and the deficits in the dysfunctional "personality" of the culture will not permit it. Were they to heed Solzhenitsyn's call to supplant authoritarian ideologies with their traditional Orthodox Christian faith, they could perhaps realize their potential for massive achievement. But they remain hobbled by their psychology, generations of enforced indoctrination in atheism, and a *modus operandi* that is dysfunctional. They have achieved what they have achieved in spite of themselves; they are their own worst enemy.

East Asians, particularly the Chinese, on the other hand, have a long history of a sense of cultural and social superiority. They will not therefore be as inclined to waste resources in aggressive conduct intended primarily to prove themselves or shore up an exaggerated sense of vulnerability. This translates into more stable, usually more predictable, behavior with less brinksmanship, all of which works to their advantage over the long term. Simultaneously, this nurtures a propensity to pragmatism. Deng Xiaoping's declaration that it does not matter what color the cat is as long as he catches mice was more than a homely homily; it was a statement of central principle that would stand the Chinese in good stead for as long as they honored it. Deng, more than Mao or perhaps any other figure, was perhaps the architect of what twenty-first-century China will become. He was, in the words of one Chinese author, Li, "determined to lead China onto the road of economic prosperity by deprogramming Mao's system and convincing people that reality is the only criterion for judging whether a theory represents the truth."[101] Need we draw attention to the dual concepts of "reality" and "truth," especially as connected in a single sentence—a theme we have emphasized and to which we will return repeatedly? Affirming another point made herein, Li further noted that "Deng stressed that Marxism was a century-old theory imported from the West. To expect Marxism to reflect China's reality in the twentieth century would simply be unrealistic. Deng defended the market economy as having no contradiction with socialism, because it was simply an economic tool that may serve any ideological cause."[102] The latter was surely a clever politician's ploy intended to manipulate—for socialist and communist theory displayed no such pragmatic malleability—but the broader recognition of the need to see "reality" realistically and respond to it accordingly is a potential feature of modern Chinese political and social thought that may carry them far.

As a result of these two central features of thought and belief, the Chinese are likely to gain greater and greater economic power far more rapidly and extensively than the insecure Russians did or could.

Ganesh festival. *India possesses formidable human resources— millions of hard-working, superbly intelligent young people are her greatest asset. Looking at this resource alone, considerable weight would have to be given to the notion of India as possibly the next world power. However, consistent with a key theme of this work, this is unlikely due to the cultural belief systems. Hinduism will never be the foundation for dynamic achievement in the modern world. Its tenets are out of touch with reality.*

CC

With economic power will come advanced technology and military power. Coupled with their cultural propensities for a "the-individual-is-nothing-the-nation-is-all" viewpoint, the result may be largely a very compliant mass of people, working very hard, producing in great quantity, all controlled by a pragmatic—as contrasted with purely ideological—authoritarian government. This is potentially a formula for economic and military achievement—albeit at the expense of the individual and the human soul. These latter deficiencies—were they never remedied—are the seeds of its own demise; but that may not come for generations.

Unlike the Russians, who tended neither to pragmatism nor a sound sense of priorities, the Chinese are not likely to challenge the West in a significant way until they are confident of their strength. By the time they do, their power is likely to be so great and the West's so dissipated by its own internal abasement, the Chinese are more likely to win the argument. Thus, ultimately, they will be more dangerous than the Russians ever were—a far more formidable adversary.

All economic, military, demographic, and sociological perspectives—and many historical viewpoints—are reflective of a superficial view. Even in the most avowedly atheistic heart there lies a core of belief that, when scrutinized closely, harbors within it precepts and values of a quasi-religious nature. Man is religious even when he most adamantly asserts his disbelief.

The economist, the social scientist, even the philosopher who addresses the great issues of his time is usually unwittingly simply speaking of manifestations of those far deeper thoughts, beliefs, and values. Many are, as it were, fly fishing from a dinghy over the Marianas Trench. Thoreau's observation that "the mind can be permanently profaned by the habit of attending to trivial things, so that all our thoughts shall be tinged with triviality" is an explication of a common phenomenon in our time and place. Western man has been in the habit of "attending to trivial things" for a long time, so it is no wonder that when he examines himself and his world it typically lacks depth and true insight.

All that has preceded should not be read as a malediction upon the West. I am the progeny of Western civilization—neither a rebellious adolescent intent on demeaning his parentage nor a perpetual and avowed skeptic of everyone and everything. Much comfort, security, and even joy have been my lot in this cultural cradle.

But we do our civilization—we do ourselves—no service if we turn a blind eye to its degradation. Stark, courageous realism is the absolutely essential first step if our civilization is to be saved.

ARC, PD.

Deng Xiaoping's *declaration that it does not matter what color the cat is as long as he catches mice was a statement of principle that would stand the Chinese in good stead. Deng, more than Mao, was perhaps the architect of what twenty-first-century China will become. The recognition of the need to see "reality" and respond to it accordingly is a feature of modern Chinese political thought that may carry them far.*

All images on this page are PD-mil

Power of China. *The Chinese have a long history of a sense of cultural and social superiority. They will not therefore be as inclined to waste resources in aggressive conduct intended primarily to prove themselves or shore up an exaggerated sense of vulnerability. This translates into more stable, usually more predictable, behavior with less brinksmanship, all of which works to their advantage over the long term. Unlike the Russians, who tended neither to pragmatism nor a sound sense of priorities, the Chinese are not likely to challenge the West's hegemony in a significant way until they are confident of their strength. By the time they do, their power is likely to be so great and the West's so dissipated by its own internal abasement, they are more likely to win the argument. Thus, ultimately, they will be more dangerous than the Russians ever were—a far more formidable adversary.*

Photo by Patrick Gruban. CC

U.N. General Assembly. *An institution established to prevent wars, it undoubtedly has at points succeeded but more often serves as a "bully pulpit" for various forms of propaganda and is increasingly ineffectual in a fashion reminiscent of Quigley's theories about "instruments" decaying into self-serving "institutions."*

The question of whether the prognosis for Western civilization should be pessimistic or optimistic triggers recollection of a meeting the American evangelist Billy Graham had with Winston Churchill, who was then in his last term as prime minister of Great Britain. Graham later wrote that he felt that the bleakness of Churchill's worldview, as he expressed it to Graham, was perhaps the consequence of the depression, Churchill's "black dog," that had nipped at his heels throughout his long life. I believe it was more likely the consequence of decades of direct experience with the nature of man and an understanding of the course of history, all viewed from a perspective devoid of perhaps not abstract religious convictions but a deep and abiding faith—the ultimate refuge for all who see history and our world as they truly are. Churchill had a greater capacity for realism and perceptiveness than most. That, coupled with his experiences of man, would drag him, albeit reluctantly, in the direction of despair.

Western civilization is profoundly and probably mortally wounded from within by its betrayal of its own roots of faith and morality. As some of our observers declared, a moral and spiritual awakening would resuscitate and invigorate the patient, but he is resistant to what could sustain him. In that sense, our culture—to use a term resorted to explicitly by Toynbee in particular—will die of suicide, not homicide. Though it is true that some other nation, civilization, or group may wield the dagger in administering a *coup de grâce*, this will only finish what the self-ingested poisons had begun long before.

PD-art

The Siege and Destruction of Jerusalem by the Romans Under the Command of Titus, A.D. *70*; 1850, by David Roberts. *The Israelites of that day experienced what Western civilization will experience in one historical variant or another. Jesus warned, "O Jerusalem, Jerusalem, thou that killest the prophets, and stonest them which are sent unto thee, how often would I have gathered thy children together, even as a hen gathereth her chickens under her wings, and ye would not! Behold, your house is left unto you desolate. For I say unto you, Ye shall not see me henceforth, till ye shall say, Blessed is he that cometh in the name of the Lord."*

Perhaps in the fullness of time some in the West might insist, "But we did not understand. We did not know this moral law" or, perhaps, "we did not understand the law's significance." This will save no man. As surely as a corporeal being walks off a great cliff—oblivious as he might incredibly be to the law of gravity—his legs will be broken and his life forfeited. Western man's efforts to redefine God and amend or abrogate his moral law will carry far worse consequences.

In practical terms, if Western man does not alter his course, we can expect more and greater cyclical catastrophes, both in human relationships, and of nature and the environment. Whether the citizen of our civilization views the latter as the natural result of man's recklessness with his environment or the manifestations of some divine punishment, or perhaps, as corollaries of one another, the consequences will be the same.

Were the present trends to continue unabated, eventually the most likely scenario will be a final and complete tectonic shift in the center of gravity of world power away from the West (a shift that, as our observers have shown us, is already occurring) to the civilization that achieves the greatest level of dynamism coupled with technological capability of a high order. Of course for this to occur, that civilization must have parallel high orders of mental and social discipline coupled with tremendous

PD-Gov

A World War I military cemetery in Europe. *Western civilization is profoundly and probably mortally wounded from within by its betrayal of its own roots of faith and morality. A moral and spiritual awakening would resuscitate and invigorate the patient, but he is resistant to what could sustain him. In that sense, our culture will die of suicide, not homicide. Though it is true that some other nation, civilization, or group may wield the dagger in administering a* coup de grâce*, this will only finish what the self-ingested poisons had begun long before.*

motive force (i.e., a dynamic belief system). This discipline need not be purely internal to the society's members, but will likely also be externally applied through a rigorously authoritarian form of government. Though the government may even be a titular democracy, it will seek to control every aspect of its citizen's lives.

The threats that human beings perceive in this new age—especially directly or indirectly from man's own creations through science and technology—will make men ever more compliant and accepting of a social contract between the governed and the governing: in essence our submission in return for your protection.

There is another scenario—seemingly more menacing, but hardly so in its actual consequences: Wars, terrorism, and international conflict, precipitating and coupled with worldwide economic collapse—accompanied also by increasingly catastrophic natural disasters—leading to a new primitivism encircling the globe. This state of affairs would be a perverse amalgam of the vestiges of science and technology being fought over and utilized by entities scarcely identifiable as states. In this scenario, nation states as we know them in the twenty-first century would be supplanted through the ensuing chaos by aggressive aggregations that find their cohesion in common religious or ethnic bases, or simply in a mutual need to survive in a hostile and chaotic environment. This could hardly be characterized as a New Dark Age, for that would elevate its status. Rather it would reflect a human regression far beyond anything seen in history. Thus, Western civilization's Parthian shot to mankind may be its pride, faithlessness, and folly manifested in its deadly creations through science and technology.

END NOTES
CHAPTER 18

1 Oswald Spengler, *The Decline of the West* (New York: A. A. Knopf, 1926), 75.
2 Pitirim A. Sorokin, *The Crisis of Our Age* (Oneworld Publications Ltd., 1941; this edition Sergei P. Sorokin and Peter P. Sorokin, 1992), 264.
3 Immanuel Wallerstein, *The End of the World As We Know It: Social Science for the Twenty-First Century* (Minneapolis: University of Minnesota, 1999), 1.
4 Saul Bellow, *Herzog* (New York: Viking Press, 1965), 1.
5 Arnold Toynbee, *A Study of History* (New York: Weathervane Books, 1972), 158.
6 Toynbee, *A Study of History*, 158.
7 Toynbee, *A Study of History*, 158.
8 Sorokin, *Crisis of Our Age*, 263.
9 Christopher Dawson, *Religion and World History: A Selection from the Works of Christopher Dawson* (Garden City, NY: Image Books, 1975), 323–324.
10 Christopher Dawson, *Religion and the Rise of Western Culture* (New York: Image Books, 1948–1949), 37.
11 Dawson, *Religion and the Rise of Western Culture*, 87.
12 Dawson, *Religion and the Rise of Western Culture*, 87.
13 Matthew 24:36/Mark 13:32 (NIV).
14 Edward Gibbon, *Epitaph for the People of Ancient Athens* (attributed).
15 Philip Bagby, *Culture and History: Prolegomena to the Comparative Study of Civilizations* (Berkeley, University of California Press, 1963), 210–211.
16 Bagby, *Culture and History*, 211–212.
17 Bagby, *Culture and History*, 221.
18 Spengler, *Decline of the West*, 29.
19 Bagby, *Culture and History, 212.*
20 Spengler, *Decline of the West*, 75.
21 Spengler, *Decline of the West*, 83.
22 Spengler, *Decline of the West*, 220–221.
23 Spengler, *Decline of the West*, 29.
24 Spengler, *Decline of the West*, 29.
25 Alfred Louis Kroeber, *A Roster of Civilizations and Culture* (Chicago: Aldine Publishing Company, 1962), 93–94.
26 Kroeber, *A Roster of Civilizations,* 90.
27 Kroeber, *A Roster of Civilizations,* 93–94.
28 Wallerstein, *The End of the World As We Know It,* 85.
29 Wallerstein, *The End of the World As We Know It,* 1.
30 Wallerstein, *The End of the World As We Know It,* 1–2.
31 Wallerstein, *The End of the World As We Know It,* 2.
32 Wallerstein, *The End of the World As We Know It,* 10.
33 Wallerstein, *The End of the World As We Know It,* 16.
34 Wallerstein, *The End of the World As We Know It,* 16–17.
35 Wallerstein, *The End of the World As We Know It,* 32.
36 Wallerstein, *The End of the World As We Know It,* 33.
37 Wallerstein, *The End of the World As We Know It,* 35.
38 Wallerstein, *The End of the World As We Know It,* 46.

39 Wallerstein, *The End of the World As We Know It,* 84.
40 Wallerstein, *The End of the World As We Know It,* 85.
41 Wallerstein, *The End of the World As We Know It,* 86.
42 Wallerstein, *The End of the World As We Know It,* 132.
43 Wallerstein, *The End of the World As We Know It,* 133–134.
44 Wallerstein, *The End of the World As We Know It,* 219.
45 Carroll Quigley, *The Evolution of Civilizations: An Introduction to Historical Analysis* (New York: Macmillan, 1961), 141.
46 Quigley, *Evolution of Civilizations,* 139.
47 Quigley, *Evolution of Civilizations,* 139.
48 Quigley, *Evolution of Civilizations,* 141.
49 Quigley, *Evolution of Civilizations,* 144.
50 Quigley, *Evolution of Civilizations,* 144–145.
51 Quigley, *Evolution of Civilizations,* 145–146.
52 Quigley, *Evolution of Civilizations,* 411–412.
53 Quigley, *Evolution of Civilizations,* 418.
54 Samuel P. Huntington, *The Clash of Civilizations and the Remaking of World Order* (New York: Simon & Schuster, 1996), 321.
55 Huntington, *Clash of Civilizations,* 54.
56 Huntington, *Clash of Civilizations,* 54.
57 Huntington, *Clash of Civilizations,* 82.
58 Huntington, *Clash of Civilizations,* 82.
59 Huntington, *Clash of Civilizations,* 82.
60 Huntington, *Clash of Civilizations,* 82–83.
61 Huntington, *Clash of Civilizations,* 83.
62 Huntington, *Clash of Civilizations,* 83–84.
63 Huntington, *Clash of Civilizations,* 321.
64 Huntington, *Clash of Civilizations,* 321.
65 Alexander Solzhenitsyn, Text of Address at Harvard Class Day Afternoon Exercises, Thursday, June 8,1978.
66 Solzhenitsyn, Harvard Class Day.
67 Solzhenitsyn, Harvard Class Day.
68 Sorokin, *Crisis of Our Age,* 248.
69 Sorokin, *Crisis of Our Age,* 21.
70 Sorokin, *Crisis of Our Age,* 22.
71 Sorokin, *Crisis of Our Age,* 264.
72 Sorokin, *Crisis of Our Age,* 244.
73 Sorokin, *Crisis of Our Age,* 245.
74 Sorokin, *Crisis of Our Age,* 245.
75 Sorokin, *Crisis of Our Age,* 246.
76 Sorokin, *Crisis of Our Age,* 246.
77 Sorokin, *Crisis of Our Age,* 247–248.
78 Sorokin, *Crisis of Our Age,* 248–249.
79 Sorokin, *Crisis of Our Age,* 248.
80 Christopher Dawson, *The Historic Reality of Christian Culture* (New York: Harper & Brothers, 1960), 62.
81 Dawson, *Religion and World History,* 244.
82 Dawson, *Religion and World History,* 263, 265.
83 Dawson, *Religion and World History,* 302.

84 Dawson, *Religion and World History*, 322–323.
85 Dawson, *Religion and World History*, 323.
86 Dawson, *Religion and World History*, 324–325.
87 Dawson, *Historic Reality*, 27.
88 Dawson, *Historic Reality*, 40.
89 Dawson, *Historic Reality*, 62.
90 Toynbee, *Civilization on Trial* (New York: Oxford University Press, 1948), 234.
91 Toynbee, *Civilization on Trial*, 13.
92 Toynbee, *Civilization on Trial*, 13–14.
93 Toynbee, *Civilization on Trial*, 14–15.
94 Toynbee, *Civilization on Trial*, 21.
95 Toynbee, *Civilization on Trial*, 30.
96 Toynbee, *Civilization on Trial*, 38.
97 Toynbee, *Civilization on Trial*, 39–40.
98 Toynbee, *A Study of History*, 141.
99 Toynbee, *Civilization on Trial*, 234–235.
100 Lord Byron, *Childe Harold's Pilgrimage* (Chicago: W. B. Conkey, 1900), 248.
101 Li Xiaobing, *A History of the Modern Chinese Army* (Langdon, MD: University of Kentucky, 2007), 244.
102 Li, *A History of the Modern Chinese Army*, 244.

PART II

THE DECLINE OF CHRISTIANITY IN THE WEST

CHAPTERS 19–27

IN INCEPTUM FINIS EST
(THE BEGINNING FORESHADOWS THE END)

As deeply as we have probed, we have yet to reach the greatest depths. There are dramatic, unexpected, and sometimes shocking, reasons why Western civilization is imperiled by history's ultimate morbidity. To understand how we got here—especially if we hope to attempt to alter the course of our civilization—we must probe those reasons. To do so, Part II addresses these questions:

- What are the foundational beliefs and values that have historically characterized Western civilization?
- What forms the superstructure of our civilization?
- Have our institutions failed our culture?
- If so, how have they failed?

To answer these questions we must be ruthlessly honest in examining revered and sacrosanct beliefs and institutions. We cannot pander to anyone's biases, prejudices, sensitivities, or to any constituency. We *can* know how we got here. Some will balk at this confrontation with reality. For others dark corners and perplexing questions will be illuminated. A few will have already intuitively sensed the underlying causes of Western civilization's degradation.

CHAPTER 19
The Superstructure of Western Civilization

The parallels between the decline and decay of Western civilization and the decline of the civilization's dominant religion, Christianity, are striking and not coincidental. They are directly related and in large part contingent upon one another. Christianity is not only the dominant religion of Western civilization but also its cultural and social superstructure. The sense of morality, values, and worldview that have characterized the civilization throughout its history are directly attributable to the influence of this religion and the Judeo–Christian ethos. Secular realms of the culture are heavily influenced by both even while often disavowing the former as a credible belief system and the latter as a transcendent moral authority.

CHAPTER 20
The Decline of the Church in the West

Over generations, the Christian church in the West has been increasingly influenced by its host culture rather than the other way round, resulting in a secular cast to the thinking and practices of its members and its leadership, thereby gradually diluting and even nullifying its influence on the mores, beliefs and behavior of the society.

CHAPTER 21
The Death of Christendom—The Decline of the Church in Europe

In Europe, this influence has been dramatically diminished; in America it is rapidly receding. As the church has become more acculturated, Western societies have drifted further from their traditional views of morality, relationships, and spirituality to the point that today in Europe the church is near an irrelevancy and no longer a cultural force with which to reckon.

CHAPTER 22
A People Set Apart—Or Indistinguishable From?

The influence of the culture on the Christian religion manifests itself in secular values, ways of thought, and practices that have become so broadly accepted within the church that their variance from the lifestyle and teachings of the faith's founder is no longer noted. This "baptizing" of the secular as religious continues to undermine the moral and spiritual credibility and efficacy of the Western church, Catholic, Orthodox, and Protestant.

CHAPTER 23
A Romance with Numbers

The church in the West has deteriorated from a social instrument for ensuring moral guidance for the individual and society and offering spiritual and psychological security in a relationship with a

Supreme Being, to an institution focused primarily on nurturing and expanding its security, perquisites, wealth, power and social standing. It accomplishes these objectives largely through resort to secular methods appropriated from the broader culture.

CHAPTER 24
The Spirit of Competition

That most revered of Western values, "competition," has infiltrated every nook and cranny of the church, turning it from a haven of peace and serenity in the midst of a strained and self-seeking culture to a bastion of worldly values, including the practices of competing for "converts" and members and serving as the arena for endless doctrinal disputes and internal conflicts.

CHAPTER 25
The Abolition of Sin

Unable to achieve increasingly self-centered goals through its traditional spiritual and moral means, the church has gradually succumbed to syncretism and the *de facto* "amendment" or "abrogation" of long-recognized moral principles and authority. Behaviors once recognized as sin are mitigated by rationalizations calculated to relieve the practitioner of full moral responsibility—if any responsibility at all. Or, sins are simply ignored altogether on a selective basis that varies from church to church.

CHAPTER 26
By Their Works Ye Shall Know Them

The near complete erasure of significant distinctions between self-proclaimed Christians—especially as expressed by the institutional church—and the culture at large has eviscerated much of the church's credibility in the eyes of the ever-expanding segment of Western culture that is secular in its viewpoint. More and more compliant with the mores, values and practices of the broader culture, the Christian's image is increasingly one of self-centeredness and hypocrisy: self-righteous on the one hand, yet much like everyone else on the other.

CHAPTER 27
A Fate Predestined or Prescribed?

The decline and decay of Western civilization is most directly attributable to the failure of its central formative institution, the Christian church, to adhere to its professed beliefs and codex. The decline of the church and the corollary decline of the civilization are neither inevitable nor foreordained in a historically deterministic way. Each is the result of a series of choices made first within the church, particularly by its leadership, which rippled into the broader culture.

CHAPTER

19

THE SUPERSTRUCTURE OF WESTERN CIVILIZATION

...it was only as Christendom—the society of Christian peoples—that the tribes and peoples and nations of the West acquired a common consciousness and a sense of cultural and spiritual unity. Now our modern Western civilization in Europe and America is the direct successor and heir of this Christian civilization. Without the latter, it would never have existed.

Christopher Dawson[1]

Western Christianity was and remains the main constituent element in European thought—including rationalist thought, which although it attacked Christianity was also derivative from it. Throughout the history of the West, Christianity has been at the heart of the civilization....

Fernand Braudel[2]

The democratic and individualistic aspects of the Western outlook were always present, and go back, like other aspects, to the New Testament.

Carroll Quigley[3]

The West differs from other civilizations...in the distinctive character of its values and institutions...most notably its Christianity, pluralism, individualism, and rule of law, which made it possible for the West to invent modernity, expand throughout the world, and become the envy of other societies.

Samuel Huntington[4]

Perhaps no single physical edifice represents what Western civilization stands for in political and social terms as does the Statue of Liberty. Certainly this is the symbol in the eyes of much of the world of the Western values of freedom and the importance of the individual. The Chinese students in Tiananmen Square, just prior to being shot down by their government, had constructed a figure reminiscent of the Statue of Liberty. Thus, this is a particularly *apropos* symbol not only for America but liberty in the Western sense.

The metaphor can be carried further when we consider the physical structure of the Statue. Externally, it appears to be a rugged, virtually indestructible monolith. But visitors to the interior realize that it is, in fact, supported by a series of interlocking heavy iron girders that bear scant resemblance in their configuration to the external statue they support. Were any of those girders weakened

PD

Photo by Daniel Schwen. GFDL

(Left) The Statute of Liberty *appears to be a rugged, virtually indestructible monolith. But it is supported by a series of interlocking heavy iron girders. Were those girders weakened or removed, symbolically, the torch-bearing arm (representing the Light of Freedom) would probably collapse first, followed eventually by the piecemeal or abrupt collapse of the remainder.* (Right) Interior of the Statue of Liberty. *Christianity forms the very superstructure of Western civilization. Christianity's role as the great girders upon which an entire civilization was built means that its renunciation—in whole or in substantial part—will ultimately result in the collapse of the entire edifice.*

or removed this would not bode well for the impressive external figure. Probably, and symbolically, the torch-bearing arm (representing the Light of Freedom) would collapse first, followed eventually by the piecemeal or abrupt collapse of the remainder.

We will see in this chapter that Christianity forms the very superstructure of Western civilization—a powerful and all-encompassing influence that pervades not simply the religious but every realm of Western human endeavor: science, technology, economics, government, law, philosophy, military strategy and training, education, and social relationships.

Christianity's role as the great girders upon which an entire civilization was built means that its renunciation—in whole or in substantial part—will ultimately result in the collapse of the entire edifice. Contrary to what secularists would blithely assume, the girders cannot be replaced, one by one, by the secularist philosophy and worldview thereby gradually reinforcing the structure with what they regard as more sound supports. Were that attempted—and that process has been well underway for more than a century—all external appearances would, at least initially, remain unchanged. But at the first strong wind or geotectonic shift, visible cracks in the structure would begin to appear. The physics of history dictate that the edifice must fall.

THE CENTRAL DEFINING FEATURE OF WESTERN CIVILIZATION

Western Christianity, first Catholicism and then Catholicism and Protestantism, is historically the single most important characteristic of Western civilization.
Huntington[5]

Civilizations are constructed, more than anything else, around a series of coherent and unifying ideas and beliefs that are usually religious, or at least carry the quality and fervor of religious beliefs. Adda Bozeman, in a passage that reminds us again of Toynbee's "surface of the stream of life" dictum, stated the case this way: "International history richly documents the thesis that political systems are transient expedients on the surface of civilization, and that the destiny of each linguistically and morally unified community depends ultimately upon the survival of certain primary structuring ideas around which successive generations have coalesced and which thus symbolize the society's continuity."[6]

Samuel Huntington, quoting Dawson and Alfred Weber, viewed religion as "a central defining characteristic of civilizations, and, as Christopher Dawson said, 'the great religions are the foundations on which the great civilizations rest.' Of Weber's five 'world religions,' four—Christianity, Islam, Hinduism, and Confucianism—are associated with major civilizations. The fifth, Buddhism, is not."[7]

That religion would play the central role in man's interactions and in history should hardly be a surprise. Christopher Dawson, in *Christianity and the New Age*, identified two fundamental human needs that pervade all of human experience: "God, the supernatural, the transcendent…[and]…deliverance, salvation, eternal life."[8] Dawson concluded that "both these two elements are represented in some form or other in any given religion."[9]

Dawson noted that "primitive man had already found the Transcendent immanent in and working through nature as the supernatural"[10]—a recognition seemingly lost on urbanized Western man. Furthermore, the Oriental religions "isolated [the transcendent] and set it over against the world of human experience…as Reality against Appearance, and as the Spiritual against the Sensible."[11]

Unlike any other world religion, Christianity embraced the transcendent character of the Absolute yet declared that this Absolute had come to the tactile world as a man. Dawson observed, "This conception of the Incarnation as the bridge between God and Man, the marriage of Heaven and Earth, the channel through which the material world is spiritualized and brought back to unity, distinguishes Christianity from all the other Oriental religions, and involves a completely new attitude to life."[12]

This "new attitude to life" was essential to the formation and growth of Western civilization. Ironically, Braudel referred to the atheist Karl Marx to describe the dual meaning of the word civilization. Civilization, Braudel asserted, suggests both "moral and material values." Karl Marx made a similar distinction in referring to the *infrastructure* (meaning the material values) and the *superstructure* (spiritual values) with the latter "depending heavily on the former."[13]

Braudel affirmed a virtually identical view of civilizations as described by Adda Bozeman.

> In every period, a certain view of the world, a collective mentality, dominates the whole mass of society.... Dictating a society's attitudes, guiding its choices, confirming its prejudices and directing its actions, this is very much a fact of civilization.... A society's reactions to the events of the day, to the pressure upon it, to the decisions it must face, are less a matter of logic or even self-interest than the response to an unexpressed and often inexpressible compulsion arising from the collective unconscious.
>
> These basic values, these psychological structures, are assuredly the features that civilizations can least easily communicate one to another. They are what isolate and differentiate them most sharply. And such habits of mind survive the passage of time. They change little, and change slowly, after a long incubation which itself is largely unconscious too.
>
> Here religion is the strongest feature of civilizations, at the heart of both their present and their past.[14]

That Braudel was correct was illustrated in a practical way by Sorokin in his description of the destruction of sensate Graeco–Roman culture by the higher values of Christianity: "The respective societies were preserved from dissolution...not so much through the 'practical and expert' manipulation of economic, political, genetic or other factors, but mainly through the transmutation of values, the spiritualization of mentality, and the socialization of conduct and ennoblement of social relations effected through the medium of religion."[15]

In this sense, Gibbon was correct in his view that Christianity brought down the Roman Empire —not through military, political, or economic power, but through "the transmutation of values" and the proffering of a higher, nobler, and eternal reality. The sensate values of Rome were wholly incompatible with the beliefs of Christianity; one had to displace the other. Yet, said Dawson, Christianity also embodied an inherent tension between the spiritual and the practical.

> But this higher type of religion, with its clear realisation of the distinction between matter and spirit, also contained the seeds of a conflict between religion and life. There was no room for common humanity on the icy summits to which the path of contemplation led, and yet it was at the same time the only way to deliverance and spiritual life. This contrast is seen in its most striking and paradoxical form in Buddhism, for Buddhism is, above all, a direct and straightforward attempt to solve the problem of human life, and it does this by a radical denial of life itself. The Buddha professed to teach man the secret of happiness and the way of spiritual deliverance, but his noble, ethical teaching has its beginning in the realization that existence is suffering and its end in the peace of Nirvana.[16]

The inherent pessimism about life that was characteristic of the great religions of the ancients was in large measure nullified by the Jewish belief in a "Living God." "Jewish religion differed from all the rest in the dynamic realism of its conception of God. The God of Israel was no metaphysical abstraction, like the Platonic Idea of the Good, or the universal Brahmin, or the Chinese Tao, "not the God of the philosophers and savants, but the Living God, God of Abraham, God of Isaac, God of Jacob, *Deus meus et Deus vester.*"[17] This led ultimately to the Christian view—a view unlike any other world religion and having an unprecedented impact on world history. Christianity did not require "deliverance from the body and from the sensible world" for salvation; rather, it offered salvation "of the whole man, body and soul, by the coming of a new life. In no other religion is the conception of life so central and so characteristic as in Christianity."[18]

Francis Schaeffer analyzed this historical process—and the reasons for Christianity's tremendous impact—more completely.

> The Greeks and later the Romans also tried to build society upon their gods. But these gods were not big enough because they were finite, limited. Even all their gods put together were not infinite.
>
> The gods were amplified humanity, not divinity. Like the Greeks, the Romans had no infinite god. This being so, they had no sufficient reference point intellectually; that is, they did not have anything big enough or permanent enough to which to relate either their thinking or their living. Consequently, their value system was not strong enough to bear the strains of life, either individual or political. All their gods put together could not give them a sufficient base for life, morals, values,

PD-old

The persecution of Christians by Rome. In one sense, Gibbon was correct in his view that Christianity brought down the Roman Empire—not through military, political, or economic power, but through "the transmutation of values" and the proffering of a higher, nobler, and eternal reality. The sensate values of Rome were wholly incompatible with the beliefs of Christianity; one had to displace the other.

> and final decisions. These gods depended on the society that had made them, and when this society collapsed the gods tumbled with it.[19]

Schaeffer's description of these gods as "amplified humanity," might be appropriately applied to modern Western man's view of himself—an ironic and interesting juxtaposition. Schaeffer explained why this made Christianity not only resilient as a world historical force but Christians individually better able to face the adversity of life.

> It is important to realize what a difference a people's world view makes in their strength as they are exposed to the pressure of life. That it was the Christians who were able to resist religious mixtures, syncretism, and the effects of the weaknesses of Roman culture speaks of the strength of the Christian world view. This strength rested on God's being an infinite personal God and his speaking in the Old Testament, in the life and teaching of Jesus Christ, and in the gradually growing New Testament. He had spoken in ways people could understand. Thus the Christians not only had knowledge about the universe and mankind that people cannot find out by themselves, but they had absolute, universal values by which to live and by which to judge the society and the political state in which they lived. And they had grounds for the basic dignity and value of the individual as unique in being made in the image of God.[20]

Schaeffer's description is revealing of much of the true power—the unique power—of Christianity as a belief system. Christopher Dawson in *Religion and the Rise of Western Culture* noted another significant way in which Christianity is different from any other world religion. The great world religions, he declared, were "great rivers of sacred tradition which flow down through the ages and through changing historical landscapes which they irrigate and fertilize." But these rivers could not be traced to their sources in the distant past.

> It is rare indeed to find a culture in which the whole course of this religious development can be traced from beginning to end in the full light of history. But the history of Christendom is an outstanding exception to this tendency. We know the historical environment in which Christianity first arose: we possess the letters of the founders of the Churches to the first Christian communities in Europe, and we can trace in detail the successive stages by which the new religion penetrated the West.[21]

But perhaps the most powerful and eloquent affirmation of what makes Christianity unique—and conspicuous among all religions of all times—was expressed by Oswald Spengler, who gave his own assessment of Christianity's power in the person of Christ himself.

> Here was no matter of philosophy. Jesus' utterances, which stayed in the memory of many of the devoted, even in old age, are those of a child in the midst of an alien, aged and sick world. They are not sociological observations, problems, debatings. Like a quiet island of bliss was the life of these fishermen and craftsmen by the Lake of Gennesareth in the midst of the age of the great Tiberius, far from all world-history and innocent of all the doings of actuality, while round them glittered the Hellenistic towns with their theatres and temples, their refined Western society, their noisy mob-diversions, their Roman cohorts, their Greek philosophy. When the friends and disciples of the sufferer had grown grey and his brother was president of their group in Jerusalem, they put together, from the sayings and narratives generally current in their small communities, a biography so arresting in its inward appeal that it evolved a presentation-form of its own, of which neither the Classical nor the Arabian Culture has any example—the Gospel. Christianity is the one religion in the history of the world in

PD-art

Ancient Roman Myth of Mars and Rhea by Rubens. *Schaeffer wrote, "The Greeks and later the Romans also tried to build society upon their gods. But these gods were not big enough because they were finite, limited. Even all their gods put together were not infinite. The gods were amplified humanity, not divinity…they had no sufficient reference point intellectually; that is, they did not have anything big enough or permanent enough to which to relate either their thinking or their living. Consequently, their value system was not strong enough to bear the strains of life, either individual or political. All their gods put together could not give them a sufficient base for life, morals, values, and final decisions. These gods depended on the society which had made them, and when this society collapsed the gods tumbled with it." Similarly, Western man has incrementally—and at an ever-increasing pace—rejected the omniscient, omnipotent God of the Christian faith and substituted for Him other "gods" that are as vacuous as those of the ancients.*

> which the fate of a man of the immediate present has become the emblem and the central point of the whole creation.[22]

We now should understand, without equivocation or doubt, that religion is central to the very concept of civilization. That Christianity is distinctive from all other world religions should also be apparent. But the questions that now present themselves are, What role has Christianity played in Western civilization? To what extent has Christianity's distinctive characteristics influenced the growth and power of Western civilization?

Without exception our observers—in one of their great common denominators—view Christianity as central to Western civilization. All of Western civilization can be likened to a great mountain range elevated above the plains and swamps of history by its unique faith and that faith's unique impact. America, in particular, juts above the landscape of history like an Everest as the only nation that was founded so clearly on the vision of a Christian future and sustained by the eternal stamina of the Christian faith.

Samuel Huntington described Christianity as not only the "single most important characteristic" of Western civilization but noted that, at one time, it provided the other name for Western civilization—Western Christendom. This distinct identity among Western Christians held them as separate from "Turks, Moors, Byzantines, and others" and it was as much "for God as well as gold that Westerners went out to conquer the world in the sixteenth century." "The Reformation and Counter-Reformation and the division of Western Christendom into a Protestant north and a Catholic south are also distinctive features of Western history, totally absent from Eastern Orthodoxy and largely removed from the Latin American experience."[23] As late as the era of Winston Churchill, Western political leaders referred to Western civilization as "Christendom."

Kroeber, likewise, reached similar conclusions and declared, "Western civilization has throughout been multinational and Christian." During its early centuries "all higher achievements were meshed" into the religion of Christianity.[24]

Anticipating the twentieth- and twenty-first-century clashes between secularism and Christianity, Dawson made a distinction between purely man-created beliefs and the transcendent.

> An ideology in the modern sense of the word is very different from a faith, although it is intended to fulfill the same sociological functions. It is the work of man, an instrument by which the conscious political will attempts to mould the social tradition to its purpose. But faith looks beyond the world of man and his works; it introduces man to a higher and more universal range of reality than the finite and temporal world to which the state and the economic order belong. And thereby it introduces into human life an element of spiritual freedom which may have a creative and transforming influence on man's social culture and historical destiny as well as on his inner personal experience. If therefore we study a culture as a whole, we shall find there is an intimate relation between its religious faith and its social achievement. Even a religion which is explicitly other-worldly and appears to deny all the values and standards of human society may, nevertheless, exert a dynamic influence on culture and provide the driving forces in movements of social change. "Religion is the key of history," said Lord Acton, and today, when we realize the tremendous influence of the unconscious on human behaviour and the power of religion to bind and loose these hidden forces, Acton's saying has acquired a wider meaning than he realized.[25]

Dawson acknowledged that the cursory observer of Western civilization might conclude that religion does not play a major role in the civilization's achievements. But this, he said, would be highly superficial, and Western civilization's achievements could not be accounted for through economic or political stimuli alone.

> The great changes that have transformed the conditions of human life in every continent and have gone a long way towards the creation of a single world society seem at first sight to be the result of purely secular and economic causes. Yet none of these causes seems adequate to explain the magnitude of the European achievement.
>
> How did it come about that a small group of peoples in Western Europe should in a relatively short space of time acquire the power to transform the world and to emancipate themselves from man's

> age-long dependence on the forces of nature? In the past this miraculous achievement was explained as the manifestation of a universal Law of Progress which governed the universe and led mankind by inevitable stages from apehood to perfection. Today such theories are no longer acceptable, since we have come to see how much they depend on an irrational optimism which was part of the phenomenon they attempted to explain. Instead we now tend to ask ourselves what were the factors in European culture which explain the peculiar achievement of Western man? or to use the brutal and expressive American phrase, "What makes him tick?"...we shall find the religious factor does have a very important bearing upon the question.[26]

That "irrational optimism" has characterized, and still characterizes, the thinking of many in the West as we addressed in the chapter "Progress and Optimism." However, just as that line of thought is "irrational," so too is the conclusion that aggression and economic exploitation are the reasons for the West's success: "...[A]ggression and exploitation are nothing new in world history, and if they suffice to explain the European achievement, it might have been realized hundreds or thousands of years earlier by any of the world empires that have successively held the stage of history."[27] The "peculiar achievement of Western culture in modern times" was due to a "new element which was not present in the older type of imperialism." For though there was a "natural aggressiveness and the lust for power and wealth" evident in European history, there were also "new spiritual forces driving Western man towards a new destiny."[28]

Dawson pointed to the age of faith known as the medieval period—the era so glibly referred to as "The Dark Ages"—as the wellspring of the thinking and forces that ultimately produced the power of Western civilization.

> And this medieval culture was the matrix in which the Western type was formed and the ultimate source of the new forces that have moved and transformed the world. The older school of "enlightened" rationalist historians dismissed the thousand years of medieval history as an age of intellectual darkness and social stagnation—an aimless wandering in the wilderness between the old world of classical culture and the Promised Land of modern Enlightenment and Liberty. But thanks to the disinterested work of the historians of the last century and a half, we have now come to understand that these centuries were ages of intense social and spiritual activity and often of violent conflict and revolutionary change.[29]

> No doubt it is easy to see how the Humanist or rationalist notion of the Dark Ages arose. From the economic point of view the early Middle Ages were indeed a period of retrogression and stagnation; there were long periods in which commercial activity was at a standstill and city life had almost disappeared.[30]

Despite these limitations, Western culture "preserved a spiritual energy which was independent of political power or economic prosperity." This "dynamic principle continued to operate. For what distinguishes Western culture from the other world civilizations is its missionary character—its transmission from one people to another in a continuous series of spiritual movements."[31]

Dawson noted that unlike other civilizations borne on the backs of great religions, Western civilization, even in the medieval period, was never a true theocracy despite religion's role then—and its more subtle role now—as the single unifying force. Christianity was distinguishable from all other religions here also in its unique "dualism between the spiritual and the temporal powers, which produced an internal tension in Western society and was a fertile source of criticism and change."

Throughout the history of Western Europe "the absence of unitary organization and of a single uniform source of culture did not destroy the spiritual continuity of the Western tradition. Behind the ever-changing pattern of Western culture there was a living faith which gave Europe a certain sense of spiritual community, in spite of all the conflicts and divisions and social schisms that marked its history."

We see the most dramatic manifestation of this phenomenon in the American Civil War, in the wake of which, despite its hatreds and bloodletting, the American people, North and South, fell back upon shared values and beliefs—essential core ideas that had their origin in the Christian faith. In our own time in American history, blood does not flow in the streets, yet the schism that exists in American society is of a far more profound and dangerous nature than that which precipitated the Civil War—precisely because of the absence of spiritual community. The erosion of a unifying belief in the Christian faith and the Judeo-Christian ethic simultaneously with the corollary ascendancy of secularist views has produced sets of values and beliefs that are poles apart—even antithetical. The unity Dawson described has broken down significantly, as I describe elsewhere in this book, and is a classic harbinger of cultural decline. Toynbee's "social discord" manifested in "vertical" and "horizontal" schisms will increasingly dictate social interaction.

Dawson believed it was often difficult to trace the relationship between faith and the secular movements that denied "any common spiritual basis." However, he declared, when these movements are closely studied the connections can usually be discerned. "In fact, nowhere is the dynamism of Western religion more strikingly manifested than in the indirect and unconscious influence it has exercised on the social and intellectual movements which were avowedly secular."[32]

That dynamism was most apparent in the teachings of the great leaders of the early Christian church, some of whom were also eventually recognized among the greatest philosophers in Western thought.

> The beginnings of Western culture are to be found in the new spiritual community which arose from the ruins of the Roman Empire owing to the conversion of the Northern barbarians to the Christian faith. The Christian Church inherited the traditions of the Empire. It came to the barbarians as the bearer of a higher civilization, endowed with the prestige of Roman law and the authority of the Roman name. The breakdown of the political organization of the Roman Empire had left a great void which no barbarian king or general could fill, and this void was filled by the Church as the teacher and law-giver of the new peoples. The Latin Fathers—Ambrose, Augustine, Leo and Gregory—were in a real sense the fathers of Western culture, since it was only in so far as the different peoples of the West were incorporated in the spiritual community of Christendom that they acquired a common culture. It is this, above all, that distinguishes the Western development from that of the other world civilizations.[33]

Biblical accounts of early missionary journeys provide the historical nexuses linking Christ himself to the ensuing centuries of Western civilization's development.

> When St. Paul, in obedience to the warning of a dream, set sail from Troy in A.D. 49 and came to Philippi in Macedonia he did more to change the course of history than the great battle that had decided the fate of the Roman Empire on the same spot nearly a century earlier, for he brought to Europe the seed of a new life which was ultimately destined to create a new world. All this took place underneath the surface of history, so that it was unrecognized by the leaders of contemporary culture, like Gallio the brother of Seneca, who actually saw it taking place beneath their eyes. But it

PD-old PD-old

(Left) *Paul Preaching,* by Gustave Doré (1832–1883). *St. Paul's obedience to a dream leading him to Macedonia and then Greece fundamentally altered the course of European and Western history. More than any other decision, this determined the nature and future of Western civilization.* (Right) *Paul Addresses the Crowd After His Arrest,* by Gustave Doré. *Dawson described the result of St. Paul's mission: "As the mob at Salonika protested: these men have turned the world upside down, proclaiming another king than Caesar—Jesus. And so indeed they did, and this act of creative revolution marks the beginning of a new era in world history, and, above all, in the history of the West...."*

> is impossible to read the contemporary account of these journeys and the letters that St. Paul wrote to the first Christian communities of Europe and Asia Minor without realizing that a new principle had been introduced into the static civilization of the Roman world that contained infinite possibilities of change. As the mob at Salonika protested: these men have turned the world upside down, proclaiming another king than Caesar—Jesus. And so indeed they did, and this act of creative revolution marks the beginning of a new era in world history, and, above all, in the history of the West. ...In the course of centuries this latter division was finally overcome by the conversion of the Empire, so that Roman and Christian became almost synonymous terms.[34]

Displaying the resilience and durability that Toynbee characterized as "the toughest and the most enduring of any that we know," Christianity not only survived that which destroyed the Roman Empire but throve in the face of adversity.

> Thus it was in those parts of the West where the material destruction of the barbarian invasions had been greatest that the new development took place. The spiritual resources of the Church had not been seriously impaired by the fall of the Empire. Indeed in certain respects they were strengthened, since the Church now united the social traditions of Roman culture with its own spiritual traditions

> and thus fulfilled a double function in a society which needed social as well as religious leadership. The new barbarian kingdoms had taken over the military and political functions of the Empire—they held the sword, they levied the taxes, they administered justice—of a sort—but everything else belonged to the Church—moral authority, learning and culture, the prestige of the Roman name and the care of the people. A man's real citizenship was not to be found in his subjection to the barbarian state, but in his membership of the Christian Church, and it was to the bishop rather than to the king that he looked as the leader of Christian society.[35]

Dawson explained that the transformation of the whole of Europe by Christianity was apparent even in the corners formerly seen as the most barbaric.

> The wholehearted acceptance of Christianity in Norway and Denmark gradually transformed the spirit of Scandinavian culture.
>
> Adam of Bremen, who is a contemporary witness and was well informed of Northern affairs through his friendship with King Sweyn Estrithson of Denmark, has described the change in a remarkable passage. After speaking of their former piracy, he goes on:
>
>> But after their acceptance of Christianity, they have become imbued with better principles and have now learned to love peace and truth and to be content with their poverty; even to distribute what they have stored up and not as aforetime to gather up what was scattered ....Of all men they are the most temperate both in food and in their habits, loving above all things thrift and modesty. Yet so great is their veneration for priests and churches, that there is scarcely a Christian to be found who does not make an offering on every occasion that he hears Mass....In many places of Norway and Sweden, the keepers of the flocks are men of noble rank, who after the manner of the patriarchs live by the work of their hands. But all who dwell in Norway are most Christian with the exception of those who dwell far off beside the Arctic Seas.[36]

The vestiges of this transformation remain evident in our time throughout Scandinavia. Despite rampant secularization, Scandinavian nations have distinguished themselves in many respects as models of civilized behavior. I have been impressed many times in visits to the world's war zones by the presence of Scandinavian peacekeepers and aid workers. Relative to their numbers and wealth, Scandinavian countries give disproportionately to the world community. These are vestigial hallmarks of the influence of the Christian faith.

Alluding to the deterioration of the Christian culture in Denmark by the mid-nineteenth century, Dawson demonstrated how, nonetheless, the legacy of Christianity remained apparent. Though the Christian culture had "become moribund in Denmark in 1850," that "does not prove that it had never existed." "There had been a time...when 'Christendom' had meant something." Christianity "had transformed the societies with which it came into contact." Christianity "has been a creative cultural force of the first magnitude, and...it has actually created a Christian culture or a number of Christian cultures."[37]

The ubiquity of the Christian influence throughout the West has been noted many times by sociologists and historians who cite the irony of avowed atheists or agnostics supporting what are known to be Christian values or perspectives. Listening attentively to atheists, agnostics, or simply those with a secularist viewpoint, arguing for a particular position on public policy, legislation, or judicial decisions will often result in the perceptive listener being struck by their resort—to which the enunciators seem oblivious—to reliance on essentials of Christian origin. In other instances they may argue for a position (aborticide, for example) for which they must resort to concepts that are antithetical to Christian principles. Significantly, in each instance, they state their supporting principles with equal authority—citing them with a certainty equivalent to a Christian's reliance, for example, on the Ten Commandments. Thus they move back and forth from Christian-derived concepts to purely man-inspired thinking, revealing inadvertently that their under-girding philosophy is founded on a doctrine of expediency.

Braudel commented on this "forgetfulness":

> ...the West seems forgetful of its Christian sources....Christianity is an essential reality in Western life: it even marks atheists, whether they know it or not. Ethical rules, attitudes to life and death, the concept of work, the value of effort, the role of women and children—these may seem to have nothing to do with Christian feeling: yet all derive from it nevertheless.

Braudel continued:

> Since the development of Greek thought, however, the tendency of Western civilization has been towards rationalism and hence away from the religious life....With very few exceptions (certain Chinese sophists, and certain Arab philosophers in the twelfth century), no such marked turning away from religion is to be found in the history of the world outside the West.[38]

That Christianity is the source even of Western rationalist thought suggests the strong connection between reason and rational thought and the precepts of the Christian faith. Reason and rational thought are not incompatible with the Christian faith and, indeed, are enhanced by that faith.

> Throughout the history of the West, Christianity has been at the heart of the civilization it inspires, even when it has allowed itself to be captured or deformed by it, and which it contains, even when efforts are made to escape. To direct one's thoughts against someone is to remain in his orbit. A European, even if he is an atheist, is still the prisoner of an ethic and a mentality which are deeply rooted in the Christian tradition. He remains, one might say, "of Christian descent," in the same way that Montherlant used to say that he was "of Catholic descent" although he had lost his faith.[39]

> European thought is inconceivable except in the context of a dialogue with Christianity, even when the dialogue is sharp and the dispute violent. This context is essential to the understanding of humanism, one of the fundamental aspects of Western thought.[40]

As Braudel noted, the influence of pagan Rome was apparent in the church, though there was a conflict of views as to the propriety of that influence. In part, what we are seeing in the Western church today is a continuation of this dispute.

> To tell the truth, pagan Rome never died out in the West. Ernst Curtius, in a technically meticulous study, has shown how amazingly tenacious the civilization of the Lower Empire proved to be, and how the West relied on it to an unheard-of degree for its literary themes, its ways of thought, its metaphors, and even its clichés.
>
> It was natural for Christian Europe to accept this day-to-day contact with ancient Rome, because there was no alternative, no rival civilization to tap. Equally, Christianity had acquiesced in such co-existence before the Roman Empire fell. In the second century, St. Justin had declared that any noble thought, "wherever it comes from, is the property of Christians." St. Ambrose said: "All truth, whoever its interpreter may be, comes from the Holy Spirit." Only Tertullian asked: "What have Athens and Jerusalem in common?" But his voice raised barely an echo.[41]

Spengler explained how Christianity became the superstructure of Western civilization, when it might just as easily have become the superstructure of a great new civilization in the east: "The important question…was: Should the gospel of Jesus be directed towards the East or the West?" This was answered by the Apostle Paul "—the first great personality in the new movement, and the first who had the sense not only of truths but of facts."[42]

Wallerstein reached much the same conclusions as our other observers on the role of Christianity—using the term "the Judeo-Christian heritage"—in Western civilization:

> Whenever one posed the question of the origin of civilized values, how it was that they have appeared originally (or so it was argued) in the modern Western world, the answer almost inevitably was that they were the products of long-standing and unique trends in the past of the Western world—alternatively described as the heritage of antiquity and/or of the Christian Middle Ages, the heritage of the Hebrew world, or the combined heritage of the two, the latter sometimes renamed and respecified as the Judeo-Christian heritage.
>
> One could after all make the case that Christianity, far from representing continuity, marked a decisive break with Greece, Rome, and Israel. Indeed Christians, up to the Renaissance, made precisely this argument. And is not the break with antiquity still today part of the doctrine of Christian churches?[43]

Dawson in *Religion and World History* asserted that the very notion of progress (i.e., the belief that mankind is continually advancing through the ages and advancing to some goal) is "because Christianity had first put these ideas into his head and he still clung to them even when he had lost his faith." Christianity, Dawson declared, "has had an incalculable influence on Western history, because it has formed the minds of the historians—the men who wrote our histories—and the philosophers—the men who reflected on the meaning of history—from St. Augustine and the Venerable Bede to Hegel and Ranke and Acton."[44]

Dawson, in *The Historic Reality of Christian Culture*, spoke again of the "moral unity" that Christianity gave Western civilization.

> It was the principle of moral unity which gave the Western peoples their spiritual values, their moral standards, and their conception of a divine law from which all human laws ultimately derive their validity and their sanction. Without Christianity there would no doubt have been some kind of civilization in the West, but it would have been quite a different civilization from that which we know: for it was only as Christendom—the society of Christian peoples— that the tribes and peoples and nations of the West acquired a common consciousness and a sense of cultural and

Lord Acton *observed, "Religion is the key of history." Dawson affirmed this by adding, "…when we realize the tremendous influence of the unconscious on human behaviour and the power of religion to bind and loose these hidden forces, Acton's saying has acquired a wider meaning than he realized." Samuel Huntington—stating one of the great common views of many historians—declared Christianity as the "single most important characteristic" of Western civilization.*

PD-old

> spiritual unity.... It is admitted just as much by historians who have no sympathy with Christianity. Edward Gibbon, for example, was notoriously hostile to the whole Christian tradition. Yet he never denied that the Church was the maker of Europe and he concludes his highly critical survey of Christian origins by showing how religious influences and "the growing authority of the Popes cemented the union of the Christian republic; and gradually produced the similar manners and the common jurisprudence which has distinguished from the rest of mankind the independent and even hostile nations of modern Europe."[45]

Likewise, Dawson declared, understanding Britain and America cannot be achieved outside a comprehension of Christianity. Yet this "underworld of sectarian Christianity" has been "so neglected by the political and economic historian" even though it "contributed so many vital elements to the complex pattern of nineteenth-century society."[46] Dawson's point is valid today. This recognition is a primary impetus for this book. We cannot understand Western civilization without understanding Christianity. Any efforts to do so otherwise—and they are now legion—are certain to fail.

Dawson rejected the notion of pure objectivity in studying history and declared that since Christianity is the source of Western culture, everything the Western mind comprehends, it comprehends through this prism. The Western views of the rest of the world are "inevitably...seen through this medium. For the idea that the historian or the sociologist is in a privileged position, from which he can study any and every culture and religion in Olympian detachment, is really an absurdity and the source of countless errors and absurdities in thought and practice."[47] This of course is completely consistent with the thinking of Toynbee. Christian culture "was identical with Western culture during the centuries of formation and growth, and...it was the integrative force which first united the different peoples of Western Europe in a new community. What Hellenism was to the ancient world, Christendom has been to the modern. So that to attempt to understand the modern world without any study of Christian culture is as difficult as it would be to understand the Roman world without any knowledge of Hellenism."[48]

EVERY WESTERNER—WHETHER ATHEIST, AGNOSTIC, OR ARDENT SECULARIST—IS A "CHRISTIAN"

...the West seems forgetful of its Christian sources.
Christianity is an essential reality in Western life: it even marks atheists, whether they know it or not. Ethical rules, attitudes to life and death, the concept of work, the value of effort, the role of women and children—these may seem to have nothing to do with Christian feeling: yet all derive from it nevertheless.
Fernand Braudel[49]

Having acknowledged that Christianity is the edifice upon which all of Western culture is supported, our observers turned their attention to the practical ways in which Christian belief and practice impacted Western civilization.

Kroeber, in *A Roster of Civilizations*, noted how Christianity achieved an imprint on Western culture unlike anywhere else. The medieval period saw Christianity reach "an organization and domination of society that were not only extraordinarily effective but were culturally productive and concordant. Mediaeval philosophy, architecture, and art are thoroughly religious and at the same time embody secular values of a high order." Christianity in other branches—Greek, Slavic, Nestorian—though "equally sincere and fervid," nonetheless, "failed to produce even rudiments of anything comparable either aesthetically or intellectually."[50]

Focusing from the broad to the particular, Fernand Braudel described how the Protestant branch of Christianity was largely responsible for the settling of the American West.

> Protestantism was alone in facing the settlers' difficult human situation when they were so quickly scattered over such an expanse of land. There they were, without pastors, reduced simply to reading the Bible—if that. True, many of the settlers lived in a kind of medieval simplicity, and their spontaneous religious life was lively: it was sometimes fertile in inventing new beliefs, like those of the Mormons, the founders of Utah. It is to the credit of American Protestantism that it kept alive and quickened the flame of faith: that was one of its finest achievements.[51]

Braudel wrote that these "Western preachers fashioned—without knowing it—the American way of life. This was the ideal, the model, the pattern of civilization to which immigrants in the second half of the nineteenth century, Protestant or not, found themselves obliged to adapt."[52] This insightful conclusion—documentable and historically sound to the point of being self-evident—would nonetheless be resisted strenuously by secular forces in modern American society. Like rebellious children determined to deny their parentage despite the DNA evidence, contemporary secularists cannot afford to acknowledge the roots and foundation of American culture, for this inevitably leads to the obvious conclusion that America's achievements are surely founded on these beliefs and values. But then this denial is further evidence that truth is not their goal.

Samuel Huntington demonstrated how the beliefs of the Christian faith contributed—unlike any other religion anywhere in the world—not to theocracy but to the development of freedom. This reality conflicts fundamentally with the arguments of Western secularists who condemn Christianity as the usurper of freedoms rather than their guarantor.

> Throughout Western history first the Church and then many churches existed apart from the state. God and Caesar, church and state, spiritual authority and temporal authority, have been a prevailing dualism in Western culture. Only in Hindu civilization were religion and politics also so distinctly separated.

PD-art

Peter Cartwright *was, in most respects, an archetypal of the frontier preacher, though distinguished by the fact that he once unsuccessfully opposed Abraham Lincoln in a race for political office. Fernand Braudel wrote that these "Western preachers fashioned—without knowing it—the American way of life. This was the ideal, the model, the pattern of civilization to which immigrants in the second half of the nineteenth century, Protestant or not, found themselves obliged to adapt."*

> In Islam, God is Caesar; in China and Japan, Caesar is God; in Orthodoxy, God is Caesar's junior partner. The separation and recurring clashes between church and state that typify Western civilization have existed in no other civilization. This division of authority contributed immeasurably to the development of freedom in the West.[53]

The belief in the value, dignity, and worth of the individual that—also unlike any other world religion—is central to Christianity and contributed what became the West's salient characteristic, at least as viewed by much of the world.

> Many of the above features of Western civilization contributed to the emergence of a sense of individualism and a tradition of individual rights and liberties unique among civilized societies. Individualism developed in the fourteenth and fifteenth centuries and acceptance of the right of individual choice—what Deutsch terms "the Romeo and Juliet revolution"—prevailed in the West by the seventeenth century. Even claims for *equal* rights for all individuals—"the poorest he in England has a life to live as much as the richest he"—were articulated if not universally accepted. Individualism remains a distinguishing mark of the West among twentieth-century civilizations.....Again and again both Westerners and non-Westerners point to individualism as the central distinguishing mark of the West.[54]

Every feature that makes Western civilization unique in world history is directly attributable to the influence of the Christian faith.

> The West differs from other civilizations...in the distinctive character of its values and institutions ...most notably its Christianity, pluralism, individualism, and rule of law, which made it possible for the West to invent modernity, expand throughout the world, and become the envy of other societies. In their ensemble these characteristics are peculiar to the West. Europe, as Arthur M. Schlesinger, Jr., has said, is "the source—the unique source" of the "ideas of individual liberty, political democracy, the rule of law, human rights, and cultural freedom....These are European ideas, not Asian, nor African, nor Middle Eastern ideas, except by adoption." They make Western civilization unique, and Western civilization is valuable not because it is universal but because it is unique.[55]

Huntington, as we related in the chapter "A House Divided," warned of a "more immediate and dangerous challenge" to "the American creed," a set of beliefs that is fundamentally Christian in its principles and values.

> Historically American national identity has been defined culturally by the heritage of Western civilization and politically by the principles of the American Creed on which Americans overwhelmingly agree: liberty, democracy, individualism, equality before the law, constitutionalism, private property. In the late twentieth century, both components of American identity have come under concentrated and sustained onslaught from a small but influential number of intellectuals and publicists.[56]

Christopher Dawson in *Christianity and the New Age* argued that Christian humanism and scientific investigation have never been at odds but are mutually supporting. In a passage typical of his efforts to demonstrate the compatibility between science and the Christian faith, Dawson insisted that "the material organization of the world by science and invention is in no sense to be refused or despised by the Catholic tradition, for to the Catholic philosopher no less than to the scientist the progressive *rationalization* of matter by the work of scientific intelligence is the natural vocation of the human mind."[57]

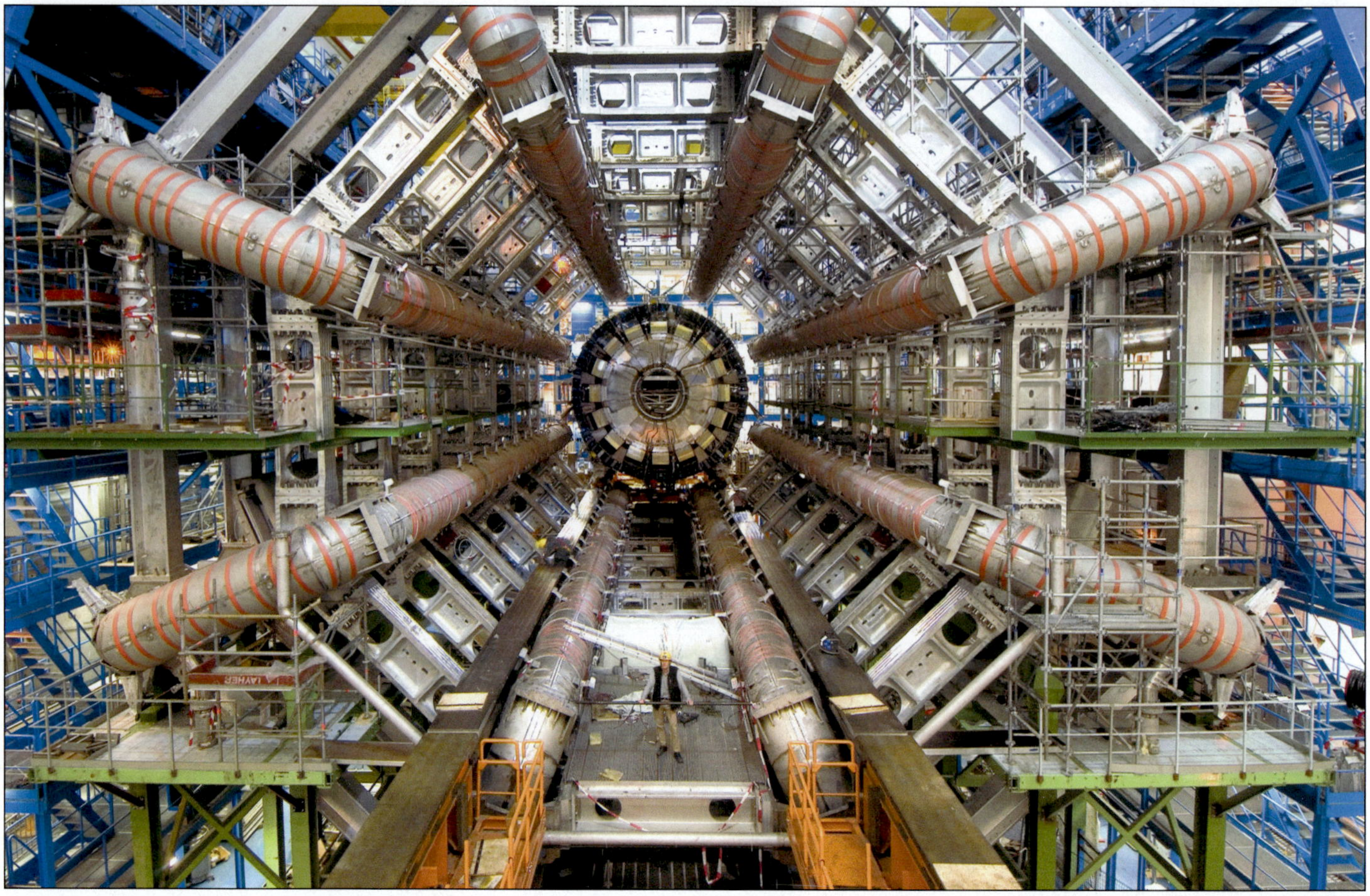

Courtesy of CERN, European Organization for Nuclear Research

Atlas Experiment facility within the seventeen-mile-circumference Large Hadron Collider in Switzerland. *Mankind has reached his present zenith of scientific discovery and technological advancement under the aegis of Western civilization—all the natural outgrowth of values and views taught by Christianity. Dynamic and stimulative of change, Christianity is the fertile soil in which creative ideas originate and flourish.*

That science and technology have reached their ultimate expression in Western civilization is not only not an irony, but predictable as a natural outgrowth of values and beliefs espoused in Christianity. Dawson continued the same line of thought by noting that Christianity—unlike most of the world's great religions, which rely heavily on tradition and the backward gaze—is dynamic and stimulative of change.

Christendom, Dawson declared, "cannot escape from the contagion of the divine fire that has been kindled in its midst. Why is it that Europe alone among the civilizations of the world has been continually shaken and transformed by an energy of spiritual unrest that refuses to be content with the unchanging law of social tradition which rules the Oriental cultures? It is because its religious ideal has not been the worship of timeless and changeless perfection, but a spirit that strives to incorporate itself in humanity and to change the world."[58]

In a passage multiculturalists should heed, Dawson explained the dynamic nature of Christianity and its role as the lifeblood of Western civilization.

> Europe is not a true racial or geographical unity; it is, in its essence, a spiritual community, and even its vast material expansion in modern times would have been impossible without the moral force and spiritual inspiration that it owes ultimately to the Christian faith.
>
> However secularized a civilization may become, it can never entirely escape from the burden of its spiritual inheritance....
>
> In the West the spiritual power has not been immobilized in a sacred social order like the Confucian State in China or the Indian caste system. It has acquired social freedom and autonomy, and consequently its activity has not been limited to the religious sphere but has had far-reaching effects on every aspect of social and intellectual life.
>
> These secondary results are not necessarily of religious or moral value from the Christian point of view, for they may be deflected and distorted by the social medium through which they pass or contaminated by materialism and selfishness. But the fact remains that they are secondary and dependent on the existence of a spiritual force, without which they either would not have been or would have been utterly different.[59]

Christian principles, priorities, and values still underpin much that is Western while the West increasingly denies the spiritual power behind them. Dawson cited the Industrial Revolution as an example of the Christian influence even though it is "at first sight one of the most materialistic aspects of Western civilization" yet it "would have been impossible without the moral earnestness and sense of duty that were generated by the Puritan ideal."[60]

Dawson's exposition is useful also for Christians who frequently look for some mystical nexus between faith and achievement—often referred to as "being blessed." But the mechanism—if we may call it that—of God's order and economy is often more direct, and even observable, if the observer will patiently seek to understand. For example, material gain is founded in large measure on principles well-established in biblical teaching, particularly hard work, diligence, a willingness to learn and to seek truth, and, above all, to assume responsibility. As several of the authors quoted herein have noted, these are all basic tenets of Christianity, finding their most pronounced expression in Puritanism and Calvinism. These partially explain the success of the West economically and in science and technology.

Weber made similar pronouncements about the impact of Christian belief on capitalism, particularly the impact of Puritanism and, especially, the highly dynamic Calvinism that called for an activism exceeding anything found in any other religious belief system. Labor discipline in the West was largely the product of these beliefs.

Quoting Montesquieu, Weber advanced a question that has been answered repeatedly in the affirmative by a variety of historians and sociologists. "Montesquieu says of the English that they 'had progressed the farthest of all peoples of the world in three important things: in piety, in commerce, and in freedom.' Is it not possible that their commercial superiority and their adaptation to free political institutions are connected in some way with that record of piety which Montesquieu ascribes to them?"[61]

PD-art

Puritans at worship. *Success, including material gain, is founded in large measure on principles well-established in biblical teaching, particularly hard work, diligence, a willingness to learn and to seek truth, and, above all, to assume responsibility. These are all basic tenets of Christianity, finding their most pronounced expression in Puritanism and Calvinism. These in part explain the success of the West economically and in science and technology. Puritanism and, especially, the highly dynamic Calvinism called for an activism exceeding anything found in any other religious belief system. Labor discipline in the West was largely the product of these beliefs.*

The avidity with which capitalism was embraced in the West did not occur, however, without some reluctance or resistance. Ironically, earlier interpretations of Christian belief militated against the dynamics of capitalism, which "both in ancient times and in the Middle Ages" would have been "proscribed as the lowest sort of avarice and as an attitude entirely lacking in self-respect."[62]

Max Weber noted the impact of human nature, in its self-centeredness and its acquisitiveness, on the early Christian ideals—an impact felt throughout the Western church today.

> To be sure, these Puritanical ideals tended to give way under excessive pressure from the temptations of wealth, as the Puritans themselves knew very well. With great regularity we find the most genuine adherents of Puritanism among the classes which were rising from a lowly status, the small bourgeois and farmers, while the beati possidentes, even among Quakers, are often found tending to repudiate the old ideals. It was the same fate which again and again befell the predecessor of this worldly asceticism, the monastic asceticism of the Middle Ages.... In the latter case, when rational economic activity had worked out its full effects by strict regulation of conduct and limitation of consumption, the wealth accumulated either succumbed directly to the nobility, as in the time before the Reformation,

or monastic discipline threatened to break down, and one of the numerous reformations became necessary.

In fact the whole history of monasticism is in a certain sense the history of a continual struggle with the problem of the secularizing influence of wealth.[63]

This diagnosis bears directly on conclusions reached in this book about the state of the church in the modern West. The phrase "the secularizing influence of wealth" is not only an understatement but of course puts a sociological slant on what should also be seen, more fundamentally, as a spiritual and moral problem.

Weber notes even John Wesley well understood the paradox affecting the church:

> I fear, wherever riches have increased, the essence of religion has decreased in the same proportion. Therefore I do not see how it is possible, in the nature of things, for any revival of true religion to continue long. For religion must necessarily produce both industry and frugality, and these cannot but produce riches. But as riches increase, so will pride, anger, and love of the world in all its branches. How then is it possible that Methodism, that is, a religion of the heart, though it flourishes now as a green bay tree, should continue in this state? For the Methodists in every place grow diligent and frugal; consequently they increase in goods. Hence they proportionately increase in pride, in anger, in the desire of the flesh, the desire of the eyes, and the pride of life. So, although the form of religion remains, the spirit is swiftly vanishing away. Is there no way to prevent this—this continual decay of pure religion? We ought not to prevent people from being diligent and frugal; we must exhort all Christians to gain all they can, and to save all they can; that is, in effect, to grow rich.[64]

It would appear that the "prosperity doctrines" espoused particularly in the modern American church, and especially among televangelists, have older antecedents than might be assumed. This neglects, however, the more important question that will be addressed in later chapters: Are these attitudes and behaviors consistent with the teachings and model of Christ?

Significantly, Weber noted that attitudes and behavior tended to follow patterns that changed over time and were reflected in somewhat predictable phases. When the peak of religious zeal and spiritual seeking passed, "the intensity of the search for the Kingdom

PD-art.

John Wesley *understood the problem of material well-being affecting the church. "I fear, wherever riches have increased, the essence of religion has decreased in the same proportion…as riches increase, so will pride, anger, and love of the world in all its branches.…So, although the form of religion remains, the spirit is swiftly vanishing away."*

PD-art

Great Awakening, 1839. *The impact of Christianity on the United States was profound, sweeping and foundational. The Founding Fathers were not all Christians—some were Deists—but as Schaeffer observed, "The word Christian can legitimately be used two ways. The primary meaning is* an individual who has come to God through the work of Christ. *The second meaning must be kept distinct but also has validity. It is possible for an individual to live within the circle of that which a Christian consensus brings forth, even though he himself is not a Christian in the first sense." Thus, many of the Founding Fathers were not Christians under the first connotation but surely were under the second.*

of God commenced gradually to pass over into sober economic virtue; the religious roots died out slowly, giving way to utilitarian worldliness." Then with interesting literary metaphors, Weber noted that "as in *Robinson Crusoe*, the isolated economic man who carries on missionary activities on the side takes the place of the lonely spiritual search for the Kingdom of Heaven of Bunyan's pilgrim, hurrying through the market-place of Vanity."[65] Clearly the modern Western church is not "hurrying through," but loitering in, "the market-place of Vanity."

> A specifically bourgeois economic ethic had grown up. With the consciousness of standing in the fullness of God's grace and being visibly blessed by Him, the bourgeois business man, as long as he remained within the bounds of formal correctness, as long as his moral conduct was spotless and the use to which he put his wealth was not objectionable, could follow his pecuniary interests as he would and feel that he was fulfilling a duty in doing so. The power of religious asceticism provided him in addition with sober, conscientious, and unusually industrious workmen, who clung to their work as to a life purpose willed by God.[66]

Soberingly, but with admirable honesty, Weber then noted the appalling truth that this view of the Christian faith gave the professing Christian "the comforting assurance that the unequal distribution of the goods of this world was a special dispensation of Divine Providence, which in these differences, as in particular grace, pursued secret ends unknown to men. Calvin himself had made the much-quoted statement that only when the people (i.e., the mass of laborers and craftsmen) were poor did they remain obedient to God. These rationales—which in effect denied the volitional role God had bestowed on man through the witness of Christ—not only gave credence to a ravenous materialism but laid the foundation for central ideas of capitalism. "Here also," Weber observed, "with the dying out of the religious root, the utilitarian interpretation crept in unnoticed, in the line of development which we have again and again observed."[67]

But this utilitarian interpretation is not so much unnoticed as assiduously avoided. It is the foul smell in the living room of the church that the inhabitants choose not to seek out or examine closely. Instead, strong room fresheners are often and regularly deployed from pulpits to distract from the stench.

Weber believed that the transmogrification of ascetic religious belief to acquisitive capitalism was an expectable metamorphosis—when belief was lost, some form of practice remained, especially that which appealed to man's baser instincts. Christian asceticism when alloyed with man's innate selfishness and greed produced what has been called "the spirit of capitalism." Modern capitalism has much of the "content of the Puritan worldly asceticism, only without the religious basis."[68]

The ascetic "calling" provided a *modus operandi* for capitalism that remained, even as the faith behind it withered. In an eloquent and profoundly insightful passage Weber tells us that the "cloak" of acquisitiveness has become "an iron cage."

> The Puritan wanted to work in a calling; we are forced to do so. For when asceticism was carried out of monastic cells into everyday life, and began to dominate worldly morality, it did its part in building the tremendous cosmos of the modern economic order. This order is now bound to the technical, and economic conditions of machine production which today determine the lives of all the individuals who are born into this mechanism, not only those directly concerned with economic acquisition, with irresistible force. Perhaps it will so determine them until the last ton of fossilized coal is burnt. In Baxter's view the care for external goods should only lie on the shoulders of the "saint like a light cloak, which can be thrown aside at any moment." But fate decreed that the cloak should become an iron cage.
>
> ...[M]aterial goods have gained an increasing and finally an inexorable power over the lives of men as at no previous period in history. Today the spirit of religious asceticism—whether finally, who knows?—has escaped from the cage. But victorious capitalism, since it rests on mechanical foundations, needs its support no longer. The rosy blush of its laughing heir, the Enlightenment, seems also to be irretrievably fading, and the idea of duty in one's calling prowls about in our lives like the ghost of dead religious beliefs. Where the fulfillment of the calling cannot directly be related to the highest spiritual and cultural values, or when, on the other hand, it need not be felt simply as economic compulsion, the individual generally abandons the attempt to justify it at all. In the field of its highest development, in the United States, the pursuit of wealth, stripped of its religious and ethical meaning, tends to become associated with purely mundane passions, which often actually give it the character of sport.[69]

Precisely so. Today the materialism of our time is in so many respects like a sport with competition at the center and the "thrill of victory" for the most "successful" and the "agony of defeat" for those who fail at the game.

Francis Schaeffer observed how the Reformation gave dignity to vocations that were earlier perceived with scant respect. This, coupled with the Protestant doctrine of the priesthood of the believer, produced an attitude of equality unparalleled in history, one that led ultimately to the American Declaration of Independence and Constitution. If man is made in the image of God then the practical implications of that notion suffuse everything in a society: law, government, economics, art, etc. Christianity declared that "in a very real sense, all people are equal as persons."[70]

But this equality could also be found in man's sinful nature; no man was free of the guilt of violating God's higher moral law. The Christian faith, Schaeffer told us, explained that which was obvious in human behavior—and that could not be explained through Renaissance humanism. Even kings and queens were human and just as guilty before God for their moral transgressions as the lowliest peasant. I would interject that this also contributed immeasurably to the line of thought that produced the American republic. Under Christian doctrine, monarchs enjoyed no special dispensation from God. This philosophical movement, not only of monarchs but the upper classes, down the rungs of the ladder of human relationships made democracy and a republic possible.

All of this was going somewhere important, though it could not be foreseen at the time of the Reformation what an impact these ideas would have on the West. Religion—at least the religion of Christianity—was trumping all other forms of thought and understanding; and the blessings that would derive therefrom for millions were as yet unfathomable. Ultimately, the most conspicuous and most immediate were in the realm of law and government.

> The clearest example of the Reformation principle of a people's political control of its sovereign is a book written by a Scot, Samuel Rutherford (1600–1661). The book is *Lex Rex: Law Is King*. . . . Here was a concept of freedom without chaos because there was a form. Or, to put it another way, here was a government of law rather than of the arbitrary decisions of men—because the Bible as the final authority was there as the base.[71]
>
> Samuel Rutherford's work and the tradition it embodied had a great influence on the United States Constitution, even though modern Anglo-Saxons have largely forgotten him. This influence was mediated through two sources. The first was John Witherspoon (1723–1794), a Presbyterian who followed Samuel Rutherford's *Lex Rex* directly and brought its principles to bear on the writing of the Constitution and the laying down of forms and freedoms. Witherspoon, educated at Edinburgh University, became president of the College of New Jersey (now Princeton University) in 1768. He was a member of the Continental Congress from 1776 to 1779 and from 1780 to 1782. The only clergyman to sign the Declaration of Independence, he played an important role on a number of the committees of the Congress.

PD-art

Samuel Rutherford (about 1647 by unknown artist). *Schaeffer observed that the Scotsman Samuel Rutherford (1600–1661) "through his book* Lex Rex: Law Is King*...presented a concept of freedom without chaos because there was a form. Or, to put it another way, here was a government of law rather than of the arbitrary decisions of men—because the Bible as the final authority was there as the base."*

> The second mediator of Rutherford's influence was John Locke (1632–1704), who, though secularizing the Presbyterian tradition, nevertheless drew heavily from it. He stressed inalienable rights, government by consent, separation of powers, and the right of revolution. But the biblical base for these is discovered in Rutherford's work. Without this biblical background, the whole system would be without a foundation.... Locke's difficulty was that he did not have Samuel Rutherford's Christian base. He stated the results which come from biblical Christianity without having the base which produced them. That is, he secularized Christian teaching.[72]

One of the most revered personages in the annals of Western political thought, Thomas Jefferson, utilized these ideas to create documents as the foundation for a government unlike any other. As noted earlier, the Founding Fathers were not all Christians—some were Deists—but as Schaeffer observed, "the word *Christian* can legitimately be used two ways. The primary meaning is: an individual who has come to God through the work of Christ. The second meaning must be kept distinct but also has validity. It is possible for an individual to live within the circle of that which a Christian consensus brings forth, even though he himself is not a Christian in the first sense." Thus many of the Founding Fathers were not Christians under the first connotation but surely were under the second.[73]

The rediscovery of the true meaning of Christ that took place during the Reformation also produced another critically important concept that for generations secured Western man from the usurpation of power by any majority. If there is a transcendent authority that supersedes man's laws then "51 percent of the vote never becomes the final source of right and wrong in government because the absolutes of the Bible are available to judge a society. The 'little man,' the private citizen, can at any time stand up and, on the basis of biblical teaching, say that the majority is wrong. So, to the extent to which the biblical teaching is practiced, one can control the despotism of the majority vote or the despotism of one person or group." Similarly, to the extent biblical teaching is ignored or rejected one of the hedges against despotism is removed.

So it was for at least a century: Western man acknowledged a higher moral law that was subject neither to opinion nor vote. This realism about man—which is what it was most completely: an honest recognition of human nature—annihilated any romantic notions about man and his character. This in turn directly contributed to the political concept of "checks and balances."[74]

Significantly, the impact of the Christian faith on England and America spared both not only from tyrannies but also the misery of massive internal disorder that the Enlightenment not only could not prevent, but actually contributed to. Schaeffer quoted Cambridge historian J. H. Plumb as noting

PD-art

George Whitefield's *dynamic preaching and evangelism redirected much of Western culture in his time, making it fairer, more benevolent and thus less likely to foment bloody revolution.*

that without the influence of the George Whitefield and John Wesley revivals of the eighteenth century —which called for foundational social reform—"it is doubtful whether England would have avoided its own version of the French Revolution."[75]

Schaeffer continued his analysis by demonstrating how Christianity not only profoundly influenced legal, governmental, and social institutions in the West, but also that other realm for which the West was to become so well known: science and technology. Three historical phenomena all occurred more or less simultaneously: the Renaissance, the Reformation, and the Scientific Revolution. Not only, Schaeffer declared, was science not seen to be in conflict with the Christian Bible, but the latter was the foundation for the former.

PD-old

Alfred North Whitehead, *mathematician and philosopher, stressed that Christianity made modern science possible. Whitehead declared that Christianity is the "mother of science because of 'the medieval insistence on the rationality of God.'"*

> The rise of modern science did not conflict with what the Bible teaches; indeed, at a crucial point the Scientific Revolution rested upon what the Bible teaches. Both Alfred North Whitehead (1861–1947) and J. Robert Oppenheimer (1904–1967) have stressed that modern science was born out of the Christian world view. Whitehead was a widely respected mathematician and philosopher, and Oppenheimer, after he became director of the Institute for Advanced Study at Princeton in 1947, wrote on a wide range of subjects related to science, in addition to writing on his own field on the structure of the atom and atomic energy. As far as I know, neither of the two men were Christians or claimed to be Christians, yet both were straightforward in acknowledging that modern science was born out of the Christian world view.[76]

Whitehead declared that Christianity is the "mother of science because of 'the medieval insistence on the rationality of God.'"[77] Because of this rationality, the early scientists had an "inexpugnable belief that every detailed occurrence can be correlated with its antecedents in a perfectly definite manner, exemplifying general principles. Without this belief the incredible labors of scientists would be without hope."[78] This reality made discovering truths about nature and the universe possible; without it all such endeavors would be impossible

PD-art

Robert Oppenheimer, *who directed the team of physicists that developed the atom bomb. Francis Schaeffer, citing Alfred North Whitehead and Oppenheimer, wrote, "As far as I know, neither of the two men were Christians or claimed to be Christians, yet both were straightforward in acknowledging that modern science was born out of the Christian world view."*

and science itself therefore could not exist. Thus science itself was founded on the Christian belief in a knowable and rational God.

Carroll Quigley in *Evolution of Civilizations* saw the progression similarly and recognized the impact of Christianity on Western views of what law and government should be. Going further, he declared that Christianity provided "the basis for science, religion, and social action as the West has known these."

> The democratic and individualistic aspects of the Western outlook were always present, and go back, like other aspects, to the New Testament. They rest on the belief that all men have souls fit for salvation and, in the long run, have equal opportunity to achieve salvation. These ideas also appear in Christ's concern with the downtrodden and oppressed, in the belief that the first and greatest sin was pride (the sin of Lucifer) and that the greatest virtue was humility, in the Beatitudes and in many parables (such as that of the lost sheep). It is worthy of note that all these points are concerned not only with the individual's relationship to himself and to God but also with his relationship to his fellow men. All these, along with the emphasis on good works and the importance of sacraments, show the significance of the social element in Western thought.[79]

This is a stunning declaration of the sweeping influence of Christianity on the building of Western civilization in every aspect. Quigley noted also that this viewpoint assumed that "there is a truth or goal for man's activity," a viewpoint that we demonstrate throughout this work has largely been lost in the frenzy of Western man's other pursuits. But we must remember Quigley pointed out that this view of life "rejects despair, solipsism, skepticism, pessimism, and chaos. It implies hope, order, and the existence of a meaningful objective external reality." The irony in the juxtaposition of these statements with the reality of modern Western man is prodigious. The very thing Quigley is pointing out, that gave Western man a unique hope and great reason for optimism, has progressively been rejected. Western man has largely left behind the one real hope that first built his world and which now could renew and revitalize it. The answer is not only right before him but suffuses every aspect of his culture. Finally, Quigley made the same blanket declaration common to our observers: "[Christianity] provides the basis for science, religion, and social action as the West has known these."[80]

DISMANTLING THE SUPERSTRUCTURE

...as Christianity goes, so goes the West.
Said of Christopher Dawson's viewpoint by John J. Mulloy[81]

In Europe, Western civilization could also be undermined by the weakening of its central component, Christianity.
Samuel Huntington[82]

We now see from myriad perspectives the astonishing role of Christianity as the superstructure of Western civilization. The most ardent secularist, rabid atheist, or skeptical agnostic who is thinking at all must ask the question *What will be the consequences of the dismantling of Christian belief and values for Western civilization?* The answer should be self-evident, but in view of our repeated emphasis on the delusional nature of Western thought and behavior, we will have our observers state it explicitly.

Not incoincidentally, Dawson in *Religion and World History* referred to the Western liberalism growing out of the Enlightenment—and affirming Karl Marx in the process!—as an example of a belief system that would not stand because it was devoid of any internal supports. Founded—like virtually everything else in Western civilization—on some aspects of Christian belief and practice, nineteenth-century liberalism, however, did not rely on Christianity for its *raison d'etre* or its motive force. Dawson acknowledged that Christians might bridle at any form of idealism founded on any basis other than faith.

> We, however, as Christians, may well take a diametrically opposite view of all this development. We may condemn the ruthless subordination of human life to economic ends and the wholesale secularisation of culture as evil; and we may look on the faith of the nineteenth century in liberal ideals, in freedom and justice and humanity and progress as a redeeming trait in the harsh and unlovely features of bourgeois civilisation.... This faith was no sign of conscious hypocrisy—indeed, men like Adam Smith and John Stuart Mill were just as sincere as any idealists who have ever lived.
>
> On the other hand, we may well agree with Marx in his belief that it is the material element in bourgeois culture that is the permanent one and that the idealist liberal element is incapable of maintaining itself by its own inherent resources. For European liberalism is a temporary phenomenon which belongs to the phase of transition between a Christian culture and one that is completely secularised. European culture had already ceased to be Christian in the eighteenth century, but it still retained the inherited moral standards and values of a Christian civilisation. And so it attempted to erect these standards into an independent system by providing a rational philosophical justification for them. This was the Liberal idealism that was the faith of the nineteenth century not a religious faith, but a quasi-religious substitute for one.[83]

Thus this liberalism was not Christian but reflected a mutated compilation of Christian principles that were the legacy of the collapsing Christian culture. But the "quasi-religious" edifice of Liberal idealism created was artificial—without a transcendent religious base it was also quixotic—and, thus, could not last. Liberalism did not create these ideals and could not preserve them. It lives, Dawson observed, "on the spiritual capital that it has inherited from Christian civilisation, and as this is exhausted, something else must come to take its place. Once society is launched on the path of secularisation, it cannot stop in the halfway house of liberalism; it must go on

PD-old

Karl Marx. *John Stuart Mill, like Adam Smith a founder of Western liberalism, was, in Dawson's words, "sincere." Dawson added, "We may well agree with* Marx *in his belief that it is the material element in bourgeois culture that is the permanent one and that the idealist liberal element is incapable of maintaining itself by its own inherent resources. For European liberalism is a temporary phenomenon which belongs to the phase of transition between a Christian culture and one that is completely secularised."*

to the bitter end, whether that end be Communism or some alternative type of 'totalitarian' secularism."[84]

I have noted before that some of our observers could not bring themselves to a fully pessimistic conclusion about the destiny of Western civilization despite the fact that they invariably offer deeply pessimistic analyses. That these are incompatible should be obvious. We see in this final prediction of a bitter end by Dawson a recognition that belies any optimistic or hopeful prognoses.

In like manner, Dawson, in *Christianity and the New Age*, saw secular humanism as ultimately a nonentity. He demonstrated how secular humanism in Western culture was built upon Christian values. Thus, for Dawson, "any attempt to eliminate Christianity or restrict its social influence cuts the roots of humanism's own source of life."[85]

Sorokin expressed this similarly, but more broadly and bluntly, and, in doing so, gave what should be an obvious warning: without Christianity even that which you value most will ultimately be lost: "This paradise sounded quite scientific, plausible and convincing. Being insensible to underground tremors, society was insensible also to the underground forces that were undermining the very well springs of its material prosperity."[86]

In one of Dawson's most compelling passages he described precisely the state of Western civilization today: The Statute of Liberty minus most of its original supporting iron girders.

> In the past, Western Civilisation was based on the assumption that man had an immortal soul, and however much the state demanded, it admitted, at least in theory, that the destiny of every human being reached beyond the extreme limits of political society, so that human conduct was ultimately governed and judged by super-social laws. The secularisation of Western society did not immediately destroy the consequences of this belief. On the contrary, the more men lost their faith in God, the more desperately did they cling to the belief in the *liberty* and value of human personality which was the fruit of a thousand years of Christian culture.[87]

This view is virtually identical to that of Sorokin, who observed that had the vestigial remains of Christianity not been present, the misery factor for the modern West would be much higher.

> More than that, if the ethical system of Christianity had not continued to linger during these sensate centuries, the disastrous results of our sensate ethics would probably have occurred much earlier than they occurred in fact, and their destructive effect would probably have been more terrible than it has been up to the present day. Without the background of an absolute system of ethics, the purely relative ethics of utilitarianism and hedonism go to pieces much more quickly and lead to moral anarchy faster than when they have such a background.[88]

What then has been the long term impact of Western man's continuing rejection of all or part of the Christian faith? Max Weber, in *The Protestant Ethic and the Spirit of Capitalism*, observed how modern Western man is no longer capable of implementing religious teachings for his own benefit. Indeed, he is moving away from them at a faster and faster clip: "The modern man is in general, even with the best will, unable to give religious ideas a significance for culture and national character which they deserve."[89]

But Dawson, in *Christianity and the New Age*, recognized that though Western man may try to obliterate deep religious conviction from his world, if not his life, this will not remove the "permanent human need" that history shows will be forever present.

> It is only by accepting the religious point of view, by regarding religion as an end in itself and not as a means to something else, that we can discuss religious problems profitably. It may be said that this point of view belongs to the past, and that we cannot return to it. But neither can we escape from it. The past is simply the record of the experience of humanity, and if that experience testifies to the existence of a permanent human need, that need must manifest itself in the future no less than in the past.[90]

Dawson declared repeatedly, "The whole spiritual inheritance of European civilization is based upon Christianity, and even today whatever there is of religious life and spiritual aspiration in the West still draws its vitality from Christian sources."[91] Then he asked one of the most critical and momentous questions of our time—one upon which the fate of Western civilization will in large measure hang:

> But is there no alternative between Americanism and Orientalism, between a spiritual order that takes no account of human needs and a material order that has no regard for spiritual values? There still remains the traditional religion of our own civilization: Christianity, a religion that is neither wholly metaphysical nor merely ethical, but one that brings the spiritual world into vital and fruitful communion with the life of man.[92]

We saw in "The Path to a New Dark Age" how Christianity was "progressively losing its hold on Western culture, and both its doctrines and its moral ideals have fallen into discredit."[93] This, Dawson observed, had causes that

> lie deep in that process of the humanization and rationalizing of Western culture....Ever since the Renaissance the centrifugal tendencies in our civilization have destroyed its spiritual unity and divided its spiritual forces. The Western mind has turned away from the contemplation of the absolute and the eternal to the knowledge of the particular and the contingent. It has made man the measure of all things and has sought to emancipate human life from its dependence on the supernatural. Instead of the whole intellectual and social order being subordinated to spiritual principles, every activity has declared its independence, and we see politics, economics, science and art organizing themselves as autonomous kingdoms which owe no allegiance to any higher power.[94]

Dawson's words may in time prove to be an obituary for Western civilization. In *Historic Reality of Christian Culture*, Dawson described the deterioration. Our modern Western civilization is "the direct successor and heir of this Christian civilization" without which Western civilization "would never have existed." Writing in the mid-twentieth century Dawson declared, "...our modern civilization is not a Christian one." What, we may speculate, would he say were he alive today? Here again we see evidence that any tentatively hopeful projections of our observers have lost—certainly not gained —any objective basis with the passage of time. Western man has proven himself inclined to act consistently with our observers' pessimistic analyses rather than any hopeful or optimistic prognosis.

Observing the church in America, Dawson wrote, "It was the first country in the Christian world to inaugurate the complete separation of the State from the Church. But this did not at first involve the secularization of culture. Throughout the greater part of the nineteenth century it was the churches rather than the State that were responsible for education and culture...."[95]

In what for many, including many professing Christians, was a shocking declaration—which, we must remember, was made in the mid-twentieth century, not recently!—Dawson told us the state of the civilization: "The traditional Christian civilization has now become a part of history and can only be understood by a considerable effort of study and imagination, while the whole Western world is coming to share a common secular technological civilization which it has transmitted and is in the course of transmitting to the rest of the world—to the old civilizations of Asia and to the new peoples of Africa and Oceania."[96] However, even as the civilization has increasingly denied its origins, it "still bears marks of its Christian origins and contains living Christian traditions and institutions, though these are, so to speak, scattered and no longer integrated into the organic structure of the civilization."[97]

As might be expected, no one spoke to the consequences of the rejection of Western civilization's superstructure like Christopher Dawson in *Christianity and the New Age*, yet he often expressed this in a weighing or comparison: on the one hand, what Western man can expect if he continued on his course; on the other, what he could gain if he turned to faith. Wisely and insightfully, Dawson did not express these results purely in spiritual or moral terms but in practical effects.

> ...[I]f our own civilization is to recover a spiritual principle, it is here that we must seek it. The essential achievement of our culture—the conquest of material order—is not, as we have seen, inconsistent with this ideal. In fact it may be regarded as its natural complement, for the restoration of man to his true position as the master of nature and the organizer of the material world, which is the function of science, corresponds in the natural order to the spiritual restoration of human nature in itself, which is the work of Christianity in the supernatural order.
>
> In a Christian civilization the scientific order would no longer offer, as it does at present, the tragic spectacle of vast resources of power and intelligence devoted to producing unsightly and unnecessary objects, and to endowing mankind with new means of self-destruction; it would become an instrument for the realization of man's true destiny as the orderer of material things to spiritual ends.[98]

Dawson asserted that it is "the function of the Church to sow this divine seed, to produce not merely good men, but spiritual men—that is to say, supermen."[99] But as the Apostle Paul observed, the "natural man" rejects "the things of the Spirit of God"; they are "foolishness to him, and he cannot understand them, because they are spiritually appraised" (1 Corinthians 2:14). What then of the "natural" men of the West? Put succinctly by John J. Mulloy, Dawson's answer was simply, *"as Christianity goes, so goes the West."*

With that in mind, we close with Toynbee, first from *A Study of History*, where he spoke of the "erosion of the corner-stones of personal discipline" that was the direct result of the growing rejection of the Christian faith.

> Can we see any signs of these conflicting ways of behaviour in the Western Society of our own day? Certainly, the invitation to "return to Nature" has been clearly audible since it was first uttered by Jean-Jacques Rousseau two centuries ago; and the clamour has reached an unprecedented volume in the claims by initiates of a contemporary "drug culture" that they have recovered the lost faculty of spontaneous and uninhibited creativity and have found the true model for a society of human perfection. To some extent the progress of the recent science of psychology has also reinforced this modern tendency towards abandon, in consequence of its attempt to probe through the layers of acquired social and personal experience which are alleged to mask an inner core of true selfhood and to inhibit its expression. This erosion of the cornerstones of personal discipline may manifest itself in the relatively innocuous form of an individual rejection of the traditional Judaeo-Christian code of sexual morality which, in one shape or another, has been embedded in the Western Society throughout the course of its history. More seriously, it may compose itself into a dangerous reduction *ad absurdum* of the principle of relativity on the social and political plane, undermining the apparently valid concept that an irreducible minimum of fixed poles of orientation is a necessary element in the psychological

> health of both individuals and societies. On the other hand, the counter-movement of asceticism does not seem to have made much headway in the present-day Western World, though perhaps the first faint stirrings of self-denial, albeit in a somewhat shallow and debased form, can be detected in what is fashionably described as the "backlash" against "moral pollution."[100]

Once again we recall that Toynbee, like Dawson and Sorokin, was writing in the mid-twentieth century. It is highly dubious that were he writing today he would view "an individual rejection of the traditional Judaeo-Christian code of sexual morality" as "relatively innocuous." In the era of AIDS, STDs, the massive fragmentation of the family unit in the West, and the proliferation of births to the unwed, he would recognize these trends for what they are: further confirmation of the decay and decline he had already documented in the mid-twentieth century. He correctly identified the "dangerous reduction *ad absurdum*" of relativism, which in our time has produced psycho-social pathologies of the worst sort. Furthermore, any "counter-movement of asceticism"—if such exists in the West—is so weak, so minimalist, so obscure, as to be irrelevant. And what can we say about Toynbee's mid-twentieth century "backlash" against "moral pollution"? It was not much of a backlash; supremely ineffective—as evidenced by the condition of the twenty-first-century West—this too was a reflection of the hard reality not simply that the culture was going down but that the church in the West had no real power to stop it, perhaps in part because it had no great desire to stop it.

Yet Toynbee, for all his dismay about the course of Western civilization, recognized that which had proven to be

Pompeius Magnus in the Temple of Jerusalem, by Jean Fouquet, 1470. *The desecration of the temple by the military might of Rome was not—as history so often suggests—the end of the story. Ultimately, faith was to prevail. In one sense, Gibbon was correct in his view that Christianity brought down the Roman Empire—not through military, political, or economic power, but through "the transmutation of values" and the proffering of a higher, nobler, and eternal reality. The sensate values of Rome were wholly incompatible with the beliefs of Christianity; one had to displace the other.*

PD-art

PD-gov

The Statue of Liberty on the morning of 9-11. *We began this chapter with the metaphor of the Statue as symbolic of the Christian superstructure of Western civilization; a superstructure that the West's own members are rapidly disassembling. Ironically, those who would destroy the West through violent means find their greatest allies in the secularists of Western culture. Their internal attacks will do more to bring the West to its knees than all the West's external enemies combined.*

the most durable and lasting of all: "If we survey all the institutions of which we have knowledge in the present and in the past, I think that the institutions created, or adopted and adapted, by Christianity are the toughest and the most enduring of any that we know and are therefore the most likely to last—and outlast all the rest."[101]

The benefits of those institutions will be enjoyed only to the extent Western man chooses to embrace them. As the superstructure—constructed from the principles of trust and morality of the Christian faith—which supports the edifice of our civilization is dismantled, the edifice itself will sag and eventually collapse. Not just morality and spirituality will suffer. Ultimately, achievement in war, law and government, economics, arts and literature, science, technology and learning will be recognized by more perceptive observers to be in decline as well. The process is not always subtle, but it will occur in such a way, over an attenuated period of time, that few will notice until it is too late. That process is well advanced.

END NOTES
CHAPTER 19

1 Christopher Dawson, *The Historic Reality of Christian Culture* (New York: Harper and Brothers, 1960), 35–36.
2 Fernand Braudel, *A History of Civilizations* (New York: Penguin Group, 1995), 333.
3 Carroll Quigley, *The Evolution of Civilizations: An Introduction to Historical Analysis* (New York: Liberty Press, 1961), 338.
4 Samuel P. Huntington, *The Clash of Civilizations and the Remaking of World Order* (New York: Simon & Schuster, 1996), 311.
5 Huntington, *Clash of Civilizations,* 70.
6 Adda Bruemmer Bozeman, *Strategic Intelligence and Statecraft* (Washington, D.C.: Brassey's Press, 1992), 26.
7 Huntington, *Clash of Civilizations,* 47.
8 Christopher Dawson, *Christianity and the New Age* (New York: Sophia Institute Press, 1985), 22.
9 Dawson, *Christianity and the New Age,* 22.
10 Dawson, *Christianity and the New Age,* 38.
11 Dawson, *Christianity and the New Age,* 38.
12 Dawson, *Christianity and the New Age,* 82–83.
13 Braudel, *History of Civilizations,* 5.
14 Braudel, *History of Civilizations,* 22.
15 Pitirim A. Sorokin, *The Crisis of Our Age* (Oneworld Publications Ltd., 1941; this edition Sergei P. Sorokin and Peter P. Sorokin, 1992), 261.
16 Christopher Dawson, *Religion and World History: A Selection from the Works of Christopher Dawson* (Garden City, NY: Image Books, 1975), 303–304.
17 Dawson, *Religion and World History,* 304.
18 Dawson, *Religion and World History,* 305.
19 Francis A. Schaeffer, *How Should We Then Live? The Rise and Decline of Western Thought and Culture* (Wheaton, IL: Crossway Books, 1976), 21.
20 Schaeffer, *How Should We Then Live?,* 22.
21 Christopher Dawson, *Religion and the Rise of Western Culture* (Garden City, NY: Image Books, 1948–1949), 12.
22 Oswald Spengler, *The Decline of the West* (New York: Alfred A. Knopf, 1926), 285.
23 Huntington, *Clash of Civilizations,* 70.
24 A. L. Kroeber, *Configurations of Culture Growth* (Berkeley: University of California Press, 1944), 92.
25 Dawson, *Religion and the Rise of Western Culture,* 14–15.
26 Dawson, *Religion and the Rise of Western Culture,* 15.
27 Dawson, *Religion and the Rise of Western Culture,* 16–17.
28 Dawson, *Religion and the Rise of Western Culture,* 17.
29 Dawson, *Religion and the Rise of Western Culture,* 18.
30 Dawson, *Religion and the Rise of Western Culture,* 18.
31 Dawson, *Religion and the Rise of Western Culture,* 18–19.
32 Dawson, *Religion and the Rise of Western Culture,* 22.
33 Dawson, *Religion and the Rise of Western Culture,* 26.
34 Dawson, *Religion and the Rise of Western Culture,* 27–28.
35 Dawson, *Religion and the Rise of Western Culture,* 31–32.

36 Adam of Bremen [*Descriptio Insularum Aquilonis*, 30–31], cited in Dawson, *Religion and the Rise of Western Culture*, 98–99.
37 Dawson, *Historic Reality*, 68.
38 Braudel, *History of Civilizations,* 23.
39 Braudel, *History of Civilizations*, 333–334.
40 Braudel, *History of Civilizations*, 339.
41 Braudel, *History of Civilizations*, 342.
42 Spengler, *Decline of the West*, 290.
43 Immanuel Wallerstein, *The End of the World As We Know It: Social Science for the Twenty-First Century* (Minneapolis: University of Minnesota Press, 1999), 174.
44 Dawson, *Religion and World History*, 276–277.
45 Dawson, *Historic Reality*, 35.
46 Dawson, *Historic Reality*, 76.
47 Dawson, *Historic Reality*, 77.
48 Dawson, *Historic Reality*, 78.
49 Braudel, *History of Civilizations*, 23.
50 A. L. Kroeber, *A Roster of Civilizations and Culture* (Chicago: Aldine Publishing Company, 1962), 90.
51 Braudel, *History of Civilizations*, 472.
52 Braudel, *History of Civilizations*, 473.
53 Huntington, *Clash of Civilizations*, 70.
54 Huntington, *Clash of Civilizations*, 71.
55 Huntington, *Clash of Civilizations*, 311.
56 Huntington, *Clash of Civilizations*, 305.
57 Dawson, *Christianity and the New Age*, 94–95.
58 Dawson, *Christianity and the New Age*, 86–87.
59 Dawson, *Christianity and the New Age*, 86–87.
60 Dawson, *Christianity and the New Age*, 87.
61 Max Weber, *The Protestant Ethic and the Spirit of Capitalism* (New York: Scribner and Sons, 1958), 45.
62 Weber, *Protestant Ethic*, 56.
63 Weber, *Protestant Ethic*, 174.
64 Weber, *Protestant Ethic*, 175.
65 Weber, *Protestant Ethic*, 176.
66 Weber, *Protestant Ethic*, 176–177.
67 Weber, *Protestant Ethic*, 177.
68 Weber, *Protestant Ethic*, 180.
69 Weber, *Protestant Ethic*, 181–182.
70 Schaeffer, *How Should We Then Live?,* 87.
71 Schaeffer, *How Should We Then Live?,* 108.
72 Schaeffer, *How Should We Then Live?,* 109–110.
73 Schaeffer, *How Should We Then Live?,* 110.
74 Schaeffer, *How Should We Then Live?,* 112.
75 J. H. Plumb, cited in Schaeffer, *How Should We Then Live?,* 119.
76 Schaeffer, *How Should We Then Live?,* 132.
77 Albert North Whitehead, cited in Schaeffer, *How Should We Then Live?,* 132.
78 Albert North Whitehead, cited in Schaeffer, *How Should We Then Live?,* 133.
79 Quigley, *Evolution of Civilizations,* 338–339.
80 Quigley, *Evolution of Civilizations,* 338–339.
81 John J. Mulloy, "Introduction" in Dawson, *Christianity and the New Age*, 103.

82 Huntington, *Clash of Civilizations*, 305.
83 Dawson, *Religion and World History*, 243–244.
84 Dawson, *Religion and World History*, 244.
85 Dawson, *Christianity and the New Age*, ix.
86 Sorokin, *Crisis of Our Age*, 190–191.
87 Dawson, *Religion and World History*, 295.
88 Sorokin, *Crisis of Our Age*, 212.
89 Weber, *Protestant Ethic*, 183.
90 Dawson, *Christianity and the New Age*, 22.
91 Dawson, *Christianity and the New Age*, 59.
92 Dawson, *Christianity and the New Age*, 58–59.
93 Dawson, *Christianity and the New Age*, 59.
94 Dawson, *Christianity and the New Age*, 59–60.
95 Dawson, *Historic Reality*, 36–37.
96 Dawson, *Historic Reality*, 38.
97 Dawson, *Historic Reality*, 37–38.
98 Dawson, *Christianity and the New Age*, 101.
99 Dawson, *Christianity and the New Age*, 103.
100 Arnold Toynbee, *A Study of History* (New York: Weathervane Books, 1972), 242–243.
101 Arnold Toynbee, *Civilization on Trial* (New York: Oxford University Press, 1948), 242–243.

CHAPTER

20

THE DECLINE OF THE CHURCH IN THE WEST

If the salt itself loses its savor, then indeed the world sinks back into disorder and death, for a despiritualized Christianity is powerless to change anything; it is the most abject of failures, since it serves neither the natural nor the spiritual order.
Dawson[1]

But in the United States culture has transformed Christ.... In every aspect of the religious life, American faith has met American culture—and American culture has triumphed.
Alan Wolfe[2]

Most people did not give up being committed Christians because they became convinced that religion was false. It simply ceased to be of any great importance to them; they became indifferent.
Steve Bruce[3]

In tragic life, God wot,
No villain need be! Passions spin the plot:
We are betray'd by what is false within.
George Meredith, *Modern Love*[4]

The wheel of history has made another near-complete revolution. The fervency, nonconformity, and self-sacrifice of the Christian church of the first century—which eventually made it the superstructure of the new and most powerful of all civilizations—have been dramatically dissipated in the geographic area of the West. With great—but perhaps appropriately just—irony, the Western church has courted the culture and now faces rejection—nearly completely so in Europe and decidedly so in terms of influence in America. The church's assignation with the Western world's power and wealth has brought it in a great circle—now closer to the catacombs than to the cathedral.

Philip Bagby observed, "Western-European Christianity has...now taken on a secular and rationalist cast in accordance with the character of the present age."[5] Christopher Dawson made much the same observation: "Christianity seems to many a thing of the past, part of the vanishing order of the old Europe, and the new powers that are shaping the world are non-Christian or even anti-Christian."[6] How much more true this is half a century later!

How did the church in Europe arrive here? Christopher Dawson provided part of the answer.

> It is the result of two hundred years of progressive secularization during which the distinctively Christian institutions and social standards have been gradually eliminated. This process was a complex one. On the continent of Europe, especially in France, it was a violent and catastrophic change, which involved political revolutions and religious persecutions. In England on the other hand it was extremely gradual and piecemeal and even today some of the typical institutions of the old Christian order, like the State establishment of the national Church and the solemn religious consecration of the monarch, still survive.[7]

PD-art

William Blake *expressed faith through the mystery of nature.*

Tyger! Tyger! burning bright
In the forest of the night,
What immortal hand or eye
Could frame thy fearful symmetry?

We do not wish to sound dismissive of it for, to be sure, the European church, Catholic and Protestant, is alive, though no longer dominant in European culture. Indeed, the church in Europe has so atrophied as a force to be reckoned with by the culture at large that its practitioners have little to gain socially, politically, or financially by affiliation. This contrasts with the American church, portions of which still operate in a milieu that is more "religious" if not "devout." For an American—especially in the environs of the Bible Belt—church affiliation can have some secular (e.g., financial, social, political, etc.) benefit. And for an American politician, churches are a prime hunting ground for votes: liberal mainline denominations and black churches if a liberal Democrat; conservative and evangelical churches if a conservative Republican.

The church has failed its progeny and ward, Western civilization. For generations it has been losing the battle—to the extent it has even mustered for the fight—to influence Western society. Aborticide, homosexuality, sexual immorality, pornography, pedophilia, children born out of wedlock, divorce, materialism, drug and alcohol abuse, debased entertainment, and rejection of the very notion of a just God and an immutable higher moral law to which all men will be accountable—these have suffused Western civilization, making it a hotbed of cultural and social pathologies and stripping it of the dignity and moral authority with which to earn the respect—a genuine respect, not one born of power and fear—of the other civilizations of the world. Here is where the focus must be and where it will be in our efforts: *We must measure the vitality and spiritual depth of the church not in statistics reflecting membership, money contributed, buildings constructed, or social or media attention, but in the impact of the church on individual lives and the culture. All other measures are at best misleading, if not outright fallacious.*

As we will see, the church itself is split into a multiplicity of camps often disputing and competing with one another. One of the most distinct schisms separates those with a leftist ideological slant from those with a rightist viewpoint. The left seeks accommodation with the culture—and with it to gain spiritual "credentials" through social action. The right also seeks accommodation with the culture, albeit of a different sort, and with it to regain influence on the course of the culture by raising moral issues politically and through the courts. The latter is compelling evidence—though it is not recognized as such—of a rear-guard, defensive action. This segment of the church is struggling through primarily political and legal means to salvage the church's waning position of influence in the culture. But wars cannot be won on the defensive—and spiritual warfare will never be won through temporal strategies.

HOW COULD—HOW DID—THIS HAPPEN?

Religion became a specialized activity which was confined to church and chapel and limited to one day in the week. Thus the destruction of Christian culture was the work of the Christians themselves who allowed the new Babylon of modern materialist civilization to be built on the soil of Christendom.

Dawson[8]

The great overarching *Question* is rarely asked and is certainly never fully and deeply answered: Why, with all the advantages the Christian church enjoyed in nineteenth- and twentieth-century Western civilization, is it now in this position? Was this inevitable? Was this decline beyond the church's control?

I believe, and will strive to demonstrate, that the honest answer is no. The failure is the result of a decline and decay within the church itself that not only paralleled but nurtured the decline and decay of Western civilization as described earlier. This decline and decay within the church is now so pervasive and insidious that most Western Christians—even the most sincere among them—don't recognize many of its manifestations. Indeed, the polarities have in many ways been reversed: that which would have once been rightly perceived as secular and worldly has now been baptized as examples of spiritual success.

We can understand the historical course of events better if we go back in time. By doing so, we can also see glaring earlier examples of the culture's dominance in the church—rather than the other way round, the way it should be—and the resultant apostasies and often horrendously evil behavior of professing Christians. All of this is but a history lesson and an object lesson to illustrate how the modern Western church has come to its own apostasies and often egregious behavior before the culture.

The secularization of the church in the West and its corollary compromises with the culture, its moral lapses, and its indifference to human suffering, were all apparent two centuries ago in Britain. Then, as now, the church was largely and callously oblivious to its shortcomings—and the extraordinary gulf between the life and teachings of its reputed leader and its own conduct. William Wilberforce understood well that only on a Christian base could opposition to slavery be built. He equally understood that the Christian base had been eroding for generations and increasingly was supplanted by a highly secularized mutation of Christianity. This prompted him to write in 1797 one of the only two books he authored: *A Practical View of the Prevailing Religious System of Professed Christians in the Higher and Middle Classes of This Country Contrasted with Real Christianity*. Though the ponderous title might suggest something daunting, the book is in fact an analysis of—and an appeal to—the Christian church of that time as contrasted with the example and teachings of Christ.

Abraham Lincoln's and the abolitionists' efforts to destroy slavery in America while preserving the Union were likewise founded on a Christian base. The words of his most eloquent references to either have a distinctly biblical authority and high moral tone. Lincoln also understood, as Wilberforce before him, that all moral laws must be founded on the transcendent and the eternal, otherwise they are specious, without lasting authority. In continuing parallel, Lincoln lived in a time in which large segments of the Christian church were bastions of support for the very thing that Lincoln resorted to the Bible's authority to destroy. Lines from Yeats would just as readily apply to thousands of churches, plantation homes, and businesses constructed with the sweat and blood of slaves owned by men claiming allegiance to Almighty God:

> Some violent bitter man, some powerful man
> Called architect and artist in, that they,
> Bitter and violent men, might rear in stone
> The sweetness that all longed for night and day,
> The gentleness none there had ever known…
> —*Meditations in Time of Civil War*

These violent, bitter, powerful men (and women) are a species alive and thriving in our time. Though their depredations more often manifest themselves in greed, materialism, self-seeking, the pursuit of power and pleasure, and the ruthlessness of competition, there are victims individually and in the form of a culture that all too often looks upon them as models of "success" to be emulated rather than the destroyers of the "sweetness" and "gentleness" that many human beings around the world will never know.

These paradoxes are only explained by the honest recognition that there is Christianity in name only and Christianity in fact. That these same conditions exist in the church in the West today therefore should not come as a surprise. The blindness and hypocrisy that allowed sin—even horrendous evil—to flourish unchallenged in the churches of Wilberforce's and Lincoln's time exist today; they simply come in other guises, typically appealing and beguiling.

Comporting fully with the study of human behavior as well as the teachings of Scripture, we recognize that everything begins in the heart and mind of individual man. Through the realm of ideas came the seeds of secularization. They in turn were fertilized by man's own selfishness and tendencies to depravity so that which is first presented as "a good idea," no matter how scripturally ill-conceived, gains a ready foothold when the "good idea" lands in the midst of the manure pile of human pride, self-centeredness, and cowardice. Everything henceforward in this book is an exposure of—and an attack upon—ideas and behaviors that have become broadly accepted in the modern Western church, Catholic, Orthodox, and Protestant, for just these reasons.

European and American Christians have displayed a marked obtuseness as to where and how these ideas originate in the culture and find their way into the church. Only perhaps in the last generation or so have some American Christians—and they remain limited quantitatively and as to breadth of comprehension—awakened to the realization that the culture is saturated with many poisons, not just to faith and morality but to a sense of reality and the fundamental soundness of reasoning and observation that prevent a culture from sliding into an abyss. Dawson described "complacent and uncritical" attitudes in the nineteenth century British church to the culture that surrounded them, "…so long as men went to church and read the Bible and abstained from gambling and drunkenness and open immorality, it did not matter that they were at the same time helping to turn England into a hideous and disorderly conglomeration of factories and slums in which the chapel and the gin palace provided the only satisfaction for man's spiritual and emotional needs."[9]

This is descriptive of the Christian church in our own time: fastidious in speaking out about the sins it chooses to condemn, yet derelict in the extreme about even acknowledging, must less opposing, sins that it chooses to see through its own version of rose-colored moral glasses—or not see at all.

Dawson's indictment of the church in the West resounds with the authority of the evidence of history. *The church has lost credibility because it has abdicated the moral and spiritual responsibility placed upon it by Christ.* Unwittingly (recall Dawson's observation: "[I]t is very seldom that a society is clearly conscious of what is at stake."), the European church gave way to values and views that were the legacy of the Renaissance and Enlightenment. No longer did it distinguish itself as "the light of the world" or a "city on a hill" that "cannot be hidden." (Matthew 5:14) *That compromise—the bridge the church itself built between the corrupt culture and its own ministry—allowed the barbarians to enter the holy gates.*

> This secularisation has been the great scandal of modern Christendom. For the Christian cannot deny the crying evils of that nineteenth-century industrial society from which the ordinary man has been delivered by the social reforms of the last fifty or one hundred years, while at the same time he is forced to reject the purely secular idealism which has inspired the new culture. Nevertheless, this has been a salutary experience for Christians. It has made us examine our conscience to see how great has been our responsibility for this decline of Christian culture and for the conversion of our society to a new kind of paganism.[10]

Here Dawson was unduly optimistic. In the interval between Dawson's writing of these words in the mid-twentieth century and the twenty-first century, no such self-examination has swept the church. Indeed, the church's compromise is bearing more and more of the poisonous fruit of syncretism, moral decline, complacency, and a propensity for believing that the course of the culture can be changed through political, judicial, and social action.

PD-old

Charles Haddon Spurgeon by Alexander Melville. *Ironically juxtaposed in time and space with the fervency of the great Victorian preacher Charles Haddon Spurgeon, the English experience is of precisely the kind of spiritual and moral complacency and compromise that has helped to decimate Christian values in American culture.*

This corrosive process was set in dynamic motion by the Enlightenment. But it was the time-servers, cowards, and security seekers of the church's leadership that made—and make—it possible.

> The goal of the Liberal Enlightenment and Revolution had been reached, and Europe at last possessed a completely secularized culture. The old religion had not been destroyed; in fact throughout Protestant Europe the churches still possessed a position of established privilege. But they held this position only on the condition that they did not interfere with the reign of Mammon. In reality they had been pushed aside into a backwater where they were free to stagnate in peace and to brood over the memory of dead controversies which had moved the mind of Europe three centuries before.[11]

This state of affairs would describe the church throughout the West today, not just the nineteenth-century European church. Charles Dickens's novels can, in many respects, be read as an indictment of the church of Victorian England, just as Mark Twain's *War Prayer* can be read similarly—though with a different theme—in the America of the same age. Ironically juxtaposed in time and space with the fervency of the great Victorian preacher Charles Haddon Spurgeon—just as similar complaints about the church in America have been juxtaposed with the comparable fervency of evangelist Billy Graham—the English experience is of precisely the kind of spiritual and moral complacency and compromise that has helped to decimate Christian values in American culture.

Surrounding for miles, if not yards, every church and cathedral in every European and American city are individuals who, in one way or another, reflect a reaction to these abysmal failures of the church. It is not so much the appeal of secularism, or atheism, or agnosticism that draws them away—for in most respects these belief systems are more desolate and unrewarding than other ideologies of our age—but rather the abject failure of the church to live up to what it has professed. The church has lost credibility and influence because it has abdicated the moral, spiritual, and social responsibility placed upon it by Christ. Professing Christians have yet to be fully awakened to the magnitude of this loss and the concomitant shift of the culture.

Tragically, shamefully, the defeat of some of Western civilization's worst social ills—though profoundly influenced by Christian thought and values—was wrought not through the leadership of the church but through secular forces with largely secular outlooks on how to reform society. Dawson referred to this as "...the great scandal of modern Christendom."[12] These afflictions of society were obvious to all but the most callous, and we must reluctantly acknowledge that it was often "secular idealism" that led the way in their reform.

But callous, hard-hearted attitudes—how striking the words when used to describe Christians!—were reinforced by a deliberate unwillingness to see, to admit, to confess. At the end of Mark Twain's *War Prayer*, after the church has just been visited by an emissary of the Almighty to point out the significance, the real import, of their patriotic prayer, Twain ended with "It was believed afterward that the man was a lunatic, because there was no sense in what he said." *Christians throughout the West are in effect declaring "there is no sense" in what Christ actually said and lived.*

Professor Dawson was unduly sanguine in his mid-twentieth-century view that Christians were examining their conscience "to see how great has been our responsibility for this decline."[13] The church has not, in the meantime, examined its conscience. Along with the culture, it has more often accelerated its pace away from that which could be its redemption. Since Dawson wrote those words, we might inquire, Can evidence be gleaned in contemporary Britain of the kind of soul-searching they imply? We would be hard-pressed to find it. Can we expect much the same apathy from the

PD-LOC

Child laborers. *Hughestown Breaker Boys,* by Lewis Wickes Hine. *"Christian" Victorian England permitted squalor and human suffering to subsist throughout the nation.*

church in America into the twenty-first century? If British history—and obvious trends—are any guide, we cannot be optimistic about the American church.

Dawson outlined the progression of ideas and movements that effectively eviscerated Christianity as the social and moral force that once forged, guided, led, indeed dominated, British culture. For Dawson, only one individual in that age, Cardinal Newman, recognized the threat from what Newman called "Liberalism," his term for a form of "progressive secularism," which became "the dominant force in nineteenth-century civilisation and shaped the world in which we live today." Neither "revolutionary" nor "anti-religious" initially, it "advocated religious toleration, the diffusion of useful knowledge, social reform, and economic progress. Nevertheless, behind the innocuous platitudes...Newman felt the...rising tide that was to submerge 'that goodly framework of society which is the creation of Christianity.'"[14]

The effect was a seismic shift of a thousand years of British history from one continent—the continent of faith in the Christian god—to another continent, the continent of faith in man and his "good works." This rebellion—for indeed that is what it was, a quiet, subtle rebellion—carried over into the twentieth century with many striking examples of its more extreme manifestations, such as the secret defection of four young Cambridge students, Donald McLean, Guy Burgess, Anthony Blunt, and Kim Philby, to communism and a lifetime of spying. Disillusioned with the Britain of their time—and certainly not

Charles Dickens's novels can, in many respects, be read as an indictment of the church of Victorian England that callously neglected the great social problems of its time. Similarly, the modern Western church in Europe and America has lost credibility and influence because it has abdicated the moral, spiritual, and social responsibility placed upon it by Christ. Professing Christians have yet to be fully awakened to the magnitude of this loss and the concomitant shift of the culture.

PD

disposed to see the church as a prospective outlet for their idealism—the notion that man through his ideologies could achieve a utopia appealed to them so much that they would betray their country.

Thus the individualistic English liberalism, a product of the Enlightenment, became the dominant belief system in the European world —and fostered the heady man-as-heroic-figure atmosphere in which Marx then reflected, contrived, and composed. It then manifested itself in the collective slant of essentially the same basic ideas in French and German Socialism. The latter claimed as one of its 46-million-plus victims a 39-year-old German minister, Dietrich Bonhoeffer, who was executed in Buchenwald days before the collapse of the Third Reich. I declare with supreme confidence: Had the Western and German church of the preceding generations adhered to the precepts of scripture as later expressed eloquently by Bonhoeffer in his classic, *The Cost of Discipleship*, none of this evil would have occurred.

Making this obvious and inescapable is imperative: All of these shifts in thought and belief were the direct consequence of the failure of the church. Having failed to meet the most fundamental needs of their fellowman, professing Christians themselves, through their own self-centeredness, callousness, and cowardice, made not only possible, but probable, a chain of choices that would lead Western man away from the love of the Cross and toward the gas chambers of Auschwitz, the torture cells of the Lubyanka, and, in our time, the many and extravagant dissipations of a decaying civilization. None of this was foreordained.

In words that almost sound sarcastic in view of what we know now—or should know—Dawson observed that nineteenth-century British "Christian opinion was slow to realise the implications...."[15] British Protestants "evolved that concordat" with capitalism, which exists today and has been replicated many times over in America, the DNA for its ever-increasing vigor having been refined through generations of rabbit-like breeding. In Catholic Europe, Dawson stated, the trends were more obvious as to their character and intent but the consequences much the same.

The religious among the British "put their faith in the restoration of the Christian state and the defeat of the revolution by an alliance with political conservatism"—a choice that should sound very familiar to American ears and to which we will return. Newman was "almost the only Christian thinker who realised the anti-Christian character of the trend to secularism without indulging in wishful thinking or identifying the Church with that of the political reactionaries." Because he would not choose sides in this fashion, Newman "...was rejected by both sides and was condemned by the leaders of the Catholic revival as a Liberal and compromiser and by the Victorian Liberals as an arch-reactionary...."[16]

Lest there be rigid skeptics about the foolhardiness of blind optimism—or the notion that history does not predict—this brief history sheds a scintillating ray of light. Change the names of the political figures and social movements and the passage could apply just as readily to the last 100 years in America. The "concordat" of the church with materialism and capitalism in America has made most American manifestations of Christianity subscribers to its terms in one fashion or another. Furthermore, the church in America, especially its conservative branches, has, to a considerable degree, "put their faith in the restoration of the Christian state and the defeat of the revolution by an alliance with political conservatism"—a theme addressed in the later chapter "Fighting Pyrrhic Battles at Points of Little Strategic Consequence."

Unlike Britain of a few generations ago, modern America has no Cardinal Newman to see through the propaganda and raise the alarm. If there were a Newman, he would likely not only suffer Newman's fate and be "rejected by both sides" but also the proverbial fate of prophets: stoning—though of the uniquely American sort, through shallow, glib statements made by even more shallow cultural arbiters, with the eager complicity of the mass media.

Insightfully, Dawson was writing over half a century ago of the loss of true faith in the church in the West, in part because it was seen—and is by many today—as "a servant of the established order" (i.e., hypocritical and self-serving) with "no real power" or "will to change the world." I believe that the first component of that skepticism was, and is, at least partially well founded; the second was never true; and the third is the crux of the matter.

The diagnosis of serious illness for our world is broadly agreed upon; but the prognosis and the treatments to be applied remain very much at issue. The highly secularized cultural leaders of the West perceive true Christianity more often as part of the problem, never the solution. That this is their view is neither purely the consequence of spiritual benightedness or

PD-art

Cardinal Newman, by Sir John Everett Millais. *Newman was one of the very few Christian thinkers in Britain who recognized the "anti-Christian character of the trend to secularism without indulging in wishful thinking or identifying the Church with that of the political reactionaries." Unlike Britain of a few generations ago, modern America has no Cardinal Newman to see through the propaganda and raise the alarm.*

unreasoning prejudice; though it is both primarily. Any objective individual can look about the West of today and have some reason to react with dismay at the church's apathy and/or incompetence in the face of society's and the world's woes. The church very often truly has been "the servant of the established order" and displays little "will to change the world."[17]

There would be no stretch of the truth or straining of logic to suggest that many in the West in the last century who became communists would have become Christians had the church been as Christ intended. The wounds of sin and evil afflict every human being on the planet—some egregiously; they search for ways to escape and to fight the perpetrators of the worst of it. The church was to be the beacon of hope—the refuge for all who would change the world for the better. Illustratively, I believe it a certainty that the trend of recent generations among some African-Americans to embrace Islam rather than their parents' and grandparents' Christian heritage is a consequence of some branches of the church's indifference to—if not complicity in—racism.

A PERSONAL ILLUSTRATION OF THIS DRAMATIC CHOICE

The best lack all conviction, while the worst
Are full of passionate intensity.
"The Second Coming" by William Butler Yeats

I could have become a victim of this same defiant impulse. Born and raised in the American South, I experienced a variation on racism unusual for a white Anglo-Saxon Protestant. My father, a minister, had taken a staunch and uncompromising stand—founded exclusively on his Christian faith—against racism in America of the 1950s–60s. Assuming the role of an administrator who would begin some of the first integrated Head Start Centers in the Deep South, my father became the target—and, by extension, his family with him—of the vituperation and malice of racism. In that era, in that place, when it seemed the favored pastimes were burning crosses and destroying African-American churches, this force brooked no opposition; it voraciously sought to devour anyone who dared oppose it. Its agents and functionaries were everywhere, not just hidden beneath bed sheets in darkened fields lit by burning crosses.

Against my family, the weaponry deployed ranged from social ostracism, to threats, to bullying at school (I was 14 to 16 during this time; my only sibling, a sister, was one year younger), to violent attacks on my father's co-workers, to the arson of my father's Centers. The stress of living in such a hostile environment can only be understood by someone who has experienced it—a revelation for us of what many American blacks have faced—and is redoubled if its victims are naïve innocents unprepared by prior experience or training for the duress. We were, in the sordid vernacular of the times, "nigger-lovers," an epithet we never rejected and that, with passing years, became a badge of honor in our memories. For the uninitiated, it must be explained that though a black was hated with an unreasoning malice, the "nigger-lovers" were hated even more and with a perverse form of "reasoning": You have betrayed your race and allied with those "niggers"; hence you are even more to be despised.

All of this might have posed little threat to our sense of identity and belief had it not been for the appalling realization that many of the wielders of these weapons, and/or their supporters, were

PD-LOC

William Butler Yeats *wrote, "The best lack all conviction, while the worst are full of passionate intensity." Having failed to meet the most fundamental needs of their fellowman, professing Christians, through their self-centeredness, callousness, and cowardice, made probable a chain of choices that led man away from the love of the Cross and to the gas chambers of Auschwitz, the torture cells of the Lubyanka, and, in our time, the many and extravagant dissipations of a decaying civilization.*

active members in one or more variations of the Christian church. Many were leaders. The governor of the state, who gained national infamy for standing in a state university's doorway and blocking entry to its first black student, was a prominent deacon in an even more prominent church in that state and community where we lived during part of this era.

The shock of it all—especially this betrayal of everything Christ taught and stood for by those who professed allegiance to Him—might have been fatal to my incipient faith, had it not been for one magnificent saving grace. Though I was given already at the age of 14 and 15 to considerable existential wandering—vagaries that led me, in thought at least, sometimes far from the environs of faith—I was never lost in that wilderness, as say a Nietzsche might have been, or so many who wander the landscape of Western civilization today. My guide and rescuer was love—true love, not one of the many ersatz versions touted endlessly in our culture. I experienced what it meant to be truly and unreservedly loved by parents and grandparents for whom faith was real and honoring the example and teachings of Christ were a way of life. No gap, no tenuousness, existed between the faith my parents and grandparents professed publicly and the obedience and love I saw day in and day out privately. This was real, genuine, authentic, and an ineffable blessing, one that to this day I can neither explain nor justify. Like the surviving soldier of a great battle, the question has often emerged from the recesses of my heart: Why me? Why was I so blessed?

Had that authentic truth, that genuine love, not been present, I fear that my life might have taken a very different course. A strongly individualistic nature—with a warrior's instincts for reaching for the sword—will likely be merciless and unforgiving when affronted, if there is no saving grace of the type that uplifted me. Because of these experiences, I feel I understand better than most the choices others have made in this cruel world—whether our black brothers and sisters or millions of others who suffer from the cruelty and evil of man—to enter a "dark side," a place from which the victim becomes the victimizer, the perpetrator.

None of us is excused for making such a choice; the wrongs committed against us never justify the wrongs of attitude or action we commit in return—hence all arguments that crime and cruelty

Mississippi Governor Ross Barnett, Lieutenant Governor Paul Johnson, and others walking on to the University of Mississippi campus intent on stopping African-American James Meredith from enrolling. *The governor gained national infamy for his conduct, yet he was a prominent deacon in a prominent Mississippi church. In that era, especially in the American South, when it seemed the favored pastimes were burning crosses and destroying African-American churches, racism brooked no opposition; it voraciously sought to devour anyone who dared oppose it. Its agents and functionaries were everywhere, not just hidden beneath bed sheets in darkened fields lit by burning crosses.*

PD-gov

James Meredith walking to class under protection of U.S. marshals. U.S. Marshal James McShane (left) and John Doar of the Justice Department (right) accompany James Meredith on the campus of the University of Mississippi. *In the sordid vernacular of the times, whites who stood against racism were "nigger-lovers." Though a black was hated with an unreasoning malice, the "nigger-lovers" were hated even more and with a perverse form of "reasoning": You have betrayed your race and allied with those "niggers"; hence you are even more to be despised.*

By Marion S. Trikosko, U.S. News & World Report

The inevitable confrontation—one that had to take place many times between the hatred of racism and the sense of justice that stood against it. Mississippi Lt. Gov. Paul Johnson (left) confronts U.S. Marshal McShane (center) and James Meredith (right). *The important point of this historical episode was the role of the church in providing sanctuary and acceptance to the opposing sides. White churches, by and large, did not forcefully oppose racism; black churches were the only places African-Americans could coalesce.*

PD-LOC

might be somehow magnanimously minimized because of prior victimhood are without moral foundation. But we can understand the choices better when we display the sensitivity to perceive the suffering that nurtured them.

I hope that by now, this vignette has served its purpose: to illustrate how the failures of Christians and the church to live up to what they profess can lead to consequences for individuals, or a nation, or a civilization that reverberate with misery, violence, hatred and disorder for generations to come. "...yet He will by no means leave the guilty unpunished, visiting the iniquity of fathers on the children and on the grandchildren to the third and fourth generations." (Exodus 34:7) Such massive sins of omission not only permit evil to flourish but serve to nourish it. When Burke's "good man" does nothing in the face of evil it is questionable how "good" he is. He who perpetrates evil, or perpetuates the milieu in which it can thrive, or averts his eyes in its presence is not "good," even if he has so labeled himself.

I have already declared my agreement with Dawson that "it is hardly too much to say that it is Christian culture that has created Western man and the Western way of life." But I also strongly agree that "Western man has not been faithful to this Christian tradition. He has abandoned it...again and again." Christianity is a dynamic, living faith, not a dry set of doctrines, laws or beliefs. Christianity is relational: God with man, man with God. For these reasons "Christendom must be renewed in every generation, and every generation is faced by the responsibility of making decisions, each of which may be an act of Christian faith or an act of apostasy."[18] Each decision likely *will be* a choice between true faith and apostasy; that is why it is critical that none be made lightly or in glib conformity to cultural norms or practices.

How the church arrived in this condition and stooped position was facilitated by the thinking and values that originated in the Enlightenment. The Enlightenment achieved its objective of a secular Europe. Like a neutron bomb, it destroyed much of the life and spiritual vitality of the church but left the edifices and institutions themselves largely intact. The church acquired, as Dawson put it, "a position of established privilege," which they were permitted "to hold on the condition that they did not interfere with the reign of Mammon."[19] The similarities with the modern Western church are great, though it could be more honestly said, with one variation: the modern Western church is *in league with* "the reign of Mammon," not simply standing aside to permit it freedom of action.

The similarities with the church in America in the late twentieth and early twenty-first centuries are striking. Today, too, the church in America increasingly finds itself even deeper in "a backwater" of the culture, but it drifts there more out of apathy, self-absorption, and default than by any compulsion from the secular realm. Likewise, internally, the contemporary church often "broods over the memory of dead controversies," splitting itself apart over doctrinal disputes rather than cohesively charging forward to change the culture. Church leaders and theologians presume to think God's thoughts for Him, spilling Niagaras of words in print and voice to little lasting purpose other than their own aggrandizement.

Western man has not been faithful. Even in those subcultures of the church itself, Catholic and Protestant, "faithfulness" is often manifested in churches that might be more honestly described as social clubs or, in America in particular, even as country clubs, with religious overtones. The great values of the Christian faith—personal holiness in thought and lifestyle, self-sacrifice, humility, compassion for the suffering of others, and boldness in advancing the teachings of Christ and God's moral law in the marketplaces of the society—are not the highest values, even if they are given lip service as such. The humble soul-searching required to truly come to remorseful grips with the state of the Western church has not occurred—nor does it appear in the offing.

THE SELLING OF INDULGENCES

It does not matter how small the sins are, provided that their cumulative effect is to edge the man away from the Light and out into the Nothing. Indeed the safest road to hell is the gradual one—the gentle slope, soft underfoot, without sudden turnings, without milestones, without signposts.
C. S. Lewis, *The Screwtape Letters*[20]

A form of corruption has long taken root in the church in the West. Martin Luther, in opposing corruption in the church of his time, produced the Reformation. In Luther's day the church sold indulgences, a supernumerary in written form intended to guarantee its purchaser a speedy exit from purgatory and into heaven. That Christ's sacrifice on the cross was the only assurance of salvation—bought and paid for with His blood—was conveniently overlooked by the church of the time.

In our time, the church is selling self-indulgence. Especially in America, it measures success and service to God in numbers: numbers on the rolls, dollars in the budget, and square footage built. That this was neither what Christ taught or modeled is conveniently overlooked by the church in our age. Just as the selling of indulgences was a reflection of the temporal world's influence on the church of the Middle Ages, the marketing of various forms of self-indulgence is a reflection of a similar temporal, worldly influence on the church in our time.

The rich young man who came by night to Jesus seeking how he might be saved went away sad because Jesus set the highest and uncompromising standard of holiness and self-sacrifice, standards the young man would not accept. (Mark 10:17–31) In the Western church today there are multitudes of such rich young men (and women and older men and women) who need not go away—they find eager acceptance.

Christians in the West have allowed their heads to be turned by Western culture—its self-indulgence, hedonism, materialism, and its methods for indulging all three. So deeply engrained in the church are these attributes that simply suggesting this produces bewilderment and confusion as to what could possibly be meant. This self-deluded ambivalence mingles with anger that anyone would have the effrontery to challenge the accepted *modus operandi* and "doctrinal" views of the church.

Christians' heads are also—and unexpectedly, under the circumstances—turned by any attention the broader culture grants to them or their efforts. Wisdom would dictate a circumspect recognition that this is nothing more than the culture finding in their actions something that fits within the parameters of what the culture deems significant or appealing—invariably there is nothing spiritual or uplifting about the motive. Yet the Christian leader or layman will often be smitten in the most obsequious way by the attention of the media, political officeholders, or other prominent cultural figures.

That the spiritual cosmology calls for the earth (i.e., man and all his institutions) to properly orbit around the sun (i.e., God), rather than the other way around, is lost on many Christian leaders of our age. For over a century, and particularly in the last half of the twentieth and first part of the twenty-first centuries, the reversal of the spiritual physics has become broadly accepted as the way the church measures success. Underlying this entire panoply of self-absorption and capitulation to human nature is the failure to recognize that God owes man nothing; man owes God everything. Man does not exist for God to serve but the other way round.

The strategy has clearly failed. It was doomed to fail because it is not the strategy taught or modeled by Christ. The Great Question suspended over all of Western civilization implores an answer: "Will the church confront this failure to follow the life and teachings of Christ or will it remain in denial and self-justification?"

Those who would find acceptance, influence, success, or power in Western culture must seek accommodation with Toynbee's "dominant minority" and disavow—by actions and expressed values, if not by words—any strong uncompromising commitment to faith, especially Christianity. A "Christianity" that does not universally challenge the culture on all points of moral disobedience or disbelief may gain acceptance—even the broader culture's embrace. Professed agnosticism is perhaps the preferred form of political correctness in the midst of the anti-Christian McCarthyism of our time. Similarly, because the culture and its values are now the dominant force in most realms of the Christian faith, Catholic, Orthodox, and Protestant, in America and Europe, those who would find acceptance, influence, success, or power in the church itself must seek accommodation with the culture there as well, and disavow any strong commitment to a faith that is uncompromisingly Christ-centered in every aspect. Put another way, neither John the Baptist nor Francis of Assisi could gain any standing in the church in the West today other than as examples of radicalism, fundamentalism, zealotry or, perhaps, emotional or mental unbalance.

Many Christian leaders will defensively deny, in whole or in part, what is said here. But they cannot credibly deny that Western culture is moving rapidly away from the Christian faith and the morality of Old or New Testament teaching. That this has occurred—and is accelerating—is sufficient evidence to prompt any honest person to acknowledge the church's failure, even if these leaders do not. Thus their credibility is eviscerated by objective reality. But human rationalization and self-justification are shamelessly creative. The very church leaders who offer an *apologia* rather than a *mea culpa* are classic illustrations within the church of Toynbee's "dominant minority" upon whom the "moral responsibility" for the decline and decay will rest.

In this work, there will be no consolatory remarks, tactful, ingratiating diplomacy, or euphemistic veiling—because the moral responsibility for the decline and decay of Western civilization will rest even more heavily on these church leaders' shoulders than on those of the secular leaders of the civilization. I knew in writing this book that popularity, comradely acceptance, and acclaim by fellow Christians would have to be abandoned if the effort was at all honest. Embedded in that awareness is the better part of the rub: The Western Christian is usually more concerned with pleasing man—and ensuring his own personal peace, social acceptance, security, and material well-being—than he is with pleasing God, even as he professes otherwise.

THE VANITY OF THE MODERN—THE MERITS OF THE ANCIENT AND THE TIMELESS

For there is nothing so repulsive as dead religion; it is the deadest thing there is. As the Gospel says, it is not even good enough for the dunghill.
Dawson[21]

Much of what receives attention in Western culture ultimately proves to be, in historical terms, to borrow a phrase from the American frontier, "a flash in the pan." We are beset on all sides by fads and trends. They appear in every facet of life, including religion. They may seem important and may be accorded great attention in the media, political arenas, and even in the church. But historical retrospectives expose their ultimate meaninglessness.

I first became especially conscious of this phenomenon in Western culture as a college student. Spending many hours in the university library reading periodicals from forty to fifty or more years earlier, I sought to learn how people thought and behaved in those earlier times—as they were being experienced, rather than through the retrospective of history. I was struck by how often events, ideas, ideological issues, social concepts, and individuals were touted and rose to prominence, only to fade into oblivion, or even to become social or conceptual rejects, often in just a decade, sometimes sooner.

Much that is praised, studied, and talked about in Christian religion as it is practiced today in the West will meet the same fate. Megachurches, marketing techniques, therapeutic approaches, and any number of infusions of the culture into religion will prove to be not only shallow and temporal but, in retrospect, will be seen for what they are: impediments to the progress of the true Christian faith. But their scrutiny is necessary, not only to expose their pervasiveness within the church, but also to shed light on the true motives that often lie unseen behind them. That there are sincere and well-meaning Christians who embrace and practice them should not be questioned. But *sincerity and spiritual soundness are not synonymous.* Nor does the adjective efficacious necessarily follow the characterization "well-meaning." Evidence of the abject failure of these attitudes, values and approaches litters Western culture, but in the now banal definition of insanity, their believers and practitioners only pursue them ever more assiduously.

WHO IS TO BLAME?

...to see how great has been our responsibility for this decline of Christian culture and for the conversion of our society to a new kind of paganism...
Dawson[22]

As we saw earlier, the reality of Western civilization's decline and decay should now be disputed only by the foolish or those who are indifferent to their own credibility. Toynbee's warning to the culture is apropos to the plight of the church as much as it is to Western civilization as a whole, in large part because of their embrace as historical Siamese twins. As goes the Christian church as an institution, surely will go Western civilization.

Aerial view of church campus, courtesy of Nick Ellis.

The huge campus of an American church complete with multiple baseball and soccer fields, gymnasiums and the many comforts and amusements today considered *de rigueur* for the "successful" church. *No longer a place where sacrifice and self-effacement are taught, much less practiced, such churches are country clubs with religious overtones, intended to satisfy their members' whims and indulgences while carrying the patina of religiosity. Christians in the West—especially America—have allowed their heads to be turned by Western culture—its self-indulgence, hedonism, materialism, and its methods for indulging all three. So deeply engrained in the church are these attributes that simply suggesting this produces bewilderment and confusion as to what could possibly be meant. This self-deluded ambivalence mingles with anger that anyone would have the effrontery to challenge the accepted* modus operandi *and "doctrinal" views of the church.*

Photograph courtesy of Indigenous Outreach International

An Ethiopian church meeting. *An American evangelical layman expressed dismay to the author about the extravagance of American churches contrasted with what those churches do for followers of Christ in poor countries. He wondered what those Third-World Christians must think of American Christians. An apropos question but secondary by a large margin to another: What does God think? The great values of the Christian faith—personal holiness in thought and lifestyle, self-sacrifice, humility, compassion for the suffering of others, and boldness in advancing the teachings of Christ and God's moral law in the marketplaces of the society—are not the highest values, even if they are given lip service as such. The humble soul-searching required to truly come to remorseful grips with the state of the Western church has not occurred—nor does it appear in the offing.*

> It is always a test of character to be baffled and "up against it," but the test is particularly severe when the adversity comes suddenly at the noon of a halcyon day which one has fatuously expected to endure to eternity. In straits like these, the wrestler with destiny is tempted to look for bugbears and scapegoats to carry the burden of his own inadequacy. Yet to "pass the buck" in adversity is still more dangerous than to persuade oneself that prosperity is everlasting.... Whenever things go awry in circumstances that seem ever more intractable, we tend to accuse the enemy of having sown tares in our field and thereby implicitly excuse ourselves for the faults in our own husbandry. This is, of course, an old story.[23]

The church in our time has been both victim and perpetrator in this age-old scenario of blame and recrimination. Secularists in the West increasingly declaim the reputed speciousness of faith and divine law, citing these beliefs and practices as "primitive" causes of hatred, violence, "intolerance" and a hindrance to "progress." Accusing fingertips meet in mid-air as the church blames the secularists for the self-evident moral decay of Western civilization. The former do not—and cannot—understand the latter. The latter stubbornly refuse to humbly look into their own souls. If unrepentant, together, the institutional church (though not the authentic church) and Western civilization shall fall into history's deepest ditch.

Christian leadership often tries but cannot justly shift the blame. We have already heard Toynbee's *j'accuse*: that the "moral responsibility" is greatest with the "dominant minority." We have also learned that the Christian faith is the superstructure of Western civilization. The juxtaposition of those two realities means that the finger pointing by church leaders at the secularists, agnostics, and atheists cannot absolve them of their own grave dereliction of duty. For as Christ Himself declared, "And from everyone who has been given much shall much be required; and to whom they entrusted much, of him they will ask all the more." (Luke 12:48 NASB)

Human beings can become masters at rationalization and self-justification. The more corrupt we become in our thinking and values, the more adept we become at the skills of self-delusion. The more skilled we become at fooling others, the more we unwittingly delude ourselves. The church has rationalized its practices and attitudes for generations now, and the rationalizations have become more and more complex and ubiquitous. This has become deeply engrained in the institutions and doctrines of the Western church itself, Catholic, Orthodox, and Protestant.

In any subculture or institution there are rules or practices, often implied or tacit, by which members of that institution are expected to conduct themselves. These rules reflect the values of the institution generally, though not necessarily all of its members. Primarily they reflect the values of dominant leaders in the institution. Those who wish to advance, either in terms of influence or position within the institution, will consciously or sometimes in part unconsciously, inculcate those rules and practices and follow them. The result is a tendency to conformity and rigidity of thinking. This tendency often runs counter to what the institution and its members really need: reformation in the values, rules, and practices by which the institution conducts itself. For most of a century at least, the Christian church in the West has followed practices in significant areas of their ministries that reflect the secular world's values rather than those lived and taught by Christ.

It is a measure of how acculturated (i.e., captive to the culture) the church is that the proliferation of books and commentaries on Western civilization focus primarily on politics, law, economics, government, and social policy. Significantly, this is true of many works originating from Christian perspectives. Innumerable books tell us how the church, in one or more of its myriad manifestations

PD-art

Martin Luther, by Lucas Cranach the Elder. 1529. *Luther, in opposing corruption in the church of his time, produced the Reformation. In Luther's day the church sold indulgences. In our time, the church is selling self-indulgence. Especially in America, it measures success and service in numbers: numbers on the rolls, dollars in the budget, and square footage built. The selling of indulgences was a reflection of the world's influence on the church then; the marketing of self-indulgence is a reflection of temporal influence on the church now.*

in Western civilization, should influence the culture in these arenas and how to go about it. But few focus with relentless, in-depth, soul-searching on the church itself. Even those that do, tend to speak generically and broadly to complacency or lack of enthusiasm and commitment. Scant thought seems to be given to the church's mindset and spiritual status as an independent, transcendent expression of God's-will-not-man's in the culture and world at large.

Somewhat paradoxically, many Christians are unsettled, restless, even hostile, as they become increasingly conscious of the secular trends and values sweeping the West, displacing their values and viewpoints and shouldering them aside from their traditional positions as moral and social arbiters. This is especially true in America.

For many this unsettled, anxious, and often emotional response is in large part due to two factors—neither of them truly spiritual: First, the longstanding apathy (and resultant lack of scrupulous personal obedience and sacrificial service) of the church; and, secondly, the loss of the cultural prominence, social and political influence, comfort, and security the church enjoyed for generations in America—all of which nurtured the apathy.

Many Christians in the West, particularly in America, are in some ways like adolescents who are now faced with the prospect of having to suddenly grow up. Increasingly, they realize to their shock that the world is not as they thought and the ease and security of childhood are gone forever. But Christians will not be truly effective until they come fully to that greater maturity and then move beyond it. Their unsettling (i.e., the permanent disruption of comfortable lives) will not be their undoing—*if they choose wisely.* But the saving of the institutional church as a profound cultural influence is at best highly problematic, at worst, far too late. Jesus declared, "…if I be lifted up from the earth, I will draw all men to Myself." (John 12:32) But the church in the West is not lifting up the real Jesus, rather a facsimile fashioned by our culture through the church. Ironically, the secular world may sense this—even if they do not fully understand—more readily than does the church itself.

As evidence of the certainty of this reality, we look now in this work on the observations of historians and sociologists who have made it their business to scrutinize religion and the church in the West. Among them are Anglo-American scholars such as Steve Bruce, Hugh McLeod, Bryan Wilson, and Peter Berger, Irishman Sheridan Gilley. Continental Europeans from a variety of nations—Callum Brown, Dutchman Peter van Rooden, Sarah Williams, Lucian Hölscher, Gerard Cholvy and Yves-Marie Hilaire, who focus on French Catholic history, as well as Thomas Kselman, Eva Hamberg, Yves Lambert, Germans Martin Greschat and Werner Ustorf, and Jeffrey Cox—all contributed to this analysis.

We rely heavily on American sociologist Professor Alan Wolfe, whose *The Transformation of American Religion* offers a better or more insightful expression of the state of the Christian church in America—especially how the secular world sees it—than most observers. Early in his book, Professor Wolfe notes that "...American religion has never existed in practice the way it is supposed to exist in theory. Democratic in their political instincts, geographically and economically mobile, attracted to popular culture more than to the written word, Americans from the earliest times have shaped religion to account for their personal needs...in the United States culture has transformed Christ....In every aspect of the religious life, American faith has met American culture—and American culture has triumphed."[24]

In what should be an especially stinging observation, Professor Wolfe speculates that "If Jonathan Edwards were alive and well, he would likely be appalled; far from living in a world elsewhere, the faithful in the United States are remarkably like everyone else."[25] A parallel should be noted here between this observation by Wolfe and the common propagandistic invocation of the names of the American Founding Fathers. Though the names of great American religious and political antecedents are invoked continually to support or justify this or that, the truth is that in most cases the early religious leaders, like Edwards, and the Founding Fathers would be appalled and angry that their legacy is used to support that which they would not only dispute but probably reject fiercely. This is part of the hypocrisy of our time—a measure of the decay and decline that is manifested in deceit and manipulation to gain power and exercise control by some, and the stark, gullible ignorance of masses of others who compliantly accept.

Professor Wolfe then insists on a realistic appraisal of Christianity in America "...as strikingly similar to the society in which it flourishes as it is distant from the religion we once knew." "It is time," Wolfe says, "for Americans to stop discussing a religion that no longer exists and to concentrate their attention on the one that flourishes all around them."

Here Professor Wolfe has said something even more significant than perhaps he realizes. I would express it this way: The chasm that separates the life and teachings of Christ from the modern church in the West is so vast as to make it something completely different. Carrying the name—and selectively citing, or conveniently "interpreting," the original authority, the Bible—it is nonetheless more often, and more completely, a creature of Western culture than the true Christian faith.

That its practitioners would not recognize this is not especially significant since conduct implies thought; but pointing this out would raise a firestorm of vehement denials, objections and rationalizations. The mountain of truth juts above the landscape right before the eyes of professing Christians, but they claim only to see a plain.

However, despite its failures—and they are massive and ubiquitous—there is no other hope for Western civilization than the Christian church. Christopher Dawson of course did not believe—and I strongly affirm him—that there was ever any hope in any of the isms, ideologies, economic theories, sciences, or technologies—not even those so reverentially held to the West's bosom: "What our civilisation lacks is not power and wealth and knowledge, but spiritual vitality, and unless it is possible to secure that, nothing can save us from the fate that overtook...so many other civilisations that were brilliant and powerful in their day."[26] This blanket statement includes for me, as I believe it would for Dawson, even those most vaunted Western ideologies and institutions: democracy, capitalism, and patriotism (i.e., nationalism), as well as science and technology.

PD-old

The great early American preacher Jonathan Edwards. *In an especially stinging and appropriate observation, Professor Wolfe observes that "If Jonathan Edwards were alive and well, he would likely be appalled; far from living in a world elsewhere, the faithful in the United States are remarkably like everyone else."*

Here all secularists lose ground. Their complaints and criticisms about the church's failures cannot, by and large, be universally refuted and should be honestly acknowledged. But the alternatives they propose—with ever-greater profligacy and intensity since the Enlightenment—have been thoroughly exposed as failures. In our age, they are physically dangerous failures as well as spiritually lethal. Yet many persist in promoting them, thus leading us full circle to the question of their true motives, in their heart of hearts. Nonetheless, as Dawson made clear with specific examples, untold thousands have sought answers elsewhere than in the Christian faith because the Western church has become a monument to the truth in the words "There is nothing so repulsive as dead religion."

The notion of charity (i.e., love) as described eloquently by the Apostle Paul is one of the great distinguishing features of the Christian religion. Nothing else rivals it on the stage of world history for power to change lives. This form of love—the product of God Himself influencing human thought and attitude—in Dawson's words, "transforms human nature." Put another way, only in this sense and through this method can the human heart truly be changed; in every other sense human nature is incorrigibly and irredeemably self-centered.

But charity in our age more often carries the connotation of what Dawson said was "the most external and spiritually barren type of social beneficence." Altruism itself can be self-seeking; a kind of ritual one goes through to prove to the larger society—and to oneself—that one is "worthy" and a person of "innate goodness." Effete and self-serving, it is spiritually light years away from "He that loveth not knoweth not God, for God is love." (1 John 4:8 KJV)

Yet this is often the form of "charity" practiced by the church; a kind of tokenism intended to offset the appearances otherwise created by the lavishing of money and effort on imposing buildings, family life centers, gymnasiums, and myriad "ministries" that are really little more than other forms of human indulgence. Destructive of the spiritual life of its practitioners, it also goes a long way to explain not only the rejection of the Christian religion by millions but outright hostility toward it. All of the human calculations in terms of church membership, square footage constructed, and money raised do not nullify this truth—or the overwhelming evidence that the Christian faith is losing its influence in the civilization, which is, in truth, the only measure that really matters.

If one embraces the fundamentals of Christ's teachings at all, then there must be recognition that one day the church (especially its leadership) must give an account for this utter failure to truly and deeply love Christ and their fellowman—for that, in truth, is the self-centered indifference that lies behind the direction of our civilization. Jesus said, "If you love me you will keep my commandments." (John 14:15 NASB) Christ's commandments and example were of a very different order and direction than much of what is seen in the Western church today.

Dr. Wolfe proclaims a principle that is another manifestation of a central theme of this work—one we have heard expressed by Dawson, Sorokin, Toynbee, and other of our observers—human nature does not change. Its corollary: Men have far more common denominators than differences. "Religions can be astonishingly different, while human beings can be surprisingly the same. Study theology, and one comes away impressed by differences. Study real people and one is more likely to notice the similarities, not only among people of different faiths but also between those for whom religion matters greatly and those for whom it matters not at all."[27] I concur and would add that this is all the more true when one's religion does not significantly change one's life.

In a preliminary reference to attitudes and behaviors we will scrutinize more closely in subsequent chapters, we let Professor Wolfe help us to see not only through his eyes, but the eyes of other social observers, some of whom are Christians. What is seen has the following attributes:

> Reflecting its informal dress code, [one church] is also relaxed in the theology it offers.... [It] uses the same PowerPoint approach to sermons that many megachurches use for the lyrics of their songs; an oversize screen highlights the two or three simple conclusions to be gotten from each sermon. And the resulting sermons... "are theologically very thin." Scripture is cited but not very often, and when it is, preachers use it to buttress conclusions they have already made, which [is viewed] as a conservative Christian version of the use of religion by liberal pastors to support their political views. When all is said and done... religion... is more of a spectacle.[28]
>
> ...Generally speaking, preaching in evangelically oriented growth churches, however dynamic in delivery, has remarkably little actual content. Rarely is the congregation challenged to do anything other than give itself over to Christ, and even the pursuit of that objective is not accompanied by any sense of complexity or difficulty.... [C]onsiderable time is devoted, as one would expect in a corporate boardroom, to statements emphasizing the church's success in mission or growth. The world outside the church is usually not acknowledged.... If religion is understood as combining reason with revelation, a substantial amount of the preaching in evangelical America has a good deal of the latter and very little of the former.[29]

Here, Professor Wolfe may in part misunderstand. The message of Christ as to how a person might gain salvation is simplicity itself. This is one of the great and salient features of the Christian faith—unique not only in its simplicity, but its accessibility: Man need not worry whether he is able and worthy (through works, virtue, etc.) to achieve salvation, nor is profound intellectual understanding a prerequisite. The Christian God's beneficence and love for His children is thereby made evident even in the very way salvation is proffered.

There is, however, considerable truth in Professor Wolfe's other underlying criticisms. The evidence in support can be found in every manifestation of the institutional church in the West. Scrutiny of the curricula of major seminaries will often reveal a focus that could be variously described as banal, cloistered, or arcane. The pragmatic (i.e., sacrificially service-oriented and powerfully effective in practice) intent to understand God's message on the one hand and touch the heart of man on the other—as best either could be achieved—is not as apparent as is a bathetic attentiveness to the methods and mores of the denominational subculture. The American evangelist Billy

END NOTES
CHAPTER 20

1 Christopher Dawson, *Christianity and the New Age* (New York: Sophia Institute Press, 1985), xv.
2 Alan Wolfe, *The Transformation of American Religion: How We Actually Live Our Faith* (New York: Free Press, 2003), 2–3. Reprinted and edited with the permission of The Free Press, a Division of Simon & Schuster, Inc., from *The Transformation of American Religion: How We Actually Live Our Faith* by Alan Wolfe. Copyright 2003 by Alan Wolfe. All rights reserved.
3 Steve Bruce, *God Is Dead: Secularization in the West* (Oxford: Wiley-Blackwell, 2002), 235.
4 George Meredith, *Modern Love and Poems of the English Roadside: With Poems and Ballads* (London: Chapman & Hall, 1862), poem 47, lines 14–16.
5 Philip Bagby, *Culture and History: Prolegomena to the Comparative Study of Civilizations* (Berkeley: University of California Press, 1963), 175.
6 Christopher Dawson, *Religion and World History: A Selection from the Works of Christopher Dawson* (Garden City, NY: Image Books, 1975), 255.
7 Christopher Dawson, *The Historic Reality of Christian Culture* (New York: Harper & Brothers, 1960), 36–37.
8 Dawson, *Historic Reality of Christian Culture*, 67.
9 Dawson, *Religion and World History*, 259.
10 Dawson, *Historic Reality of Christian Culture*, 22.
11 Dawson, *Christianity and the New Age*, 3–4.
12 Dawson, *Historic Reality of Christian Culture*, 22.
13 Dawson, *Historic Reality of Christian Culture*, 22.
14 Dawson, *Religion and World History*, 289–290.
15 Dawson, *Religion and World History*, 290.
16 Dawson, *Religion and World History*, 290–291.
17 Dawson, *Religion and World History*, 302.
18 Dawson, *Religion and World History*, 256.
19 Dawson, *Christianity and the New Age*, 3.
20 C. S. Lewis, *The Screwtape Letters* (New York: HarperCollins, 1942, 2001), 60–61.
21 Dawson, *Religion and World History*, 308.
22 Dawson, *Historic Reality of Christian Culture*, 22.
23 Arnold Toynbee, *Civilization on Trial* (New York: Oxford University Press, 1948), 21.
24 Wolfe, *Transformation*, 2–3.
25 Wolfe, *Transformation*, 3.
26 Dawson, *Religion and World History*, 302.
27 Wolfe, *Transformation*, 5.
28 Wolfe, *Transformation*, 30–31.
29 Wolfe, *Transformation*, 31.
30 Carroll Quigley, *The Evolution of Civilizations: An Introduction to Historical Analysis* (New York: Macmillan, 1961), 101–102.
31 Quigley, *Evolution of Civilizations*, 110.
32 Quigley, *Evolution of Civilizations*, 115.
33 Earl Shorris, "Literary Life Among the Dinka," *Harper's Magazine* (Aug. 1972), 104–107.

CHAPTER

21

THE DEATH OF CHRISTENDOM— THE DECLINE OF THE CHURCH IN EUROPE

The decline of Christendom has meant that Christianity has been gradually losing its status as a lingua franca, and has tended to become a local language used by those who are professing Christians, but not understood by others.
Hugh McLeod[1]

[All churches in the Western world] *stake their life upon the continued existence of those social patterns into which they have so closely woven themselves, instead of upon the abiding truth of God.*
Iain Wilson[2]

How the Western church got where it is has been the focus of many historians and sociologists. Though for our purposes, a focus on how we arrived is not as important as where we are and how we rescue the church from cultural irrelevance. Nonetheless, the path out can be more readily discerned if we pay attention to the trail in.

Ironically, the moment of what seemed the church's greatest triumph in Western civilization was also the inception of its ultimate downfall. When Constantine made Christianity the religion of the Roman Empire in 312, he rescued it from three centuries of relentless persecution and elevated it to a status that most could not be blamed for perceiving as a great achievement. But this embrace by the temporal powers of the age would eventually break the sturdy bones of principle and belief and the spine of courage of the institutional church. Far from ensuring its vigor and strength it compromised its spiritual vitality and health.

As would be expected from those who love power, position and wealth, the elite of that age converted to the new faith forthwith. In every age those who savor worldly rewards always gravitate to that which is most likely to sate their hunger. The *hoi polloi*—who had less to gain in the worldly sense—were persuaded for very different reasons.

Constantine's actions initiated a phenomenon that replicated itself in a variety of ways throughout Western history: the church allied with the state; the church allied with the culture; the church as barely distinguishable from the other two in practice and behavior. This collusion—though widely accepted and even deemed meritorious—was in fact the unhinging of the church from the actual life and teachings of

Christ; a life that was supremely countercultural, which never pandered to pride, temporal power, or the favors of man.

It would be impossible to say what was genuine and what was ersatz in terms of belief for millions of succeeding generations who lived out their lives in what historians came to call "Christendom." Hugh McLeod described this as "a society where there were close ties between the leaders of the church and those in positions of secular power, where the laws purported to be based on Christian principles, and where, apart from certain clearly defined outsider communities every member of the society was assumed to be a Christian."[3] Under persecution, authenticity, sincerity, and conviction are easy to spot. In a state of culture like Christendom too much was to be gained by affiliation with the dominant order, and too much to be lost by its rejection. Here we see historical evidence that makes greater sense of Christ's warning that some would hear the startling condemnation, "Depart from me, for I never knew you." (Matthew 7:23)

Head of the colossal statue of Constantine I, Musei Capitolini, Rome. Marble, Roman artwork, A.D. 313–324. *Constantine made Christianity the religion of the Roman Empire in 312 and initiated a phenomenon that replicated itself throughout Western history: the church allied with the state; the church allied with the culture; the church was barely distinguishable from the other two in practice and behavior. This collusion was the unhinging of the church from the life and teachings of Christ, a life that was supremely countercultural, that never pandered to pride, temporal power, or the favors of man.*

It might be argued in a purely sociological sense that all of this produced something worthwhile: a concert of opinion and belief that nurtured greater unity within society. But human dissipations being what they are, even the nominal Christians found other things to fight about—including doctrinal issues that were often nothing more than mechanisms for concealing a vainglorious quest for power and prestige.

In any event, by the mid-twentieth century a transition was becoming apparent. In truth, indicia of the decline of the church in Europe were already present prior to that era, but soon it would become evident even to the most inattentive. The decline is now obvious, even egregiously so, though not uniform. As we will see, Scandinavia is now deemed the most secular part of Europe, while Ireland, at the other end of the continuum, yet retains a close attachment to the Catholic manifestation of Christianity as does Northern Ireland to Protestantism. In no place in Europe, however, are indicia apparent of *growth* in the influence of the church on society resulting in a concomitant change in the surrounding society. To the contrary, secularization is clearly afoot on every front. That is beyond dispute. It appears that sociologists and historians only disagree on whether 1) this process has an inevitability about it; and 2) it will or won't, can or cannot, be reversed at some point.

There is seeming paradox in all of this. As sociologist Steve Bruce pointed out, the last twenty years of the twentieth century saw a triumphant West in economic, political and ideological terms while it suffered a "crisis of confidence in one aspect of its culture: religion."[4] But, as we will argue later in this work, this is not as paradoxical as it might appear; it is in one sense, predictable. Nonetheless this "erosion of specifically Christian ideas has left a vague spirituality that is coincidentally similar to the more philosophical and less ritualistic traditions in Hinduism and Buddhism."[5]

A PROFILE OF SECULARIZATION

The bald statement is this: secularisation fillets the religious spine out of the body of human culture.... The churches are now less relevant; indeed, to be frank, they become increasingly irrelevant with every year.
Callum G. Brown[6]

Consistent with the declaration made in the Introduction of this book, I have made no effort to *prove* the decay and decline of our civilization was either occurring or was significant. To do so seemed to me a superfluous and specious undertaking for the simple reason that its manifestations were obvious to all but the most obtuse and the delusional. Similarly, I am not intent here in proving the decline of the church in the West, but we will utilize the findings of historians and sociologists in a way that reflects that decline, and the degree of the decline, and the areas of greater or lesser decline. Hugh McLeod provides an initial insight:

> While levels of nominal Christian affiliation and participation in the rites of passage were still very high in 1960, levels of participation in Sunday worship or in communion varied greatly. At one extreme, over 90 per cent of the population were regular church-goers in the Irish Republic, and very high levels of attendance at mass were also found among the rural populations of Brittany, the Basque Country, the Veneto, and other traditionally pious Catholic regions. At the other extreme, weekly attendance fell below 5 percent in many parts of Scandinavia, as well as in the "dechristianised" regions of central France. In the 1990s, the highest levels of church-going were still found in Ireland and in some rural regions of Italy and Portugal, but there had been a general levelling down. Quite large drops have been seen in some areas previously known for their piety, whereas there has been a more modest decline in other areas where attendance was already low.
>
> The signs were that belief in various Christian tenets and doctrines declined between the 1960s and the 1990s, though there is insufficient evidence to say whether the figures for the 1960s represent a decline from a higher level at some earlier point. Admittedly, questionnaires may be too blunt a tool to elucidate some of the complexities and ambiguities of individual belief. For instance, while about two-thirds of west Europeans will say when asked that they believe in God, this does not tell us very much, as conceptions of God vary so greatly. This is even more true of beliefs concerning the after-life, where the findings of surveys often appear to be contradictory. For instance, in a number of countries the proportion of respondents claiming to believe in heaven exceeds the proportion claiming to believe in a life after death.[7]

It should come as no surprise that the area in which the shift from traditional Christian mores to those of a secular society has been most evident is sexual behavior. Though earlier generations were often hypocritical in their attitudes and behavior, at least there was some recognition of the merit of social constraints on sexual behavior. The 1960s radically altered the social topography. Sexual controls—such as they were—were effectively removed from the purview of the church and given to government.

> Britain set the trend with the liberalisation of the laws on obscenity (1959), abortion (1967) and divorce (1969), legalisation of homosexual acts between consenting adults (1967), abolition of theatre censorship (1968), and provision of contraceptives to unmarried couples through the National Health Service (1967). In Britain, Christian opinion on all of these issues was divided. While many of the leaders in the movements for change were themselves secularists, there was also a significant degree of support for these reforms from within the churches. So the forces for change were varied, including growing secularist influence, changes in Christian opinion, and also a realisation that in an increasingly pluralistic society some compromise was needed between the various and conflicting moral standards that were current.... "abortion on demand"...was supported by many Christians on the pragmatic grounds that legal abortion was at least preferable to the widely prevalent "backstreet" abortions. The legalisation of divorce in Italy and Ireland, and of abortion in France, Belgium and Italy, marked more unequivocally a defeat for the church in those countries.[8]

The phrasing "there was also a significant degree of support for these reforms from within the churches" is significant and reflects evidence of a pattern to which we will return.

For those who fancy statistics, Yves Lambert offered the following, which will unequivocally corroborate trends and consequences across Europe.

> Essentially, the surveys concern Christianity, constituting 70 per cent of the population of the nine countries where figures for both 1981 and 1999 are available (85 per cent in 1981). In these countries we find that church attendance at least once a month has decreased from 36 per cent in 1981 to 30 per cent in 1999; 68 per cent in the nine countries believe in God, compared to 74 per cent in 1981. Only 7 per cent say they are "a convinced atheist," the maximum being in France (14 per cent), the home of positivism; this rate has increased, though very slightly (from 5 per cent in 1981). The other respondents are agnostic or hesitating. When asked what kind of God they believed in, the responses were: "a personal God" (38 per cent), "a spirit or life force" (30 per cent), "I don't really think there is any sort of spirit, God or life force" (15 per cent), "I don't know" (13 per cent), and "no answer" (4 per cent).
>
> Regarding the after-life, 43 per cent say they believe in "a life after death" (which may include reincarnation), the percentage being the same as that found in 1981; 38 per cent say they believe in heaven (39 per cent in 1981); 25 per cent in hell (22 per cent in 1981). It seems that the better side of the hereafter is preserved more willingly. Eighteen per cent believe in reincarnation (12 per cent in 1981) (1999 EVS). Belief in sin drops from 57 per cent in 1981 to 47 percent in 1999.[9]

After a long recitation of statistics marking the decline of traditional Christian beliefs in Europe, McLeod then asks, What is left of Christendom in the twenty-first century?

> A considerable proportion of west European countries retain links of one kind or another between church and state. In Germany and Scandinavia there is the church tax system, which has placed the churches in those countries in a uniquely favourable financial position. In Belgium the state pays the

> salaries of the clergy. In England twenty-six Anglican bishops have seats in the House of Lords. In Italy the church-state treaty of 1984 contained very favourable terms for the Catholic Church.[10]

This response is telling. For the committed follower of Christ these connections reflect not faith but culture, compromise rather than conviction. As we will see, in every instance in which the church has allied itself with the established political or social order its "gains" are eventually proven to be ephemeral. Such alliances corrode the integrity of the church and eventually undermine its credibility and moral authority.

There are perhaps four other noteworthy vestigial remains of Christendom that may be unearthed. McLeod continues.

> First there are the rites of passage. Even in those countries where marriage in church and the baptism of infants have seen a major decline, they remain quite widespread, and are asked for by many couples who seldom go to church at other times.... And in nearly all countries Christian funerals are heavily predominant—whether or not, as Callum Brown suggests, this is beginning to change. Second there is education. In some countries, such as England and the Netherlands, there are considerable numbers of church schools. In most countries (France being the major exception) religious education is provided in state schools. Though this education may no longer be exclusively Christian, and though there may be an increasing emphasis on "balance," it inevitably includes a major element of teaching on Christianity, often by teachers who are trained in theology.... A third area is that of welfare and charity.
>
> In Germany, a major part of the public welfare system is church-based. In every country a large proportion of private charities have religious origins, and religious motivation continues to be important for many of those working for them. A fourth area is the role of "public conscience" which churches may still perform even in apparently very secular societies. This is perhaps most evident in totalitarian societies, such as East Germany where the Protestant churches were among the very few bodies enjoying some limited degree of independence and where they accordingly became a major forum for the expression of dissent and played an important part in the protest movements culminating in the fall of the Communist regime in 1989–90. But even in democratic and pluralist societies the churches may have a unique role, because of their ability to mount a moral, rather than purely political, critique of government. For instance in the 1980s the British churches mounted a sustained attack on the policies of Margaret Thatcher's administration, to which Thatcher herself felt obliged to respond, and in France the Catholic Church has played an important part in speaking up for the rights of immigrants and combating racism.[11]

These, however, are hardly indicia of a living, vibrant personal faith. Rather, they are closer to the calciferous remains of a mollusk left behind at the creature's death, yet conveying the illusion of life. But the mollusk did not die abruptly. This was a process, drawn out over generations and identifiable, according to some sociologists and historians, in four stages:

> *First,* toleration by the state of a variety of forms of Christianity.
> *Second,* open communication of anti-Christian ideas.
> *Third,* separation of church and state.
> *Fourth,* loosening of the connections between the society and the church.

The first identified stage should produce skepticism in the observer. Religious toleration in the American colonies—the Baptists in Rhode Island, the Quakers in Pennsylvania, and the Catholics in Maryland were all required to accept religious toleration as a principle—seemed to invigorate rather than stultify the Christian faith. Thus this alone is not persuasive even if the places in which "Christian minorities first gained the right to worship were also those where the open avowal of religious scepticism first became possible." Indeed, this did lead to a proliferation of books, pamphlets and discourse on deism and atheism in ensuing years. But was religious toleration causative or merely the opening of a window through which expressions of disbelief could be heard? There is a difference.

Lucian Hölscher asserted that the eighteenth century did not stimulate a decline in Christianity but a "reinterpretation" that was salutary in that it shifted religion from an externally imposed order into the category of personal piety reflecting individual commitment rather than compulsion.

As pointed out before, conversion to Christianity cannot be achieved at the point of a sword—or through any other form of compulsion—Charlemagne's efforts notwithstanding. Among the most distinctive features of Christianity, in contrast to other religions, personal choice for personal piety cannot be imposed. Thus all efforts to do so are not Christian.

Hugh McLeod's observation is supportive of Hölscher's view.

> In so far as Christendom depended on conformism and a degree of coercion, these developments were undermining Christendom, without necessarily undermining Christianity. In so far as they made it possible to think about various aspects of the world and various areas of life without having to presuppose the existence of supernatural powers, they potentially prepared the way for a more secular society, but they did not necessarily lead in that direction.[12]

This distinction between Christendom and Christianity is reminiscent of our distinction between the institutional church and the authentic church. The former reflects the external, the shell, the mechanism; the latter reflects the internal, genuine belief. Similarly, the notion of separation of church and state as a stage in the dissolution of Christendom can only be accounted for in terms of that shell, not in terms of closely held personal convictions.

> The eighteenth century ended with further important steps in the direction of the decline of Christendom. In 1791 the Separation of church and state was written into the Constitution of the United States, and laws of Separation were also enacted in France in 1795 and the Netherlands in 1796. However, in France church and state were reunited as early as 1801—though in a novel form, since Protestants and Jews as well as Catholics were supported by and subjected to a measure of control by the state. The defeat of Napoleon in 1815 meant that the alliance of throne, altar and château was in power again across most of Europe. But Separation returned to the political agenda in the second half of the nineteenth century, when it became a normal part of Radical and later Socialist programmes. It was enacted in Ireland in 1869, in France in 1905, in Geneva in 1907, in Germany in 1919, in Wales in 1920 and in Spain in 1931. In Sweden this happened as recently as 2000, and in several countries, including Belgium, Denmark, England and several Swiss cantons, no formal Separation has taken place.[13]

Perhaps the most significant stage in the dissolution of Christendom was also the most drawn out: the loosening of ties between the culture and the church.

> In Christendom, Christianity was a common language, shared by the devout, the lukewarm and even the secretly sceptical, through which a wide range of social needs could be met, and which provided generally accepted concepts and symbols. These could be drawn upon by more or less everyone,

> especially in times of collective crisis, or in situations of personal danger or tragedy.... In "Christendom," to be baptised not only marked entry into the church: it also meant entry into society.
>
> The decline of Christendom has meant that Christianity has been gradually losing its status as a lingua franca, and has tended to become a local language used by those who are professing Christians, but not understood by others. This process began as early as the 1790s, with the short-lived but extremely intensive campaign to "dechristianise" France.[14]

McLeod declares what I believe we can enunciate as a reliable principle: "Widespread anti-clericalism is to be expected in any society where the church is wealthy and influential."[15] Similarly, the close association of the church with the established order has always proven to be a corrosive situation—for the church.

WHY THE DECLINE?

Conventional wisdom and common sense suggest that the people stopped going to church because they no longer believed what the churches taught them. Perhaps the causal mechanism was really closer to the opposite: they stopped believing because they stopped going.
Simon Green[16]

But why has Christendom declined in Western Europe? Auguste Comte, and later Emile Durkheim and Max Weber, proposed what has come to be known as the secularization (secularisation in the British spelling) thesis. Simply put, this thesis posits that religious belief and institutions generally are declining in modern societies. This line of thought was further developed by Bryan Wilson and Peter Berger in the 60s and 70s and is today defended vigorously by British sociologist Steve Bruce, whom we quote herein. Bruce argued in *Religion in the Modern World*, subtitled *From Cathedrals to Cults*, that the binding force of religion has been lost to an "irreversible" trend towards individualism. This individualism has fragmented religion and led to a consumer-oriented approach of selectivity from many options suited to the individual's preferences. (We will see in later chapters how priests and preachers pander to this.)

Not all scholars accept the secularization thesis. Some view the European experience as unique to Europe—a pattern that cannot be expected to replicate itself elsewhere. Others acknowledge the reality of secularization but reject other components of the thesis as to how it evolves. Still others insist that the state of the church is in its own hands—a view much closer to my own—and that decline is not inevitable. Some have emphasized the importance of the ideas and attitudes that originated in the Enlightenment as corrupting influences—a view that I also, in part, share and that we address.

Four reasons have been proposed for the decline of Christendom with industrialization and the growth of large cities.

> The first, and least controversial, argument is that the dramatic demographic shifts of the nineteenth century presented the churches with logistical problems which they failed to solve, or which were exacerbated by being addressed in ways that proved counterproductive. Insufficient churches

> and schools were built, and insufficient numbers of new clergy were recruited to meet the needs of fast-growing cities and industrial regions; high rates of mobility within those regions meant that migrants to the cities found it difficult to establish links with any particular clergyman or congregation.
>
> A second argument is that great cities are by their nature pluralistic: they lend themselves to the formation of numerous discrete subcultures, as supervision of morals and religion by employers, magistrates or the church is no longer possible. This in turn leads to a relativistic outlook, in terms of which all religious and moral absolutes are called in question. A third argument focuses on the major advances in living standards and life expectancy that have become possible in modern industrial societies. As a result of these advances…[t]he crises in which people feel the need to "turn to" religion have become more infrequent. Religion consequently has become less salient to most people's lives. The fourth and most ambitious argument proposes that industrialisation has brought about a mental revolution, as a result of which a rationalistic and mechanistic way of thinking has come to prevail, and all forms of supernaturalism have lost their credibility.[17]

Interestingly, for those who may have wondered how so many political parties in highly secular modern Europe ended up with "Christian" in their names, there was a pervasive outlook in the immediate wake of World War II that the way to rebuild and avoid further cataclysms would be to reconstitute the Christian basis for European society. This led to the development of Christian Democratic Parties, many of which retain great political power long after the reasons for their appellation have been abandoned.

Great trauma and fear are destructive of pride. Such upheavals nurture humility and a corollary interest in the spiritual. Both are gradually relinquished with growing material success and a sense of security. Post-war Europe clearly reflects this, as does, on a much smaller, briefer, scale, post-9-11 America.

A meeting of the German Christian Democratic Union (CDU). *In the immediate wake of World War II a pervasive view held that the way to rebuild and avoid further cataclysms would be to reconstitute the Christian basis for European society. This led to the development of Christian Democratic Parties, many of which retain great political power long after the reasons for their appellation have been abandoned.*

CDU meeting in Germany. CC

WHEN DID IT BEGIN?

For the historian of religious decline, there is no period in history as important as the 1960s.
Callum Brown[18]

A more precise question would be When did secularization accelerate in a significant and conspicuous manner so as to become irrefutable? The answer, it seems universally among historians and sociologists, is the 1960s; especially what some call the "long 60s" beginning in the mid-fifties and stretching to the mid-seventies. We will resort to Hugh McLeod's review of the writings of individual scholars on a sampling of European nations and how each scholar perceives secularization has played out in their respective nations.

BRITAIN

The historian Callum G. Brown cites 1963 as the approximate date Britain entered the "brave new world of secular secularization."[19] The 1960s in his judgment is the single most important era in the history of religious decline and, for Britain, reflected decline in "virtually all indicators."[20] One of the indicators of Britain's religious decline was church attendance: "It might be fair to estimate that the proportion of the population attending church and Sunday school in mainland Britain on a given Sunday stood at around 40–45 per cent in 1851, and fell thereafter to about 30 per cent by 1900, 15 per cent by 1950, 11.3 per cent in 1979–84, and to less than 10 per cent in the 1990s."[21]

Steve Bruce described the British experience as "naturally occurring" in contrast to Ataturk's Turkey or the Soviet Union.[22] He adds, "Britain has now been secular for long enough for us to be sure that this is an enduring trend worthy of sociological explanation and for it to serve as a test bed for theories about the obstinacy of secularization."[23] The evidence suggests to Bruce that "unless trends that have held since at least the 1950s are soon reversed, major British denominations are only a generation from extrication [*sic—extinction*]."[24]

Church Membership, United Kingdom, 1900–2000

Year	Members (000)	Population (000)	Members (as % of population)
1900	8,664	32,237	27
2000	5,862	59,122	10

Source: Brierley (1999: Tables 2.12 and 4.10.2)[25]

Bruce believes that Methodism will become extinct in Britain around the year 2031 and the "Church of England will by then be reduced to a trivial voluntary association with a large portfolio of heritage property. Regular churchgoers will be too few to show up in representative national survey samples. Perhaps then the critics of the secularization paradigm will recognize that, however convincing our explanations of decline, decline is not a sociological myth."[26]

The almost complete collapse of Methodism and evangelicalism in Britain is especially ironic when juxtaposed with their history—an extraordinary and colorful history of service—in Great

Britain. Bruce first makes the point that "Sacrifice, commitment and community are intimately related. Shared beliefs sustain the community, which in turn extracts commitment and sacrifice from the individual. Sacrifice reinforces the sense of commitment and of belonging to a community, which strengthens the beliefs."[27] He then contrasts this principle—so characteristic of evangelical behavior and belief—with the rapid burgeoning of New Age belief in Britain.

> One way to illustrate the point is to compare the impact of the New Age with that of another countercultural religious movement. In the late eighteenth and throughout the nineteenth centuries groups of British evangelicals banded together to campaign against what they believed to be un-Christian aspects of industrialization (Smith 1998). The religious motives of William Wilberforce MP and fellow reformers were so obvious that they were known (both derisively and affectionately) as the "Clapham sect." There were two aspects to the evangelical improvement of industrial society. One was philanthropic. Evangelicals gave large amounts of money and time to voluntary activity.... The second strand was legislative. Although the evangelical temperament was in favour of personal philanthropy (which was held to benefit the giver as much as the recipient), Wilberforce and his colleagues appreciated that the grossest abuses of the industrial age could be prevented only by legislation. Hence their campaign to ban slavery.
>
> New Agers and Victorian evangelicals alike condemn their worlds. But the latter were able to unite around very specific goals and devoted vast amounts of time and money to promote them. Their value-consensus meant that the movement organizations they formed exerted influence beyond

"Heroes of the Slave Trade Abolition" from the National Portrait Gallery of London at *http://www.npg.org.uk/collections/search/portrait.php?search=ap&npgno=D9338*

William Wilberforce (center) and the Clapham Sect *led the fight against slavery in Britain. Driven by their Christian faith they prompted derision from the secularists of their time—and the "religious" hypocrites—as well as affection from those who rightly perceived the compassion behind their passion and courage. The Clapham Sect was countercultural to a significant degree—an attribute that should always characterize the church and the Christian, but which rarely does in the West.*

> that of their number as individuals. New Agers are highly critical of many aspects of the modern world but make little or no effort to change it and such efforts as they do make are not amplified by being concerted. Or, to put it rhetorically, where are the New Age schools, nurseries, communes, colleges, ecological housing associations, subsistence farming centres, criminal resettlement houses, women's refuges, practical anti-racism projects and urban renewal programmes?[28]
> ...
> Methodism profoundly changed those people who adopted it and it profoundly changed their society. The New Age has changed very little.[29]

Callum G. Brown's conclusions about the future of faith in Britain are also sobering and consistent with the themes of this work.

> The bald statement is this: Secularization fillets the religious spine out of the body of human culture. When that happens, as in Britain since the 1960s, it is not possible to continue to study the subject by looking at the churches, church membership, religious observance or opinion polls. The basis of the academic subject has fundamentally changed. The churches are now less relevant; indeed, to be frank, they become increasingly irrelevant with every year. They are so marginal to the place of religion in society that the academic game has to change fundamentally.[30]

SWEDEN

According to the sociologist Eva M. Hamberg,[31] and apparently the overwhelming majority of historians and sociologists who have studied European religiosity, Sweden is perhaps the most secular of all European states.

> In 1990, only 15 per cent of the adult Swedish population (aged 16–74 years) said that they believed in the existence of a personal God, 27 per cent believed in heaven, and 19 per cent in the resurrection of the dead. Only 4 per cent attended church weekly, while another 6 per cent did so monthly. A similar pattern can be found for prayer and Bible reading. In 1990 only 10 per cent of adult Swedes said that they often prayed, while 49 per cent never prayed and 10 per cent hardly ever did so. Bible reading is even less common: according to a Swedish survey undertaken in the mid-1980s, only 8 per cent of the adult population read the Bible at least once a month.[32]

Hamberg adds, "Thus, for many of those Swedes who still believe in God, this belief is more or less unimportant."[33] Significantly, she notes that traditional Christian beliefs have been supplanted by an "interest in various occult phenomena, such as astrology, ghosts and extra-terrestrial beings visiting the earth....Thus, both a decline in traditional Christian beliefs and an increase in other types of religious faith [as well as the bizarre] characterize Swedish society today. This process may also be described as an increasing individualisation of life-philosophies or world-views."[34]

Here is another reference to the increasing "individualization" of modern Western societies. This form of individualization is simply another manifestation of the reality—or another way of saying—that the Western citizen is self-absorbed. True self-sacrifice is anathema to his thinking.

With what at first glance seems supreme irony, Hamberg notes that "While the level of church attendance is very low in Sweden, the overwhelming majority of the population, 80 per cent, are members of the Church of Sweden."[35] However, she adds, not unexpectedly, "The majority [have] little or no confidence in the church!"[36]

This is highly significant and should not surprise us. Though many scholars have taken for granted that religious pluralism undermines religiosity, others argue that the evidence suggests just the opposite: religious pluralism stimulates rather than retards religious participation. America is a classic supporting example. Eva M. Hamberg quotes a fellow sociologist: "There is ample evidence that in societies with putative monopoly faiths, religious indifference, not piety, is rife."[37]

Increased availability of services and a diversity of services have been shown in studies to correlate with higher rates of attendance. Hamberg concludes, "Thus, a rich supply of worship services seems to lead to increased attendance. Possibly, the very low levels of church attendance which generally prevail in Sweden may be due less to a general lack of demand for worship services than to a lack in demand for the types of services which usually are provided." Hamberg adds, "Although probably several factors contribute to explain the religious situation in contemporary Sweden, empirical data indicate that this situation may *at least partly* be understood as the result of a long period of religious monopoly: for centuries the religious market has been dominated by the Church of Sweden."[38]

I believe this evidence points us in the right direction. But regardless of the underlying causes, the results can be strange—even bizarre: "For instance, a world-view where human beings are no longer regarded as being intrinsically different from animals now seems to be fairly widespread in

Image taken by Henrik Sendelbach. *http://commons.wikimedia.org/wiki/File:Harnosands_domkyrka_interior.jpg*

Empty cathedral in Härnösands domkyrka (cathedral of Härnösand). *The sociologist Eva Hamberg notes about the government-supported Swedish church that "While the level of church attendance is very low in Sweden, the overwhelming majority of the population, 80 percent, are members of the Church of Sweden." However, she adds, not unexpectedly, "The majority [have] little or no confidence in the church!"*

Sweden. In recent years, several surveys have shown that only a minority of Swedes think that human beings have greater value than animals."[39] Coupled with this, studies have shown that "Swedes see good health as the most important value in life. In the 1986 survey, the respondents were asked what they regarded as most important in their lives. The value most often given (mentioned by 45 per cent) was health. About a third mentioned families or friends and about a quarter of the respondents gave answers related to their economic situation."[40] Parenthetically, it is noteworthy that health was a central value of Nietzsche's desolate worldview. When there is nothing to believe in beyond one's self, what else is there?

IRELAND

Ireland does not fit the mould. Would the Irish have it otherwise? Sheridan Gilley notes that Ireland is distinctive in two ways:

> [F]irst, in the complete identification of Irish nationalism with Irish Catholicism; and second, in the high levels of religious practice in Catholic Ireland until very recently, with over 90 per cent of the population attending mass every Sunday. Ireland has been unusual if not unique since the sixteenth century as a country in which the Counter-Reformation largely prevailed in the very teeth of persecution by a Protestant state, so that its Catholic faith was forged in the fire of suffering.[41]

But this Catholicism was different. Though De Valera wrote the Church into the new Irish Constitution in 1937, "the Constitution did not speak of the Catholic Church as 'the one true church.' ...Instead, it guaranteed 'not to endow any religion'..."[42] and recognized the Church of Ireland, as well as the Presbyterian, Methodist, and Quaker iterations of Christianity by their names—and surprisingly in view of the times—as well as Judaism. This was all the more significant when we learn that all of these non-Catholics together amounted to no more than seven percent of the Irish.

Catholicism has continued to exercise not only influence with the society but power in the state. Legislation has continually tended to uphold Catholic values and beliefs. But fissures exist, not the least of which have been caused by pedophile priests. Observers acknowledge a growing space between what at one time were inseparable terms—"Irish-Catholic."[43]

THE NETHERLANDS

Peter van Rooden speaks frankly of the toleration of pornography, prostitution, abortion, euthanasia, and drugs—all of which are legalized to some degree in the Netherlands. Van Rooden observes that in the early twentieth century the Dutch reflected a high level of religious interest and practice. Yet as the century unfolded there was a relatively rapid decline in those who openly identified with the church. Today, with the Scandinavian countries, the Netherlands is among the most secular nations in Europe. Though there has been a backlash against the dissipations alluded to above—which some Dutch now consider a national embarrassment—and a concomitant effort to limit them, these movements appear more pragmatically secular than religious in their motivations.

Amsterdam's red light district. *One of the more overt examples of the consequences of rejection of Christianity and the embrace of secularism, this district is notorious in the Western world, not simply for promiscuity and perversion but for the fact that all is legal and culturally accepted.*

Netherlands Red Light District. CC.

GERMANY

The German fall from religiosity is all the more striking inasmuch as this was the home of the Reformation and Nazism, of Adolph Hitler and Dietrich Bonhoeffer, and throughout the twentieth century, the locus of much theological thought and scholarship. Martin Greschat noted that the theologian Karl Barth profoundly influenced religious perceptions in Germany with the *Darmstädter Wort* of 1947.

In a related vein, Greschat described the views of Iain Wilson, the army chaplain to the Protestant churches in the British Occupied Zone, who, in the late forties, took a position strikingly consistent with themes of this work: "All churches in the western world, in terms of their institutions and expressions of life, were deeply rooted in their respective national, cultural and social environment, 'they stake their life upon the continued existence of those social patterns into which they have so closely woven themselves, instead of upon the abiding truth of God.'"[44]

Similarly, Paul Graf Yorck von Wartenburg, the managing director of the *Evangelisches Hilfswerk* (Protestant Aid) in the French Occupied Zone "called…a 'truly great and serious undertaking'" the efforts toward "'disentangling the Church from the secular structures and values and liberating her for her calling, to announce the good news to the poor.' However, the Declaration would not

Karl Barth. *The German fall from religiosity is all the more striking inasmuch as this was the home of the Reformation and Nazism, of Adolph Hitler and Dietrich Bonhoeffer, and throughout the twentieth century, the locus of much theological thought and scholarship. Theologian Barth profoundly influenced religious perceptions in Germany with the* Darmstädter Wort *of 1947.*

Karl Barth. Photo by Maria Netter. CC

really encourage this important and proper intention for it remained too much attached to 'the securities of a bourgeois, state-oriented existence.'"[45] So it has proven to be—and has proven to be throughout the history of the Christian church in Western civilization.

FRANCE

Unexpectedly, French sociologists and historians have examined the "dechristianisation" of France by scrutinizing its discernible effects on death. Michel Vovelle argued that the language of wills in eighteenth-century France suggested that this process was already under way that early.[46] Thomas Kselman took this further by referring to the funeral of one of France's most famous writers.

> The civil funeral and entombment of Victor Hugo in 1885 was a culminating event in the emergence of an alternative to Catholicism as the source of a sacred atmosphere for the cult of the dead. His services drew over one million Parisians to what may have been the largest demonstration in nineteenth-century France. In the twenty years following Hugo's funeral the politicians of the Third Republic continued to dismantle the Catholic hegemony over the cult of the dead.[47]

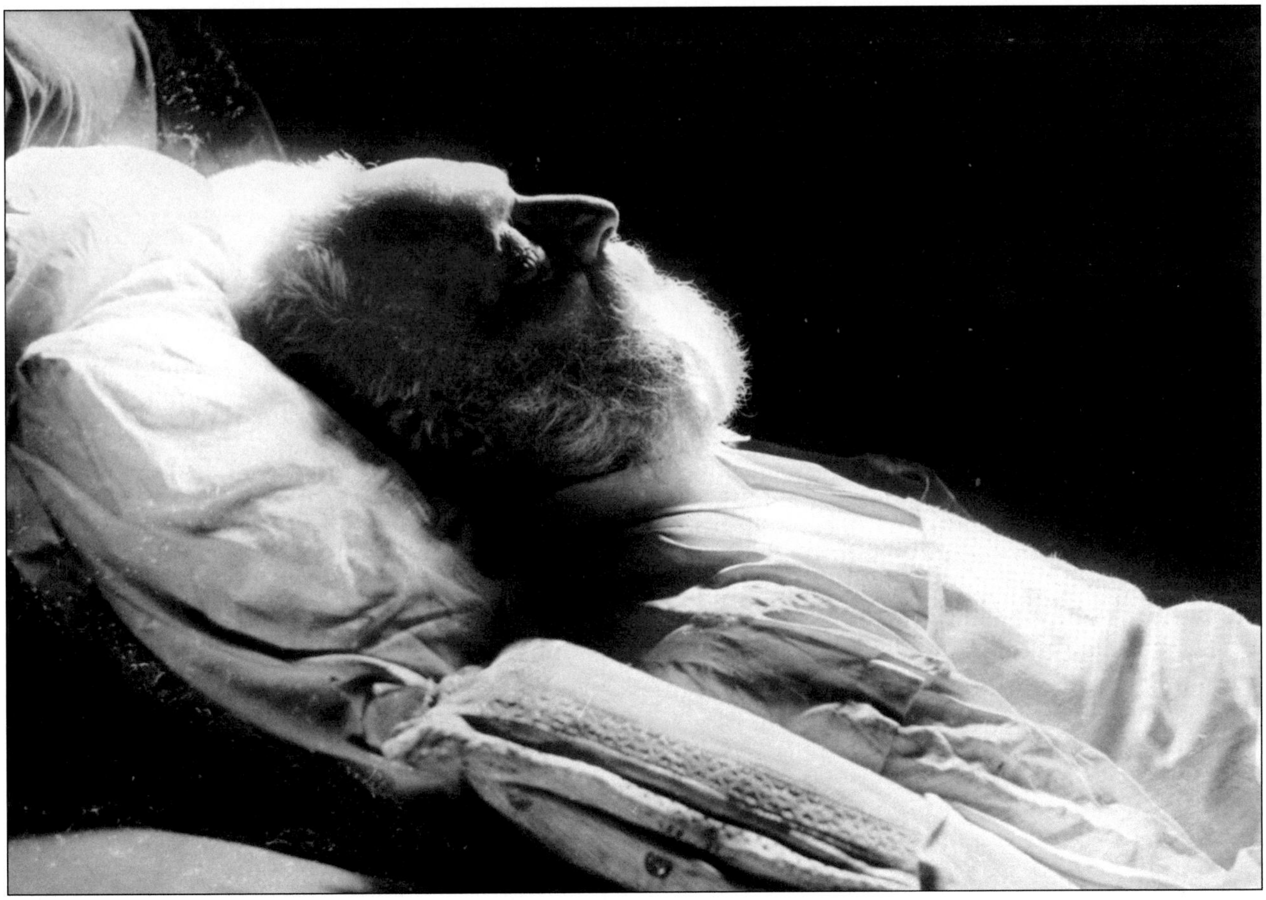

CC

Victor Hugo on his deathbed. *The one inescapable reality the atheist and the believer can agree upon—the end of man. Hugo's funeral drew perhaps a million Parisians and was significant for its rejection of Catholic ritual for a secular "cult of the dead." One of the early indicators of the decline of Christian faith in Europe, it set a precedent for other political and cultural leaders.*

In an observation we would expect—and a consummate understatement—Kselman explained, "The French Revolution clearly had a major impact on the status of Christianity in France. The process of 'stripping the altars,' to borrow a phrase from Eamon Duffy, broke traditional relations between priests and people and produced a generation more inclined to independence and scepticism."[48] Though the authority of the Church had been profoundly limited, "The French were left free to choose a Catholic service and a tomb marked by Christian symbols, and most continued to do so."[49]

World War I confronted the increasingly secular French with one of life's painful choices.

> As passed on to the twentieth century, the cult of the dead proved to be a potent force in the face of the catastrophic bloodletting that occurred in France between 1914 and 1918. Historians who look for dramatic breaks in cultural history have generally identified World War I as a crucial turning-point in the creation of "modernity," understood as a sceptical frame of mind which dissolves traditional certainties about politics, art and religion. If the Enlightenment, the Revolution and the laic legislation of the Third Republic did not "dechristianise" death, perhaps this process was at work in the trenches and battlefields of World War I. But if we follow the research of Annette Becker and Jay Winter, the carnage of the war produced not so much a modernist impulse as a reversion to principles and beliefs inherited from the past. The cult of the dead as it emerged from the war, and as displayed in cemeteries and memorial monuments, found an important place for Christianity, though not one that allowed it to monopolise the work of consolation.[50]
>
> ...
>
> Thousands of crosses, arranged in neat lines as in military formation, decorate the individual graves of the vast majority of soldiers.[51]

By the late twentieth century, France's first Socialist president faced that which confronts every individual eventually. Francois Mitterand, in a decision that would appear typical of an astute politician still intent on running for office, chose to project religion and the secular, even in his death.

> Mitterand might have been expected to honour the tradition of the French left and forego a Catholic funeral and burial service. After all, he had the precedent of Victor Hugo's civil burial a hundred years before, an event used by the anti-clericals of the Third Republic to help forge a dignified alternative to the Catholic ritual of death and burial. But as a number of recent biographies have made clear, Mitterand never entirely escaped the pious Catholic milieu of his origins, a tradition to which he showed himself faithful in arranging both a private mass for his family in his home at Jarnac, and a public mass attended by foreign dignitaries in Paris at the cathedral of Notre Dame. It was typical of Mitterand to have balanced this reversion to his Catholic past with a separate ceremony of remembrance for his associates on the political left, held appropriately at the Place de la Bastille.[52]

We might expect this of a politician, especially one so devoted to power and prestige as Mitterand. But this straddling of the fence, as it were, may not be entirely explained in terms of a lifetime of habituation to political considerations. It might be—as some human beings are wont to attempt—a hedging of one's bets: if you are not sure what to believe then at least try to appease the god you do not personally know. Then again it might reflect a longing for something not fully expressed while the person lived—and pathetically, tragically, never fulfilled.

Consistent with what we have learned of behavior in other secular European cultures, we are told, "Recent surveys indicate that, despite signs of eroding belief, a clear majority of the French still identify themselves as Catholic."[53]

Michel Lagrée raised the issue of the impact of technology on Catholicism in France. On the one hand the philosopher Henri Bergson concluded that advancements in technical progress liberated humanity from "the fear of not feeding its hunger," thereby freeing men from an externally imposed asceticism to pursue spiritual enlightenment. Subsequent history does not corroborate this view, nor was it shared by Catholic chaplains in rural 1950s France who saw in technology an inducement to turn away from, rather than toward, faith. Lagrée observed that comparing religion and technology leads to a "contradiction": "Some hope to find in technical progress a starting point for a new type of evangelization, while on the contrary others see in it a fearful dissolution of ancient Christian civilization."[54] We might query, Why can it not include elements of both? The individual response is the key. What choice does the individual make in the face of new circumstances?

A MASTER NARRATIVE?

Jeffrey Cox provided a convenient concluding summation to this review:

> One of the great stories of modern European history is the emergence of openly declared and publicly sanctioned irreligion and indifference. Popular and elite resistance to religious ideas, to religious mobilisation, to religious institutions, characterise much of modern European history. In large areas of modern Europe, religious men and women who attempt to create new religious institutions or promote religious ideas run into a brick wall of resistance and indifference.[55]

Toynbee and Sorokin would likely say this is not *one* of the great stories of modern European history but *the* great story of this era. Though historians and sociologists know *what* has happened, there is widespread dispute as to *why* it has happened. There is no broadly accepted "master narrative" to explain the decline of the Christian religion in Europe or whether it is reversible. Related to these great questions is another: Is the European experience distinct, or is it the precursor to a similar experience for America? The fact that the features of modernity are just as apparent in America, yet without the same level of secularization as in Europe, suggests that perhaps the secularization thesis is not correct insofar, at least, as it is deemed inevitable.

In an intriguing postscript—and an observation that is highly significant to the church generally and to the

By George Grantham Bain Collection. PD

The philosopher Henri Bergson *concluded that advancements in technical progress liberated humanity from "the fear of not feeding its hunger," thereby freeing men from an externally imposed asceticism to pursue spiritual enlightenment. Subsequent history does not corroborate this view, nor was it shared by Catholic chaplains in rural 1950s France who saw in technology an inducement to turn away from, rather than toward, faith. The chaplains rather than Bergson have been proven right.*

purposes of this book—Cox quotes Simon Green regarding the British religion: "Conventional wisdom and common sense suggest that the people stopped going to church because they no longer believed what the churches taught them. Perhaps the causal mechanism was really closer to the opposite: they stopped believing because they stopped going."[56]

But of course this raises the question of why they stopped going. Part of the answer almost certainly lies in the fact that the biblical injunction against being "unequally yoked" (2 Corinthians 6:14–7:1 KJV) has been passed over lightly by the church in most of its manifestations in the West. Thus the Western institutional manifestations of the Christian faith incrementally lost credibility in the eyes of millions. Hopefully, we can answer our question more fully—and will strive to do so—in the ensuing chapters.

But this we can know for sure: The relationship between exposure to religious beliefs and values and human choices to live a morally upright life of faith is not only biblical but critical—and central to the ascent or descent of morality and faith in the individual as well as the collective life of a society.

The truth in this has powerful and civilization-shaking—and -shaping—implications.

END NOTES
CHAPTER 21

1 Hugh McLeod, "Introduction," in *The Decline of Christendom in Western Europe, 1750–2000*, ed. McLeod and Ustorf (Cambridge: Cambridge University Press, 2003), 11.
2 Wilson, cited in Martin Greschatlain, "The Potency of 'Christendom': the Darmstädter Wort," in *The Decline of Christendom in Western Europe, 1750–2000*, 138.
3 McLeod, "Introduction," 1.
4 Steve Bruce, *God Is Dead: Secularization in the West* (Oxford: Wiley-Blackwell, 2002), 118.
5 Bruce, *God Is Dead*, 118.
6 Callum G. Brown, "The Secularization Decade: What the 1960's Have Done to the Study of Religious History," in *The Decline of Christendom in Western Europe, 1750–2000*, 36.
7 McLeod, "Introduction," 3–4.
8 McLeod, "Introduction," 4.
9 Yves Lambert, "New Christianity, Indifference and Diffused Spirituality" in *The Decline of Christendom in Western Europe, 1750–2000*, 69–72.
10 McLeod, "Introduction," 3–4.
11 McLeod, "Introduction," 4–5.
12 McLeod, "Introduction," 8.
13 McLeod, "Introduction," 8–9.
14 McLeod, "Introduction," 213.
15 S. J. D. Green, *Religion in the Age of Decline: Organization and Experience in Industrial Yorkshire, 1870–1920* (Cambridge: Cambridge University Press, 1996), 17.
16 McLeod, "Introduction," 13.
17 McLeod, "Introduction," 16–17.
18 Brown, "The Secularization Decade," 29.
19 Brown, "The Secularization Decade," 29.
20 Brown, "The Secularization Decade," 31.
21 Brown, "The Secularization Decade," 31.
22 Bruce, *God Is Dead*, xii–xiii.
23 Bruce, *God Is Dead*, xiii.
24 Bruce, *God Is Dead*, 60.
25 As shown in Bruce, *God Is Dead*, p. 67.
26 Bruce, *God Is Dead*, 74.
27 Bruce, *God Is Dead*, 95.
28 Bruce, *God Is Dead*, 97.
29 Bruce, *God Is Dead*, 98.
30 Brown, "The Secularization Decade," 36.
31 Eva M. Hamberg, "Christendom in Decline: The Swedish Case," in *The Decline of Christendom in Western Europe, 1750–2000*, 47.
32 Hamberg, "Christendom in Decline: The Swedish Case," 48.
33 Hamberg, "Christendom in Decline: The Swedish Case," 48–50.
34 Hamberg, "Christendom in Decline: The Swedish Case," 49.
35 Hamberg, "Christendom in Decline: The Swedish Case," 49.
36 McLeod, *The Decline of Christendom in Western Europe, 1750–2000*, 50.
37 McLeod, *The Decline of Christendom in Western Europe, 1750–2000*, 56.

38 Roger Finke and Rodney Stark, *The Churching of America, 1776–1990: Winners and Losers in Our Religious Economy*, 59.
39 Hamberg, "Christendom in Decline: The Swedish Case," 53.
40 Hamberg, "Christendom in Decline: The Swedish Case," 54.
41 Sheridan Gilley, "Catholicism in Ireland," in *The Decline of Christendom in Western Europe, 1750–2000*, 99.
42 Gilley, "Catholicism in Ireland," 107.
43 Gilley, "Catholicism in Ireland," 109.
44 Martin Greschat, "The Potency of 'Christendom': the Darmstädter Wort," in *The Decline of Christendom in Western Europe, 1750–2000*, 138.
45 Greschat, "The Potency of 'Christendom': the Darmstädter Wort," 145.
46 Michel Vovelle, *Piété baroque et déchristianisation en Provence au XVIIe siècle* (Paris: Seuil, 1978).
47 Thomas Kselman, "The Dechristianisation of Death in Modern France," in *The Decline of Christendom in Western Europe, 1750–2000*, 153.
48 Kselman, "The Dechristianisation of Death in Modern France," 149.
49 Kselman, "The Dechristianisation of Death in Modern France," 154.
50 Kselman, "The Dechristianisation of Death in Modern France," 155.
51 Kselman, "The Dechristianisation of Death in Modern France," 155.
52 Kselman, "The Dechristianisation of Death in Modern France," 157.
53 Kselman, "The Dechristianisation of Death in Modern France," 163.
54 Bergson, cited in Michel Lagrée, *The Decline of Christendom in Western Europe, 1750–2000*, 163.
55 Green, cited in Jeffrey Cox, "Master Narratives" in *The Decline of Christendom in Western Europe, 1750–2000*, 213.
56 Green, cited in Jeffrey Cox, "Master Narratives" in *The Decline of Christendom in Western Europe, 1750–2000*, 214.

CHAPTER

22

A PEOPLE SET APART—OR INDISTINGUISHABLE FROM?

...it is the sign of the dollar rather than the cross that now marshals the forces of Western civilization.
Christopher Dawson[1]

...but to understand the mass of the population it is not self-conscious irreligion that is important. It is indifference. The primary cause of indifference is the lack of religious socialization and the lack of constant background affirmation of beliefs.
Steve Bruce[2]

The Western Christian is now virtually indistinguishable from the rest of the society in appearance, tastes, entertainment, divorce and family dysfunction, and the materialistic drive to "succeed." Indeed, one of the few remaining distinctions is simply his willingness to characterize himself as a Christian when polls or surveys are taken.

A now-trite aphoristic question was once asked among evangelicals, "If you were accused of being a Christian, would there be enough evidence to convict you?" Of course the problem with the question is the standard that is applied. Were the standard to be those features of attitude or life that are accepted as norms by the Western church at large, then many could legitimately say yes. Were the standards to be those contained in Christ's life, the Sermon on the Mount, and his many teachings, many would be exculpated. That prosecutions for being a practicing Christian are the norm in some places in the world—and, if some of our quoted observers are correct, may become a feature of Western civilization soon—implies that the question may become more than a trivial test of belief. Should such prosecutions ensue, the sheep will surely be separated from the goats with rapidity.

A EUROPEAN PERSPECTIVE

European scholars like Steve Bruce have perspectives on the American church that at once share the limitations of looking in from outside, as well as some advantages. Typically, external observers see features with greater clarity while simultaneously making mistakes based on a failure to understand the unfamiliar.

But there is little we could contest in Bruce's observations: "If we leave aside the social, moral and political behaviour of its citizens, the United States has every appearance of being unusually godly. Americans are more likely than their European counterparts to go to church, for example, and American politicians routinely invoke God and lay claim to religious identities."[3] But that one statement is especially telling in the distinction drawn between the "appearance" and the actual "social, moral and political behaviour." That there is a distinction that is more than just an expression of the weaknesses of man—a view we strongly affirm herein—tells us at once why the church in America is weakening.

Bruce continued by making four points:

> First, there is ample evidence of Christianity in the USA losing power, prestige and popularity. Secondly, there is ample evidence that Christianity in the USA has changed in ways expected by the secularization paradigm: greater emphasis on individual choice, a shift from other-worldly to this-worldly salvation, and an increasing therapeutic orientation to religion. Thirdly, for all the sound and fury that accompanied the "new Christian right" (NCR), as a cluster of religious right organizations that mobilized in the late 1970s were known, there has been no significant reversal of the major trend of religion becoming marginal to the operation of the social system. Finally, to the extent that the USA does differ from Europe, the differences can be explained in ways that are perfectly consistent with the secularization paradigm. The key point is that the federal and diffuse structure of the USA allows conservative Christians the freedom to construct distinct subcultures in which their faith retains some of the hegemony that Christianity once had in pre-industrial Europe.[4]

Even as we avoid being drawn into the argument over the soundness of the secularization theory, much less its applicability to the U.S., we must acknowledge there is surely merit in all four of these observations. Bruce also cannot be refuted in even more pointed observations.

> At the same time as the faith was being stripped of its traditional supernaturalism, it was also losing its behavioural distinctiveness. Asceticism was out. Churchgoers no longer gave up smoking, drinking, dancing or going to the theatre. They wore the same clothes as other people, lived in the same kinds of houses, and had the same increasingly liberal moral and ethical standards. They got divorced.[5]
>
> A Barna survey in 2000 showed that born-again adults were more likely than others to have experienced a divorce.[6]

Bruce's conclusion: "Privatization, individualism and relativism are now affecting the U.S. churches in the way they did the British churches in the middle of the twentieth century." Those three forces, he declares, "weakened religion by undermining the cohesion of religious organizations, reducing the degree of background affirmation provided for any worldview in the flow of everyday life, and weakening the commitment of individuals to ensuring the successful transmission of their religious culture intact to their children."[7]

PD-art

Hans Holbein's portrait of Henry VIII. *Arrogant, self-centered and dissipated, Henry VIII broke with the Catholic Church and formed his own so that he might divorce his wife. This same doctrine of personal convenience and expediency is behind the appalling truth that the Western Christian is now virtually indistinguishable from the other members of the culture in appearance, tastes, entertainment, divorce and family dysfunction, and the materialistic drive to "succeed."*

THE TRUTH, THE WHOLE TRUTH, AND NOTHING BUT THE TRUTH?

Strong conceptions of sin require not only a conception of a demanding God but also the idea of a powerful, and tempting, Satan. Yet polls routinely show that while Americans frequently believe in the existence of heaven, they are not that sure about the reality of hell.
Alan Wolfe[8]

Like Bruce, Professor Alan Wolfe sees the contradictions between the professions of belief on one hand and the practice on the other. But more telling is the confusion in the modern American church between what is truly biblical and what are the sloughs of the culture. The relationship between faith and morality is of great interest to Wolfe—as it is to millions of Americans (consciously or subconsciously) who have no faith, and who wonder, Does it really mean anything to be a Christian? Is religion, Wolfe wonders, a genuine relationship with the Creator of the Universe or simply a set of beliefs?

> A debate over the [relationship between religion and personal morality] can be traced to a widely cited 1969 article; expecting to find that such variables as church attendance and belief in an afterlife would be associated with low rates of juvenile delinquency, its authors discovered that religious belief had little or no relationship to what society labeled as deviant behavior. ...The results [of subsequent studies] are inconsistent and puzzling, depending, as is often the case with such research, on the wording of questions in surveys or the samples chosen for analysis. ...there is, for example, if anything, a tendency for evangelicals to divorce in greater amounts, or to have more children out of wedlock, than other religious believers. On the other hand, many studies have found that people who attend church regularly and indicate a strong belief in God are less likely to report high rates of gambling, alcohol and drug consumption, tax cheating, and domestic violence. Perhaps the fairest way to summarize the empirical data is to say that religious faith has a slight, but nonetheless positive, effect on personal morality.[9]

We would hope that there is a "nonetheless positive" correlation between individual behavior and the Christian faith. But to characterize it as "slight" should be no consolation to the church in America; and, I suspect, Professor Wolfe, speaking broadly, has been fair in that characterization.

Professor Wolfe also mentions embarrassments any evangelical Christian or Catholic should expect. In the process, however, he fails to note a deeper infirmity than those that appear so blatantly on the surface.

> The prevalence of widespread cheating at a predominantly conservative Christian university would seem to confirm the views of those who believe that religion, far from having a positive influence on personal moral conduct, is more likely to produce hypocrisy than honesty. For all the talk of faith-based initiatives and charitable choice, they would point out, religion's record on personal morality cannot be evaluated without considering such real-world events as the financial scandals associated with Jimmy Swaggert *[sic]* and Jim and Tammy Faye Bakker, the persistence of racism or anti-Semitism among various religious denominations, or the all-too-frequent examples of pedophilia found in the Catholic priesthood and the immoral (by any standard) efforts of the Church hierarchy to keep

Shutterstock

Professor Alan Wolfe observed, "...there is...if anything, a tendency for evangelicals to divorce in greater amounts, or to have more children out of wedlock, than other religious believers," evidence again that even in the most sacrosanct institution—marriage and the family—the American church is failing. Here too, Christians are much like the culture.

them secret. If anything, people of this persuasion believe, faith is more likely to be associated with immorality than its opposite, since it causes so many people to close their eyes to the kind of self-examination that genuine morality requires.[10]

All of this points us again to the difference between true faith—and its inherent relationship of the individual with the Supreme Being—and simple religion, the professed adherence to doctrinal views and belief systems. They are not the same. The latter truly can be often "associated with immorality" and a lack of the humility that would produce the "self-examination that genuine morality requires." We are here of course talking about a central theme of this work.

The confusion in the secular world caused by the church's failure to distinguish itself as wholly in the former rather than the latter category underlies the church's failure to profoundly influence the course of Western civilization.

To be sure, "religion" offers expediency and a convenient fig-leaf of hypocrisy to cover any number of sins; and many will be drawn to it for precisely these reasons. When the church panders to these motives, wittingly or unwittingly, it is debasing the integrity of the Christian faith. The marketing, megachurches, promotional techniques, extravagance in buildings, romance with numbers, and unwillingness to speak bluntly of sin and judgment, which characterize the Western church, are all manifestations of this pandering. To use Lincoln's reputed phrasing, you "cannot fool all of the people all of the time"—and many in the secular world are not fooled, even if many in the church are.

Of far greater significance for the church are not the scandals and the scandalous behavior of high profile "Christian" leaders, but the fawning gullibility of those who follow them. Part of the problem with the attitudes Professor Wolfe has exposed is the underlying deficiency in sound biblical teaching, which is the consequence once again of the infiltration of the culture's influence. Thus many churches and Christian leaders avoid the emphatic and repeated noting of God as judgmental and a being to be feared. This abstemiousness with the biblical truth ignores the fact that Christ made many references to hell and judgment.

"Strong conceptions of sin require not only a conception of a demanding God but also the idea of a powerful, and tempting, Satan. Yet polls routinely show that while Americans frequently believe in the existence of heaven, they are not that sure about the reality of hell."[11]

The danger in this should be self-evident. For generations now in the West, the church, Protestant and Catholic, has been moving away from sin and judgment.

> The more authoritative forms of Catholicism admired by these believers are hard to find in America these days. "In the first half of the twentieth century," as the authors of one study of Catholic attitudes write, "the Church promulgated a punitive image of God. It enforced strict rules that applied to nearly all areas of social, spiritual, and moral life.... Sins varied in magnitude from venial (relatively minor) to mortal (the most serious)." Today, by contrast, "the Church hierarchy has emphasized a loving God, one characterized by unconditional love, compassion, and kindness.... According to this view, God knows people will treat one another unjustly now and then, but God also understands their human frailties. God does not punish them; God loves and forgives them." With these changes in theology, American Catholicism transformed its culture from one of suffering to one of warm acceptance, a transition that surely made it possible for the Church to retain the allegiance of ever more modern Catholics who no longer lived in the parish-bound, priest-dominated parishes of American cities. But it also made it harder for the Church to maintain even its belief in venial sins, let alone mortal ones.[12]

The turn away from a focus on the centrality of suffering and sacrifice to the Christian life has resulted in millions of weakened—if not AWOL—soldiers of the Cross, unprepared for the struggle many will surely face, and equally unprepared to carry the gospel into the world. The future of the Catholic Church on the planet is in part suggested by Professor Wolfe, in a juxtaposition that reminds us again that we are focused in this book on Western civilization. The rest of the world moves ahead into the future on its own path—sometimes a higher road: "Increasingly, it seems as if there will be two versions of Catholicism in the future: a third-world church at home in Africa and Latin America in which sin will be featured in homilies and other church practices and a North American (and European) one that will resemble the turn away from the judgmentalism characteristic of other religions."[13]

I believe this insight applies to Western Protestantism as well as Catholicism. The evidence strongly suggests that the mantle of spiritual dynamism and doctrinal sanctity has passed from the church in the West to the church in Africa, Asia, and Latin America. With that mantle passes the future of the church—and the dynamism of civilization. This is as it should be: when the true message is rejected, the "dust should be shaken from the feet." Christ's teachings in this regard should be an ever-present reminder—and another lesson in humility—for the church in the West: it holds no special place.

> If nationalism—whether in the East or the West—denies the right of the Church to exist as a universal autonomous spiritual society, it is a challenge to the law of God and the kingship of Christ. But this does not mean that the Church is essentially Western. On the contrary, the same principle that forbids us to make the Church a national organization also prevents us from identifying it with a particular civilization. The mission of the Church is essentially universal and it is common to all nations and races—to those of the East equally with those of the West.[14]

The expansive common ground Christianity has with Judaism, in terms of principles of moral behavior, makes a quick glance at their recent history of interest as well. Professor Wolfe seems to conclude that, like every form of Christianity in America, Jews have also sought refuge from sin and judgment in the broader culture's dispensations from both.

> Similar, if less visible and dramatic, developments have been taking place among American Jews. The 1960s' fascination with *havurah* resulted in the emergence of what one member of an Oregon home-fellowship group called "non-judgmental Judaism"—more concerned with creating community than

> assigning blame. And while such experiments were limited to a minority of Jewish worshipers, the nonjudgmentalism they featured has spread out to the rest of the Jewish community in the United States.
>
> ...Assimilated Jews have made their peace not only with the American melting pot but also with a general American tendency to find a comforting and rewarding God.[15]

One wonders what Rabbi Soloveitchik—who declared that the "task of man is to bring down the Divine Presence, to the lower world, to this vale of tears"—would say.[16]

Thus it would appear that the beguiling power of so much wealth, so much pleasure, and such a lulling sense of security is a temptation to politely ignore—if not forget entirely—the demands and challenges of true faith, Christian or Judaic.

> It is clear from these accounts, stemming from many religious traditions, that the God in which large numbers of Americans believe, in the words of Robert Wuthnow, "is a God of love, comfort, order, and security. Gone is the God of judgment, wrath, justice, mystery, and punishment. Gone are concerns about the forces of evil." America's God has been domesticated, there to offer solace and to engage in dialogue with the understanding that, except under the most unusual circumstances, he will listen and commiserate. In a world governed by this more accessible God, sin still exists and atonement is still possible. But the sins are less numerous, less serious, and more forgivable. The wrongs that people do are the sorts of things that can be set right by pleading to God's good side, not his commanding presence.[17]

The Protestant church in America certainly will never hear its own Tevye fiddling on any of its roofs or singing exuberantly about "tradition." To most Americans, it would appear that tradition, in religion at least, is of value only to the hidebound and the hoity-toity. "No religion can stay old-fashioned forever in a society that constantly reinvents the new."[18]

This practice of reinvention of course takes into account neither the reality that the new is not necessarily by definition better—or even good—or the principle that faith is, by definition, founded on timeless and immutable principles of belief. True faith's very immutability grants to man a stability and order he desperately needs.

Courtesy of Koren Publishers

Rabbi Soloveitchik *declared that the "task of man is to bring down the Divine Presence, to the lower world, to this vale of tears." Professor Wolfe notes that American Jews like American Christians have "made their peace not only with the American melting pot but also with a general American tendency to find a comforting and rewarding God." Jews have also sought refuge from sin and judgment in the broader culture's dispensations from both.*

Mormonism appears to be in the category of religious practice for which Professor Wolfe has at least a grudging admiration. The fact that it is one of America's fastest growing religions, and perhaps also the strictest and most consistent in moral teachings and probity, is probably no coincidence.

> Mormonism is the great exception to any suggestion that faith and traditional moral conduct have little to do with one another....Once denounced by non-Mormons as libertines for their practice of polygamy, Latter-day Saints are now widely admired by large numbers of Americans for their strict

Latter-Day Saints Salt Lake Temple in Salt Lake City, Utah, USA. *Mormonism is one of America's fastest-growing religions and also one of the strictest and most consistent in moral teachings and probity. The convergence of these facts is probably no coincidence. A distinctiveness and "separateness" from the culture may be, in Professor Wolfe's view, more important to the Mormon Church's cohesion than is its doctrine.*

> personal conduct. From time to time, stories of continued adherence to polygamy on the part of some Mormons emerge, and as they do, some less than attractive forms of moral conduct that seem oppressive to women and potentially abusive of children emerge along with them. And not all evangelical Protestants are happy with what they perceive to be Mormon deviations from Christian teachings on sin and grace. Yet in the course of a century and a half, a religion that began by challenging the central religious and moral precepts of a predominantly Protestant society has come to stand in the public mind as the embodiment of old-fashioned Christian ideals.[19]

Why is this so? Is it simply because of Mormonism's apparently greater unwillingness to lower its standards to accommodate the culture's quest for a religious imprimatur for its ever-expanding dissipations? Or is it simply the strong family orientation? But then we must be careful lest we find ourselves measuring value in terms of numbers rather than in terms of practices and principles—a propensity I condemn vehemently throughout this work.

Professor Wolfe continues his analysis of the Mormon record in contemporary America.

> Mormons, of course, are only human, which is why from time to time evidence of immoral behavior on the part of individual members of the Church comes to light. Still, considerable evidence exists that the Mormon reputation for moral probity is justified. A thorough review of survey data concludes that "more so than the average American, Mormons want children, marriage, and a more traditional division of labor; they are also less likely to have cohabited and more likely to disapprove of extramarital sex."...Not surprisingly, given their code of conduct, Saints are also less likely than members of other faiths, including conservative ones, to smoke, drink, and take drugs.[20]

A distinctiveness and "separateness" from the culture may be, in Professor Wolfe's view, more important to the Mormon Church's cohesion than its doctrine.

> Mormonism began, as we would say today, as an explicitly countercultural movement. "In direct contrast to most Protestant parishes made up of congregations whose members worshiped together on Sundays but returned during the week to a pluralistic (albeit Protestant) culture," writes the historian Jan Shipps about Mormons living in the Great Basin, "the Saints who attended sacrament meetings or heard sermons from less than imposing stands on Sundays lived out their ordinary weekday lives in close proximity to one another."...As blended in with the rest of American culture as their religious practices have been, the cultural practices of the Mormons have made them, as they call themselves, "a particular people."[21]

The term "countercultural" is *apropos* of everything addressed in this work. Christ was a revolutionary. Everything he said and did was "countercultural." Unlike the modern church in the West, he sought no accommodation with the culture of his time—a distinction in attitude, thought, and conduct that has long since been lost on many of the West's leading Christian figures.

The self-reference of Mormons as "a particular people" might sound suspiciously like "a peculiar people" to many Western Christians' ears. Yet distinguishing themselves—not out of pride, power, or anti-social proclivities—was a central feature of Christians through many centuries. Nowhere in history has that distinction been so completely blurred as in the modern West—with disastrous consequences for the church and the civilization.

Professor Wolfe also notes another feature of the Mormon Church that has undoubtedly been the source of much of its vitality—its unity. Though this might sound suspiciously like cult-conformity to some, the underlying principle of consciousness of a shared cause and shared beliefs would be of great benefit to the church in the West.

Canadian pastor Stephen Boissoin was fined and muzzled by a provincial human rights tribunal under hate speech laws for his principled stand against homosexuality. Similar trends will come to fruition in the United States soon despite that country's vaunted "freedom of speech." Yet in one sense this is not to be feared or shunned. The term "countercultural" is apropos *of everything addressed in this work. Christ was a revolutionary. Everything he said and did was "countercultural." Unlike the modern church in the West, he sought no accommodation with the culture of his time—a distinction in attitude, thought, and conduct that has long since been lost on many of the West's leading Christian figures.*

Photographer unknown

> Rarely are Mormons given to anguished confessions of disappointment or cries of woe that God has betrayed those who believe in him. Unlike small-group practices in other faith traditions, which often reach moments of emotional catharsis before harmony is achieved, Mormon testimonies tend to be harmonious from the start.[22]
>
> ...
>
> Houses of worship are constructed according to a standard plan, and "the teachings and activities are standardized so that—as far as is feasible—Mormonism is the same wherever it is in the world. Almost a religious franchise, the church remains a constant in a multicultural world." If the faithful are "scattered" rather than "gathered," one can at least gather them together in ways that emphasize not only the commonality of Mormons with each other but also their collective distinctiveness from everyone else.[23]

The susceptibility of the church to the whims and caprices of the broader culture tell us something: the tail (i.e., the church) is not wagging the dog; there has been a role reversal in the last century of the appendage and the dominant organism: "...of all the believers in the United States, Christians tend to jump on whatever cultural fad happens to be preoccupying secular people in their society, as their megachurches, which feature everything from state-of-the-art technology to shopping-mall conveniences, so often demonstrate."[24]

However, Wolfe seems to believe that Christianity cannot grow, much less flourish, if it becomes what he calls "sectarian"; thus, despite his seeming preference for church leadership that would reject the fawning after the culture, he perceives a silver lining in evangelicalism's "tacky" conduct.

> This adherence to growth can have its frustrations; watching sermons reduced to PowerPoint presentations or listening to one easily forgettable praise song after another makes one long for an evangelical willing to stand up, Luther-like, and proclaim his opposition to the latest survey of evangelical taste. Tacky as evangelicalism can be, however, sectarian it is not. Its problem, in fact, is the opposite-so strong a desire to copy the culture of hotel chains and popular music that it loses what religious distinctiveness it once had.[25]

This seemingly paradoxical perspective is repeated in another passage finding reassurance in the notion that this cultural compliance will prevent "bigotry."

> As much as we may be tempted to denounce as flighty Americans who change their faith as often as their cars, we ought to recognize that religious switching acts as a kind of insurance policy against

Photo by Richard Johnstone. CC

Political and judicial efforts to keep marriage an institution between one man and one woman are rearguard defensive actions against accelerating cultural decay. Worthwhile perhaps insofar as they go, they nonetheless reflect a failure to perceive the wellspring of such historically unparalleled decadent conceptions as homosexual "marriage."

> bigotry. If you cannot be sure today what your faith will be tomorrow—let alone the faith of the people your son or daughter bring home for the weekend—you had better not say anything too nasty about any of them. Sometimes the more seemingly frivolous of the ways Americans practice their faith turn out to be blessings in disguise.[26]

Here we see the fundamental distinguishing feature of Professor Wolfe's secularist philosophy that we can state thusly: "Ultimately, moral law is determined by man; it does not truly originate with a Supreme Being." His is a distinctively "democratic" view, not just of American society, but, in a sense, of all human society.

If faith and moral law are reduced to a human construct they become nothing more than a set of rules and constraints imposed by those with the greater power on those with the lesser. This produces a void of temporal nothingness that can sustain neither a nation nor an individual. Supremely vain, it is profoundly deficient in the humility that would recognize man's extraordinarily expansive limitations.

In any event, the days of Constantine are gone. Men are not compelled by the state in Western societies to adhere to any religion—though such compulsion remains a feature of most Islamic countries. Even so, we must ponder many questions: If I assert my belief in a Supreme Being and Jesus Christ as His human manifestation on earth, am I being intolerant? You may label me so, but does that make it true? And if you choose to define "intolerance" so broadly as to encompass the assertion of one's beliefs in public settings does that lessen my responsibility before God to assert them nonetheless?

If I also assert that I believe the moral law given in the Bible is the ultimate authority to which all of humanity will be held accountable, am I then seeking to control your life as someone who hears?

That Jesus never compelled anyone to believe—or even to obey—is one of the great distinguishing features of the Christian faith. And a mature Christian will attempt neither. But Christ did show the pathway to salvation, and He warned of the consequences of failure to honor God's moral law. A Christian who is striving to be obedient will boldly do the same. It is not a matter of discretion any more than it is an effort to ram religion down someone's throat. It is a matter of obedience and—as incomprehensible as it may sound to secularists—an act of love.

END NOTES
CHAPTER 22

1 Christopher Dawson, *Historic Reality of Christian Culture* (New York: Harper & Brothers, 1960), 38.
2 Steve Bruce, *God Is Dead: Secularization in the West* (Oxford: Wiley-Blackwell, 2002), 240.
3 Bruce, *God Is Dead,* 204.
4 Bruce, *God Is Dead,* 204.
5 Bruce, *God Is Dead,* 210.
6 Bruce, *God Is Dead,* 211, referring to G. Barna, "The year's most intriguing findings, from Barna research studies." *Barna Research Online* (2000). *www.barna.org.*
7 Bruce, *God Is Dead,* 227–228.
8 Alan Wolfe, *The Transformation of American Religion: How We Actually Live Our Faith* (New York: Simon and Schuster, 2003), 161. Reprinted and edited with the permission of The Free Press, a Division of Simon & Schuster, Inc., from *The Transformation of American Religion: How We Actually Live Our Faith* by Alan Wolfe. Copyright 2003 by Alan Wolfe. All rights reserved.
9 Wolfe, *Transformation*, 152.
10 Wolfe, *Transformation*, 153–154.
11 Wolfe, *Transformation*, 161.
12 Wolfe, *Transformation*, 162–163.
13 Wolfe, *Transformation*, 173.
14 Dawson, *Historic Reality*, 115.
15 Wolfe, *Transformation*, 173.
16 Joseph B. Soloveitchik, *Halakhic Man* (New York: Jewish Publication Society, 1984), 52.
17 Robert Wuthnow, cited in Wolfe, *Transformation*, 165.
18 Wolfe, *Transformation*, 144.
19 Wolfe, *Transformation*, 144–145.
20 Wolfe, *Transformation*, 145.
21 Wolfe, *Transformation*, 148–149.
22 Wolfe, *Transformation*, 148.
23 Wolfe, *Transformation*, 150.
24 Wolfe, *Transformation*, 250.
25 Wolfe, *Transformation*, 256.
26 Wolfe, *Transformation*, 262.

CHAPTER

23

A ROMANCE WITH NUMBERS

...[T]he rapid growth of evangelical religion in the United States can just as easily be cited as evidence of secularism's powerful appeal. Indeed, the very notion of church growth—which, in evangelical circles these days, comes complete with case studies borrowed from business schools and analyses of the success or failure of various marketing plans—suggests that there is much more than a purely religious dimension to the story of evangelical Protestantism's popularity.
Alan Wolfe[1]

Luther and Calvin would have been horrified to find that centuries after their reforms a secularized version of their ideas was being used to justify the pursuit of wealth (which, like most pious people, they saw as a major threat to the pursuit of godliness).
Steve Bruce[2]

...[T]he spirit of Jesus has existed for two thousand years and the United States for just a little more than two hundred, but whenever American popular culture clashes with that of time-tested religion, it is usually the latter that finds itself giving way.
Alan Wolfe[3]

These are all destined to perish with use, because they are based on human commands and teachings.
Colossians 2:22 (NIV)

In a culture that has had so much materially there is a common attitude, even in the church, of entitlement—and, with it, a common, unrecognized ingratitude, even for the great gift of the Christian faith: salvation. This attitude has opened one of the great hemorrhaging wounds of the Christian church in the West, particularly in America; a wound that is sometimes more evident to secularists than to Christians. Standing on the outside, a secularist like Professor Wolfe sees the spiritual hemophilia—inbred from generations of the church promiscuously cohabiting with the culture—from a viewpoint that is unquestionably sensed by others who, as a result, keep their distance. It is telling evidence of the failures and decline of the church that those on the inside evidently do not see them—or if they do, they compliantly conform and never challenge.

> As churches find themselves seeking out worship styles that feel intimate and comfortable rather than imposing and distant, it is not clear that even the best forms of contemporary worship can survive. Indeed, there is reason to believe that the way evangelicals borrow from the culture surrounding them is blowing back into the sermons offered in the evangelical world. Evangelicals have long found ways to reconcile their version of Christianity with the materialistic, consumption-driven American culture, whether reflected in the ostentatious lifestyles of the televangelists, the success-oriented preaching of a Robert Schuller, or the explicitly procapitalist prosperity theology of the Kenneth Hagin Ministries of Tulsa, Oklahoma. Critics have found such tendencies disturbing, not only because they seem to turn their backs on the poor and needy but also because prosperity theology makes so few demands on those who practice it.[4]

The "prosperity theology" or "prosperity gospel," as it is variously called, is pervasive, so much so that it is no longer conspicuous in many of its manifestations, some of which are artfully and subtly presented. Professor Wolfe cites one such example in the form of a book entitled *The Prayer of Jabez: Enlarge My Territory.*

> Christian executives, [Dr. Bruce Wilkinson] tells his readers, ask him whether they can properly ask God for more business, and his answer is "Absolutely!" Wilkinson himself has recited the prayer for years, and it certainly has increased his opportunities; he has enlarged his Jabez territory with offshoots for children and women, cassettes, self-help guides, and every other marketable device he and his publisher could think of. One searches this exceptionally thin book in vain for any statement indicating that Christian prayer is an act of sacrifice. In Wilkinson's form of Christianity, you get far more than you give.[5]

Any true Christian understands that "you get far more than you give" with God. But that recognition is bred by humility and the insight of Job that God is under no compelling obligation to do anything for his creation—man. The greater problem in evangelical circles is not that this is universally a crass, disingenuous, rationalizing materialism at work, but something far worse: a belief system for many that is completely sincere—Christ's life and teachings to the contrary notwithstanding. Otherwise, Professor Wolfe's point is well taken.

> In the way they shape their worship services to attract new members, down to consulting surveys on the right kind of music to feature, evangelical megachurches have already prepared believers for a faith

A Promise Keepers rally. *Part of the parachurch movement in America, such organizations are sometimes seen by churches as competition for limited dollars, energy, and time. Reflecting impermanence and the pronounced tendency to faddishness in the American church, the existence of such groups also suggests American Christians are seeking something they cannot find in their churches.*

Courtesy of Promise Keepers

> that puts their own needs first...simplistic sermonizing need not automatically follow when churches become so obsessed with gaining and keeping members that they modify every aspect of religious life within reach, including worship, to account for contemporary taste. But, then again, once popular taste rules, there are no barriers to the success of a book as focused on individuals and their desire for material success and personal recovery as *The Prayer of Jabez*. Worship in evangelical America may serve many needs, but otherworldly reverence is unlikely to be one of them, so determined are these churches to respond to the everyday concerns of those who attend them.[6]

SCRATCHING THE MULTITUDINOUS ITCHING EARS

Television, publishing, political campaigning, education, self-help advice—all increasingly tell Americans what they already want to hear. Religion, it would seem, should now be added to that list.
Alan Wolfe[7]

In words compellingly consistent with another major theme of this book, Professor Wolfe puts a well-aimed bullet into the very heart of contemporary American religion:

> American religion survives and even flourishes not so much because it instructs people in the right ways to honor God but because people have taken so many aspects of religion into their own hands. Because evangelicals describe themselves, and are described by others, as conservative Protestants, the increasing popularity of their worship styles ought to mean a return to the fiery preaching of Jonathan Edwards. But those who fear the consequences for the United States of a return to strong religious belief should not be fooled by evangelicalism's rapid growth. On the contrary, evangelicalism's popularity is due as much to its populistic and democratic urges—its determination to find out exactly what believers want and to offer it to them—as it is to certainties of the faith. The biggest challenge posed to American society by the popularity of megachurches and other forms of growth-oriented Protestantism is not bigotry but bathos. Television, publishing, political campaigning, education, self-help advice—all increasingly tell Americans what they already want to hear. Religion, it would seem, should now be added to that list.[8]

There is of course a biblical phrasing for this phenomenon—the "itching ears." A multitude of ministers, teachers, and sundry religious figures are ever eager to scratch them. Though some would read Professor Wolfe's indictment and my affirmation as surely not applying to them, it likely would—the only differences would be in the doctrinal slant. Each perceives its position and message as the true and correct one, but most are, in some significant way, at variance with the actual life and teachings of Christ.

Christ's example and his message are so challenging that some professing Christians in every generation have sought doctrinally "acceptable" ways to ameliorate the impact on their lives. But perhaps nowhere and in no time has that dilution been more ubiquitous and creative than in the twentieth- and twenty-first-century church in America. Each denomination, each group, each sect, tends to focus on the sins it has deemed offenses worthy of rebuke, while carefully overlooking others for which they themselves may be culpable. That many of these offenses are often sins of omission makes them no less sinful—just easier to ignore.

Lakewood Church. *Another illustration of pandering to the "itching ears" with the health, wealth, happiness, and prosperity gospel, this church's popularity, in the words of Professor Wolfe "is due as much to its…determination to find out exactly what believers want and to offer it to them—as it is to certainties of the faith. The biggest challenge posed to American society by the popularity of megachurches and other forms of growth-oriented Protestantism is not bigotry but bathos. Television, publishing, political campaigning, education, self-help advice—all increasingly tell Americans what they already want to hear. Religion, it would seem, should now be added to that list."*

Lakewood Church in Texas

To be sure, some ministers and religious leaders do, from time to time, say that which their charges—and certainly the broader culture—would not want to hear. But those forays into the dangerous ground of courage and commitment—and true leadership—are, by comparison, few and limited. Modern American preaching, Protestant and Catholic—with some notable and worthy exceptions—is significant by and large for what is not said, rather than what is said.

The certainty of this failure—and the moral responsibility that goes with it—is so great that, were John the Baptist alive today—the man whom Jesus declared "the greatest man ever born" (Luke 7:28)—he would undoubtedly be treated as leprous and ostracized by most Western religious leaders and most churches, Catholic and Protestant. His message of self-sacrifice and complete rejection of the culture's values would be regarded as radical and untenable. That he was ostracized by the religious leaders of his day should be a jarring juxtaposition for the modern Western church. John would not countenance any degree of what Professor Wolfe refers to as Americans "practicing their faith in ways so personal and individualistic that their practices blend seamlessly into the culture around them."[9]

SERVING GOD BY THE NUMBERS

I take what is worldly, and baptize it.
Dr. H. Edwin Young[10]

Professor Wolfe then notes evidence of a different kind of church vigor that is much more common in the church in America: "…the organizational life of the churches seemed healthy enough. The churches themselves were, in many cases, 'imposing structures of stone and brick'."[11]

A manifestation of the materialism of the culture having infiltrated the church, of Sorokin's "colossalism," and Toynbee's "*ad hoc* stratagem for the true creative process," this is how the church is responding to the civilization's crisis, rather than through the true "creative process" modeled and taught

Church billboard promoting networking and prosperity. *As Professor Wolfe perceptively acknowledges, "Church growth tends to be a hot topic wherever evangelical leaders gather: They judge their movement successful if it registers ever-increasing numbers of new members…churches that grow are invariably celebrated, whereas those that do not are judged to have gotten God's message wrong; and methods that work are copied and those that fail avoided. As their ranks expand, evangelicals can perhaps be forgiven for concluding that the people who join them testify to a deep desire for spiritual connection that only religion can offer. Yet the rapid growth of evangelical religion in the United States can just as easily be cited as evidence of secularism's powerful appeal."*

by Christ. This purely secular form of dynamism has become the measure by which "service" to God is gauged. A form of religious numerology, it calculates "success" the old-fashioned American way: in numbers—numbers on the rolls, dollars in the budget, and square footage built or bought.

Pastors or priests who have displayed aptitudes in these areas have more influence inside their own denominations or sects and are typically the ones chosen for leadership positions, not because of greater spirituality—the attribute we would assume God would prefer—or even more sound theology, but simply because of their ability to enhance numbers in one or more of these areas. Their power and influence should be seen then for what it is, political and economic, not spiritual.

This is highly suggestive of the lurid causes for the church's morbidity—as measured by its influence on the culture at large—which is rarely discussed with anything approaching true insight, or, for that matter, closely scrutinized at all.

That would be perilously close to soul-searching. Were that to happen, the sobering truth would become unpleasantly evident: the church's "accomplishments" and "successes" are largely worldly, and the spiritual power to change the course of a civilization is clearly not present—available, but not present.

> Ever on the lookout for a church and a pastor that feels somehow right for them, churchgoers put the denominations to which churches belong in the position of shedding whatever stands in the way of appealing to the greatest number of potential believers. The more the saints circulate, the more the building blocks upon which American Protestantism has been constructed begin to crumble.[12]

There is disquiet among some, however. Doubt, uncertainty, and skepticism about where the church is in the modern West and whether its *modus operandi* is truly biblical have resulted in a return to a first-century phenomenon—the house church.

> Roger Upton, a former Southern Baptist pastor, explains in "Grace Abounding," his website devoted to the house church movement, "[T]here simply is no scriptural basis for the church meeting in a specially constructed religious building." Institutions corrupt, he believes, and the church, understood bureaucratically, can corrupt absolutely. The house church movement aims to practice what one believer, Glenn Heller, calls "relational Christianity" rather than "accomplishment Christianity." In his view, "it is more important to focus on the being than on the doing" and "the doing will

come without any effort if one learns the being." For Glenn, like Americans attracted to the ecology movement, simpler is better.[13]

The "being" must come first, and the "doing" will surely follow. That is a prescription for spiritual growth fully supported by scripture. The notion that the church should be a great family is also scripturally supportable, and the longing for this model is a clear indication not only of the lack of intimacy in the modern Western church but the concomitant loneliness felt in the culture at large.

> ...House churchers treat even the more evangelical Protestant churches the way Luther treated Catholics, denouncing them as more interested in protecting their privileges than in expressing their piety. Jesus, after all, reached out to all who would follow him without, in the words of one believer, "pyramid structures, programs, gimmicks, marketing, psychology, advertising, titles, schedules, [and] meetings."[14]

The merit in these criticisms is unassailable, but the power (i.e., worldly, not spiritual) in the church is largely in the hands of those who believe otherwise; thus these views are given short shrift. Furthermore, there is an unsettling sense behind all of this, however, that it may be another form of rearranging the deck chairs on the Titanic. Something is still missing.

Other expedients are being tried, particularly the "parachurch," an entity that is neither a true church nor a denomination but that seeks to fulfill some of the functions of both. "Although not new, parachurch movements, especially among evangelicals, are more likely to challenge, rather than to sustain, the denominational character of American religious life."[15] And we must be ever mindful of that great American tradition and venerated value—competition: "Because its practices threaten existing denominational turf, Promise Keepers has not been well received by long-established denominations."[16]

Professor Wolfe describes one evangelical pastor who "wants to bring people into his church who have long been uncomfortable with religion, and to do so, he makes his services as non-threatening as possible."

> His particular contribution to evangelical practice has been to apply the same kind of comfort level to his church's outreach to the wider community. "You can't be an evangelist because you don't make people feel bad," is the way he describes the reaction of more old-fashioned Christians to his approach. His response has been to develop a form of witnessing that makes people feel good, a "low risk" strategy that removes the guilt and fear built into traditional evangelical encounters.[17]

> How this pastor achieves this is accomplished through a certain "inventiveness."
>
> ...Reinterpreting the Bible...[the pastor] developed a slogan that, in his words, comes "*almost* straight" from Scripture: "Where the Spirit of the Lord is, there is fun!"
>
> Committed to reaching out to the unchurched with innovative methods, however turned off from religion the unchurched may be, evangelicals like Sjogren assign considerable importance to church growth; the cover of Sjogren's book *Conspiracy of Kindness* points out that his own church is one of the twenty-five fastest-growing churches in the United States. Church growth tends to be a hot topic wherever evangelical leaders gather: They judge their movement successful if it registers ever-increasing numbers of new members; ....churches that grow are invariably celebrated, whereas those that do not are judged to have gotten God's message wrong; and methods that work are copied and those that fail avoided. As their ranks expand, evangelicals can perhaps be forgiven for concluding that the people who join them testify to a deep desire for spiritual connection that only religion can offer. *Yet the rapid growth of evangelical religion in the United States can just as easily be cited as evidence*

> *of secularism's powerful appeal* [emphasis added]. Indeed, the very notion of church growth—which, in evangelical circles these days, comes complete with case studies borrowed from business schools and analyses of the success or failure of various marketing plans—suggests that there is much more than a purely religious dimension to the story of evangelical Protestantism's popularity.[18]

Here Professor Wolfe has handed down one of many astute indictments of the church in America —one that would readily result in a conviction were the case ever brought before a reasonably objective court.

The marketing always focuses on the goal—"what will bring in the largest number of people."

> To be effective recruiters for Christ's message in a less than perfect world requires that they be open to opportunity and eclectic in method. And so, while the product—the soul—is not equivalent to a vacuum cleaner or a mutual fund, the techniques by which salvation is offered inevitably come to resemble the latest fashions in marketing and advertising.
>
> Precisely because efforts at witnessing are so important to them, evangelicals feel that there would be something amiss if they did not explore any and every method that is likely to work in bringing the largest number of people to Jesus in the shortest period of time. "I take what is worldly, and baptize it," says H. Edwin Young, pastor of the Second Baptist Church of Houston, Texas.[19]

Relating this to a personally familiar example of the same facet of human nature, Professor Wolfe also, inadvertently, leads us to understand the deeply engrained tendency to conformity in the human species.

> Every college teacher knows about both grade inflation and assignment deflation; as the amount of assigned work has decreased over the past two or three decades, the rewards students have received have increased. Much the same phenomenon—call it salvation inflation—has taken place as evangelical Christians carry out their duty to witness; as less becomes expected in order to achieve salvation, the blessings of salvation are offered with fewer strings attached.[20]

Alluding to observations dating to the beginnings of suburban sprawl in the 1950s, the deep roots of these practices in the American church become more obvious in Professor Wolfe's analysis.

> The effects of suburbanization on their religious practice could be immediately detected, for, as a number of 1950s' social critics pointed out, suburbia was as incompatible with spiritual seriousness as it was with the promotion of social justice. For these new suburbanites, as for those Jews who moved out to what was once called "the suburban frontier," fund-raising, membership drives, and construction projects, rather than a concern with, God's word, seemed to be the major focus of their religious lives.[21]
>
> ...
>
> ...Yet Bellevue Baptist [in Memphis, Tennessee] has a strong megachurch character nonetheless: "Six Flags over Jesus" was how it was described to me by another Memphis Baptist pastor with whom I spoke on a visit to the city. "You have to go where God calls you," he continued with heavy irony, "but God always seems to be calling you east," the direction middle-class Memphians generally take when they leave the city for the rewards of suburbia.[22]
>
> ...
>
> ...The Reverend Billy Vaughn, who is affiliated with mainline Idlewild Presbyterian, is proud that his church has not decamped for the suburbs, for he is not sure that thriving churches recognize "the power of God to transform the city." As he and some of his colleagues see it, suburban evangelism is

> not really evangelism at all. "Megachurches say that they are practicing the faith," Rev. Jeff Irwin, director of urban ministries for the United Methodist Church of Memphis adds, "but what they are really doing is practicing the culture." Pastor Irwin thinks that what he calls "the full service church" is a church that has forgotten that its primary obligation is service to God. For these ministers, nothing in the tradition of evangelical religion is more important than reaching out to the poor and oppressed, and newly prosperous evangelical churches, like the mainline ones that preceded them to the suburbs a generation ago, are not well positioned for the task.[23]

Perhaps a secularist would be forgiven for confusion over which of these viewpoints is biblically consistent. Even longstanding believers dispute these perspectives. However, in a sense, each suggests a shallowness of understanding of the broader state of the church in America. The greater depth has not been plumbed.

In an extraordinarily revealing passage, Professor Wolfe analyzes the marketing and the accompanying mindset that goes into so much of the contemporary American church. Using phrases like "balance of power," he illustrates a fundamental theme of this book—one that would be denied vigorously by its practitioners—the world in the church, rather than the other way round.

> At Hebron Baptist…the congregation goes out of its way to make people feel welcome rather than to make them feel bad. "Hebron," writes one sociologist, "like most megachurches, provides high-intensity experiences of communality with relatively weak systems for insuring individual religious accountability—the assurance of right without the punishment of wrong." The church does this by toning down its hellfire preaching in favor of more contemporary sensibilities.
>
> …In traditional evangelism, the church, standing in for God, is the savior and the sinner is the penitent; believing themselves to be in possession of a truth that will set others free, evangelicals seek to bring the power they possess to those whose empty spiritual lives render them weak. Lacking either downtown locations that bring them in contact with strangers or public spaces in which they can reach out to passersby, evangelical megachurches, by contrast, have little choice but to offer incentives that will bring people to their doors. That process inevitably transforms the balance of power between institution and individual. The unchurched and the newly churched know that they have something the megachurches want—their potential or continuing membership—and they are willing to drive a hard bargain before they offer it up. Savvy church officials search out savvy consumers (and vice versa), and the result is a form of religious practice capable of pleasing both parties.[24]

Continuing, Wolfe notes the "quantity rather than quality" motives and the "superficial and shallow" "security." A true family integer is not there, only the promise of one, and a promise made by those who, sadly, may not even understand what a real one would look or feel like.

> Because the evangelical efforts of megachurches attract people without much regard for doctrine, and because the people who are attracted to them are so often religious switchers perhaps on the way to yet another congregation or denomination, the commitments new members make are often as transitory as exurbia's rates of residential-home ownership. Megachurch evangelism aims for quantity rather than quality, as if an alternative conception of witnessing that pronounced itself satisfied with fewer, but more committed, converts is simply out of the question. The security such churches offer, while undeniably real, is also somewhat superficial and shallow, masking, as it does, the fact that membership so easily gained can also be easily lost. And when conflicts arise, which invariably happens at even the most family-oriented congregations, members, who tend to shy away from conflicts of any

sort, are often poorly prepared to stick with the congregation in order to work out their difficulties. Megachurches are often treated as a revolutionary new stage in the ways in which people worship, but they may also turn out to be a passing fad, their success anything but guaranteed.

No longer residing in close proximity with others, dependent on cars to get them where they want to go, time-starved and consumer conscious, impatient with complexity and ambiguity, American evangelicals live in a society that makes serious conversation about any topic, especially one as important to individuals themselves as their faith, difficult. For all the commitments to witnessing they make, therefore, evangelicals are no longer certain why they make them. The charge to win people to faith is treated by evangelical theologians as having originated in the Great Commission: "Therefore go and make disciples of all nations, baptizing them in the name of the Father and of the Son and of the Holy Spirit, and teaching them to obey everything I have commanded you." (Matthew 28:19–20) Yet in a 1994 survey, only 9 percent of Americans in general and 25 percent of self-described evangelicals could say what [Jesus'] Great Commission is. (More, but still not a majority, could place John 3:1 [*sic*]—"For God so loved the world, that he gave his only begotten Son, that whosoever believeth in him should not perish, but have everlasting life"—another important text for evangelicals, but one whose promise of life after death is less demanding than the command to evangelize.) Even when evangelicals overcome all the obstacles put in their path in order to bring people to Jesus, the majority of them, it would seem, have lost touch with the theological reasons for doing so.

..."If you put on a three-ring circus to get them in," one of the urban pastors with whom I spoke in Memphis put it, "you have to keep putting on three-ring circuses to keep them in."[25]

ELMER GANTRY'S PROGENY OR JUST CHRISTIANITY LITE?

The fact that some of these efforts ended in scandal, financial or otherwise, neglects what might have happened had more of them actually succeeded. For any success surely would have come at the expense of the religious messages being delivered.

Alan Wolfe[26]

Professor Wolfe, as one might expect, touches upon the phenomenon of televangelism and uses the term "Faustian Pact" in introducing his focus. We might preface this segment by observing that it is not the method (TV, radio, publishing, etc.) but its content that Christians must regard with unstinting and uncompromising vigilance. The former are simply means of communicating, but the way they are used in Western culture can lead to the subtle—and often not so subtle—infusion of secular values, methods, and ways of thinking, into what is ostensibly a Christian practice.

No other example of the evangelical receptivity to modern means of communication has received as much publicity as "televangelism," the effort on the part of figures such as Robert Schuller, Jimmy Swaggert [*sic*], Jim Bakker, and others to reach a mass audience for their message through television programming. The fact that some of these efforts ended in scandal, financial or otherwise, neglects what might have happened had more of them actually succeeded. For any *success* surely would have come at the expense of the religious messages being delivered. "The subtleties of theology do not carry well over television," write the sociologists who studied the phenomenon. "The medium is fundamentally visual, not cerebral." In theory, televangelists, like all evangelists, are committed to the Great Commission. But in practice, theological considerations inevitably give way to financial ones. Like exurban churches that must supply inducements to bring people to their doors, televangelists, intent on gaining and keeping their audience, preach a kind of prosperity theology on the one hand

Courtesy of photographer

The indoor pool of an American television "evangelist." *This species of "success" always comes at the expense of the gospel. It has nothing to do with the life and teachings of Christ—indeed, it is antithetical. That this reality is lost on much of the church is another powerful evidence of the supplanting of true biblical values with those of the culture. The "price to be paid" by courting the culture is always the abnegation of Christ Himself. Christians cannot have it both ways. Just as Jesus declared that "He who is not with me is against me, and he who does not gather with me scatters" (Matthew 12:30 NIV), the culture is much the same, in practice if not in overt declaration. The culture will not abide—nor long give weight or attention to—that which does not meet its own definition of "success" in the form of dollars or the social and political power that comes with numerous adherents. Yet this is the true state of much of the American church—of the culture far more than of Christ.*

> and fund-raise from their viewers on the other. As this study concludes, "fund-raising has virtually become the tail that wags the dog, even to the point of dominating, in some instances, the theologies of some of the televangelists."[27]

Here we have reference to that decidedly Western notion of success addressed earlier in this book, and, by implication, the recognition that this is the form of success that many in the institutional church pay obeisance to. This species of "success" always comes "at the expense of the religious messages"—at least those that are genuinely scriptural. That this reality is lost on much of the church is another powerful evidence of the supplanting of true biblical values with those of the culture.

> As it turns out, however, the marriage between evangelicals and commerce was not made in heaven. Like the attempts by popular-front screenwriters to slip in positive references to the Communist Party in Hollywood movies, one has to pay careful attention before the coded religious messages of *Heart in Motion* can be detected. [Amy] Grant herself said that she wanted to produce songs "about life experience without any hidden spiritual agenda," and with her 1997 release of *Behind the Eyes* she achieved her goal, for this album, in the words of one communications scholar, "contained no explicit references to God or Jesus." There is always a price to be paid by those who cross over into the mainstream, and for evangelicals, the price is self-effacement. To meet the standards of commerce, Grant had to tone down her evangelism, and while the result was profitable, it left more conservative Christians wondering what the fuss was all about. Grant may have reached the top of the Billboard charts with *Baby, Baby,* but religious radio stations, appalled by its soft-edged sexuality, refused to play the song, and before long, conservative Christian watchdogs were just as likely to denounce Christian rock for its satanic content as they were any other kind of rock. (Nor, by the way, were they off base in doing so; Christian rock groups such as Stryper and singers like Steve Taylor really are often indistinguishable from heavy-metal bands and sometimes go out of their way to mock rightwing fundamentalism.)[28]

The "price to be paid" by courting the culture is always much more than simple "self-effacement"; it is the abnegation of Christ himself. Christians cannot have it both ways. Just as Jesus declared that "He who is not with me is against me, and he who does not gather with me scatters" (Matthew 12:30 NIV), the culture is much the same, in practice, if not overt declaration. The culture will not abide—nor long give weight or attention to—that which does not meet its own definition of "success" in the form of dollars, or the social and political power that comes with numerous adherents.

Though Professor Wolfe's insights here, once again, help us to see realities that are typically overlooked, it is some measure of how far the church has strayed that these realities are in fact actually quite conspicuous. An even greater depth has yet to be seen. A Christian who has genuinely come to a reckoning with God over his own sinfulness and his ultimate destiny without Christ should sense in much of contemporary Christian music a spiritual hollowness, if, indeed, the adjective "spiritual" could accurately be deployed at all. The contrast between "Amazing Grace," "Great Is Thy Faithfulness," "How Great Thou Art," and "Holy God, We Praise Thy Name" on one hand and much that is touted as contemporary Christian music on the other should be apparent to the intellectually astute and even more so to the spiritually sensitive. The profound reverence, other-worldly focus, and abject humility of the former could not be more alien to the tenor and tones of the latter had they been created by distinct species of mankind, unrelated by ethnicity, geography, blood and thought—much less spiritual belief. In the former slave-trader John Newton's profound humility and tear-stained gratitude for an "amazing grace" that he cannot comprehend, we hear the groanings of self-abnegation and the exaltation of an adored, loving, and all-powerful God. Nothing in contemporary Christian music can approach it—and there are reasons for that falling short.

Highly imitative as it is of secular music, much of contemporary Christian music would be indistinguishable were it not for the occasional references to God, Christ, or religious jargon. Its lack of originality in lyrics and melodies gives away its intellectual aridity and void of spiritual passion. At times an almost mindless repetition of words or phrases, the "sound and fury" of the secular merges with the language of the pietistic, all signifying very little. Money motivates, pride propels, and ego enthuses.

Couched and designed as it is for the marketplace, most contemporary Christian music is replete with the words, phrases, the "Christianese" of modern views of Christianity, as if each were inserted to give the piece spiritual authenticity. And the music itself...well, that is indistinguishable from the tones, rhythm and noise of the various genres of popular music of the age.

Professor Wolfe then asks an important question—a worldly question, to be sure, but one wonders why it has not been asked by Western Christians, particularly evangelicals.

> What did evangelicals gain by overcoming their suspicion of popular entertainment in favor of contemporary rock? The answer seems to be very little. For one thing, the notion that young people were going to be lured into stronger faith commitments after listening to watered-down gospel music seems rather naive. And just to set the record clear, the firm that conducts survey research for evangelicals asked those who considered Jesus their savior and found that none of them mentioned Christian music as responsible for their conversion. (Thirty-eight percent cited families and upbringing, 14 percent cited a sermon, and 10 percent a conversation with a friend about Jesus.)[29]

The compelling need to point out that a professing agnostic is making these observations keeps resurrecting. The point should be obvious: You need not be a person of faith to see this—but if you

1780. PD-old.

John Newton, author of "Amazing Grace." *The contrast between "Amazing Grace" and much of contemporary Christian music should be apparent to the intellectually astute, and even more so to the spiritually sensitive. In the former slave-trader's profound humility and gratitude for an "amazing grace" that he cannot comprehend, we hear self-abnegation and the exaltation of an adored, loving, and all-powerful God. Nothing in contemporary Christian music can approach it—and there are reasons for that "falling short."*

are a person of professed faith and you do not see, that awareness should be profoundly troubling.

Parenthetically, we should note the thirty-eight percent—it is a reality we will return to later.

> Conservative Christians also find their own religious practices being transformed by the very popular entertainment they were seeking to emulate. As he concluded his travels throughout evangelical America, historian Randall Balmer was "astounded at how the media, especially television, have permeated evangelical worship. Soloists and musical ensembles gyrate to 'canned' orchestra music from cassette tapes played over elaborate sound systems. Applause regularly punctuated Sunday morning services almost everywhere I went, as though each congregation was a studio audience. God apparently likes applause, a fact that had eluded me as I grew up within the evangelical subculture." When evangelicals search for God in popular culture, not only does faith give way before commerce but also commerce, in the form of popular entertainment, reaches down into the inner sanctums of faith. "Turning mass recordings and rock tours into a form of 'ministry' took church pastoring from the world of local, personal relationships, premised on trust and familiarity, into the impersonal world of entertainment, characterized by the market-driven terms of production and consumer choice," as one professor at Calvin College, an evangelical institution, puts it.[30]

As Mr. Balmer astutely noted, the church seems persuaded it can appease and please the Supreme Being by admonitions to "Give God a hand." This line of thought borders—if not trespasses across—the line of sacrilege. Do we honor God by the slapping of our appendages together or by reverential obedience? Professor Wolfe then pierces once again the armor of self-deception and rationalization worn by the American evangelical church:

> Pleased by their success at bringing in new members, the leadership of fast-growing evangelical churches is busy counting filled pews, tabulating the sales of their CDs, and raising funds for the next church construction on the new ring road being completed as part of the interstate highway program. Yet one has to wonder whether their efforts are worth it. As conservative Christians change their attitudes toward popular culture away from ambivalence to active involvement, the results seem suspiciously like the kinds of Faustian pacts against which Christians often warn. For the truth is that there is increasingly little difference between an essentially secular activity like the popular entertainment industry and the bring-em-in-at-any-cost efforts of evangelical megachurches. As evangelicals since the days of popular revivalist George Whitefield learn over and over again, the spirit of Jesus has existed

PD. Source: *http://en.wikipedia.org/wiki/File:Stryper_Concert_1986.jpg.*

Professor Alan Wolfe asked, "What did evangelicals gain by overcoming their suspicion of popular entertainment in favor of contemporary rock? The answer seems to be very little. For one thing, the notion that young people were going to be lured into stronger faith commitments after listening to watered-down gospel music seems rather naive...survey research for evangelicals...found that none of them mentioned Christian music as responsible for their conversion." Emulating the world is not the way.

> for two thousand years and the United States for just a little more than two hundred, but whenever American popular culture clashes with that of time-tested religion, it is usually the latter that finds itself giving way.[31]

Wolfe is correct: In the modern West, when culture clashes with religion the former is nearly always the victor. This can only be explained one of two ways: Either we are seeing a clash between culture and the institutional church (as contrasted with the authentic church mentioned earlier), in which case the two are really the same—not adversaries, but adherents to largely identical value systems simply jockeying for power; or, the weakness and spiritual shallowness of the church is pervasive. Of course, it can be explained—and surely is—as an amalgam of both.

The utter purposelessness of this—a "bitter truth" yet unrecognized—is suggested by the following passage.

> As is true of so much else of their approach to modernity, evangelicals swing back and forth from rejecting popular culture to embracing it. The bitter truth seems to be that neither makes much of a difference. American popular culture is both amazingly indifferent to those seeking to shape its direction and astonishingly competent at absorbing and transforming anyone who tries. There is, contrary to what evangelicals sometimes think, no systematic bias against religious believers in the media because they are run by liberal elites ensconced in Manhattan; nor is there a rush on the part of the media to embrace Christian themes as a way of tapping into new sources of advertising revenue. Popular culture

> is instead about itself; it has its own imperatives, its own forms, and its own priorities. As willing to feature Jesus as it is Satan, it will reduce both to the lowest common denominator of its deeply entrenched conception of popular taste. Evangelicals are free to use the media to gain adherents, but in the process, they are likely to be used by media outlets desperate to fill twenty-four-hour programming. The whole unseemly process makes one think that perhaps those fundamentalists who warned against the temptations of popular culture may have known a thing or two. At least Faust was aware of the consequences of the pact he signed.[32]

Faust, in his faithless pride, did understand more than it would appear the leadership of the church in America understands. Popular culture is about itself, just as politics in the West is about itself. The values of each are inimical to the kingdom of God. The resistance to the values and principles of faith among the many "Philistines at the Helm" of American culture as described earlier is less about an elaborate conspiracy and more about an utter indifference. At the risk of creating an oxymoron, it is a hostile indifference to be sure, but indifference more accurately characterizes their attitude because these forces do not feel seriously threatened by faith and belief—except in the arena of law and politics, in other words, the loci of governmental power. Indeed, to the extent they can, they will use professed faith and belief (i.e., religion) to further their own interests—which are ultimately about wealth, status, and power.

The view of church growth I have described is corroborated by the corollary decline in the moral standards of the culture. Thus it illustrates a central theme of this work: The church's "success"—as measured primarily in numbers of any kind (attendance, members, media exposure, books sold, square footage, dollars, etc.)—bears no genuine relationship to honoring the life of Christ or obeying His commandments. *Were the church successful in the true biblical and spiritual sense, the true measures of that success would be found in dramatically changed lives and Western civilization headed in an entirely different direction.*

CHAPTER

25

THE ABOLITION OF SIN

Such a sense of personal sin presents the sharpest contrast imaginable to the passive sense of drift; for, while the sense of drift has the effect of an opiate in instilling into the soul an insidious acquiescence in an evil that is assumed to reside in external circumstances beyond the victim's control, the sense of sin has the effect of a stimulus because it tells the sinner that the evil is not external after all, but is within him, and hence subject to his will.
Arnold Toynbee[1]

Things rot through evils native to their selves,
And all that injures issues from within.
Menander[2]

When psychology reigns, sin is driven out.
Alan Wolfe[3]

Dissatisfied with his status as a private in God's army and chafing at the thought that anyone should rebuke him, Western man attempts to, if not abolish the classification of sin for much of what he wants to do, at least reduce his sins from felonies to misdemeanors. Of course he cannot abolish all sin outright—that would expose his temerity. Nor would he want to. Selectively choosing what conduct he will regard as sinful and what he will regard as sinless carries with it the best of both worlds: On the former hand he can ensure his status as "good" or "principled" or even "righteous" by not overtly committing the designated offenses; yet through the expedient of the latter he can remove, or at least diminish, the stigma for committing the sins he holds dear.

The church in America has tended to define its "righteousness" by what it does not do in certain respects and what it does in others—neither classification having complete biblical breadth and depth. Significantly, the lists for each category are, on the one hand, limited, and, on the other, specific to the ideological slant of the denomination or church. The more conservative churches will assert vigorously the moral obligation to abstain from sex outside of heterosexual marriage, drug abuse, pornography, aborticide, perhaps alcohol use, and most of the other elemental vices that plague human nature. That many of their members—and indeed some of their most prominent leaders—spend much of their time and energy in materialistic acquisitiveness not only goes unindicted

Western man does not accept his accountability to a higher moral law. Thus he characterizes all references to this reality as "dogma," "intolerance," "judgmentalism" or some other such propagandistic labeling designed to undermine the credibility of those who assert such views. Thus in just two generations, Western man has produced views of life that reflect this regression: "God, an absolute higher moral law, man's innate sinfulness and accountability" to "God, a 'misunderstood' moral law, man's innate goodness" to "man is his own god, absolute moral law does not exist, no one is accountable except to himself." At this rate, in just a few more generations, Western man will be, metaphorically at least, swinging from the vines of the jungle in a reversal of his favorite explanation of his existence.

PD

—but is actually rather often treated as evidence of God's beneficence for their virtue—is never acknowledged. A compelling sense of compassionate urgency to be in the forefront of treating and healing the various social, relational, and psychological infirmities of their community cannot be found. Readily deferring to government or other secular agencies to address those infirmities, they spend their wealth on family life centers, gymnasiums, larger and more imposing buildings and elaborate sanctuaries, and bureaucratically devised programs of dubious efficacy—at least efficacy as defined in biblical terms.

In similar manner, but with a reversal of values in many respects, the more left-leaning denominations and churches may feel the need to display their convictions through social action—though these are typically limited, rarely extensive or truly sacrificial—while either not rebuking the practice of elemental vices by its members or doing so with a tepidity that would not unsettle an infant. The killing of an unborn child may be as morally acceptable to them as the self-centered materialism would be to the conservative.

This selectivity about sin is common and typically suggestive of cultural ideological biases and prejudices—although, in truth, indicative of much more deep-seated traits of human nature. We note below the predisposition of some left-leaning churches to expunge all guilt for homosexual behavior—arguing disingenuously and with bizarre illogic that the conduct is neither abnormal nor a violation of God's law as to sexual expression. But the rightist-leaning churches often display similar inclinations, rarely raising their voices, much less their fingers, over the social injustices all around them. Though said somewhat facetiously, it could be observed with all truth that one will never hear a sermon on the sin of gluttony in an evangelical or fundamentalist church—albeit one of the "seven deadly sins" and a primary cause of morbidity in the West—even as the pews groan and creak under the ponderous weight of excess flesh.

The historian Arnold Toynbee observed that a key distinction between a healthy, vibrant civilization and one in marked decay can always—and should always be sought—within the "inner world" of the individual citizen. This is completely consistent with the teachings of Christ, who insisted that man is fully and individually responsible not only for what he does, but who he becomes in this "inner world." Awareness of his responsibility through the concept of sin is central.

What route must the individual take to arrive at his destination of self-realization in his inner world? He experiences, after all, the same crisis as his fellows in their common ordeal of life in a disintegrating

> society; yet what is a stumbling-block to them becomes for him a supreme challenge. When the *élan* of growth in a healthy society seems to have given out, the passive individual loses his bearings upon the uncharted seas of the Universe; but the alternative reaction to this sense of a loss of control is, not to look outwards upon a macrocosm engulfed by evil, but to look inwards to the soul's own self and to recognize the moral defeat as a failure of self-mastery. Such a sense of personal sin presents the sharpest contrast imaginable to the passive sense of drift; for, while the sense of drift has the effect of an opiate in instilling into the soul an insidious acquiescence in an evil that is assumed to reside in external circumstances beyond the victim's control, the sense of sin has the effect of a stimulus because it tells the sinner that the evil is not external after all, but is within him, and hence subject to his will.
>
> There is here the whole difference between the Slough of Despond and the faith that moves mountains; at the same time, though, we can see that there may be a margin of common ground between the mountains and the slough in practical life—an intermediate Zone of feeling and conduct across which the tormented soul in an age of social disintegration may make, if it will, the arduous passage from resignation to endeavour.[4]

The great question for multitudes in our age is "Will" the "tormented souls" in our "age of social disintegration" make that "arduous passage"? If those souls have no help, no encouragement, no sense of direction, from a pusillanimous, weak, insensitive, or self-seeking church leadership, can we expect that they likely will? This is precisely the role of the church—to neither nurture a sense that his conduct is beyond his control nor permit him to assume he can evade ultimate accountability, but to empower him with the recognition that he does have a choice in thought and deed, and he will be held accountable for both. This is the church's duty, a duty that the Western church is failing miserably to discharge.

The British sociologist Steve Bruce described the American pattern this way:

> ...in 1984 Gallup reported that the percentage of those asked who believed that the Bible is "literally true" had fallen from 65 per cent in 1964 to just 37 per cent (Wuthnow 1988: 165). Although heaven remains popular, belief in hell has also declined....[T]he change has actually been greater than a simple report of survey data would suggest, because what the churches (and, we have to presume, their members) mean by these terms has itself undergone a considerable reinterpretation.
>
> The simplest way of describing the changes in content is to say that the supernatural has been diminished and it has been psychologized or subjectivized. Religion used to be about the divine and our relationship to it. God was a real force external to us. The Bible was his revealed word. Miracles actually occurred. Christ really was the son of God and he did actually die to atone for our sins. Heaven and hell were real places. Gradually over the last hundred years a quite different interpretation of these things has affected much of mainstream Christianity. God is no longer seen as an actual person but as some sort of vague power or, in the final reduction, our own consciences. The Bible is no longer the word of God but a historical book with some useful ethical and moral guidelines for living. Miracles are explained away; either they did not really happen or they were natural phenomena misunderstood by ignorant peasants. Christ was not actually God's son but an exemplary prophet and teacher. Heaven and hell are not real places but psychological states.[5]

But of course, two lines of thought should occur to the astute reader: First, the conservative elements of the Christian church in America will tend to rejoin, "Yes, but that is about them (i.e., the liberals), not about us." Second, many American Christians will still see themselves as much more pious than their European brethren. But, as to the first, Bruce is pointing out what we have striven to demonstrate throughout this work: the corrupting influence of Western culture is at work throughout the Western church in all its manifestations, the differences being a matter of type and degree. Second, the other difference is not only about degree but about timing; it is just a matter of time—should the present trends continue—that many more of the precedents set by the European church will become obvious in the American.

YOU'RE OKAY, I'M OKAY—WHY THEN IS THE CULTURE *NOT* OKAY?

The hungry sheep look up and are not fed....
Dante

This abdication of responsibility is so ubiquitous that Professor Wolfe found much evidence—common, not rare—of the minister and priest resorting to the culture's authorities to determine matters of right and wrong!

> On one occasion, sinful acts are explained away when the preacher invokes the classification of diagnostic disorders assembled by the American Psychological Association to describe the elder brother's narcissism. Rare is the sermon that dwells on sin if doing so leaves a gloomy message that leaves little reason to feel joy in the presence of the Lord.[6]
>
> ...
>
> Sin existed long before psychology. When God called down his wrath on those who had been led astray, or when preachers, speaking in the name of God, singled out sinners for special treatment in hell, no one thought that a better way of framing the problem was to explore whether conduct deemed sinful from a religious perspective could more appropriately be labeled dysfunctional from a psychological one. Now nearly everybody does, none more so than religious believers themselves.
>
> ...These days psychological language routinely permeates the sermons, publications, appeals, and small-group efforts of mainline American religion. "Low self-esteem can keep us from achieving our goals, forming solid friendships, and seeing the good in others," suggests an article in a Methodist magazine aimed at teenage readers, before going on to add that "it can even hinder our relationship with God."
>
> When psychology reigns, sin is driven out.[7]

Thus man's creation, the "science" of psychology, can be used to obliterate sin. Of course, to do this successfully—at least with theoretical logic—surgery must be performed to remove the indeterministic power of choice—of man's will—from the mix. If it is still present in the formulation—even in a diluted or attenuated form—then the volitional choice that the Bible calls sin is still present.

These practices are consistent with the trends in the West to not only disavow notions that homosexual behavior is a forbidden exercise of sexuality, but also a perverse behavior that subjects the individual and society to an array of problems—most of which are roundly ignored by arguments in favor of "tolerance." The proponents of this "tolerance"—it could be far more accurately christened "irrationality"—would be hard pressed to explain—having looked into a pasture and seen two stallions (or two mares) engaging in the same homosexual acts humans engage in—that this was not abnormal.

PD

Dante and the Divine Comedy; fresco from the nave of the Duomo of Florence, Italy, by Domenico di Michelino, 1465. *Dante wrote, "The hungry sheep look up and are not fed...." Preachers and priests all across the West are not truly feeding the sheep. Sin and punishment are either diluted, some sins not addressed, or obliterated. One of Western man's creations, the "science" of psychology, can be used to obliterate sin. Of course, to do this successfully—at least with theoretical logic—surgery must be performed to remove the indeterministic power of choice—of man's will—from the mix. If it is still present in the formulation—even in a diluted or attenuated form—then the volitional choice that the Bible calls sin is still present.*

Any attempt to do so would shred their credibility. Yet, as Professor Wolfe's vignette suggests, what is "credible" can be a self-deluding matter of choice.

The dissipated sense of moral responsibility—and the Western desire to be free to sin without real moral accountability—when merged with the hubris of some psychologists and psychiatrists, results not only in a perversion of morality but of logic, and the partial destruction of the credibility of a social science that might otherwise have great utility even within the church.

> To this day, psychology is looked upon as a dubious, if not diabolical, enterprise in some quarters of conservative Christianity...."Psychoheresy" is the integration of secular psychological counseling theories and therapies with the Bible. Psychoheresy is also the intrusion of such theories into the preaching and practice of Christianity, especially when they contradict or compromise biblical Christianity

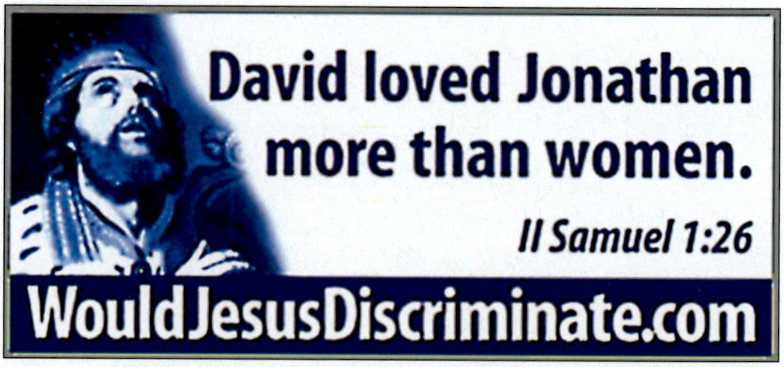

PD

The lust in the West to sin without accountability is so great resort is made to distorting biblical passages in order to justify the behavior. When the focal point of an individual's life is sexuality then everything becomes subject to manipulation and tailoring to accommodate that sexuality. These practices are consistent with the trends in the West to not only disavow notions that homosexual behavior is a forbidden exercise of sexuality, but also a perverse behavior that subjects the individual and society to an array of problems—most of which are roundly ignored by arguments in favor of "tolerance." The proponents of this "tolerance"—it could be far more accurately christened "irrationality" —would be hard pressed to explain, having looked into a pasture and seen two stallions (or two mares) engaging in the same homosexual acts humans engage in, that this was not abnormal. Any attempt to do so would shred their credibility. Yet what is deemed "credible" can be a self-deluding matter of choice.

in terms of the nature of man, how he is to live, and how he changes." Groups like this know the appeal of psychology and have made it clear that they want nothing to do with it.

Evangelicals, however, have proven themselves far more responsive to psychology than fundamentalists.[8]

Psychologists have something of value to offer to people of faith. People of faith have much more of value to offer to psychologists. One need not reject the other even as each may be selective in what to embrace.

Wolfe notes the pervasive practice of Americans seeking help in self-help guides.

> Somebody, it is clear, is buying all those self-help guides, and whether or not those who do formally share a religious designation matters less than the fact that few if any of them contain much language about sin and the damage it can do to people, God, and society.
>
> Popular psychology is bound to influence churches more than the other way around, if for no other reason that, in their attempts to reach the "unchurched," religious leaders have to pay attention to what Americans are buying and reading in such copious amounts.
>
> This blending of psychology and religion has its positive side, for there is no necessary reason to conclude that those who focus on their own needs will automatically neglect the needs of others. Still, the psychologizing of American religion makes it difficult for the faithful to emphasize classic religious themes such as duty and responsibility.[9]

It makes it difficult to know what is sin and what is not; but is that not the crux of the matter? Western man, as I have repeatedly declared, seeks license not moral constraint, absolute freedom not accountability. Western man, in the favorite phrasing of advertisements and marketing ploys, has been told—and is convincing himself—"you deserve it."

Some sociologists, including Steve Bruce, believe that the dramatic, foundational shift away from a biblical viewpoint in American Protestantism began in the 1930s, reaching its pinnacle in the writing and preaching of Norman Vincent Peale.

Photo by Nathan Williams. CC

Psychology and self-help books fill rows of shelves, but no Bibles are found in this section. *Western publishers make billions from self-help guides. Evidently Western man is looking for answers much as was said in the old song about searching for love in all the wrong places. Authors of these self-help books typically are a reflection of Western culture itself—the same culture that is thrashing about in a chaos of dysfunctionality nurtured by pride and vanity. As Alan Wolfe observed, "Somebody, it is clear, is buying all those self-help guides, and whether or not those who do formally share a religious designation matters less than the fact that few if any of them contain much language about sin and the damage it can do to people, God, and society."*

> Peale was a liberal Presbyterian minister, pastor of one of the biggest churches in New York (which he built from just forty souls to over 900) and the originator of what he called "the power of positive thinking" (George 1994). In the first two years after its publication, the book of the same name sold over two million copies. For Peale the Christian message was reduced to a battle between good and evil, but these were no longer realities external to us. Evil was a lack of self-confidence; good was positive thinking. Those people who think positively (while conforming to the norms of suburban middle-class 1950s America) will be successful; this is salvation. Those who do not will be damned that is, they will be unhappy.[10]

To the observant, it is striking to note the parallels between Peale's "gospel" and that of the New Age. In substance little has changed, except—and this is a very important exception—New Agers are overt in their rejection of notions like God, preferring instead to cast man as his own god. But in the essentials of attitude and behavior, Peale and those like him are, in many respects, kith and kin with the New Agers, and those like them.

Thus in just two generations, Western man produced views of life that reflect this regression: "God, an absolute higher moral law, man's innate sinfulness and accountability"—to "God, a 'misunderstood' moral law, man's innate goodness"—to "man is his own god, absolute moral law does not exist, no one is accountable except to himself." At this rate, in just a few more generations, Western man will be, metaphorically at least, swinging from the vines of the jungle in a reversal of his favorite explanation of his existence.

As we might expect, anything so "successful" in the midst of a culture smitten with "success" will surely be emulated. Bruce carries the narrative forward one generation to one of Peale's evolutionary progeny and the spectacle of "church" as Sorokin's colossalism and human pride and vanity enshrined in glass and steel.

> The spirit of Peale lives on in the theology of Robert Schuler [*sic*], who in the 1950s started preaching at a drive-in cinema in Garden Grove, California. He stood on the roof of the snack bar; his congregation sat in their cars. Televising the service as *The Hour of Power* brought a growing congregation

Norman Vincent Peale. *Some sociologists believe the foundational shift away from a biblical viewpoint of sin in American Protestantism began in the 1930s, reaching its pinnacle in the writing and preaching of Norman Vincent Peale. The evolutionary regression continues with others who would tell Americans what they wish to hear. The focus is not on sin, what we would do for God or on the hereafter but on man's indulgence and on the here-and-now—what "God" will do for you if....*

PD-LOC

> and in 1980 the Garden Grove Community Church abandoned the drive-in for the $16 million Crystal Cathedral, a modernist edifice walled and roofed in glass. Schuler [*sic*] did not forget his roots: one end of the building was designed to slide open and the car park was fitted with headphones so that those who wanted to stay in their cars could still enjoy the service. In the mid-1980s, *The Hour of Power* was the most popular religious programme on US television. Schuler preaches a Pealean gospel that he called "possibility theology." The extent to which this differs from traditional Christianity is very neatly symbolized in the title of his most popular book. The Beatitudes (so-called from the Greek word for "blessed") are the promises given by Christ in the Sermon on the Mount: "Blessed are the poor in spirit: for theirs is the kingdom of heaven. Blessed are they that mourn: for they shall be comforted" and so on (Matthew 5:3–11). The contract is clear (and it has for centuries been recited as a central part of the liturgy of most Christian churches). Christ promised the poor, the mournful, the meek, the righteous, the merciful, the pure in heart, the peacemakers, and the oppressed that they will attain the kingdom of heaven. With no trace of irony, Robert Schuler's *The Be-Happy-Attitudes* promises that those who "believe in Christ" will be rewarded with health, prosperity and happiness in this world.[11]

The temptations to pursue "success"—and we all know "nothing succeeds like success"—readily overwhelmed the ramparts of self-possession and humility to compromise not just American liberal Christians but the conservatives as well.

> An important element of Peale's psychologizing of religion was its positive valuation of the self. Conservatives were bitterly critical of liberals for abandoning the idea of sin and for turning salvation from another-worldly destination to therapeutic improvement in this life. Yet, a generation later, evangelicals were rewriting the gospel in precisely the same way. Hunter makes the point economically by listing the titles of best-selling evangelical books of the 1980s: *You Can Become the Person You Want to Be*; *The Healthy Personality and the Christian Life*; *How to Become Your Own Best Self;* and *Self-Esteem: The New Reformation* (J. D. Hunter 1987: 69–70). God is still there, but he is no longer the strict father who crushes our pride and brings us to see our worthlessness. He is the psychotherapist who can help us to be more fulfilled and to achieve more in this life.[12]

The evolutionary regression continues with others who would toady. A Texas youngster named Joel Osteen is the latest to take up the mantle and tell Americans what they wish to hear. All of it leaves the discerning Christian with many perplexing and dismaying questions of great theological and philosophical import, and one that is decidedly practical: Do the honest and insightful secularists and agnostics in American culture have unusually strong stomachs or just remarkable self-possession?

Features of these forms of "ultra-modern Christianity" include "this-worldly" salvation, as reflected in sociological studies: Central to all is what Yves Lambert calls "this-worldly salvation." In "the study of a Breton parish, I observed that Catholicism had been *de facto* reinterpreted as a transcendental humanism, aimed towards earthly fulfillment, while being open to an after-life devoid of eternal damnation; the evocation of hell disappeared slightly after Vatican II (1962–65)."[13] This of course is completely consistent with the "health, wealth and prosperity" gospels of many American preachers and priests. "On the extreme side, televangelists put forth an analogous argument by showing that the expiation of sin and fidelity to God are infallible ways of assuring heavenly grace and benediction, especially in matters of health, family and employment."[14] The focus is not on the hereafter but the here-and-now—what "God" will do for you *if*....

"An important consequence of 'this-worldliness' is the *dissociation between sin and one's fate after death*, the desoteriologisation of guilt (hence, the collapse of the practice of confession in Catholicism?) or a more worldly interpretation: sin distances one from God and prevents one from benefiting from His grace, from being fully happy, from communicating with others." Thus it is not man's salvation with which we need be so concerned, but with his happiness, his fulfillment.

All of this contrasts significantly with New Testament teaching about joy in the face of pain, adversity and suffering. "Joy," in the biblical sense—not to be confused with "happiness"—is a state of mind and heart that for the true Christian comes *with*

PD release

Vatican II. *Sociologists note what has been called "this-worldly salvation." In the study of a Breton parish, writes Yves Lambert, "I observed that Catholicism had been* de facto *reinterpreted as a transcendental humanism, aimed towards earthly fulfillment, while being open to an after-life devoid of eternal damnation; the evocation of hell disappeared slightly after Vatican II (1962–65)." This of course is completely consistent with the "health, wealth and prosperity" gospels of many American preachers and priests. "On the extreme side, televangelists put forth an analogous argument by showing that the expiation of sin and fidelity to God are infallible ways of assuring heavenly grace and benediction, especially in matters of health, family and employment."*

the panoply of problems and griefs associated with the human experience—especially those that are the peculiar burden of the true Christian.

These observations are fundamentally consistent with those of Wolfe; the trends in the Western church all reflect the same elements: this-worldliness, an obsession with comfort, personal gain, personal security and individual happiness, an absence of significant sacrifice, greater freedom to sin without the burden of guilt or the fear of social or Divine accountability; in a sentence—the elevation of man to the center stage of life and the world and the reduction of God to not much more than an unchallenging, avuncular sugar daddy.

All is accomplished under the cover of a pietistic religiosity. The rapidity and ease with which the church moves away from sin and judgment is facilitated by religious teachings—taken out of context and even sugar-coated, but religious nonetheless. Alan Wolfe explains it this way:

> But there are religious origins to the culture of nonjudgmentalism in the United States as well as secular ones, as anyone who recalls Jesus' admonition to "judge not" will understand. Believers who have a warm and personal relationship with the deity will probably want to have a warm and personal relationship with everyone else, and this precludes them from being ever on the lookout for behavior to condemn. Once specific behaviors have been removed from a category called sin, there is no place for them to go other than to a category called understanding—and understanding, along with empathy, warmth, and friendship, is what a large number of faithful Americans seek.[15]

One potential test of an individual's interpretation of scripture can be expressed thusly: Is their interpretation trendy, politically correct, convenient, self-serving, or easy? Most Christians who stand for obedience to God's moral law do so at their own risk and cost. They take positions that restrict their own behavior on one hand and make them more vulnerable to criticism from those who do not wish to be so confined on the other.

God's moral law is confining in the sense that it sets high and clear standards of behavior. Those who choose to interpret scripture to their own gain or ease can typically be easily spotted: their interpretations focus on notions such as "tolerance," "diversity," "inclusiveness," "forgiveness," "mercy," and "understanding," but the connotations they give to each of those terms is often at variance with Scriptural dictates when read with stringent objectivity. This is striving to make the Bible say what man wants it to say; what is expedient for him. Many people—the Bible refers to them as those having "itching ears"—will be taken in by this practice because it offers license for that which they desire, and the course of least resistance.

No human being is as understanding as is God. Yet God told man of an event called judgment and a place called hell. Why would an "understanding" God mention such unpleasantness—much less make them so prominent in his revelation of Himself—unless they are central to man's fate?

The agnostic Professor Wolfe acknowledges—in a passage that will gratify the wise and frustrate the foolish—the value of immutable standards of human behavior and personal accountability as critically necessary to the health of an individual and a society. In brief, he astonishes—perhaps most other agnostics and secularists, and not a few professing Christians—by declaring that the concept of sin is essential.

> But there is something to be said for belief in sin if it is accompanied by the ability to focus on matters outside the self. In the ways in which they dispense with doctrine, reinterpret tradition, and transform worship, Americans have long ago left behind ways of practicing religion that would satisfy the prophets and martyrs who shaped their faiths, yet in no other area of religious practice, especially for evangelicals, is the gap between the religion as it is supposed to be and religion as it actually is as great as it is in the area of sin. As a nonbeliever, I ought to be encouraged by this development, for it suggests that we will be less likely to point invidious fingers of shame at those who do not happen to agree with the majority's determination of what is acceptable morality and what is not.
>
> But somehow I am not pleased with this retreat from sin, for the ease with which American religious believers adopt nonjudgmental language and a psychological understanding of wrongdoing is detrimental to anyone, religious or not, who believes that individuals should judge their actions against the highest possible ideals of human conduct, however those ideals are established. One need not be a Calvinist preoccupied with the dark side of human nature to recognize that covenants exist and that we break them only at great cost to ourselves and to others with whom we share our society.[16]

Wolfe's views remind one of Christ's remark to the inquisitive scribe: "You are not far from the Kingdom of God." (Mark 12:34 NIV) It is difficult to know for certain whether Wolfe's seeming longing for an authentic faith and practice is largely that of a sociologist who has reasonably concluded that this is a needed and benevolent influence on society, or, whether there is in it an undercurrent of searching that transcends academic inquisitiveness and social concern. Either way the pathos is apparent: if the former case, because of intellectual assent to myth; if the latter case because the pride of intellect has so far been a stumbling block to faith.

His comprehension of the dangers for our civilization of a diluted, effete, reinterpretation of Christian teaching is very close to the mark.

The exigency of the perilous situation of the West requires a willingness to speak forcefully and uncompromisingly about human attitudes and behavior. The practices of many ministers and priests, in abstaining from offending their listeners, reflect a self-centered focus. Their pusillanimity—if not their heretical unbelief in what the Bible says and clearly means—makes a dangerous complement to Western man's self-absorbed quest for moral autonomy. But man does not leave the environs of hazardous circumstances or the need for external accountability once he exits childhood. The dangers are all the greater with maturity—and especially so in a world of ever-burgeoning temptations, problems and threats. The hubris of Western man has convinced him that he should be the ultimate arbiter of his own morality. Yet the fatuity and folly in this is self-evident from the state of his world—faith and belief in a Supreme Being notwithstanding.

END NOTES
CHAPTER 25

1 Arnold Toynbee, *A Study of History* (New York: Weathervane Books, 1972), 249.
2 Menander, cited in Toynbee, *A Study of History*, 161.
3 Alan Wolfe, *The Transformation of American Religion: How We Actually Live Our Faith* (New York: Simon and Schuster, 2003), 176. Reprinted and edited with the permission of The Free Press, a Division of Simon & Schuster, Inc., from *The Transformation of American Religion: How We Actually Live Our Faith* by Alan Wolfe. Copyright 2003 by Alan Wolfe. All rights reserved.
4 Toynbee, *Study of History*, 249.
5 Steve Bruce, *God Is Dead: Secularization in the West* (Oxford: Wiley-Blackwell, 2002), 208–209.
6 Wolfe, *Transformation of American Religion*, 170.
7 Wolfe, *Transformation of American Religion*, 176.
8 Wolfe, *Transformation of American Religion*, 177–178.
9 Wolfe, *Transformation of American Religion*, 183.
10 Bruce, *God Is Dead*, 209.
11 Bruce, *God Is Dead*, 209–210.
12 Bruce, *God Is Dead*, 211–212.
13 Yves Lambert in *The Decline of Christendom in Western Europe, 1750–2000*, ed. McLeod and Ustorf (Cambridge: Cambridge University Press, 2003), 75.
14 Lambert, *Decline of Christendom*, 75.
15 Wolfe, *Transformation of American Religion*, 176.
16 Wolfe, *Transformation of American Religion*, 184.

CHAPTER

26

BY THEIR WORKS YE SHALL KNOW THEM

...[W]e must admit that Western man has not been faithful to this Christian tradition. He has abandoned it not once, but again and again. For since Christianity depends on a living faith and not merely on social tradition, Christendom must be renewed in every generation, and every generation is faced by the responsibility of making decisions, each of which may be an act of Christian faith or an act of apostasy.
Christopher Dawson[1]

The stone which the builders rejected, the same is become the head of the corner.
Arnold Toynbee, quoting Matthew 21:42 (KJV)[2]

Preach the gospel at all times. If necessary, use words.
Francis of Assisi

There are two compelling offenses human beings can commit against one another that involve no theft and no violence but that are universal in their adverse impact. They can be found in every social relationship from marriage, to the church, to society as a whole. The first is an offense against another's pride and self-image when he feels himself looked down upon in any way by another who regards himself as superior. Individuals will put up with a lot if they feel they are on—and perceived by their milieu to be on—an equal footing with others. Deny them that and resentment is bred.

The second and related offense is against a person's intellect, their understanding, through the hypocrisy of others. Though they may never voice their feelings—and may even be complicit in the charade—here disrespect and contempt are bred.

The Western church has sometimes been an offender in both respects—reflecting the worst of both worlds—appearing self-righteous on the one hand, yet much like everyone else on the other. The permutations of these offenses are as many and varied as the mutations of the church that have strayed from the actual life and teachings of Christ. No one will influence anyone in a significant and profound way through such attitudes.

Some avoid the church because of the "hypocrites" there. Many Christians respond with an equally glib, now trite, riposte: "Churches are hospitals for sinners, not museums for saints." This is certainly true as far as it goes, but it often smacks of rationalization and excuse. What the critics may be telling us is that they would only give credence to a church where people actually fully lived their faith not just talked it. Perfection is not usually the issue; sincere and complete commitment certainly is.

Abraham Lincoln, who never joined a church, declared, "When any church will inscribe over its altar, as its sole qualification for membership, the Saviour's condensed statement of the substance of both law and Gospel, 'Thou shalt love the Lord thy God with all thy heart, and with all thy soul and thy neighbor as thyself,' that church will I join with all my heart and all my soul."[3] Lincoln's skepticism about the church is a species of incredulity even more common in our time.

Credibility and respect can only be nurtured by integrity, consistency, authenticity, and unflagging commitment to principle. Trust is bred when these three are then complemented by compassion and humility.

As I have already suggested, there is a poignancy and pathos to Professor Wolfe's analysis of the church in America. One cannot help but believe that despite his agnosticism, Professor Wolfe feels deep disappointment and something akin to disillusionment about what he sees in the American church. It would seem that an agnostic would be indifferent—if you do not believe, why does it matter?—one senses, however, that Professor Wolfe, like so many people in Western civilization, is searching. In that sense, Wolfe is illustrative of what I believe is a common phenomenon among many agnostics and secularists: Some may prefer to find reasons for belief, but the church they see is often bereft of inspiration, revelation, and hope.

Since the very term "church" conjures up mental images in the West of a structure, rather than an aggregation of highly cohesive and motivated individuals, those structures are significant in the message they send to the wider world. The nature of that message will reflect the nature of those who initiate and devise construction. In medieval times, Catholic churches were often designed by architects and artists at the behest of the Church, with no expectancy that the identities of the individuals behind the edifices would ever even be relevant, much less known. In that sense, an element of humility before God and man was blended with the mortar that cemented the stones together. To be sure, the Catholic Church typically had another motive: to remind the populace of its grandeur and power and thereby ensure their deference to the Church. Only God could know for certain the proportions of each set of motives that went into the construction of the greatest cathedrals of Western civilization.

In our time, similar motives are at play in the construction of the physical edifices of churches throughout the Western world, but nowhere would some worldly motives be suggested more emphatically than in the construction of some of the larger and leading churches' edifices in America. Standing before, or in, some of these palatial monuments to Western man's wealth and technical skill, the contemplative observer might gaze upward at their towering, immaculate façades and have reason to question the motives of those who caused them to come to pass. Is this really about God or is it more about man?

The contrast, we earlier noted, that Yeats observed between the splendor of the architectural expression he described in Ireland in his time and the conditions of the hearts that made them is a penetrating gaze into the soul of man[4]—a gaze not unlike that displayed by Christ himself.

Emblematic more of the material plenitude of the church and its concomitant human pride, the church's edifices rest in proximity to unrelieved suffering, much of which continues day in and day out within a stone's throw of their emplacement. Just as some of the imposing churches of the American

Used by permission. *http://www.therestorationmovement.com*

CC

(Top) Cane Ridge Meeting House, Kentucky, where the Second Great Awakening in American history began. *In an unprepossessing and humble log church one of the most powerful and sweeping religious awakenings in world history erupted. Historians and sociologists have observed the positive social impact of what is now usually referred to as the Great Awakenings.* (Left) *No such individual or social exaltation of any significant magnitude has ever originated in the* Crystal Cathedral *or any of its pretentious ilk. Emblematic more of the material plenitude of the Western church and its concomitant human pride, the church's edifices rest in proximity to unrelieved suffering, much of which continues day in and day out within a stone's throw of their emplacement. It is no mere coincidence that one of America's Great Awakenings began in the humble log structure, not the gaudy edifice.*

South were constructed with slave labor, the imposing churches of today often reflect sacrifices, not on the altar of God, as they are invariably touted, but sacrifices of the "sweetness," "gentleness," and "humility" of Christ that many of the suffering in the communities near them have never known.

Christ told those who profess to follow him, "If you love me, you will obey what I command" (John 14:15 NIV) without anywhere ever suggesting that this encompassed erecting edifices from brick and mortar contrived by the hand of man. That man cannot, in his pathetic way, construct anything to rival, or even symbolize, the love, grace and justice that Christ offered humankind is lost on so many. The efforts would be pathetic yet cause for sympathy were they not illustrative of misbegotten motives.

The only edifice with which man may truly honor God is the edifice of obedience—in sacrifice, love for one's fellowman, and humility. Furthermore, nothing ever has—and nothing ever will—rival this intangible monument in its impact on human beings or the course of history.

As so often seems to be the case, the dubiousness of the church's "works" is rarely questioned by its leadership. If uncertainty is expressed, this will likely be from the laity. A Baptist deacon, who had no theological training, once confessed to me his persistent unease of conscience at the wealth expended by his church in buildings and property—which, he pointed out, contrasted greatly with the money spent on missions, evangelism, and service in their community. Noteworthy was the deacon's concern not with the expenditure of money, but the priority given to those expenditures. He sensed rightly that anyone's true priorities can be discerned, not by listening to them recount them, but by watching how they use their resources—time, thought, energy, and money. This is true of ministers, priests, Christian leaders, and the church itself. Raising this concern with his pastor, who was a doctoral graduate of a major Protestant seminary, he was summarily told—significantly, without biblical support—that this was what the church should do, and thereafter treated coolly. "…and a little child will lead them." (Isaiah 11:6 NIV)

Like the violence referred to in Yeats' poem, there is a "slippered contemplation" about the way the church's wealth is expended. Little deep—much less biblically centered—thought is given to it. It thus becomes, to use Yeats's words again, a "servile shape—at others' beck and call." Serving very human purposes and motives, it becomes also a "stumbling block" to millions who sense—perhaps less analytically, more intuitively—that these practices are inconsistent with the life of Christ (i.e., true selfless and absolute love). Tactilely emblematic more than anything else of the church's condition in the West, it reflects not spiritual success, but failure—and why for generations that failure has been increasingly telling in the culture at large.

THE VAUNTED AMERICAN "INDIVIDUALISM"—WHAT IT TRULY MEANS

We know what a person thinks not when he tells us what he thinks, but by his actions.
Isaac Singer

Two things are infinite: the universe and human stupidity; and I'm not sure about the universe.
Albert Einstein

Professor Wolfe cites attitudes and behavior that serve as additional illustrations of the theme of "hypervelocity" in Western culture in—a place you would not expect—religion. Western man is in such a hurry that even the reputedly most profound and significant value in his life is one he has little time to tend.

"American society is a nonliturgical society, its pace of life too fast, its commitments to individualism too powerful, its treatment of authority too irreverent, and its craving for innovation too intense to tolerate religious practices that call on believers to repeat the same word or songs with little room for creative expression."[5]

The "individualism" Wolfe cites here, sadly, is not the individualism of earlier generations of Americans, given as they were to insisting on thinking and deciding for themselves and on the relentless exercise of self-reliance. The modern American conforms—and seeks the support of government or any number of other institutions upon which he can lean for this or that. True self-reliance is not in his repertoire any more than is truly independent thought or bold action in defiance of the norms of the culture or his fellows.

Modern American individualism, such as it is, smacks of the individualism of self-centeredness: "I want my rights, my share of the pie, my expectations met, and my sense of security ensured." This species of "individualism" breeds a doctrine of personal convenience that permits Western man to rationalize even the killing of his unborn young and construct a massive, imperious legal regime designed to tend to his "rights"—including the "right" to kill those unborn young.

The quest to make their religion efficient, so as to neither consume much of their time nor impose significant burdens on thought or conscience, manifests itself in religious services that have the weight and power of Toynbee's "flare of cotton waste."[6] The hard work of spiritual growth is outsourced to the Sunday preacher or priest.

Professor Wolfe relentlessly points again to reasons why, in America, faith is less faith in God than in man. "Will Herberg claimed that Americans were naïve to believe that they could create a religion 'so innocently *man-centered*.' But he may have been naive to think that people could continue to believe in the power of the religious doctrines that once inspired their ancestors when their society chews up ideas of any sort in order to digest them for widespread public consumption."[7]

Lest naysayers to Professor Wolfe's insights assert that the afflictions he points to are not characteristic of their church or their denomination, we affirm them as not only true but perceptive and comprehensively so. To a greater or lesser extent, every American church has been profoundly influenced by the bull-in-the-china-shop of Western materialist consumer culture. A powerful, domineering force, it has never been fully recognized by the church as the threat to faith and morality that it is. No one is immune to its influence or its consequences.

Wolfe continues by noting the ubiquity of this force. Doctrinal controversies seem pedestrian in comparison to other manifestations of the church's near complete integration into the culture.

> For all their (often quite legitimate) denunciation of sex and violence in the popular media, evangelicals flourish amidst the celebrity-drenched, lowest-common-denominator, highly sentimentalized world of romance novels, daytime soaps, NASCAR races, and Opry-knockoff music that dominates America's entertainment industry.[8]
>
> ...But such efforts [to market directly to evangelicals through religious programming] often failed, and one of the reasons why they failed was because there was no appreciable difference between the religious subculture and the general culture of popular media programming; conservative Christians are too busy watching the same sitcoms enjoyed by other Americans to support a highly profitable network of their own.[9]

This is a profound indictment of the church in America—not only of its faith and morality, but of its intellect. That ministers, priests, Christian leaders, and the lay church would feel no need of absolution for many of these practices says more in one sense than rampaging crime statistics, illegitimate births, millions of aborticides, and a surfeit of addictive behaviors could.

> In one of the most comprehensive efforts to characterize Protestant religious beliefs, Nancy Ammerman found similar patterns of theological unpreparedness nationwide. She classified believers into three categories: activist, those who put considerations of social justice at the heart of their faith; evangelical, those who identify with born-again forms of conservative Christianity; and "Golden Rule Christians," for whom faith involves trying to lead a good life and making the world a better place by doing for others as they would do for you. Ammerman is persuaded that Golden Rule beliefs "may in fact be the dominant form of religiosity among middle-class suburban Americans," including many of those who might also be classified (by others) as evangelical. Yet even though such beliefs are meant to define the essence of faith for moderate Christians, Golden Rule principles are theologically fuzzy. They outline, not a set of correct assertions, but a coterie of good practices.[10]

Since each of these categories of professed belief clearly is lacking something, we must ask how that comes to pass in a society that ostensibly sees itself as religious. The answer can be found in part in the tactical thinking, oriented to marketing, of some church leaders.

> But hoping to bring into worship the unchurched, they also are reluctant to identify with any of Protestantism's many traditions and, even to some degree, with Christianity itself. For example, Willow Creek, America's most famous megachurch, located outside Chicago, displays no cross on its building, but this does not mean it lacks one. "We do have a cross," as a tour guide explained. "We bring it out for special occasions, like baptism." This openly strategic way of thinking about religious identity is fairly common in evangelical circles; one survey of megachurches found that more than half of them refrain from placing religious symbols in prominent places.[11]

Wolfe quotes one pastor, "We don't have a statement that says we'll only go this far. I think we'll do whatever it takes, as long as it's biblical."[12]

This revealing declaration prompts obvious questions: What does the speaker consider "biblical"? Is this "biblical"? Reminiscent of a pettifogging lawyer's search for any angle to justify dubious conduct, it all suggests that should the trend continue, before long the Western church will have regressed to Pilate's question: "What is truth?"

The underlying "romance with numbers" seen here and dealt with more fully in the chapter by that name, reflects a major historical shift for evangelicals. More gravely it reflects a dramatic thinning of belief and conviction such that now these lie lightly on the surface of the church like a veneer. This would be denied by countless ministers, but the evidence is compelling.

> Evangelicals can be accused of many things, including their relative failure (until recently) to take questions of social justice seriously, their flirtations with anti-Catholicism and anti-Semitism, and their suspicion of modern science, including Darwinism. But they cannot be accused of being stick-in-the-muds determined to turn their back on progress in favor of old-fashioned ways. Early in their history, evangelicals were prepared to abandon tradition for the sake of doctrinal purity. Now they are prepared to abandon tradition for the sake of organizational growth.[13]

However, evangelicals abandoning "tradition" is not the truly important issue. Evangelicals are—bit by bit, increment by increment—abandoning the great features of Christ's life and words—self-sacrifice, willingness to face persecution and adversity, pursuit of personal holiness—all of which separate a true Christian from the culture at large in any age. The gimmickry, shallowness, promotion, and obsession with entertainment that panders to self-indulgence has spilled over from the culture, where it might be expected, into the practices, and the thinking, of the church, where it never should be found.

FAILURE AS "SUCCESS"; WEAKNESS AS "STRENGTH"

American religion has been so transformed that we have reached the end of religion as we have known it. This does not mean religion no longer has meaning. It means we will have to know it in new ways.
Alan Wolfe[14]

Professor Wolfe turns his focus to another dimension of America's religiosity—the political movement to faith-based initiatives.

> The idea that religion can have positive benefits for personal morality would be something of a purely academic question were it not for efforts on behalf of faith-based initiatives: programs that enable churches and other religious organizations to use government money for charitable and social-welfare purposes. Where the welfare state failed, the reasoning behind these policies holds, religion might succeed; the best cure for poverty and its persistent social pathologies is not to throw money at people but to encourage them to turn around their lives by discovering the power of faith.
>
> ...It seems safe to predict that over the next few decades, a national sociological experiment will be conducted to see if it is true that people who are devout religious believers are more likely to lead lives of greater moral responsibility.[15]

Unfortunately, faith-based initiatives are evidence not of the American church's success but of its failure. Were churches marshalling resources to serve their fellowman in the manner of Christ's example, none of this would be necessary—much less politically initiated. The entire array of services that are potentially at the disposal of a modern Western society—medical care, psychological care, addiction treatment, family counseling, rehabilitation therapy, financial counseling, etc.—to treat the infirmities of a complex culture, and its often equally complex pathologies, could be implemented by churches in every community across the land.

Had that one form of Christ's example and teaching been honored by the church in the last two generations, the salutary impact on the broader culture would have been incalculable. But the church responds to the pathologies and compelling needs of Western man as if it were on another planet, one whose gravitational force was many times that of earth: with a ponderousness that is far removed from the dynamism and vitality of warfare—the dynamism it should project.

In a revealing passage, one finds paradox and ambivalence in Professor Wolfe. Having decried the flaccidity of the Christian religion in America, he then suggests this is also a redeeming quality; to the extent it adapts in certain ways to the culture it is less a threat and more a blessing. "Still, believers who prefer a God of love to a God of truth are not going to kill for their beliefs—or to give their support to those who do. It is because Americans do not treat religion as a battle for the soul that the conservative Christians who denounced Islam as a false religion received very little hearing for their views; if anything, they embarrassed themselves and marginalized their message."[16]

This fails to take into account a central tenet of Christ's life and teaching: the absolute absence of compulsion. Unlike Islam, where compulsion is not just permissible but central, true Christianity is a faith of purely volitional choice. To be sure, *professing* Christians over the centuries have attempted to compel or coerce, but gaining a personal relationship with Christ can *never* happen that way.

Those who persist in that approach either will be among the hypocrites to whom Christ will declare, "Then I will tell them plainly, 'I never knew you. Away from me, you evildoers!'" (Matthew 7:23 NIV), or, perhaps, they are sincere Christians for whom the human temptation to assert worldly power has overwhelmed scrupulous obedience to Christ's example.

"If one needed evidence of why Americans so often make a distinction between their faith, which they treat with reverence, and the institutions within which faith is traditionally practiced, about which they are usually less enthusiastic, the pedophilia crisis provides it."[17] And well they should be. Those Catholics who were stung to fury—not only about the multitudinous abuses by priests, but the Church's complicity in concealing these most debased offenses against the most innocent of humanity—represented the remnant in the Church that perhaps understood the grave significance of these acts and omissions. The evil in both—the sacrifice by reputed "servants of God" of children to their depraved lusts, and the Church's obsession with its power and image—is beyond expression. This is *Catholicism without Christianity.*

That Pope John Paul II never addressed this reality forcefully, openly, and compellingly was the only obvious blemish on an otherwise remarkable papacy and exalted life. At present, evidence is

PD-gov

Bernard Cardinal Law, one of many priests, bishops, and archbishops who put their reputations and the image of the church above the protection of innocent children from pedophile priests. *This was and is Catholicism without Christianity. One of the junctures where the depravity and selfishness of man intersects with the institutional church, these individuals' conduct not only sacrificed youthful bodies to debased lusts but also sacrificed the credibility of Christianity on the altar of their benighted minds and hard hearts.*

not apparent that the hierarchy of the Church has resolved to sacrifice careers, power, and the church's "image" on the altar of holiness—though this and this only will produce true redemption before God and man.

Wolfe then gives voice to perceptions of secularists who use such evil to support and justify their rejection and contempt for the church.

> As these examples of strife and secrecy suggest, the first year of the twenty-first century has not been a good one for people of faith. For some, this may merely mean that religion is getting what it deserves. Religion, they would point out, has always been a force for discord and intolerance, and we can hardly be surprised when it reverts to form. As tragic as all these events are, they may have a positive outcome. By reminding us of the degree to which strong forms of faith are incompatible with liberal principles, September 11 and its aftermath, from this perspective, underscores the need to protect democratic societies against ways of life it is poorly prepared to accommodate.
>
> ...Understanding how religion is actually practiced in the United States offers the more optimistic scenario that religion need not be an enemy of democracy and can in many cases be its friend.[18]

Here Wolfe has advanced the argument secularists clearly believe is their strongest against dynamic faith (as contrasted with the flaccid, unassertive religious views they find non-threatening): "it is the historical source of conflict and discord." But like most such glib conclusions, it is neither fair nor objective. Christ said, "Do not suppose that I have come to bring peace to the earth. I did not come to bring peace, but a sword." (Matthew 10:34 NIV) But he was referring to the reaction of those who would oppose him and all he taught. He was clearly not referring to his methods or those taught his disciples—all of which emphasized patience, non-violence, and loving conduct. Jesus was powerless in the worldly sense—a powerlessness assumed rather than imposed. In that sense he was not a threat to anyone. Yet his teaching ran contrary to the pride and self-interest of those who had worldly power. They did the violence to him, not the other way round.

The depth of commitment Wolfe seems to long for in earlier observations may readily be mistaken for, or deliberately propagandized as, bigotry. Christians have literally lost their heads over the centuries for expressions and actions that many in the West today would eagerly label "bigotry." Wolfe's analysis is closer to the reality of the church in the West when he focuses on its self-indulgence rather than its self-assertion.

His next observation is far more suggestive of the former than the latter. "Americans are more likely to identify with their faith, which they consider personal to them, than with the institutions, including denominations and congregations that have historically represented their faith to them."[19]

Why? Is this not a subconscious or implicit acknowledgment of the ineffectuality of the American church as an institution? Does it not indicate a profound credibility deficit not simply among unbelievers but among professing Christians themselves?

As we near the end of Professor Wolfe's analysis, the failure to grasp and understand that characterizes agnosticism is more patent.

> The more we refrain from treating religion as if it has some status that makes it different from everything else in the world, holier and more moral if you like it, more sectarian and divisive if you do not, the greater our chances of avoiding religion's ugly legacies while still being able to appreciate its benefits for the individuals who practice it and for the democratic society they inhabit. American religion has been so transformed that we have reached the end of religion as we have known it. This does not mean religion no longer has meaning. It means we will have to know it in new ways.[20]

If the professor is correct—and his conclusion is more or less consistent with what we have already heard from our observers in the first part of this book—and "we have reached the end of religion as we have known it," this corroborates the axial warning at the core of this book. The difference is in the interpretation of the significance to be attributed to this dissolution of the church in the West. Once again, Arnold Toynbee displayed an insight and understanding lost on other observers and on much of the church itself.

> And the actors in the reversal of roles are, in this context, neither Pharisees-and-Publicans nor Jews-and-Gentiles, but are adults-and-children:
>
> > Except ye be converted and become as little children, ye shall not enter into the kingdom of heaven. Whosoever, therefore, shall humble himself as this little child, the same is greatest in the kingdom of heaven. And whoso shall receive one such little child in my name, receiveth me.
>
> This paradoxical *peripeteia* between sophistication and simplicity was affirmed by Jesus in a quotation from Jewish Scripture:
>
> > Out of the mouth of babes and sucklings thou hast perfected praise.
>
> The mystery symbolized here in the reversal of roles between children and adults flashes out of its sheath of allegory in the exultant phrases of Saint Paul:
>
> > God hath chosen the foolish things of the world to confound the wise; and God hath chosen the weak things of the world to confound the things which are mighty; and base things of the world, and things which are despised, hath God chosen, yea, and things which are not, to bring to nought things that are: that no flesh should glory in his presence.[21]
>
> Moreover, since the rise of the higher religions, Man's never-ceasing spiritual quest has not been fruitless. It has borne out Aeschylus's dictum that "suffering is the key to learning." During the age of human history that the rise of the higher religions has inaugurated, recurrent mundane catastrophes have been the occasions for successive spiritual advances.
>
> The "sorrowful round" of the recurrent vicissitudes of civilization has carried the higher religions forward in a spiritual movement that has been, not cyclical, but progressive. If we ask ourselves why the descending movement in the revolution of the wheel of civilization has carried the chariot of religion forward and upward, we shall find our answer in the truth that religion is a spiritual activity; for spiritual progress is governed by the law proclaimed by Aeschylus in the words already cited, and by the author of the Epistle to the Hebrews in the verse: "Whom the Lord loveth he chasteneth, and scourgeth every son whom he receiveth."[22]

Yet despite the accuracy of Toynbee's analysis, much of the Christian church in the West will not be carried "forward and upward" as the wheel of Western civilization descends; it is more part and parcel of that secular civilization than it is of the spiritual realm. Lincoln reputedly and famously observed that you cannot fool all the people all the time, but the church in the West has succeeded best perhaps at fooling itself.

Like a great oak, the church is entangled by the vines of Western culture that are choking out its life. But there will always be the faithful remnant so often referred to throughout the Bible. As Toynbee declared, a catastrophe will bring about a fresh rebirth of that church—the authentic church.

END NOTES
CHAPTER 26

1 Christopher Dawson, *Religion and World History: A Selection from the Works of Christopher Dawson* (Garden City, NY: Image Books, A Division of Doubleday & Company, Inc., 1975), 255–256.
2 Arnold Toynbee, *A Study of History* (New York: Weathervane Books, 1972), 167.
3 Abraham Lincoln, *Wisdom and Wit* (White Plains, NY: Peter Pauper Press, Inc., 1965), 12.
4 W. B. Yeats, *The Collected Poems of W. B. Yeats: Meditations in Time of Civil War*, 2d edition (Macmillan, 1958), 198.
5 Alan Wolfe, *The Transformation of American Religion: How We Actually Live Our Faith* (Simon and Schuster, 2003), 17. Reprinted and edited with the permission of The Free Press, a Division of Simon & Schuster, Inc., from *The Transformation of American Religion: How We Actually Live Our Faith* by Alan Wolfe. Copyright 2003 by Alan Wolfe. All rights reserved.
6 Arnold Toynbee, *Civilization on Trial* (New York: Oxford University Press, 1948), 86.
7 Wolfe, *Transformation*, 95.
8 Wolfe, *Transformation*, 83.
9 Wolfe, *Transformation*, 83.
10 Wolfe, *Transformation*, 86–87.
11 Wolfe, *Transformation*, 113.
12 Wolfe, *Transformation*, 117.
13 Wolfe, *Transformation*, 116–117.
14 Wolfe, *Transformation*, 264.
15 Wolfe, *Transformation*, 138.
16 Wolfe, *Transformation*, 261.
17 Wolfe, *Transformation*, 260.
18 Wolfe, *Transformation*, 260–261.
19 Wolfe, *Transformation*, 263.
20 Wolfe, *Transformation*, 264.
21 Toynbee, *A Study of History*, 167.
22 Toynbee, *A Study of History*, 350.

CHAPTER

27

A FATE PREDESTINED OR PRESCRIBED?

. . . [A] Western Christian bishop reached the same conclusion in the fourth century of the Christian Era: "The enemy is right inside you, the cause of your erring is there inside, I say, shut up in ourselves alone."
Arnold Toynbee[1]

But we, blinded by the love of the world, have forsaken the True Law.
Pope Gregory VII[2]

Every Christian mind is a seed of change so long as it is a living mind, not enervated by custom or ossified by prejudice. A Christian has only to be in order to change the world, for in that act of being there is contained all the mystery of supernatural life. It is the function of the Church to sow this divine seed, to produce not merely good men, but spiritual men—that is to say, supermen. In so far as the Church fulfills this function it transmits to the world a continuous stream of spiritual energy.
Dawson[3]

As early Christians were persecuted by the Roman state and Christ's teachings came sharply into focus against the backdrop of a powerful, materialistic, and sensualist culture, many Christians faced the second greatest choice of their lives: whether they would remain as "Christians" or become "followers of Christ." The distinction is relevant again today—as in truth it has been throughout the centuries. The former denotes professed embrace of a belief system; the latter absolute commitment. One such true "follower," Maurice, ironically a Roman military commander, when ordered to participate in a persecution, made his choice in a dramatic and unequivocal manner: "he handed his insignia to his assistant in order to join the Christians and be killed as a fellow believer."[4]

This great Christian, so worthy of respect and emulation, contrasts starkly with the proud preachers and priests of Western societies standing before TV cameras in large and elaborate church buildings blandly and ritualistically exhorting largely complacent members to sacrifice little, distinguish themselves less, and risk not at all. The *de facto* motto of the church in Western civilization, *ad captandum vulgus*, though not engraved on the cornerstones of countless striking edifices, echoes through the cavernous centuries of the Christian era—and surely is heard in heaven.

PD

The Martyrdom of Maurice by El Greco. *Maurice, a Roman military commander ordered to participate in a persecution, joined the Christians in their martyrdom. A follower of Christ, not just a "Christian," his example contrasts starkly with the proud preachers and priests of Western societies standing before TV cameras in large and elaborate church buildings blandly and ritualistically exhorting largely complacent members to sacrifice little, distinguish themselves less, and risk not at all.*

How has it come to this? How does a faith that would inspire a Maurice become the chrysalis, not for a beautiful butterfly, but for any number of subspecies that flit about in, rather than above, worldliness, self-absorption, and a materialistic culture's dissipations?

The problem remains the same in every generation: the human species, by and large, does not learn—and this is as true for those professing to be Christians as for the rest of humanity.

The temptations have not changed in millennia and the choices to give in to them are just as common. Differences are seemingly apparent in the historical record in only two respects: first, in the nature and extent of the casuistry and self-deceptions deployed to conceal the sins; and second, in the presence, or dearth, of leaders with the courage and commitment to expose the folly and exhort to a different course. Due to a surfeit of rationalizations and self-delusions, and a deficit of true leadership, the modern Western church has become the province of spiritual dilettantes. I have spoken in previous chapters to the former; here I will address the latter by first contrasting the spiritual leadership that, in past ages, has truly led.

Christopher Dawson, in *Religion and the Rise of Western Culture*, spoke of the fervency of some of those earlier leaders who strove to bring reform to the Catholic Church.

> It is in the Bible and, above all, in the Prophets that the real source of Gregory VII's inspiration is to be found; and the primary scriptural doctrines of divine judgment, the divine law of justice and the prophetic mission provide the recurrent theme of all his thought and teaching. His sense of the urgency of his mission and the terrible predicament of the Christian world finds its most striking expression in the last appeal he addressed to the Christian people from his exile in Salerno before his death.
>
> To me also, though unworthy and a sinner, that word of the Prophet has come, "Go up into the mountain and cry aloud: spare not," and so whether I will or no, setting aside all fear and all affection, I cry, I cry and I cry again. The Christian religion, the true faith taught to our fathers by the Son of God, has fallen so low that it is an object of scorn, not only to the Evil One, but even to the Jews, the Saracens and the pagans. These have laws that profit them not to salvation and yet they are faithful to them. But we, blinded by the love of the world, have forsaken the True Law.
>
> Every day we see men who go to death in thousands for their lords or their fellows, but those who fear God, few as they are, think only of their own souls and forget their brethren.[5]

A love of status and prestige, an unwillingness to truly offend, a desire to please, and a fear of facing the onslaught that comes with the uncompromising stating of one's convictions—all infect the church's leadership with an enervating fever.

Willing to stand in one area or on some issues, they quiver and quake at uncompromising commitments on others. What should we say about fear? Well, that should be obvious, though the two, the fear and the affection, are closely related. The great evangelist Billy Graham, in discussing his seeming anti-Jewish comments found on White House tapes from the Nixon administration, later humbly admitted his recognition that he was trying to please. This confessional, coming as it did from a man of such obvious depth of commitment, should be a warning and an object lesson for any number of preachers and priests. The warning: you are vulnerable to this temptation as well. The object lesson: this is the way to respond when you realize you have succumbed.

Dawson carried us forward to a later age—the cusp of the revolution in thought and attitude that began to undermine the search for truth in the West—and another reform-minded Christian leader.

Artist (between 1073 and 1085) unknown. PD-art

Pope Gregory VII. *Evidenced by his remarkable life, Gregory was one of the true Christian popes. In words apropos for our own time, he declared, "The Christian religion, the true faith taught to our fathers by the Son of God, has fallen so low that it is an object of scorn, not only to the Evil One, but even to the Jews, the Saracens and the pagans. These have laws that profit them not to salvation and yet they are faithful to them. But we, blinded by the love of the world, have forsaken the True Law. Every day we see men who go to death in thousands for their lords or their fellows, but those who fear God, few as they are, think only of their own souls and forget their brethren."*

Courtesy of BGEA

Billy Graham. *The great evangelist of the twentieth century demonstrated that it is possible for a Christian leader to live a life of humility and integrity. When he spoke of biblical morality and a God of accountability he clearly meant it. In that sense, his example has been a more powerful message than his sermons.*

> And in the twelfth century this tradition of monastic reform finds its supreme representative in St. Bernard, who was at once the embodiment of the ascetic ideals of Cistercian monasticism and the greatest public figure in the life of his time. In spite of his profound devotion to the monastic ideals of contemplation and penance, he was also a great man of action of the type of Gregory VII.... Above all, he was the champion of the Gregorian ideal of uncompromising spiritual reform, and applied the principles of the eleventh-century reformers to the changed circumstances of a new age. For, as we have seen, the victory of the Church created new problems and new temptations.[6]

The "victory of the Church" and the similar seeming victory of the Christian church in the nineteenth century West only led to "new problems and new temptations" to which the Church then, and the more modern church of the nineteenth, twentieth, and twenty-first centuries, succumbed. Dawson related the anguish of the German reformer Gerhoh of Reichersberg (1093–1169) who "saw the coming of the end, not in the external distress and persecution of the Church, but in its corruption" and "in despair he looks to the speedy coming of Christ as the only hope of the Church":

> Come then, Lord Jesus, he prays, come to Thy ship, the Holy Church, which is labouring heavily in this Fourth Watch of the Night; come O Lord, rule in midst of Thine enemies, the false priests who sell and rob in Thine house and the princes who tyrannize in the name of Christ. Come, Saviour Jesus, working salvation in the midst of the earth and the midst of the Church, making peace between the Kingdom and the Priesthood.[7]

This is the heart's cry of those who honestly confront what has taken place in the church. But the timing of the terminus of history is "known only to the Father," and Christians must seek to fulfill their duty rather than escape it, or the suffering, through a focus on the possible imminence of Christ's return.

Dawson noted that the sense of urgency among the more spiritually sensitive and committed was common in this earlier era, but it "came too late."

> That century which seems to us the Golden Age of medieval Catholicism—the age of St. Anselm and St. Bernard, the age of the Crusades and the Cathedrals, of the new religious Orders and the new schools—appeared to contemporaries dark with the threat of the coming doom.[8]
>
> ...
>
> But unfortunately it came too late: the great age of the reforming movement was over, and the Popes who did most to favour and make use of the Friars were not men of the type of Gregory VII or St. Bernard but able lawyers and statesmen like Gregory IX himself and Innocent IV and Martin IV who were preoccupied with the intense political conflict with the Hohenstaufen and the fatal entanglements of the Angevin alliance.[9]
>
> ...
>
> Hence it came about that the prophetic and evangelical vocation of the early Friars became subordinated to the demands of ecclesiastical power politics, and this produced a rift in the reforming movement from which medieval Christendom never recovered. The Papacy issued from the conflict with the Hohenstaufen victoriously, but with a serious loss of moral prestige. In the following century it never regained the universal European position that Innocent III had held. Above all, it lost the leadership of the movement of reform. Henceforward during the later Middle Ages the reformers were predominantly anti-Papal in spirit, as were the Spiritual Franciscans and Wycliffe, or supporters of the secular power like William of Ockham and Marsiglio of Padua.[10]

Typically, Dawson, as a devout Catholic, was more generous than an objective rendering of the personalities and events of the age would perhaps dictate. But his essential themes ring true and apply in so many ways equally to our own age. There is nothing new under the sun.

Toynbee alluded to many of the same failures that ultimately led to the Reformation—and called them what they were: an "obsession with worldly success." There is that ugly word again—*success*—heavy with the ponderous burdens of unacknowledged sin.

> ...the "Babylonish Captivity" of the Papacy under the French kings at Avignon, which began during Clement's pontificate in 1309....and the ensuing Great Schism were the sequel to a disastrous series of misjudgments by successive Popes, whose obsession with worldly success tempted them to overreach themselves. The Papacy's decline as a spiritual force, culminating in the Reformation, is a classic example of the catastrophic effects of blinding ambition.[11]

Intriguingly, Francis Schaeffer observed the creeping corruption during the same centuries described by Dawson and Toynbee and saw evidence in the art of those ages of the change in the underlying attitudes and thinking:

> The Byzantine style...had a real beauty, but increasingly only religious themes were given importance, and people were depicted not as real people but as symbols. This came to its climax in the ninth, tenth, and eleventh centuries. The portrayal of nature was largely abandoned, and even more unhappily, the living, human element was removed. This, we should stress once more, was in contrast to the early Christian catacomb paintings in which, though simply portrayed, real people lived in a real world which God had made.
>
> Nevertheless, the pristine Christianity set forth in the New Testament gradually became distorted. A humanistic element was added: Increasingly, the authority of the church took precedence over the teaching of the Bible.[12]

as with the culture at large, has not only remained unchanged, the pursuit has accelerated. Clearly he was either not truly heard and understood, or, having heard him, the church leadership quietly rejected the message.

This is the favored initial tactic of all who seek to keep their sins and simultaneously maintain their cloak of propriety: quietly ignore the charges, perhaps even give some tepid lip service to the message, but otherwise patiently wait until the challenge has passed. This would have been the preferred course for the Pharisees, but Jesus would have none of it. Thus, as always in history, personality trumps ideas. So it will be in the church; so it will be until the end of time.

The ability to see the nexus between the distortions in belief and thought on the one hand and the elemental failures and sins on the other was one of Schaeffer's gifts. Coupled with his similar gift for relating this to the many disparate manifestations of man's life on earth, he produced an insight that should have been universally heeded within the church.

> Gradually, that which had become the basic thought form of modern people became the almost totally accepted viewpoint, an almost monolithic consensus. And as it came to the majority of people through art, music, drama, theology, and the mass media, values died. As the more Christian-dominated consensus weakened, the majority of people adopted two impoverished values: *personal peace* and *affluence*.
>
> Personal peace means just to be let alone, not to be troubled by the troubles of other people, whether across the world or across the city—to live one's life with minimal possibilities of being personally disturbed. Personal peace means wanting to have my personal life pattern undisturbed in my lifetime, regardless of what the result will be in the lifetimes of my children and grandchildren. Affluence means an overwhelming and ever-increasing prosperity—a life made up of things, things, and more things—a success judged by an ever-higher level of material abundance.[20]

Yet seeing through this folly requires neither the accumulated experiences of modernity nor a deeply biblical perspective. Thoreau observed a century and a half ago, "It is not enough to tell me that you worked hard to get your gold. So does the devil work hard."[21] But these values have infiltrated every nook and cranny of the church,

PD-old

Henry David Thoreau at age 39, Maxham daguerreotype made in 1856. *Thoreau observed, "It is not enough to tell me that you worked hard to get your gold. So does the devil work hard." But materialism has infiltrated the church, leading men to pursue education, not in a selfless effort to become a better servant of God, but in order to make more money and have more possessions. The greatest sacrifices of Christian lives in terms of energy expended, time spent, thoughts devoted, goals pursued, are regularly made on the altar of Western materialism.*

leading men to pursue education, not in a selfless effort to become a better servant of God, but in order to make more money, gain status, and have more possessions.

> All too often when the students of the early sixties asked their parents and others, "Why be educated?" they were told, in words if not by implication, "Because statistically an educated man makes so much more money a year." And when they asked, "Why make more money?" they were told, "So that you can send *your* children to the university." According to this kind of spoken or implied answer, there was no meaning for man, and no meaning for education.[22]

Throughout his writings, Schaeffer slid the sword of truth right into the heart of the dragon of self-deception—and a salient point of corruption of the church by a declining civilization: materialism. The thinking of millions of professing Christians is awash in one or more of its manifestations.

The greatest sacrifices of Christian lives in terms of energy expended, time spent, thoughts devoted, goals pursued, are regularly made on the altar of Western materialism.

Yet, as Schaeffer noted, this is neither condemned nor treated as sinful. Indeed, often these dissipations are carried forward on values that are exalted within the church—and practiced by the church as an organization. "The work ethic, which had meaning within the Christian framework, now became ugly as the Christian base was removed. Work became an end in itself—with no reason to work and no values to determine what to do with the products of one's work."[23]

But, worst of all, the church is spiritually paralyzed by the pursuit of personal peace and affluence and inclined to largely keep its wealth to itself—professed belief in sacrifice notwithstanding.

> If industrialization had been accompanied by a strong emphasis on the compassionate use of accumulated wealth and on the dignity of each individual, the Industrial Revolution would have indeed been a revolution for good. But all too often in England and other countries the church was silent about the Old and the New Testament's emphasis on a compassionate use of wealth. Individual efforts of charity did not excuse this silence. Following industrialization, the noncompassionate use of accumulated wealth was particularly glaring.[24]

Government is expected to do in the West what Christ clearly expected the church to do. The result: the former does poorly what the latter largely will not do at all.

Christopher Dawson, in *The Historic Reality of a Christian Culture*, reached much the same conclusions about materialism within the church and the abdication of moral responsibility.

> The secularization of Western Christendom…involved the abdication by Christians of their responsibilities with regard to certain fields of social activity, so that we may say that nineteenth-century England was still a Christian society, but a Christian society that had diverted its energies to the pursuit of wealth. And finally it involved a loss of belief, which was to a certain extent involuntary and inevitable, since the stability of faith had already been undermined by the two processes which I have mentioned.
>
> To state the problem in a simplified form, if one century has destroyed the unity of Christendom by religious divisions, and a second century has confined the Christian way of life to the sphere of individual conduct and allowed the outer world of society and politics to go its own way, then a third century will find that the average man will accept the external social world as the objective standard of reality and regard the inner world of faith and religion as subjective, unreal and illusory.[25]

Of course, this is precisely the state of affairs in twenty-first-century Western civilization—Dawson's prescient analysis was right on point. He continued.

> Thus the process of secularization arises not from the loss of faith but from the loss of social interest in the world of faith. It begins the moment men feel that religion is irrelevant to the common way of life and that society as such has nothing to do with the truths of faith. It is important to distinguish this secular separation between religion and society from the traditional opposition between the Church and the World—or between the present world and the world to come—which has always been so deeply rooted in the Christian tradition.[26]

Max Weber, in *The Protestant Ethic and the Spirit of Capitalism*, observed the historical genesis of obeisance to the materialistic and its subtle and insidious effects not only on the church, but an entire civilization.

> To be sure, these Puritanical ideals tended to give way under excessive pressure from the temptations of wealth, as the Puritans themselves knew very well.... It was the same fate which again and again befell the predecessor of this worldly asceticism, the monastic asceticism of the Middle Ages. In the latter case, when rational economic activity had worked out its full effects by strict regulation of conduct and limitation of consumption, the wealth accumulated either succumbed directly to the nobility, as in the time before the Reformation, or monastic discipline threatened to break down, and one of the numerous reformations became necessary.
>
> In fact the whole history of monasticism is in a certain sense the history of a continual struggle with the problem of the secularizing influence of wealth.[27]
>
> We may hence quote here a passage from John Wesley himself...:
>
>> I fear, wherever riches have increased, the essence of religion has decreased in the same proportion. Therefore I do not see how it is possible, in the nature of things, for any revival of true religion to continue long. For religion must necessarily produce both industry and frugality, and these cannot but produce riches. But as riches increase, so will pride, anger, and love of the world in all its branches. How then is it possible that Methodism, that is, a religion of the heart, though it flourishes now as a green bay tree, should continue in this state? For the Methodists in every place grow diligent and frugal; consequently they increase in goods. Hence they proportionately increase in pride, in anger, in the desire of the flesh, the desire of the eyes, and the pride of life. So, although the form of religion remains, the spirit is swiftly vanishing away. Is there no way to prevent this—this continual decay of pure religion? We ought not to prevent people from being diligent and frugal; *we must exhort all Christians to gain all they can, and to save all they can; that is, in effect, to grow rich.*[28]
>
> There follows the advice that those who gain all they can and save all they can should also give all they can, so that they will grow in grace and lay up a treasure in heaven. It is clear that Wesley here expresses, even in detail, just what we have been trying to point out.
>
> As Wesley here says, the full economic effect of those great religious movements, whose significance for economic development lay above all in their ascetic educative influence, generally came only after the peak of the purely religious enthusiasm was past. Then the intensity of the search for the Kingdom of God commenced gradually to pass over into sober economic virtue; the religious roots died out slowly, giving way to utilitarian worldliness. Then, as Dowden puts it, as in *Robinson Crusoe*, the isolated economic man who carries on missionary activities on the side takes the place of the lonely spiritual search for the Kingdom of Heaven of Bunyan's pilgrim, hurrying through the market-place of Vanity.

Thus even Wesley seemed stumped and bewildered by the seeming paradox. But it is not a paradox at all when scrutinized closely through the prism of Christ's life and teachings.

Therein lies the failure not only of action but of simple understanding—the unwillingness to return over and over with relentless devotion to what Christ said and did with no dilution, no rationalization, no compromise, and no abstention.

But the spiritual *contretemps* that this failure has produced in the Western church in the modern age all sprang, as Weber revealed, from a process of thought that would strike certainly any Western Christian as plausible—even laudable.

> With the consciousness of standing in the fullness of God's grace and being visibly blessed by Him, the bourgeois business man, as long as he remained within the bounds of formal correctness, as long as his moral conduct was spotless and the use to which he put his wealth was not objectionable, could follow his pecuniary interests as he would and feel that he was fulfilling a duty in doing so.[29]

Such logic is common in the Western church—and rarely challenged. Thus it supplants a higher order of reasoning from scripture as "the spiritual authority" and provides the imprimatur for a deliberately materialistic lifestyle. Worse still, it forms the rationale for the "noncompassionate" use of wealth that Schaeffer so eloquently and soundly condemned.

Over time, church leadership provided the rationales for attitudes and behaviors that were—and are—completely contrary to the example and teachings of Christ. Presuming to think God's thoughts for Him they devised theories that led to circumventions of God's law. As Steve Bruce noted, Calvin was among them.

> By insisting that God had already divided all people into the saved and the unsaved, the chosen and the rejected (that is, our fate is *predestined*), John Calvin and his followers inadvertently created a climate in which the Puritans could see worldly success, provided it was achieved honestly and diligently by pious people, as proof of divine favour. These elements combined to produce a new "ethic."[30]

This played right into the hands of those who would make material acquisitiveness a paramount feature of their lives; and, in so doing, it provided a philosophical basis for some of the most ruthless aspects of Western capitalism. Marx should have been grateful for Calvin, for the latter aided in the creation of a state of affairs that the former built an international reputation defying. Weber described the nefarious process:

> Finally, it gave him the comforting assurance that the unequal distribution of the goods of this world was a special dispensation of Divine Providence, which in these differences, as in particular grace, pursued secret ends unknown to men. Calvin himself had made the much-quoted statement that only when the people, i.e. the mass of labourers and craftsmen, were poor did they remain obedient to God. In the Netherlands (Pieter de la Court and others), that had been secularized to the effect that the mass of men only labour when necessity forces them to do so. This formulation of a leading idea of capitalistic economy later entered into the current theories of the productivity of low wages. Here also, with the dying out of the religious root, the utilitarian interpretation crept in unnoticed, in the line of development which we have again and again observed.[31]

Oswald Spengler, generations before Schaeffer and Dawson, saw the regression similarly:

> Religious-ascetic fundamentals such as "selfless," "sinless," are without meaning in the economic life. For the true saint business in itself is sinful, and not merely taking of interest, or pleasure in riches, or the envy of the poor. The saying concerning the "lilies of the field" is for deeply religious (and philosophical) natures unreservedly true. The whole weight of their being lies outside economics and politics and general facts of "this world." We see it in Jesus' times and St. Bernard's and in the Russian soul of today; we see it too in the way of life of a Diogenes and a Kant. For its sake men choose voluntary poverty and itinerancy and hide themselves in cells and studies. Economic activity is never found in a religion or a philosophy, always only in the political organism of a church or the social organism of a theorizing fellowship; it is ever a compromise with "this world" and an index of the presence of a will-to-power.[32]

We should soberly note Spengler's use of the term "will-to-power" and remember Nietzsche and all he stood for—or, more precisely, did not stand for. This is starkly honest insight and points up that capitalism, materialism, and virtually every other ism has to do with worldly power.

We have heard what one great church father of an earlier age, Tertullian, asked, "What have Athens and Jerusalem in common?" The modern Western church should be asking—what does the church and the pursuit of power and wealth have in common? Any answer that does not take fully into account the surrender of self, taught and modeled by Christ, is of Athens (or perhaps more precisely, of Rome), not of Jerusalem.

But the grotesquely materialistic and self-centered Western culture is the breeding ground of so much dissimulation, deceit, and artificiality that reality and truth are blurred and distorted, if not lost entirely. The church, through its absorption of the culture, has not only not helped humanity strip away this falsity and see beyond it, but has become complicit to some degree in perpetuating it, through its own marketing, self-promotion, and glib sermons. The artificial trappings of contemporary culture are now such a pervasive part of the church that few notice any more—other than on an intuitive, instinctual level where a longing can be sensed for they know not what.

These failures of recognition and acknowledgment of the true meaning and clear intent of Christ's words and conduct are reinforced in religious schools, universities, seminaries, churches and denominational bureaucracies throughout the West. They are now so pervasive—and so mutually and reciprocally self-reinforcing—that priests and pastors are ubiquitously imbued with a theology that they accept without question. Thus, sincerity of belief is often not the issue, but spiritual blindness surely is.

All of this, in turn, has nurtured a shallowness and immaturity in the church's understanding of faith and the true significance of obedience to God. Preferring now a safer course as opposed to that which challenges, or calls to sacrifice and risk, many churches and Christians resort to a mystical interpretation of scripture that effectively nullifies their duty to act, and to act boldly. They wait for "the opening door," "God's leading," the "sign" of what they should do—all the time ignoring the commands and the example of Christ Himself.

Prayers are prayed less with the expectancy of God's help and guidance in facing formidable challenges, than with the assumption that this is, in itself, the doing of one's duty. An army with this mindset would be overwhelmed by its enemies—and thus it is with this one.

Weber revealed through these themes further evidence of just how much Western civilization is the progeny of the Christian faith—often an illegitimate progeny but the "descendent of" nonetheless.

> The Puritan wanted to work in a calling; we are forced to do so. For when asceticism was carried out of monastic cells into everyday life, and began to dominate worldly morality, it did its part in building

> the tremendous cosmos of the modern economic order. This order is now bound to the technical, and economic conditions of machine production which today determine the lives of all the individuals who are born into this mechanism, not only those directly concerned with economic acquisition, with irresistible force. Perhaps it will so determine them until the last ton of fossilized coal is burnt. In Baxter's view the care for external goods should only lie on the shoulders of the "saint like a light cloak, which can be thrown aside at any moment." But fate decreed that the cloak should become an iron cage.[33]

More than this, the cloak, which should lie on the saint's shoulders so lightly, became the screen behind which is hidden the betrayal of the heart and soul of Christ's teaching—with the institutional church serving as co-conspirator. How propitious this was—and has been ever since—for the forces of greed and materialism that prowl the earth: the church itself provided not only the philosophical basis for exploitation and avarice but the imprimatur of "God's blessing."

> Since asceticism undertook to remodel the world and to work out its ideals in the world, material goods have gained an increasing and finally an inexorable power over the lives of men as at no previous period in history. Today the spirit of religious asceticism—whether finally, who knows?—has escaped from the cage. But victorious capitalism, since it rests on mechanical foundations, needs its support no longer. The rosy blush of its laughing heir, the Enlightenment, seems also to be irretrievably fading, and the idea of duty in one's calling prowls about in our lives like the ghost of dead religious beliefs. Where the fulfillment of the calling cannot directly be related to the highest spiritual and cultural values, or when, on the other hand, it need not be felt simply as economic compulsion, the individual generally abandons the attempt to justify it at all. In the field of its highest development, in the United States, the pursuit of wealth, stripped of its religious and ethical meaning, tends to become associated with purely mundane passions, which often actually give it the character of sport.[34]

A bloody, ruthless sport it has become. The rules of the game are forever being liberalized such that what was once deemed a foul becomes just another form of the venerated practice called competition. From strikes and gun battles in the coal fields of places like Matewan, West Virginia, to the covert exploitation of illegal immigrants just about anywhere in the United States today, the sport is pursued assiduously and the most rewarded of cultural leaders are those who demonstrate the greatest avidity in winning at the game. The selfless and the self-sacrificing, with few exceptions, can lay claim to neither wealth nor fame—the culture, with often the at least tacit complicity of the church, having decreed what is truly worthy of reward and recognition in its eyes.

Where will it all lead? Weber was honest about his uncertainty; but there are only two courses open and the one chosen, for good or ill, will largely be the result ultimately of choices made by the church (i.e., professing Christians) in Western civilization.

> No one knows...whether at the end of this tremendous development entirely new prophets will arise, or there will be a great rebirth of old ideas and ideals, or, if neither, mechanized petrification, embellished with a sort of convulsive self-importance. For of the last stage of this cultural development, it might well be truly said, "Specialists without spirit, sensualists without heart; this nullity imagines that it has attained a level of civilization never before achieved."[35]

The church in our time in Western civilization does not, by and large, stand above this shallowness and profligacy, nor does it attempt to rescue Western man from it; it is more often part and

PD

The Capture of Christ by Michael Merisi da Caravaggio. *Christ betrayed by a kiss. The Western church, through its absorption of the grotesquely materialistic and self-centered Western culture, has not only not helped humanity strip away this falsity and see beyond it, but has become complicit in perpetuating it. These failures of recognition and acknowledgment of the true meaning and clear intent of Christ's words and conduct are reinforced in religious schools, seminaries, churches, and denominational bureaucracies throughout the West. They are now so pervasive—and so mutually and reciprocally self-reinforcing—that priests and pastors are ubiquitously imbued with a theology that they accept without question. Thus, sincerity of belief is often not the issue, but spiritual blindness surely is. Though they may not knowingly betray Christ, the effect is the same—on the church and on the broader culture.*

parcel of it. "The modern man is in general, even with the best will, unable to give religious ideas a significance for culture and national character which they deserve."[36]

Indeed, he is moving away from them at a faster and faster clip. No longer a dynamic entity of divine warriors intent on carrying the message of Christian love to the world no matter what the risks or sacrifice, the church in Western civilization has more often modeled the phenomenon described by Carroll Quigley: an organization that has moved from selfless service to self-serving self-preservation as an institution—and increasingly one of the less effectual institutions of Western culture, particularly when viewed in the context of its prodigious size.

> When instruments become institutions, as they all do, the organization achieves its function or purpose in society with decreasing effectiveness, and discontent with its performance begins to rise, especially among outsiders. These discontented suggest changes, which they call reforms.... When these suggestions are not accepted or are rejected by the established groups who control the criticized organization, conflicts and controversies begin, the discontented seeking to change the organization, while the vested interests seek to maintain their accustomed methods of operation.... From this tension and its ensuing controversy, there may emerge any one (or combination) among three possible outcomes: reform, circumvention, or reaction. In the first case, reform, the institution is reorganized and its methods of action changed so that it becomes, relatively speaking, more of an instrument and achieves its purpose with sufficient facility to reduce tension to a socially acceptable level. In the second case, circumvention, the institution is left with most of its privileges and vested interests intact, but its duties are taken away and assigned to a new instrument within the same society.[37]
>
> ...
>
> In the third possible outcome, reaction, the vested interests triumph in the struggle, and the people of that society are doomed to ineffective achievement of their needs on that level for an indefinite period.[38]

Sorokin noted in the mid-twentieth century that some saw the "salvation" of Western civilization in "a mild religious therapy: making the churches more comfortable, the services more attractive, and the sermons more entertaining."[39] That approach clearly has been tried and found wanting—if tested by the ultimate and only true standard of the impact on individual lives and the complete redirection of a civilization. Sorokin saw that this has all been tried before in other permutations. Referring first to the opposite extreme of monasticism and asceticism, he described the seeming inability of man to get it right—to do anything other over generations than propel himself to extremes.

> This uncompromisingly ideational system of ethics began to give way to the less rigorous idealistic ethics of the thirteenth to the fifteenth century. In the fourteenth and fifteenth centuries sensate ethics re-emerges, flourishing apace during the next century—that of the Renaissance and the Reformation. The hedonism, sensuality and paganism of the ethics of the Renaissance are well known. The period was notoriously sensuous and utilitarian, cynical and nihilistic in the teachings as well as in the conduct of its leaders.... Though masked by its ideational phraseology, the real character of the ethics of Protestantism was largely utilitarian and sensate. Money-making was declared the sign of God's grace; it was elevated to the rank of a primary duty.[40]
>
> ...
>
> Early and medieval Christianity had denounced wealth.... "On Sundays he [the Puritan] believes in God and Eternity; on week days, in the stock exchange. On Sundays the Bible is his ledger, and on week days the ledger is his Bible." Hence the parallel growth of Protestantism, paganism, capitalism, utilitarianism and sensate ethics during the subsequent centuries. The last four centuries have witnessed the supremacy of sensate ethics in Western society.[41]

We see of course a continuation of this view in the mindset of much of the church in the West today. It undergirds the "prosperity gospel" so often touted by television preachers in America, but in an only slightly subtler form it pervades the church, manifesting itself in the "doctrine of numbers," and millions of professing Christians obeisance to materialism. Sorokin agreed that the salvation of the West could be found only in religion, but of a very different sort—not unlike what had preceded in man's history in its essentials; it nonetheless might also have a unique character.

The history of the church and the behavior of individual Christians are always highly predictable as long as the life and words of Christ are not the paramount authority in either. This is so because the church then is nothing more than another human organization—given to all of the weaknesses of the human species. The individual then is nothing more than another human being given also to those same weaknesses. Unless and until either sets itself apart by the complete surrendering of self to the power and guidance of God it can be and do no other. Thus the lessons of history apply wholly to the behavior and the ultimate destiny of the church or the man who has not made that choice—and who does not daily continue to make it. Nothing exalted or transcendent can ever be found in human flesh or thought; only the power of the Divine working in and through man can so elevate.

BETRAYED BY WHAT IS FALSE WITHIN

In tragic life, God wot,
No villain need be! Passions spin the plot:
We are betray'd by what is false within.
George Meredith[42]

This recognition leads us to turn once again to Arnold Toynbee's astute analysis of decay and decline. He expressed the process in a fashion unique to him—and one worthy of respect and attentiveness. Toynbee returned repeatedly to a central theme—the willingness to humbly acknowledge that the fault lies within, not without, and that all of mankind's prospects hinge on the willingness to change self. Toynbee made this point eloquently by resort to the writings of others, including George Meredith in our epigram above.

And Meredith's flash of insight is not a new discovery of nineteenth-century Western wisdom, like the Origin of Species or the Law of the Conservation of Energy. A century earlier the genius of Volney had casually exploded the eighteenth-century doctrine of the natural goodness and automatic improvement of human nature by testifying that "the source of his calamities…resides within Man himself; he carries it in his heart." The same truth is declared in a fragment of Menander, which almost anticipates Meredith's own words:

Things rot through evils native to their selves,
And all that injures issues from within.

PD-Project Gutenberg

George Meredith *told Western man where the fault really lay: "In tragic life, God wot, No villain need be! Passions spin the plot: We are betray'd by what is false within." Preceding him was Menander: "Things rot through evils native to their selves, And all that injures issues from within." And an early Christian bishop: "The enemy is right inside you, the cause of your erring is there inside, I say, shut up in ourselves alone."*

> And a Western Christian bishop reached the same conclusion in the fourth century of the Christian Era: "The enemy is right inside you, the cause of your erring is there inside, I say, shut up in ourselves alone."[43]

But as we have noted, Western man and the Western church tend to see the afflictions and evils of our time as largely someone else's fault or, more often—in the abdication of personal responsibility so fashionable in our times—the fault of systems, institutions, and circumstances. Man is not at fault—not he of innate goodness—but something else, something perhaps in his circumstances or his institutions. The church is culpable through a variation in this folly and moral abdication: tending to look outside itself at the more conspicuous sources and promoters of moral decay and faithlessness—and there are many, to be sure—rather than questioning its own role in this state of affairs.

Toynbee noted that far more "primitive" civilizations than ours have come to the wise recognition that man must always look inward, first and foremost.

> The concept of self-determination as a religious issue is also found in the philosophies of the African Civilizations, which see the misfortunes that befall a man or his community as the fruits not of fate but of sin; in other words, as the results of irresponsible behaviour. '*Onipa ne asem*, say the Akan [a West African people]: it is mankind that matters—meaning, in this context, that any man can always be responsible for himself.'
>
> This truth about the lives of human beings is equally true of the lives of societies. A Hellenic philosopher, Dicaearchus, is reported to have maintained—in a lost work called *How Men Go to Destruction*—that the greatest danger to Man is Man.[44]

Then Toynbee became even more unsettling—saying something that suggests an important historical/psychological principle about the nature of leadership required to achieve true reform and a dramatic change of course.

> Another aspect of that failure of self-determination which we have been considering is the apparent nemesis of creativity. It looks as if it were uncommon for the creative responses to two or more successive challenges in the history of a given society to be achieved by one and the same minority or individual. So far from this being the rule, the party that has distinguished itself in dealing with one challenge is apt to fail conspicuously in attempting to deal with the next. This ironical and disconcerting yet apparently normal inconstancy of human fortunes is one of the dominant motifs of the Attic drama, and *it* is discussed by Aristotle,

Constantin Francois de Volney, 1757–1820. *Toynbee alluded to Volney when he pointed to the wisdom of the ages that man is the author of his own problems: "A century earlier the genius of Volney had casually exploded the eighteenth-century doctrine of the natural goodness and automatic improvement of human nature by testifying that 'the source of his calamities...resides within Man himself; he carries it in his heart.' "*

PD-old

in his *Poetics*, under the name of *peripeteia*, or 'the reversal of roles,' it is also one of the principal themes of the New Testament.

In the drama of the New Testament a Christ whose epiphany on Earth in the person of Jesus is, in Christian belief, the true fulfilment of Jewry's long-cherished Messianic hope is nevertheless rejected by a school of Scribes and Pharisees which, only a few generations back, has come to the fore at a critical juncture by leading an heroic Jewish revolt against the triumph of Hellenization. Yet now, in this far more momentous crisis, the Jews that comprehend and accept the—in Christian eyes—authentic Jewish Messiah's message are the least within the community, the publicans and the harlots.[45]

The stone which the builders rejected, the same is become the head of the corner.

...God loves to cut short everything that overtops its kind. In this way a great army is destroyed by a small army in certain circumstances—as, for instance, when God in His envy sends down panic upon them, or thunder. Then they perish, and their last state is unworthy of their first. God suffers no one to be proud except Himself.[46]

Medea performance at the Teatro Greco (Syracuse 2009). *Toynbee wrote that the greatest danger to man was man, a recognition common even to primitive societies. "This ironical and disconcerting yet apparently normal inconstancy of human fortunes is one of the dominant motifs of the Attic drama, and it is discussed by Aristotle, in his* Poetics, *under the name of* peripeteia, *or 'the reversal of roles,' it is also one of the principal themes of the New Testament." Yet modern Western man and the Western church tend to see the afflictions and evils of our time as largely someone else's fault or, more often—in the abdication of personal responsibility so fashionable in our times—the fault of systems, institutions, and circumstances. Man is not at fault—not he of innate goodness—but something else, something perhaps in his circumstances or his institutions. The church is culpable through a variation in this folly and moral abdication: tending to look outside itself at the more conspicuous sources and promoters of moral decay and faithlessness—and there are many, to be sure—rather than questioning its own role in this state of affairs.*

In the following passages, we can see reasons why the church in the West, so "successful" for so long, lapsed into its own "nemesis of creativity."

> It was a Greek and not a Jew who, with an insight reaped from his own spiritual travail, first proclaimed the truth that the cause of *peripeteia* is not to be found in the intervention of any external power but is an aberration in the soul of the sufferer himself, and that the name of this fatal moral evil is not envy but sin.
>
> But I hold my thought alone and by others unbeguiled;
> 'Tis the deed that is unholy shall have issue, child on child,
> Sin on sin, like his begetters; and they shall be as they were.
> But the man, who walketh straight, and the house thereof,
> Tho' Fate Exalt him, the children shall be fair.
>
> The sinner is brought to destruction not by God's act but by his own.... His offence lies, not in rivalling his Creator, but in deliberately making himself utterly unlike him; and God's part in this human tragedy is not active but passive. The sinner's bane is not a divine envy, but a divine inability to continue to use as an instrument of creation a creature that has insisted upon alienating itself from the life of its Creator. The sinful soul comes to grief because, so long as it wills to sin, God's grace is unable to inspire and inform it. According to this view, *peripeteia*—the reversal of roles—is produced by the inward spiritual working of a moral law, and not by the impact of some external agency; and, if we examine the plot of this psychological tragedy, we shall discern two variations on it. In one version the subject errs through an untimely passivity, while in the other he rushes actively to seek his doom.[47]

This view of scripture reflects a more sound understanding of the utter, absolute, incomprehensible power of God. **Rather than the primitive notion of a paternalistic figure sitting in heaven flinging the metaphorical equivalent of lightning bolts down upon erring humanity, it suggests an extraordinary, ineffable, incomprehensibly complex order God has given to the universe that dictated *ab initio* the inevitable consequences of certain choices individual men may make throughout the millennia. Nothing escapes the Divine power or the Divine law.** In this sense, and this sense only, perhaps the Deists were partially correct—God set this awesome Creation in motion with irrefragable laws that shall play out the cause and effect, the choices and consequences, to the "last syllable of recorded time" (*Macbeth* V, v, 19).

Toynbee then described a tendency of human nature that always comes to the fore in the wake of "success," comfort, security, and apparent achievement.

> The passive aberration to which a creative human being is prone in the sequel to an achievement is to "rest on his oars" in a fool's paradise where he dreams that, by having exerted himself once upon a time, he has won a title to "live happily ever after." Short of this degree of folly, the victor in yesterday's battle is apt to dream that, if time does refuse to stand still, then he has merely to repeat mechanically the motions that served him so well last time in order to be sure of overcoming any new challenge. It is plain that the creative individual who yields to this passive mood is falling into the posture of the arrested society which has achieved so exact an equilibrium with its environment that it becomes its slave instead of remaining its master. In the case of an arrested society this posture is only tenable so long as the environment happens to remain constant, and it spells disaster as soon as the environment begins to change. The same fate awaits a creative individual or minority which has become infatuated with his own works.[48]

PD

Woe unto You, Scribes and Pharisees!, 1894, by James Tissot. *Toynbee wrote, "In the drama of the New Testament a Christ whose epiphany on Earth in the person of Jesus is, in Christian belief, the true fulfilment of Jewry's long-cherished Messianic hope is nevertheless rejected by a school of Scribes and Pharisees which, only a few generations back, has come to the fore at a critical juncture by leading an heroic Jewish revolt against the triumph of Hellenization. Yet now, in this far more momentous crisis, the Jews that comprehend and accept the—in Christian eyes—authentic Jewish Messiah's message are the least within the community, the publicans and the harlots." There are analogues to the Scribes and Pharisees in the Western church today, exemplified by religious leaders who clearly love their prestige, power and perquisites and are unwilling to risk any of them.*

The church's "posture" was "only tenable so long as the environment" remained "constant." But the environment (i.e., Western civilization) began changing dramatically many generations back—and the complacent church was, at first at least, largely unaware. "Disaster" now looms, yet the church, so long "infatuated with [its] own works" remains oblivious to the fact that those works failed then—even though they gave the appearance of "success" (in truth a worldly version)—and repeating them will certainly fail now.

> If the moral of this passive aberration that overtakes some creative spirits is 'let him that thinketh he standeth take heed lest he fall,' we shall find that 'pride goeth before destruction, and an haughty spirit before a fall' is the epitaph of those others who rush to seek their doom.
>
> In Plato's words:
>
>> If one sins against the laws of proportion and gives something too big to something too small to carry it—too big sails to too small a ship, too big meals to too small a body, too big powers to too small a soul—the result is bound to be a complete upset. In an outburst of *hybris* the overfed body will rush into sickness, while the jack-in-office will rush into the unrighteousness that *hybris* always breeds.[49]

Toynbee's analysis of history suggests that leadership that could bring the church out of its great dismal swamp can only come from new "creative spirits." The old leadership "lodged…in key positions" will only "thwart and hinder."

> We can see that in the drama of social life this nemesis of creativity would bring on social breakdowns directly in two distinct ways. First, it would seriously diminish the number of candidates for the creator's role in the face of any given challenge, since it would tend to rule out those who had responded successfully to the last challenge; and these, *ex hypothesi*, were potential creators before their very success threatened to sterilize their creativity in the act of demonstrating it. In the second place, this frequent sterilization of the *ci-devant* creators would handicap the society in its next ordeal out of all proportion to the mere numerical ratio between a handful of lost leaders and a host of creative spirits; for, *ex hypothesi* again, the very past achievement which has fatally disqualified them from achieving anything further has also brought them to the front and lodged them in key positions where their senile impotence to create is aggravated by their lasting potency *ex officio* to thwart and hinder.[50]

This view fits of course with Quigley's concept of institutionalization. The validity of Toynbee's insights, and Quigley's concept, as applicable to the Western church can be found in the growing evidence alluded to earlier that the mantle of missions and evangelism has passed to the church in Asia and Africa and no longer rests on the shoulders of the church in Western civilization. In places like China, and even some of the more remote parts of Africa, the church possesses a dynamism, a fervency, and a commitment not unlike those in the first-century church.

THE POWER IS PRESENT

It is the will, not the power, that is lacking.
Christopher Dawson[51]

Toynbee then focused on the individual who finds himself or herself in the midst of a society that has lost its creative dynamism.

> The social schism which we have been examining…is an experience which is collective and therefore superficial. Its significance lies in its being the outward sign of a spiritual rift which scars the souls of the individuals who "belong" to a disintegrating society. Beyond the social expressions of disintegration lie the personal crises of behaviour and feeling and life which are the true essence and origin of the visible manifestations of social collapse. Individual souls which have lost the opportunity (though not of course the personal capacity) for initiating the creative actions by which the growth of a society is sustained are apt to take refuge in a series of alternative reactions to the pressures of disintegration, and these reactions are as it were pathological inversions of some of the growth processes which we tried to identify earlier in this Study.[52]

We should remember Toynbee's observation about the relative inconsequence of dramatic events that are actually on the surface of life and relate this to what Schaeffer observed in quoting the scripture that what a man "thinks in his heart, so is he." (Proverbs 23:7 NKJV) Noteworthy also is the relationship between this line of thought and Sorokin's observation that social decay is reflected in an obsession with the pathological. Toynbee used the phrasing "take refuge in" "alternative reactions"—which is almost perfectly congruous with Sorokin's thinking. Would not all of this also apply to the church—taking refuge in secular values and secular forms of achievement and security?

> There are two types of personal behaviour which seem to represent alternatives to the exercise of the general faculty of creativeness, in the sense that both of them are attempts at self-expression. The passive attempt consists in an *abandon* in which the soul lets itself go utterly, believing that creativeness comes as the reward of a natural and wholly undisciplined spontaneity—a state of mind in which antinomianism is accepted as a substitute for creativity. The active counterpart to this attempt to "live according to Nature" is an effort at stringent self-discipline, based on the inverse belief that Nature is the bane of creativity and not its source, and that a rigorous restraint of the natural passions is the only way to recover the lost faculty.[53]

Here we see a strong correlation with Schaeffer's thinking and his concern that most Christians simply seek refuge in their own small world and focus on their pursuit of personal peace and affluence. In our own time, the obsession with buildings, numbers, materialism, and the general acquiescence to the culture at large rather than creative resistance, all reflect these tendencies.

> When individual creativity has been replaced by spurious modes of self-expression in this way, we should also expect that the mechanism of mimesis, by which the mass of society is induced to follow its leaders in an age of growth, will be equally unable to operate satisfactorily. The effect of a sudden collapse of social drill is to deprive the individual of his sense of social identity and mutual obligation, and to encourage wholly individualistic reactions to the crisis. In this frame of mind the truant will attempt to escape the consequences of a social breakdown by repudiating his duty to his fellows and deserting the disordered majority in the selfish hope of securing his personal safety at any price.[54]

PD-gov

A communist propaganda poster of the idealized Soviet or Communist man looking up at the murderous Lenin and Stalin. *Communism is a manifestation of what Toynbee referred to as "futurism," the escape to an idealized future which is wholly out of touch with reality. I debated Russian intellectuals in Moscow over this concept; they were bereft of any historical evidence to support its plausibility. Yet futurism is a common theme in the modern West, which tends to believe that between the innate goodness of man, his institutions, such as capitalism and democracy, and the continued growth of science and technology, the future is bright and promising.*

U.S. Army Center of Military History, Washington, D.C.

Lanzinger's propaganda poster was an attempt to glorify Hitler and Nazism by associating both with a glorious, mythological German past. This is a manifestation of what Toynbee called "archaism": "...archaism" and "futurism" are both attempts to escape from a crushing present, which has become manifestly unserviceable as a medium for growth, by pointing to an alternative goal. Yet both these attempts are vitiated by the fundamental error of believing that the soul can be saved from that spiritual sickness which the breakdown of a civilization brings to light without any change of spiritual clime or dimension.... The bankruptcy of the archaistic and futuristic experiments derives from a stubborn refusal to acknowledge the necessity of that shift from macrocosm to microcosm which we have already recognized as the sine qua non of growth in a healthy civilization; yet the illusion that this can be avoided may be shattered at last by the reality of a spiritual defeat which, if it is not accepted as irretrievable, can lead to a new departure in life."

Here too, we hear echoes in Schaeffer: individuals "hiding out" rather than confronting the problems of the culture. In the following passage, Toynbee stated directly the critical nature of the "perception" of the "individual soul" and the absolute necessity of a "change" in the "spiritual clime" if there is to be any hope.

> The path of growth which is closed by those whose capacity for life and feeling exhausts itself on the mundane level may be reopened by a soul that can see beyond the veil of mundane appearance to the distant view of an "other world" of a supra-mundane spiritual order. The social catastrophe of disintegration thus reveals itself finally as a crisis of perception in the individual soul. In their very limited way, the modes of life which we have called "archaism" and "futurism" are both attempts to escape from a crushing present, which has become manifestly unserviceable as a medium for growth, by pointing to an alternative goal. Yet both these attempts are vitiated by the fundamental error of believing that the soul can be saved from that spiritual sickness which the breakdown of a civilization brings to light without any change of spiritual clime or dimension; and this is as much as to say that the life of Man on Earth is a mere temporal mechanism, a chronological sequence which fulfils itself in the macrocosm of the material world. The bankruptcy of the archaistic and futuristic experiments derives from a stubborn refusal to acknowledge the necessity of that shift from macrocosm to microcosm which we have already recognized as the sine qua non of growth in a healthy civilization; yet the illusion that this can be avoided may be shattered at last by the reality of a spiritual defeat which, if it is not accepted as irretrievable, can lead to a new departure in life.[55]

Thus, the thinking and choices of the individual are everything—and the only place where change for the better can begin or continue. That there are so few who can "see beyond the veil of mundane appearance to the distant view of an 'other world'" is the bane of the Western church in terms of leadership. Stunted as they have been by the influences of generations of teaching and belief influenced far more by the culture than they can see, much of the church's leadership is permanently deformed—even hypocritical on a grandiose scale—while others are simply maimed but might once again walk. But the real hope will only be in the courageous cries of a John the Baptist, Elijah, or Jeremiah demanding that all look to Christ, and Christ only, and not to any other authority, form, value, or belief.

Dawson, in *The Historic Reality of Christian Culture*, put the choices in the following fashion:

> But society cannot remain stationary in this kind of spiritual no man's land. It will inevitably become a prey to the unclean spirits that seek to make their dwelling in the empty human soul. For a secular civilization that has no end beyond its own satisfaction is a monstrosity—a cancerous growth which will ultimately destroy itself. The only power that can liberate man from this kingdom of darkness is the Christian faith. *For in the modern Western world there are no alternative solutions, no choice of possible other religions. It is a choice between Christianity or nothing. And Christianity is still a live option....* Thus the revival of Christian civilization does not involve the creation of a totally new civilization, but rather the cultural reawakening or reactivization of the Christian minority....It is the intellectual and social inertia of Christians that is the real obstacle to a restoration of Christian culture....Christians can hardly say that they are powerless to influence society. It is the will, not the power, that is lacking.[56]

END NOTES
CHAPTER 27

1 Arnold Toynbee, *A Study of History* (New York: Weathervane Books, 1972), 161.
2 Pope Gregory VII, cited in Christopher Dawson, *Religion and the Rise of Western Culture* (Garden City, NY: Image Books, 1948–1949), 132.
3 Christopher Dawson, *Christianity and the New Age* (Manchester, NH: Sophia Institute Press, 1985), 103.
4 Francis A. Schaeffer, *How Should We Then Live? The Rise and Decline of Western Thought and Culture* (Wheaton, IL: Crossway Books, 1976), 32–33.
5 Dawson, *Religion and the Rise of Western Culture*, 132–133.
6 Dawson, *Religion and the Rise of Western Culture*, 201–202.
7 Dawson, *Religion and the Rise of Western Culture*, 203–204.
8 Dawson, *Religion and the Rise of Western Culture*, 204.
9 Dawson, *Religion and the Rise of Western Culture*, 215.
10 Dawson, *Religion and the Rise of Western Culture*, 215–216.
11 Toynbee, *A Study of History*, 153.
12 Schaeffer, *How Should We Then Live?*, 31.
13 Kierkegaard, cited in Christopher Dawson, *The Historic Reality of Christian Culture* (New York: Harper & Brothers, 1960), 68.
14 T. S. Eliot, cited in Dawson, *Historic Reality*, 38–39.
15 Dawson, *Historic Reality*, 38–39.
16 Dawson, *Historic Reality*, 68–70.
17 Schaeffer, *How Should We Then Live?*, 176.
18 Schaeffer, *How Should We Then Live?*, 176.
19 Schaeffer, *How Should We Then Live?*, 227.
20 Schaeffer, *How Should We Then Live?*, 205.
21 Henry David Thoreau, *Life without Principle* (1863, Reprint: Forgotten Books, 2008), 9.
22 Schaeffer, *How Should We Then Live?*, 205–206.
23 Schaeffer, *How Should We Then Live?*, 206.
24 Schaeffer, *How Should We Then Live?*, 114.
25 Dawson, *Historic Reality*, 19.
26 Dawson, *Historic Reality*, 19–20.
27 Max Weber, *The Protestant Ethic and the Spirit of Capitalism* (New York: Charles Scribner and Sons, 1958, 2003), 174.
28 John Wesley, cited in Weber, *Protestant Ethic*, 176.
29 Weber, *Protestant Ethic*, 176–177.
30 Steve Bruce, *God Is Dead: Secularization in the West* (Oxford: Wiley-Blackwell, 2002), 7.
31 Weber, *Protestant Ethic*, 177.
32 Oswald Spengler, *The Decline of the West* (Oxford: Oxford University Press, 1991), 401.
33 Weber, *Protestant Ethic*, 181.
34 Weber, *Protestant Ethic*, 181–182.
35 Weber, *Protestant Ethic*, 182.
36 Weber, *Protestant Ethic*, 183.

37 Carroll Quigley, *The Evolution of Civilizations: An Introduction to Historical Analysis* (New York: Macmillan, 1961), 115–116, 117.
38 Quigley, *Evolution of Civilizations,* 117.
39 Pitirim A. Sorokin, *The Crisis of Our Age* (Oneworld Publications Ltd., 1941; this edition Sergei P. Sorokin and Peter P. Sorokin, 1992), 251.
40 Sorokin, *Crisis of Our Age*, 115.
41 Sorokin, *Crisis of Our Age*, 116.
42 George Meredith, cited in Toynbee, *A Study of History*, 161.
43 Toynbee, *A Study of History*, 161.
44 Toynbee, *A Study of History*, 161.
45 Toynbee, *A Study of History*, 167.
46 Toynbee, *A Study of History*, 167.
47 Toynbee, *A Study of History*, 169.
48 Toynbee, *A Study of History*, 169.
49 Toynbee, *A Study of History*, 169.
50 Toynbee, *A Study of History*, 169–170.
51 Dawson, *Historic Reality*, 46.
52 Toynbee, *A Study of History*, 241
53 Toynbee, *A Study of History*, 241.
54 Toynbee, *A Study of History*, 243.
55 Toynbee, *A Study of History*, 249.
56 Dawson, *Historic Reality*, 45.

PART III

WESTERN CIVILIZATION'S ONLY HOPE

CHAPTERS 28–40

Part III offers a strategy for saving Western civilization—the only strategy that has any prospect of success. We address the following questions:

- Can our civilization be rescued from the fate of all preceding civilizations?
- If so, what must be done?
- Who must do it?

Here we empower the individual member of our civilization by demonstrating how the fate of our civilization is in his hands and millions like him—not in the hands of Western governments, ideologues, economists, military forces, scientists, or engineers.

In times of great crisis and transition, the creative individual—the man or woman of great character—can have far greater impact on their fellowman and their world than they ever could in a more sanguine or tranquil age. The Crisis of Western Civilization in our age will prove to be the spiritual and intellectual birthplace of especially noble, unselfish, creative, and courageous souls.

CHAPTER 28
The Way Out of the Wilderness

Since true civilization is essentially a spiritual order and since Western civilization's spiritual order and superstructure have been the Christian religion, the only force that can now alter the moribund state of the civilization is the Christian faith. The destiny of the civilization will not be determined by mass movements, nor by governmental, political, ideological, military, social, or economic action, but by the inner choices of a minority: Christians.

CHAPTER 29
The Cobblestones of Humility on the Path to God

Pride, self-centeredness and hubris are the underlying attitudes that have most contributed to the decline and decay of Western civilization. The overweening sense of "success" that has increasingly characterized Western man has led him further from the wellsprings of his true successes and into the desolate places of unbelief and a misguided conviction that he can shape and control his own destiny. These attitudes have infiltrated the Christian church and fomented practices far removed from its founder's teachings. The starting point for altering the tragic course of Western civilization is a transformation from this prideful thinking to humility.

CHAPTER 30
The Christian's Legal Domicile

Related to the Western Christian's pride is his loss of an eternal perspective. Smitten with the activities and apparent rewards of the temporal world, he forgets that he is merely a sojourner whose true "legal domicile" is eternal. This absorption with the material and temporal world undermines his morality, service, courage, hope and sense of meaning and purpose.

CHAPTER 31
Jesus Christ—The Central Point of History

Christianity is the only religion in which the fate of a single individual became the symbol and the central point of all of creation. Other religions have formed the superstructure of other civilizations, but none have this unique heritage, nor have any risen to such power and scope as has Western civilization on this distinctive foundation.

CHAPTER 32
The Triumph of Evil through the Weakness of the Good

The triumph of evil invariably occurs—and always only occurs—in the vacuum created by the failures, cowardice, or the weaknesses of the "good." Man blames God, other men, faulty institutions or ideologies or even "circumstances" for the ascendancy of evil. But the truth is that man's world is evil because he wills it so by his own choices. Man's folly, cowardice, complacency, and self-centeredness are behind the depredations of evil and most of the misery, suffering and tyrannies of history.

CHAPTER 33
The Individual and the Power of Choice

Every event in human history, every act of evil or good, every achievement, the sum of all that is history and life, devolve from the individual—his or her core beliefs and choices. History is nothing more than the sum of those choices. The course of history will not be determined by mass movements but by critical, often obscure, choices of individuals. Therein lays a vast power that the individual of faith, conviction and courage can wield to influence an entire civilization.

CHAPTER 34
The Christian Soldier

The crisis and foreboding future of Western civilization can be altered only by individuals who embrace the ethos of the soldier: self-sacrifice, courage, a compelling sense of duty, and a willingness to suffer; and who realize the vital and central importance of the spiritual issue to the survival and renewal of the civilization.

CHAPTER 35
A Distinction of the Highest Order—The Christocentric Life

The church's tendency to bear the central mark of its progeny and host civilization rather than the central mark of its founder's life and teachings must be reversed. The despiritualized and self-centered Christianity of Western civilization must be supplanted by a vibrancy of moral purpose, self-sacrifice, and compassion that make it a conspicuous and attractive alternative to the effete Western lifestyle.

CHAPTER 36
Faith without Actions Is Dead

Passivity, complacency, cowardice and a propensity for turning to government or other cultural institutions to address the grievous problems and pathologies of the civilization must be substituted within the church for a willingness to unselfishly serve the members of the civilization in every conceivable way. The church must become the primary cultural force for addressing society's myriad problems and needs.

CHAPTER 37
Fighting Pyrrhic Battles at Points of Little Strategic Consequence

Resources must be directed primarily at the individual in the culture rather than the culture's powerful institutions, for only by changing the individual can the broader culture be fundamentally changed. Efforts that focus on politics, government and law to alter the civilization's course or resolve its problems are addressing the surface rather than the foundation and will ultimately prove inefficacious, if not preceded and superseded by a change of thought and belief of the individual members of the civilization. The macrocosm will be changed only via the microcosm.

CHAPTER 38
Seeking Truth—Through a Glass Darkly

All thought, belief and action must be preceded by a diligent seeking of the truth—an endeavor that is neither as facile nor as readily achieved as is generally assumed. Much of what Western man thinks and believes is a product of his prejudices and powerful cultural influences rather than a deep, fervent, independent quest for truth. His confusion and ignorance are compounded and exacerbated by a culture in which manipulation and deceit have risen to their zenith as art forms. There are methods by which this may be overcome and something more than simple knowledge gained: insight, understanding and wisdom.

CHAPTER 39
The Greatest of These Is Love

Everything of lasting and real importance is summed up in the word "relationships": man's relationship with God and man's relationship with his fellowman. The imperative of love—the unselfish, sacrificial love as expressed in the teachings and life of Christ, not the ersatz substitutes of Western culture—is critical to the individual's and the civilization's "success" in the absolute and most exalted sense of the word.

CHAPTER 40
More Things in Heaven and Earth

CHAPTER

28

THE WAY OUT OF THE WILDERNESS

Have I now become your enemy by telling you the truth?
Galatians 4:16 (NIV)

True civilization is essentially a spiritual order,
and its criterion is not material wealth, but spiritual vision.
Christopher Dawson[1]

…[T]he spiritual progress of individual souls in this life will in fact bring with it much more social progress than could be attained in any other way. It is a paradoxical but profoundly true and important principle of life that the most likely way to reach a goal is to be aiming not at that goal itself but at some more ambitious goal beyond it.
Toynbee[2]

For it is time for judgment to begin with the family of God; and if it begins with us, what will the outcome be for those who do not obey the gospel of God?
1 Peter 4:17a (NIV)

We have seen that Western civilization was built on the superstructure of the Christian faith. That awareness alone should be persuasive, even to the most ardent secularist, that the dismantling or destruction of that superstructure will inevitably have inimical and eventually catastrophic effects on Western civilization. This is the central issue for our civilization in our age.

The only force that can now alter the dismal course of Western civilization is the Christian faith. The destiny of our civilization will be determined not by mass movements, nor by governmental, political, military, social, or economic action, nor by ideologies, even those so venerated as democracy, but by the inner choices of a minority—Christians.

The need, therefore, is for the Western church—or, more precisely, the individual Western Christian—to look inward far more than outward in humble soul-searching for the source of this Nile of cultural and moral decline. We have no prospect for altering the course of our civilization until we do. We will instead witness the continued abasement of an entire civilization with a corollary increase in misery that we cannot now comprehend. Innumerable books have been written on the need for the church to influence the culture, and how it should go about it. But few focus on the soul of the church itself. Even those that do, speak primarily to complacency or lack of enthusiasm and tepid commitment.

Scant thought is given to the church's adherence, or lack thereof, to the example and teachings of Christ and its spiritual status as an independent, transcendent expression of God's-will-not-man's in the culture and world large. The profound humility necessary for the true, deep, starkly honest soul-searching required has been gradually supplanted over generations by an affectation. Pervading the Western church, Catholic, Orthodox, and Protestant, there is, at best, a Fabian reluctance to face its failures and the reasons therefor, or, at worst, a conscious, flagrant, prideful, rationalizing disobedience.

The natural consequence of this deficit has been a continuation of a pattern of ever-deepening worldliness within the church—a worldliness that church leaders are typically complicit in nurturing. A shallow, largely meaningless preciosity enshrouds the church. Christians themselves are spiritually and morally compromised in ways they do not perceive, in large part because of the failures of their leadership. Yet the secular world often does perceive—or at least intuitively sense—the gulf between the professed and the real.

A simple family incident impressed itself upon me as a metaphor of the significance of this reality in our age. When my younger daughter, Lane, was 16, our family prepared to leave home one morning for a round of errands. I stood waiting, distractedly reflecting, while my wife Mona locked the door. Dressed the way I prefer to dress, in old jeans, boots, and an outdoorsman's shirt, I was retrieved from my reverie by something tugging at the bottom of my jeans. Lane was kneeling beside me, pulling my jeans neatly over my boots. Perplexed, I asked, "Honey, what are you doing?" She answered, "Remember, Dad, how you look reflects on me."

How we as Christians look to the rest of the world reflects on our God. The image is often unattractive—and, worse still, very misleading about Jesus. Christ said, "When…I am lifted up from the earth, I will draw all men to Myself." (John 12:32 NASB) If we understand that verse literally, Christ lifted up on the cross, and figuratively, the life and teachings of Christ being lifted up before mankind, we should, if we are at all honest, acknowledge that the church has often not lifted up the true Jesus. Rather it has diluted and attenuated his teachings and is "lifting up" an ersatz Son of God fashioned from an unholy blending of the biblical figure with the traits and characteristics of our culture. Generations ago, the Western church began to gradually succumb to these practices through its complacency and self-centeredness. The church, so to speak, first let the Devil himself in by the back door. Today, due to ever deepening weakness, self-centeredness, and now cowardice, within the church, he strides confidently in through the front.

Evil gains strength in direct proportion to the weakness of its opposition. Thus moral weakness, self-centeredness, and cowardice on the part of those who profess to be Christians make us accessories to the advances of secularism, unbelief, moral decline, and the spasms of horrific evil seen in the last century of Western civilization.

(Opposite) *Lifting Up Christ* by Rubens. *Christ said, "And I, if I am lifted up from the earth, will draw all men to Myself." (John 12:32 NASB) If we understand that verse literally, Christ lifted up on the cross, as well as figuratively, the life and teachings of Christ being lifted up before mankind, we should, if we are at all honest, acknowledge that the church has often not lifted up the true Jesus. Rather it has diluted and attenuated his teachings and is "lifting up" an ersatz Son of God fashioned from an unholy blending of the biblical figure with the traits and characteristics of our culture. Generations ago, the Western church began to gradually succumb to these practices through its complacency and self-centeredness. The church, so to speak, first let the Devil himself in by the back door. Today, due to ever deepening weakness, self-centeredness, and now cowardice, within the church, he strides confidently in through the front.*

PD-art

"Bundesarchiv, Bild 183-R0211-316. Foto: o. Ang. | 1932 Frühling." ADN-ZB/IML-ZPA. Bonhoeffer, Dietrich. Antifaschistischer Widersstandskämpfer, geb. 4.2.1906; ermordet: 9.4.1945 in Flossenburg. UBz.: Dietrich Bonhoeffer mit Schülern im Frühjahr 1932.

Dietrich Bonhoeffer (front) *declared, "The life of discipleship can only be maintained so long as nothing is allowed to come between Christ and ourselves—neither the law, nor personal piety, nor even the world. The disciple always looks only to his master, never to Christ and the law, Christ and religion, Christ and the world.…If the heart is devoted to the mirage of the world…the disciple is lost." Bonhoeffer lived his faith and died at the hands of the Nazis.*

A man who had intimate knowledge of these trends—and indeed was destroyed by them—Dietrich Bonhoeffer, understood—or, perhaps more precisely, was willing to face—the reality, the ultimate duty of the Christian life:

> The life of discipleship can only be maintained so long as nothing is allowed to come between Christ and ourselves—neither the law, nor personal piety, nor even the world. The disciple always looks only to his master, never to Christ *and* the law, Christ *and* religion, Christ *and* the world. He avoids all such notions like the plague. Only by following Christ alone can he preserve a single eye. His eye rests wholly on the light that comes from Christ, and has no darkness or ambiguity in it. As the eye must be single, clear and pure in order to keep light in the body, as hand and foot receive light from no other sources save the eye, as the foot stumbles and the hand misses its mark when the eye is dim; so the follower of Christ is in the light only so long as he looks simply to Christ and nothing else in the world. Thus the heart of the disciple must be set upon Christ alone. If the eye sees an object which is not there, the whole body is deceived. If the heart is devoted to the mirage of the world, to the creature instead of the Creator, the disciple is lost.[3]

PD

The Prophet Jeremiah by Michelangelo (1475–1564). *Jeremiah never focused on numbers but on the truth. He was condemned as unpatriotic and traitorous for his attacks on the behavior of the people of Israel and was repeatedly at risk of being killed. He persisted in carrying the message of God's truth to the people of Israel even though roundly and almost universally rejected. The Western church is filled with leaders who are the antithesis of Jeremiah, yet it desperately needs men and women who are like him.*

For this reason, the central theme of this work is the absolute necessity of Western man's choosing to honor and obey God. We may ask many questions: What is the significance of Christ to the church—and indeed all of history? What can we glean from the New Testament about what Christ was telling mankind by His words and His deeds? How are these truths to be applied to Christians' lives in all times?

What we learn will change nothing unless the pride—which is not only epidemic but seems at times endemic—in Western civilization is rejected. This is particularly true for the church and its leadership. We shall see how the attribute of humility is foundational to any successful quest for truth and any seeking after God. Without the repentance of pride and the embrace of a profound and authentic humility, the Western church itself will continue to degenerate into increasing ineffectuality and effete irrelevancy.

We also answer the questions How would the church that Christ taught us to build look? How would it function? What would be its ministries? What would characterize the attitudes of its members?

Contrary to the image created by the Western church—sometimes grandiose, imposing, often pretentious, focused on numbers, and largely self-serving, though with a veneer of altruism—a metaphor will be summoned up from my childhood to describe the authentic church. My grandmother made frequent use of a milk stool—plain and unpretentious, yet very sturdy and with just three legs. That stool was small but very stable and could support a lot of weight for its size. In like manner, the church Christ described and modeled was plain and unpretentious; it had none of the prideful trappings that so often characterize the church in Western civilization. Yet that church was the most enduring institution the world has ever seen.

END NOTES
CHAPTER 28

1 Christopher Dawson, *Christianity and the New Age* (Manchester, NH: Sophia Institute Press, 1985), 98.
2 Arnold Toynbee, *Civilization on Trial* (New York: Oxford University Press, 1948), 247.
3 Dietrich Bonhoeffer, *The Cost of Discipleship* (SCM-Canterbury Press Ltd., 2001), 118–119.
4 Pitirim A. Sorokin, *The Crisis of Our Age* (Oneworld Publications Ltd., 1941; this edition Sergei P. Sorokin and Peter P. Sorokin, 1992), 24–25.
5 Francis A. Schaeffer, *How Should We Then Live? The Rise and Decline of Western Thought and Culture* (Wheaton, IL: Crossway Books, 1976), 22.
6 Christopher Dawson, *The Historic Reality of Christian Culture* (New York: Harper & Brothers, 1960), 101–102.
7 Dawson, *Historic Reality*, 103.
8 Dawson, *Historic Reality*, 103.

CHAPTER

29

THE COBBLESTONES OF HUMILITY ON THE PATH TO GOD

Human arrogance has been humanity's greatest self-imposed limitation. This, it seems to me, is the message of the story of Adam in the Garden of Eden.
Immanuel Wallerstein[1]

For everyone who exalts himself will be humbled,
and he who humbles himself will be exalted.
Luke 14:11 (NIV)

There is no remembrance of men of old, and even those who are yet to come will not be remembered by those who follow.
Ecclesiastes 1:11 (KJV)

The fear of the Lord teaches a man wisdom, and humility comes before honor.
Proverbs 15:33 (NIV)

As wisdom grows, pride diminishes. Humility is a condition God desires for all men, regardless of their understanding. It is striking and profoundly significant that true understanding and wisdom always displace pride and vanity. This truth bears heavily on the state of Western man and the Western church. The historical, philosophical, and practical twists and turns in our daunting pilgrimage thus far can easily lead us off the trail—or to a frustrated and fearful rejection of all or part of the lessons this trek has taught us. Regardless of whether those lessons are ever fully understood, much less appreciated, there is one lesson from this historical pilgrimage, above all others, that should be ever before humanity: the lesson of humility.

Knowledge and understanding are to be desired and sought, but man will never achieve completeness in either. As a Christian and a human being with a strong bent to the analytical, the seeking, and the probing, I have long since recognized what an extraordinary gift faith is in this respect alone. It does not require great knowledge or complete understanding, or sophistication, or erudition, or certainty. It is faith—simply that—the willingness to believe that there is a God and that a higher moral law transcends everything. St. Augustine declared, "*Credo ut intelligam*"—"I believe in order to understand." Man will never perceive or reach God through his intellect. For me at this point in my life it is abundantly clear that that is impossible in any event. Yet God has made it possible for us to approach Him if we will do so as "a little child" trusting that "He is and that He is a rewarder of those who seek him."[2] But the absolute essential antecedent to seeking and finding God is humility —for Western man as a civilization, for the Western church, and for the individual.

WESTERN MAN

This brain that fills the skull with schemes,
And its humming hive of dreams,
These today are proud in power and lord it in their little hour:
The immortal bones obey control
Of dying flesh and dying soul.
"The Immortal Part" by A. E. Housman

The insidious, ubiquitous cancer eating away the soul of Western civilization can be diagnosed in one word—pride. This infirmity, which has afflicted man from Adam, is a raging epidemic in the West. Blinding Western man to the greatest truths of the universe and of life, pride has nurtured within him a hubristic, overweening sense of self. Western man cannot countenance the thought that he is fundamentally and profoundly wrong, or that his entire civilization is in decay and decline because of his skewed values and beliefs. To be sure, he cannot because he will not, for he will not humble himself. Thus, his involuntary humbling is in the offing. "For everyone who exalts himself will be humbled, and he who humbles himself will be exalted." (Luke 14:11 NIV)

God has exalted his tiny, frail creature, man, by making his soul immortal and investing him with a free will. But this is the extent of man's exaltation—and this is, in truth, the only exaltation that truly matters. But man tries to exalt himself through his intellect—benighted and profoundly limited as it is, at best—and by assuming a mantle of moral, as well as intellectual, superiority often expressed in such non-sequiturs of history as the "innate goodness" of man.

Were his pride and vanity not distorting his view of reality, man would immediately recognize his own conspicuous limitations—all of which militate against any notion that he perceives, reasons, or understands to the length, breadth and depth he assumes. Philosophers have speculated for centuries on the ability of man to "know" reality or, even, the nature of reality, or, as we might put it, the reality of reality. Implicit in those questions is a recognition that is of more value to man than the product of the speculations: Man's capacities to know, understand, and reason are all far more limited than he recognizes; subtle evidence of this is inherent in his presumptions to the contrary.

The physical universe is merely God's backyard—and a small backyard at that. The Greater World, the Greater Reality, is beyond all measure. We stare out at the physical universe and are awed—as well we should be—but this is but a hint of an unfathomable, limitless, dimensionless, timeless universe beyond our senses and our intellects.

Even when addressed from a secular standpoint, the wiser will recognize man's limitations and, as a consequence, the need for humility. Immanuel Wallerstein declared, "We must turn ourselves around, if we are to have any hope of helping everyone else (or indeed anyone else) to turn the world around. We must most of all lower our arrogance decibels."[3] Dawson asserted that the "only lesson we can learn" from much of history is "that which the Greeks had learnt—the lesson of humility—that man is a drop in an endless stream, but he cannot see where the stream is going."[4]

Constrained as he is by his four score years (a grain of sand in the unending desert of a timeless universe), and the fragility of a few pounds of flesh embedded in his uppermost appendage, man lacks the resources to declare—with any degree of true authority—there is no God and no transcendent law to which he will be held accountable. Resort to his meager resources would suggest more readily the contrary, if for no other reason than the remarkable, irrefragable order of the universe, such as he can perceive it—or believes he does. Thus faith is his only hope for meaning, but not "faith in faith," or faith in a falsity, for everything he can perceive suggests an order: "There is a certain order to be seen in all things apprehended by man,"[5] compellingly evincing that there is "a way" and "an order" and "a law" that govern the seen and unseen, the known and unknown, the comprehensible and the ineffable. But man's pride is an impermeable membrane, separating him from the greatest and most rewarding truths of his evanescent life.

Ironically, as C. S. Lewis observed, this pridefulness is often offensive to the individual when observed in others, while he tenaciously holds it close to his own bosom.

> There is one vice of which no man in the world is free; which every one in the world loathes when he sees it in someone else; and of which hardly any people, except Christians, ever imagine that they are guilty of themselves. I have heard people admit that they are bad tempered, or that they cannot keep their heads about girls or drink, or even that they are cowards. I do not think I have ever heard anyone who was not a Christian accuse himself of this vice....There is no fault... which we are more unconscious of in ourselves. And the more we have it ourselves, the more we dislike it in others.
>
> The vice I am talking of is Pride or Self-Conceit...Pride leads to every other vice: it is the complete anti-God state of mind.[6]

For our purposes, the disease of pride is of particular significance because its salient symptom is unteachableness. Sorokin identified this critical deficiency as a precursor to disaster for Western civilization.

> This unteachableness manifests itself also in the current hope of extricating ourselves from the crisis by means of a variety of facile but shallow artifices, without any fundamental re-orientation of values, any thoroughgoing change of mentality and conduct, any persistent personal effort to realize man's divine creative mission on earth instead of acting merely as a "reflex mechanism," or an organism endowed with digestive and sex functions and controlled by its "residues," "drives" and "prepotent reflexes." Hence the crisis itself, and hence the inevitability of a fiery ordeal as the only available means of teaching the otherwise unteachable....The more unteachable we are, and the less freely and willingly we choose the sole course of salvation open to us, the more inexorable will be the coercion, the more pitiless the ordeal, the more terrible the *dies irae*, the days of wrath, of the transition. Let us hope that the grace of understanding may be vouchsafed us and that we may choose, before it is too late, the right road—the road that leads not to death but to the further realization of man's unique creative mission on this planet! *Benedictus qui venit in nomine Domini....* [7]

The humility implicit throughout Sorokin's observation is particularly significant—originating as it does from an intellect of extraordinary scope and experience. Yet this is a fundamental characteristic of most of our key observers, as suggested by Toynbee in a remarkably self-effacing passage.

> The only personal advantage that he can claim to possess is that he happens also to be a historian, and is therefore at least aware that he himself is a piece of sentient flotsam on the eddying surface of the stream of time. Realizing this, he knows that his fleeting and fragmentary vision of the passing scene is no more than a caricature of the surveyor's chart. God alone knows the true picture.[8]

Man as sentient protoplasm might be another way to express what honest objectivity demands—a truly novel, even radical, notion in the supremely self-absorbed West. But of course man is more than protoplasm—though in truth that would be the only accurate assessment if the secular materialistic view, so in vogue in the West, were taken to its logical conclusion. Ironically, the Western humanistic view of man is, as we have seen, fundamentally materialist, yet attributes to man vaunted abilities and understanding he clearly does not possess. Humanism tries to have it both ways in an oxymoronic concept: man as the heroic center of a purely materialist domain. That this is not only illogical but extraordinarily vain is telling. But there surely is something more, something unexplained by the various humanistic theories propounded as de facto gospel throughout the West. Malcolm Muggeridge displayed the wise man's intellectual contempt for Western humanism.

> Religious faith is the acceptance of the mystery of our existence here on earth, science being the antithesis of this—the conviction that somehow, sometime the alleged "facts of life," how we came to be, what we are, and to what end, will all be elucidated. Hence the ludicrous theories propounded and expounded, and the wild controversies about them—as, the Big Bang against the notion of continuous creation, and, above all, Darwinian evolution, a very rickety hypothesis based on some old bones or a tooth discovered in Kenya or Nanking, and infiltrating all the different disciplines of learning, and making an ultimate nonsense of them all.[9]

Just as the Docetists would not believe that the Son of God inhabited a human body, Western man will not believe that he is nothing more than a frail aggregation of cells, invested with importance and significance *only* by the existence of a Creator. The Russian philosopher Berdyaev uttered a Western secular heresy, the truth of which however stands up under logical scrutiny: "For man exists only if he is an image and reflection of God, he exists only if God exists. Let God be nonexistent, let man make of himself a God and no longer a man—his proper image will perish. The only solution to the problem of man lies in Christ."[10]

The imperative of such humility in order to perceive the greater verities of life has not been lost on those willing to humble themselves. It is obscure only to those who will not kneel before the conspicuous, looming void. Thomas à Kempis saw the truth with a vividness that could be vouchsafed to any denizen of the West if he would only humble himself.

> God arises because we cannot do anything alone. We are too weak and variable and helpless. Even just to take charge of our own bodies is impossible without outside help. Existence itself becomes impossible without God. To the minute degree that I have been able to lift my head out of the trough round which we humans so furiously and so avidly gather, it has been entirely due to God's help. If this had been lacking (and of course it never is) I should have lived wholly in darkness, in "licking the earth!"[11]

À Kempis's graphic language is precisely *apropos* for the modern West that licks the earth continually and has its head so deep in the trough of materialism and hedonism it is in danger of choking with each ravenous gulp. It does not see its utter dependence on the Being behind it all.

PD-old

Nikolai Berdyaev. *The Russian philosopher declared what today is a Western secular heresy: "For man exists only if he is an image and reflection of God, he exists only if God exists. Let God be nonexistent, let man make of himself a God and no longer a man—his proper image will perish. The only solution to the problem of man lies in Christ."*

> There is no holiness, Lord, if you withdraw your hand. No wisdom is of any use if you no longer guide it. No strength can avail if you do not preserve it. No purity is safe if you do not protect it. No watchfulness on our part can affect anything unless your holy vigilance is present with us. If you abandon us, we sink and perish; but if you come to us we are raised up and we live.[12]

What Muggeridge and à Kempis saw analytically, William Blake perceived more intuitively.

> Tyger! Tyger! burning bright
> In the forest of the night,
> What immortal hand or eye
> Could frame thy fearful symmetry?[13]

But Western man, positioned as he is for a brief, ticking moment at the apex of world history, cannot see the utter meaninglessness of the worldview he has created for himself. A Solomonic humility would lead him to precisely the same perceptions of reality reached millennia ago by a man who was truly seeking the truth.

> "Meaningless! Meaningless!" says the Teacher. "Utterly meaningless! Everything is meaningless." What does man gain from all his labor at which he toils under the sun? Generations come and generations go, but the earth remains forever. The sun rises and the sun sets, and hurries back to where it rises.
>
> The wind blows to the south and turns to the north; round and round it goes, ever returning on its course. All streams flow into the sea, yet the sea is never full. To the place the streams come from, there they return again. All things are wearisome, more than one can say. The eye never has enough of seeing, nor the ear its fill of hearing. What has been will be again, what has been done will be done again; there is nothing new under the sun. Is there anything of which one can say, "Look! This is something new"? It was here already, long ago; it was here before our time. There is no remembrance of men of old, and even those who are yet to come will not be remembered by those who follow.[14]

Indeed, there is "nothing new under the sun." History—the nightmare from which James Joyce longed to awaken—a seemingly endless litany of man's foolishness expressed in a markedly limited array of methods, leads inevitably—when honestly observed from a perspective of humility—to an appalling realization: everything endlessly recurs with monotonous meaninglessness.

A drama acted out with different players, in different costumes, on different stages, in different eras, it is nonetheless a reprise of the same scripts. Malcolm Muggeridge described how Western man

Thomas à Kempis on Mount Agnes, artist unknown, 1569. *Thomas à Kempis acknowledged, "To the minute degree that I have been able to lift my head out of the trough round which we humans so furiously and so avidly gather, it has been entirely due to God's help. If this had been lacking (and of course it never is) I should have lived wholly in darkness, in 'licking the earth!'" The West licks the earth continually and has its head deep in the trough of materialism and hedonism. It does not see its utter dependence on the Being behind it all.*

Stedelijk Museum Zwolle. PD-art.

unwittingly responds to this meaninglessness: "Then anguish seizes him. What is he doing, he asks himself, but filling in time? Bored here, he must go there; tired of such a person, he must cultivate some other person. So his life has no real meaning, is all spent wandering about the world, only to find that its variety is an illusion; that everywhere, everyone and everything endlessly recur."[15]

But this painful recognition is one of the major signposts on the cobblestoned path to the truth and away from the self-absorbed pansophism of modern Western civilization. Thus it is not desolate—unless one collapses on the trail in utter despair, like a Bertrand Russell, stubbornly refusing in another paroxysm of pride to move ahead on hands and knees to the higher ground, the spectacular view.

But the obsession with the avidity of knowledge and learning as an expression of man's self-will and power is another of the many manifestations of pride that has been tried before—and found wanting.

> I thought to myself, "Look, I have grown and increased in wisdom more than anyone who has ruled over Jerusalem before me; I have experienced much of wisdom and knowledge." Then I applied myself to the understanding of wisdom, and also of madness and folly, but I learned that this, too, is a chasing after the wind. For with much wisdom comes much sorrow; the more knowledge, the more grief. (Ecclesiastes 1:16–18 NIV)

Such is always the ultimate result of knowledge without faith and transcendent purpose, no matter how it may be concealed from the mind's eye. But the spiritually feral among us reach that appalling state not by chance or adverse circumstance, but by choice.

> What then? What Israel sought so earnestly it did not obtain, but the elect did. The others were hardened, as it is written: "God gave them a spirit of stupor, eyes so that they could not see and ears so that they could not hear, to this very day." And David says: "May their table become a snare and a

PD

King Solomon Receiving the Queen of Sheba. *Western man, positioned as he is for a brief, ticking moment at the apex of world history, cannot see the utter meaninglessness of the worldview he has created for himself. A Solomonic humility would lead him to precisely the same perceptions of reality reached millennia ago by a man who was truly seeking the truth: "'Meaningless! Meaningless!' says the Teacher. 'Utterly meaningless! Everything is meaningless.' …Generations come and generations go, but the earth remains forever. The sun rises and the sun sets, and hurries back to where it rises.…All things are wearisome, more than one can say. The eye never has enough of seeing, nor the ear its fill of hearing. What has been will be again, what has been done will be done again; there is nothing new under the sun. Is there anything of which one can say, 'Look! This is something new'? It was here already, long ago; it was here before our time. There is no remembrance of men of old, and even those who are yet to come will not be remembered by those who follow."*

©Jorge Salcedo

Harvard University. *Western man's obsession with the avidity of knowledge and learning as an expression of man's self-will and power is another of the many manifestations of pride that has been tried before—and found wanting. Solomon expressed it, "I thought to myself, 'Look, I have grown and increased in wisdom more than anyone who has ruled over Jerusalem before me; I have experienced much of wisdom and knowledge.' Then I applied myself to the understanding of wisdom, and also of madness and folly, but I learned that this, too, is a chasing after the wind. For with much wisdom comes much sorrow; the more knowledge, the more grief." (Ecclesiastes 1:16–18 NIV) Such is always the ultimate result of knowledge without faith and transcendent purpose, no matter how it may be concealed from the mind's eye. But the spiritually feral among us reach that appalling state not by chance or adverse circumstance, but by choice.*

> trap, a stumbling block and a retribution for them. May their eyes be darkened so they cannot see, and their backs be bent forever." (Romans 11:7–10 NIV)

The evangelist Billy Graham—supported in this view by the writings of John Paul II—observed that an individual's failure to believe is not ultimately a deficiency of intellectual knowledge or perception but a problem of the heart.

Among the greatest of biblical themes is the blinding effect of sin—the ultimate barrier to God. The man who will not relinquish his sin—especially the sin of pride—will not be able to see.

In large part for this reason, the vaunted position of humility in God's order is also one of the greatest themes of the Bible; it is an attribute highly esteemed. This principle is even understood on the more pedestrian planes of human experience. William Wordsworth observed, "Wisdom is oftentimes nearer when we stoop than when we soar."[16]

But truly, men only hear what they are ready to hear and, in the words of Emerson, "only see what they are ready to see." But when—and if—the surrender of self comes—and should it continue, for the submission is progressive and unending—everything one learns is continually more humbling such that the seeker's frustration then becomes that he cannot get lower on his knees. His own innate pride becomes anathema to him—for he recognizes that it is the high wall between God and him, true understanding and foolish assumption, peace and trouble. Man is born to trouble "as sparks fly upward" (Job 5:7 NIV)—but only because of his foolish pride.

Portrait by Benjamin Robert Haydon, 1842 (Yorck Project)

William Wordsworth *observed, "Wisdom is oftentimes nearer when we stoop than when we soar." Among the greatest of biblical themes is the blinding effect of sin—the ultimate barrier to God. The man who will not relinquish his sin—especially the sin of pride—will not be able to see.*

THE CHURCH

The sinner is brought to destruction not by God's act but by his own. His offence lies, not in rivalling his Creator, but in deliberately making himself utterly unlike him; and God's part in this human tragedy is not active but passive. The sinner's bane is...a divine inability to continue to use as an instrument of creation a creature that has insisted upon alienating itself from the life of its Creator. The sinful soul comes to grief because, so long as it wills to sin, God's grace is unable to inspire and inform it.

Arnold Toynbee[17]

If only C. S. Lewis had been fully correct in his observations of the consciousness of the dangers of pride within the church. If only it were true that among professing Christians could be found the recognition of the bane of pride. But as we have repeatedly observed, Western culture so infects the Western church that the two are largely indistinguishable.

Though admonished a multitude of times and ways—and surfeited with the example of Christ—the church will not see or hear. Looking to its own interests rather than those of millions of the spiritually, emotionally, and physically desperate that surround it, the church covertly considers itself better than others but without the authentic credentials of self-sacrifice and the surrender of sin to "prove" it. It has not come to the recognition about itself that was implied by Stephen Crane in his poem "I Stood Upon a High Place":

I stood upon a high place,
And saw, below, many devils
Running, leaping,
And carousing in sin.
One looked up, grinning,
And said, "Comrade! Brother!"[18]

Standing upon its own "high place," the church often becomes the worst—and least attractive—of two worlds: self-righteous in its religiosity on the one hand yet largely indistinguishable from the rest of the world in most other respects. Giving, perhaps, lip service to the expectations of God, it nonetheless indulges self.

> Do nothing out of selfish ambition or vain conceit, but in humility consider others better than yourselves. Each of you should look not only to your own interests, but also to the interests of others. Your attitude should be the same as that of Christ Jesus.... (Philippians 2:3–5 NIV)

But the attitude common in the church in the West is not that of Christ Jesus. For millions of professing Christians, and their leaders, this glorious name is merely the Potemkin façade for a lifestyle, an attitude, and a belief system that only superficially bear a resemblance to the one they declare as their Savior.

As a consequence, that which is truly valued and praised within the church can often actually be perceived as an incestuous mutual backslapping that serves to affirm the motives and purposes each wishes to sustain and pursue. The attitude is one of a focus on temporal authority (e.g., If the church, if my pastor, if my priest, if my denomination, says it is important or of value then surely it must be true—it is certainly easier to believe so.) rather than God's expectations. The numbers, so esteemed in Western culture, become the measure of merit. And the true call to selfless sacrifice is ignored for a tepid, spiritual dilettantism. The church dabbles in Christianity, then praises its practitioners for their "successes," completely overlooking Christ's declaration, "How can you believe if you accept praise from one another, yet make no effort to obtain the praise that comes from the only God?" (John 5:44 NIV)

But Christ told us that God will not be mocked nor manipulated. "Indeed there are those who are last who will be first, and first who will be last." (Luke 13:30 NIV) The shock of realizing who is first and who is last in the kingdom of God may prove to be the ultimate trauma for many in the Western church today. Many Western Christians blindly choose to believe the church's own propaganda—since that is not only the course of least resistance, but the most promising in terms of affluence, pleasure, security, and pride—and stray far from the great reality of who Christ really was, and what he truly meant.

Malcolm Muggeridge pointed out that man has been here before. The church has been here before. Francis Schaeffer noted what it took to turn the tide:

> But from the critical attitude toward the traditions which had been accepted without question, the Reformers turned not to man as beginning only from himself, but to the original Christianity of the Bible and the early church. Gradually they came to see that the church founded by Christ had since been marred by distortions. However, in contrast to the Renaissance humanists, they refused to accept the autonomy of human reason, which acts as though the human mind is infinite, with all knowledge within its realm. Rather, they took seriously the Bible's own claim for itself—that it is the only final authority. And they took seriously that man needs the answers given by God in the Bible to have adequate answers not only for how to be in an open relationship with God, but also for how to know the present meaning of life and how to have final answers in distinguishing between right and wrong. That is, man needs not only a God who exists, but a God who has spoken in a way that can be understood.[19]

Christopher Dawson expressed one of the salient and unique features of Christianity that man desperately needs as well: the hope beyond suffering and death.

> [Christianity] did not free from suffering and death, but it subordinated them to vital ends. This is the greatest psychological victory of Christianity: the spiritual reconquest of that great part of life that had hitherto lain under the shadow of death.
>
> This heroic acceptance of suffering is, of course, rare. It is the mark of a saint. But it is only in the saints that the Christian life is completely realised. We cannot judge Christianity by statistics or by striking an average. One saint can do more than a thousand average men, however active and well organised they may be. In this respect Christianity is essentially aristocratic, since the quality of the

> individual is the only thing that matters. And yet, on the other hand, it is the most democratic of religions, for an uneducated beggar who is a saint counts more than a thousand scholars or organisers. As St. Francis says, the brilliant preacher may congratulate himself on the effects of his sermons, when their success is really due to the prayers of some unknown saint, whose importance is realised neither by himself nor by others.[20]

St. Francis of course understood well the significance of Christ's declaration that in the kingdom of God "The first shall be last and the last first." Would that there was a Francis in the Western church of our age! Instead, fretting and feuding over ancient doctrinal controversies or modern tactics for gaining greater standing in the culture or within the subcultures of the institutional church itself, church leaders presume to think God's thoughts for Him and are smitten with their own knowledge and "insights." Humility becomes, unwittingly for many, an affectation that could easily be recognized as such by a saintly "uneducated beggar" who possessed genuine humility and not the ersatz or counterfeit form.

But the church in the West has turned this truth on its head by not only striving to free its members from suffering, but inculcating an acceptance of the broader culture's assiduous passion for material comfort, pleasure, and position. The prosperity gospel is only one, more obvious, manifestation of this perversion of the faith; far more subtle distortions inhabit every nook and cranny of the church. For this reason the Western church, as it presently exists, affords Western man little hope.

Toynbee speculated in *Civilization on Trial* that the apparent historical evolution (if we might use that word) of man's experience on this planet might lead to a third state of development characterized by a universal Christian Church. Would this, he asks, be a good thing?

> As the primitive species of societies has given place to a second species known as the civilizations within the brief period of the last six thousand years, so this second species of local and ephemeral societies may perhaps give place in its turn to a third species embodied in a single world-wide and enduring representative in the shape of

PD-old

Stephen Crane, author of the highly realistic Civil War novel *Red Badge of Courage, acknowledged man's true nature in his poem "I Stood Upon a High Place":*

I stood upon a high place,
And saw, below, many devils
Running, leaping,
And carousing in sin.
One looked up, grinning,
And said, "Comrade! Brother!"

> the Christian Church. If we can look forward to that, we shall have to ask ourselves this question: Supposing that this were to happen would it mean that the Kingdom of Heaven would then have been established on Earth?[21]

I believe the answer is unquestionably no. The church itself has demonstrated its own flawed nature throughout the last two millennia. The Kingdom of Heaven will be known only within the hearts of men in this world—but only fully experienced in the next. Toynbee concluded similarly.

> I think this question is a very pertinent one in our day, because some kind of earthly paradise is the goal of most of the current secular ideologies. To my mind the answer is emphatically "NO," for several reasons which I shall now do my best to put before you. One very obvious and well-known reason lies in the nature of society and in the nature of man. Society is, after all, only the common ground between the fields of action of a number of personalities, and human personality, at any rate as we know it in this world, has an innate capacity for evil as well as for good. If these two statements are true, as I believe them to be, then in any society on Earth, unless and until human nature itself undergoes a moral mutation which would make an essential change in its character, the possibility of evil, as well as of good, will be born into the world afresh with every child and will never be wholly ruled out as long as that child remains alive.[22]

THE INDIVIDUAL

Humble yourselves therefore under the mighty hand
of God, that he may exalt you in due time.
1 Peter 5:6 (NIV)

In so many ways, who we are as human beings, fundamentally, is beyond our control. Our gender, race, ethnicity, physical attributes, intelligence, place of birth, circumstances of birth, etc. are all random (if you lean to atheism and agnosticism) or the permissive will of God (if you choose to believe)—but truly beyond our control regardless of the viewpoint. The absence of our control over those circumstances is another powerfully compelling argument for humility—for each of us could have been dealt a very different set of circumstances. It is also a powerful argument for loving one's fellowman for the same reasons. The overused expression "There, but for the grace of God, go I" is extraordinarily *apropos* of man's most fundamental experiences.

As a youth, I wanted to achieve many things, one of which was to reach the height of 6'6". Carefully marking off a measure behind the door of my room, I watched attentively through my teen years for all signs of progression. By the age of 18, the goal had been achieved; by 21 it had been exceeded to 6'7". But with maturity—that of humility and understanding, less that of chronology—I came to recognize I had little say in the matter. Outside of exercise, sound nutrition, rest and the avoidance of deleterious behaviors, my physical size would be determined largely by what our era of scientists has denoted as the "genetic code." This awareness contributed to my realization that my race, my nationality, the extraordinarily loving family into which I had been born, my intellectual aptitudes, any access to wealth and material possessions, and—at least early on—my very way of perceiving reality, were all a matter of chance or divine orchestration, depending on your view of life. But in any event they were not the result of my power, my wisdom, my choice.

CHAPTER

30

THE CHRISTIAN'S LEGAL DOMICILE

Consequently, you are no longer foreigners and aliens, but fellow citizens with God's people and members of God's household.
Ephesians 2:19 (NIV)

Since you call on a Father who judges each man's work impartially, live your lives as strangers here in reverent fear.
1 Peter 1:17 (NIV)

By faith [Abraham] lived as an alien in the land of promise, as in a foreign land, dwelling in tents with Isaac and Jacob, fellow heirs of the same promise; for he was looking for the city which has foundations, whose architect and builder is God.
Hebrews 11:8–10 (NIV)

....they desire a better country, that is a heavenly one. Therefore God is not ashamed to be called their God; for He has prepared a city for them.
Hebrews 11:16 (NIV)

One of the great ironies of the Christian faith—and the wellspring of much of its benevolence and magnanimity—is its assertion of the individual Christian's citizenship in an eternal realm far removed from the brief abode in the temporal, material world he or she presently occupies. The irony is found in the impact this belief and that status have on the Christian's attitudes and actions. When one views the temporal world as an alien setting and merely a preliminary stage to a far greater, more powerful, more meaningful, eternal world, then one's "investments," to use a favored Western concept, in time, energy, wealth, and resources of any kind are shifted dramatically. The true Christian lays up treasures in Heaven and has much less interest in the more pedestrian variety that consumes Western man. This produces benignity, unselfishness, hope, courage, even boldness—all atypical of the human species—becoming one of the great features distinguishing the Christian from all others. It also leads to a nobility of thought and action beyond compare. For the true Christian, the world is not his home, it is his workplace.

One may have many "residences" but only one "domicile"—the place, defined in the law, as the one place to which he repeatedly returns and intends to continue to return. The Western church's weakness and decline can be couched in terms of this loss of an other-world focus on the eternal that is supplanted by a myopic this-world focus. No longer perpetually conscious of an acknowledged "legal domicile" in the Kingdom of God and an eternal hereafter, the typical Western Christian is fully—often obsessively—engaged with the here-and-now. His energies are absorbed with the marketplace, the Colosseum, the parliament. The temporal is in residence in his brain—though he does not recognize it, much less acknowledge it—almost to the exclusion of anything else. Thus his thoughts become shallow, his insights dry up, his heart hardens, his spirit withers, his loftier aspirations atrophy, his innocence is corrupted, and he becomes only a few degrees removed from the faithless from whom he—in his mind—always distinguishes himself. But he is more like them than dissimilar, more of their world than any other. They may sense this even as he does not.

From this derives his romance with numbers, his pyrrhic battles, his materialism, his competitive spirit, his elaborate church buildings, his passion for pleasure, his drive to abolish sins—or at least ameliorate their penalties—his cowardice, and, ultimately, his absolute failure to alter the course of his community, his state, his nation, his civilization, and even sometimes his own family. Perplexed as to the reasons for these failures, he assumes they are the result of external forces over which he has no control—which he then rails against. He does not recognize that directing his gaze to eternity will dramatically clarify his vision of the temporal. Short-sightedly focused on the proximate, his spiritual and intellectual eyes cannot focus on the grand, the noble, the lofty, the transcendent.

WHICH PASSPORT SHALL THE CHURCH CARRY?

As is the earthly, so also are those who are earthly; and as is the heavenly, so also are those who are heavenly. And just as we have borne the image of the earthly, we shall also bear the image of the heavenly. Now I say this, brethren, that flesh and blood cannot inherit the kingdom of God; nor does the perishable inherit the imperishable.
1 Corinthians 15:48–50 (NIV)

There is great danger for the church in its assumption of an earthly legal domicile. We have been here before. As we saw earlier, Toynbee spoke of the growth of the church in Roman times leading to its embrace by the culture around it as a victory: "The true beneficiary of the temporary Roman Peace was the Christian Church" that "seized this opportunity to strike root and spread; it was stimulated by persecution until the Empire, having failed to crush it, decided, instead, to take it into partnership."[1] It was a victory of sorts—one that impressed the world and the writers of histories. But "when even this reinforcement failed to save the Empire from destruction, the Church took over the Empire's heritage." The convergence of earthly success with innate human weakness, in time, bred defeat and failure.

This "partnership" proved to be in many respects the most corrupting of influences in much the same way that a similar partnership has existed between the church and late Western culture. The prospects for true revitalization and spiritual growth of the church will be greater—as they were two millennia ago—when a polarity is once again struck with the temporal powers. Every movement toward partnership has eventually become complicity; the church has been weakened, compromised, and corrupted by its assignations with the culture and human government.

The support of European churches by the state was guaranteed to weaken further what was clearly already weak, thus producing further evidence of the product of compromise with the culture and a this-world focus. The ardent patriotism (read "nationalism" or "tribalism," etc.) of the conservative branches of the American church will in time prove more and more to be incipient evidence that for many American Christians the question of "legal domicile" has, in reality, long since been settled. When push comes to shove, their allegiances will be with the temporal rather than the eternal. They already often are; they just do not recognize it.

But this is not the order described by Scripture or the allegiances taught by Christ. Christopher Dawson understood what being a Christian truly meant when it came to one's ultimate authority: "But East or West, it is basically the same conflict, and alike in East and West the Church stands neither for East nor West but for the universal spiritual society which is destined to embrace them both."[2]

Thus we have patriotism and nationalism versus the universalism of the church. Many Christians have never given serious thought to where their duty lies or to the choice they make, consciously or unconsciously, deliberately or inadvertently.

THE PURSUIT OF STATUS

Am I now trying to win the approval of men, or of God? Or am I trying to please men? If I were still trying to please men, I would not be a servant of Christ.
Galatians 1:10 (NIV)

The pursuit of status and recognition can be either that of an elevated position in the church or society—these are the more extreme manifestations of the underlying temptation—or the more pedestrian, commonplace, and rarely questioned desire of the church and Christians for recognition and approval by the society at large. The world is not the Christian's home, it is his workplace, but all biblical admonishments to this effect have largely been lost in the Western church.

Studies have repeatedly shown that individuals will betray their own principles and deny what their own senses tell them in an effort to conform and be accepted by their group. The perils in succumbing to this impulse to conform—to strive to be accepted—should be obvious to all but a fool, and even more so when viewed in the historical context of tyrants and ideologies that exploited this propensity in order to control millions. The craving for acceptance was a primary dynamic of the power of fascism and communism, but all humanity should be forewarned: This same drive has brought millions to their moral knees and rendered them the victims of all forms of obsequious conformity and addictions known to man—even in democracies and supposedly "free" nations. But no individual is ever truly free outside of Christ. For when he seeks to be accepted by any group he necessarily forfeits some degree of his freedom to be different, to think and act with individuality. He becomes dependent on the group for affirmation; he is, indeed, dependent on his own need for acceptance.

The phenomenon of peer group pressure, now tritely recognized in the West as a major aggravation of the life experience we call adolescence, never in truth passes from the human psyche with the passage of time. Though the human being who grows wiser also grows commensurately freer, it will ever be a bane of human existence to want to be accepted—and to be expected to conform. But the only acceptance that should matter to the Christian is that of God; and the only conformity he should desire is to God's moral law and commandments. Any other impulse is sure to lead him astray. In a famous passage St. Paul set the standard for conformity: "Do not conform any longer to the pattern of this world, but be transformed by the renewing of your mind. Then you will be able to test and approve what God's will is—his good, pleasing and perfect will." (Romans 12:2 NIV)

The Christian should ever be mindful that his citizenship is elsewhere.

> For, as I have often told you before and now say again even with tears, many live as enemies of the cross of Christ. Their destiny is destruction, their god is their stomach, and their glory is in their shame. Their mind is on earthly things.
>
> But our citizenship is in heaven. And we eagerly await a Savior from there, the Lord Jesus Christ. (Philippians 3:18-20 NIV)

The true Christian is an "alien" and a "stranger" on earth, so then what truck has he with the awards and recognition of man? In the most famous biblical list of men and women of faith the reader is told, "All these people were still living by faith when they died. They did not receive the things promised; they only saw them and welcomed them from a distance. And they admitted that they were aliens and strangers on earth." (Hebrews 11:13 NIV)

The reality behind the Christian's focus on his distinctive status is summed up by what is ultimately meaningful: "So we fix our eyes not on what is seen, but on what is unseen. For what is seen is temporary, but what is unseen is eternal." (2 Corinthians 4:18 NIV) In any event, the Christian seeking acceptance and a home already has that beyond measure, as Paul described:

> ...you are no longer foreigners and aliens, but fellow citizens with God's people and members of God's household, built on the foundation of the apostles and prophets, with Christ Jesus himself as the chief cornerstone. In him the whole building is joined together and rises to become a holy temple in the Lord. And in him you too are being built together to become a dwelling in which God lives by his Spirit. (Ephesians 2: 19–22 NIV)

The problem of course is that very often the Western church is truly little more than a bureaucracy and a building; the physical edifice—which, as we have relentlessly noted, is an obsession of the materialistic Western church—and the true "dwelling," whereof Paul spoke, cannot be found there. If the Christian cannot find the intimacy, the solace, the support—in a word, the love—that is implicit in Paul's description, how can the church expect the desperate, seeking stranger to find it there either? Churches of this nature are churches in name only, best left behind as the seeker finds the comfort and encouragement of the true church. The void of love and dearth of intimacy that often characterizes the Western church is a primary stimulant to the drive for acceptance by the culture at large pursued by many. Like an unloved child who cannot find what he needs in his home, he will seek it elsewhere.

BOUND TO THE WORLD OR LIBERATED CHILDREN OF GOD

Do not be bound together with unbelievers;
for what partnership have righteousness and lawlessness,
or what fellowship has light with darkness?
Or what harmony has Christ with Belial,
or what has a believer in common with an unbeliever?
Or what agreement has the temple of God with idols?
For we are the temple of the living God....
Therefore, come out from their midst and be separate," says the Lord.
"And do not touch what is unclean; And I will welcome you.
And I will be a father to you, And you shall be sons and daughters to Me,"
says the Lord Almighty.
2 Corinthians 6:14–18 (NIV)

The above passage was never intended to apply solely in the context of marriage—as it is often taken and surely would include—but rather, in the words of Oxford theology student Nicholas Ellis, "of dwelling with or participating with the ungodly and unfaithful of this world." But the desire for acceptance makes every human being susceptible to influences—if not outright manipulation—that are not necessarily consistent with his own best interests, much less his adherence to a transcendent code of behavior and expansive view of life. It is no wonder that the temptations in this regard are so readily surrendered to by Western Christians: The praise of the secular world turns many a religious leader's head. We are at regular intervals treated to the spectacle of ministers and priests pandering to the media, political figures, business leaders, and celebrities. Recognition or plaudits from any of these sources should be cause for concern and soul-searching rather than satisfaction. Yet it is apparent that many religious leaders who are the beneficiaries of secular praise or attention interpret this as suggesting that their ministries are being "blessed." Pulpits are surrendered to political figures—can we fathom Christ doing this in the Temple after his violent rejection of the money changers?—and the attention garnered is deemed another recognition of the importance and success of that church's ministry.

Christian universities and ministries fill their boards with individuals whose achievements are notably worldly, not spiritual. The businessman who has shown himself adept at the techniques and tactics of material acquisition has only to deposit sufficient funds into the pockets of the church, university, ministry, etc., to gain status and perhaps a prestigious role in governance of the Christian institution. Little more is expected except some display of assent to the doctrines of the entity. The sports figure, celebrity, media figure who would bestow their prestige on one of these institutions will hardly be shunned. The church and its institutions are so often on their knees before the culture and the world's values that hardly anyone notices; the rationalizations and justifications—astutely contrived—are extensive and plausible to anyone except someone who has both studied the life of Christ and the early church and who insists on thinking humbly, contritely, and independently for himself.

Jesus Christ does not need Western media, politicians, celebrities, or affluent businessmen to advance the cause of faith and redemption. Indeed, they are a stumbling block to the church in advancing the cause of Christ. The integrity, credibility, and spiritual vitality of the church have been massively eroded by the sycophancy of Christian leaders to the shallow, temporal, materialistic, and vainglorious.

WHERE ARE THE MEN OF WHOM THE WORLD IS NOT WORTHY?

...and others were tortured, not accepting their release, in order that they might obtain a better resurrection; and others experienced mockings and scourgings, yes, also chains and imprisonment. They were stoned, they were sawn in two, they were tempted, they were put to death with the sword; they went about in sheepskins, in goatskins, being destitute, afflicted, ill-treated (men of whom the world was not worthy), wandering in deserts and mountains and caves and holes in the ground. And all these, having gained approval through their faith, did not receive what was promised.

Hebrews 11:35–39 (NIV)

In my experience many depictions of the church and religious leaders in the Western cinema are an indicator of how the broader secular culture views both. The Christian is often depicted at any point on a continuum from hypocritical fanatic to effete fool to the pathologically deranged. Similarly, intrusions by movie villains into the setting of a church or cathedral are often met by the script writer having the priest or pastor declare, "This is the house of God!" with an authority and efficacy comparable to a child responding to a school yard bully. Often the result of this cinematic confrontation is sanguinary in the worst way for the priest, preacher, and many of his acolytes as it proved to be in *Tears of the Sun* and, in another variation, in *The Patriot.* Typically, the resolution of the crisis, the vindication of the injustice, is accomplished by the man with the sword, who may or may not—more often not, Sergeant Alvin York notwithstanding—show any obeisance to faith and God. This can be revealing of how the secular world often views the church and its leadership—shockingly perhaps, we might confess there can be degrees of validity to this perception—as weak, ineffective, sometimes parasitic on the society (a view noteworthily advanced by the Nazis and Communists) and, ultimately, something of an anachronism.

It is no historical accident that the contemporaries William Wilberforce and Napoleon Bonaparte were awarded extravagantly disproportionate levels of fame—and even attention by succeeding generations of historians—despite their equally disproportionate achievements for—or against—humanity in entirely different directions. The former pursued life and freedom for millions; the latter pursued death and domination for countless others. Need we juxtapose the motives? Need we point out the degree of disparity in fame accorded each? Few in the West today even know who Wilberforce was, much less what he did; but most have heard of Napoleon and are aware of his "triumphs" at the cost of hundreds of thousands of lives.

In like manner, the examples of men like Alvin York or Dietrich Bonhoeffer—both of whom not only rejected acceptance by the broader culture but defied it in their efforts to honor God—are, today, rarely acknowledged. The reasons, I believe, are twofold: First, they are not consistent with the image of the church and its leadership held by much of the West's cultural arbiters and leaders; and, secondly, there is admittedly a dearth of such bold Christian iconoclasts to be found in the Western church. Many are either falling over themselves to gain recognition and approval of the broader culture—or, for that matter, within the subculture of their own denomination, church hierarchy, etc.—or, like the dogs that bark only in their own yard, they are cautiously circumspect in what they say and where, much less what they will courageously do.

All concern with acceptance by the broader culture—much less its awards or accolades—is misplaced for the true Christian. At worst this constitutes pandering to those who are contemptuous of the church and the moral law of God. At best, it validates an imprimatur founded on criteria other than those that are purely biblically based. The money changers did not care for the significance of the Temple—a reality Christ was implicitly acknowledging as he threw them out. The church in the West should follow His example. It will not matter who praises whom or who gets what awards or recognition or place of prestige or power. Ultimately, the only opinion that matters for any of us is God's. The sooner a man or woman learns to focus on pleasing God and not man, the sooner that person is truly free. Better to be the target of the stones of Stephen than the vainglorious accolades and praise of a culture in decline and decay.

THE WRONG TURN ON OUR WAY HOME

Should it be ours to drain the cup of grieving
Even to the dregs of pain, at thy command,
We will not falter, thankfully receiving
All that is given by thy loving hand.
"New Year 1945" by Dietrich Bonhoeffer, written in a Gestapo prison[3]

A fundamental philosophical/theological/attitudinal wrong turn for the Western church was—and remains—its this-world focus rather than the biblically mandated next-world focus. Put another way, the typical Western Christian has never recognized the significance of Christ's teaching—followed by St. Paul and the Apostles—that we are merely sojourners here with a task to perform. Our "legal domicile" is in the world to come. We are not to place emphasis and ultimate reliance on what happens in this world, nor are we to seek solace in any worldly outcome. The irony of this perspective is that it produces a

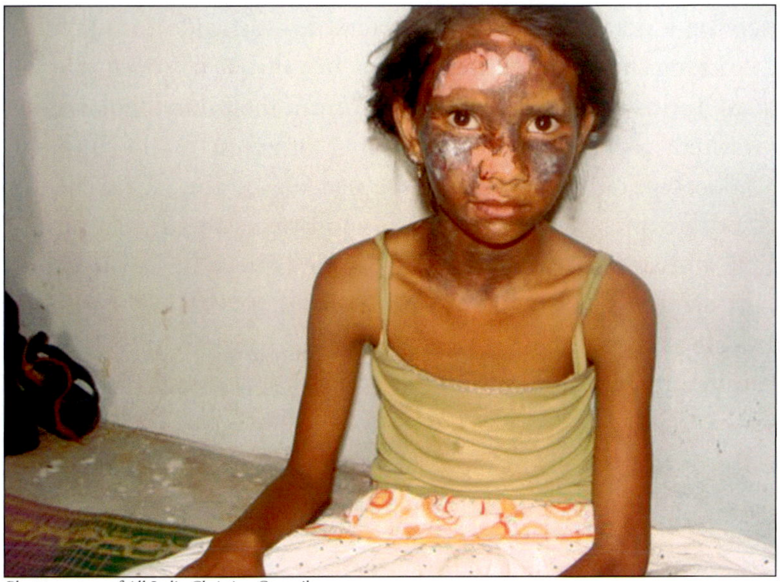

Photo courtesy of All India Christian Council

This little Christian girl was bruised and burned during anti-Christian violence by Hindu nationalists in India in 2008. *Anti-Christian violence has worsened and spread since the Hindu nationalist Bharatiya Janata Party came to power in March 1998, including arson of churches, forced "re-conversion" of Christians to Hinduism, distribution of threatening literature, burning of Bibles, raping of nuns, murder of Christian priests, and destruction of Christian schools, colleges, and cemeteries. Ultimately, the only opinion that matters for any of us is God's. The sooner a man or woman learns to focus on pleasing God and not man, the sooner that person is truly free. Better to be the target of the stones of Stephen than the vainglorious accolades and praise of a culture in decline and decay.*

PD-old

William Wilberforce. *The British parliamentarian and devout Christian was a contemporary of Napoleon and led the fight to end slavery in Britain and its colonies. Yet each was awarded extravagantly disproportionate levels of fame —and even attention by succeeding generations of historians—despite their equally disproportionate achievements for—or against—humanity in entirely different directions.*

character that more profoundly influences this temporal world for good and great than any other more earthly perspective ever could.

As Christopher Dawson expressed it, "There can be no doubt that Christianity in the past has been a creative cultural force of the first magnitude...."[4] All of what has been wrong with the Western church for generations can prospectively be stated in these terms.

This awareness is another reason why, throughout this work, I have so vigorously and frequently condemned the Western passion for optimism. On the one hand, from a purely intellectually objective standpoint it is invalid in any search for the truth and reality, nor do I believe it is warranted. The "optimism" proclaimed in our culture is actually a species of self-delusion and vanity. On the other, for the Christian, there is another, perhaps even more compelling reason: notions of optimism, even hope, should always and only be founded on the next-world eternal focus whereof we speak. Not for the Christian any attachment to the "security blankets" of man, his devices, his intellect, his character. All such reliance will prove to be investments in the ephemeral.

None of this should be read as implying a detached—much less remote—attitude to our temporal world and our fellow inhabitants. Nothing should be clearer by now from what has been written heretofore in this book. But there are many forms of "escape and evasion" from their duty deployed by Western Christians. As I have already warned, for example, all thinking oriented to the implicit escapism of what some have called the Apocalyptic theology should be rejected by the Christian. As philosopher and theologian Dr. Randall Bush expresses it, this is "...false prophecy, because it promises the Christian escape from tribulation and suffering. No wonder people believe it! But it is not only Christianity without a cross; it also deludes Christians into believing that they can continue their complicity with the world system while at the same time failing to be 'salt' and 'light' in a decadent and dark world." This is a way to evade rather than confront, and Christ never evaded the great issues.

Toynbee noted the historical evidence of the power of Christians who sought not security but service.

PD

Napoleon Crossing the Alps, equestrian portrait of Napoleon Bonaparte, by Jacques-Louis David between 1801 and 1805. *Napoleon has been awarded extravagant levels of fame in the West. By contrast, few even know who his contemporary William Wilberforce was, much less what he did in ending slavery in the British Empire. But most have heard of Napoleon and are aware of his "triumphs" at the cost of hundreds of thousands of lives.*

Nazi book burnings *included Bibles, Torah, and other Christian philosophy books. For the Christian, notions of optimism, even hope, should always and only be founded on the next-world eternal focus whereof we speak. Not for the Christian any attachment to the "security blankets" of man, his devices, his intellect, his character. All such reliance will prove to be investments in the ephemeral.*

PD-gov

> To detach oneself spiritually from the world is an easier option than to take on the travail of sharing God's love for the world and participating in his work of transfiguring it. . . . Many, perhaps a majority, of the aspirants to sainthood fell by the wayside; yet the few who did live up to the Christian ideal in some measure sufficed to secure the survival of the Christian society when Roman hands failed to save the Hellenic Civilization from the final consequences of its own past suicidal acts.[5]

Where then should the Christian choose to be? A metaphor from a much earlier time in Western civilization's history—a time when just being a Christian could get you killed—offered up by perhaps one of the greatest earthly rulers ever to live, Alfred the Great, provides a remarkable answer.

> . . . [O]n the axle-tree of a wagon the wheel turns, and the axle-tree stands still, and yet supports the whole wagon and regulates its progress. . . . Now the axle is as it were the highest Good, which we call God, and the best men move nearest to God just as the hub moves nearest to the axle. . . .
>
> The most numerous class of men is nearest to the rim. . . . Though they turn all their love towards this world, they are not able to rest there, nor do they come to anything, if they are not in some measure attached to God, any more than the rim of the wheel can make any progress if it is not fastened to the spokes, and the spokes to the axle. The hub goes nearest to the axle, therefore it goes the most-securely. So do the best men. In proportion as they place their love nearer to God, so are they more free from care. . . .
>
> —Alfred the Great,
> translation of Boethius[6]

Thus Alfred's metaphor comports closely with the traditional metaphor of the wheel of history. Immediately next to that Great Axle is the safest and most momentous place to be—bound for Home.

CC

Alfred the Great's statue at Winchester by Hamo Thornycroft. *Alfred, perhaps the greatest earthly ruler ever to live, observed, "[O]n the axle-tree of a wagon the wheel turns, and the axle-tree stands still, and yet supports the whole wagon and regulates its progress.... The most numerous class of men is nearest to the rim.... Though they turn all their love towards this world, they are not able to rest there, nor do they come to anything, if they are not in some measure attached to God, any more than the rim of the wheel can make any progress if it is not fastened to the spokes, and the spokes to the axle. The hub goes nearest to the axle, therefore it goes the most securely. So do the best men. In proportion as they place their love nearer to God, so are they more free from care."*

END NOTES
CHAPTER 30

1 Arnold J. Toynbee, *Civilization on Trial* (New York: Oxford University Press, 1948), 13–14.
2 Christopher Dawson, *The Historic Reality of Christian Culture* (New York: Harper & Brothers, 1960), 120.
3 Dietrich Bonhoeffer, "New Year 1945," in *Letters and Papers from Prison* (New York: Macmillan, 1962), 249.
4 Dawson, *Historic Reality*, 68.
5 Arnold Toynbee, *A Study of History* (Oxford: Thames and Hudson, 1972), 331–332.
6 Peter J. Helm, *Alfred the Great* (New York: Crowell, 1965), 173.

CHAPTER

31

JESUS CHRIST—THE CENTRAL POINT OF HISTORY

Christianity is the one religion in the history of the world in which the fate of a man of the immediate present has become the emblem and the central point of the whole creation.
Oswald Spengler[1]

...the Bible tells men and women true things about God. Therefore, they can know true things about God. One can know true things about God because God has revealed himself.
Francis Schaeffer[2]

If I be lifted up from the earth, I will draw all men unto me.
Jesus Christ (John 12:32 KJV)

Nikolai Rimsky-Korsakov captured the moods and the mystery of a world seeking ultimate meaning—a quest for a savior—in his masterpiece, the *Russian Eastern Overture.* Beginning with melancholy, somber brooding, the overture suggests a world in despair and darkness, searching for it knows not what. Yet in the midst of desolation and purposelessness something inexplicable and profoundly mysterious manifests. The mood melodically shifts to a musical interrogatory, a tone of quizzical bewilderment tinged with wonder. Then on, as it were, "the third day," the despair and brooding, the mystery and anguished wonderment are swept away, and the listener is lifted onto a wave of joy, carried forward exultantly to a crescendo of faith and hope. Perhaps no better expression of the life, sacrifice, and resurrection of Christ can be experienced in music. Man has striven many times in many ways over the centuries to express the absolute significance of Jesus Christ. There can be no greater task.

Through generations, the Western church in all of its manifestations has diluted and distorted the image and teachings of Christ to the point that the authentic Christ and the genuine law have been in whole or in part obscured. But even the slightest transgression in this respect is a grave wrong against God and man. There can be no room for relativism here, no latitude for men to stretch, manipulate, or amend the Great Truth. Jesus Christ was either the Son of God, or he was a liar. Every human being who hears the name Jesus is faced with a choice: to assume the latter or accept the former. Christ himself left no other alternative. Mankind's hope—the only hope—is in the real Jesus Christ. I have surveyed the topography of history and man's world in every direction and found only desolation every where I have looked—except when I look in the direction of Jesus Christ.

THE EMBLEM AND THE CENTRAL POINT OF THE WHOLE CREATION

Jesus answered, "My kingdom is not of this world. If My kingdom were of this world, then My servants would be fighting, that I might not be delivered up to the Jews; but as it is, My kingdom is not of this realm."
John 18:36 (NASB)

Oswald Spengler described "the incomparable thing which lifted Christianity out above all religions": "In all the great creations of those years there is nothing which can be set beside it. Tame and empty all the legends and holy adventures of Mithras, Attis and Osiris must have seemed to any man reading or listening to the still-recent story of Jesus' sufferings—the last journey to Jerusalem, the last anxious supper, the hours of despair in Gethsemane and the death on the cross."[3]

Christianity is no mere philosophy, no artificial religious construct designed to comfort man, no mere regimen of morality. Nor is it subject to debate, only to choose to believe or not believe.

> Here was no matter of philosophy. Jesus' utterances, which stayed in the memory of many of the devoted, even in old age, are those of a child in the midst of an alien, aged and sick world. They are not sociological observations, problems, debatings. Like a quiet island of bliss was the life of these fishermen and craftsmen by the Lake of Gennesareth in the midst of the age of the great Tiberius, far from all world-history and innocent of all the doings of actuality, while round them glittered the Hellenistic towns with their theatres and temples, their refined Western society, their noisy mob-diversions, their Roman cohorts, their Greek philosophy. When the friends and disciples of the sufferer had grown grey and his brother was president of their group in Jerusalem, they put together, from the sayings and narratives generally current in their small communities, a biography so arresting in its inward appeal that it evolved a presentation-form of its own, of which neither the Classical nor the Arabian Culture has any example—the Gospel.[4]

PHARISAISM—THEN AND NOW

It angered [Jesus] that this wilderness of cold-hearted [Pharisaical] formulae was reputed to be the only way to salvation.
Oswald Spengler[5]

With superb insight, Spengler saw the relationship between Rome and the Pharisees; a similar relationship to that which we declare in this work exists today between Western culture and the Western church. Pharisaism, as I use the term and as I believe Spengler also used it, encompasses more than a cold-blooded doctrinaire legalism. Pharisaism is a view of life that deals with—and only acts upon—actuality, not the true otherworldliness of Christ's teachings and life. Thus the Pharisees had much in common with the Romans, though neither would perceive the relationship, much less acknowledge it. Similarly, the Western church often perceives and acts upon actuality and, in this respect, is kith and kin of the broader culture; yet it, too, is oblivious to the relationship.

PD-old

The Pharisees and Sadducees Come to Tempt Jesus by James Tissot. *Spengler wrote, "[Jesus'] repugnance for the stiff and selfish ideal of [Pharisaism]...is the hallmark of all his discourses from first to last. It angered him that this wilderness of cold-hearted formulae was reputed to be the only way to salvation." A modern version of Pharisaism is alive in the Western church today. The reality of a world that the shallow minds and hardened hearts of modern Western culture cannot comprehend —given as they are to faith in the material world as defined and measured by material gain, scientific "proof," and a moral license to do as "seems right in [their] own eyes"—is often just as elusive in the church.*

> So he went, proclaiming his message without reservation, through his country. But this country was Palestine. He was born in the Classical Empire and lived under the eyes of the Judaism of Jerusalem, and when his soul, fresh from the awful revelation of its mission, looked about, it was confronted by the actuality of the Roman State and that of Pharisaism. His repugnance for the stiff and selfish ideal of the latter....is the hallmark of all his discourses from first to last. It angered him that this wilderness of cold-hearted formulae was reputed to be the only way to salvation. Still, thus far it was only another kind of piety that his conviction was asserting against Rabbinical logic.
>
> Thus far it is only the Law versus the Prophets.[6]

"Cold-hearted formulae" is a term we could readily apply to much that characterizes the modern Western church. In the confrontation that ensued between those who believed in actuality, the Romans and the Pharisees on the one hand, and the representative of the greater reality, Christ on the other, hidden realities were exposed to the discerning, as can be seen in this infamous exchange: "But they shouted, 'Take him away! Take him away! Crucify him!' 'Shall I crucify your king?' Pilate asked. 'We have no king but Caesar,' the chief priests answered." (John 19:15 NIV) This declaration was at once hypocritical and unwittingly revealing. The chief priests and Pharisees did not truly deem Caesar their king but, in one of history's supreme ironies, they worshipped the same values Caesar worshipped, money, prestige, and power, even as they hated their philosophical kindred, the Romans, as their oppressors. Thus their declaration was both a manipulative lie and a revelation of their true motives.

In this sense, a modern version of pharisaism is alive in the church today. The reality of a world that the shallow minds and hardened hearts of modern Western culture cannot comprehend—given as they are to faith in the material world as defined and measured by material gain, scientific "proof," and a moral license to do as "seems right in [their] own eyes"—is often just as elusive in the church.

A KINGDOM NOT OF THIS WORLD

...the unthinkable as a certainty, the supernatural as a fact, life as existence in a world that is non-actual, but true. Jesus never lived one moment in any other world but this.
Oswald Spengler[7]

Spengler saw the absolute and complete separation of the two worlds: actuality and "the divine world-order."

> *My kingdom is not of this world.* This is the final word which admits of no gloss and on which each must check the course wherein birth and nature have set him. There is no bridge between directional Time and timeless Eternity, between the *course* of history and the *existence* of a divine world-order, in the structure of which the word "Providence" or "dispensation" denotes the form of causality. *This is the final meaning of the moment in which Jesus and Pilate confronted each other.* In the one world, the historical, the Roman caused the Galilean to be crucified—that was his Destiny. In the other world, Rome was cast for perdition and the Cross became the pledge of Redemption—that was the "will of God."[8]

Ultimately, Rome could not "win," just as Western culture—despite its historic hubristic optimism and zealous competitive spirit—cannot win. So the issue becomes the magnitude of suffering that will follow upon its efforts to do so. In the world of actuality it may appear for some period of time to prevail, but in the greater reality it will be reduced to the same ruins that now are the last meaningless vestiges of the Roman Empire.

In another telling insight, Spengler declared the true nature of Christ and Christianity as neither just another religion—as it is wont to be seen in our time in the relativistic West—nor as simply a moral teaching and code. In so doing, he echoed the biblical passage, "Now faith is being sure of what we hope for and certain of what we do not see." (Hebrews 11:1 NIV)

> *Religion is metaphysic and nothing else—"Credo quia absurdum"*—and this metaphysic is not the metaphysic of knowledge, argument, proof (which is mere philosophy of learnedness), but *lived and experienced* metaphysic—that is, the unthinkable as a certainty, the supernatural as a fact, life as existence in a world that is non-actual, but true. Jesus never lived one moment in any other world but this. He was no moralizer, and to see in moralizing the final aim of religion is to be ignorant of what religion is. Moralizing is nineteenth-century Enlightenment, humane Philistinism. To ascribe social purposes to Jesus is a blasphemy.[9]

PD-old

Christ in front of Pilate by Mihály Munkácsy, 1881. *Spengler saw the absolute and complete separation of the two worlds: actuality and "the divine world-order." "'My kingdom is not of this world.' This is the final word that admits of no gloss and on which each must check the course wherein birth and nature have set him. There is no bridge between directional Time and timeless Eternity, between the course of history and the existence of a divine world-order, in the structure of which the word 'Providence' or 'dispensation' denotes the form of causality. This is the final meaning of the moment in which Jesus and Pilate confronted each other. In the one world, the historical, the Roman caused the Galilean to be crucified—that was his Destiny. In the other world, Rome was cast for perdition and the Cross became the pledge of Redemption—that was the 'will of God.'"*

Spengler here exposed one of modern Western man's interpretations of the Christian faith, and, in so doing, placed the terms "Enlightenment" and "Philistinism" in the same sentence. The significance of Spengler's insight is relevant not only to our earlier examination of the Renaissance and the Enlightenment but also to the state of the church in the West as we addressed it earlier herein. "No moralizer"? Yes, Christ and all He stood for go far beyond that thin veneer. If there is no God, there is no law. But if there is a God, He is the absolute divine legislator and the ultimate judge. If Christ was, as he claimed, the Son of God, then everything he uttered, everything He did, was a manifestation of that Absolute Law. Only that which is fully and completely consistent with those actions and those words can be granted the status of "legal" or "moral." Deny that and you deny Him.

By this definition, Western civilization is, has been, and likely will continue to be, a flagrant and remorseless law breaker. By this definition, the Western church, is, has been, and perhaps will be, the greatest of sinners. Knowing the law, having ready access to the Truth, it nonetheless turned aside from it and committed adultery with its mistress, Western culture. She sits in all her meretricious finery, an honored guest, in church and cathedral throughout Western civilization and listens attentively even as her lover professes devotion to *the one* she would supplant entirely. Her conquest, the Western church, does not recognize its obsession with this simpering, beguiling temptress. Were it ever to pull back the veil and rub away the makeup, it would be shocked to recognize that this creature is indeed hideous.

But the spiritual—and, yes, intellectual—insensitivity bred by this illicit relationship makes it difficult for the church to fully come to grips with its sin, even to see it. As Spengler suggested, even the *capacity* to conceive of the glory and beauty of the other and greater world may be lost entirely by this hardening of the heart.

> His *teaching* was the proclamation, nothing but the proclamation, of those Last Things with whose images he was constantly filled, the dawn of the New Age, the advent of heavenly envoys, the last judgment, a new heaven and a new earth. Any other conception of religion was never in Jesus, nor in any truly deep-feeling period in history. *Religion is, first and last, metaphysic,* other-worldliness *(Jenseitigkeit),* awareness of a world of which the evidence of the senses merely lights the foreground. It is life in and with the supersensible. And where the capacity for this awareness, or even the capacity for believing in its existence, is wanting, real religion is at an end.[10]

Disturbingly, this may be where Western civilization now rests. If so, its doom is certain and its collapse will be exquisitely painful.

> "Consider the lilies" means: "Give no heed to riches *and poverty,* for both fetter the soul to cares of this world." "Man cannot serve both God and Mammon"—by Mammon is meant the *whole* of actuality. It is shallow, and it is cowardly, to argue away the grand significance of this demand. Between working for the increase of one's own riches, and working for the social ease of everyone, he would have felt no difference whatever. When wealth affrighted him, when the primitive community in Jerusalem—which was a strict Order and not a socialist club—rejected ownership, it was the most direct opposite of "social" sentiment that moved them. Their conviction was, not that the visible state of things was all, but that it was nothing: that it rested not on appreciation of comfort in this world, but on unreserved contempt of it.[11]

THE PURPOSE OF IT ALL

The greatest new event will then not be the monotonous rise of yet another secular civilization out of the bosom of the Christian Church in the course of these latter centuries; it will still be the Crucifixion and its spiritual consequences.
Arnold Toynbee[12]

Toynbee speculated, "The breakdowns and disintegrations of civilizations might be stepping-stones to higher things on the religious plane."[13] If, Toynbee wondered, we juxtapose Aeschylus' observation that it is only through suffering that learning comes, with "the New Testament…verse 'whom the Lord loveth, He chasteneth; and scourgeth every son whom He receiveth'"; and if we then "apply that to the rise of the higher religions" then we might conclude "that the Passion of Christ was

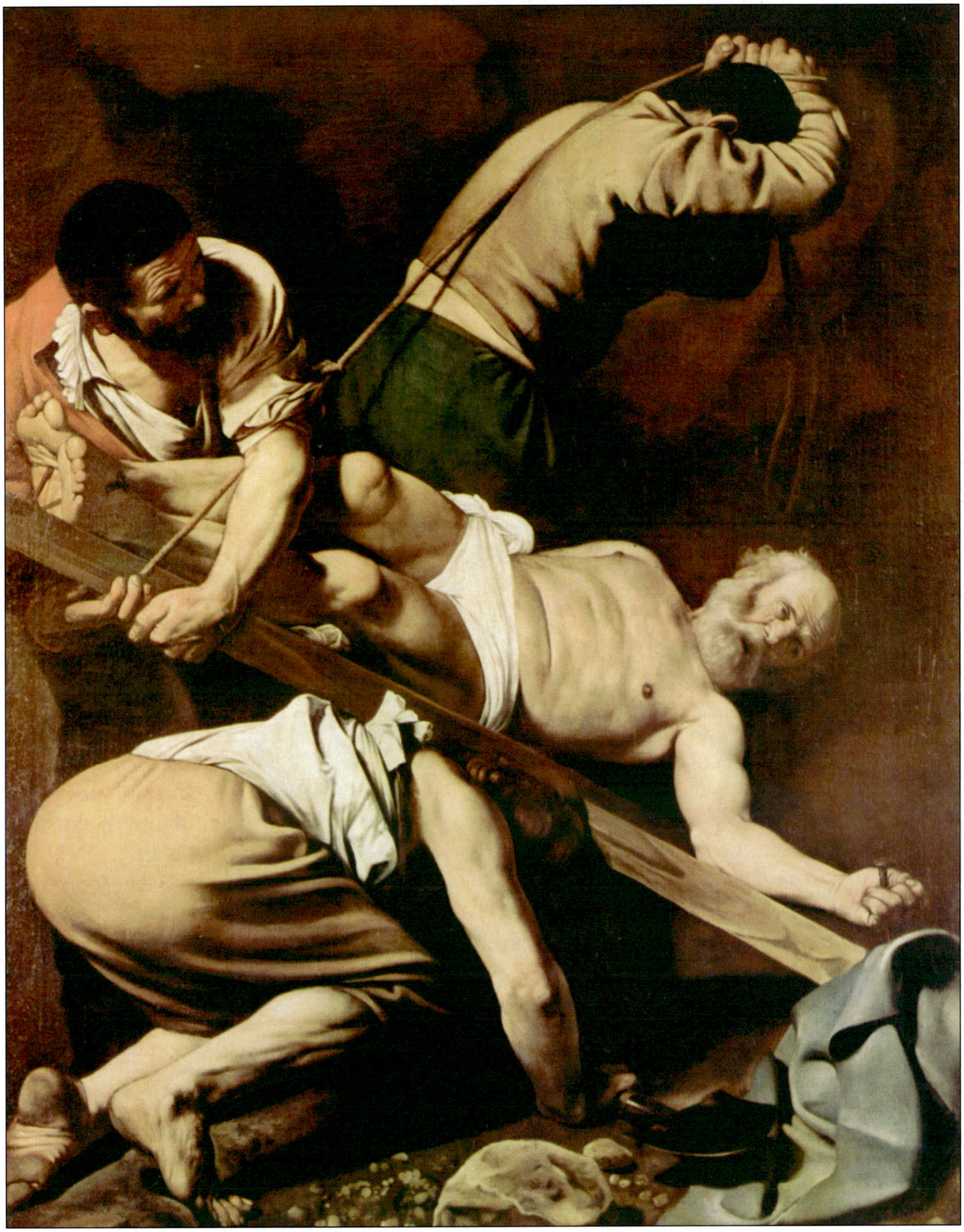

PD-old

The Crucifixion of St. Peter by Caravaggio. *Peter asked to be crucified upside down, proclaiming he was not worthy to be crucified as Jesus was. Francis Schaeffer noted that the early Christians' suffering at the hands of the culture of that age was a direct consequence of their belief that John 1:9 was true. "If they had worshiped Jesus and Caesar, they would have gone unharmed, but they rejected all forms of syncretism.... They allowed no mixture: All other Gods were seen as false gods." "All other Gods" would include the gods of materialism, pride, worldly prestige, pleasure, vanity, self-seeking, and power. The modern Western Christian has been, for generations, in effect, worshipping Jesus and Caesar (i.e., the values and mores of the broader culture) and thus far, by virtue of his syncretism, has eluded serious persecution. He is not a threat to the* status quo; *he is part and parcel of it. The time is upon us—has indeed already passed—when the Western Christian must clearly and decisively break with one or the other, Christ or Caesar, Christ or the culture.*

the culminating and crowning experience of the sufferings of human souls in successive failures in the enterprise of secular civilization."[14]

This viewpoint is consistent with my own, namely, that history is not a meaningless redundancy nor an ascension through progressive steps to a utopian world created by man. Rather it is the repetitive teaching of a great lesson—there is a God and a transcendent, immutable law and only through these can man find what he most needs—peace, love, and salvation—leading inevitably to the complete final revelation of God. Jesus Christ "...was the true Light, which lighteth every man that cometh into the world." (John 1:9 KJV)

Francis Schaeffer noted that the early Christians' suffering at the hands of the culture of that age was a direct consequence of their belief that John 1:9 was true. "If they had worshiped Jesus *and* Caesar, they would have gone unharmed, but they rejected all forms of syncretism....They allowed no mixture: All other Gods were seen as false gods."[15]

"All other Gods" would include the gods of materialism, pride, worldly prestige, pleasure, vanity, self-seeking, and power. The modern Western Christian has been, for generations, in effect, worshipping Jesus and Caesar (i.e., the values and mores of the broader culture) and thus far, by virtue of his syncretism, has eluded serious persecution. He is not a threat to the *status quo*; he is part and parcel of it. The time is upon us—has indeed already passed—when the Western Christian must clearly and decisively break with one or the other, Christ or Caesar, Christ or the culture.

Toynbee declared what was truly significant in all of history.

> Our present view of modern history focuses attention on the rise of our modern Western secular civilization as the latest great new event in the world. As we follow that rise, from the first premonition of it in the genius of Frederick II Hohenstaufen, through the Renaissance to the eruption of democracy and science and modern scientific technique, we think of all this as being the great new event in the world which demands our attention and commands our admiration. If we can bring ourselves to think of it, instead, as one of the vain repetitions of the Gentiles—an almost meaningless repetition of something that the Greeks and Romans did before us and did supremely well—then the greatest new event in the history of mankind will be seen to be a very different one. The greatest new event will then not be the monotonous rise of yet another secular civilization out of the bosom of the Christian Church in the course of these latter centuries; it will still be the Crucifixion and its spiritual consequences.[16]

Therefore, he who would call himself a follower of Christ must—without reservation, compromise, or hesitation—say with the Apostle Paul, "I glory in Christ Jesus in my service to God." (Romans 15:17 NIV)

(Opposite) *Crucifixion of Jesus* by Peter Paul Rubens. *Toynbee declared, "Our present view of modern history focuses attention on the rise of our modern Western secular civilization as the latest great new event in the world....We think of all this as being the great new event in the world which demands our attention and commands our admiration. If we can bring ourselves to think of it, instead, as one of the vain repetitions of the Gentiles—an almost meaningless repetition of something that the Greeks and Romans did before us and did supremely well—then the greatest new event in the history of mankind will be seen to be a very different one. The greatest new event will then not be the monotonous rise of yet another secular civilization out of the bosom of the Christian Church in the course of these latter centuries; it will still be the Crucifixion and its spiritual consequences."*

PD-old

END NOTES
CHAPTER 31

1 Oswald Spengler, *The Decline of the West* (New York: A. A. Knopf, 1926), 285.
2 Francis A. Schaeffer, *How Should We Then Live? The Rise and Decline of Western Thought and Culture* (Wheaton, IL: Crossway Books, 1976), 84.
3 Spengler, *Decline of the West,* 285.
4 Spengler, *Decline of the West,* 285.
5 Spengler, *Decline of the West,* 287.
6 Spengler, *Decline of the West,* 287.
7 Spengler, *Decline of the West,* 288.
8 Spengler, *Decline of the West,* 288.
9 Spengler, *Decline of the West,* 288.
10 Spengler, *Decline of the West,* 289.
11 Spengler, *Decline of the West,* 289.
12 Arnold J. Toynbee, *Civilization on Trial* (New York: Oxford University Press 1948), 237.
13 Toynbee, *Civilization on Trial,* 234.
14 Toynbee, *Civilization on Trial,* 234–235.
15 Schaeffer, *How Should We Then Live?,* 26.
16 Toynbee, *Civilization on Trial,* 237.

CHAPTER

32

THE TRIUMPH OF EVIL THROUGH THE WEAKNESS OF THE GOOD

When Pilate saw that he could prevail nothing, but that rather a tumult was made, he took water, and washed his hands before the multitude, saying, I am innocent of the blood of this just person: see ye to it.
Matthew 27:24 (KJV)

...the Roman world-dominion was a negative phenomenon, being the result not of a surplus of energy on the one side—that the Romans had never had since Zama—but of a deficiency of resistance on the other.
Oswald Spengler[1]

Anyone, then, who knows the good he ought to do and doesn't do it, sins.
James 4:17 (NIV)

We are all ready to be savage in some cause.
The difference between a good man and a bad one is the choice of the cause.
William James

The power of evil is manifest only in relation to the weakness of the good. The absence of the light produces darkness. Thus Man's world is evil because he wills it so.

Attributed, perhaps erroneously, to Edmund Burke, "the only thing necessary for evil to triumph is for good men to do nothing" is now an iconic maxim in the West. But is such a creature not an oxymoron? If "good men" are good, why do they do nothing? Do "good" men's failures to stand not say that they are not good after all—except in their own minds and in terms of not actively "participating" with the evil? Is passivity in the face of evil or acquiescence in the presence of injustice not evil itself? Is such a moral pacifist not then an accessory to evil?

From the twenty-first century henceforward the notion that one can be passive, or even simply disengaged, from the battle against all forms of evil and injustice and remain righteous or "good" is not tenable. The dangers for the world are now so great that no one can claim, "But I had nothing to do with it" or "I don't agree with it" and still assume the mantle of moral propriety. Just as the defense "I was ordered to do it" did not work at Nuremberg, nor certainly would any Pilate-like

A Sudanese Christian whose arm had been hacked off by Islamic soldiers. *Sudan remains today a place of misery and persecution for Christians. Slavery is still practiced. A classic illustration of the consequences of the world's indifference, Sudan reflects the triumph of evil.*

Photo courtesy of Frontline Fellowship

washing of the hands suffice to absolve anyone in our time and henceforth, neither can man continue his denial of his moral duty.

The triumph of evil invariably occurs—and always only occurs—in the vacuum created by the absence or weakness of the good. Every void in the heart and mind of man will be filled—it is man's choice whether it will be filled by good or evil. One will necessarily displace the other as dictated by the individual's choice. For millennia, man has chosen sin and evil—individual tragedy is then followed by collective tragedy and earth's gravity draws the blood of millions deep into its bosom. The tears are stanched only by death or the hardest of hardening of the heart. The monotonous litany is like the chanting of a fool, oblivious to the obvious and blind to the course upon which he has set his feet.

Yet man blames God. Western man, in particular, is wont to deploy this rationalization; against God, if he professes belief in a Supreme Being; against faith, if he professes agnosticism or atheism. Either way it is "someone else's fault, but not mine." "I am," he declares—if not overtly then impliedly—"superior. I see where the fault lies." But this too is nothing new. Indeed, noting this tactical circumvention of personal responsibility by man even before the advent of Christianity, the historian Barbara Tuchman, in *The March of Folly*, observed that "The gods' interference does not acquit man of folly; rather it is man's device for transferring the responsibility for folly."[2] Cycling from brief intervals of

PD-gov

(Left to right) Field Marshall Alan Brooke, Churchill, and Field Marshall Montgomery. *The French, apparently stronger militarily than the British at the outset of World War II, were in fact, psychologically and spiritually weaker. Brooke confided to his diary his fears that the Maginot Line not only suggested a spiritual and moral complacency but nurtured a false sense of security. These weaknesses meant that Hitler would not be stopped early, rather than after millions of lives were forfeited.*

Photo by Theo Eisenhart. PD

German President Paul Von Hindenburg (right) called Hitler to the chancellorship of Germany on 30 January 1933. *Von Hindenburg had the power and prestige to have successfully banned the Nazi Party and spared Germany the worst infamy in world history. But he did not. Similarly, with a few exceptions, such as Dietrich Bonhoeffer, professing Christians in Germany not only did not oppose Hitler but, in many instances, sang his praises. Austrians, predominantly Catholic, were largely as enthusiastic about National Socialism as were the Lutheran Germans.*

against Nazism, made them more likely to embrace it."[11] So much for the institutional church. So much for that much venerated Western value—education.

The weakness of what should have been the countervailing forces to Nazism in Germany and Austria was complemented by the weakness of the external forces that might have stopped Hitler early, rather than after millions of lives were forfeited. "Appeasement," in the words of Ferguson, "did not lead to war. It was war that led to appeasement." Put another way, the cowardice of the West in the face of Hitler's aggressive behavior made his ascendancy a certainty.[12] Capitulation by Chamberlain to Hitler allowing the Germans to take the Czechoslovakian Sudetenland undercut the internal resistance to Hitler led by General Ludwig Beck. Thus the weakness of the "good" not only gave evil what it wanted—making it much stronger—it undermined the efforts of others to destroy the evil.

Throughout these early years leading up to World War II, every conceivable limp-wristed tactic the West could devise was attempted, but the only stratagem that had any prospect of success was a preemptive strike against Hitler before he became too powerful. The psychological effect alone of this on Hitler and the German people would have been incalculable. But the dallying of the West bought Hitler time, precious time in which to build his military and economic base. Contrary to the received conventional wisdom, appeasement did not buy the British time—the British were economically stronger at the onset of the crisis than later—it worked in Hitler's favor. He became stronger while the British weakened. Once again, Niall Ferguson put his finger on a profound mistake: "The British nightmare was a German-Italian-Japanese combination. Yet the more they sought to avert it by diplomatic expedients rather than military counter measures, the more likely it became."[13]

The French, apparently stronger militarily than the British, were in fact, psychologically and spiritually even weaker. British Lieutenant General Alan Brooke confided to his diary his fears that the Maginot Line not only suggested a spiritual and moral complacency but nurtured, by its very existence, a false sense of security.[14] The Nobel Laureate Roger Martin du Gard wrote of the statements of a German officer after the defeat of France that the French "did not know what they were

War-ravaged Kosovo from the gunport of a Blackhawk helicopter; 1999. *In the cases of Rwanda, Bosnia, and Kosovo, the evidence existed for some time of genocide but the West dallied, its weakness and self-centeredness on abject display. We live in a culture that is becoming more self-indulgent and, with it, cowardly and complacent. Western man does not realize that he is unwittingly making it more and more possible for evil to flourish on this benighted orb.*

Photograph by Ivy Scarborough

H. S. Wong, photographer; United States Office of War Information, 1926–1951. PD-gov

Chinese baby in bombed-out Shanghai railway station in the early phase of World War II. *Historian Niall Ferguson observed, "The European empires had simply caved in, as if the Japanese had exposed a fundamental loss of self-belief."*

fighting for"—a pronouncement also consistent with what our observers have told us of the characteristics of civilizational decline and decay.

Simultaneously, on the other side of the world, the Japanese were running amok, stepping on and over the bodies of the weaker nations that they saw as chickens for the plucking. Significantly, the Japanese were nonetheless successful in securing collaboration even as they committed atrocities. "The key to securing collaboration turned out to have little, if anything, to do with the cruelty or kindness of the invading forces. The decisive factor was the extent to which the invaded people were divided among themselves."[15] Once again, Ferguson perceived an underlying cause: "The European empires had simply caved in, as if the Japanese had exposed a fundamental loss of self-belief."[16]

Then, in the same part of the world, immediately after the Japanese were vanquished, the obtuse West made similar mistakes by supporting the corrupt and inept Kuomintang against the ruthless but capable Mao and the Chinese Communists. In the aftermath, the slow students then stridently

Bodies of Rwandan refugees wrapped in straw mats and blankets line the roadside. *In 1993 in Burundi, thousands of civilians were slaughtered. The West paid no attention. Their neighbors in Rwanda correctly concluded that a genocide of their own could be effected with resulting similar apathy from the West. Thousands died and—in a boon to the world's incipient and future tyrants—evil was emboldened.*

PD-gov

engaged one another over "Who lost China?"—never considering that there was ample blame—and incompetence—to go around.

The litany of vain, meaningless words and conduct continued into the second half of the twentieth century. Secretary of State Dean Acheson publicly declared that South Korea was outside "our defense perimeter," signaling to the North that perhaps aggressive action would not be resisted. Saddam Hussein, a *de facto* ally of the U.S. in the 1980s, was assured by the American ambassador that the U.S. would not intervene in quarrels among Arabs. Kuwait was invaded shortly thereafter.

In the cases of Rwanda, Bosnia, and Kosovo, the evidence existed for some time of genocide but the West dallied, its weakness and self-centeredness on abject display for anyone who would but look. In 1993 in Burundi, thousands of civilians were slaughtered. The West paid no attention. Their neighbors in Rwanda concluded that a genocide of their own could be effected with resulting similar apathy from the West.

In Bosnia in 1993 and then Kosovo in 1998, I saw first-hand the consequences of these moral failures. Thousands died and—in a boon to the world's incipient and future tyrants—evil was emboldened.

THE PSYCHOLOGY OF WEAKNESS

We have not the freedom to reach to this or to that, but the freedom to do the necessary or to do nothing. And a task that historic necessity has set will be accomplished with the individual or against him.
Oswald Spengler[17]

Man, it seems, is wont to draw the wrong conclusions from his experiences. For example, pain in some form often produces fear and, in many people, this in turn produces timidity and anxiety (what psychologists would call *neuroses*). We all tend to this, but some people see the threat and resist it. There are indissoluble links between this response and an individual's spiritual views—most of which would either be deficient or stunted. In Christian theology, "Perfect love casts out fear." But if that faith is weak, Christians, as with other human beings, may hold their fear close to their bosoms in the vain hope that this will somehow protect them from future pain and danger.

Just the reverse is true. Were human beings disposed to choose to hate fear and to become relentlessly angry when confronted with injustice or cruelty—and to become very aggressive in the face of these evils—the world would be safer and more secure, not less so. There are times when, as was said of an implacably pugnacious Confederate general, we should draw the sword and throw away the scabbard. Most people don't understand a reaction like this—indeed they may fear it—but it is only when we become angry—righteously angry—that we will rise to the occasion and take the stand that needs to be taken.

The absence of righteous anger, of the species that prompts an individual to feel outrage intensely and act upon it, is a deficit of faith and conviction in the hormone and immune systems of Western civilization. We live in a culture that is becoming more and more self-indulgent and, with it, spiritually and morally cowardly and complacent. The philosophy of life embodied in these attitudes and behaviors is sad; for Western man clearly does not realize that he is unwittingly making it more and more possible for evil to flourish on this benighted orb. As for the Christian, God truly does not give us a spirit of fear, and what a glorious thing it is to be free of it!

THE DEARTH OF BOLD LEADERSHIP

He's going around the country stirring up apathy.
William Whitelaw, British MP[18]

Mr. Whitelaw's sarcastic reference to a political adversary would aptly apply to many ministers and priests. Predisposed to tell their parishioners what they want to hear (e.g., how good they are, how deserving, how victimized, how God wishes to make them wealthy, comfortable, popular, etc.) they are loath to challenge, much less courageously lead, their flock into the spiritual battle of our times, thereby entreating them to seek neither material gain nor happiness but instead embrace sacrifice, exertion, and danger.

Even among those who might give lip service to volunteering for dangerous duty in God's army, there is an ironic trait of passivity that undermines the resolution of problems in their own lives, and certainly does not prompt them to tackle the problems of the culture. The rationalized assumption seems to be that if Christians act in a dynamic, assertive way this suggests a lack of faith and takes matters out of God's hands.

But the old maxim "God helps those who help themselves" is, in many respects, theologically sound, and it is certainly applicable to many of life's problems. The Christian's duty is to seek God's will through prayer and Bible study, get the wise counsel of others, and then act as action is needed. The most eloquent statement of demonstrating faith by actions is found in James: "What good is it my brothers, if a man claims to have faith but has no deeds?...As the body without the spirit is dead, so faith without deeds is dead." (James 2:14, 16 NIV)

The passive response in the face of a daunting challenge is not unknown, even among the great heroes of faith. The Old Testament book of Exodus relates that as Moses led the Israelites out of Egypt, the people became ever more fearful. Apparently, so was Moses. With the Red Sea (or the Reed

PD

The Crossing of the Red Sea by Nicholas Poussin. *A passive response in the face of a daunting challenge is not unknown, even among the great heroes of faith. The Old Testament book of Exodus relates that as Moses led the Israelites out of Egypt, the people became ever more fearful—apparently, so was Moses. With the Red Sea to their front and thousands of Egyptian soldiers bearing down on them in chariots from the rear, Moses "fell on his face" and began to pray. God's response is fascinating and profoundly instructive for the man or woman who would lead the life of faith: "Then the Lord said to Moses, 'Why are you crying out to me? Tell the Israelites to move on.'" (Exodus 14:15 NIV) God told Moses to quit praying and get moving! Often we demonstrate our faith best by acting. Concealing our fear even from ourselves behind a façade of false faith weakens Christians in their confrontations with life's adversities and in their Christian witness. No one admires fear, but what a powerful force and attraction is courageous action. Prayer is in part asking the Commander for His orders and support. It should never be a substitute for boldly taking to the field on the offensive.*

Sea, depending on your interpretation) to their front and thousands of Egyptian soldiers bearing down on them in chariots from the rear, Moses "fell on his face" and began to pray. God's response is fascinating and profoundly instructive for the man or woman who would lead the life of faith: "Then the Lord said to Moses, 'Why are you crying out to me? Tell the Israelites to move on.'" (Exodus 14:15 NIV) God told Moses to quit praying and get moving!

This was not a subordination of prayer to action, but simply a clear lesson that there is a time for faithful, bold action. Often we demonstrate our faith best by acting. Concealing our fear, even from ourselves, behind a façade of false faith weakens Christians in their confrontations with life's adversities and in their Christian witness. No one admires fear, but what a powerful force and attraction is courageous action. Prayer is, in part, asking the Commander for His orders and support. It should never be a substitute for boldly taking to the field on the offensive.

A minister or priest who is truly challenging his flock to serve—and not just be served—and demanding of them holy, nonconforming lives—and not just acceptance of what is common to the culture (even within the church)—will compel a spiritual growth that will leave little time or inclination for self-indulgence or internecine conflict. As any good military officer knows, the best troops are those who are fighting; or when not fighting they are training in weapons and tactics; or when not training they are exercising vigorously to gain strength and stamina; and when not exercising they are resting so as to begin the next day with renewed commitment and vigor for what will follow. There is no place for casualness with the true warrior; there is no place for casualness with the true Christian.

THE CHRISTIAN'S CHOICE

At no time can we expect this work to be unopposed, for the very fact that the Church represents something entirely different—the intervention of a supernatural principle and the coming of a divine Kingdom—must inevitably arouse the fierce opposition of all those human societies and powers which claim absolute power over man and refuse to admit a superior or rival.

Christopher Dawson[19]

None of our observers wrote more fully or more pointedly about the challenge before the Christian church in the West than did Christopher Dawson. Before our time, Dawson saw over the horizon of history. "Hence we can hardly doubt that when ultimately a conflict takes place between the new state and the Christian Church, it will be far more severe in character than anything that has been known before."[20] It is not a stretch to say that were he to view the landscape of Western civilization today he would be grievously disappointed at both the course of the civilization and the failure of the church to more profoundly influence that course.

Unlike the Christians of the early church who saw that "nothing was clearer" than that "the mystery of iniquity that was already at work in the world would come out into the open and claim to stand in the place of God Himself," Christians of today largely do not yet recognize what is upon them. This is because they have been conditioned by the church not only to accept many of the values and mores of the broader culture, but to be complicit in bringing them into the middle of their hearts, homes, and churches. Hence the church today is not prepared as were the early Christians "for vast and immediate historical changes" and the battle that is already being waged all about it. In that former age when the church was the outcast of the culture, it was strong and ready for the persecutions that followed. Because of that strength "the world suddenly awoke to find that the Empire itself had become Christian." Unlike the church of our age, which at best concluded generations ago, "if you can't beat 'em, join 'em," the reverse was true and the powerful, worldly culture succumbed to the church.[21]

The committed Christian recognizes that this was not something to marvel at as an impossible dream but precisely what can be expected if the Christian "strategy" is truly honored. But the Western church, forgetful as it remains of that true biblical strategy, still struggles to use the weapons and tools of the culture—money, political power, prestige, legal recourses, etc.—to fight the battle. As long as it persists in this misbegotten—and heretical—approach, it will be decimated and defeated. Dawson declared what could be:

> It is true that we do not know where the world is going. We cannot say it must go towards a Christian culture any more than towards destruction by atomic warfare. All we know is that the world is being changed from top to bottom and that the Christian faith remains the way of salvation, that is to say, a way to the renewal of human life by the spirit of God, which has no limits and which cannot be prevented by human power or material catastrophe.[22]

There is even greater reason for hope for the church were it to repent of its course and change its strategy. Dawson, speaking here of principles applicable to the Catholic Church that we assert as applicable to all true followers of Christ, explained why continued failure and defeat need not be the church's lot.

> Inevitably in the course of history there are times when this spiritual energy is temporarily weakened or obscured, and then the Church tends to be judged as a human organization and identified with the faults and limitations of its members. But always the time comes when she renews her strength and once more puts forth her inherent divine energy in the conversion of new peoples and the transformation of old cultures....The intervention of a supernatural principle and the coming of a divine Kingdom—must inevitably arouse the fierce opposition of all those human societies and powers which claim absolute power over man and refuse to admit a superior or rival.[23]

These forces, led in our time as in all ages by those with the will-to-power are not simply of the right or left, or the East or West, or North or South. So long as the Western church perceives reality in ideological, political, or geographic terms it will fail.

> But the conflict is not really one between East and West: it is the old conflict between the spiritual and temporal powers, which was formerly confined largely to the Western world and has now emerged as a burning question in the East, largely owing to the introduction of the political ideologies of the West into Asia and Africa. But East or West, it is basically the same conflict, and alike in East and West the Church stands neither for East nor West but for the universal spiritual society which is destined to embrace them both.[24]

"For we wrestle not against flesh and blood, but against principalities, against powers, against the rulers of the darkness of this world, against spiritual wickedness in high places." (Ephesians 6:12 KJV) And their power grows only because we, the body of believers in Christ, have permitted it.

END NOTES
CHAPTER 32

1 Oswald Spengler, *The Decline of the West* (New York: A. A. Knopf, 1926), 27.
2 Barbara Wertheim Tuchman, *The March of Folly: From Troy to Vietnam* (New York: A. A. Knopf, 1984), 46.
3 Andrew Roberts, *Salisbury: Victorian Titan* (London: Weidenfeld & Nicholson, 1999), 435.
4 Spengler, *Decline of the West*, 414.
5 Spengler, *Decline of the West*, 27.
6 Niall Ferguson, *The War of the Worlds* (New York: Penguin Books, 2006), 313.
7 John Keegan, *An Illustrated History of the First World War* (New York: A. A. Knopf, 2001), 360.
8 Ferguson, *War of the Worlds*, 183.
9 Ferguson, *War of the Worlds*, 183.
10 Ferguson, *War of the Worlds*, 229.
11 Ferguson, *War of the Worlds*, 243.
12 Ferguson, *War of the Worlds*, 312–313.
13 Ferguson, *War of the Worlds*, 332.
14 Ferguson, *War of the Worlds*, 389.
15 Ferguson, *War of the Worlds*, 481.
16 Ferguson, *War of the Worlds*, 494.
17 Spengler, *Decline of the West*, 415.
18 John Ransley, *Chambers Dictionary of Political Biography* (Edinburgh: Chambers, 1991), 379.
19 Christopher Dawson, *The Historic Reality of Christian Culture* (New York: Harper & Brothers, 1960), 119.
20 Christopher Dawson, *Religion and World History: A Selection from the Works of Christopher Dawson* (Garden City, NY: Image Books, 1975), 265.
21 Dawson, *Religion and World History*, 265.
22 Dawson, *Religion and World History*, 265–266.
23 Dawson, *Historic Reality*, 119.
24 Dawson, *Historic Reality*, 119–120.

CHAPTER

33

THE INDIVIDUAL AND THE POWER OF CHOICE

Mankind? It is an abstraction. There are, always have been, and always will be, men and only men.
Goethe[1]

Jesus replied, "If anyone loves me, he will obey my teaching."
John 14:23 (NIV)

There is no limit to the efficacy of faith and to the influence of...acts of spiritual decision, which are ultimately the response of particular men to God's call, as revealed in particular historical and personal circumstances.
Christopher Dawson[2]

The father of the legendary explorer Marco Polo had been to Cathay (China) long before his son's more famous journeys and was perhaps the first Westerner welcomed at the court of the Mongol emperor Kublai Khan. The Khan, ruler of one of the great empires known to history, gave Polo a commission: travel to his home in the West and return with one hundred Christian missionaries and oil from the Holy Sepulcher in Jerusalem. For this, he granted Polo his seal ensuring his safety in all the lands of the vast empire. Polo, the evidence suggests, made plans to return, albeit for commercial motives. He attempted to honor his commission but could recruit only two priests who would go with him. Both of them turned back due to the rigors of the journey.

Like so many junctures in world history where individual choices made a decisive difference, the failure of the Christians of Polo's time to rise to the challenge profoundly influenced world history thereafter. One wonders what the world would have been like had one hundred committed Christian missionaries—or even two—returned to satisfy the emperor's curiosity about Christianity.

The Christians who heard of the opportunity presented by Kublai Khan through Polo undoubtedly never considered that their decision not to act would have profound effects on the course of history. Surely, many rationalized to themselves that someone else would follow through, or that their Christian duty lay in tending to the rituals, functions, and buildings of their churches.

The church in the West faces a similar great challenging question today: Will professing Christians display the courage, self-sacrifice, and love of God and fellowman to do what must be done to alter the tragic course of a civilization? Or will they continue to display the weakness and indifference of the "ninety-eight" missionaries-who-never-were or the lack of resolve of the two who failed to persevere?

The value and the power of the individual are at the forefront of the Christian faith. Recognition of the innate worth of each individual human being—precisely because they are the creation of God—is fundamental to the love that is central to Christian belief and Christ's sacrifice on the cross.

Everything hinges on the individual's inner choices: For good or ill, each person writes the script for his own destiny—and, in so doing, shapes the destiny of their family, their tribe, their nation, their civilization. Everything of consequence is determined in the heart and mind of each individual, not through a collective consciousness or within the powerful institutions of human society.

Every human being is an actor in more than one of the many great dramas of history. The greatest and most significant of these performances is often the most obscure: the individual's inner life and each individual's choices of belief and values. Only the choices of individuals—what to believe and what not to believe, whom to love and whom not to love, what to value and what not to value, whether to act or not to act—ultimately matter in the great tapestry of life. These threads, woven together, produce what we call history.

This understanding takes us first to its most powerful expression in the realm of the spiritual: what we will call "The Gideon Principle."

Kublai Khan, 1294, by Nepalese artist and astronomer Anige. *The Khan, ruler of one of the great empires known to history, gave Marco Polo's father a commission: travel to his home in the West and return with one hundred Christian missionaries and oil from the Holy Sepulcher in Jerusalem. Polo, the evidence suggests, made plans to return, albeit for commercial motives. He attempted to honor his commission but could recruit only two priests who would go with him. Both of them turned back due to the rigors of the journey. Like so many junctures in world history where individual choices made a decisive difference, the failure of the Christians of Polo's time to rise to the challenge profoundly influenced world history thereafter. One wonders what the world would have been like had one hundred committed Christian missionaries —or even two—returned to satisfy the emperor's curiosity about Christianity.*

PD-art

THE GIDEON PRINCIPLE

But the Lord said to Gideon, "There are still too many men. Take them down to the water, and I will sift them for you there. If I say, 'This one shall go with you,' he shall go; but if I say, 'This one shall not go with you,' he shall not go."
Judges 7:4 (NIV)

The Gideon Principle: God works through the committed individual and the faithful "remnant," not through mass movements, large numbers, or powerful human institutions.

Gideon was a reluctant warrior, doubting himself and, by implication, doubting God. But his individual choice to say yes to God, and by so doing become an instrument by which God would effect dramatic change in the history of Gideon's time—as well as subsequent centuries—was the axis upon which all of that history was to turn.

The Old Testament's historical accounts of early Jewish history are a litany of cycles: first of obedience to God, followed by national achievements, followed by disobedience and dissipations, and then ultimately victimization by a conquering power. These cycles bear a striking—and expectable—resemblance to the cycles that lead to the decline and decay of civilizations as described earlier in this book. One such cycle's downward turn was reversed through the leadership of Gideon, whom the Bible describes as one of Israel's "judges," a form of leader prior to the investiture generations later of Israel's first monarch, Saul.

Painting by Joseph Karl Stieler (1781–1858). PS-art

The German writer Goethe *declared, "Mankind? It is an abstraction. There are, always have been, and always will be, men and only men." This observation lends weight to the recognition that each person is individually responsible. There can be no hiding behind the culture or collective attitudes, beliefs or behaviors.*

Gideon, a farmer, certainly did not see himself as a leader or a soldier; he balked when confronted with God's command to lead the Israelites in an uprising against their oppressors the Midianites. Even when told "The Lord is with you, mighty warrior," (Judges 6:12b NIV) Gideon responded, "But

PD-old

Gideon Inspecting his Army by Johann Heinrich Schonfeldt, c. 1640. *The Gideon Principle: God works through the committed individual and the faithful "remnant," not through mass movements, large numbers, or powerful human institutions. Everything noble and spiritually exalted originates first in the mind of God from whence it finds root in the heart and mind of a single individual. God's focus is on the small numbers of the committed and the faithful, not the large numbers of the vacillating or lukewarm.*

sir…if the Lord is with us, why has all this happened to us? Where are all His wonders that our fathers told us about…?" (Judges 6:13a NIV)

Gideon's question and implicit complaint—in one form or another—recurs in Scripture and throughout history, into our own time.

Man blames God for what man himself has brought about by his own disobedience and folly. He asks, "Where is God? Why would he permit this (evil, suffering, etc.)? Why doesn't he care? Why won't he help us?" Though, to be sure, it could be said there is no "complete" answer—complete in the sense of being fully explicative or fully comprehensible by man—there is certainly a substantial answer to these questions: Man is responsible for his destiny and many of his dilemmas.

Even the innocent (i.e., those who did not disobey or commit acts of folly) who become victims are nonetheless victims of others' disobedience and folly, not the callous indifference or willful caprice of God. The blame for suffering and evil lies at the feet of man, but he bridles at acknowledging it, much less assuming full accountability. Whether we individually are guilty of blatant disobedience that brings about calamity, we all become victims of others' selfishness and evil; thus man is fully accountable for the state of his world and what happens not only in his own life but to other men.

Gideon did not know it yet, but God would use him to demonstrate how one individual assuming responsibility—in keeping with God's will and His moral law—can change his world dramatically. Instead of receiving a direct answer to his question Gideon was told, "Go in the strength you have….Am I not sending you?" (Judges 6:14 NIV)

At this point Gideon asks a question that, on its surface, seems to reflect humility, but in fact reflects fear and a lack of faith: "But Lord...how can I save Israel? My clan is the weakest in Manasseh, and I am the least in my family." (Judges 6:15 NIV) This response—in myriad versions, untold languages, and a variety of syntaxes—has been uttered countless times throughout history; and, in one form or another, has become the *de facto*—and often unspoken—rationalization for millions of Christians in modern Western civilization.

Despite being reassured, "Do not be afraid. You are not going to die," Gideon remained skeptical to the point of asking for a "sign." Gideon received the indicator he wanted—in the form of a dew-laden sheep's fleece once; then once again, through a dry fleece. (Judges 6:23 NIV) Having thus been doubly reassured, to his credit Gideon then acted. After assembling an army of 32,000 men, Gideon, to his shock, was told by God, "You have too many men for me to deliver Midian into their hands. In order that Israel may not boast against me that her own strength has saved her, announce now to the people, 'Anyone who trembles with fear may turn back.'" (Judges 7:3 NIV) As a consequence, 22,000 left!

This winnowing demonstrates yet another biblical principle: God's focus is on the small numbers of the committed and the faithful, not the large numbers of the vacillating or lukewarm.

To his dismay, Gideon was then told to truncate his army even further—by another test requiring his men to drink from a stream—this time to 300 men! Self-sufficiency was to play no role in Israel's battle. Gideon, now facing an army of 15,000 with 300, remained fearful; and, significantly, God did not excuse him of his duty even as God reassured him. The culmination of this exercise in faith and boldness was a great victory and "the land enjoyed peace forty years." (Judges 8:28 NIV)

Gideon's story became one of the most famous examples from the Bible in which individual choices and personal commitment are keys in God's order. Furthermore, we see the corollary that though there may be a dearth of committed Christian warriors, there will never be a void. The Apostle Paul recounted the Old Testament story of the prophet Elijah, who, in the aftermath of an extraordinary victory against the prophets of Baal, ran for his life and hid in the wilderness. Lapsing into despair—Western man would label it "clinical depression"—Elijah sat under a juniper tree and, in essence, said to God, "If you are going to treat me thusly then just kill me. I am alone, pursued by my enemies and no one cares!" But God's response to Elijah's self-pity was telling. "'I have reserved for myself seven thousand who have not bowed the knee to Baal.' So too, at the present time there is a remnant chosen by grace." (Romans 11:4–5 NIV)

The theme of the faithful remnant appears throughout the Bible. The prophet Ezekiel, while a captive of the Babylonians, prophesied that a faithful remnant would restore Israel to vitality as a God-oriented people. Yet this optimism was couched in condemnation of the apostasy of Judea, a condemnation even more strident than that of the prophet Jeremiah. Put in the vernacular of our time, Ezekiel's message was "Our nation is a spiritual and moral mess; its only hope will be found in a return to faith and honoring God and His moral law. Though the majority will not make this choice, a minority of faithful citizens will, and that will make all the difference."

The "faithful remnant" and the committed individual are the keys in terms of methodology to understanding how God works in human history.

The Christian walk is replete with surprises. The seeking Christian will be repeatedly reminded through the events of his life of the extent of God's power by the remarkable way in which prayers

PD-art

The Prophet Elijah, by Daniele da Volterra (between 1550 and 1560). *Elijah, one of the Old Testament's greatest prophets, nonetheless, in the aftermath of an extraordinary victory against the prophets of Baal, ran for his life and hid in the wilderness. Lapsing into despair—Western man would label it "clinical depression"—Elijah sat under a juniper tree and, in essence, said to God, "If you are going to treat me thusly then just kill me. I am alone, pursued by my enemies and no one cares!" But God's response to Elijah's self-pity was telling: "I have reserved for myself seven thousand who have not bowed the knee to Baal." St. Paul resorted to this account and then added, "So too, at the present time there is a remnant chosen by grace." (Romans 11:4–5 NIV) This remains true even in the dissipated, secular Western civilization.*

are answered, problems overcome, and objectives achieved. It seems to me that God nurtures our trust by deliberately doing the unconventional, the unexpected, and the seemingly illogical.

The Gideon Principle—as old as Scripture itself—did not change in the twentieth century. It will not change in the twenty-first. The American Marine Corps slogan that all they want is "a few good men" is similar to a message of the Bible. God wants men and women who are deeply committed to Him, not masses who are shallow.

Having spent time in several war zones I came to the conclusion that were I in peril of death, I would rather face that prospect with a dozen highly motivated, elite Special Forces soldiers than a company of complacent recruits. The analogy in the spiritual realm, for our purposes, is simply that the special operations soldiers are the committed few; the company is the mass of churches and Christians in Western civilization.

PD-art

Ezekiel by Michelangelo (1475–1564). *The theme of the faithful remnant appears throughout the Bible. The prophet Ezekiel, while a captive of the Babylonians, prophesied that a faithful remnant would restore Israel to vitality as a God-oriented people. Yet this optimism was couched in condemnation of the apostasy of Judea, a condemnation even more strident than that of the prophet Jeremiah. Put in the vernacular of our time, Ezekiel's message was "Our nation is a spiritual and moral mess; its only hope will be found in a return to faith and honoring God and His moral law. Though the majority will not make this choice, a minority of faithful citizens will, and that will make all the difference." The "faithful remnant" and the committed individual are the keys in terms of methodology to understanding how God works in human history.*

THE POWER OF THE INDIVIDUAL

Life is a sum of all your choices.
Albert Camus

In a declaration that is profoundly at variance with most popular thought—and certainly the focus of politics, government, and media—Christopher Dawson alluded to the vain modern tendency to "control the development of culture" by "external methods":

> The return from a secular civilization to a Christian way of life no doubt involves a reversal of many historical forces that transcend the limits not only of our personal experience but even of our particular society. But in spite of the modern totalitarian tendency to control the development of culture by the external methods of legislation and international organization and the control of parties and political police, it is still the individual mind that is the creative force which determines the ultimate fate of cultures. And the first step in the transformation of culture is a change in the pattern of culture within the mind, for this is the seed out of which there spring new forms of life which ultimately change the social way of life and thus create a new culture.[3]

The macrocosm can be truly changed only through the microcosm. Dawson understood the congruence between biblical teaching on the significance of the individual's mind and thought and what we can observe of world history—if we look beneath the surface. Francis Schaeffer placed the same line of thought in a specifically biblical context.

> People are unique in the inner life of the mind—what they are in their thought world determines how they act. "As a man thinketh, so is he," is really most profound. An individual is not just the product of the forces around him. He has a mind, an inner world. Then, having thought, a person can bring forth actions into the external world and thus influence it. People are apt to look at the outer theater of action, forgetting the actor who "lives in the mind" and who therefore is the true actor in the external world. The inner thought world determines the outward action.[4]

Heraclitus declared similarly, "The soul is dyed the color of its thoughts. Think only on those things that are in line with your principles and can bear the light of day. The content of your character is your choice. Day by day, what you do is who you become. Your integrity is your destiny—it is the light that guides your way."

Christ's declaration that "as a man thinketh, so is he" not only tells us everything about history but strips man—including man as often expressed within the church—of his pretensions.

Arnold Toynbee was undoubtedly referring to government and nationalism when he declaimed against the subsuming of the individual heart and mind to the group: "In religious terms, this treatment of the individual as a mere part of the community is a denial of the personal relation between the soul and God and is a substitution, for the worship of God, of a worship of the human community—Leviathan, the abomination of desolation, standing in the place where it ought not...."[5]

Man approaches God as an individual only; the collective emphasis leads man away from understanding his ultimate accountability—and his ultimate power.

As we have seen, Toynbee shared Dawson's disdain and alarm at the thought of the individual's being lost within the group: "We may also conclude that individuality is a pearl of great moral price, when we observe the moral enormities that occur when this pearl is trampled in the mire."[6] As Toynbee noted, there is great hope in recognizing that the power is vested in the individual not the group; and that even in the midst of chaos and decay the individual has the means not only to rise above it but to grow.

> The path of growth which is closed by those whose capacity for life and feeling exhausts itself on the mundane level may be reopened by a soul that can see beyond the veil of mundane appearance to the distant view of an "other world" of a supra-mundane spiritual order. The social catastrophe of disintegration thus reveals itself finally as a crisis of perception in the individual soul....The bankruptcy of the archaistic and futuristic experiments derives from a stubborn refusal to acknowledge the necessity of that shift from macrocosm [the broader physical world] to microcosm [the individual soul] which we have already recognized as the sine qua non of growth in a healthy civilization....[7]

As Sorokin noted, "Faced by the catastrophe brought about by his misdeeds, [sensate man] is once more reminded that liberty is not so much external as internal; that it cannot endure without cogent values and moral norms; and, finally, that it demands self-control and the punctilious fulfillment of one's obligations.[8]

WHO THEN CAN DO THIS?

I can do nothing alone; my own will, however hard I exert it, does not suffice;
my own plans, however astutely and systematically devised, all fail. So, there is
nothing for it but to hand myself over to God, truly and wholly, so that He may use, or,
for that matter, in His wisdom, not use, whatever capacity I possess to serve Him.
"Behold, O Lord, my poor heart which through your goodness has conceived many great desires
but is too weak and wretched to put them into practice unless You grant Your heavenly grace."
St. Francis de Sales[9]

Anyone can do this. Anyone, that is, who is willing to trust and obey can change himself—and, by extension, change his world. Francis Schaeffer put it simply—there must be an absolute, uncompromising internal commitment to truth—not a relative "truth" or "truth" fashioned from the mores and values of our age.

> The biblical message is truth and it demands a commitment to truth....It means the acceptance of Christ as Savior and Lord, and it means living under God's revelation. Here there are morals, values, and meaning, including meaning for people, which are not just a result of statistical averages. This is neither a utilitarianism, nor a leap away from reason; it is the truth that gives a unity to all of knowledge and all of life. This second alternative means that individuals come to the place where they have this base, and they influence the consensus. Such Christians do not need to be a majority in order for this influence on society to occur.[10]

It is always the individual—not the mass, not the great movements, not powerful institutions—who achieves the zenith of human experience. Toynbee observed that, though the evidence suggested civilizations were efforts to rise above the primitivism of man, only the individual has ever demonstrated the capacity to actually achieve this.

> In each of these civilizations, mankind, I think, is trying to rise above mere humanity—above primitive humanity, that is—towards some higher kind of spiritual life. One cannot depict the goal because it has never been reached—or, rather, I should say that it has never been reached by any human society. It has, perhaps, been reached by individual men and women.... But if there have been a few transfigured men and women, there has never been such a thing as a civilized society.... No known civilization has ever reached the goal of civilization yet.[11]

Only the individual has any prospect of achieving the loftiest aspirations. Having chosen this course, the truly "Christian mind," in Dawson's phrasing, becomes "a seed of change so long as it is a living mind, not enervated by custom or ossified by prejudice." A true Christian in belief and practice "has only to be in order to change the world, for in that act of being there is contained all the mystery of supernatural life." This, Dawson declared, is "the function of the Church":

> ...to sow this divine seed, to produce not merely good men, but spiritual men—that is to say, supermen. In so far as the Church fulfills this function it transmits to the world a continuous stream of spiritual energy. If the salt itself loses its savor, then indeed the world sinks back into disorder and death, for a despiritualized Christianity is powerless to change anything; it is the most abject of failures, since it serves neither the natural nor the spiritual order.[12]

The absolute divorce between church and state imposed by the secularists of Western civilization is a reflection of practical as well as spiritual blindness. We see great examples of alternative views in the life of Alfred the Great and, in the eighteenth and early nineteenth century, in the life of William Wilberforce. Both derived their moral authority from their Christian faith; and both understood that the principles of that faith should penetrate every area of human existence.

This meant that the beliefs of the Christian faith, especially as interpreted with greater maturity and honesty as a consequence of the Reformation, vested man—now recognized as made in the image of God—with new power and new significance. The priesthood and the ministry was no longer the sole repository of virtue and the spiritual life; instead a broad range of vocations came to acquire a new dignity. With this understanding of Christianity came the recognition that the housewife, the businessman, the laborer, the factory worker all had dignity insofar as their lives were a reflection of Christ and God's moral law. Position means nothing; trust and obedience mean everything.

Dawson traced the *de facto* realization of these truths to the medieval culture:

> What gave mediaeval culture its Christian character was not that the Church enforced a universal Christian standard on everybody to the exclusion of all scandal and evil, but that it turned men's eyes to a vision of spiritual perfection that could be attained by all sorts of people in all sorts of ways; a man might be a contemplative monk, like St. Bernard, or a tough fighting man, like a Knight Templar; he might be a philosopher, like St. Bonaventure and St. Thomas, or a politician, like Simon de Montfort the Younger. He might be a beggar, like St. Francis, or a king, like St. Louis; a poet, like Wolfram von Eschenbach, or a scientist, like Roger Bacon. All shared a common faith and a common purpose, and each had his own personal goal of spiritual perfection, which had its allotted place in the completed order of the city of God.[13]

Hendrick ter Brugghen (1588–1629). PD-art

Heraclitus *declared, "The soul is dyed the color of its thoughts. Think only on those things that are in line with your principles and can bear the light of day. The content of your character is your choice. Day by day, what you do is who you become. Your integrity is your destiny—it is the light that guides your way." Schaeffer placed this in a Christian context: "'As a man thinketh, so is he,' is really most profound....The inner thought world determines the outward action."*

In a real sense, Dawson said, Christianity is "essentially aristocratic," not due to birth, beauty, talent, wealth, or status, but due to "the quality of the individual":

> [The] heroic acceptance of suffering is, of course, rare. It is the mark of a saint. But it is only in the saints that the Christian life is completely realised. We cannot judge Christianity by statistics or by striking an average. One saint can do more than a thousand average men, however active and well organised they may be. In this respect Christianity is essentially aristocratic, since the quality of the individual is the only thing that matters.[14]

The message of Toynbee, Dawson, and Schaeffer could be illustrated by reference to American popular culture through the film *It's a Wonderful Life.* Frank Capra's classic not only demonstrated the impact of one individual's life on his time and place, but what would have followed had he not been there to make positive, unselfish choices for good. The principle could just as readily be extended to what happens—or does not happen—in every community, every city, and in Western civilization itself, when professing Christians never make the courageous, self-sacrificing choices to trust, obey and serve.

THE POWER OF POSITIVE CHOICES IN TIMES OF CRISIS

A common soldier, a child, a girl at the door of an inn, have changed the face of the future and almost of Nature.
Edmund Burke[15]

In this sense we may adapt Burke's saying and assert that the prayer of some unknown Christian or some unrecognised and unadmitted act of spiritual surrender may change the face of the world.
Christopher Dawson[16]

The choice is the individual Christian's. He can either ascribe his circumstances and those of his civilization to chance or to forces beyond his influence or to some other essentially deterministic cause, or he can accept individual responsibility. Chance has nothing to do with the state of Western civilization; choice has everything to do with it.

Many will strive to reconcile themselves—and by extension attempt to absolve themselves of their personal responsibility—to the decline and decay of Western civilization by characterizing it as historical chance, an inevitability, or, perhaps more often, the consequence of choices made by others; choices of which he disapproves but is unwilling to confront or challenge.

Central to Christian doctrine—though the doctrine of original sin teaches man's predispositions—is the belief that Adam volitionally brought his world down around him and that therefore Man's free will is inescapable.

Many in the Western church would argue that choices have been made, and choices are being made, to stem the tide of decay and decline. But, upon close examination, much of what they refer to could be characterized by Toynbee's phrase "the substitution of stratagem for creation." This "may arguably bring in gains on the short-term account,"[17] but ultimately it is a prescription for failure—as the circumstances of the West already demonstrate. Yet Toynbee believed that "the supreme crisis of social collapse, which proves an insuperable challenge to most, has also the power of evoking a supreme response in others."[18]

Far more that is exalted can be achieved by individual choices to trust and obey in such a dismal time of crisis than would be possible in a more sanguine age. Immanuel Wallerstein argued that in times of historical crisis and dramatic transition, "human struggle takes on the most meaning," and "free will"[19] has greater opportunity to dramatically change one's world than at any other stage of history.

Dawson put the Christian church's conduct in the modern West in blunt terms: "It is the intellectual and social inertia of Christians that is the real obstacle to a restoration of Christian culture...." Dawson concluded, "It is the will, not the power, that is lacking."[20]

PD-old

Frank Capra's classic film *It's a Wonderful Life demonstrated not only the impact of one individual's life on his time and place but what would have followed had he not been there to make positive, unselfish choices for good. The principle could just as readily be extended to what happens—or does not happen—in every community, every city, and in Western civilization itself, when professing Christians never make the courageous, self-sacrificing choices to trust, obey and serve.*

SPIRITUAL SELF-REALIZATION— THE CREATIVE RESPONSE OF CHOOSING TO TRUST AND OBEY

The path of growth which is closed by those whose capacity for life and feeling exhausts itself on the mundane level may be reopened by a soul that can see beyond the veil of mundane appearance to the distant view of an "other world" of a supra-mundane spiritual order. The social catastrophe of disintegration thus reveals itself finally as a crisis of perception in the individual soul.
Arnold Toynbee[21]

Toynbee, in *A Study of History*, observed that the individual in the midst of a disintegrating society has, fundamentally, only two choices: to remain passive, swept to and fro by the forces in his dying culture, or to rise to "the supreme challenge" by looking inward past the "stumbling-block" of a "disintegrating society" and seeking self-mastery.

> When the élan of growth in a healthy society seems to have given out, the passive individual loses his bearings upon the uncharted seas of the Universe; but the alternative reaction to this sense of a loss of control is, not to look outwards upon a macrocosm engulfed by evil, but to look inwards to the soul's own self and to recognize the moral defeat as a failure of self-mastery. Such a sense of personal sin presents the sharpest contrast imaginable to the passive sense of drift; for, while the sense of drift has the effect of an opiate in instilling into the soul an insidious acquiescence in an evil that is assumed to reside in external circumstances beyond the victim's control, the sense of sin has the effect of a stimulus because it tells the sinner that the evil is not external after all, but is within him, and hence subject to his will.[22]

This insight is a perceptive statement of the church's duty. The battle will be won or lost in "the soul's own self"—nowhere else.

Toynbee was not unmindful of the perils; nor is his observation an idealistic ephemera. He acknowledged the difficulties.

> There is here the whole difference between the Slough of Despond and the faith that moves mountains; at the same time, though, we can see that there may be a margin of common ground between the mountains and the slough in practical life—an intermediate Zone of feeling and conduct across which the tormented soul in an age of social disintegration may make, if it will, the arduous passage from resignation to endeavour.
>
> If thus the passive sense of drift may be turned in the life of an individual soul to an active and potentially creative sense of sin, so also the social feeling of helpless *pammixia* may rise to a positive sense of cultural unity. When it can attain to this perception, a soul will react to the loss of a distinctive cultural style in a disintegrating civilization, not by shrinking from a chaos void of any form at all, but *by embracing a cosmos which partakes of what is eternal and universal*.... This awakening to a sense of unity broadens and deepens as the vision expands from the unity of Mankind, through the unity of the cosmos, to the unity of a spiritual presence within and beyond both Man and the whole of the Universe.[23]

> I have dealt in some detail with the events of these years, because they were of such decisive importance in the history of the West. There has never been a war which so directly threatened the existence of Western Christendom as a whole; indeed the Christian resistance has more right to the name of a crusade than the Crusades themselves. It subjected the inchoate order of Western Christendom to a terrible test which burnt away anything that was weak and superfluous and left only the hardest and most resistant elements which were inured to insecurity and violence.[9]

Such violent, grief-laden adversity can hardly be compared with the bloodless calumnies against the Christian faith that have multiplied in Western thought and behavior in the last century. Yet the Western church of today faces, nonetheless, a "terrible test" that it will either fail or that will burn "away anything that" is "weak and superfluous," leaving "only the hardest and most resistant elements."

Dawson continued by noting the ultimate result of the courage and commitment of the Christians of that era.

> But in so far as these changes lessened the distance between the Christians and the barbarians, they made it easier for the latter to become assimilated by Christian society. The Viking conquerors on Christian soil in England, Normandy and Ireland often became Christian from the moment of their settlement, thus forming an intermediate zone between Christendom and the pagan world through which Christian influence gradually penetrated back to the homelands of the conquerors and prepared the way for the conversion of Scandinavia.[10]

But would the Western church today, weak and self-serving as it is, be able to influence modern-day conquerors of Western civilization—whether conquered by military might or the relative accretions and losses of economic power?

Dawson discovered in this earlier period a political leader who not only fought the invaders militarily but understood the "vital importance of the spiritual issue." "Yet King Alfred, unlike his contemporaries on the Continent, such as Eudes in France, Arnulf in Germany and Boso in Provence, was not content to organize a successful military resistance. Alone among the rulers of his time, he realized the vital importance of the spiritual issue and devoted no less energy to the recovery of the tradition of Christian culture than to the defence of national existence."[11]

If only we had a leader of this caliber and wisdom in Western civilization today!

The theme of suffering and the model of the soldier, as we have suggested, is found throughout Scripture. In the following passage, Paul uses the latter to prepare Timothy for the former: "Endure hardship with us like a good soldier of Christ Jesus. No one serving as a soldier gets involved in civilian affairs—he wants to please his commanding officer." (2 Timothy 2:3–4 NIV)

Earlier, a similar theme is expressed regarding Paul himself as the new convert waiting patiently on the street called Straight for what, he knew not. "But the Lord said to Ananias, 'Go! This man is my chosen instrument to carry my name before the Gentiles and their kings and before the people of Israel. I will show him how much he must suffer for my name.'" (Acts 9:15–16 NIV)

Yet Paul, previously known as Saul, had been the instigator of the murder of Christianity's protomartyr, Stephen, and the source of much suffering.

> And Saul was there, giving approval to his death. On that day a great persecution broke out against the church at Jerusalem, and all except the apostles were scattered throughout Judea and Samaria. Godly men buried Stephen and mourned deeply for him. But Saul began to destroy the church.

> Going from house to house, he dragged off men and women and put them in prison. Those who had been scattered preached the word wherever they went. (Acts 8:1–4 NIV)

In a reference to Old Testament martyrs, the first-century church was forewarned of the bitter cup they would have to tilt heavenward—not even being spared the dregs: "Some faced jeers and flogging, while still others were chained and put in prison. They were stoned; they were sawed in two; they were put to death by the sword. They went about in sheepskins and goatskins, destitute, persecuted and mistreated—the world was not worthy of them." (Hebrews 11:36–38 NIV)

Paul himself declared to Timothy much later that this was the lot of anyone who would truly love Christ. "In fact, everyone who wants to live a godly life in Christ Jesus will be persecuted, while evil men and impostors will go from bad to worse, deceiving and being deceived." (2 Timothy 3:12–13 NIV)

The "imposters" of whom Paul spoke are a subspecies that can be found throughout the Western church of the twenty-first century. Inured to the teachings of Paul, the Apostles, or Christ himself regarding the necessity of obedience, humility, and suffering, they preach instead the contrarian view and call it "Christian." Protean in their behavior and theology, their true doctrine is one of expediency and personal convenience. Prestige, if not popularity, is important to them despite their reputed master's declaration:

> This is my command: Love each other. If the world hates you, keep in mind that it hated me first. ...Remember the words I spoke to you: 'No servant is greater than his master.' If they persecuted me, they will persecute you also. If they obeyed my teaching, they will obey yours also. They will treat you this way because of my name, for they do not know the One who sent me. If I had not come and spoken to them, they would not be guilty of sin. Now, however, they have no excuse for their sin. He who hates me hates my Father as well. If I had not done among them what no one else did, they would not be guilty of sin. But now they have seen these miracles, and yet they have hated both me and my Father. But this is to fulfill what is written in their Law: 'They hated me without reason.' (John 15:17–25, quoting Psalms 35:19; 69:4 NIV)

Reliance, for the true Christian, must be on Christ Himself, not the culture, its values, institutions, or most sacrosanct beliefs. "'You believe at last!' Jesus answered. 'But a time is coming, and has come, when you will be scattered, each to his own home. You will leave me all alone. Yet I am not alone, for my Father is with me. I have told you these things, so that in me you may have peace. In this world you will have trouble. But take heart! I have overcome the world.'" (John 16:31–33 NIV)

The Western church has already, in some of its manifestations, reached the debased condition that Christ spoke of when he warned that truly following Him would be tantamount to inviting rejection and even murder—all in the name of faith and belief: "...They will put you out of the synagogue; in fact, a time is coming when anyone who kills you will think he is offering a service to God. They will do such things because they have not known the Father or me." (John 16:1–4 NIV)

PD

Arthur Wellesley, First Duke of Wellington, by Sir Thomas Lawrence, 1818. *The Duke of Wellington displayed acuity about human nature. "Asked if he were pleased to have been mobbed by the ecstatic population of Brussels on his return from Waterloo, he rejoined, 'Not in the least; if I had failed, they would have shot me.'" The fickleness of human nature was not lost on the Duke but is lost on millions of Western Christians. A realistic view of the value of human acclaim or simple social acceptance recognizes it is shallow, fragile, feckless, and absolutely of no eternal value.*

This unsettling reality drives us —if we will go—further toward an even greater challenge; not since the age of Luther has there been a more compelling need for the attributes that follow.

NONCONFORMITY

If the world hates you, keep in mind that it hated me first.
John 15:18 (NIV)

We might validly modify Emerson's dictum that "whoso would be a man, must be a nonconformist" to an edifying declaration of the true nature of the Christian walk: "Whoso would be a Christian, must be a nonconformist." The approbation of our fellowman is neither to be coveted nor sought.

For the realist about human nature there are practical reasons for this form of self-integration. British war historian John Keegan noted the Duke of Wellington's acuity in this regard. "Asked if he were pleased to have been mobbed by the ecstatic population of Brussels on his return from Waterloo, he rejoined, 'Not in the least; if I had failed, they would have shot me.'"[12] The fickleness of human nature was not lost on the Duke even if it is lost on millions of Western Christians. A realistic view of the value of human acclaim or simple social acceptance recognizes that it is shallow, fragile, feckless, and of absolutely no eternal value. Only what God thinks truly matters. And it is only when we strive to conform to God's expectations—not man's—that the Christian triumphs.

We might validly modify Ralph Waldo Emerson*'s dictum that "whoso would be a man, must be a nonconformist" to an edifying declaration of the true nature of the Christian walk: "Whoso would be a Christian, must be a nonconformist." Only what God thinks of each human being will truly matter. And it is only when we strive to conform to God's expectations, not man's, that the Christian triumphs.*

PD-old

Immanuel Wallerstein observed—with a depressing acknowledgment of its ubiquity—"Most people live day by day and are reluctant to engage in the dangerous path of defying authority. Many persons are 'free riders,' ready to applaud quietly the actions of the brave and the bold, but waiting to see whether others among their peers are joining in active support of the movement."[13]

The Western church is filled with these. While on patrol with Salvadoran Commandos during the Communist guerrilla wars of the mid and late eighties, I was privy to the recounting of an incident that could serve as a metaphor for these tendencies among Christians. The young Salvadoran lieutenant in command of this patrol, "MacArthur" Montoya, told of a night attack that took place a few weeks prior in the village where we were bivouacked this night. Without radio equipment to maintain contact with all of his men positioned around the perimeter of the village, Montoya had to run from point to point, guiding and encouraging them. As he raced through the dark, narrow streets, his boots clicking on the cobblestones in counterpoint to automatic weapons' fire, he could hear the villagers praying loudly behind their bolted doors. None dared even peer out. Montoya related this with transparency—and with no apparent bitterness toward the villagers who were quite prepared to let him and his men do the suffering and dying for them.

This view of the Christian's role (i.e., let us pray) devoid of the willingness to boldly stand or to personally suffer and sacrifice must be rejected outright by the church as unbecoming of him who would claim to love Christ and of him who would claim to love his fellowman.

This form of nonconformity—to the world, and, if need be, to the Western church, such as it is, is part and parcel of an exalted view of life eloquently described by Toynbee.

> Seeking God is itself a social act.
>
> …
>
> Only, the Christian soul…is a citizen of the Kingdom of God, and therefore his paramount and all-embracing aim is to attain the highest degree of communion with, and likeness to, God Himself; his relations with his fellow men are consequences of, and corollaries to, his relations with God; and his way of loving his neighbour as himself will be to try to help his neighbour to win what he is seeking for himself—that is, to come into closer communion with God and to become more godlike.[14]

Photograph by Ivy Scarborough

While I was on patrol with Salvadoran Commandos during the Communist guerilla war, the young Salvadoran lieutenant in command of this patrol, "MacArthur" Montoya (front; author standing in center), *told of a night attack. Montoya raced through the dark, narrow streets of the village under attack, his boots clicking on the cobblestones in counterpoint to automatic weapons' fire. He could hear the villagers praying loudly behind their bolted doors. None dared even peer out. The villagers were prepared to let him and his men do the suffering and dying for them. Many Western Christians manifest this same attitude, but this view of the Christian's role (i.e., let us pray) devoid of the willingness to boldly stand or to personally suffer and sacrifice must be rejected outright by the church as unbecoming of him who would claim to love Christ and of him who would claim to love his fellowman.*

COURAGE

Courage is resistance to fear and mastery of fear, not the absence of fear.
Mark Twain[15]

There are other attributes, some more often associated with the soldier, that must characterize the true Christian. If "perfect love drives out fear" (1 John 4:18 NIV), then one attribute will always be apparent in the Christian who loves Christ.

Courage is the hinge upon which every other virtue pivots. Without courage all that is noble will ultimately fail.

Here the faithful Christian can take solace: few themes are as pervasive throughout Scripture as the theme of courage, even boldness. The actor Jim Caviezel, who portrayed Christ in the movie *The*

Jim Caviezel meeting with Pope John Paul II. *Few themes are as pervasive throughout Scripture as the theme of courage, even boldness. The actor, who portrayed Christ in the movie* The Passion of the Christ, *described his meeting with Pope John Paul II and the Pope's immediate and fervent admonition, "Jim Caviezel, do not be afraid!" Courage is the hinge upon which every other virtue pivots. Without courage, all that is noble will ultimately fail.*

Photo courtesy of the Vatican Photographic Service

Passion of the Christ, described his first meeting with Pope John Paul II and the Pope's immediate and fervent admonition, "Jim Caviezel, do not be afraid!" This was, in so many respects, the motto of Karol Wojtyla's life; and what a powerful impact that central conviction had, not simply on his life but on his time. The reasons for the Pope's focus on this theme can be easily gleaned from his past. With the death of his mother when he was small, the Nazi invasion of Poland in September of 1939, the oppressive years of occupation, the most violent war known to man, another oppressive regime in the form of communism, and an ever present choice between conforming and defying, Karol Wojtyla repeatedly chose to defy—and, in so doing, chose to act courageously, believing what God told the man or woman of faith, when He repeatedly declared from Genesis to Revelation, "Do not be afraid." This is not simply a common biblical theme, but a spiritual litany.

- Do not be afraid, Abram. I am your shield, your very great reward. (Genesis 15:1 NIV)
- The Lord said to Moses, "Do not be afraid of him, for I have handed him over to you, with his whole army and his land." (Numbers 21:34 NIV)
- Then the Lord said to Joshua, "Do not be afraid; do not be discouraged." (Joshua 8:1 NIV)
- Be on your guard; stand firm in the faith; be men of courage; be strong. (1 Corinthians 16:13 NIV)
- You came near when I called you, and you said, "Do not fear." (Lamentations 3:57 NIV)
- "Do not be afraid, O man highly esteemed," he said. "Peace! Be strong now; be strong." (Daniel 10:19 NIV)
- Fear of man proves to be a snare, but whoever trusts in the Lord is kept safe. (Proverbs 29:25 NIV)
- He said to his disciples, "Why are you so afraid? Do you still have no faith?" (Mark 4:40 NIV)
- But the angel said to him, "Do not be afraid, Zechariah; your prayer has been heard." (Luke 1:13 NIV)

- But the angel said to her, "Do not be afraid, Mary, you have found favor with God." (Luke 1:30 NIV)
- But the angel said to them, "Do not be afraid. I bring you good news of great joy that will be for all people." (Luke 2:10 NIV)
- Then Jesus said to Simon, "Do not be afraid, from now on you will catch men." (Luke 5:10 NIV)
- I tell you, my friends, do not be afraid of those who kill the body and after that can do no more. But I will show you whom you should fear: Fear him who, after the killing of the body, has power to throw you into hell. Yes, I tell you, fear him. (Luke 12:4–5 NIV)
- Don't be afraid; you are worth more than many sparrows. (Luke 12:7 NIV)
- Do not be afraid, Paul. (Acts 27:24 NIV)
- Then he placed his right hand on me and said: "Do not be afraid. I am the First and the Last." (Revelation 1:17 NIV)
- Do not be afraid of what you are about to suffer....Be faithful, even to the point of death.... (Revelation 2:10 NIV)

Focusing on our fears is a natural tendency. However, having lived a little, we learn, if we are honest and observant, that, like Mark Twain, we "had a lot of troubles in our life" most of which "didn't happen." The truth in that notwithstanding—and though the coward does die a thousand deaths to the brave man's once—sometimes those troubles do "happen." They certainly will for anyone who stands for the noble cause or the great principle.

The world is a vicious place that strives to drag down to its level all that would stand above it; and, having failed that, to destroy the paragon whose virtue and belief hold it up to shame. Such has it been throughout history, such it will be in the Western church in the twenty-first century; so it will be until the end of time.

A central question then confronts all Christians in all times: Will you stand?

Having chosen to stand we naturally tend to see only the battle just before us; and withal fail to remember that our comrades in arms around the world are ferociously engaged as well; and, even more importantly, that God's order and His power are transcendent. Even nature itself—the omnipresent grandeur of God in tactile form—defies the worst that man can conjure. The young soldier in Stephen Crane's *Red Badge of Courage* perceived this to his astonishment.

> As he listened to the din from the hillside, to a deep pulsating thunder that came from afar to the left, and to the lesser clamors which came from many directions, it occurred to him that they were fighting, too, over there, and over there, and over there. Heretofore he had supposed that all the battle was directly under his nose.
>
> As he gazed around him the youth felt a flash of astonishment at the blue, pure sky and the sun gleaming on the trees and fields. It was surprising that Nature had gone tranquilly on with her golden process in the midst of so much devilment.[16]

CONTRA MUNDUM—CONFRONT

...the very fact that the Church represents something entirely different—the intervention of a supernatural principle and the coming of a divine Kingdom —must inevitably arouse the fierce opposition of all those human societies and powers which claim absolute power over man and refuse to admit a superior or rival.
Christopher Dawson[17]

But the devilment that the twenty-first-century Western church must confront is far more subtle and intractable than cannons and a clearly defined enemy army. In a real sense that form of enemy would be much easier to confront and defeat. In that form too, Western man has failed, but in an unexpected and historically obscure way. Hearkening back to a time when belief was the central theme of Western civilization—a depth of belief and commitment that led to an antiwar posture—we learn that this noble and biblically sound conviction was largely decimated by the barbarian invasions. Western civilization ever since has embraced the ethos of war. But this is not the kind of soldier of which we speak here; the true Christian soldier must often oppose these very traits in Western civilization—not unlike the uneducated but spiritually astute Sergeant Alvin York. Though pacifism cannot be supported by resort to New Testament teaching, peacemaking certainly can.

The Apostle Paul had reconnoitered the spiritual battlefield and declared the true nature of the battle and the enemy that every Christian who has volunteered for God's army must fight: "For we wrestle not against flesh and blood, but against principalities, against powers, against the rulers of darkness of this world, against spiritual wickedness in high places." (Ephesians 6:12 KJV) That the "high places" might include the church would not have been lost on Paul; certainly the enemy would seek to dominate and control the high ground, wherever it may be.

Significantly, this passage is one of the many places in Scripture where allusions to war, battle, and soldiering are most prominent. Just prior and subsequent to this verse Paul, in a famous passage, declared the preparations the Christian soldier must make—and then followed that with very specific orders.

> Put on the whole armour of God, that ye may be able to stand against the wiles of the devil. (Ephesians 6:11 KJV)
>
> ...
>
> Wherefore take unto you the full armour of God, that ye may withstand in the evil day, and having done all, to stand. Stand therefore, having your loins girt about with truth, and having on the breast plate of righteousness; and your feet shod with the preparation of the gospel of peace; above all, take the shield of faith wherewith ye shall be able to quench all the fiery darts of the wicked. And take the helmet of salvation, and the sword of the Spirit, which is the word of God. (Ephesians 6:13–17 KJV)

In what appears a paradoxical statement, Christ declared, "Think not that I am come to send peace on earth: I came not to send peace, but a sword." (Matthew 10:34 KJV) But the conflict he referred to was one of belief and practice. The foolish Christian—who believes that he can be faithful to Christ and yet always be a peacemaker and always live in peace with all men—is a subspecies more akin to the coward than to the true Christian soldier. Lincoln not only understood this concept but had to implement it in his life in one of the great tragedies of history: "The man does not live who is more devoted to peace

PD-art

Man in Armor, by Rembrandt, 1655. *The Western Christian has forgotten—if he ever really knew—that the Christian life is that of a warrior. The foolish Christian—who believes that he can be faithful to Christ and yet always be a peacemaker and always live in peace with all men—is a subspecies more akin to the coward than to the true Christian soldier. The Christian must be willing to sacrifice peace and personal security to stand for moral principle and religious conviction.*

than I am, but it may be necessary to put the foot down firmly."[18] So must the individual Christian be willing to sacrifice peace and personal security to stand for moral principle and religious conviction.

The only people who would oppose this are like those who opposed what Jesus said and did—and for the same reason: they have a vested interest in the *status quo.* In taking a strong but risk laden position within the church, the Christian soldier will find himself running aground on the shoals of human nature. What may be self-evident to him, as supremely supported by the teachings and life of Christ, may be genuinely—or disingenuously professed to be—obscure to the very individuals who should be most sympathetic.

After returning in 1985 from my time with the Afghan mujahedeen during their war against the Soviet Union, I made many television, radio, and public appearances encouraging Americans to support their cause. Most telling of these were the direct contacts with large audiences. To my dismay—and confessing here to being completely unprepared for this—I slowly realized that in any given group there were roughly three categories of thought and perception. The first, a group I came to think of as the cynics, could not comprehend an American, with neither the compulsion of a military order nor financial gain to be had, traveling to a war zone in support of an underdog, especially one so alien to Western culture. This group invariably assumed there was some hidden motive or clandestine connection: money to be had from some source for taking the risk, or an intelligence network relationship such as with the CIA.

The second group, which could be referred to as the passive and the bewildered, clearly could not make heads or tails of any of it. Though the cynical theories might not jump immediately to the forefronts of their minds, the more idealistic notions were lost to them also.

Only in the third group—the group with which I found affinity and common cause—was some semblance of understanding to be gained. Having some well-developed sense of principle, as well as a concern for their fellow human beings, they could readily comprehend the idealistic appeal of aiding these suffering and courageous people. Among these more noble souls the cause was carried forward. A few undertook their own lobbying campaigns with the American government.

Years later I discovered a parallel expression of much the same phenomenon. Two friends, both highly decorated combat veterans (one who had served in World War II, Korea, and Vietnam; the other with four tours of duty in Vietnam, and an aggregate of over two dozen medals for valor between them), in separate conversations about the reliability of soldiers in combat, gave strikingly similar descriptions. One group, perhaps a third, could not be counted on; another group, again perhaps a third, might act but would not initiate and tended to passivity; the final group, perhaps a third, would aggressively fight.

Some similar pattern might be expected of any challenge to the church, but this should not dismay or discourage, since we have already seen that God works through the faithful individual and the faithful remnant, never the mass. As Dawson and Toynbee observed, and as Schaeffer—in a passage reminiscent of Andrew Jackson's declaration, "One man with courage is a majority"—put it: "Christians do not need to be in the majority in order to influence society."[19]

The Western church has lost touch with the authoritative ways and methods of those it deems its greatest leaders. Can we imagine a Western priest or minister uttering "You are a child of the devil and an enemy of everything that is right! You are full of all kinds of deceit and trickery. Will you never stop perverting the right ways of the Lord?" (Acts 13:10 NIV) Yet these were the words of the Apostle Paul!

And there is still another deterrent the Western Christian must surely face. Though it might not take the form of that which followed for Paul—later perhaps, if not soon—there will be consequences nonetheless: "Then some Jews came from Antioch and Iconium and won the crowd over. They stoned Paul and dragged him outside the city, thinking he was dead. But after the disciples had gathered around him, he got up and went back into the city. The next day he and Barnabas left for Derbe." (Acts 14:19–20 NIV)

Paul had committed to do what every Christian soldier is duty bound to do: "Fight the good fight of the faith. Take hold of the eternal life...." (1 Timothy 6:12 NIV) The great question faced by every Western Christian is, Will I do my duty, the expression of God's will on earth through me?

END NOTES
CHAPTER 34

1 Christopher Dawson, *Religion and the Rise of Western Culture* (Garden City, NY: Image Books, 1975), 88.
2 Jennifer Viegas, *William James: American Philosopher, Psychologist, and Theologian* (New York: Rosen Publishing, 2006), 6.
3 Theodore Roosevelt, "The Man in the Arena," speech at the Sorbonne (Paris, April 23, 1910).
4 Francis A. Schaeffer, *How Should We Then Live? The Rise and Decline of Western Thought and Culture* (Wheaton, IL: Crossway Books, 1976), 24.
5 Schaeffer, *How Should We Then Live ?*, 26.
6 Christopher Dawson, *The Historic Reality of Christian Culture* (New York: Harper & Brothers, 1960), 28.
7 Kent Gramm, *Gettysburg: A Meditation on War and Values* (Bloomington, IN: University of Indiana Press, 1994), 107.
8 Dawson, *Religion and the Rise of Western Culture*, 87.
9 Dawson, *Religion and the Rise of Western Culture*, 87–88.
10 Dawson, *Religion and the Rise of Western Culture*, 88.
11 Dawson, *Religion and the Rise of Western Culture*, 88.
12 John Keegan, *An Illustrated History of the First World War* (New York: A. A. Knopf, 2001), 163.
13 Immanuel Wallerstein, *The End of the World As We Know It: Social Science for the Twenty-First Century* (Minneapolis: University of Minnesota Press, 1999), 23.
14 Arnold J. Toynbee, *Civilization on Trial* (New York: Oxford University Press, 1948), 246–247.
15 Mark Twain, *Pudd'nhead Wilson and Those Extraordinary Twins,* ed. with introduction by Malcolm Bradbury (New York: Penguin Classics, 1969), 138.
16 Stephen Crane, *The Red Badge of Courage* (New York: Read How You Want Classics Library, 1960), 60–61.
17 Dawson, *Historic Reality*, 119.
18 Abraham Lincoln, "Address to New Jersey Assembly, Feb. 21, 1861," in *Complete Works* (New York: F. D. Tandy, 1894), 39.
19 Schaeffer, *How Should We Then Live?*, 256.

CHAPTER

35

A DISTINCTION OF THE HIGHEST ORDER—THE CHRISTOCENTRIC LIFE

Do not conform any longer to the pattern of this world, but be transformed by the renewing of your mind. Then you will be able to test and approve what God's will is—his good, pleasing and perfect will.
Romans 12:2 (NIV)

I know your deeds; you have a reputation of being alive, but you are dead. Wake up! Strengthen what remains and is about to die, for I have not found your deeds complete in the sight of my God. Remember, therefore, what you have received and heard; obey it, and repent. But if you do not wake up, I will come like a thief, and you will not know at what time I will come to you.
Revelation 3:1–3 (NIV)

Among the most unsettling of Christ's teachings is a passage that distinguishes between professed commitment and genuine obedience.

> A man had two sons. And he went to the first and said, "Son, go and work in the vineyard today." And he answered, "I will not," but afterward he changed his mind and went. And he went to the other son and said the same. And he answered, "I go, sir," but did not go. Which of the two did the will of his father?' They said, 'The first.' Jesus said to them, 'Truly, I say to you, the tax collectors and the prostitutes go into the kingdom of God before you. For John came to you in the way of righteousness, and you did not believe him, but the tax collectors and the prostitutes believed him. And even when you saw it, you did not afterward change your minds and believe him." (Matthew 21:28–32 NIV)

The church has, in myriad ways, attempted to force Christ into the Procrustean bed of the culture and its values. But such prideful efforts do not diminish Christ or alter one whit who He is and what He stands for—nor does it aid man. It deprives man of exactly what he desperately needs: the authentic Christ. So smitten is Western man by his achievements he cannot conceive that his values are anything other than sound, laudable, even sacrosanct, much less that Christ was leading man toward a very different path.

The failure to question, much less scrutinize closely, the possibility that the church and millions of professing Christians have gone astray suggests unwillingness—a carefully concealed and rationalized disobedience. The true seeking pilgrim, should he begin soul-searching, will sense that his quest will lead to the disruption of his life in a fashion he may be unwilling to countenance.

This will be true of the priests and pastors as surely as of the laity—more so. The reminder of Christ's admonition that he who would lead must be servant of all will inevitably be a conspicuous signpost they must pass along the way. The comfort, security, pride of place, prestige, and standing will have to go for many ministers, priests and religious leaders, if they sincerely and humbly begin that pilgrimage and see it through to the end.

The Western church's failure to honor Christ, his words and his witness, in all respects, not just those that are convenient, has been the instrument of its own decimation. As Malcolm Muggeridge bluntly observed, the most effective enemies of Christianity in the West have been Christians themselves.

> It is, indeed, among Christians themselves that the final decisive assault on Christianity has been mounted. All they had to show was that when Jesus said that His kingdom was not of this world, He meant that it was. Then, moving on from there, to stand the other basic Christian propositions similarly on their heads. As, that to be carnally minded is life; that it is essential to lay up treasure on earth in the shape of a constantly expanding Gross National Product; that the flesh lusts with the spirit and the spirit with the flesh, so that we can do whatever we have mind to; that he that loveth his life in this world shall keep it unto life eternal. And so on....[1]

Millions of professing Christians who read Muggeridge's words will protest, inwardly or outwardly, that this is not true, that they do honor Christ. But their lives belie their words. This of course is nothing new, though it is likely far more a feature of our time than any that preceded it. Augustine, in the midst of the obsessions and chaos of the collapsing Roman Empire, chose to distinguish himself by continuing to offer what Muggeridge referred to as "the alternative reality of Christ to a bored, sick, decomposing world of fantasy" and "to go on to the very end proclaiming in the shambles of the once great Roman Empire the everlasting glory and availability of the City of God."[2] Muggeridge perceptively observed that "some twenty centuries later a tawdry presentation of the obscenities of the Emperor Claudius on a television screen provides a diversion for another decomposing world of fantasy. Some future Gibbon will surely

PD-art

A great prophetic voice of our time, Malcolm Muggeridge *declared that Christians themselves were the worst enemy of Christianity: "It is...among Christians themselves that the final decisive assault on Christianity has been mounted. All they had to show was that when Jesus said that His kingdom was not of this world, He meant that it was.... As....it is essential to lay up treasure on earth...that he that loveth his life in this world shall keep it unto life eternal. And so on...."*

note that in the last twilight of Christendom the advanced technology then available is used to bring in the decadence of the old world to complete the decadence of the new."[3]

We have stressed the dangerous two-edged sword of Western technology and science, but the greater danger it poses is the one exposed here by Muggeridge: the compelling and ubiquitous dissemination of self-deluding thought and decadence. Should civilization of some sort survive to see a new century, some latter-day Gibbon or de Tocqueville may note that the most destructive inventions of the twentieth century were not the nuclear bomb or the chemical weapon but the television and the Internet.

Mentioned earlier was a book published in England in 1797 under the extraordinary and unwieldy title *A Practical View of the Prevailing Religious System of Professed Christians, in the Higher and Middle Classes in this Country Contrasted with Real Christianity.* The title's length was in large part an effort on the part of the author, William Wilberforce, to make his central theme inescapable—and incapable of being rationalized around, dodged, ignored, or synthesized into a more palatable and less onerous understanding for the Christians and the church of that age. A supremely articulate politician and close friend of Prime Minster William Pitt the Younger, Wilberforce led the crusade that eventually abolished the slave trade and slavery itself in Great Britain, founding his campaign on a relentless honesty and realism. His book, rejected initially by publishers as a work no one would be interested in, eventually went through several printings on its way to influencing the thought and feeling of a nation.

Wilberforce, with the insight and wisdom that characterized much of his life, correctly perceived, in the words of his biographer Eric Metaxas, that "real Christianity had evaporated from England principally because it was woven into the social fabric," an observation in harmony with one of the major themes of this work: Christianity in Western civilization in the twenty-first century is largely no longer true Christianity primarily because it has permitted itself to become part and parcel of the broader culture. This massive and insidious compromise has resulted in our pulpits filled, as they were in Wilberforce's time, with "lukewarm professors" preaching a "lukewarm faith that thrilled no one and challenged no one."[4] The blandness, mediocrity, pusillanimity, and banality emanating from thousands of Western pulpits every Sunday morning is more calculated to harden arteries than inspire hearts, more

http://www.oneyearbibleblog.com/2008/01/january-7th-one.html

Highly representative of the professing Christian in the West, most cast two shadows. Weber explained the rationale: "With the consciousness of standing in the fullness of God's grace and being visibly blessed by Him, the...business man, as long as he remain[s] within the bounds of formal correctness, as long as his moral conduct [is] spotless and the use to which he put[s] his wealth [is] not objectionable, could follow his pecuniary interests...and feel that he was fulfilling a duty in doing so."

certain to nurture complacency and lethargy than stimulate a zeal that rebels against the world, its injustices, callousness, and faithlessness.

Rebelling against the "faux Christianity" of his time, an uncompromising Wilberforce "couldn't stand this tepid version of the real thing" and "labored to show that this practice that everyone thought was Christianity was in fact not Christianity at all."

How *apropos* for our time! Wilberforce saw the truth and courageously, relentlessly confronted it. He understood that if the professing Christians in Britain actually "believed the doctrines" they "claimed to believe" they "could never have countenanced the slave trade or the institution of slavery itself." Eventually, it was probably more shame than conviction that brought about legislative extinction of the slave trade.

True Christianity changes the heart and perceptions; no longer can callousness, suffering, the taking of unborn human life, the toleration of sexual immorality, or other myriad ways in which man is cruel to man and indifferent to God be countenanced.

The fervent, courageous leadership that brought down the slave trade emanated from the man who saw Christ and Christianity in uncompromising terms. This is no coincidence. The cyanosis of the Christian church in the twenty-first century West that makes it incapable of altering the course of a civilization is the result of the absence of the oxygen of authentic Christianity. The former is effete, sterile, and enervating; the latter is dynamic, powerful, and invigorating. The momentum toward greater and greater civilizational abasement will continue unabated with the former; it can conceivably only be halted and completely redirected with the latter. Wilberforce understood this in his time; sincere Christians must grasp it and embrace it in our age.

Wilberforce was imploring, importuning, pleading for his nation to—in that most religious of terms—"repent"; to embrace the true faith that it had gradually supplanted with an ersatz version. The former was magnificent, imposing, and exalting; the latter fit only to be "spewed out of the mouth."

Wilberforce "knew that many people didn't know what real Christianity was; though they attended church, they'd never seen it and though they'd heard hundreds of sermons they had never heard it preached." Two centuries later, Western man is faced with the same state of affairs. All of Western civilization in our age suffers from similar confusion and deficiencies. Authentic Christianity, the Christianity of Christ in word and deed, can now largely only be found in undiluted form in the very places in the world where it is most difficult, and even dangerous, to be a Christian. Wilberforce acknowledged this reality in his time, observing, "Christianity...has always thrived under persecution. For then it has no lukewarm professors."

None of this should come as a surprise. Christ himself said that many would profess to be Christians, even with the expectancy of an eternal destiny in the kingdom of heaven, yet—in some of the most chilling words in the Bible—he warned of their true fate. "Not everyone who says to me, 'Lord, Lord,' will enter the kingdom of heaven, but only he who does the will of my Father who is in heaven. Many will say to me on that day, 'Lord, Lord, did we not prophesy in your name, and in your name drive out demons and perform many miracles?' Then I will tell them plainly, 'I never knew you. Away from me, you evildoers!'" (Matthew 7:21–23 NIV)

For there to be genuine, deep, and meaningful change in Western civilization, that distinction of the highest order that is the hallmark, the *sine qua non*, of the Christian life must be present in the lives of those who profess faith in Christ. This will require individual Christians to confront the values and pursuits of Western culture. Salient among these are the pursuit of money and possessions, the pursuit of pleasure, the pursuit of status, and the pursuit of self-interest at the expense of the self-sacrifice called for and demonstrated by Christ.

THE PURSUIT OF MONEY AND POSSESSIONS

...so often times it happens, that we live our lives in chains,
and we never even know we have the key.
Glenn Frey[5]

Jesus made it clear that the pursuit of money and possessions was at enmity with God and the ennobled spiritual life. Yet that teaching has been turned on its head within the Christian church in the West. The pursuit of dollars—even by the church itself, for use on itself—is central to much of the effort expended by churches, denominations, and religious leaders, not just individual Christians. Neither frowned upon nor even questioned it is more often deemed, when successful, an indicator of virtue rewarded. None of this is consistent with Christ's teachings. "No one can serve two masters. Either he will hate the one and love the other, or he will be devoted to the one and despise the other. You cannot serve both God and Money." (Matthew 6:24 NIV) Material gain more often reflects nothing more vaunted than a singularity of focus and expenditure of substantial effort in gaining the material, not any higher spiritual purpose—despite any expedient "spiritual" characterization otherwise.

Yet the broad obeisance to the pursuit of money is, and has been, flagrant in Western culture for generations and has become more pervasive and deeper rooted with its prodigious success in achieving its object. The speciousness of this viewpoint is rarely questioned even by leaders in the church and then only with glancing blows tendered not to disable or fully undermine that line of thought but to convey some semblance of duty done in the face of such dissipation of individual lives and energies.

Anyone's priorities can be perceived—listening to them recount them is a naïve endeavor—only by observing how they use their resources: time, thought, energy and money. Individual Christians would perhaps be dismayed to recognize that the bulk of their energy, waking hours, and efforts are focused on making money and material gain—not serving God or sacrificing for one's fellowman. This is an apostasy when measured by the life and teachings of Christ but fully compatible with the model and teachings of the Western church.

This extravagant and blind dissipation of life in the shallowest of pursuits has been obvious to some over the centuries of Western civilization—even to those who do not necessarily view it from a religious perspective. The English poet William Wordsworth observed two centuries ago:

The world is too much with us; late and soon,
Getting and spending, we lay waste our powers;
Little we see in nature that is ours;
We have given our hearts away, a sordid boon![6]

Western Christians have given their "hearts away" without compunction—not even striking a good bargain. This "sordid boon" could only be possible if the church itself was not speaking out emphatically, unequivocally, and relentlessly about where one should lay up one's treasures. But the heresy is much worse than one of omission. The church itself is engaged in the active commission of behaviors that are contrary to everything Christ taught and lived. As in most realms, the Western church has not realized that swimming upstream—against the current of the culture—is the only way *uphill*, or, having perceived it, has chosen not simply to drift but to paddle vigorously downstream.

In the history of the Catholic Church, no figure, no saint, more clearly exemplified this understanding than St. Francis. Christopher Dawson observed that Francis's life has a unique appeal in our time precisely because of its "Christocentric character" and doctrine. "What impressed his contemporaries and still impresses us today is the 'conformity' of St. Francis to the pattern of the divine humanity, so that, in the words of a mediaeval writer, 'St. Francis became as it were the picture of Christ, and was transformed at all points into Jesus, the Lord Himself....'"[7] Significantly, St. Francis "was not only a master of the spiritual life, he was also among the greatest of the leaders of the reforming movement."[8] He could not have been the latter without having first become the former.

But "conformity" to "the pattern of the divine humanity" was precisely what the Gospels dictated as the ultimate goal of Christian man on earth—as preparation for the Christian soul's abode in heaven. Rising to live the Christocentric life is the purpose of the individual Christian in the world.

Evidence suggests that many Western Catholics today treat Francis as a venerated saint, but little more, his example having no real application to themselves, in their time, in their culture. But Francis is a reminder of Spengler's observation: "...it is personality that counts....The martyr derived his strength not from doctrines, but from the example of the Man on the Cross."

Protestants would do well to pay attention to the life of Francis. In his rags and destitution—so despised by our proud and materialistic time—he stands above our age like a colossus.

Francis Schaeffer put his finger on what that earlier Francis understood and acted out—being "in the world but not of it": "[T]his challenged Christians in their attitude toward material possessions and style of living. Not only in the time of Peter and Paul but for generations after believers were noted for openhanded generosity. Even their enemies admitted it."[9]

The two are bound inextricably together. The earlier Francis's point—as modeled on the life of Christ—was not simply an anathema on possessions, but a declaration of the Christian's duty to remember in what world he is a citizen: in the material world he is a visitor, just passing through; in the kingdom of God, he is permanently domiciled. If this is so, then he should act like it. If he does not, then perhaps there is reason to pause and consider where his domicile truly may be. Perhaps he is an illegal alien trying to crawl through the basement window of the kingdom of God that is being wedged open by the Western church. But what the church in the West may tell him—or the church rolls to which his name is added—will never supplant the authentic passport and visa required by God.

The consequences of this deferral by the church to the values of the culture are an extreme poverty for Western man—including millions of professing Western Christians who are rich yet poor: "You say, 'I am rich; I have acquired wealth and do not need a thing.' But you do not realize that you are wretched, pitiful, poor, blind and naked." (Revelation 3:17 NIV)

Christ warned of the dangers in selecting the wrong repository for the wrong treasure.

PD

St. Francis in Prayer before the Crucifix, by El Greco. *Protestants would do well to pay attention to the life of Francis. In his rags and destituion—so despised by our proud and materialistic time—he stands above our age like a colossus. Deferral by the church to the values of the culture has resulted in an extreme poverty for Western man—who is rich yet poor: "You say, 'I am rich; I have acquired wealth and do not need a thing.' But you do not realize that you are wretched, pitiful, poor, blind and naked." (Revelation 3:17 NIV)*

> ..."Watch out! Be on your guard against all kinds of greed; a man's life does not consist in the abundance of his possessions."..."The ground of a certain rich man produced a good crop. He thought to himself, 'What shall I do? I have no place to store my crops.' Then he said, 'This is what I'll do. I will tear down my barns and build bigger ones, and there I will store all my grain and my goods. And I'll say to myself, "You have plenty of good things laid up for many years. Take life easy; eat, drink and be merry."' But God said to him, 'You fool! This very night your life will be demanded from you. Then who will get what you have prepared for yourself?'
>
> "This is how it will be with anyone who stores up things for himself but is not rich toward God." (Luke 12:15–21 NIV)

Tellingly, Christ made the distinction between those who inhabit so fully this "lower world" and those who are trusting in God. "For the pagan world runs after all such things, and your Father knows that you need them." (Luke 12:30 NIV) But nowhere was Christ more explicit about the status of materialism in the Kingdom of God than when he spoke of it as the idol that it remains in our day. "No servant can serve two masters. Either he will hate the one and love the other, or he will be devoted to the one and despise the other. You cannot serve both God and Money." The Pharisees, who loved money, heard all this and were sneering at Jesus. He said to them, "You are the ones who justify yourselves in the eyes of men, but God knows your hearts. What is highly valued among men is detestable in God's sight." (Luke 16:13–15 NIV)

If the truth were known—the thoughts of the heart heard—many Western religious leaders today, in effect, sneer at this teaching of Jesus. Others would not consciously defy, yet—with more than the ordinary human being's opportunity to understand and know what Christ taught—they persist in laying waste to the spiritual edifice of which Christ spoke and erect in its place material edifices of considerable cost, and often of extravagance and evident pretentiousness. Reflecting the norms of the culture and the values of man, they have not, and surely cannot, succeed in altering the course of a civilization. "But," these practitioners argue, "we need our family life centers, our gymnasiums, our sports programs, our theatres, etc., for Christian fellowship." No, we do not. True service and fellowship are not a function of activities, but of human beings sharing in a transparent and open way. The bond of fellowship and brotherhood is strengthened most through shared trials, adversity, and strenuous efforts to achieve demanding goals.

The first-century church had none of these extravagant features, or anything analogous, but the evidence suggests that fellowship among these Christians was deep and moving. Even in the early to mid-twentieth century, especially in the rural areas of America, fellowship within the church was not perceived as a product of activities, place, or material gain. Survivors from that era often recalled glowing accounts of church gatherings that featured "dinner on the ground" as a favored form of fellowship. In that time, the material possessions regarded today as so necessary to a successful church did not exist. The unacknowledged—and, worse yet, even unperceived—truth is that these temples the Western church has proliferated across the West's landscape are for man himself, not for God, who made it clear where He truly dwells.

> The God who made the world and everything in it is the Lord of heaven and earth and does not live in temples built by hands. (Acts 17:24 NIV)
>
> However, the Most High does not live in houses made by men. As the prophet says: "Heaven is my throne, and the earth is my footstool. *What kind of house will you build for me?* says the Lord. *Or where will my resting place be?*" (Acts 7:48–49 NIV)

The rejection of the materialistic view of life must be central to the awakening of the individual Christian and the church in Western civilization. Since this one feature of Western culture is so dominant, so all-consuming, any compromise on this point will ultimately mean continued failure for the church.

THE PURSUIT OF PLEASURE

...if we ourselves bear the central mark of our generation, we cannot at this moment in history be the voice we should be to our poor and fractured generation....
Schaeffer[10]

To see and listen to the wicked is already the beginning of wickedness.
Confucius[11]

The great Scottish Christian teacher Oswald Chambers perceptively observed that most sin is the consequence of a legitimate need being met in an illegitimate way. My various life roles have affirmed the truth in this over and over. That man would pursue his needs illicitly is hardly surprising, but that the Christian would should be shocking. The Christian has been scripturally assured that God knows his needs and will supply them, but he must patiently pursue their fulfillment in God's way and consistent with His laws. Having pursued my needs through both the biblical and the worldly methods, I can speak with experience as to the pleasures and the consequences of each. Though, to be sure, even Scripture acknowledges there is "pleasure in sin for a season," we must not omit the trailing caveat that "the end thereof is death." The pleasurable experience gained illegitimately will eventually produce misery, and, for the Christian, the misery will be redoubled, trebled, and quadrupled.

Therein lies another form of loss hidden from all but the most perceptive: the loss of innocence, of sensitivity of the mind and heart, of trust and trusting, of lofty, grand feeling and thought, of a species and character only God could craft—and man can destroy by his disobedience. In its place come hardening of the heart, mistrust and mistrusting, and an inability to feel and think on the

PD

The great Scottish Christian teacher Oswald Chambers *perceptively observed that most sin is the consequence of a legitimate need being met in an illegitimate way. The Christian has been scripturally assured that God knows his needs and will supply them, but he must patiently pursue their fulfillment in God's way and in keeping with His laws.*

Used by permission

Confucius, *writing before the time of Christ, could have been referring to twenty-first century Western entertainment and media when he declared: "To see and listen to the wicked is already the beginning of wickedness." It is not enough to decry that which is outright pornographic. Much of what is regarded as entertainment in Western culture should be regarded as suspect; too much sewage has gone under the social bridge for us to now assume anything flowing beneath is pristine and we can just jump in.*

highest planes. Not only is sin a barrier between man and God, it is also the chief obstacle to man's even perceiving God. Man wonders if He exists, and, if so, why he cannot perceive evidence of Him; yet man's own pride—which underlies and supports all of his sins—and his willful disobedience blind him.

The poet William Butler Yeats alluded to the value of innocence in lines from "A Prayer for My Daughter":

The soul recovers radical innocence
And learns at last that it is self-delighting,
Self-appeasing, self-affrighting,...

Having walked on both sides of the divide that separates the pursuit of needs through God's way on the one hand, and the world's way on the other, I can affirm also that there is no comparison. Any pleasure enjoyed in the latter cannot rise to the rewards afforded by the former. They are two separate and distinct species of experience: one on a spectacular, lofty mountaintop, the other in the swamps and thickets at the foot. One is exalting, the other debasing.

Here too, in this pursuit of needs and pleasures, we see manifold evidence of the church's complicity in leading man down the mountain rather than up it. There is an ample range of options for failure of the church, and it is highly dubious that any Western church has not availed itself of one or more of them. Man will sin. Christians will sin. But when the church does not stand, does not condemn, does not act, it has abdicated the most fundamental duty lain at its feet by Christ. When the church pleases man, it will likely displease God. "Those who live according to the sinful nature have their minds set on what that nature desires; but those who live in accordance with the Spirit have their minds set on what the Spirit desires. The mind of sinful man is death, but the mind controlled by the Spirit is life and peace; the sinful mind is hostile to God. It does not submit to God's law, nor can it do so. Those controlled by the sinful nature cannot please God." (Romans 8: 5–8 NIV)

But one may declare, "we do declaim against sin." But which sins? All of them as cited in Scripture? Or is your exercise of moral authority selective? More precisely, is it compromised by the culture's views and values? If you can honestly declare that it is not, then the remoteness of your location must be so great as to obscure your very existence from the rest of Western society—and you from the reach of its multitudinous tentacles. It is not credible that any Western church has not, and is not, failing somehow in this respect.

The first-century church's failure to sometimes confront sin suggests strongly that, in our age and place, this is not simply a weakness but a pandemic of failures. Paul anticipated as much: "For I am afraid that when I come I may not find you as I want you to be, and you may not find me as you want me to be. I fear that there may be quarreling, jealousy, outbursts of anger, factions, slander, gossip, arrogance and disorder." (2 Corinthians 12:20 NIV)

But we must be specific and concrete rather than abstract; otherwise, the latitude for rationalization to keep and pursue sins will be exploited even more. Perhaps the most obvious place to begin is with those forms of communication utilized for entertainment that are most pervasive in Western society: television, movies, magazines, and the Internet. We have already seen how each of these reflects the culture from which it springs and how a civilization in decline and decay will produce the debased and label it as art and entertainment.

The fatuity in this should be obvious even to the secularist who is using his or her head, but it is the blindness within the church and its own abysmally low standards we are concerned with here. It is not enough for pastors and priests to decry that which is outright pornographic. Much of what is regarded as entertainment in Western culture should be regarded as suspect; too much sewage has gone under the social bridge for us to now assume anything flowing beneath is pristine and we can just jump in.

The culture's standards for what is appropriate or acceptable should be rejected outright by the church. Nor should anyone, in America at least, be gulled by the shrieks about censorship and the First Amendment that emanate from any number of cultural arbiters. As a lawyer, I can affirm it is neither difficult to demonstrate how censorship already exists—and always has—or that the First Amendment was never intended to shield the perverse, the debased, and the pathological. Not to have some forms of censorship is the social equivalent of continually ingesting poisons with one's food. No society will survive it. Censorship always exists—it is simply a matter of where a society draws the line. Western civilization has drawn it so low that tons of garbage must be displaced just to find it.

None of this should be taken as a call to shift to the end of the spectrum of social involvement that, for example, the Amish have chosen. But any Christian and any priest and preacher should know that our Amish brethren are surely closer to the truth of the New Testament in this respect than is the church generally in Western civilization. Fellow Christians could do worse than to contemplate their example.

By implication, the Internet, that more recent technology—which was to expand man's knowledge but has managed to shrink his character—is also a conspicuous offender in the bringing down (we would be fortunate if it were just "dumbing down" but it is surely both) of the standards of an entire civilization. Millions of young people are exposed to that which no human being should ever be exposed to, regardless of age. Marriages are destroyed through the ready accessibility of the salacious and the perverse. Here too, the society goes lemming-like off the cliff—swooned by the mantras of self-serving fools talking about "freedom," "the right to know," and the virtues of "information."

Where are church leaders in the midst of this? Many of them are at their computer terminals. Others are simply terminally cowardly—understanding to some degree their duty, they do it not and survive in their sinecures. Then they preach tepid sermons that are useless—Sisyphean in their effect and the spiritual stupor they nurture. Their sheep are thus willing to consume more and more of the poisons.

Inevitably, the subject of sex should follow closely on the heels of an analysis of the moral quicksand fashioned from modern technology. Sexual sins are perhaps the most intractable of the sins of the flesh, precisely because they exploit a natural and God-given human impulse

Photo by Perov Stanislav © used by permission

Television, movies, magazines, and the Internet all reflect the culture from which they spring. A civilization in decline and decay will produce the debased and label it as art and entertainment—or even education. Where are church leaders in the midst of this? Unfortunately, many of them are at their computer terminals or in front of their televisions.

of considerable power. For that reason alone, without mention of the destructiveness of sexual sins, sexual attitudes and behaviors should be treated with the utmost discipline and respect for their dangers, not unlike the handling of an unstable explosive.

These sins were of course not unknown in the first-century church: the New Testament makes several candid references to their ubiquity. "I am afraid that when I come again my God will humble me before you, and I will be grieved over many who have sinned earlier and have not repented of the impurity, sexual sin and debauchery in which they have indulged." (2 Corinthians 12:21 NIV) But lest the modern church take perverse comfort in the failures of ancient members—we should be forewarned: "The body is not meant for sexual immorality, but for the Lord, and the Lord for the body." (1 Corinthians 6:13b NIV)

The distinction is critical because the primary difference between the first-century church and the modern Western church was not a dearth of hormones among the former's members and an excess among the members of the latter. Rather it was the stand the church of that time took assertively against sexual immorality; and its willingness to exclude those who practiced or taught that any of its manifestations should be tolerated. "...we have renounced secret and shameful ways; we do not use deception, nor do we distort the word of God. On the contrary, by setting forth the truth plainly we commend ourselves to every man's conscience in the sight of God." (2 Corinthians 4:2 NIV)

In a passage that galls Western purveyors and practitioners of the perverse—and one that they work diligently to rationalize away—we are told, "Do you not know that the wicked will not inherit the kingdom of God? Do not be deceived: Neither the sexually immoral nor idolaters nor adulterers nor male prostitutes nor homosexual offenders nor thieves nor the greedy nor drunkards nor slanderers nor swindlers will inherit the kingdom of God." (1 Corinthians 6:9–10 NIV)

This is neither a priggish frigidity nor an attempt to control other people's lives—as it would so shallowly be characterized in our time. This was a stand on principle that said, in effect, "If you breach these moral laws you will be hurt and you will hurt others—often in ways you will never foresee." This of course is true, but in our time, often even in the church, much sexual immorality is seen as a "victimless" sin, if it is characterized as sin at all. King David's plaintive acknowledgment in Psalm 51 that against God and God only had he sinned would not be understood by many professing Christians in our time.

Anyone honestly searching the Scriptures for an answer to the question, What is sexually permissible? will be rewarded by a clear and straightforward answer that can be stated: No sexual relationship is permitted except that between one husband and one wife within the bonds of matrimony. Many efforts are being made in Western civilization to "amend" this law. Even within the church, heterosexual behavior outside marriage and homosexual behavior are not only often tolerated but sometimes treated as a *cause célèbre.* The consumption of intellectual and moral carrion by a culture in decay might be expected; that it is being served up by the church is one of the indicia of an advanced stage of decomposition.

The apostle Paul, in a passage mirrored many times in different places in Scripture, admonished the church to maintain a distinction of the highest order—no compromise, no exceptions, no tolerance, no fear:

> But among you there must not be even a hint of sexual immorality, or of any kind of impurity, or of greed, because these are improper for God's holy people. Nor should there be obscenity, foolish talk

PD from Yorck

David and Bathsheba, by Paolo Veronese, sixteenth century. *In the wake of history's most famous adultery, David's plaintive acknowledgment in Psalm 51 that against God and God only had he sinned would not be understood by many professing Christians in our time. Anyone honestly searching the Scriptures for an answer to the question,* What is sexually permissible? *will be rewarded by a clear and straightforward answer that can be stated, "No sexual relationship is permitted except that between one husband and one wife within the bonds of matrimony." Many efforts are being made in Western civilization to "amend" this law. Even within the church, heterosexual behavior outside marriage and homosexual behavior are not only often tolerated but sometimes treated as a* cause célèbre. *The consumption of intellectual and moral carrion by a culture in decay might be expected; that it is being served up by the church is one of the indicia of an advanced stage of decomposition.*

CHAPTER

36

FAITH WITHOUT ACTIONS IS DEAD

Preach the gospel at all times. If necessary, use words.
St. Francis of Assisi[1]

Again Jesus said, "Peace be with you! As the Father has sent me, I am sending you."
John 20:21 (NIV)

Only one life, it will soon be past, only what's done for Christ will last.
C. T. Studd[2]

In the classic war movie *Patton*, the actor George C. Scott, in the title role, stands in his staff car and gazes back at a seemingly endless line of armored vehicles, trucks, and jeeps snaking toward the front. War, he declaims, makes all other forms of human endeavor pale by comparison.[3] Man has never committed the resources and energy to any other endeavor on the scale and with the zeal that he commits his absolute most and best to war. Yet this could and should be said about the advancement of the Christian faith.

The Western church—Catholic, Orthodox, and Protestant—should be making all other forms of human endeavor pale in comparison, by battling the ills that afflict mankind and telling humanity about their greatest hope. This is not an abstract ideal to which lip service may be given with no sincere belief in its accessibility. Nor is it beyond the wit of man to achieve—certainly not faithful man, believing man.

Christ's most powerful statement on this Christian duty reflected the gravity and significance of obeying this command:

> Then the King will say to those on his right, "Come, you who are blessed by my Father, inherit the kingdom prepared for you from the foundation of the world. For I was hungry and you gave me food, I was thirsty and you gave me drink, I was a stranger and you welcomed me, I was naked and you clothed me, I was sick and you visited me, I was in prison and you came to me." Then the righteous will answer him, saying, "Lord, when did we see you hungry and feed you, or thirsty and give you drink? And when did we see you a stranger and welcome you, or naked and clothe you? And when did we see you sick or in prison and visit you?" And the King will answer them, "Truly, I say to you, as you did it to one of the least of these my brothers, you did it to me." (Matthew 25:34–40 ESV)

PD-gov

Omaha Beach, D-Day, 6 June 1944. *In the classic war movie* Patton, *the actor George C. Scott, in the title role, stands in his staff car and gazes back at a seemingly endless line of armored vehicles, trucks, and jeeps snaking toward the front. War, he declaims, makes all other forms of human endeavor pale by comparison. Man has never committed the resources and energy to any other endeavor on the scale and with the zeal that he commits his absolute most and best to war. Yet this could and should be said about the advancement of the Christian faith. The Western church should be making all other forms of human endeavor pale in comparison, by battling the ills that afflict mankind and telling humanity about their greatest hope.*

WILL WE CONTINUE TO TEND TO OUR INTERESTS—OR GOD'S?

For everyone looks out for his own interests, not those of Jesus Christ.
Philippians 2:21 (NIV)

When faced with an implicit appeal to its Christian duty by the advent of the Great Depression, the American church largely demurred. Seeing it not as an opportunity but a daunting imposition, like most in American society, the church looked to government. There has been no turning back since. Recent "faith-based initiatives" in America, though certainly not tokenism, are inconsequential relative to the needs of the society and relative to the ubiquitous role of government in simultaneously addressing, and sometimes aggravating, social pathologies. The church's failure to question this assignment of duties implies its unwillingness to shoulder the burden. Just as power abhors a vacuum and megalomaniacs often fill it, human needs produce a vacuum as well—and values will be taught, consciously or unconsciously, by whoever or whatever fills it. Sorokin recognized the impact the church had on another decaying civilization through the "transmutation of values." "...the crisis of sensate Graeco–Roman culture was terminated by the growth of Christianity. The respective societies were preserved from dissolution, be it noted, not so much through the 'practical and expert' manipulation of economic, political, genetic or other factors, but mainly through the transmutation of values, the spiritualization of mentality, and the socialization of conduct and ennoblement of social relations effected through the medium of religion."[4]

PD-LOC

One of Dorothea Lange's famous portraits of a migrant mother in America during the Great Depression. *When faced with an implicit appeal to its Christian duty by the advent of the Great Depression, the American church largely demurred. Seeing it not as an opportunity but a daunting imposition, like most in American society, the church looked to government. There has been no turning back since. Recent "faith-based initiatives" in America are a drop in the bucket relative to the needs of the society and relative to the ubiquitous role of government in simultaneously addressing, and sometimes aggravating, social pathologies. The church's failure to question this assignment of duties implies its unwillingness to shoulder the burden. Just as power abhors a vacuum and megalomaniacs often fill it, human needs produce a vacuum as well—and values will be taught, consciously or unconsciously, by whoever or whatever fills it.*

But the crisis of Western civilization will not be terminated by the modern Western iteration of Christianity unless the church profoundly transforms itself first. Churches in every community should be seen by all as *the place* to go for help. The responsibility is not "out there"—it is in the Christian church in the West. God has laid these duties at Christians' feet.

"Faith-based initiatives" proposed by the American government are not successes but evidence of the American church's failure. The church should have been doing these things—and much, much more—for generations, and not looking to government for help.

TO WHOM MUCH HAS BEEN GIVEN, MUCH WILL BE EXPECTED

From everyone who has been given much, much will be demanded; and from the one who has been entrusted with much, much more will be asked.
Luke 12:48b (ESV)

Dawson, like Sorokin, recognized that not only can the church alter the very course of a civilization, it will have that effect—if it is doing its duty at all—regardless of any conscious strategy. Choosing to take the actions commanded and demonstrated by Christ inevitably leads to massive and foundational change. This is the Christian's responsibility regardless of the outcome and regardless of any deliberate intent or strategy.

> Indeed it is this vital tension between two worlds and two planes of reality which makes the Christian way of life so difficult but which is also the source of its strength. To live for eternal truths, to possess the first fruits of eternal life, while facing every practical responsibility and meeting the demands of the present moment and place on their own ground—that is the spirit by which a Christian culture lives and is known. For Christian culture involves a ceaseless effort to widen the frontiers of the Kingdom of God—not only horizontally by increasing the number of Christians but vertically by penetrating deeper into human life and bringing every human activity into closer relations with its spiritual center.[5]

During the course of a political event at a country club not far from our home, the wealthier and more politically influential leaders of that county gathered to discuss issues and hear speeches. During the discussion, a member of the audience decried the fact that government was intruding into every area of life. The comment appeared to come from a man of religious belief. A political leader from the community responded, "That's because churches aren't serving people. They aren't taking care of social problems. Instead, they are building bigger buildings and gymnasiums and family life centers."

This observation was telling. It exposed not only a great shortcoming of the church in our time, but it also evidenced how the secular world perceives the church. The church has little influence and is a poor example in their eyes—and not without cause. This is partly true because the church has tended to define itself in terms of a doctrinal belief system. If you believe this or that you are a "true" Christian, particularly of that denomination, group or sect. But nothing in Christ's life suggested that He was only about doctrine, beliefs, or ideas. His life was full of action; action that influenced every aspect of the culture of that time and place. Francis Schaeffer explained how this model should influence all Christians in all times: "…as Christians we are not only to know the right world view, the world view that tells us the truth of what is, but consciously to act upon that world view so as to influence society in all its parts and facets across the whole spectrum of life, as much as we can to the extent of our individual and collective ability."[6]

Nothing should remain unaffected by the Christian in his or her walk through this temporal world. Modern Western notions about faith being a "private" matter—the rationalizing and propaganda of a decaying civilization intent on limiting the impact of religious belief and one's responsibility before God—are to be rejected. That was never what Christ taught, much less demonstrated. It is its antithesis.

Even "separation of church and state" should only be respected in the limited sense of the absence of compulsion. Christ never compelled; thus the church and the Christian should never compel. But this does not imply that church (i.e., religious belief and practice) and state (i.e., the making of laws and the exercise of governance over a people) can be, in the final analysis, separated. This is an impossibility in any event. Men are influenced in everything they do by what they believe at the core of their being. Artificial walls or philosophical constructs can never separate them or their actions from those beliefs.

To what extent then is the individual Christian to deploy his faith and beliefs? Schaeffer's answer: "…as much as we can to the extent of our…ability." This implies no limits, no rationalizations, no excuses. That is precisely the way the disciples and the first-century church lived their lives. That is the way millions of Christians across the ages lived theirs as well.

WHY?
BECAUSE TRUE LOVE = SACRIFICIAL SERVICE

If you love me, you will obey what I command.
John 14:15 (NIV)

Even with his own disciples, Christ had need not only of making his expectations abundantly clear but of explaining the reasons. The reasons are central. Near the end of his ministry a strange form of confrontation took place, instigated by Christ, with Peter, the apostle of boisterous certainty and confidence.

Jesus said to Simon Peter, "Simon son of John, do you truly love me more than these?" "Yes, Lord," he said, "you know that I love you." Jesus said, "Feed my lambs." Again Jesus said, "Simon son of John, do you truly love me?" He answered, "Yes, Lord, you know that I love you." Jesus said, "Take care of my sheep." The third time he said to him, "Simon son of John, do you love me?" Peter was hurt because Jesus had now asked him three times, "Do you love me?" He said, "Lord, you know all things; you know that I love you." Jesus said, "Feed my sheep." (John 21:15–17 NIV)

Peter surely never forgot the point Christ had made so forcefully. But the Western church very often has. The reason for sacrificial service is love: love of Christ; love of our fellowman. If we truly love Christ we will obey. If we truly love our fellowman, we will serve. If we love ourselves more than Christ and our fellowman we will engage in tokenism and altruistic dilettantism, but the bulk of our time, thoughts and resources will be committed to that which pleases us, which makes us more comfortable, which makes us feel more secure, which exalts our pride. We may fool others; we may even fool ourselves, but we will not fool God.

NO AFFECTATION, NO TOKENISM, NO SHOW

[Jesus said,]"Thus, when you give to the needy, sound no trumpet before you, as the hypocrites do in the synagogues and in the streets, that they may be praised by others. Truly, I say to you, they have received their reward. But when you give to the needy, do not let your left hand know what your right hand is doing, so that your giving may be in secret. And your Father who sees in secret will reward you."
Matthew 6:2–4 (ESV)

There is a seeming tension inherent between our Christian duty to be self-effacing and Christ's admonition to let our light shine before men. But selfless service will never go unnoticed. It is the surest method by which Christ's love will be recognized as real and mankind's only hope. Straying over the line into vanity and personal pride is the danger of which Christ warns. Ironically in my experience, though most of humanity operates not on an analytical but an intuitive plane, that intuitiveness will detect the self-centered motive in the seemingly selfless service thus destroying the credibility of the offending Christian and undermining the witness for Christ.

SURRENDER SELF

When Jesus heard this, he said to him, "You still lack one thing. Sell everything you have and give to the poor, and you will have treasure in heaven. Then come, follow me."
Luke 18:22 (NIV)

If a pastor or priest announced, "Our church has raised one million euros (dollars, etc.), and we believe God would have us spend it for a new gym, family life center, and sanctuary," then we may—and should—be skeptical of the motives and the wisdom reflected in that decision. Observers have little choice but to accept the decision and with it whatever example, implications, or doubts it may create in their minds or the minds of the secular world.

However, if the pastor or priest said, "We believe God would have us give this one million euros, dollars, etc. to missions (or evangelism, or to provide medical care to the poor in our community, or counseling for the troubled or the addicted, or training and education for the underprivileged, or for a Christian education, or security for the aged and poor)," then the sacrificial nature of that act erases doubt about motives, and eliminates reasons for skepticism. The credibility gained thereby is powerful—with an impact perhaps even greater than the services rendered.

Yet the buildings—seemingly always the buildings—are among the central indicators of the "success" of a church or religious institution, especially in America. The buildings should be, church members conclude, imposing and impressive. But of course, this is how we "honor" God. In truth, we honor ourselves, conveniently forgetting what we were told, "However, the Most High does not live in houses made by men. As the prophet says, 'Heaven is my throne, and the earth is my footstool. What kind of house will you build for me? says the Lord. Or where will my resting place be?'" (Acts 7:48–49 NIV)

US National Archives

St. Paul's Cathedral, London, during the great fire raid of Sunday 29 December 1940. *Buildings—seemingly always the buildings—are among the central indicators of the "success" of a Western church or religious institution. The buildings should be, church members conclude, imposing and impressive. But of course, this is how we "honor" God. In truth, we honor ourselves, conveniently forgetting what we were told: "However, the Most High does not live in houses made by men. As the prophet says, 'Heaven is my throne, and the earth is my footstool. What kind of house will you build for me? says the Lord. Or where will my resting place be?'" (Acts 7:48-49 NIV) St. Paul's is a classic illustration of the meaninglessness of buildings. This majestic structure survived the Blitz and is standing today, but the edifice of faith in Christ that once characterized the hearts of the British people is now in near-total collapse.*

When traversing the Hindu Kush to the China border not far from K2, I was struck by the significance of this verse. The majesty and grandeur of those, the earth's greatest mountains, seemed fitting as God's "footstool." There was nothing man could do that rivaled them. How then can we truly honor God with mortar, brick, and stone?

Ruth Graham observed, "God's work is not in buildings but in transformed lives. Buildings fall into decay and eventually disappear. The transformed life goes on forever."[7] This principle is directly related to another: "Yet a time is coming and has now come when the true worshipers will worship the Father in spirit and truth, for they are the kind of worshipers the Father seeks. God is spirit, and his worshipers must worship in spirit and in truth." (John 4:23–24 NIV)

Ruth Bell Graham, the daughter of missionaries to China and the wife of evangelist Billy Graham, *incisively wrote, "God's work is not in buildings but in transformed lives. Buildings fall into decay and eventually disappear. The transformed life goes on forever."*

Ruth Bell Graham courtesy of BGEA

But true sacrifice is as foreign to most Western churches as is true humility. We honor and value the big, the imposing, the impressive, the comfortable. The humble and the sacrificial are largely ignored, Christ's teachings notwithstanding. "…Jesus saw the rich putting their gifts into the temple treasury. He also saw a poor widow put in two very small copper coins. 'I tell you the truth,' he said, 'this poor widow has put in more than all the others. All these people gave their gifts out of their wealth; but she out of her poverty put in all she had to live on.'" (Luke 21:1–4 NIV)

One of the most famous confrontations in Scripture occurred between Christ and the rich young ruler, or, more precisely, between Christ and the worldly values of wealth, status, and prestige. St. Luke identified this man as a "ruler"; this suggests once more that nothing in history has changed: wealth brings prestige and power; prestige and power bring wealth; those who seek one usually fawn for the others.

> A certain ruler asked him, "Good teacher, what must I do to inherit eternal life?" "Why do you call me good?" Jesus answered. "No one is good—except God alone. You know the commandments: Do not commit adultery, do not murder, do not steal, do not give false testimony, honor your father and mother." "All these I have kept since I was a boy," he said. When Jesus heard this, he said to him, "You still lack one thing. Sell everything you have and give to the poor, and you will have treasure in heaven. Then come, follow me." When he heard this, he became very sad, because he was a man of great wealth. Jesus looked at him and said, "How hard it is for the rich to enter the kingdom of God!" (Luke 18:18–24 NIV)

Yet the modern Western church, and its many institutional manifestations, would not only welcome this rich man eagerly but see his joining as a "blessing" that would enhance the church's every material prospect and its "ministries." The state of his heart notwithstanding, the modern church's true—albeit often unspoken—viewpoint is "surely we can find a place for the philanthropy which will certainly follow upon his admission to the rolls."

Yet the state of our hearts, not the parameters of our pocketbooks, is the issue that concerns Christ. Not only is the church not well served by such attitudes, the rich men and women are misled—dangerously so. Even that which appears on the surface to be spiritual or a form of service

PD-old

Jesus and the Rich Young Ruler, by Heinrich Hofmann. "A certain ruler asked him, 'Good teacher, what must I do to inherit eternal life?' 'Why do you call me good?' Jesus answered. 'No one is good—except God alone. You know the commandments: Do not commit adultery, do not murder, do not steal, do not give false testimony, honor your father and mother.' 'All these I have kept since I was a boy,' he said. When Jesus heard this, he said to him, 'You still lack one thing. Sell everything you have and give to the poor, and you will have treasure in heaven. Then come, follow me.' When he heard this, he became very sad, because he was a man of great wealth. Jesus looked at him and said, 'How hard it is for the rich to enter the kingdom of God!'" (Luke 18:18–24 NIV) Yet the modern Western church, and its many institutional manifestations, would not only welcome this rich man eagerly but see his joining as a "blessing" that would enhance the church's every material prospect and its "ministries." But the state of our hearts, not the parameters of our pocketbooks, is the issue that concerns Christ. Not only is the church not well served by such attitudes, the rich men and women are misled—dangerously so. Even that which appears on the surface to be spiritual or a form of service can in fact be a reflection of self-interest and a this-world value system—and a perilous form of self-delusion.

can in fact be a reflection of self-interest and a this-world value system—as well as a perilous form of self-delusion.

The apostle Peter confronted just such a circumstance as described in the book of Acts:

> When Simon saw that the Spirit was given at the laying on of the apostles' hands, he offered them money and said, "Give me also this ability so that everyone on whom I lay my hands may receive the Holy Spirit." Peter answered: "May your money perish with you, because you thought you could

The Widow's Mite, by Gustave Doré. *True sacrifice is as foreign to most Western churches as is true humility. We honor and value the big, the imposing, the impressive, the comfortable. The humble and the sacrificial are largely ignored, Christ's teachings notwithstanding. "...Jesus saw the rich putting their gifts into the temple treasury. He also saw a poor widow put in two very small copper coins. 'I tell you the truth,' he said, 'this poor widow has put in more than all the others. All these people gave their gifts out of their wealth; but she out of her poverty put in all she had to live on.'" (Luke 21:1–4 NIV)*

PD-art

> buy the gift of God with money! You have no part or share in this ministry, because your heart is not right before God. Repent of this wickedness and pray to the Lord. Perhaps he will forgive you for having such a thought in your heart. For I see that you are full of bitterness and captive to sin." (Acts 8:18–23 NIV)

There is a strong parallel in this story with the state of the modern Western church and its predilection for erecting extravagant buildings, seeking recognition, and generally measuring its success and service by human standards. But the perceptiveness of Peter and the spiritual sensitivity required to detect and address these manifestations do not typically exist in the modern church primarily because these measures of success are broadly embraced.

IN JESUS' NAME

Jesus said, "I tell you, whoever acknowledges me before men, the Son of Man will also acknowledge him before the angels of God. But he who disowns me before men will be disowned before the angels of God."
Luke 12:8–9 (NIV)

But before we take one step further a strong admonition should be made. Any ministry, any service, any good deed by the Christian or the church must be "in Jesus' name" as in the famous promise from Christ about giving only a "cup of cold water." (Mark 9:41) Churches and ministries sometimes evade this, or, having once done it at the inception of their ministry, they have long since failed to remember—much less tell others—of the love and hope behind their original benevolent intent. I have seen aid groups in Third World countries and war zones like this: originally founded to honor Christ's commission and His example, they transmogrify into something that is of man, for man's glory, and with no serious mention of the name Jesus Christ—much less an appeal to their beneficiaries to recognize that the greater gift they bring is eternal, not temporal.

"GO YE THEREFORE" EVANGELISM

He who is not with me is against me, and he who does not gather with me, scatters.
Luke 11:23 (NIV)

Whoever acknowledges me before men, I will also acknowledge him before my Father in heaven, but whoever disowns me before men, I will disown before my Father in heaven.
Matthew 10:32–33 (NIV)

The nineteenth-century American Protestant evangelist Dwight L. Moody was once criticized by a man for the "way he talked about God and tried to persuade people to follow God." Moody responded that he wasn't always pleased with his methods either and asked what methods the man used. His critic said that he did not talk publicly about religion. Moody rejoined, "Well, in that case I like my methods better than yours."

The Western church has not only succumbed in large measure to the heretical position of Moody's critic but increasingly over generations has bureaucratized its every function—including evangelism. It is as if married couples were to forego the most central and traditional functions of their unique relationship and began to procreate solely by the joining of sperm and egg in a test tube! Nothing could or should be more personal, more human, more an expression of love, than one-to-one individual evangelism. For that reason alone, evangelism should not be primarily through "professionals" but predominantly through individuals.

All Christians are charged with the duty to go into the world and influence those with whom they have contact. The church must train the troops in the ranks for this, not simply the "professionals." "I solemnly charge you in the presence of God and of Christ Jesus, who is to judge the living and the dead, and by His appearing and His kingdom: preach the word; be ready in season and out of season; reprove, rebuke, exhort, with great patience and instruction." (2 Timothy 4:1–2 ESV) True evangelism is the natural consequence of the joy that comes from discovering a genuine relationship with Christ and the zeal engendered by that joy to share it with others.

PD-LOC

Dwight L. Moody. *The nineteenth-century evangelist was once criticized for talking publicly and forthrightly outside the church about religion. The Western church has not only succumbed in large measure to the heretical position of Moody's critic but increasingly over generations has bureaucratized its every function—including evangelism. In the West today, "religion is a private matter" has become a mantra not only of secularists but of many professing Christians.*

Evangelist Billy Sunday, 1921. *The American church in particular has focused much time and emphasis on what one might call "professional" evangelism—from Charles Finney, through Dwight L. Moody, Billy Sunday and to Billy Graham. Yet ironically, each of these men believed nothing could or should be more personal, more human, more an expression of love, than one-to-one individual evangelism. For that reason alone, evangelism should not be primarily through "professionals" but predominantly through individuals. All Christians are charged with the duty to go into the world and influence those with whom they have contact. The church must train the troops in the ranks for this, not simply the "professionals."*

PD-old; LOC

SPEAK BOLDLY

[Jesus said,] "When you are brought before synagogues, rulers and authorities, do not worry about how you will defend yourselves or what you will say, for the Holy Spirit will teach you at that time what you should say."
Luke 12:11–12 (NIV)

A ubiquitous theme of this book has been the need for courage within the Western branch of Christianity, but not courage alone—boldness. Compromised and corrupted as Western Christianity has become, its resuscitation from a near-moribund state will be possible only if professing Christians display bold courage.

In every area of human experience, Christians must remember their faith and act in reliance upon it with the abiding conviction that their faith is neither misplaced nor unstable ground upon which to take a firm and permanent stand. Courage can and should come more readily for the Christian.

Yet we see all about us in the West examples of the opposite. Some of this is couched in plausible rationales that range from "you must be diplomatic and gracious in order to get people to listen," or "you do not beat up on the sheep," to an especially flagrant denial of what is right under their noses in the New Testament—"Jesus was gentle, meek and forgiving; we must be the same." Thinking like this characterizes much that is said and written within the Western church, but it conceals a multitude of sins of omission, foremost among them the failure to honor the absolute duty to tell the truth, the whole truth, and nothing but the truth. Reading the New Testament in multiple translations will reveal to the discerning reader a pattern: neither Christ nor the apostles spoke in diplomatic code, veiled euphemisms, or ingratiating language. They—Christ above all—were models of transparency, forthrightness, and absolutely uncompromising expressions. Could we have it any other way and truly grant them credibility?

Yet Western Christians—especially, it seems, many of their leaders—are masters of the euphemistic, the banal, the coded, the disingenuous, the deliberately indirect. This blunted spear of conviction and communication will never slay any Western dragons. It is all far removed from "So have no fear of them, for nothing is covered that will not be revealed, or hidden that will not be known. What I tell you in the dark, say in the light, and what you hear whispered, proclaim on the housetops." (Matthew 10:26–27 AMP)

The pandering, fawning, abject, sometimes sycophantic fear that characterizes so much in the Western church has reached depths that would offend even an ardent secularist with a strong sense of integrity. A priest, bishop, or preacher who manages only tepid clichés and banal utterances before the media or his congregation in the face of sexual molestations of children by other priests or ministers is revealing his true nature. Such horrors should evoke—in all but the hardest of hearts—deep anger! Having represented well over one hundred children over the years who were the victims of abuse or sexual molestation, I have been repeatedly dismayed by the actions or inertia and attitudes of professing Christians who had some contact with the child or offender. While representing four little girls who had been sexually molested by their fifth-grade school teacher, I learned that the perpetrator was not only a Sunday School teacher and choir member in a local Protestant church, but that he suffered no disapprobation—even remaining in his roles, with members of the church testifying as character witnesses for him!—until he finally was sent to prison.

Catholicism is by no means the sole branch of the Christian church plagued by such depredations in our decadent time. But neither is it, especially its hierarchy, exempt from the most vociferous of condemnations for its failures to 1) prevent further crimes when they were first exposed; 2) speak out boldly, relentlessly, and fiercely against perpetrators and their accessories regardless of their status within the Church; and 3) act to permanently strip guilty priests of their status as representatives of the Church. The damage done to the credibility of the Church by all of these failures is incalculable. The damage done to the credibility of the Christian faith in the eyes of secularists, agnostics, and seekers cannot be measured. And we speak only of damage to the credibility of individuals, churches, and a religion; what of the damage done to the victims? Where is the compassion? Where is the outrage that would compel action?

The condemnations should be loud, long, and very public. The rest of the world must hear and understand that no amount of worldly power, no status in any church bureaucracy, no religious institution, and no individual is free of accountability of the most forceful sort for this evil.

These sins of commission and omission are compelling, inescapable evidence of the charge raised in this book of the Western church as a bastion of cultural influences and norms rather than the very ramparts of a transcendent faith and morality. But for the obtuse—and, more likely, those who choose comforting, appeasing self-delusion over reality—let it be said that nothing in our time proffers greater evidence of the Western church's failure.

The point of this contemporary historical illustration of sexual depravity within the church is the urgent need not simply for forthrightness from Christians in the West but for boldness with the truth. All of the biblical admonitions to "fear not," "be not afraid," "be of good courage" and to speak and act "boldly" notwithstanding, Western Christians often fear open, overt, courageous stands of conviction. To the extent they will stand, their voices typically reverberate only against the walls of their churches and other venues that are "safe" and from which they are unlikely to draw significant fire. The Christian and the church trade temporal peace and gain for the eternal—the worst of all bargains.

Paul's admonitions to Timothy are relevant reminders to the Western church today:

> Preach the Word; be prepared in season and out of season; correct, rebuke and encourage—with great patience and careful instruction. For the time will come when men will not put up with sound doctrine. Instead, to suit their own desires, they will gather around them a great number of teachers to say what their itching ears want to hear. They will turn their ears away from the truth and turn aside to myths. But you, keep your head in all situations, endure hardship, do the work of an evangelist, discharge all the duties of your ministry. (2 Timothy 4:2–5 NIV)

CHRISTIAN EDUCATION

Every Christian mind is a seed of change so long as it is a living mind, not enervated by custom or ossified by prejudice. A Christian has only to be in order to change the world.
Christopher Dawson[8]

Education is perhaps the one area in which Western churches have, over the life span of our civilization, taken significant and broad initiatives to profoundly influence the culture. Roman Catholicism has particularly distinguished itself in this regard. As early as the ninth century, Alfred the Great supported monasteries devoted to learning. Many of the renowned universities of Europe, including Oxford and Cambridge, and in America, encompassing the Ivy League universities, were founded by Christians of a deep faith that they believed, rightly, should suffuse every aspect of human experience. No compartmentalization of faith from learning for them! Both were part of the great search for truth.

But precisely because man's tendency is always toward pride, learning—without the constant inculcation and reminders of the need of, and reasons for, humility—inevitably leads man to a man-centric viewpoint. Thus in a multiplicity of ways these famed universities have become bastions of the arrogance and vanity of man; oracular abodes where those who perceive themselves as the cognoscenti and the elite make judgments and forge world views untrammeled by the exigencies of humility or faith.

The Western church should make providing a Christian education from kindergarten through graduate school a central priority. The church should never defer to the state in this task. The American church in particular, with resort to prodigious resources, should completely preempt government in this field.

Furthermore, the church should provide the best educations—not just the values and convictions but the scaffolding of thought and knowledge upon which each student can erect a life of achievement and morality. Many American Christians complain about the intrusiveness of government on the one hand and the lack of moral values found in the public schools on the other. They declaim against the absence of prayer in the schools and the presence of so much else that is debased. But the answer to their concerns is obvious: Stop looking to government. Do these things for yourself, your children, and other people's children.

Many church buildings sit largely idle for six days a week. There is no reason why every church building cannot be used for some form of education.

Earlier, we analyzed the dismal state of education in the West. Now, we say that none of this need remain so; the church in the West has within its means the power to alter the face of education in Western civilization from the dissipated, man-absorbed profile to a noble visage.

In time, the very best educations should originate on campuses where the Christian faith provides the order, the purposes, and the methods for everything that takes place. The quality of secular education in the West is declining. It is increasingly detached from reality, bereft of critical and discriminatory thought, and devoid of any moral superstructure that is essential to authentic creative achievement.

Today, all across America in particular, churches or groups of Christians have founded private schools to educate their own, or, in the absence of such schools, parents home school their children. These are usually wise and self-reliant decisions that reflect some dimensions of the attitudes and frame of mind that this book encourages.

Yet something more need be said: The church's initiatives to educate should not be solely aimed at benefiting its own. In the first instance, not all Christians have the means to send their children to private schools. They are left with resort only to the decaying schools run by government. Every conceivable means should be exploited to make certain that education is accessible to others. The doors of the Christian kindergarten, grade school, high school, university, and graduate school should be open to those who will respect and honor their founding principles. Christian education can dramatically offset the damage done to minds and hearts sequestered in a decaying culture.

THE GREAT MISSION—THE MODEL OF CHRIST'S MINISTRIES

Some like to live within the sound of church or chapel bell—
I want to run a rescue shop within a yard of hell.
C. T. Studd[9]

How then do we practically implement these principles? We first must look to the example of Christ Himself. How did He minister? How did He serve? When those questions are answered truthfully and fully, the flagrant sins of omission of the Western church are exposed. As Schaeffer suggested, no aspect of human experience was untouched by Christ. The listing offered below does not approach the breadth or impact of His life.

TEACHING AND TRAINING

So for a whole year Barnabas and Saul met with the church and taught great numbers of people.
Acts 11:26 (NIV)

The church's mission does not end with leading others to Christ. Indeed, this should be but the beginning. The church should not cease its efforts at leading others to Christ but intensively teach and train them what it means to be a Christian—to surrender all aspects of one's life to God—and how that translates into an activist's life of dynamic service. I do not refer here to the typical "Sunday School," many of which display a passionless insipidity that deadens rather than enlivens the mind and inspires the heart. Rather I refer to a new form of teaching, a new approach with a dynamism and fervency rarely seen in the Western church today.

Some churches teach by implication and actions that salvation is the only thing that is important; subsequent personal growth, service, and obedience to God are neglected. Many have the effect of leading people to think this way even if they give lip service otherwise.

When holiness and personal obedience are not emphasized in the pulpit or in the actions of the church through church discipline, the implication is that making God the Lord of one's life is not central to the Christian life. This is religion, not true faith. Belief—and with it God—become a compartment of man's life. For this reason, many who presume to embrace Christ wander into the Western wilderness and do great harm to themselves, their lives, their loved ones and their witness. I believe that this is one of the most sweeping and dangerous of the many afflictions of the Western church: millions of professing Christians who have no idea what it truly means to be a follower of Christ. Thus they wander through the minefields of Western civilization and invariably end up casualties—in their marriages, their morality, their mental and physical health, and their work—indeed, even their sense of life's true purpose.

As a corollary, the church must train its members in how to address the proliferating needs and pervasive pathologies of Western civilization. Years of grappling with those needs and pathologies as a lawyer have repeatedly exposed the naïveté and ignorance of many ministers and priests, who have no idea of the scope and depth of these problems and the needs, much less how to address them. If the leaders themselves are unprepared then the troops surely will be lost.

Teaching was a dominant feature of Christ's ministry, which should tell the church something significant. The greatest recorded example is His sermon preached outdoors to thousands who gathered to hear Him speak.

MATTHEW 5–7 (NIV)—THE SERMON ON THE MOUNT

Blessed are the poor in spirit, for theirs is the kingdom of heaven.

Blessed are those who mourn, for they will be comforted.

Blessed are the meek, for they will inherit the earth.

Blessed are those who hunger and thirst for righteousness, for they will be filled.

Blessed are the merciful, for they will be shown mercy.

Blessed are the pure in heart, for they will see God.

Blessed are the peacemakers, for they will be called sons of God.

Blessed are those who are persecuted because of righteousness, for theirs is the kingdom of heaven.

Blessed are you when people insult you, persecute you and falsely say all kinds of evil against you because of me. Rejoice and be glad, because great is your reward in heaven, for in the same way they persecuted the prophets who were before you.

You are the salt of the earth. But if the salt loses its saltiness, how can it be made salty again? It is no longer good for anything, except to be thrown out and trampled by men.

You are the light of the world. A city on a hill cannot be hidden. Neither do people light a lamp and put it under a bowl. Instead they put it on its stand, and it gives light to everyone in the house. In the same way, let your light shine before men, that they may see your good deeds and praise your Father in heaven.

Do not think that I have come to abolish the Law or the Prophets; I have not come to abolish them but to fulfill them. I tell you the truth, until heaven and earth disappear, not the smallest letter, not the least stroke of a pen, will by any means disappear from the Law until everything is accomplished. Anyone who breaks one of the least of these commandments and teaches others to do the same will be called least in the kingdom of heaven, but whoever practices and teaches these commands will be called great in the kingdom of heaven. For I tell you that unless your righteousness surpasses that of the Pharisees and the teachers of the law, you will certainly not enter the kingdom of heaven.

You have heard that it was said to the people long ago, "Do not murder, and anyone who murders will be subject to judgment." But I tell you that anyone who is angry with his brother will be subject to judgment. Again, anyone who says to his brother, "Raca," is answerable to the Sanhedrin. But anyone who says, "You fool!" will be in danger of the fire of hell.

Therefore, if you are offering your gift at the altar and there remember that your brother has something against you, leave your gift there in front of the altar. First go and be reconciled to your brother; then come and offer your gift.

Settle matters quickly with your adversary who is taking you to court. Do it while you are still with him on the way, or he may hand you over to the judge, and the judge may hand you over to the officer, and you may be thrown into prison. I tell you the truth, you will not get out until you have paid the last penny.

You have heard that it was said, "Do not commit adultery." But I tell you that anyone who looks at a woman lustfully has already committed adultery with her in his heart. If your right eye causes you to sin, gouge it out and throw it away. It is better for you to lose one part of your body than for your whole body to be thrown into hell. And if your right hand causes you to sin, cut it off and throw it away. It is better for you to lose one part of your body than for your whole body to go into hell.

It has been said, "Anyone who divorces his wife must give her a certificate of divorce." But I tell you that anyone who divorces his wife, except for marital unfaithfulness, causes her to become an adulteress, and anyone who marries the divorced woman commits adultery.

Again, you have heard that it was said to the people long ago, "Do not break your oath, but keep the oaths you have made to the Lord." But I tell you, Do not swear at all: either by heaven, for it is God's throne; or by the earth, for it is his footstool; or by Jerusalem, for it is the city of the Great King. And do not swear by your head, for you cannot make even one hair white or black. Simply let your "Yes" be "Yes," and your "No," "No"; anything beyond this comes from the evil one.

You have heard that it was said, "Eye for eye, and tooth for tooth." But I tell you, Do not resist an evil person. If someone strikes you on the right cheek, turn to him the other also. And if someone wants to sue you and take your tunic, let him have your cloak as well. If someone forces you to go one mile, go with him two miles. Give to the one who asks you, and do not turn away from the one who wants to borrow from you.

You have heard that it was said, "Love your neighbor and hate your enemy." But I tell you: Love your enemies and pray for those who persecute you, that you may be sons of your Father in heaven. He causes his sun to rise on the evil and the good, and sends rain on the righteous and the unrighteous. If you love those who love you, what reward will you get? Are not even the tax collectors doing that? And if you greet only your brothers, what are you doing more than others? Do not even pagans do that? Be perfect, therefore, as your heavenly Father is perfect.

Be careful not to do your "acts of righteousness" before men, to be seen by them. If you do, you will have no reward from your Father in heaven.

So when you give to the needy, do not announce it with trumpets, as the hypocrites do in the synagogues and on the streets, to be honored by men. I tell you the truth, they have received their reward in full. But when you give to the needy, do not let your left hand know what your right hand is doing, so that your giving may be in secret. Then your Father, who sees what is done in secret, will reward you.

And when you pray, do not be like the hypocrites, for they love to pray standing in the synagogues and on the street corners to be seen by men. I tell you the truth, they have received their reward in full.

But when you pray, go into your room, close the door and pray to your Father, who is unseen. Then your Father, who sees what is done in secret, will reward you. And when you pray, do not keep on babbling like pagans, for they think they will be heard because of their many words. Do not be like them, for your Father knows what you need before you ask him.

This, then, is how you should pray:

Our Father in heaven,
hallowed be your name,
your kingdom come,
your will be done
on earth as it is in heaven.
Give us today our daily bread.
Forgive us our debts,
as we also have forgiven our debtors.
And lead us not into temptation,
but deliver us from the evil one.

For if you forgive men when they sin against you, your heavenly Father will also forgive you. But if you do not forgive men their sins, your Father will not forgive your sins.

When you fast, do not look somber as the hypocrites do, for they disfigure their faces to show men they are fasting. I tell you the truth, they have received their reward in full. But when you fast, put oil on your head and wash your face, so that it will not be obvious to men that you are fasting, but only to your Father, who is unseen; and your Father, who sees what is done in secret, will reward you.

Do not store up for yourselves treasures on earth, where moth and rust destroy, and where thieves break in and steal. But store up for yourselves treasures in heaven, where moth and rust do not destroy, and where thieves do not break in and steal. For where your treasure is, there your heart will be also.

The eye is the lamp of the body. If your eyes are good, your whole body will be full of light. But if your eyes are bad, your whole body will be full of darkness. If then the light within you is darkness, how great is that darkness!

No one can serve two masters. Either he will hate the one and love the other, or he will be devoted to the one and despise the other. You cannot serve both God and Money.

Therefore I tell you, do not worry about your life, what you will eat or drink; or about your body, what you will wear. Is not life more important than food, and the body more important than clothes? Look at the birds of the air; they do not sow or reap or store away in barns, and yet your heavenly Father feeds them. Are you not much more valuable than they? Who of you by worrying can add a single hour to his life?

And why do you worry about clothes? See how the lilies of the field grow. They do not labor or spin. Yet I tell you that not even Solomon in all his splendor was dressed like one of these. If that is how God clothes the grass of the field, which is here today and tomorrow is thrown into the fire, will he not much more clothe you, O you of little faith?

So do not worry, saying, "What shall we eat?" or "What shall we drink?" or "What shall we wear?" For the pagans run after all these things, and your heavenly Father knows that you need them. But seek first his kingdom and his righteousness, and all these things will be given to you as well. Therefore do not worry about tomorrow, for tomorrow will worry about itself. Each day has enough trouble of its own.

Do not judge, or you too will be judged. For in the same way you judge others, you will be judged, and with the measure you use, it will be measured to you.

Why do you look at the speck of sawdust in your brother's eye and pay no attention to the plank in your own eye? How can you say to your brother, "Let me take the speck out of your eye," when all the time there is a plank in your own eye? You hypocrite, first take the plank out of your own eye, and then you will see clearly to remove the speck from your brother's eye.

Do not give dogs what is sacred; do not throw your pearls to pigs. If you do, they may trample them under their feet, and then turn and tear you to pieces.

Ask and it will be given to you; seek and you will find; knock and the door will be opened to you. For everyone who asks receives; he who seeks finds; and to him who knocks, the door will be opened.

Which of you, if his son asks for bread, will give him a stone? Or if he asks for a fish, will give him a snake? If you, then, though you are evil, know how to give good gifts to your children, how much more will your Father in heaven give good gifts to those who ask him! So in everything, do to others what you would have them do to you, for this sums up the Law and the Prophets.

Enter through the narrow gate. For wide is the gate and broad is the road that leads to destruction, and many enter through it. But small is the gate and narrow the road that leads to life, and only a few find it.

Watch out for false prophets. They come to you in sheep's clothing, but inwardly they are ferocious wolves. By their fruit you will recognize them. Do people pick grapes from thornbushes, or figs from thistles? Likewise every good tree bears good fruit, but a bad tree bears bad fruit. A good tree cannot bear bad fruit, and a bad tree cannot bear good fruit. Every tree that does not bear good fruit is cut down and thrown into the fire. Thus, by their fruit you will recognize them.

Not everyone who says to me, "Lord, Lord," will enter the kingdom of heaven, but only he who does the will of my Father who is in heaven. Many will say to me on that day, "Lord, Lord, did we not prophesy in your name, and in your name drive out demons and perform many miracles?" Then I will tell them plainly, "I never knew you. Away from me, you evildoers!"

Therefore everyone who hears these words of mine and puts them into practice is like a wise man who built his house on the rock. The rain came down, the streams rose, and the winds blew and beat against that house; yet it did not fall, because it had its foundation on the rock. But everyone who hears these words of mine and does not put them into practice is like a foolish man who built his house on sand. The rain came down, the streams rose, and the winds blew and beat against that house, and it fell with a great crash.

When Jesus had finished saying these things, the crowds were amazed at his teaching, because he taught as one who had authority, and not as their teachers of the law.

PD-art

Sermon on the Mount, by Carl Heinrich Bloch, 1890. *The most powerful and influential teaching about man's relationship with God and man's relationship with his fellowman ever uttered, it dominated the philosophical formation of Western civilization's moral codes but has increasingly been relegated to the status of an anachronistic irrelevancy.*

OTHER INSTANCES OF CHRIST'S TEACHING NOTED BY MATTHEW

Matthew 9:10–13 (ESV)

And as Jesus reclined at table in the house, behold, many tax collectors and sinners came and were reclining with Jesus and his disciples. And when the Pharisees saw this, they said to his disciples, "Why does your teacher eat with tax collectors and sinners?" But when he heard it, he said, "Those who are well have no need of a physician, but those who are sick. Go and learn what this means, 'I desire mercy, and not sacrifice.' For I came not to call the righteous, but sinners."

Matthew 11:1 (ESV)

When Jesus had finished instructing his twelve disciples, he went on from there to teach and preach in their cities.

MINISTRY OF HEALING

[Jesus said,]"Heal the sick, raise the dead, cleanse lepers, cast out demons.
You received without paying; give without pay."
Matthew 10:8 (ESV)

Christ's ministries were probably most often perceived in terms of healing, healing of the body, the mind and emotions, and the spirit. This focus on the entire person is significant and should not be forgotten by the church, which sometimes tends to define "ministry" in narrow terms. A left-leaning American church may expend considerable verbiage and some effort on the physical; a more right-leaning church may declaim frequently on the spiritual and the moral to the neglect of the physical and emotional. Representative passages follow with citations for other examples of healing at the end of this segment.

HEALING OF THE BODY

Matthew 8:2–17 (NIV)

A man with leprosy came and knelt before him and said, "Lord, if you are willing, you can make me clean." Jesus reached out his hand and touched the man. "I am willing," he said. "Be clean!" Immediately he was cured of his leprosy. Then Jesus said to him, "See that you don't tell anyone. But go, show yourself to the priest and offer the gift Moses commanded, as a testimony to them." When Jesus had entered Capernaum, a centurion came to him, asking for help. "Lord," he said, "my servant lies at home paralyzed and in terrible suffering." Jesus said to him, "I will go and heal him." The centurion replied, "Lord, I do not deserve to have you come under my roof. But just say the word, and my servant will be healed. For I myself am a man under authority, with soldiers under me. I tell this one, 'Go,' and he goes; and that one, 'Come,' and he comes. I say to my servant, 'Do this,' and he does it." When Jesus heard this, he was astonished and said to those following him, "I tell you the truth, I have not found anyone in Israel with such great faith...." Then Jesus said to the centurion, "Go! It will be done just as you believed it would." And his servant was healed at that very hour. When Jesus came into Peter's house, he saw Peter's mother-in-law lying in bed with a fever. He touched her hand and the fever left her, and she got up and began to wait on him. When evening came, many who were demon-possessed were brought to him, and he drove out the spirits with a word and healed all the sick.

PD-art

Christ Healing the Sick at Bethesda, by Carl Heinrich Bloch, 1883. *Healing was central to Jesus' ministry—and therefore to his model for Christians—but healing the infirmities (physical and psychological) of increasingly pathological and dysfunctional Western societies is not central to the Western church's ministries. Western Christians more often choose to leave these burdens to government.*

This was to fulfill what was spoken through the prophet Isaiah: "He took up our infirmities and carried our diseases."

Matthew 9:2–7 (NIV)

Some men brought to him a paralytic, lying on a mat. When Jesus saw their faith, he said to the paralytic, "Take heart, son; your sins are forgiven." At this, some of the teachers of the law said to themselves, "This fellow is blaspheming!" Knowing their thoughts, Jesus said, "Why do you entertain evil thoughts in your hearts? Which is easier: to say, 'Your sins are forgiven,' or to say, 'Get up and walk'? But so that you may know that the Son of Man has authority on earth to forgive sins...." Then he said to the paralytic, "Get up, take your mat and go home." And the man got up and went home.

Matthew 9:18–31 (NIV)

While he was saying this, a ruler came and knelt before him and said, "My daughter has just died. But come and put your hand on her, and she will live." Jesus got up and went with him, and so did his disciples. Just then a woman who had been subject to bleeding for twelve years came up behind him and touched the edge of his cloak. She said to herself, "If I only touch his cloak, I will be healed." Jesus turned and saw her. "Take heart, daughter," he said, "your faith has healed you." And the woman was healed from that moment. When Jesus entered the ruler's house and saw the flute players and the noisy crowd, he said, "Go away. The girl is not dead but asleep." But they laughed at him. After the crowd had been put outside, he went in and took the girl by the hand, and she got up. News of this spread through all that region. As Jesus went on from there, two blind men followed him, calling out, "Have mercy on us, Son of David!" When he had gone indoors, the blind men came to him, and he asked them, "Do you believe that I am able to do this?" "Yes, Lord," they replied. Then he touched their eyes and said, "According to your faith will it be done to you"; and their sight was restored. Jesus warned them sternly, "See that no one knows about this." But they went out and spread the news about him all over that region.

Matthew 12:9–13 (ESV)

He went on from there and entered their synagogue. And a man was there with a withered hand. And they asked him, "Is it lawful to heal on the Sabbath?"—so that they might accuse him. He said to them, "Which one of you who has a sheep, if it falls into a pit on the Sabbath, will not take hold of it and lift it out? Of how much more value is a man than a sheep! So it is lawful to do good on the Sabbath." Then he said to the man, "Stretch out your hand." And the man stretched it out, and it was restored, healthy like the other.

Matthew 14:35–36 (ESV)

And when the men of that place recognized him, they sent around to all that region and brought to him all who were sick and implored him that they might only touch the fringe of his garment. And as many as touched it were made well.

Matthew 15:30–31 (ESV)

And great crowds came to him, bringing with them the lame, the blind, the crippled, the mute, and many others, and they put them at his feet, and he healed them, so that the crowd wondered, when they saw the mute speaking, the crippled healthy, the lame walking, and the blind seeing. And they glorified the God of Israel.

Luke 7:12–16 (ESV)

As he drew near to the gate of the town, behold, a man who had died was being carried out, the only son of his mother, and she was a widow, and a considerable crowd from the town was with her. And when the Lord saw her, he had compassion on her and said to her, "Do not weep." Then he came up and touched the bier, and the bearers stood still. And he said, "Young man, I say to you, arise." And the dead man sat up and began to speak, and Jesus gave him to his mother. Fear seized them all, and they glorified God, saying, "A great prophet has arisen among us!" and "God has visited his people!"

Luke 7:21–22 (NIV)

At that very time Jesus cured many who had diseases, sicknesses and evil spirits, and gave sight to many who were blind. So he replied to the messengers, "Go back and report to John what you have seen and heard: The blind receive sight, the lame walk, those who have leprosy are cured, the deaf hear, the dead are raised, and the good news is preached to the poor.

Luke 13:11–13 (ESV)

And there was a woman who had had a disabling spirit for eighteen years. She was bent over and could not fully straighten herself. When Jesus saw her, he called her over and said to her, "Woman, you are freed from your disability." And he laid his hands on her, and immediately she was made straight, and she glorified God.

Luke 17:11–18 (ESV)

On the way to Jerusalem he was passing along between Samaria and Galilee. And as he entered a village, he was met by ten lepers, who stood at a distance and lifted up their voices, saying, "Jesus, Master, have mercy on us." When he saw them he said to them, "Go and show yourselves to the priests." And as they went they were cleansed. Then one of them, when he saw that he was healed, turned back, praising God with a loud voice; and he fell on his face at Jesus' feet, giving him thanks. Now he was a Samaritan. Then Jesus answered, "Were not ten cleansed? Where are the nine? Was no one found to return and give praise to God except this foreigner?"

Luke 22:50–51 (ESV)

And one of them struck the servant of the high priest and cut off his right ear. But Jesus said, "No more of this!" And he touched his ear and healed him.

John 9:1–11 (ESV)

As he passed by, he saw a man blind from birth. And his disciples asked him, "Rabbi, who sinned, this man or his parents, that he was born blind?" Jesus answered, "It was not that this man sinned, or his parents, but that the works of God might be displayed in him. We must work the works of him who sent me while it is day; night is coming, when no one can work. As long as I am in the world, I am the light of the world." Having said these things, he spat on the ground and made mud with the saliva. Then he anointed the man's eyes with the mud and said to him, "Go, wash in the pool of Siloam" (which means Sent). So he went and washed and came back seeing.

Other accounts of Christ's healing ministry can be found in Matthew 4:23–25; Matthew 9:35; Matthew 10:1; Matthew 10:5–8; Matthew 11:5; Matthew 15:21–28; Matthew 20:29–34; Matthew 21:14; Mark 1:33–34; Mark 1:40–42; Mark 5:25–34; Luke 6:17–19.

PD-art

The Good Samaritan, by Rembrandt. *The religious leaders passed the robbed and beaten victim on the side of the road, carefully averting their eyes in order to not see the suffering and the need. A Samaritan, an outcast among the Jews, was the only person with the compassion to stop and aid the man. Western Christians are carefully averting their eyes from much suffering and need all about them and are diligent in finding rationales why they should expend resources in time, energy and money elsewhere.*

HEALING OF THE MIND AND EMOTIONS

As a lawyer coping with the problems of human behavior and relationships common to our increasingly dysfunctional culture, the value of mental health professionals and trained counselors, whether psychiatrists, clinical psychologists, or masters-level therapists and nurses has become increasingly evident. This training, when merged with a mature faith and an experienced, wise outlook on life and human nature, produces an asset of inestimable value for relieving suffering and saving not only relationships but sometimes lives. This is a point of great need and opportunity for service that is not being exploited by the church in the West to any significant degree. As with education, the church could become a dominant institution in our culture for providing these therapeutic services. Churches in every community should make it a priority of their ministries to provide Christian counseling, psychological, and therapeutic services, either as individual churches, or in collective efforts.

But individuals with this combination of attributes are rare, and just finding, much less recruiting, such professionals will continue to be difficult until churches and Christian universities emphasize training them. Skilled and wise therapists cannot be produced in less than ten years from the inception of their university education, and even that is optimistic because this professional role, more than most, demands not only a high level of training but an equally high level of spiritual and personal maturity, none of which come easily or quickly.

Biblical references to Christ's ministry in this area of human experience include the following:

Luke 6:17–19 (ESV)

And he came down with them and stood on a level place, with a great crowd of his disciples and a great multitude of people from all Judea and Jerusalem and the seacoast of Tyre and Sidon, who came to hear him and to be healed of their diseases. And those who were troubled with unclean spirits were cured. And all the crowd sought to touch him, for power came out from him and healed them all.

Luke 8:27–32 (ESV)

When Jesus had stepped out on land, there met him a man from the city who had demons. For a long time he had worn no clothes, and he had not lived in a house but among the tombs. When he saw Jesus, he cried out and fell down before him and said with a loud voice, "What have you to do with me, Jesus, Son of the Most High God? I beg you, do not torment me." For he had commanded the unclean spirit to come out of the man. (For many a time it had seized him. He was kept under guard and bound with chains and shackles, but he would break the bonds and be driven by the demon into the desert.) Jesus then asked him, "What is your name?" And he said, "Legion," for many demons had entered him. And they begged him not to command them to depart into the abyss. Now a large herd of pigs was feeding there on the hillside, and they begged him to let them enter these. So he gave them permission.

MINISTRY TO CHILDREN

Children are the most vulnerable in any culture but all the more so in a decaying and dysfunctional culture. Millions of children are either born into, or raised in, one-parent homes, or have no parents, or survive in homes dominated by emotionally unstable, immature, addicted, or mentally or physically ill adults. The damage done to fragile emotions and malleable young personalities is incalculable. The unwillingness to see and come to grips with this in Western culture is, in itself, compelling evidence of the decline of our civilization.

Shortly after law school I took a position as an attorney for the state of Tennessee. One of my primary duties was to take legal action to protect children who were neglected, abused, or sexually molested. The confrontation with reality was shocking. The shock was trebled by the realization that this was neither that rare nor limited to certain social subcultures. It affected every stratum of life.

To that point I would have said that I understood that some children were not loved. But I truly only understood that as an abstract concept that is, unfortunately, the way most of us understand the hard realities of life. Soon I understood it on a deep and visceral level, the level of reality, like someone who once declared, "Yes, people die in war," but who had no idea whereof they spoke until they saw their friends atomized by artillery or screaming in agony as they died on a battlefield.

My first-hand experience with these tragedies is one of the reasons I give no credibility to those who try to argue that our culture is fundamentally sound. No culture with these features is anything other than pathologically ill. The refusal or inability to see this is evidence in and of itself of the illness.

The church could have a direct role in addressing these circumstances, becoming a bastion of hope for generations of children to come.

Following are references to Christ's ministry specifically to children:

Mark 10:13–16 (NIV)

People were bringing little children to Jesus to have him touch them, but the disciples rebuked them. When Jesus saw this, he was indignant. He said to them, "Let the little children come to me, and do not hinder them, for the kingdom of God belongs to such as these. I tell you the truth, anyone who will not receive the kingdom of God like a little child will never enter it." And he took the children in his arms, put his hands on them and blessed them.

Luke 9:47–48 (NIV)

Jesus, knowing their thoughts, took a little child and had him stand beside him. Then he said to them, "Whoever welcomes this little child in my name welcomes me; and whoever welcomes me welcomes the one who sent me."

Other illustrations of Christ's ministry to children include Matthew 19:13–15; Mark 9:36–37; Luke 18:15–17.

MINISTRY TO THE POOR AND NEEDY

Matthew 14:16–21 (ESV)

But Jesus said, "They need not go away; you give them something to eat." They said to him, "We have only five loaves here and two fish." And he said, "Bring them here to me." Then he ordered the crowds to sit down on the grass, and taking the five loaves and the two fish, he looked up to heaven and said a blessing. Then he broke the loaves and gave them to the disciples, and the disciples gave them to the crowds. And they all ate and were satisfied. And they took up twelve baskets full of the broken pieces left over. And those who ate were about five thousand men, besides women and children.

Matthew 15:32–38 (ESV)

Then Jesus called his disciples to him and said, "I have compassion on the crowd because they have been with me now three days and have nothing to eat. And I am unwilling to send them away hungry, lest they faint on the way." And the disciples said to him, "Where are we to get enough bread in such a desolate place to feed so great a crowd?" And Jesus said to them, "How many loaves do you have?" They said, "Seven, and a few small fish." And directing the crowd to sit down on the ground, he took the seven loaves and the fish, and having given thanks he broke them and gave them to the disciples, and the disciples gave them to the crowds. And they all ate and were satisfied. And they took up seven baskets full of the broken pieces left over. Those who ate were four thousand men, besides women and children.

Matthew 19:21 (NIV)

Jesus answered, "If you want to be perfect, go, sell your possessions and give to the poor, and you will have treasure in heaven. Then come, follow me."

MINISTRY TO OUTCASTS AND FOREIGNERS

Matthew 9:10–13 (NIV)

And as Jesus reclined at table in the house, behold, many tax collectors and sinners came and were reclining with Jesus and his disciples. And when the Pharisees saw this, they said to his disciples, "Why does your teacher eat with tax collectors and sinners?" But when he heard it, he said, "Those who are well have no need of a physician, but those who are sick. Go and learn what this means, 'I desire mercy, and not sacrifice.' For I came not to call the righteous, but sinners."

Matthew 22:1–10 (NIV)

Jesus spoke to them again in parables, saying: "The kingdom of heaven is like a king who prepared a wedding banquet for his son. He sent his servants to those who had been invited to the banquet to tell them to come, but they refused to come. "Then he sent some more servants and said, 'Tell those who have been invited that I have prepared my dinner: My oxen and fattened cattle have been butchered, and everything is ready. Come to the wedding banquet.' But they paid no attention and went off—one to his field, another to his business. The rest seized his servants, mistreated them and killed them.

"The king was enraged. He sent his army and destroyed those murderers and burned their city. Then he said to his servants, 'The wedding banquet is ready, but those I invited did not deserve to come. Go to the street corners and invite to the banquet anyone you find.'

"So the servants went out into the streets and gathered all the people they could find, both good and bad, and the wedding hall was filled with guests."

John 4:7–15 (NIV)

A woman from Samaria came to draw water. Jesus said to her, "Give me a drink." (For his disciples had gone away into the city to buy food.) The Samaritan woman said to him, "How is it that you, a Jew, ask for a drink from me, a woman of Samaria?" (For Jews have no dealings with Samaritans.) Jesus answered her, "If you knew the gift of God, and who it is that is saying to you, 'Give me a drink,' you would have asked him, and he would have given you living water." The woman said to him, "Sir, you have nothing to draw water with, and the well is deep. Where do you get that living water? Are you greater than our father Jacob? He gave us the well and drank from it himself, as did his sons and his livestock." Jesus said to her, "Everyone who drinks of this water will be thirsty again, but whoever drinks of the water that I will give him will never be thirsty again. The water that I will give him will become in him a spring of water welling up to eternal life." The woman said to him, "Sir, give me this water, so that I will not be thirsty or have to come here to draw water."

Further illustrations of Christ's ministry to outcasts and foreigners can be found at Matthew 25: 35–40.

MINISTRY TO THE WEARY AND OPPRESSED

Matthew 11:28–30 (NIV)

"Come to me, all you who are weary and burdened, and I will give you rest. Take my yoke upon you and learn from me, for I am gentle and humble in heart, and you will find rest for your souls. For my yoke is easy and my burden is light."

CHURCH DISCIPLINE

But now I am writing you that you must not associate with anyone who calls himself a brother but is sexually immoral or greedy, an idolater or a slanderer, a drunkard or a swindler. With such a man do not even eat.
1 Corinthians 5:11 (NIV)

The failure to practice church discipline as taught in the New Testament is yet another illustration of the Western church's straying from the model given. This has vastly contributed to the weakening of churches both in the internal integrity and cohesion of the church and the external example. Though it is certainly true that churches are "hospitals for sinners, not museums for saints" this worn cliché does not address the point. The church must stand for morality and its own professed beliefs. When it does not, it betrays both. Significantly, St. Paul never minced words or actions when addressing breaches of morality within the church.

> It is actually reported that there is sexual immorality among you, and of a kind that does not occur even among pagans: A man has his father's wife. And you are proud! Shouldn't you rather have been filled with grief and have put out of your fellowship the man who did this?... [H]and this man over to Satan, so that the sinful nature may be destroyed and his spirit saved on the day of the Lord.... I have written you in my letter not to associate with sexually immoral people—not at all meaning the people of this world who are immoral, or the greedy and swindlers, or idolaters. In that case you would have to leave this world. But now I am writing you that you must not associate with anyone who calls himself a brother but is sexually immoral or greedy, an idolater or a slanderer, a drunkard or a swindler. With such a man do not even eat. What business is it of mine to judge those outside the church? Are you not to judge those inside? God will judge those outside. Expel the wicked man from among you. (1 Corinthians 5:1–13 NIV)

The New Testament contains many lessons of church discipline. It is there, if the modern Western church will heed. When sin is allowed to characterize the church, like a cancer it will metastasize.

MAKE PEACE WHENEVER POSSIBLE

Blessed are the peacemakers, for they will be called the sons of God.
Matthew 5:9 (NIV)

Churches and Christians are frequently drawn into the legal arena and deal with their conflicts through secular methods and with anything but Christian attitudes. This contravenes St. Paul's teaching: "If any of you has a dispute with another, dare he take it before the ungodly for judgment instead of before the saints?...but instead one brother goes to law against another—and this in front of unbelievers! The very fact that you have lawsuits among you means you have been completely defeated already." (1 Corinthians 6:1, 6–7 NIV) A similar theme is found in the Old Testament: "What you have seen with your eyes, do not bring hastily into court, for what will you do in the end if your neighbor puts you to shame?" (Proverbs 25:7–8 NIV) Yet, as a lawyer, I have repeatedly watched—even as I advised against it—individual Christians, churches, and Christian institutions violating these principles. Many react with surprise that an American trial lawyer would tell them to stay out of the courts. Yet pastors and parishioners reveal their capitulation to the culture by turning in that direction, despite the biblical prohibitions.

I can tell you from much experience, "resolving" conflict through the courts often exacerbates the relational aspects of conflict and makes its consequences worse. Western legal systems function on the premise that justice is accomplished through adversarial proceedings pitting one party against the other in what amounts to more conflict, albeit regulated by prescribed procedures. This approach not only often aggravates the conflict but also contributes to emotional wounding. The reality goes unnoticed—the adversarial system is only one short logical and historical step removed from trial by combat as a method for achieving "justice." The legal system is complex but not sophisticated, competitive rather than relational, more palliative than curative. Above all, the adversarial legal system is the worst system for dealing with disputes among family members and conflicts among Christians and Christian institutions.

When conflicts arise, particularly if they are intense enough to lead to legal action, anyone involved would be wise to consider peaceful methods of resolving their dispute or at least methods that would allow them to avoid the courts. On the practical plane alone, the legal system, at least in America, is needlessly complex, extravagantly expensive, ponderously slow, and unnervingly stressful. When these factors are coupled with the biblical teaching, the arguments for finding a "better way" are overwhelming.

However, the church typically provides no means, no method or process by which disputes could be settled outside the courts. Here again, the church defers to the culture rather than setting the pace for society. There are other options. The church throughout Western civilization should exploit them and become known as *the place* to go when justice and peace are sought.

There are forms of professional practice designed to help people reach resolutions of disputes without resort to the courts, an approach known as Alternative Dispute Resolution or ADR. ADR techniques should be the first option considered by Christians involved in conflict. Among these, mediation is certainly the preferable method for dealing with conflict related to the family and church. Another form of ADR, arbitration, is closely related to the legal process. Yet it is faster, cheaper, more informal and usually less hostile. All churches' bylaws should contain a provision that any dispute among members should be resolved by mediation, and in the event that does not succeed, by church-sponsored and -managed arbitration.

Resort to the courts should be avoided by all means available. This may in part sound like a call for a return to ecclesiastical courts—and something similar should be seriously considered for limited purposes—but it certainly is a call for the church to be instrumental not only in encouraging non-litigious ways of resolving conflicts but in actually training the professionals who can provide such services. Few ministries could have as sweeping effect on our culture as offering peaceful, non-litigious ways by which differences can be settled.

PRISON MINISTRY AND PRISON REFORM

The quality of mercy is not strained.
It droppeth as the gentle rain from heaven
Upon the place beneath. It is twice blest:
It blesseth him that gives and him that takes.
'Tis mightiest in the mightiest; it becomes
The throned monarch better than his crown.
His sceptre shows the force of temporal power,
The attribute to awe and majesty,
Wherein doth sit the dread and fear of kings.
But mercy is above this sceptred sway;
It is enthroned in the hearts of kings;
It is an attribute to God himself;
And earthly power doth then show likest God's
When mercy seasons justice.

William Shakespeare, *The Merchant of Venice*

The United States has the highest imprisonment rate in the world, according to one study by the Research, Development and Statistics Directorate of the Home Office of Great Britain: 686 people per 100,000 population. The U.S. Department of Justice figures for 2007 indicate 2,299,116 prisoners were held in federal or state prisons or in local jails. Those same studies show "there were an estimated 509 sentenced prisoners per 100,000 U.S. residents—up from 501 at year end 2006." Regardless of which estimate is closest to the mark, the figures are stunning. But this is only the tip of the iceberg. The report adds, "An estimated 60,500 inmates (or 4.5% of all State and Federal inmates) experienced one or more incidents of sexual victimization involving other inmates or staff." The report continued, "At year end 2005, an estimated 18,953 males and 1,935 females in State prisons were HIV-infected or had confirmed AIDS." We will not attempt to get into speculation about unreported sexual offenses and unreported violence, which any discerning person could readily assume are much more common than the reported cases suggest. Nor do these figures reflect suicides.

To say that American prisons are snake pits is to slander the serpent. These universities of evil continually bestow advanced degrees in debased thought and sinister skills. The most depraved of human behavior runs rampant in these "classrooms" and among the members of their respective "fraternities" and "sororities." Students—some of whom may be reluctant to participate in the "educational" process—are victims, not simply of the justice system in its clumsy, inept zeal to punish the guilty but of the callousness of a society that shallowly perceives solutions to crime in longer prison sentences under the most debased conditions.

The quality of mercy is not strained for many American Christians in this realm of thought—or abdication of thought—it is extinguished. Nor will it be "twice blest," for though it has dropped "as the gentle rain from heaven" upon every Christian, so many American Christians see no need and feel no impulse to give it, even as they readily partake of it.

The majority of the inmates of prisons and jails have not simply victimized others, sometimes repeatedly and often viciously, but are often themselves victims, most often of child abuse and sometimes other forms of maltreatment, not the least of which is simply not being loved. Centuries before the modern disciplines of psychology and sociology, Shakespeare, through the voices of the two murderers in *Macbeth*, displayed remarkable insight into the significance of this in any human being's life.

Second Murderer: I am one, my liege,
Whom the vile blows and buffets of the world
Have so incensed that I am reckless what
I do to spite the world.
First Murderer: And I another
So weary with disasters, tugg'd with fortune,
That I would set my lie on any chance
To mend it or be rid on't.

Be advised, my urgings here are not founded on the typical limp-wristed, vapid assertions about "victimization" that have so often characterized some in the West. Nor does the awareness and sensitivity I call for in any way excuse the criminal's behavior. It certainly does not relieve him of accountability. But a measure of our own willingness to honor the example of Christ will be found in how much we strive to understand the malformed in our culture and display some sensitivity to them.

No nation that considers itself just—much less moral, and even less so Christian—can

To say that American prisons are snake pits is to slander the serpent. These universities of evil continually bestow advanced degrees in debased thought and sinister skills. The most depraved of human behavior runs rampant in these "classrooms" and among the members of their respective "fraternities" and "sororities." Students—some of whom may be reluctant to participate in the "educational" process—are victims, not simply of the justice system in its clumsy, inept zeal to punish the guilty but of the callousness of a society that shallowly perceives solutions to crime in longer prison sentences under the most debased conditions. No nation that considers itself just—much less moral, and even less so Christian—can justify the conditions that exist in American prisons. We may choose to almost literally "lock 'em up and throw away the key," rationalizing our behavior and our attitudes by reference to their crimes. But the choice to show no mercy will be revisited upon us and our children, and our children's children, as it surely already has now for generations—and will be cause for accountability before God.

Photo by Lou Oates (C) used by permission

justify the conditions that exist in American prisons. We may choose to almost literally "lock 'em up and throw away the key," rationalizing our behavior and our attitudes by reference to their crimes. But the choice to show no mercy will be revisited upon us and our children, and our children's children, as it surely already has now for generations—and will be cause for accountability before God.

NO EXCUSES, NO COMPROMISE, NO FEAR—JUST ACTION

The breadth, depth and scope of Christ's teachings and demonstrations of love for mankind leave no room for excuse by the modern Western church. There is nothing in the New Testament implying that Christians should look to government or secular entities to meet any of these human needs.

To the extent that resources limit them, churches can nonetheless serve in two ways: First, by selecting one or two needs for which to provide special service—a concentrated focus for their community. Each church can become known for its own ministry specialty or specialties, something that perhaps it and it alone in that community does.

Second, churches across denominational lines should pool their resources in joint efforts to provide specific ministries for their community. Their goal: to be the place where everyone in that community may go to receive help for specific needs. Churches should be using resources, not for themselves, but to provide Christian counseling, save marriages and families, see that the physically and mentally sick receive care, and that the poor are never left homeless or destitute. They should be striving to prevent aborticide, child abuse, drug and alcohol abuse, and offering solace and refuge to the abandoned and the lonely. Paramount above all, they should demonstrate through sincere, loving service that there is a God who loves them, and through Him there is hope.

END NOTES
CHAPTER 36

1 St. Francis of Assisi, cited in David W. Augsburger, *Dissident Discipleship: A Spirituality of Self-Surrender, Love of God, and Love of Neighbor* (Grand Rapids, MI: Brazos Press, 2006), 171.

2 C. T. Studd, cited in John Barnett, *Discipline Yourself for Godliness: The Power of a Word Filled Life* (Tulsa, OK: BFM Books, 2004), 70.

3 *Patton* (film), directed by Franklin J. Schaffner (Hollywood, CA: 20th Century Fox Entertainment, 1970).

4 Pitirim A. Sorokin, *The Crisis of Our Age* (Oneworld Publications Ltd., 1941; this edition Sergei P. Sorokin and Peter P. Sorokin, 1992), 261.

5 Christopher Dawson, *The Historic Reality of Christian Culture* (New York: Harper & Brothers, 1960), 20.

6 Francis A. Schaeffer, *How Should We Then Live? The Rise and Decline of Western Thought and Culture* (Wheaton, IL: Crossway Books, 1976), 256.

7 Ruth Bell Graham, "Our Old Home," *Decision* (Charlotte, NC: Billy Graham Evangelistic Association, 2007).

8 Christopher Dawson, *Christianity and the New Age* (Manchester, NH: Sophia Institute Press, 1985), xv.

9 Norman Percy Grubb, *C. T. Studd, Athlete and Pioneer* (Atlantic City, NJ: World-Wide Revival Prayer Movement, 1947), 170.

CHAPTER

37

FIGHTING PYRRHIC BATTLES AT POINTS OF LITTLE STRATEGIC CONSEQUENCE

I'd driven with every ounce of energy in my body to do the things in government that I believed might make people's lives better. But in all that time, I could not point to one single person, not one life, that had actually been changed for the better.
Charles Colson[1]

...the spiritual man is at a disadvantage in the world of politics and business. The eyes that have looked upon the sun can no longer distinguish the shadows of the cave. The man who cares only for eternal things, who seeks to fly hence and to become assimilated to God by holiness and justice and wisdom, is unable to strive for political power with the mean cunning of the ordinary "man of affairs."
Dawson, quoting Plato[2]

Ere I had learnt that the world was a welter of futile doing...
Thomas Hardy[3]

Paradoxical" may seem the only appropriate adjective for much of what is said here about Christians and their involvement in politics, government, and law. This will seem all the more so when uttered by someone who has spent years as a trial lawyer, who was active in politics both behind the scenes and as a candidate, and who repeatedly called fellow Christians to their duty in these realms. But it is precisely because of these experiences that a challenge will be made to the mindset that anything of great consequence and lasting spiritual import will come from it. The issue is not passivity versus bold action, but rather insight and perspective on the nature of the battle, the terrain, and the appropriate weapons. So, before we go further—and lest there be a misunderstanding—a clarification is in order.

Charles de Gaulle displayed his passionate interest in military matters and leadership in a 1932 autobiography with the memorable title *Le Fil de l'Epée (The Edge of the Sword).* That title should be *apropos* for the Christian church in the West. Every Christian should strive to be the edge of the sword, the tip of the spear. Nor should an inch ever be conceded to the enemy or the Christian ever be on the defensive. The famous military maxim attributed to Frederick the Great is applicable to the Christian life: *"L'audace, L'audace, Toujours L'audace"* ("Audacity, Audacity, Always Audacity").

THE TRUE OBJECT OF PERSUASION

"...if Christianity is true, then the individual is not only more important but incomparably more important, for he is everlasting and the life of a state or a civilization, compared with his, is only a moment."
C. S. Lewis[4]

Where, when, and how a Christian should be boldly on the offensive is a critical strategic issue. To grasp the answer, the Christian must first understand the Divine perspective as reflected in the Bible. Seen this way, it becomes immediately apparent that the teachings and ministry of Christ were focused on the individual, not the culture at large.

The culture at large is changed not from the top down through government, ideology, and law, but from the bottom up through radical changes in the individual human heart.

C. S. Lewis in *Mere Christianity* clarified what should be a Christian's priorities in an insightful passage that put the lie to the notion that any state, any government, any ideology, any laws, or even an entire civilization, is of great importance relative to the individual. "If individuals live only seventy years, then a state, or a nation, or a civilization, which may last a thousand years, is more important than an individual. But if Christianity is true, then the individual is not only more important but incomparably more important, for he is everlasting and the life of a state or a civilization, compared with his, is only a moment."[5] So much for the specious notions closely held for generations in the West of man carrying forward his ideas, his philosophies, his ideologies to the secular nirvanas, Valhallas, utopias—or whatever he conceives as the ultimate states of society and mankind.

The ultimate, transcendent value of the individual is a uniquely Christian concept, one of those fundamental beliefs that underpin Western civilization and make it unlike any other. Recognition of this great truth dramatically reorders a Christian's view of life and what is truly meaningful. We will recall that Toynbee shared the essential truth in Lewis's declaration, "...this treatment of the individual as a mere part of the community is a denial of the personal relation

C. S. Lewis from *LIFE* magazine.

C. S. Lewis *declared, "If individuals live only seventy years, then a state, or a nation, or a civilization, which may last a thousand years, is more important than an individual. But if Christianity is true, then the individual is not only more important but incomparably more important, for he is everlasting and the life of a state or a civilization, compared with his, is only a moment." The individual's value is a uniquely Christian concept that makes Western civilization unlike any other.*

between the soul and God and is a substitution, for the worship of God, of a worship of the human community—Leviathan, the abomination of desolation, standing in the place where it ought not...."[6]

The Watergate defendant and Christian victor Charles Colson came belatedly to a recognition that many Christians in the West have not yet achieved, surfeited as they are with notions of political power: "For eleven years of my life I'd driven with every ounce of energy in my body to do the things in government that I believed might make people's lives better. But in all that time, I could not point to one single person, not one life, that had actually been changed for the better."[7]

In this man's humble confession not only do we see the dawning of a new and greater reality, we find another implicit suggestion of the infiltration of the world's values and views into the church, for though Colson was not a Christian at the time of his supreme efforts to "make people's lives better" through government and law, many Christians pursue this same goal with alacrity, never recognizing the speciousness of their undertaking or its marked drift from the teachings and model of Christ. In time they become more and more enamored with power; the centripetal forces of politics and government pull them into their orbit rather than they pulling that world into Christ's orbit. This result is inevitable, because these are not the tools, weapons, and strategies that Christ taught and modeled for changing our world; they are human, purely so, often abasedly so.

True faith changes morality by changing the individual human heart. This—and this alone—is the only change that ultimately matters. Change through government, law, and politics is at best ancillary, never primary; it is superficial rather than deep. The failure to grasp this truth unreservedly is the mistake many Christians have made when seeing answers for our civilization in politics, government, and law.

Charles Colson. PD-gov

The Watergate defendant and Christian victor Charles Colson *came belatedly to a recognition that many Christians in the West have not yet achieved, surfeited as they are with notions of political power: "For eleven years of my life I'd driven with every ounce of energy in my body to do the things in government that I believed might make people's lives better. But in all that time, I could not point to one single person, not one life that had actually been changed for the better." In this man's humble confession not only do we see the dawning of a new and greater reality, we find another implicit suggestion of the infiltration of the world's values and views into the church, for—though Colson was not a Christian at the time of his supreme efforts to "make people's lives better" through government and law—many Christians pursue this same goal with alacrity, never recognizing the ultimate speciousness of their undertaking or its marked drift from the teachings and model of Christ. In time they become more and more enamored with power; the centripetal forces of politics and government pull them into their orbit rather than they pulling that world into Christ's orbit. This result is inevitable, because these are not the tools, weapons, and strategies that Christ taught and modeled for changing our world; they are human, purely so, often abasedly so.*

The folly of this approach is abetted by naïveté, itself fostered by a failure to understand the true nature of power and the instruments ruthlessly and deceitfully deployed to gain and sustain it.

Taken on the tide of man's innate vanity, pride, and lust to dominate others, this faulty compass heading carries the unsuspecting Christian off the edge of spiritual cartography and into regions intended for the primal creature—man-without-faith, man-as-his-own-god, man-doomed-to-a-monotonous-repetition-of-his-debased-history. There the professing Christian must adapt if he is to survive—much less gain any degree of dominance in the jungle—and his adaptation will threaten to destroy that which he professes to uphold within himself.

THE TRUE NATURE OF POWER

...unholy alliances between naked power and "true" religion...
only go to prove the utter subservience of religion to the state.
R. C. Zaehner[8]

The forms of power that are recognized as such and accorded any standing in Western civilization are almost exclusively political and economic. Political power, as we use the term here, does not mean solely that which relates to government and law, but the ability to influence large numbers of people. Hence many media, entertainment, and sports figures, and some religious figures, have political power. The Geiger counter of political power can most clearly detect its radiation by the efforts of politicians to become associated with these figures. The coziness the American church has felt with politics and government was illustrated perhaps most conspicuously in our time by the relationship between Billy Graham and Richard Nixon, a relationship that led ultimately to the exploitation of Dr. Graham and his belated recognition—especially upon release of the Watergate tapes—of the ruthlessness of those who seek power.

An acknowledgment of this harsh reality can be found in the foreword by R. C. Zaehner to Christopher Dawson's work *Religion and World History*: "...unholy alliances between naked power (Realpolitik, if you like) and 'true' religion...only go to prove the utter subservience of religion to the state." He then added, "...Christians are drawing together as they have never done before, but that is scarcely surprising since, by the mere fact of being 'a thing of the past'—a 'righteous remnant,' if you like—they have little choice but to stand or fall together."[9]

In the former point, the subservience of religion in the West to the state, the writer is largely correct. But on the latter point, as we see in another chapter, his conclusion seems anticipatory rather than objective; it is falsely optimistic and entirely too "logical" in what he expects Christians will do. Christians still find ways—despite the extraordinary and growing adversity facing them—of neither standing nor falling together. Unity is neither present, nor a foregone conclusion for the future. Phrases like "unholy alliance" and "utter subservience" may seem harsh, particularly if they are not seen as intended. I believe the Christian church in the West has deferred to the state, cooperated with the state, and sometimes praised the state when none of this is appropriate, wise, or biblical.

The church must stand above the state, not in a haughty, prideful, or legally more powerful fashion, but with the implicit recognition that the church is God's instrument on earth and as such it is undertaking a task and fulfilling a duty that is both sanctified and transcendent above all other human endeavors no matter how imposing. By comparison with the gravitas of the church, the state is neither consequential, nor eternal, nor to be venerated.

Throughout the West, delusions are fostered and nurtured that pander to the interests of those with power and serve to manipulate those without it. Truly critical political decisions are made by a relative handful of intellectually bright, ruthlessly ambitious individuals in concert with the centers of wealth in the respective societies. Everything and everyone beneath them become simply tools or instruments by which they implement their will. In the early twentieth century, Oswald Spengler described the concealed reality: "…the great political parties nevertheless cease to be more than reputed centres of decision. A small number of superior heads, whose names are very likely not the best-known, settle everything, while below them are the great mass of second-rate politicians—rhetors, tribunes, deputies, journalists—selected through a provincially conceived franchise to keep alive the illusion of popular self-determination."[10] Though this may strike the idealistic (naïve?) as entirely too cynical and impossible—an attitude more likely to exist among Americans than Europeans—it is far closer to the truth than most would ever imagine.

Nothing has changed since Spengler's time; indeed, it has only worsened. But the greater danger for the church is the failure of Christians to see and fully comprehend. The truly powerful are not typically conspicuous, nor are they vociferous in the way that most would assume power manifests itself. They are extraordinarily pragmatic in a purely cynical way: that which gets the results we want is what we will do. But of course they invariably dress their initiatives in habiliments that would be attractive to those beneath them—especially the political *hoi polloi*, the "cannon fodder" if you will, of political struggle. They are, as Immanuel Wallerstein described them, in a word—"Machiavellian." Yet their exercise of power is typically subtle: "They know that their ability to use force in the future usually is diminished by the very process of actually using it in the present, and they are therefore quite sparing and prudent in such use."[11]

The deceitfulness, ruthlessness, and manipulativeness of those who seek power are often obvious to those inoculated to power's charms—having perhaps gazed upon its monstrous true visage—but completely lost on those enamored with its glories. There has for some time in America existed a political marriage—discreetly morganatic in the eyes of the political powers that be—between conservative political ideologues, particularly in the Republican Party, and conservative Christians. The former are primarily interested in power for power's sake and the ascendancy of fiscally conservative policies that, in one way or another, protect and enhance their wealth; the latter are focused on moral issues, particularly as expressed in social policy. That this alliance should not exist should go without saying, but by now many of these Christians have been so completely co-opted and compromised they often do not even think about what they are doing, what they are being told—and its relative merits or truthfulness—much less what they should be doing.

Ironically, and perhaps appropriately, this alliance has brought relatively little benefit for the conservative Christians while it has strengthened the secular conservatives in the Republican Party. In the words of British sociologist Steve Bruce, "For all the noise it generated," the conservative Christian political movement has "failed to achieve any of its specific goals. Rather, it has merely reinforced the secular conservative wing of the Republican Party but it has not reduced the number of abortions, cut the proportion of mothers working outside the home, restored male hegemony, made divorce more difficult, put religious ceremonies back into state schools, required biology classes to teach 'creation science,' or forced homosexuals back into the closet."[12]

ARC Identifier 194597

Nixon's farewell to his cabinet and members of the White House staff, 9 August 1974. *The deceitfulness, ruthlessness, and manipulativeness of those who seek power are often obvious to those inoculated to power's charms—having perhaps gazed upon its monstrous true visage—but completely lost on those enamored with its glories. There has, for example, for some time in America, existed a political marriage—discreetly morganatic in the eyes of the political powers that be—between conservative political ideologues, particularly in the Republican Party, and conservative Christians. The former are primarily interested in power for power's sake and the ascendancy of fiscally conservative policies that, in one way or another, protect and enhance their wealth; the latter are focused on moral issues, particularly as expressed in social policy. The former's true objectives are inconsistent with the latter's social issue agenda, of which they are, in truth, disdainful. That this alliance should not exist should go without saying, but by now many of these Christians have been so completely co-opted and compromised they often do not even think about what they are doing, what they are being told—and its relative merits or truthfulness—much less what they should be doing.*

Bruce further observed, "The legislative record parallels the electoral one: initial success in small arenas followed by defeat in larger ones. Despite conservative Republican influence in Congress in the last two decades of the twentieth century, the [conservative Christian political movement] has signally failed to make progress on its agenda. Many legislators find it advantageous to make supportive noises but then fail to commit their political capital to the cause."[13] But even should conservative Christian political groups achieve in whole or in part any of these goals, that does not nullify the truth: This is not where the war will be won, for it is not where the battles are to be fought.

One noteworthy illustration in American politics of the co-opting of Christians by the secular right is the many conservative Christians who have kept their distance from the ecological movement—or even displayed overt hostility toward it—sometimes because they profess to detect a pantheistic tenor in that movement's thinking and actions. There is some evidence to support that criticism, and, insofar as such attitudes and views exist, they must be rejected by Christians. Christians worship the Creator, not the creation.

But such concerns should not result in abdication of our moral duty to stand against the exploitation, waste, pollution, or degradation of our environment and natural resources. These should be viewed honestly for what they are: illustrations of the selfishness of man, indifference to the well-being of others, greed, and defiance of God's moral law, defiance that is condemned throughout the Bible. Thus, unholy political alliances are formed that lead the Christian away from God's law and toward man's methods in the quest for temporal power.

This kind of prejudice and propaganda can be another barrier between Christians and the larger society. It appears to the observer to pander to self-centered powerful interests on the one hand, and seems primitively backward on the other. We already observed how alliances between the church and powerful vested interests eventually undermined the church and its credibility in European societies. A similar process is afoot here.

Ignoring, or even disputing, the evidence of ecological and environmental degradation is a form of recklessness and self-centeredness by the right—a practice that may lie heavily on the shoulders of those professing Christians as future generations, their own children and grandchildren, bear the brunt of these choices. Responsibility and concern for future generations dictates that we be willing to consider the evidence, recognizing that were we to err in one direction the consequences would be expensive and dislocating to society, but if we err in the other direction the consequences will be catastrophic for all mankind. Leftists, being—as they are—children of the Enlightenment, are alarmed at the prospect of environmental degradation. Their sense of reality (i.e., the material world—as perceived through science) is the only one to which they give ultimate validity and significance and is, in truth, all they know. That there is, and has been for generations, a spiritual and moral degradation of Western culture—a decay in which their complicity has been great—is lost on them despite that form of degradation's central role as the underlying cause of the material degradations of the environment. Man is where he is on this planet precisely because of his defiance of God's laws—moral and physical.

Politically active Christians commingle their political capital with that of their allies in a mutual quest for power and are often co-opted into supporting policies that, were they scrutinized closely, are at variance with Christian thought and values. This is most obvious in the areas of social justice, foreign policy, and concern for the environment. In like manner, there is a similar unholy alliance and exploitation of the church by the left and the Democratic Party—that seeks the direct involvement of African-American churches and their leaders, as well as more left-leaning denominations—in their efforts to gain and hold power.

For those incorrigible Christians who either will not see or refuse to heed—a form of idol-worship having crept stealthily into their hearts—a blunt caveat is in order. Be forewarned: those who oppose Christian values (whether they openly acknowledge that opposition or not) will fight especially vigorously against all efforts by Christians to assert their values in the political, legislative, or judicial arenas. To the extent Christians remain compliant, quiescent, or passive in these areas overt attacks will not be as prevalent or as vicious. But the human will-to-power will be the dynamic driving their reactions to all perceived "Christian" initiatives in these arenas. They will not feel as readily threatened when Christians advance their faith through other means, but here they will perceive a threat and respond accordingly.

Ironically, as a central theme of this book declares, the greater threat—and only real threat—to their dominance in the culture will come from Christians following, with fervent commitment, the model and teachings of Christ in the exercise of their faith. Yet, having the secular, materialist view of life and human experience, the power seekers will be guarding and looking to secure their position in other areas, especially the political, judicial, economic, entertainment, and media dimensions of Western society. Seen from the spiritual perspective, this is a serious strategic mistake—albeit one that many Christians in the West have been repeatedly making—and one that will ultimately ensure the defeat of all those whose values and view of life are worldly. We can safely surmise that the Creator of the Universe will be neither stymied nor frustrated in His ultimate goals, even if Christians abandon the field or collaborate with the enemy.

Any wielding of the sword of faith and the spear of morality that threatens these powers that be will result first in a cry of "foul"—uttered most infamously by the nineteenth-century English politician and twice prime minister Lord Melbourne, in opposition to William Wilberforce and his efforts to abolish the slave trade in Britain: "Things have come to a pretty pass when one should permit one's religion to invade public life."[14] Many of the political figures of our time—who would rush headlong to associate their names with Wilberforce's effort in that age—concurrently sound much like Melbourne in the political arenas of the West about "mixing religion and politics."

If the foolishness of this line of thought were not exposed by the historical record, it should be by any discerning analysis of human behavior. Everyone is driven by something, prioritizes by some standard, chooses values according to that which he believes has greatest merit; thus all is influenced by religion—or the absence thereof—in every realm of life.

To separate religion from political and public life is the logical equivalent of obtaining a paper divorce decree while continuing to not only cohabit with the erstwhile spouse but rear children with them as well. A pretense is present—but that is all, a pretense. Thus we see the smoke, mirrors, and Potemkin façades Western man has deployed in his world and that he no longer can—if he ever could—distinguish from reality.

Western politicians—at least those who make any claim to religiosity themselves—typically deal with this by the expedient of declaring, "Faith is a private matter."

Nineteenth-century British politician and prime minister Lord Melbourne, *in opposition to William Wilberforce's efforts to abolish the slave trade, complained, "Things have come to a pretty pass when one should permit one's religion to invade public life." Western politicians typically deal with the issue of religion by the expedient of declaring, "Faith is a private matter." No, when you become a public figure, your faith, or the lack thereof, is very much a public matter, for it will tell much about you.*

PD-art

the church's failure and the culture's decay bear upon one another God only knows, but the negative symbiosis is certain. This moral and religious deconstruction could take place only with the complicity, complacency, and cowardice of the church. We cannot say which is the greatest factor—even if that were now relevant—but in the way the church deals with the culture at large all three are in play.

To the extent the church does not acknowledge (a religious word would be more *apropos*, "confess") this regression and turn from it in self-sacrificing advocacy for Christ, it becomes the dupe, the gullible fool who is complicit in his own demise. The downward trajectory of the civilization will continue—the apogee for the West has long since been reached and passed—and further decline can be abated only by a turn to faith and the recognition of an immutable, transcendent Higher Law. Thus Christians who hitch their wagon to the star of political or legal power will eventually see their hopes and aspirations (even those that are noble and unselfish) crash and burn with it.

For American Christians in particular a reckoning is imminent. Lincoln observed, "A nation may be said to consist of its territory, its people and its laws. The territory is the only part which is of certain durability."[23] Many American Christians in particular—if they do not "worship" their country—are in love with an America that no longer exists to any significant degree and, to some extent, never was. They have not come to grips with the reality that Lincoln's observation suggests. Nor do they recognize fully how much their own culture and some of its major institutions are now in mortal conflict with the faith they espouse.

Western Christians truly are now closer to the catacombs than to the cathedral. Yet, for many, allegiances remain unwittingly divided. They continue to commingle their professed passion for Christ with their patriotism and produce a force that is neither one thing nor the other. Though useful to politicians, it is useless to Christ.

Ironically, the enthusiastically patriotic American Christian is at risk of helping to kill the object of his affections, America.

I have offered many speeches standing on podiums or behind pulpits with a Christian flag over one shoulder and an American flag over the other. Conscious as I was of the already significant conflicts between those two symbols, I have often felt dismay that my audience either did not perceive the choice that faced them or, having perceived it, chose nation over God—*de facto* if not expressly.

One's nation can be an idol supplanting God in one's affections and devotions. The devotee, thus compromised, is convinced of his goodness by virtue of his patriotism, never questioning the significance of the priorities he has embraced.

Christians must be conscious of where their true allegiances lie and why. Western democracies, including the United States, are moving ever more rapidly away from the earlier consensus that biblical principle is the ultimate authority. It seems hopelessly nostalgic to suggest this is still true even in a vestigial sense. The tyranny of the majority spoken of earlier is an increasing threat, and will inevitably surge forward like a massive barbarian horde so long as Western civilization stays its present course. The high-sounding phrases and pronouncements surrounding the word "democracy" will metamorphose into increasingly propagandistic casuistry used by politicians, judges, media, and various influence peddlers to support that which is neither free nor just.

With this collapse of the foundations of the culture there will always be power in some form, whether a titular democracy or not. An ever-amplifying desperation to maintain order in the decaying culture will require increasingly heavy-handed action by government. The choice Christians face—now more inchoate and subtle, by then obvious—will be between continued allegiance to the state—including obeisance to its laws no matter how at variance with transcendent moral law—or a courageous stand.

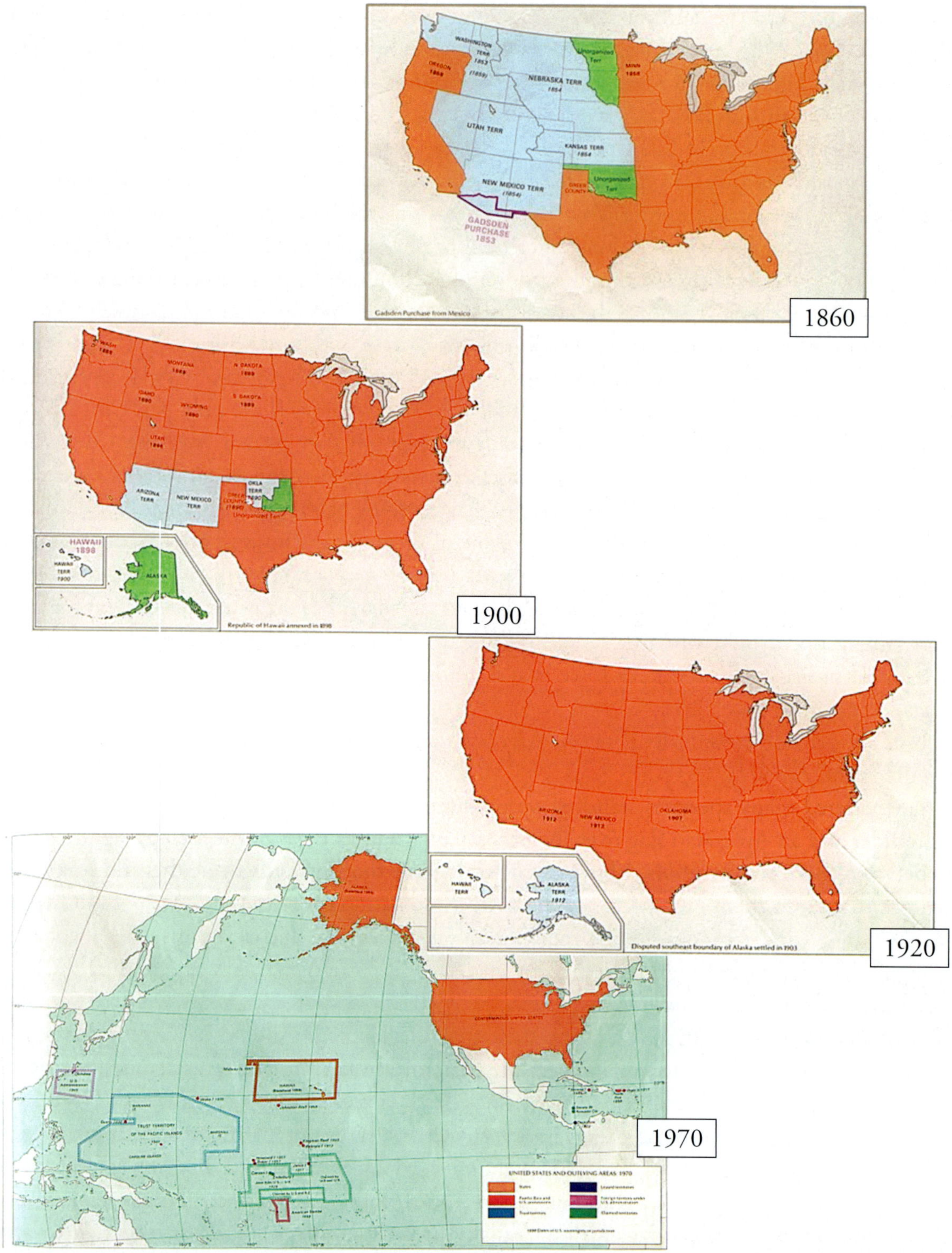

CC

These maps show the change in the boundaries of the American nation over the last two centuries. *But a far more important change has taken place over that period in the nature and character of the American people. Lincoln observed, "A nation may be said to consist of its territory, its people and its laws. The territory is the only part that is of certain durability." This distinction is critically important. We tend as Americans to speak of ourselves as part of the same people going back over two centuries. But we are not. America is an entirely new nation populated by a very different citizenry than, for example, during World War II.*

Christians' credibility—and by far their most powerful influence on a society and hence its government—is nurtured by allegiance to the teachings and model of Christ, not by allegiance to any particular nation, form of government, ideology, or party, no matter how attractive they may seem to dazzled eyes. Indeed, the greatest service—the most patriotic duty—Christians can perform for their nation is to fervently lift up Christ and God's transcendent moral law. This sacred duty will do more for a nation and a civilization than all of the combined legal, social, and political initiatives imaginable.

If the church lifts up Christ, He "will draw all men" to Him. If, instead, energies are focused on lifting up a government, a nation, a party, an ideology, or any form of governance, the church will fail—and ultimately will be betrayed in the process. Lincoln in a sense approached the importance of this distinction when he declared that he was not so much concerned with whether God was on his side, but with whether he was on God's side. Christians, in like manner, should understand the choices they must make in their allegiances. Wrapping ourselves in the flag of any nation—including the United States—is not synonymous with allegiance to Christ. Indeed, it can be a betrayal of our relationship with Christ.

The Old Testament prophet Jeremiah made the choice to defy the similarly ubiquitous strain of patriotism in his own nation in his own time in an appeal to the people to change course. A latter-day Jeremiah might fare no better than the original and face violent rejection from the church in the West—and a similar despair.

THE CHRISTIAN'S CHOICE

...the famous doctor Gamaliel is profoundly impressed by the striking contrast between the powerful moral resistance to persecution of Jesus' Apostles, and the sterile conventional militancy of the contemporary epigoni of Judas Maccabeus.
Arnold Toynbee[24]

There are what we might term varying degrees of obliviousness among Christians (i.e., the ones who did not hear or heed about being "clever as a serpent") who not only allow themselves to be manipulated by the forces we describe herein—especially those they perceive as supportive of their viewpoint—but who unwittingly, through their own actions in politics, government, the media, and the legal system, become collaborators in manipulation. To be sure, many are not so unwitting; they have succumbed to the temptation to themselves manipulate—and then rationalize it all by dint of the "virtue," "morality," or "righteousness" of their cause. The Devil himself has won the issue, but they do not see; and the ends have "justified" the means.

A conspicuous expression of this mindset—one that can readily be debunked, but there are others, far more subtle—was one heard repeatedly by this writer when once I ventured a misbegotten candidacy for the American Congress. The litany of rationale was always the same. In the face of many campaign decisions—some of which were of dubious merit—the reminder was trotted out: "To change anything you must get elected!" Never mind that the changes would first be to the candidate and his campaign; the question was never seriously asked: In that, what would we have achieved? In this experience I learned that a reasonably well-formed sense of right and wrong, truth and deceit, selflessness and selfishness, would always conflict with the methods and mores of the political arena.

Photo by Reverend Bobby Russ. Used by permission.

*Many speeches and sermons are made at podiums or pulpits with a Christian flag over the speaker's one shoulder and an American flag over the other. There are already significant conflicts between those two symbols, yet most of the time an audience either does not perceive the choice that faces them or, having perceived it, chooses nation over God—*de facto *if not expressly. The choice Christians increasingly face will be between continued allegiance to the state—including obeisance to its laws no matter how at variance with transcendent moral law—or a courageous stand.*

Having prepared myself beforehand for the ruthlessness and deceit I knew I would encounter in that setting, I could not readily be ambushed. But the shallowness that pervaded every nook and cranny of that arena and, with it, the superficiality of thought and perception—to refer to it as "smoke and mirrors" grants it a substance it does not deserve—were deeply disappointing.

It was a lesson virtually identical to one I had learned before in the courtroom that could now be broadly expressed thusly: Be advised, when you step into these arenas you will have to make a choice—consciously or unconsciously—whether to honor the Marquis of Queensbury Rules attendant to that arena or honor a standard far higher—one that may tie at least one hand behind your back in the heat of a very aggressive competition. To be sure, you can gainsay those rules as low and demeaning standards and be marked as an idiosyncratic nonconformist, or you can embrace them and, having done so—should you prevail in the competition—be honored and touted. A thumb raked slowly across the throat might signal an ignominious end for the Roman gladiator who did not please; but many a professing Christian has left—and is leaving—Christ's example and words hemorrhaging on the floor of Western civilization's most celebrated arenas.

There is an alternative: the Christian can lose, and, having lost, win. Or, with even greater wisdom, the would-be warrior can choose to fight his battles where it truly matters: in the hearts and minds of his fellowman, with the most powerful weapons ever known—those taught and demonstrated by Christ himself. Anything else is a pyrrhic battle fought at a point of little or no strategic consequence.

The choice to "fight the good fight" in the political, legal, and governmental arenas will carry a related price: debilitation of one's own spiritual advancement. All of the expostulations for engaging in this warfare cannot nullify the truth that it is not apposite to the eternal, it is opposite. Christopher Dawson used the words of Plato to make this point.

> Plato...saw that it was necessary on the one hand to drag humanity out of the shadow world of appearances and false moral standards into the pure white light of spiritual reality, and, on the other hand, that the contemplative must be forced to leave his mountain of vision and "to descend again to these prisoners and to partake in their toils and honors." But, as he says, the spiritual man is at a disadvantage in the world of politics and business. The eyes that have looked upon the sun can no longer distinguish the shadows of the cave. The man who cares only for eternal things, who seeks to fly hence and to become assimilated to God by holiness and justice and wisdom, is unable to strive for political power with the mean cunning of the ordinary "man of affairs."[25]

Thus success in these arenas is, at best, problematic for the true Christian, and surely inimical to the exalted goal of becoming "assimilated to God by holiness and justice and wisdom." Any argument to the contrary is either evidence of the mean manipulation spoken to herein or of an anesthetized spiritual sensitivity made so by a too-ready willingness to heed the trumpeting call of the temporal at the expense of the whispering eternal.

Arnold Toynbee, in *A Study of History*, made much the same point—about the manner, methods and means of true triumph—but in a very different way in his analysis of early church history.

> ...the famous doctor Gamaliel is profoundly impressed by the striking contrast between the powerful moral resistance to persecution of Jesus's Apostles, and the sterile conventional militancy of the contemporary epigoni of Judas Maccabeus. Here, then, are two responses to an identical challenge which are not only different but are actually contradictory and incompatible....[F]rom the second century BC onwards we see violence and gentleness striving for the mastery of souls, until violence annihilates itself and leaves gentleness alone in the field.
>
> ...[A] few months after the crucifixion Gamaliel was already taking note of the executed leader's miraculously rallied disciples as men who might prove to have God on their side; and a few years later Gamaliel's own disciple Paul was preaching a crucified Christ. This vastly painful but infinitely fruitful conversion of the first generation of Christians from the way of violence to the way of gentleness had to be purchased at the price of a shattering blow to their material hopes....[26]

Clearly, Gamaliel was a man who used his head—an uncommon trait in any age—and perceived the incredible power in the early Christians' use of their hearts—as Christ had taught and shown them.

Just as the earth still revolves around the sun, nothing has since changed in the spiritual cosmology: the light is to be found only in one place and through the very specific means demonstrated by Christ. Western man—and the Western church—will never improve upon this Divine navigational route or upon biblical cartography.

THE HAZARDS AND THE GLORIES OF BOLD FAITH

[We are on] a mission that suggests the heavy labour of the peasant rather than the pomp of a ruler.
St. Bernard[27]

Ironically, as I noted earlier, advocacy for Christian values and beliefs in the political and legal arenas will raise the ire and draw the fire of those who oppose them, yet this is still—even at its most vigorous and aggressive—far removed from the forms of advocacy Western civilization desperately needs: faith and belief professed openly, courageously, lovingly, relentlessly, in the marketplace, the workplace, and every place, not simply by the "professionals" (i.e., priests and preachers) but by the Christian Everyman. Yet many Christians—even the "professionals"—are like guard dogs that will bark only in their own yard—or the yard of a sympathetic listener. Boldness about faith and belief before the culture is treated as if it is stigmatic, when in truth its absence is reflective of two sordid traits: a lack of love (for Christ and our fellowman) and a lack of courage.

Schaeffer warned of the consequences of this selfishness and cowardice:

> ...as Christians we are not only to *know* the right world view, the world view that tells us the truth of what *is,* but consciously to *act* upon that world view so as to influence society in all its parts and facets across the whole spectrum of life, as much as we can to the extent of our individual and collective ability.[28]

But Western Christianity has been largely corralled in convenient enclaves of human experience—not so much because of intimidation or adversity at the hands of secularists, but because of a lack of courage and love of ease within the church. The church literally runs the risk of effectively making a Faustian bargain with government and the broader culture: Leave us alone to pursue our ministries and the maintenance of our subculture, and we will stay in that subculture. This, to a considerable degree, is precisely the state of affairs.

I disagree with Schaeffer on one point—use of the relatively narrow term of "authoritarian government." Christian faith and belief will increasingly be opposed by political, legal, and judicial fiat that does not originate from anything resembling the usual connotation of the term "authoritarian government." The more dangerous threats will likely originate from that which is deemed the will of the people—not necessarily just the government—in titular "republics" and "democracies."

A price must be paid. The *bête noire* that inhabits the breast of man, the will-to-power, will not brook a serious challenge without first an ungodly roar and then a vicious bite. The early Christians were sometimes literally torn joint and marrow asunder by this monster for precisely that reason. *The stronger it grows, the more implacable its will to dominate and the more forceful its means.* If the church in our age would avoid its own baptism of suffering it must act before it is too late. The willingness to sacrifice is central to the Christian faith. If professing Christians continue to instead sacrifice the willingness, there will be no hope for the Western church or the civilization.

True sacrifice is never a gift from pride, but a boon from humility. As St. Bernard declared, we are on "a mission that suggests the heavy labour of the peasant rather than the pomp of a ruler. For if you are to do the work of a prophet you need the hoe rather than the scepter."[29] Vaunted places in politics, government, and law are not the strategically commanding positions from which the Christian will achieve victories. Similarly, prestigious churches, cathedrals, and the self-adulation the church gives to success in numbers are of the scepter, not the humble hoe.

WHERE THE BATTLE MUST BE JOINED

...having a form of godliness but denying its power.
2 Timothy 3:5

The Christian church cannot compete with the Titans of our culture on their own terms using their methods. To the extent it tries, it has "stooped to conquer" and that is never the posture to be assumed by the church in the world. In that position the church opens itself to ridicule—sometimes subtle, sometimes not—and it risks becoming the very thing it should oppose in the pridefulness, materialism, and self-absorption of our age. This pragmatic assessment does not encompass the greater spiritual considerations that militate even more forcefully against Christians competing via any forms of mass culture. But neither perspective, the pragmatic nor the spiritual, has stopped many churches from trying; their skill in the effort not typically as great as the "mean cunning" of Plato's ordinary

PD-old

Bernard of Clairvaux. *St. Bernard declared we are on "a mission that suggests the heavy labour of the peasant rather than the pomp of a ruler. For if you are to do the work of a prophet you need the hoe rather than the scepter." Vaunted places in politics, government, and law are not the strategically commanding positions from which the Christian will achieve victories. Similarly, prestigious churches, cathedrals, and the self-adulation the church gives to success in numbers are of the scepter, not the humble hoe.*

"man of affairs." One wonders why they never seem to stop and contemplate this—or bridle, rather than stampede forward, at the thought of stooping to conquer in the culture's manner. But then, Christ himself used the term "sheep" when referring to mankind—though it would seem he would expect His sheep to follow Him in manner and deed, not just name and professed belief.

Our concern as followers of Christ must be with where the legal and political struggle is engaged and, most especially, how it is fought. I believe in the efficacy of bold action in every dimension of our society, but there will be areas in which maximum force must be deployed. Among the oldest of military maxims apply even here: Never engage the enemy on his terms—only on yours.

Numbers are not the key. To the contrary, recognition of minority status—and eschewing any notions of being part of a "Moral Majority"—is not just useful, but essential. All such thinking to the contrary imperils the cause of faith; it does not enhance it.

Should Christians continue to place their faith in the legal or political processes and government, they will not only be disillusioned, but will ultimately either permit themselves to be manipulated by the centers of power in the culture—a phenomenon that is already occurring—or find themselves eventually overwhelmed by the ruthlessness of raw power. Having resorted to the world's stratagems, they become its victims.

Controversy ensued over the absence of any Academy Award nominations for the movie *The Passion of the Christ*, despite its obvious and extraordinary artistic achievement. This was not a slight—though probably intended so—but a gain. To have juxtaposed this exceptional cinematic creation—and this incomparable substance—with the frivolous and meretricious cinematic "art" of a decaying culture, would have demeaned it. It stood alone.

In like manner—and even more so—the association of the Christian faith with political, ideological, legal, or governmental actions does not enhance but demeans it. Above all things—above all history—it stands alone.

God has given Christians the greatest weapons to win spiritual and moral warfare, yet many choose to go into battle with the primitive clubs of human culture—politics, legal processes, and economics. Christians have got the cart before the horse—or, more aptly, the garbage wagon before the thoroughbred steed. Should the church reverse that arrangement—asserting through its actions the faith and compassion found in the Sermon on the Mount—it will revolutionize Western civilization.

Behind all of this—behind the propensity of Christians to view law, politics, government, and ideology as places to stand and vehicles to propel forward their convictions—is the festering reality that many of these Christians really do not believe Christ. Though they might never say it, their covert conclusion is that Christ's way cannot work because it is, implicitly, out of touch with reality, an idealistic paragon set up to profess allegiance to but never to be sincerely modeled or taken too seriously. They betray their own lack of faith by their actions, or, perhaps for some, they betray their determination to have it their way (i.e., man's way).

Politics, government, law, and human ideology are not devoid of significance and meaning such that the Christian should disdain them. Nor could it be said that nothing good could come of them; William Wilberforce and Abraham Lincoln disproved such notions. Yet even they succeeded only because of seeds of faith and belief planted in thousands of hearts for generations before they were born.

The issues, ideas, and beliefs upon which all of history ultimately turns are only distantly expressed in the realms of politics, government and law, as of a man who can be heard shouting from far away. Only part of what he says—or truly means—is discernible. The shouts are not the great message; the quiet whispers of the human heart tell all.

Political, legal, ideological, and governmental battles are skirmishes on the periphery of the main battlefield of history. They are for Christians, as it were, distractions of the troops who, having been ordered to take the high ground, dally on the flanks or in the rear. The great battles of man's experience are *always* fought within the heart and soul of each human being. Win the battle at that decisive point and everything else will follow.

END NOTES
CHAPTER 37

1 Charles W. Colson, *Born Again* (Grand Rapids, MI: Baker Publishing Group, 2004), 172.
2 Plato, cited in Christopher Dawson, *Christianity and the New Age* (New York: Sophia Institute Press, 1985), 52–53.
3 Thomas Hardy, "In Tenebris III," in *Collected Poems of Thomas Hardy* (Hertfordshire: Cumberland House, 1994), 155.
4 C. S. Lewis, *Mere Christianity* (New York: HarperCollins, 2001), 75.
5 Lewis, *Mere Christianity*, 75.
6 Arnold J. Toynbee, *Civilization on Trial* (New York: Oxford University Press, 1948), 256.
7 Colson, *Born Again*, 172.
8 Christopher Dawson, from "Foreword" to *Religion and World History* (New York: Image Books, 1975), 9–10.
9 Dawson, *Religion and World History*, 10–11.
10 Oswald Spengler, *The Decline of the West* (New York: A. A. Knopf, 1926), 27.
11 Immanuel Wallerstein, *The End of the World As We Know It: Social Science for the Twenty-First Century* (Minneapolis: University of Minnesota Press, 1999), 61.
12 Steve Bruce, *God Is Dead: Secularization in the West* (Oxford: Wiley-Blackwell, 2002), 214.
13 Bruce, *God Is Dead*, 215.
14 Eric Metaxas, *Amazing Grace* (New York: HarperCollins, 2007), xix.
15 Doris Kearns Goodwin, *Team of Rivals: The Political Genius of Abraham Lincoln* (New York: Simon and Schuster, 2005), 700.
16 Goodwin, *Team of Rivals*, 700.
17 Francis A. Schaeffer, *How Should We Then Live? The Rise and Decline of Western Thought and Culture* (Wheaton, IL; Crossway Books, 1976), 241–242.
18 Christopher Dawson, *The Historic Reality of Christian Culture* (New York: Harper & Brothers, 1960), 189.
19 Schaeffer, *How Should We Then Live?*, 228.
20 Schaeffer, *How Should We Then Live?*, 230.
21 Schaeffer, *How Should We Then Live?*, 245.
22 Saint Augustine, *The Confessions of St. Augustine* (Oxford: James Parker and Co., 1968), 104.
23 Abraham Lincoln, *Wisdom and Wit* (White Plains, NY: Peter Pauper Press, 1965), 40.
24 Arnold Toynbee, *A Study of History* (New York: Weathervane Books, 1972), 232.
25 Christopher Dawson, *Christianity and the New Age*, 52–53.
26 Toynbee, *A Study of History*, 232.
27 St. Bernard of Clairvaux, cited in Christopher Dawson, *Religion and the Rise of Western Culture* (New York: Image Books, 1948–1949), 202.
28 Schaeffer, *How Should We Then Live?*, 256.
29 St. Bernard, cited in Dawson, *Religion and the Rise of Western Culture*, 202.

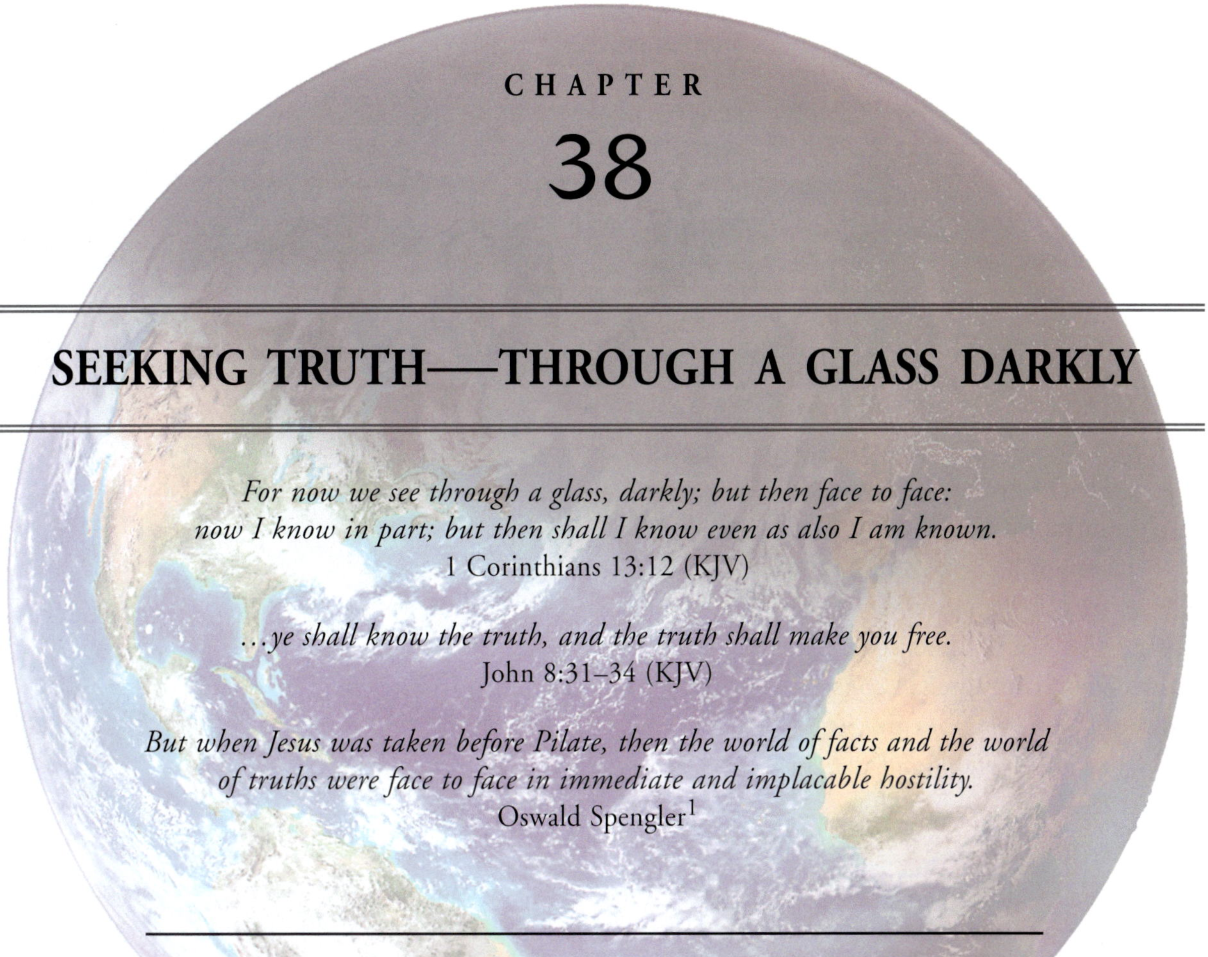

CHAPTER

38

SEEKING TRUTH—THROUGH A GLASS DARKLY

For now we see through a glass, darkly; but then face to face:
now I know in part; but then shall I know even as also I am known.
1 Corinthians 13:12 (KJV)

...ye shall know the truth, and the truth shall make you free.
John 8:31–34 (KJV)

But when Jesus was taken before Pilate, then the world of facts and the world
of truths were face to face in immediate and implacable hostility.
Oswald Spengler[1]

We have seen the plight of Western civilization and explored how it arrived at this dismal and dangerous point in history. We have seen too the integral, foundational role of the Christian faith as the superstructure of Western civilization, and the church's profound failure to stand above the corrupting influences of humanism, materialism, and other isms of our age, thus permitting the civilizational decline and decay. But we must not stop there. Perceiving is not enough. Understanding is not enough. Discussion and exposition are not enough. Preaching and speaking are not enough. Duty requires we strive to alter this course.

But to do so, we must first engage in profound and painful soul-searching. We cannot just move forward from where we are because the historical evidence of the failure of our thinking, our values, our perceptions of reality, is all about us. Before we act—before we even consider how we should act—we must examine how it is that we can know the truth, for we have surely not known it before—not truly known it—or, having once known it, we have turned aside from it. We have seen through a glass darkly, not simply the opaque glass of man's finite nature, but a glass distorted by the myriad reflections of our time and place.

The path to the truth is the path to God. Seeking the truth is synonymous with seeking God. You cannot do one without in effect doing the other. We shall not disavow the human intellect. Man must think, but he must think on his knees. His attitude must reflect supreme consciousness of his limitations and his need for knowledge of God.

God gave us intellects and with them a curiosity. This implies His intention that we use them to search and seek. But we "think on our knees" by being ever mindful of the limitations of human senses

The path to God and His wisdom is paved with the cobblestones of humility. It is littered on its sides with the castoffs and detritus of pride, self-reliance, self-will, and self-assurance. They are too heavy; no one can carry them and ascend.

Used by permission

and intellects: we perceive, grasp, and understand much less than we might presume.

The cacophony of noise, the blur of images, the hypervelocity of activity, the internal intensities that define Western culture, all conspire to keep its citizens from the reflection, quiet observation, and patient pursuit that lead to truth. There is therefore a vicious cycle: the sensory and mental overload borne by Western man keeps him focused on tending to it all, on coping, and, most of all, pursuing the values and priorities Western civilization has proclaimed important. But this takes him further from the light and the truth that might save him from his afflictions and give his life meaning, purpose, and serenity.

None of this is new. Thoreau noted a century and a half ago, "We are provincial, because we do not find at home our standards; because we do not worship truth, but the reflection of truth; because we are warped and narrowed by an exclusive devotion to trade and commerce and manufactures and agriculture and the like, which are but means, and not the end."[2] Neither discerning nor discriminating, Western man is sheeplike in conforming to views and values that he has not closely examined in the stark, penetrating light of history and reason. Any society that continues to distance itself from reality, as Western man does, is engraving its own tombstone.

The science and technology of which we warned earlier, and the dangers implicit in both, that run like a scarlet thread through the pages of modern history, manifest themselves also in dangers not readily perceived as dangers. Spengler made the connections:

> Gunpowder and printing belong together—both discovered at the culmination of the Gothic, both arising out of Germanic technical thought—as the two grand means of Faustian distance-tactics. The Reformation in the beginning of the Late period witnessed the first flysheets and the first field-guns, the French Revolution in the beginning of the Civilization witnessed the first tempest of pamphlets in the autumn of 1788 and the first mass fire of artillery at Valmy.

Dupont Circle Escalators, Washington, D.C. Photo by Owen Byrne. CC

The stark, bloodless sterility of the world Western man has created through his materialism, science, and technology leads him further from the timeless repositories of truth. The cacophony of noise, the blur of images, the hyper-velocity of activity, the internal intensities that define Western culture, all conspire to keep its citizens from the reflection, quiet observation, and patient pursuit that lead to truth. There is, therefore, a vicious cycle: the sensory and mental overload borne by Western man keeps him focused on tending to it all, on coping, and, most of all, pursuing the values and priorities Western civilization has proclaimed important. But this takes him further from the light and the truth that might save him from his afflictions and give his life meaning, purpose, and serenity. This is the state of our age: millions believing, often with great conviction, that which will not stand up to the scrutiny of reason, the rigors of reality, or the lessons of history. It is an age-old story repeated with languorous monotony through the centuries. Only if we come to the truth shall we be free of the curse of history and the ineffable misery that awaits us.

> Today we live so cowed under the bombardment of this intellectual artillery that hardly anyone can attain to the inward detachment that is required for a clear view of the monstrous drama. The will-to-power operating under a pure democratic disguise has accomplished its task so well that the object's sense of freedom is actually flattered by the most thorough-going enslavement that has ever existed.[3]

Few probe for the truth, preferring instead the perceived security and the comfortable conformity of the community of bias and prejudice rather than the stark, often lonely, wilderness of those frontiers. Real change in a person's thinking, for most, typically only comes about through a shock, through fear, pain, and suffering. Yet, even so, many will still "go to the gallows" clinging to a lie. As Solzhenitsyn correctly perceived, "…truth eludes us if we do not concentrate with total attention on its pursuit. And even while it eludes us, the illusion still lingers of knowing it and leads to many misunderstandings. Also, truth is seldom pleasant; it is almost invariably bitter."[4]

While we in the modern West, in our retrospective of history, look with dismay and a supercilious contempt at a people who would, for example, permit the sacrifice of their children and their land to a belief system that left Berlin a smoking cinder in May 1945, we are set upon a not dissimilar path. We see—or think we do—the folly in them and their thinking and smugly assume we stand above all of that from our vantage point in modern Western civilization at the summit of reason and wisdom. But the night is near when our very souls will be demanded of us. That which infected Germany under the Nazis is not unlike—indeed in many respects is synonymous with—that which infects us.

This is the state of our age: millions believing, often with great conviction, that which will not stand up to the scrutiny of reason, the rigors of reality, or the lessons of history. It is an age-old story repeated with languorous monotony through the centuries. Only if we come to the truth shall we be free of the curse of history and the ineffable misery that awaits us.

Freedom, true freedom, is the great boon to the successful seeker of truth. This freedom is expansive, encompassing most connotations of the word freedom save that of literal physical, as well as political, freedom. Even there, the prospects for gaining those forms of freedom are better for the seeker, the American experience as a result of the quests of their forefathers being a classic example. But the first freedom is the most important and was explicated by Christ:

> If ye continue in my word, *then* are ye my disciples indeed; And ye shall know the truth, and the truth shall make you free. They answered him, We be Abraham's seed, and were never in bondage to any man; how sayest thou, Ye shall be made free? Jesus answered them, Verily, verily, I say unto you, Whosoever committeth sin is the servant of sin. And the servant abideth not in the house for ever: but the Son abideth ever. If the Son therefore shall make you free, ye shall be free indeed. (John 8:31–36 KJV)

The religious leaders saw themselves as free; Jesus saw their bondage. The religious leaders did not hear the truth because they could not. They believed themselves righteous, primarily because of their positions and their status, but their minds were closed and their hearts hard. They practiced deceit—including deceiving themselves, at every turn—and by so doing cut themselves off from the truth.

This is a phenomenon common to the church in the West in our time: many supremely confident they have found "the way" yet their lives and their thoughts far removed from those of Christ. This is the essence of this book: challenging the reader to honestly question who he or she is and what he or she believes.

Embrace of Christ's message requires of course an act of faith. But even the skeptic who resists all notions of a spirit realm or of a loving God, must acknowledge—if he or she is at all honest—that the depredations visited on man throughout history by the forces to which Christ alludes have been not only ubiquitous but devastating.

THE FUNDAMENTALS OF THE SEARCH FOR TRUTH

Wisdom is supreme; therefore get wisdom. Though it cost all you have, get understanding.
Proverbs 4:7 (NIV)

Seeking truth requires humility, courage, and a rigorous tough-minded realism. There is a deficit of all three. For the first inevitably leads to a belief in God. The most obvious failures are in the latter; men seek what shores up and affirms their biases and prejudices, permits their favored sins, and says what they simply want (the itching ears must be scratched) to hear.

How, then, does man successfully seek truth?

For the answer, we must return to the rudiments, the attitudes of mind and heart, the disciplines of thought, which man has found countless times in his history only to lose again amidst his dissipations.

This tripod of truth includes absolute uncompromising honesty (a facet of which is intellectual integrity), humility (intellectual, moral, and relational), and courage (of the species that will not falter in the face of the looming void, the sometimes frightening and often lonely wilderness of the unfamiliar, nor balk at the risk of losing social standing and acceptance—pariah status often being the lot of the true seeker—and even life itself in pursuit of truth).

This quest is the most important we will undertake, for bound up in the mission is the search for God, for authentic love, for meaning and purpose, and for wisdom. How far and in which direction we go in this pilgrimage will determine the state of our minds: the characteristic most defining of who we truly are.

We have seen how Francis Schaeffer explained it as the unique feature (contrary to assumptions, this uniqueness is not found in biology or physiology) of our being. "People are unique in the inner life of the mind—what they are in their thought world determines how they act. 'As a man thinketh, so is he,' is really most profound. An individual is not just the product of the forces around him.... The inner thought world determines the outward action."[5]

But the tragedy for millions is their method of building their unique selves, as Schaeffer explained:

> Most people catch their presuppositions from their family and surrounding society the way a child catches measles. But people with more understanding realize that their presuppositions should be chosen after a careful consideration of what world view is true. When all is done, when all the alternatives have been explored, "not many men are in the room"—that is, although world views have many variations, there are not many basic world views or basic presuppositions.[6]

Toynbee, in *Civilization on Trial*, shared very similar views on how we acquire our perceptions of reality—and what it takes to change them. "On matters which do not happen to come within the range of our adult experience, all of us are apt to retain, uncriticized and unrevised, the crude and simple-minded conceptions that were suggested to us in childhood."[7]

For the seeking person, all of life can be described as one lengthy disabusement of fallacious and often naïve notions about man and the world. Though many people, if not most of humanity, will, in William James' words, simply "rearrange their prejudices"[8] in lieu of realistic thought and courageous searching, others can, to a considerable degree, measure the *success* of their lives in terms of how well they distinguished truth from falsehood, reality from fiction, objectivity from prejudice.

ONLY *REALITY* IS REALITY

With the degradation of truth, man is debased from the sublime seeker after truth as an absolute value to that of the hypocrite who uses "truth" as a beautiful smoke screen for the justification of his impulses and lust, profit and greed.
Pitirim Sorokin[9]

We must insist on recognizing what would seem self-evident but is not: Only reality is reality. The director of the war movie *The Big Red One*, a combat veteran of World War II, was once asked if the film was realistic. He acknowledged it was not and that the only way to make a war movie remotely realistic was to blind the audience with smoke, deafen them with explosions and gunfire, and shoot at least a few people in the theatre.

We cannot find truth if we persist in the bifurcation of knowledge that we have already condemned as the twisted intellectual legacy of the Renaissance and the Enlightenment. Truth is neither severable nor subject to compartmentalization. Truth is an eternal, unending, great whole.

Immanuel Wallerstein described the search for knowledge as "a singular enterprise, and there are no fundamental contradictions between how we may pursue it in the natural and in the human world, for they are both integral parts of a singular universe. Nor is knowledge separate from creativity or adventure or the search for the good society."[10] In like vein, trying to comprehend life and history by giving credence only to the highly superficial perceptions of material reality—the foundation of contemporary science and technology—is like the cave dweller who, because he cannot see anything beyond its walls, acknowledges no greater reality. Western man thus far has been unwilling to come out of his cave; he retreats yet deeper and deeper into it.

Seeking truth has nothing to do with argument, debate, controversy, or contention. All of these reflect prideful competition and sometimes hypocritical, but always spurious, dedication to the notion that winning explicates truth. In fact, **seeking truth is a solitary exercise in self-abnegation and profound humility.** As we quoted Wordsworth earlier regarding wisdom, it "is oftentimes nearer when we stoop than when we soar."

Human beings tend to fall intellectually into one of three categories: conformists, competitors, or explorers (we might also refer to them as "seekers"). One individual may at various times occupy simultaneously or congruently the categories of conformist and competitor. All competitors are to some degree conformists, though not all conformists are competitors. Conformists are the largest group, primarily because they reflect two common traits in human nature: a tendency to sheep-like thought and behavior and a lack of courage.

The competitors may not perceive themselves as conformists—inasmuch as they are often vociferous and argumentative in their views—but when closely analyzed their thinking proves to be more of the same regimented thought that characterizes various groups (ideological, religious or otherwise). Rather than original and insightful they are a reflection of William James's "rearranging of prejudices." These individuals will debate with alacrity and do not truly comprehend what it means to seek. Often ready upon the slightest stimulus to argue their case or attack another's, they perceive themselves as thinkers when in fact their greater motives are to defend and nurture values or views to which they have chosen to subscribe out of blind conformity or from self-centered motives.

The competitor *wants something*. Although he may tell you, and even himself, that it is "truth" he is seeking, it will invariably be prestige, or power, or money, or vindication, or attention, or a mixture. It would appear that most politicians, lawyers, judges, media figures, and many scientists—contrary to assertions, or even their perceptions of themselves—fall into the competitive category. Atheists, by definition, are in this category. They have asserted that their sensory capacities, intellects, and reason are sufficiently robust to make the unequivocal determination that there is no God. Many agnostics fall into this category—albeit disingenuously claiming objectivity and a seeking attitude—and give themselves away by asserting what are clearly atheistic tendencies. It is fashionable in the West of our time for many *de facto* atheists to refer to themselves euphemistically as agnostics.

As a young trial lawyer, I learned that the search for truth, even of the most pedestrian variety (such as is typically pursued in a courtroom) can be very problematic. This search is difficult in part

Used by photographer permission.

Oxford Union debate hall. *Debate—so often touted and immensely popular in Western civilization—is a specious method of getting at the truth. Debate, especially as it is practiced in the West, resembles an intellectual form of professional wrestling: sound, fury, strutting, and a surfeit of the testosterone of egoism, all signifying very little. If someone's argument appears to be thrown from the ring, it may or may not be due to its weakness—or the strength of the opposition's position. A put-down expertly executed or a thrust deftly parried will likely stimulate the typical jaded Western audience to applause—or perhaps even to marveling (gullibly) at the champion's skill—not unlike the primitive emanations from the Colosseum in ancient Rome. But none of it contributes to a true, objective, commonsense understanding of the issue. It is more closely akin to flummery and hot air in its effect on nurturing a fair-minded and insightful scrutiny of the question. Only the seekers have any hope of discovering the truth. They will do so only as the result of a humble, honest, courageous, individual, iconoclastic, and unselfish effort.*

because one or more of the participants (often most) are not sincerely searching for a revelation of the truth, the whole truth, and nothing but the truth despite their declarations of commitment to that goal. The courtroom is a clear example of the competitive mindset. Were those commitments genuine and complete on everyone's part (e.g., lawyers, judges, juries, witnesses, etc.), justice would often be achieved in the courtroom rather than the ersatz variety, or miscarriages of justice, more often arrived at. The practices and mores of the legal system are often so deleterious to a search for the truth—and so deeply engrained that they are rarely questioned—that they often inhibit and frustrate finding it.

The competitive approach is inimical to finding truth. This is part of the reason why debate—so often touted and immensely popular in Western civilization—is a specious method of getting at the truth. Debate, especially as it is practiced in the West, is reminiscent of an intellectual form of professional wrestling: sound, fury, strutting, and a surfeit of the testosterone of egoism, all signifying very little. If someone's argument appears to be thrown from the ring, this may or may not be due to its weakness—or the strength of the opposition's position. A put-down expertly executed or a thrust deftly parried will likely stimulate the typical jaded Western audience to applause—or perhaps even to marveling (gullibly) at the champion's skill—not unlike the primitive emanations from the Colosseum in ancient Rome. But none of it contributes to a true, objective, commonsense understanding of the issue. It is more closely akin to flummery and hot air in its effect on nurturing a fair-minded and insightful scrutiny of the question.

Only the explorers (i.e., seekers) have any hope of discovering the truth. They will do so only as the result of a humble, honest, courageous, individual, iconoclastic, and unselfish effort.

THE COMPLEXITY OF TRUTH

Everything affects everything, and as time goes on, what is everything expands inexorably.
Immanuel Wallerstein[11]

> Why is truth complex? Because reality is complex. And reality is complex for one essential reason: the arrow of time. Everything affects everything, and as time goes on, what is everything expands inexorably. In a sense, nothing is eliminated, although much fades or becomes blurred. The universe proceeds—it has a life—in its orderly disorder or its disorderly order. There are of course endless provisional orderly patterns, self-established, holding things together, creating seeming coherence. But none is perfect, because of course perfect order is death, and in any case enduring order has never existed. Perfect order is what we may mean by God, which is by definition beyond the known universe.[12]

I have emphatically stressed what I have called the Bayeux Tapestry principle (i.e., that everything is connected to everything else and neither reality nor truth can be separated into parts or categories). But not only is Wallerstein correct in his statements, there are also depths of truth. Emerson's dictum that "beneath each depth, a greater depth lies" suggests that not only is truth, in many of its manifestations, continually becoming more complex, it is not always readily discernible at those greater depths.

But the *truth* with which we are concerned here has the redeeming feature of *timelessness.* Never altered by events or the ticking of any clock, it was always true, it is true, and it always will be true. *The paradox of this truth is its utterly incomprehensible scope, depth, and complexity on the one hand yet its simplicity in application to man's existence.* One need not be an intellectual or copiously erudite to understand how this truth can and should be applied in one's life. This is an implied but often unexpressed theme of the Bible, particularly in that most profound of books, Job, and to some extent, in Ecclesiastes.

Wallerstein also observed that human relationships are even more complex than physical and mathematical realities.

> If physical scientists and mathematicians are now telling us that truth in their arena is complex, indeterminate, and dependent on an arrow of time, what does that mean for social scientists? For, it is clear that, of all systems in the universe, human social systems are the most complex structures that exist, the ones with the briefest stable equilibria, the ones with the most outside variables to take into account, the ones that are most difficult to study.[13]

We should consider the means and the tools by which we can pursue the truth. How facile are they? How reliable?

FACTA FACTORUM CAUSAE (FACTS FOR FACT'S SAKE): EDUCATION AND THE SEARCH FOR TRUTH

The words of the wise are as goads, and as nails fastened by the masters of assemblies, which are given from one shepherd. And further, by these, my son, be admonished: of making many books there is no end; and much study is a weariness of the flesh.
Ecclesiastes 12:11–12 (KJV)

The avidity for knowledge in Western civilization contributes to Western man's misapprehension—he who is so easily misapprehending because of his vanity and pride—of the spurious conviction that he is advanced, sophisticated, perceptive and, in a word, superior, in one way or another, to all others, and all who have gone before. "Information is not knowledge" declared Albert Einstein. No, and it is certainly not insight, nor is it wisdom.

Yet in the West there is an accretion of knowledge that is sometimes superfluous and hence often useless. As an oyster coats the irritating grains of sand well beyond what is needed to smooth its hard edges, so do some social scientists, commentators, and physical scientists laboriously add to their field. The "pearl" may be valued, primarily by those in the discipline, but it contributes little or nothing to true understanding or the revelation of eternal verities. Spengler touched upon a facet of this when he declared, "For me, therefore, the test of value to be applied to a thinker is his eye for the great facts of his own time."[14]

This eye is darkened in our own time as evidenced by a plethora of writings explicating the specious, the superficial, or the meaningless. The ability to discern that which is important from that which is trivial is critical to a successful search for truth.

Central in the West to this, what we might call "frivolous learning," is the artificial division of knowledge and the search for truth that we have already vilified as a philosophical and intellectual fallacy. Wallerstein noted that "No other historical system has instituted a fundamental divorce between science and philosophy/humanities, or what I think would be better characterized as the separation of the quest for the true and the quest for the good and the beautiful."[15]

Yet man resisted this approach: "However hard scholars worked to establish a strict segregation of the two activities, it ran against the psychological grain, especially when the object of study was social reality."[16] There is clearly a reason for that resistance: many will instinctively sense that the distinction is false, artificial and an impediment to achieving understanding or discovering truth. The narrowness of learning and the blinkered perspective of physical scientists especially, but also now social scientists, in the West is a direct consequence of this foolishness. This is in part why the better part of one's education must be autodidactic: the one we give ourselves in a personal quest for "the nature of true reality and true values."

WESTERN MAN—SENSORILY AND RATIONALLY PRETERHUMAN? HUMAN LIMITS AND THE SEARCH FOR TRUTH

...some divine truths are attainable by human reason,
while others altogether surpass the power of human reason.
St. Thomas Aquinas[17]

Man lacks the sensory capability and the intellectual capacity to deny God, the spiritual dimension—or, for that matter, to make unequivocal judgments or assertions regarding much that he assumes he understands. This is a primary reason why atheism and even agnosticism are untenable. We may, for example, doubt God (hell, heaven, a transcendent moral law, etc.) with the hubris of those who assume their intellects will bring them to all knowledge, but our doubting is more often a manifestation of our limitations—real or self-imposed—than of any accurate, insightful assessment of reality.

Our family dog Abraham, a wolf–German shepherd hybrid with extraordinary sensory acuity, sees what I do not see, hears what I cannot hear, smells what I cannot smell. Those gifts are but one simple illustration of why man should be humble about his empirical comprehensions. Even a creature that man considers his inferior excels him in some respects. There is a world beyond what we can empirically perceive that is far greater and more significant than even the vastness of our universe suggests. Sorokin, referring to the development of the sensate culture in the wake of the Renaissance and Enlightenment, declared, "The rude and imperfect human organs of sense were made the supreme arbiter of what was real and what was not, what was value and what was not." This way of viewing reality "clipped the wings of man with which he could soar to the vision of more sublime values and the less coarse aspects of reality."[18]

Couple this with the limitations of a few pounds of neurological matter whose life span at best is measured in years—milliseconds on the clock of the universe—rather than millennia, and man's intellectual restrictions should be obvious. St. Thomas Aquinas expressed a dimension of this, appropriately centuries ago, in an insight that would be impliedly if not expressly refuted by many today.

> Sensory cognition is occupied with external, sensible qualities, but intellectual knowledge penetrates to the very essence of the things. In the things which we hold about God there is truth in two ways. For certain things that are true about God wholly surpass the capability of human reason; for instance, that God is three and one; while there are certain things to which even natural reason can attain, for instance, that God is… Accordingly some divine truths are attainable by human reason, while others altogether surpass the power of human reason.[19]

Dawson noted centuries later "if we once admit the possibility of a mode of spiritual consciousness or being which transcends the biological, there seems no reason to regard the human mind as its only field of manifestation."[20] Yet it is not self-evident in our time precisely because of the vain, man-centric attitudes that prevail in the West.

"It would indeed be strange if reality did not transcend man's comprehension qualitatively as well as quantitatively. The refusal to admit this possibility rests not so much on reason as on the humanist prejudice which insists that the human mind is the highest of all possible forms of existence and the only standard of reality."[21]

When honestly approached, the question even of the existence of God cannot be answered by dint of empirical knowledge and human reason; though the evidence and the arguments in those realms in favor vastly outweigh any against. On a purely rational plane—without resort to faith—the existence of God is, I believe, a certainty; only God's attributes cannot be discerned with clarity. This is certainly so if we grant the human intellect the weight and ascribe to it the capacities posited by the modern Western viewpoint. *But it is a certain certainty that man lacks the wherewithal to deny the existence of God—he has not the means.*

The atheist cannot describe for us the back side of the most remote galaxy, yet he presumes to declare that a being who conceivably created that galaxy, and who is by definition not of the material realm, does not exist! "The fool hath said in his heart, There is no God." (Psalms 14:1 KJV) Such "reasoning" is nonexistent; and the motives profoundly suspect. Hence it is the atheist, not God, in whom we cannot believe.

Yet the significance of these two disparate ways of looking at reality is far greater than simply whether one or the other is more efficacious in the search for truth. If abstract understanding and knowledge were all that was at stake, the consequences would not be as grave. Dawson explained why the choice Western man has made to believe in himself, first and foremost, has also been the cause of so much misery: "Man cannot worship himself, nor can he adore a Time God that is the creation of his own mind. As soon as he recognizes its fictitious character such an idea loses all its religious power. And for the same reason every attempt to create a new religion on purely rational and human foundations is inevitably doomed to failure."[22] This leads then to "The more religious a man is, the more is he sensitive to the common need of humanity. All the founders of the world religions—even those, like Buddha, who were the most uncompromising in their religious absolutism—were concerned not merely with their private religious experience, but with the common need of humanity."[23] Western man professes to be concerned with "the common need of humanity," yet his belief system makes such a concern meaningless; there is no Higher Being, no Higher Law behind it.

Whether a man's belief system is God and otherworldly-centered or man-centered is critical to the meeting of his most fundamental needs. His most essential religious needs, based on what we can see from history, are a need for God, the transcendent, and for salvation or eternal life. Dawson observed that there was "an extraordinary degree of unanimity" on this and that "both these elements are represented in some form or other in any given religion." In the ancient Jewish faith the focus seems to be almost "entirely on the first of these two elements—the reality of God" and has little or "nothing to say about the immortality of the soul and the idea of eternal life" even though the Old Testament prophets were speaking essentially of "a doctrine of salvation—a social and earthly salvation, it is true, but nevertheless a salvation which is essentially religious and related to the eternal life of God." Buddhism, on the other hand, "seems to leave no room for God and to put the whole emphasis of its teaching on the second element—deliverance."[24]

These religious perspectives are highly significant to the actual living of man's life and how he interacts with his fellowman, because they "produce an attitude to life totally opposed to the practical utilitarian outlook of the ordinary man." The ordinary man "regards the world of man—the world of sensible experience and social activity—as the one reality, and is sceptical of anything that lies beyond, whether in the region of pure thought or of spiritual experience, not to speak of religious faith." His counterpart, the religious man, "on the contrary, turns his scepticism against the world of man. He is conscious of the existence of another and greater world of spiritual reality in which we live and move and have our being, though it is hidden from us by the veil of sensible things."

Intriguingly, Dawson reminded us of Cardinal Newman's speculations that "the knowledge of the senses has a merely symbolic value" and that "the whole series of impressions made on us by the senses may be but a Divine economy suited to our need, and the token of realities distinct from them, and such as might be revealed to us, nay, more perfectly, by other senses as different from our existing ones as they are from one another."[25] Newman may well be right. If he was, then man's deference to his own senses and intellect is then twice removed from reality.

THE LIMITATIONS OF MAN'S COLLECTIVE EXPERIENCE

Yet it is of the very nature of a mystery that it should so transcend our experience and the reasoning that is based on experience.
Dawson[26]

Here we seize on a phrase resorted to by Christopher Dawson, "based on experience." This truth, that human reasoning is always founded on human experience, is, or should be, central to the recognition of the need for humility in all of man's intellectual endeavors. For this is a primary weakness of reason: it *is* based on experience, which is always limited. Thus reasoning itself perforce is always limited, if not imperceptibly flawed, *ergo* the necessity of faith.

Augustine expressed this insight with the phrase "*Credo ut intelligam*"—"I believe in order to understand." Braudel alluded to the "exceptional brilliance" of Augustine's works (*The City of God, The Confessions*), and "his contradictory nature, his desire to bring together faith and intelligence, classical and Christian civilization, the old wine and the new—these deliberate efforts made him in some ways a rationalist." Some of us would assert that this is not contradictory at all. This approach

Fernand Paul Braudel. PD released

Fernand Braudel *alluded to the "exceptional brilliance" of Augustine's works* (The City of God, The Confessions)*, and "his contradictory nature, his desire to bring together faith and intelligence, classical and Christian civilization, the old wine and the new—these deliberate efforts made him in some ways a rationalist." This approach is congruent with Sorokin's ideal culture, the "idealistic" who sees faith and the spiritual on the one hand, and the physical world on the other, as simply two existing realms in which to seek truth. But it is important to add Braudel's additional observation that for Augustine "faith came first." Despite his imposing intellect—one of the leading minds of Western civilization—Augustine appeared contemptuous of any tendency to place the human intellect at the head of the class; his humility and spiritual insights would not permit it.*

is congruent with Sorokin's ideal culture, the "idealistic" who sees faith and the spiritual on the one hand and the physical world on the other, as simply two existing realms in which to seek truth. But it is important to add Braudel's additional observation that for Augustine "faith came first."[27] Despite his imposing intellect—one of the leading minds of Western civilization—Augustine appeared contemptuous of any tendency to place the human intellect at the head of the class; his humility and spiritual insights would not permit it.

Dawson declared that "the idea of mystery" was essential before man had any hope of perceiving a greater reality. "Yet if we reject the idea of mystery, the religious point of view itself becomes impossible. A mystery is not contrary to reason or without relation to reality. It forms part of a system of reality, but not of that system which is familiar to our experience. As Newman says somewhere, it is like an island which seems lost in a world of waters, but which is really a peak of a hidden range of mountains."[28]

Dawson here makes two more critically important points: First, we cannot know all, will never know all, but can acknowledge that there is Truth beyond which we know. Here we can interject Wallerstein's observation, "To be sure, knowledge will always remain a pursuit, never a point of arrival."[29] Second, that simply because we do not "know" does not suggest that the mystery is "contrary to reason or without relation to reality."

Francis Schaeffer affirmed the notion that religious knowledge was not all there was. In a viewpoint also consistent with Sorokin's "idealistic" culture, Schaeffer declared that "the Bible tells us true things about people and about nature. It does not give men and women *exhaustive* truth about the world and the cosmos, but it does give truth about them." This means that "one can know many true things about nature, especially *why* things exist and why they have the form they have" from study of the Bible. Yet "because the Bible does not give exhaustive truth about history and the cosmos, historians and scientists have a job to do, and their work is not meaningless." Schaeffer rejected the modern Western materialist view of the world by observing, "there is a total break between God and his creation, that is, between God and created things; God is infinite—and created things are finite." Nonetheless, man can know truth about God and "about the things of creation" because of the Bible's revelation of God and "the key to understanding God's world" given in the Bible.[30]

Of particular irony are the views expressed by our observers about the search for truth through the discipline of history that they, many of them historians themselves, note is of lesser utility than one might presume, highly useful but limited. Dawson, a historian, in *Religion and World History*, described these limitations.

> For the knowledge of history, however exhaustive, is not a panacea that will solve all our political problems and cure all our social ills. That is the fallacy of historicism, of which we have heard so much in recent years. For during the nineteenth century the intoxication of the new knowledge and the influence of evolutionary theories led men to believe that history was a kind of progressive revelation which would gradually lead us to a wider knowledge, to larger moral values, and ultimately to universal truth. This view was propagated, on the one hand, by the French and English and of course American, liberal philosophers who believed in the theory of social progress, and on the other by the German philosophers who constructed their vast systems of speculative idealism and their philosophies of history.
>
> Now it is true enough that history leads us to wider knowledge, but only to a knowledge of historical phenomena. It does not create truth or moral values. The historical world left to its own resources is a world of pure relativism, and the more completely we immerse ourselves in it, the more difficult it is to see beyond it or to grasp any ultimate truth to which we can hold fast.[31]

Wallerstein, as we previously saw, affirmed the limitations and hence errors of the study of history in referring to "the Whig interpretation of history, the presumption that the present is the best time ever and that the past led inevitably to the present."[32] Significantly, Toynbee, asserted late in his career:

> Of one thing we can be fairly confident: religion is likely to be the plane on which [a] coming centripetal counter-movement will first declare itself; and this probability offers us a further hint for the revision of our traditional Western methods of studying history. If our first precept should be to study our own history, not on its own account but for the part which the West has played in the unification of mankind, our second precept, in studying History as a whole, should be to relegate economic and political history to a subordinate place and give religious history the primacy.[33]

Toynbee then added, "For religion, after all, is the serious business of the human race."[34]

THE LANGUAGE OF EVIL IS DECEIT

When he lies, he speaks his native language, for he is a liar and the father of lies.
John 8:44b (NIV)

The language of evil is deceit. When a liar lies, he is speaking his native tongue. (John 8:44) Any form of deceit is a manifestation of the communications of the forces of evil in human experience. Thus deceit should never be taken lightly, or the deceiver granted any reprieve from absolute accountability. All that is good in human experience is built upon the truth; thus the clouding, concealing, misrepresenting, or refutation of the truth is among the greatest of wrongs against mankind.

THE ELYSIAN FIELDS OF WESTERN CIVILIZATION—TELEVISION, CINEMA, THE INTERNET, AND OTHER SUBSTITUTES FOR REALITY

They never open their mouths without subtracting from the sum of human knowledge.
Thomas Brackett Reed[44]

Citing the great sinister light that glows in millions of Western living rooms and bedrooms, Francis Schaeffer perceived correctly how dangerous this Orwellian instrument truly is for purposes of altering thought and manipulating behavior. Since Schaeffer's time, the advent of the Internet has expanded exponentially the opportunities for—and the actual practice of—manipulation. The typical Western citizen, and certainly the typical Western young person or child, does not understand how completely this medium is controlled for the purpose of manipulating the audience. Schaeffer noted that "Many viewers seem to assume that when they have seen something on TV, they have seen it with their own eyes....He knows, because his own eyes have seen. He has the impression of greater direct objective knowledge than ever before. For many, what they see on television becomes more true than what they see with their eyes in the external world."[45]

Even those who would insist as an abstract principle that they recognize this do not behave as if that awareness truly existed.

Every news program, every documentary, every movie, every program is a highly edited and controlled presentation—the like of which is historically unprecedented in its scope, its power and its reach—and is profoundly influenced by the values and motives of its designers. It is, Schaeffer declared, "the image someone has decided we should see...what can a properly managed TV schedule, with its edited illusion of reality, be as it enters every home and is watched for endless hours by both young and old?"[46]

This writer—having entered eight war zones on four continents and seeing the television and media coverage of each, before and after the fact, and having been on the inside of domestic

Released by photographer

The typical Western citizen, and certainly the typical Western young person or child, does not understand how completely the medium of television is controlled for the purpose of manipulating the audience. Western man is beset on all sides by the unctuous blandishments of politicians, marketers, advertisers, public relations specialists, entertainers, and even many priests and preachers. His ability— not to mention his will—to become highly discriminating so he might see through this shall in large part determine his future. If he continues to acquiesce and view these manipulations as an acceptable, perhaps even useful, part of his society then he will remain an unwitting victim and become more and more complicit in the degradation and decay of his culture.

political and other news stories—can attest from personal experience to the accuracy of Schaeffer's insights.

Absolutely nothing substitutes for reality. From this first principle we then are compelled—if we are seeking truth at all—to ask questions: If it is not reality, what then is it?

If what you see has been edited—as it surely has—what has been kept and what discarded, and why? Lastly, and most important of all, what is the nature of its creator, a Dr. Frankenstein or perhaps a Dr. Goebbels, or simply someone who is profoundly limited in some area or unbalanced—a lightweight in intellect, experience, morality, or wisdom?

The answers to these questions would prove unsettling were they known, but the product, packaged as it is, so attractively, so professionally, and with such seeming credibility, is never really unwrapped and scrutinized closely. The damage then is done, the public "informed," and the purveyor successful in his goals—and thence emboldened.

This need not be, and usually isn't, a conspiracy—the treatment of political and ideological issues sometimes an exception—but that is often beside the point in any event. The consequences are the same: contrived presentation or illusion controls behavior. The manipulation is often the product of a highly materialistic culture determined to sell, sell, sell (i.e., transfer the money in the audience's pockets to the bank accounts of the producers and corporate sponsors) and to advance political, social, and ideological agendas with a ruthless efficiency that bears no relationship to objectivity or getting at the truth. Conspiracy theories may distract from what Schaeffer called "a much greater danger":

> With an elite providing the arbitrary absolutes, not just TV but the general apparatus of the mass media can be a vehicle for manipulation. There is no need for collusion or a plot. All that is needed is that the world view of the elite and the world view of the central news media coincide.....It is natural that they act upon this viewpoint, with varying degrees of consciousness of what they are doing, and even varying degrees of consciousness of who is using whom. Their world view is the grid which determines their presentation.[47]

Collusion and conspiracy are not needed in order to achieve manipulation of thought and behavior. If many of the gatekeepers of the media have much the same value systems and worldview, this can be achieved almost effortlessly. As Schaeffer explained, "...rarely would all the media be involved. *It is always unfair to say simply "the press" or "the media" do this or that.* They are never to be all lumped together as though they were a monolithic whole. Nonetheless, the media can be a vehicle of manipulation."

In an analysis congruent with that of the journalist Malcolm Muggeridge, Schaeffer pointed out that many of these gatekeepers have the ability to manipulate through news-making (i.e., by choosing to "puff" this or that story, individual, idea, etc.):

> There are certain news organizations, newspapers, news magazines, wire services, and news broadcasts which have the ability to generate news. They are the *news makers,* and when an item appears in them it *becomes* the news....The influence is not necessarily based on circulation, but rather on its reputation with the right people. This is at times consciously cultivated; for example, certain news outlets release their big stories to the wires and the radio and TV networks before the "big story" hits the newsstands.[48]

I first became fully aware of how powerful just the choosing of the topics and the information to be published or broadcast can be while in El Salvador during the communist guerrilla wars there in the 1980s. Interviews with governmental figures and ordinary citizens coupled with Commando patrols into the heart of the guerrillas' territory revealed to me that the "news" coming out of El Salvador was more an ideological battle than a revelation of objective reality. Outright lies were not necessary to slant a story. That could be achieved simply by selectivity as to the information to be conveyed—or withheld.

Francis Schaeffer observed another source of manipulation, one that we would be less likely to anticipate: "The next step is that these highly motivating religious words out of our religious past, but separated from their original content and context in the Bible, are then used for manipulation. The words became a banner for men to grab and run with in any arbitrary direction—either shifting sexual morality from its historic Christian position based on the Bible's and Christ's teaching, or in legal and political manipulation."[49]

This is yet another form of scratching "itching ears." At the present rate of growth in its use, many churches will soon seem like kennels of flea-infested dogs seeking relief from the demands of biblical morality and transcendent truth.

Western man is beset on all sides by the unctuous blandishments of politicians, marketers, advertisers, public relations specialists, entertainers, and even many priests and preachers. His ability—not to mention his will—to become highly discriminating so he might see through this shall in large part determine his future. If he continues to acquiesce and view these manipulations as an acceptable, perhaps even useful, part of his society then he will remain an unwitting victim and become more and more complicit in the degradation and decay of his culture.

THE HIGHEST WESTERN ART FORM—PRETENDING

He is not only dull himself, he is the cause of dullness in others.
Samuel Johnson[50]

Few seem to notice—fewer still seem to care—that the most powerful media in the West, movies and television in particular, are almost exclusively the domain of the unreal. Thousands of actors, actresses, and entertainers spend their professional lives standing in front of a camera or audience *pretending.* That this would more appropriately be the province of children is a psychological phenomenon rarely noted. What does it say about individuals who devote their lives to this behavior? What does it say about a culture so transfixed by this same behavior that it spends billions of dollars and millions of life hours for its creation and consumption? Granted, artistic expression is surely possible through these means; Western man has known this since at least the time of the Greek playwrights.

But the distinction in our time between reality and pretense is now so blurred that actors, actresses, and entertainers have long since joined the pantheon of "heroes" of Western culture. True heroes (i.e., those who courageously and unselfishly stand for principle, and sacrifice for the well-being of their fellowman in the harsh and unforgiving real world) are accorded secondary status in this pantheon—or, very often, consigned to oblivion.

(Top) 2008 Super Bowl. *On the same day of the Super Bowl, a special operations unit stormed an al Qaeda stronghold in Iraq. Two of their number, Nathan Hardy and Michael Koch, died the following day from the fusillade of bullets that met them. This was a great and ultimate sacrifice for the well-being of Western civilization. But it was eclipsed by a child's game, the making of millions of dollars, and a torrent of shallow thoughts, banal words, and frivolous images endlessly reviewing the game, the plays, and the players over the ensuing weeks. Millions know the names of key players; very few have ever heard of Nathan Hardy and Michael Koch. This is not simply a perverse set of values; it is supremely out of touch with reality. In so many respects, adolescence for Western man has been extended to the grave.*

Used by permission of photographer.

PD-mil

On the same day of the 2008 Super Bowl, a special operations unit stormed an al Qaeda stronghold in Iraq. Two of their number, Nathan Hardy and Michael Koch, died the following day from the fusillade of bullets that met them. This was—it is absurd that we even need to declare it—a great and ultimate sacrifice for the well-being of Western civilization. But, as we could have anticipated, it was eclipsed by a child's game, the making of millions of dollars, and a torrent of shallow thoughts, banal words, and frivolous images endlessly reviewing the game, the plays, and the players over the ensuing weeks. Millions know the names of key players on each of the participating football teams; very few have ever heard of Nathan Hardy and Michael Koch.

This is not simply a perverse set of values; it is supremely out of touch with reality. In so many respects, adolescence for Western man has been extended to the grave.

THERE IS ABSOLUTE TRUTH OR THERE IS NO TRUTH AT ALL

"You are a king, then!" said Pilate. Jesus answered, "You are right in saying I am a king. In fact, for this reason I was born, and for this I came into the world, to testify to the truth. Everyone on the side of truth listens to me." "What is truth?" Pilate asked.
John 18:37–38a (NIV)

In our relativistic Western world the notion of absolutes is accepted in the material realm, yet rejected in any area not subject to empirical observation and "scientific" measurement or testing. This is of course certainly the case with notions of spirituality or morality. But just because a human being can choose between two or more options or courses of behavior does not mean that all are true.

Spengler, with extraordinary profundity, spotlighted the great issue of all of history.

> But when Jesus was taken before Pilate, then *the world of facts and the world of truths were face to face in immediate and implacable hostility.* It is a scene appallingly distinct and overwhelming in its symbolism, such as the world's history had never before and has never since looked at. The discord that lies at the root of all human life from its beginning, in virtue of its very *being*, of its having both existence *and* awareness, took here the highest form that can possibly be conceived of human tragedy. In the famous question of the Roman Procurator: "What is truth?" lies *the entire meaning of history*, the exclusive validity of the deed, the prestige of the State and war and the all-powerfulness of success and the pride of ancestry in an exalted destiny. The silence of Jesus answers this question by that other which is decisive in all things of religion—*What is actuality?* For Pilate actuality was all; for Him nothing. Were it anything, indeed, pure religiousness could never stand up against history and the powers of history, or sit in judgment on active life; or if it does, it ceases to be religion and is subjected itself to the spirit of history.[51]

In the film *King of Kings*, the screenwriters took Pilate's question to its next logical step and had the character of Pilate utter explicitly the implications of his question, "Can there not be more than one truth?" **No longer Christ, but now Pilate is the philosophical father of Western civilization. His belief system, rather than Christ's teachings, dominates Western culture.**

PD-old

Antonio Ciseri's depiction of Pontius Pilate presenting a scourged Christ to the people. *Ecce homo!* (Behold the man!), painted in the nineteenth century. *In the film* King of Kings, *the screenwriters took Pilate's question to its next logical step and had the character of Pilate utter explicitly the implications of his question, "Can there not be more than one truth?" No longer Christ, but now Pilate is the philosophical father of Western civilization. His belief system, rather than Christ's teachings, dominates Western culture.*

MODUS OPERANDI IN THE SEARCH FOR TRUTH

...truth eludes us if we do not concentrate with total attention on its pursuit. And even while it eludes us, the illusion still lingers of knowing it and leads to many misunderstandings.
Solzhenitsyn[52]

Sorokin's three main systems of truth corresponding to his "three main super systems of culture," the ideational, sensate, and idealistic systems, help us to understand the different approaches man has taken in the search for truth. As we will see, one is profoundly flawed, another significantly so, and the third is man's best prospect.

> Ideational truth is the truth revealed by the grace of God...disclosed in a supersensory way through mystic experience, direct revelation, divine intuition and inspiration. Such a truth may be called the truth of faith. It is regarded as infallible, yielding adequate knowledge about the true-reality values.
>
> Sensate truth is the truth of the senses, obtained through our organs of sense perception. If the testimony of our senses shows that "snow is white and cold," the proposition is true; if our senses testify that snow is not white and not cold, the proposition becomes false.

> Idealistic truth is a synthesis of both, made by our reason. In regard to sensory phenomena, it recognizes the role of the sense organs as the source and criterion of the validity or invalidity of a proposition. In regard to supersensory phenomena, it claims that any knowledge of these is impossible through sensory experience and is obtained only through the direct revelation of God.[53]

Though the last declaration may be absolute, there is, I believe, a real prospect for man to move further *toward* God and "supersensory" truths through reason. Sound reasoning always takes us *toward* God even if it cannot take us all the way *to* God.

The conceivable advancements in this, the most exalted of realms, may in time become obvious should civilization—some form of authentic, realistic, and healthy civilization—survive and head in an entirely different direction. Such advancements will not occur—not without massive and foundational change—under the tutelage of Western civilization, for all the reasons cited in this book. But I believe it is possible. God, I believe, will permit it, if man's approach is as God would have it.

Sorokin described these "three principal systems of truth" as the methods by which the "eternal question, 'What is truth?'" has been answered by the "great thinkers of mankind." There are, he observed, periods in history in which "purely negative, sceptical answers" are given but then only by "a comparatively small circle of thinkers." Man, he explained, "cannot live and act under the conditions of such a scepticism."[54] Of course, these systems of truth derive from the broader "supersystems of culture" or what we today might call "worldviews."

> Each dominates its respective culture and society. If we have a preponderantly ideational culture, its dominant truth is always a variety of the revealed truth of faith; in a sensate system of culture the truth of the senses will prevail; in an idealistic culture the idealistic truth of reason will govern men's minds. With a change of the dominant cultural supersystem, the dominant truth undergoes a corresponding change.[55]

Sorokin explained more specifically how this has played out over the millennia, and in doing so, inadvertently reminds us once more that there truly is "nothing new under the sun"; we have heard all of this before and are hearing much of it again today in Western civilization. Modernity is not truly modern at all, but in many respects quite primitive. Western man is back where he began.

> To the pagan Graeco–Roman thinkers, swayed by the truth of the senses, Christian revealed truth appeared but mere superstition and ignorance. The foremost intellectuals of the time, like Tacitus, called it "dangerous superstition," "infamous and abominable." Pliny characterized it as "nothing but a debased superstition carried to an extreme." To Marcus Aurelius it was only an unreasoned and intemperate spirit of opposition; to Suetonius it was "a novel and maleficent superstition." Celsus regarded the Christians as "illogical folk....They will not reason or listen to reason about their faith, but stick to their 'Ask no question but believe,' or 'Thy faith shall save thee,' or 'The wisdom of the world is a bad thing and the foolishness a good.'" To Celsus, as to other partisans of sensory truth, the Christians, with their truth of faith, were mere charlatans, ignoramuses, prestidigitators and the like. Even Christ and the Apostles were ignorant and "notorious vagabonds"; the Virgin Mary, a girl with an illegitimate child; and so on. From the point of view of sensory truth, the Christian truth of faith, revelation and God—indeed the whole Christian religion and movement—could not appear other than an absurdity and superstition.[56]

Yet as Sorokin repeatedly observed, this "infamous and abominable" "superstition" changed the world and is the one mechanism by which it could be changed further for the good. That which is "impossible or untrue from the sensate standpoint may be possible and quite true from the standpoint of the Christian truth of faith, and vice versa."[57] Thus the Christian faith—or ideational perspective—does not deny the truth of the senses even as the sensate perspective denies the truth of faith and the possibility of a transcendent reality. Now, which is narrow-minded?

Western education is dominated by the sensate system and thus is—whether it wishes to acknowledge it or not—seriously limited in its breadth, scope, and depth. One cannot advance far in this system because of the towering concrete walls erected in every direction. These walls are not hard and fast, insurmountable obstacles to man's advancement but artificial impediments created by Western man himself. He cannot venture further because he will not. These impediments manifest themselves in three primary ways.

> **The Sensate System of Truth and Knowledge.** Since, according to the major premise of sensate culture, the true-reality value is sensory, cognition is obviously derived only through the sense organs. Sensate truth is mainly the truth of the senses. John Locke's dictum, *Nihil esse in intellectu quod non fuerit prius in sensu*—nothing is in the mind that was not already in the sense—is its exact formula. In this system of truth the sense organs become the principal source of cognition of sensory reality; their testimony decides what is true and what is false; they become the supreme arbiters of the validity of any experience and proposition. Another name for this truth of the senses is empiricism. From the basic character of sensory truth are derived its other characteristics.
>
> A. Any system of sensate truth and reality implies a denial of, or an utterly indifferent attitude toward, any supersensory reality or value..... Being unknowable, it is irrelevant and devoid of interest (Kantian criticism, agnosticism, positivism, etc.). Hence it follows that the sensory cultures regard investigations of the nature of God and supersensory phenomena as superstitious or fruitless speculation. Theology and religion, as a body of revealed truth, are at best tolerated, just as many hobbies are tolerated, or are given mere lip service, or are transformed into a kind of scientific theology, and sensory religion reduced to the level of empirical disciplines devoid of revealed truth.
>
> B. If the sensate system disfavours any preoccupation with the supersensory aspects of reality, it most strongly favours the study of the sensory world, with its physical, chemical and biological properties and relationships. All the cognitive aspirations are concentrated on the study of these sensory phenomena, in their materiality and observable relationships, and on the technological inventions that aim to serve our sensory needs. Knowledge becomes equivalent to the empirical knowledge represented by the natural sciences. Hence in a sensate society natural science replaces religion, theology and even speculative philosophy.[58]

There is the story, perhaps apocryphal, of a lecture by Einstein to graduate students in physics and cosmology. Struck by their zeal and self-confidence, Einstein reputedly asked, "What percentage of the universe's natural laws would you speculate we have discovered?" The most conservative answer was 4%, to which Einstein responded this was certainly hopelessly optimistic and far beyond the actual figure.

Apocryphal or not, this makes a profoundly important point, one stated more succinctly by Immanuel Wallerstein, who observed that "Science is at its earliest moments."[59] Western man, intent on blindly worshipping his Molech, does not perceive how the infant of truth is being sacrificed on the altar of the sensate.

Scientific truth (i.e., sensory truth) then, in the words of Sorokin, "...when made exclusive, inevitably develops into a kind of illusionism in which it undermines itself. Instead of valid cognition of the true reality and values, it increasingly gives us relative and conditional hints respecting the ever-fleeting shadows of ever-changing sensory impressions, which differ with different individuals, groups and conditions."[60]

Here Sorokin resorts to one of the "four-letter words" so inimical to the search for truth: "relative." But also he uses the word "illusionism," which comports fully with our preference for delusion or self-delusion. If God is supersensate and the physical world merely a shadow of a greater reality, why would God create a physical, tactile world? Perhaps the author of Acts gives us the best answer we can find: "God did this so that men would seek him and perhaps reach out for him and find him, though he is not far from each one of us." (Acts 17:27 NIV)

In a damning indictment of Western man's treatment of truth, Sorokin gave us the underlying reasons for so many untruths in Western thought and attitude.

> With the degradation of truth, man is dragged down from his lofty pedestal as a seeker after truth, as an absolute value, to the level of an animal who tends, by means of various "ideologies," "rationalizations," and "derivations," to exalt his greed, his appetites and his egoism. When he does this unwittingly, he becomes a simpleton; when he deliberately resorts to such rationalizations, appealing to "truth" and other high-sounding names, he becomes a downright hypocrite who employs "truth" as a mere smoke screen in order to justify his "residues" and complexes. In either case the result is disastrous to the dignity of man and to the cause of truth and science.[61]

Perhaps masses of inhabitants of our civilization are the simpletons, compliantly conforming to the conventions and guidance of Toynbee's "dominant minority." But others—perhaps most especially in that "dominant minority"—are surely the worst of hypocrites. Passing through life they "exalt" their "greed," "appetites" and "egoism" through their "ideologies" and "rationalizations." This is not a social disease restricted to the secular realms of the culture, but readily found within the church.

Sorokin observed the consequences of the foolishness of man using "truth" as a "beautiful smoke screen" to justify "his impulses and lust, profit and greed."

PD-old

John Locke. *According to Sorokin, "John Locke's dictum,* Nihil esse in intellectu quod non fuerit prius in sensu— *nothing is in the mind that was not already in the sense—is [the] exact formula. In [the sensate] system of truth the sense organs become the principal source of cognition of sensory reality; their testimony decides what is true and what is false; they become the supreme arbiters of the validity of any experience and proposition. Another name for this truth of the senses is empiricism."*

Similar dualism pervades our minds, our conduct and our social relationships. We aspire for happiness and prepare wretchedness for ourselves. The more we try to improve our well-being, the more we lose our peace of mind, without which no happiness is possible. Instead of being serene, at peace with God, the world and his fellow men, contemporary man is a boiling pot of desires that are at war with one another, and with those of his fellows. He is torn between them, cannot control them, and is in a state of perpetual dissatisfaction and restlessness.[62]

This comports fully with the 2,000-year-old message from the New Testament:

What is the source of quarrels and conflicts among you? Is not the source your pleasures that wage war in your members? You lust and do not have; so you commit murder. And you are envious and cannot obtain; so you fight and quarrel. You do not have because you do not ask. You ask and do not receive, because you ask with wrong motives, so that you may spend it on your pleasures. (James 4:1–3 NASB)

The theologian Reinhold Niebuhr observed man's critical role as the nexus between the two worlds.

There is a point at which the "world of spirit comes into conscious contact with the world of matter. That point is man. It is surely rational to suppose that the world of thought and of spiritual values, on the threshold of which man has the consciousness of standing, is a real world, an order no less great than the material order, and that it is in this alone that we shall find a solution to the otherwise hopeless conflict of man's spiritual aspirations and the limitations of his material existence."[63]

But if man foolishly rejects his role and denies even the reality of one or the other, there will be no solution. "There is a way that seems right to a man, but in the end it leads to death." (Proverbs 14:12 NIV)

PD-old

Reinhold Niebuhr *wrote, "There is a point at which the world of spirit comes into conscious contact with the world of matter. That point is man. It is surely rational to suppose that the world of thought and of spiritual values...is a real world, an order no less great than the material order, and that it is in this alone that we shall find a solution to the otherwise hopeless conflict of man's spiritual aspirations and the limitations of his material existence."*

STAY CLOSE TO DEATH

The heart of the wise is in the house of mourning; but the heart of fools is in the house of mirth.
Ecclesiastes 7:4 (KJV)

Truth is often most readily found in proximity to death, whether the awareness of one's own demise or consciousness of the death of others. Passage through the threshold of death will be the ultimate revelation. Yet on this side of that threshold, when we shun seeing death, when we seek to avoid evidence of it, when we evade the reminder of it, we deny ourselves the afflatus that will lift us above the mendacity, mediocrity, and temporality of human experience. *The hunting grounds for truth are the forests of suffering and the fields of mourning.*

PD-gov

Used by permission

Modern funerals isolate the participants from the realities of the death of the body as much as possible. Our culture averts its eyes from death. Modern burials seek to cloak death and the grave in velvet, shielding the family from direct confrontation with mortality. Much money is spent on the funeral industry, at once an effort to sanitize and ameliorate the impact of the reality of death on the one hand and allay our guilt for all we did not do for the deceased when they were alive on the other. In each instance the truth is evaded and a falsehood erected as a screen in its place, separating us from a greater reality, a reality that, if confronted, would make us a better and wiser person. Yet Solomon declared, "The heart of the wise is in the house of mourning; but the heart of fools is in the house of mirth." Proximity to death—awareness of death—will lead one to a higher plane and a more fulfilled life, not the perpetual gloom of depression and despair. Just as Aeschylus taught us that suffering is the only true teacher of wisdom, awareness of death compels us to acknowledge what is important.

Solomon came to understand.

> A good name is better than precious ointment; and the day of death than the day of one's birth. It is better to go to the house of mourning, than to go to the house of feasting: for that is the end of all men; and the living will lay it to his heart. Sorrow is better than laughter: for by the sadness of the countenance the heart is made better. (Ecclesiastes 7:1–5 KJV)

Death, the great absolute truth that the believer and the atheist can agree upon, is truly the "end of all men." If that is so, then it is clear that knowing about death is essential to understanding the meaning and purposes of life. When shadowed by the great darkness we are compelled to search for the light. That is why "the heart of the wise is in the house of mourning" rather than the house of mirth. We scarcely need point out that our civilization—the situs of so much death, the designer of weapons that deal massively in death—nonetheless constantly seeks to revel in the "house of mirth" and never darken the doors of the "house of mourning" except when compelled to do so. Were citizens of Western civilization predisposed to visit the "house of mourning," much actual death would have been avoided.

Neither Solomon nor I counsel morbidity. For the proximity to death of which I speak will lead one to a higher plane and a more fulfilled life, not the perpetual gloom of depression and despair. Just as Aeschylus taught us that suffering is the only true teacher of wisdom, awareness of death compels us to acknowledge what is important.

In my life every exposure to the specter of death—whether the fear on a foreign battlefield that my life may be at its last syllable or witnessing the death of others—has made me a better person. I now nurture the awareness of death. Visiting cemeteries, one may ponder over many a grave the significance of a body in repose, the wisdom or foolishness of its original inhabitant's choices, the meaningfulness or meaninglessness of his or her existence—and how quickly and stealthily death may have crept upon them.

Our culture averts its eyes from death. Much aversion to war in the modern West is less about compassion for its victims than the distaste for being forcefully reminded of the ultimate end of life. Much money is spent on the funeral industry, at once an effort to sanitize and ameliorate the impact of the reality of death on the one hand and allay our guilt for all we did not do for the deceased when they were alive on the other. In each instance the truth is evaded and a falsehood erected as a screen in its place, separating us from a greater reality, a reality that, if confronted, would make us a better and wiser person.

SKEPTICISM AND THE SEARCH FOR GOD

And without faith it is impossible to please God, because anyone who comes to him must believe that he exists and that he rewards those who earnestly seek him.
Hebrews 11:6 (NIV)

When man approaches the quest to understand himself, his universe, and his history with an attitude of unalloyed skepticism—bordering, if not entering, prejudice—about God, he has already blinded his eyes, proscribed his potential view of reality and checked the creative afflatus.

The great truth that has been lost in our time is the truth of Job: man's true status relative to an all-powerful God.

This is the underlying principle beneath the warning by Dawson et al that Western man, especially since the Enlightenment, has entered into the New Dark Age. **An ant has better prospects of understanding man than man has of understanding God. Yet Western man has asserted his intellectual powers with supreme confidence that he can make determinations about God, a universal moral law, human experience, and his universe without deference to faith. To be sure, God has granted us insight into His character and, in part, His will. But the Old Testament writer described what man can know about the mind of God, "For my thoughts are not your thoughts, neither are your ways my ways, saith the Lord." (Isaiah 55:8 KJV) It should be self-evident that this is an understatement unparalleled in human experience.**

There is a legitimate question for the true seeker: With so many religions and belief systems, how do you find the way if you are a skeptic? That question was answered with simple beauty by a missionary to South America in the course of an interview on a major American television network. His wife and child had been killed over the Amazon jungles, the victims of a careless attack on the family's small plane by the pilot of a Peruvian government jet fighter who mistook them for drug smugglers. When asked by his interviewer, who was clearly a skeptic, how someone could come to believe in God as he did, and continue to believe—especially in view of what had happened to him—he responded simply, **"Seek God." God wants us to seek Him, he told the interviewer, and He wants to be found. He will honor a sincere and humble quest for the truth. Of course any diligent student of the Bible will immediately recognize that this humble and faithful Christian was stating one of the great themes of scripture.**

The greatest questions that have haunted man will never be answered purely through human reason. Dawson explained, "The mystery of death, which has always lain so heavy on the human race—the despair of Ecclesiastes before the emptiness of life, the agony of Job in face of the apparent injustice of God—find

AP photo by Paul Warner

Missionary Jim Bowers speaking at his wife's memorial service. *Bower's wife and child were killed over the Amazon jungles, the victims of a careless attack on the family's small plane by the pilot of a Peruvian government jet fighter who mistook them for drug smugglers. When asked by an American TV news interviewer, who was clearly a skeptic, how someone could come to believe in God and continue to believe—especially in view of what had happened to him—he responded simply, "Seek God." God wants us to seek Him, he told the interviewer, and He wants to be found. He will honor a sincere and humble quest for the truth. Of course any diligent student of the Bible will immediately recognize that this humble and faithful Christian was stating one of the great themes of scripture.*

Consciousness of death is a great leveler. Men are stripped of their pride when faced with imminent death, which is why it is said "There are no atheists in foxholes." Exposure to the specter of death—whether the fear on a foreign battlefield or witnessing the death of others—can make an individual a better person.

PD

their solution in the yet more profound mystery of the Cross, in the darkness of Calvary, not in the light of human philosophy and science."[64]

But the quest in search of these answers is not of course limited to the skeptic, but is shared by the believer. Here, however, we see the massive failure described in upcoming chapters of this book.

The ultimate authority for true followers of Christ will not be the writings of theologians, the teachings of the church, or the model of what is being done in other churches, but the example and teachings of Christ. In every age men have lost sight of this. Confusion, error, and suffering have been the inevitable result. If you resist going to the life and teachings of Christ as your ultimate guide then you can know that your authority is man, not God.

What could have been—and perhaps still could be—the alternative for Western civilization? More than any of our observers of the decay and decline of Western civilization, Dawson pondered this question and offered some answers. In *Religion and the Rise of Western Culture,* Dawson resorted to one of the classics of the literature of Western civilization to describe a worldview that is far broader and more hopeful than that offered by Western thought today.

> William Langland's poem [*Piers Plowman*] is the last and in some respects the most uncompromising expression of the medieval ideal of the unity of religion and culture. He realized more clearly than the poets and more intensely than the philosophers that religion was not a particular way of life but the way of all life, and that the divine love which is "the leader of the Lord's folk of heaven" is also the law life upon earth.[65]

> For Heaven might not hold it: it was so heavy of himself,
> Till it had upon earth eaten his fill.
> And when it had of this fold—flesh and blood taken,
> Was never leaf on a linden—lighter thereafter,
> As light and as piercing—as the point of a needle,
> That no armour may hold it—nor no high walls.
> Therefore these words—be written in the Gospel,
> Ask and it shall be given you—for I give all things,
> And that is the lock of love—that letteth out my grace,
> To comfort the careworn—cumbered with sin.

> This vision of Christendom as a labour of love is embodied in the great central figure of Piers Plowman who represents the threefold state of humanity. First he appears as man, the child of nature, the peasant who sustains the world by his labour. Secondly he is the Son of Man and the Son of God who saves the world by his blood,

> Who comes in with a cross—before the common people,
> Like in all limbs—to our Lord Jesus.

And thirdly he is the figure of the Church, the new spiritual humanity, anointed and enlightened by the Holy Ghost to carry on the work of unity and salvation.

> Hence the symbolism of the poem leads Langland necessarily to view human life according to the pattern of the earth as a work of spiritual tillage and harvest. In this he is returning to the imagery of the Gospel and to the words of St. Paul, "We are fellow workers with God. You are God's tillage. You are God's building"; or, to use the words of the Vulgate which were so familiar to him, *Dei agricultura estis.*

All of life is intended to be a search for truth and the application of that truth to one's life so that all of life is simply a choice between self and selfless growing, becoming a better and better person consistent with the model of Christ.

Dawson decried the loss of such a grand and expansive worldview as Langland's—a view that encompasses the material and the spiritual in one incomprehensible, magnificent tapestry.

> What have we done with this inheritance? At least we have *had* it. It has been part of our own flesh and blood and the speech of our own tongue.
>
> And the importance of these centuries of which I have been writing is not to be found in the external order they created or attempted to create, but in the internal change they brought about in the soul of Western man—a change which can never be entirely undone except by the total negation or destruction of Western man himself.
>
> If there is any truth in what I have been saying…such moments of vital fusion between a living religion and a living culture are the creative events in history, in comparison with which all the external achievements in the political and economic orders are transitory and insignificant.[66]

In his rejection of "the external order" as important and his focus on "the internal change they brought about in the soul of Western man," Dawson saw man and history as did Toynbee and is acknowledging once more that most of man's focus is "on the surface of the stream of life."

Only the spiritual ultimately matters. If Western man rediscovers this truth alone, he will have at least taken the first step toward the saving of his civilization. If the Western Christian rediscovers this truth—and his duty in propagating it throughout his world—he will have done his part as well.

St. Paul described the circumstances of man in this regard two millennia ago in passages that remind us again—nothing really changes.

> Where is the wise man? Where is the scholar? Where is the philosopher of this age? Has not God made foolish the wisdom of the world? For since in the wisdom of God the world through its wisdom did not know him, God was pleased through the foolishness of what was preached to save those who believe. Jews demand miraculous signs and Greeks look for wisdom, but we preach Christ crucified: a stumbling block to Jews and foolishness to Gentiles, but to those whom God has called, both Jews and Greeks, Christ the power of God and the wisdom of God. For the foolishness of God is wiser than man's wisdom, and the weakness of God is stronger than man's strength....God chose the foolish things of the world to shame the wise; God chose the weak things of the world to shame the strong. (1 Corinthians 1:20–27 NIV)

END NOTES
CHAPTER 38

1 Oswald Spengler, *The Decline of the West* (New York: A. A. Knopf, 1926), 287.
2 Henry David Thoreau, *Life without Principle* (Forgotten Books, 1902), 19.
3 Spengler, *The Decline of the West,* 394.
4 Alexander Solzhenitsyn, Harvard Class Day Afternoon Exercises, Thursday, June 8, 1978.
5 Francis A. Schaeffer, *How Should We Then Live? The Rise and Decline of Western Thought and Culture* (Wheaton, IL; Crossway Books, 1976), 19–20.
6 Schaeffer, *How Should We Then Live?,* 20.
7 Arnold Toynbee, *Civilization on Trial* (New York: Oxford University Press, 1948), 132.
8 William James, cited in David George Plotkin and David Kin, *Dictionary of American Maxims* (New York: Philosophical Library, 1955), 421.
9 Pitirim A. Sorokin, *The Crisis of Our Age* (Oneworld Publications Ltd., 1941; this edition Sergei P. Sorokin and Peter P. Sorokin, 1992), 200.
10 Immanuel Wallerstein, *The End of the World As We Know It: Social Science for the Twenty-First Century* (Minneapolis: University of Minnesota Press, 1999), 212.
11 Wallerstein, *The End of the World As We Know It,* 213.
12 Wallerstein, *The End of the World As We Know It,* 213.
13 Wallerstein, *The End of the World As We Know It,* 214.
14 Spengler, *Decline of the West,* 32.
15 Wallerstein, *The End of the World As We Know It,* 183.
16 Wallerstein, *The End of the World As We Know It,* 187.
17 St. Thomas Aquinas, cited in Sorokin, *The Crisis of Our Age,* 66.
18 Sorokin, *The Crisis of Our Age,* 253.
19 St. Thomas Aquinas, cited in Sorokin, *The Crisis of Our Age,* 66.
20 Christopher Dawson, *Christianity and the New Age* (New York: Sophia Institute Press, 1985), 48.
21 Dawson, *Christianity and the New Age,* 49.
22 Dawson, *Christianity and the New Age,* 50.
23 Dawson, *Christianity and the New Age,* 51.
24 Dawson, *Christianity and the New Age,* 311.
25 Dawson, *Christianity and the New Age,* 311–312.
26 Christopher Dawson, *Religion and World History: A Selection from the Works of Christopher Dawson* (Garden City, NY: Image Books, 1975), 344.
27 Fernand Braudel, *A History of Civilizations* (New York: Penguin Books, 1995), 334.
28 Dawson, *Religion and World History,* 344.
29 Wallerstein, *The End of the World As We Know It,* 212.
30 Schaeffer, *How Should We Then Live?,* 86.
31 Dawson, *Religion and World History,* 271– 272.
32 Wallerstein, *The End of the World As We Know It,* 172.
33 Toynbee, *Civilization on Trial,* 94.
34 Toynbee, *Civilization on Trial,* 94.
35 Schaeffer, *How Should We Then Live?,* 242.
36 Dawson, *Religion and World History,* 324–325.
37 Dawson, *Religion and World History,* 325.
38 Dawson, *Religion and World History,* 325–326.
39 Quote commonly attributed to Mark Twain.

40 Malcolm Muggeridge, *Confessions of a Twentieth-Century Pilgrim* (New York: HarperCollins, 1988), 67.
41 Muggeridge, *Confessions*, 121.
42 Spengler, *Decline of the West*, 394–395.
43 Schaeffer, *How Should We Then Live?*, 243.
44 Thomas Brackett Reed, American politician, 1839–1902.
45 Schaeffer, *How Should We Then Live?*, 240.
46 Schaeffer, *How Should We Then Live?*, 240–242.
47 Schaeffer, *How Should We Then Live?*, 242.
48 Schaeffer, *How Should We Then Live?*, 242–243.
49 Schaeffer, *How Should We Then Live?*, 178.
50 James Boswell, Arnold Glover, et al, *The Life of Samuel Johnson, LL.D.* (London: J. M. Dent & Co., 1901), 222.
51 Spengler, *Decline of the West*, 287–288.
52 Solzhenitsyn, Harvard Class Day.
53 Sorokin, *Crisis of Our Age*, 67.
54 Sorokin, *Crisis of Our Age*, 68.
55 Sorokin, *Crisis of Our Age*, 68.
56 Sorokin, *Crisis of Our Age*, 69.
57 Sorokin, *Crisis of Our Age*, 70.
58 Sorokin, *Crisis of Our Age*, 71–72.
59 Wallerstein, *The End of the World As We Know It*, 219.
60 Sorokin, *Crisis of Our Age*, 81–82.
61 Sorokin, *Crisis of Our Age*, 101.
62 Sorokin, *Crisis of Our Age*, 200.
63 Reinhold Niebuhr, *The Nature and Destiny of Man* (New York: Charles Scribner, 1920), 253.
64 Dawson, *Religion and World History*, 342.
65 Dawson, *Religion and the Rise of Western Culture*, 221.
66 Dawson, *Religion and the Rise of Western Culture*, 224.

CHAPTER

39

THE GREATEST OF THESE IS LOVE

He that loveth not knoweth not God; for God is love.
1 John 4:7–8 (KJV)

The hunger for love is much more difficult to remove than the hunger for bread.
Mother Teresa[1]

And now these three remain: faith, hope and love. But the greatest of these is love.
1 Corinthians 13:13 (NIV)

Behind most of the problems that beset humanity is the absence of love. Were man to have any hope of making his world more just, more peaceful, more sanguine, more meaningful, he must confront his failure to love. This is especially so within the church, and the fact that we Christians often do not love is an indictment of the church like no other. Even those who profess to love—who tout the virtues and blessings of love, who extol the church's duty to love—are often the hypocritical covert proponents of materialism, personal security, comfort, self-centeredness, and complacency, all of which are in profound conflict with love.

During my sojourn with the mujahadeen during the Soviet–Afghan war, I passed through a village in Pakistan in the tribal areas, now lost to memory, that was the scene of one of those epiphanies that change one's view of reality. The memory of such an experience, once formed in the mind, becomes emblematic of a broader truth. We had stopped to pick up supplies and other mujahadeen when I noticed two children, a boy and a girl, perhaps two and three years of age, lying side by side in the middle of the dusty street. Their eyes closed, and with flies crawling into their mouths, noses and ears, I first thought these were corpses. A woman dressed in a full-length *chador* stepped alongside the children, knelt and began waving a tattered cloth over their faces, apparently to repel the flies.

The children were not dead even though their well-being was clearly in doubt. Despair and a sense of helplessness swept over me. That any child, any mother, would be left in this predicament was a tragic wrong. Yet two unsettling thoughts followed in rapid succession: this scene, or something akin to it, was neither unique nor rare, and most of humanity—including all those passing this sad tableau on a busy street—did not care. The pathetic scene became representative to me of the state of our world. The suffering and tragedy are all about us but the professions of concern and the desultory acts of compassion ring hollow.

Mother Teresa *observed, "The hunger for love is much more difficult to remove than the hunger for bread." Yet there are few in the Western church willing to sacrificially offer it. Even those who profess to love—who tout the virtues and blessings of love, who extol the church's duty to love—are often the hypocritical covert proponents of materialism, personal security, comfort, self-centeredness, and complacency, all of which are in profound conflict with love.*

Photo courtesy of the Vatican

The world truly does not care. In light of biblical teaching, that is an expectable reality; but the church's indifference is an affront to the teachings and sacrifice of Christ.

Here, with the help of Oswald Spengler, we confront that first terrible truth; momentarily we confront the second.

> The world in general—meaning the world-as-history—is base. It fights instead of renouncing; it does not possess the idea of sacrifice. It prevails over truth by means of facts. And therefore the highest sacrifice that intellectual man can offer is to make a personal present of it to the powers of nature. *Every moral action is a piece of this sacrifice,* and an ethical life-course is an unbroken chain of such sacrifices. Above all, the offering of sympathy, compassion, in which the inwardly strong gives up his superiority to the powerless. The compassionate man kills something within himself. But we must not confuse this sympathy in the grand religious sense with the vague sentimentality of the everyday man, who cannot command himself, still less with the *race-feeling of chivalry,* which is not a moral of reasons and rules at all, but an upstanding and self-evident *custom* bred of the unconscious pulsations of a keyed-up life. But Compassion likewise demands inward greatness of soul, and so it is those self-same springtimes that produce the most saintly servants of pity, Francis of Assisi, Bernard of Clairvaux, in whom renunciation was a pervading fragrance, to whom self-offering was bliss, whose *caritas* was ethereal, bloodless, timeless, historyless, in whom fear of the universe had dissolved itself into pure, flawless love, a summit of causal moral of which Late periods are simply no longer capable.[2]

We have examined man and Western culture from complex and sophisticated perspectives: history, sociology, theology, and psychology. But all that we might conclude—all that is meaningful and eternal at least—can be reached by a very simple approach: that of Scripture and what it teaches about love.

A person need not be highly educated, analytically gifted, or broadly experienced to reach mountaintops of human understanding. There is a way by which any human being can ascend to the summit of an Everest of morality and spiritual enlightenment: faith in, and obedience to, the life and teachings of Christ. The ultimate expression of that faith and obedience is love.

THE CHRISTIAN DEFINITION OF LOVE

Since man and his values are sacred, the relationship of man to man should be guided by sublime love, as the categoric imperative....they all are one and all serve one purpose: the unfolding of the Absolute in the relative empirical world, to the greater nobility of Man and to the greater glory of God.
Pitirim Sorokin[3]

Our culture says love is emotional fulfillment, romantic feelings, erotic passion, etc. But what is love really? Love is the most beautiful truth in the universe—something we all desperately need and through which we are deeply blessed. Yet we rarely stop to consider what it is or how it manifests itself in our world, or who gives it.

"Love" is perhaps the most misused and abused word in the English language. Love, in most of the languages found in Western civilization, may carry many connotations from fondness for an object, or activity, to sex. The ancient Greeks had a better idea. Three Greek words with three distinct meanings encompass most of the concepts embodied in the singular word, love, in English: *eros* (sexual "love"); *philos* (brotherly love or the love of one friend for another); and *agape* (God's love for man or altruistic love). The failure of English to make such important and salutary distinctions has contributed to the confusion over the concept of love. Even among Christians its meaning is often clouded and confused by our culture's misuse of the term. Much of the actual use of the word in the West carries connotations of self-interest, self-indulgence, and unreality in relationships, even lust—all notions and attitudes that are antithetical to true love as Christ used the term.

It can also be a shallow conformity to a faddish social norm. Robert Frost declared, "I have none of the tenderer-than-thou, collectivistic regimenting love, with which the modern world is being swept."[4] This is the kind of "love" of which many people speak in Western culture, an ersatz variety born of the same pattern of self-delusion and affinity for the artificial that we recognized earlier in this study as one of the major indicia of cultural decline.

Neither is love, as Jesus spoke of it and as appears most places in the New Testament, some maudlin sentiment. Christ's definition and demonstration of love is our primary concern. The Christian understanding of love should reflect an unselfish desire to take into account the interests of others in the same way we would wish others to take into account our welfare and interests. This understanding of love has nothing to do with sex, romance, or sentimentality. It is a choice—an act of the will—and purely unselfish.

However, by making that choice of the will—to love as Christ spoke of it—we often find that our emotions follow. There is a therapeutic school of psychology built entirely around this premise: we become in our minds and hearts what we choose to act out and demonstrate in our lives. This understanding of human nature has been with us for centuries and is now understood to a high degree. Theodore Roosevelt described how learning to act unafraid helped him to defeat fear and actually *be* unafraid.

Ultimately, we must not search for sentiment or emotion in order to show love. True Christian love will forever remain a choice of the will that translates into unselfish and caring actions toward others. A person may "speak with the tongues of men and angels," but if he does not truly love his fellowman, and if he will not stand for them and for his convictions, he is worthless to the cause of freedom, justice, and faith.

The classic description of Christian love is found in the eloquent verses of 1 Corinthians 13:

> If I speak in the tongues of men and of angels, but have not love, I am only a resounding gong or a clanging cymbal. If I have the gift of prophecy and can fathom all mysteries and all knowledge, and if I have a faith that can move mountains, but have not love, I am nothing. If I give all I possess to the poor and surrender my body to the flames, but have not love, I gain nothing. Love is patient, love is kind. It does not envy, it does not boast, it is not proud. It is not rude, it is not self-seeking, it is not easily angered, it keeps no record of wrongs. Love does not delight in evil but rejoices with the truth. It always protects, always trusts, always hopes, always perseveres. Love never fails.... When I was a child, I talked like a child, I thought like a child, I reasoned like a child. When I became a man, I put childish ways behind me. Now we see but a poor reflection as in a mirror; then we shall see face to face. Now I know in part; then I shall know fully, even as I am fully known. And now these three remain: faith, hope and love. But the greatest of these is love. (1 Corinthians 13:1–13 NIV)

When we speak of love, however, we must not make another error that is so common in our culture. The kind of love that is largely devoid of accountability (i.e., we must be "understanding," "forgiving," "tolerant," etc.) is not true love. A world without accountability would be wretched and chaotic. This underlies much of the world's misery now. Just as the natural world would immediately become chaotic by the suspension of just one natural law, the world of human relationships becomes chaotic when God's moral laws are not obeyed.

The notion that love means tolerance or acceptance of what the Bible condemns is not only propagandistic and rationalizing, it is heretical. We do not show love to others by in any way countenancing their sins. Precisely the opposite is true: Genuine love will make the hard choices to stand, to confront, to rebuke. Loving is not about love without law. Nor is it about grace without repentance.

God wants to forgive; this is surely true. Yet it is a heresy when we extend this to the notion that there is forgiveness without repentance. Just as love is not some maudlin sentiment or gushy feeling, as is the perception of many in our culture, nor does it mean that God's moral law can be ignored or amended because "God is a god of love." When we hear such utterances we can know that the speaker has no understanding of the God of the Bible or for that matter the God of the universe. Law is integral to the teachings of Christ: "Do not think that I came to abolish the Law or the Prophets; I did not come to abolish, but to fulfill." (Matthew 5:17 NIV) Men and women of our age in the West want to believe that God's grace is unconditional. This view panders to their desire to sin with impunity. But a world in which grace was unconditionally given would be a place of even greater misery than we have seen in human history. Men readily understand that the physical laws of the universe that produce its remarkable order are critical to our existence. Yet, Western man foolishly asserts that moral law is relative and not absolute.

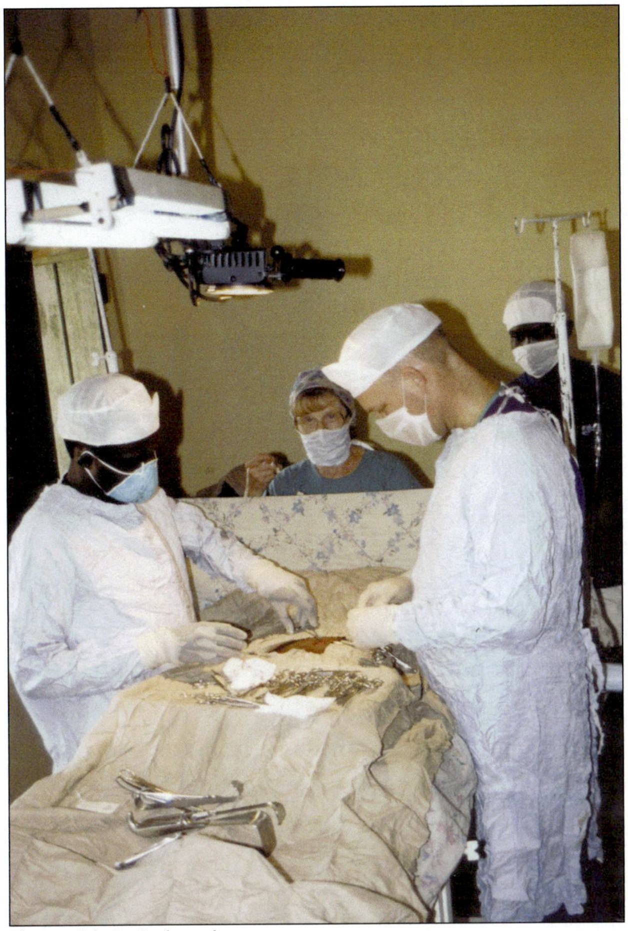

Photograph by Ivy Scarborough

Dr. Bill Greiser, with Samaritan's Purse, performing surgery at Lui in the war zone of Sudan. *Christian love is not some maudlin sentiment. The Christian understanding of love should reflect an unselfish desire to take into account the interests of others in the same way we would wish others to take into account our welfare and interests. This understanding of love has nothing to do with sex, romance, or sentimentality. It is a choice—an act of the will—and purely unselfish.*

Toynbee spoke of the significance of man's conception of law generally and contrasted it with the concept of love.

> The vision of a unity of the cosmos—foreshadowed in the pedestrian and limited unification of human society in the universal states—has presented itself to men in a series of variations on the theme of a Universe governed by law. The Babylonian astrologer—and the modern Western scientist—has been captivated by a mathematical law; the Buddhist ascetic by a psychological law; the Hellenic philosopher by a social law. Such beliefs have at least the merit of acknowledging the existence of a common principle behind the multiple appearances of the mundane world, but the identification of the unifying principle with law ignores the role of love, and love, as well as law, is an aspect of reality that we encounter in our human experience. We know law as the imposition of unity by the fiat of a sovereign legislator. We know love as the quest for unity by a living being whose divisive self-centredness—another name for life itself—has been overcome by an irresistible impulse to give instead of taking. Our acquaintance with both love and law is in the tiny field of human affairs. The belief that love and law are also aspects of an ultimate spiritual reality is an act of faith....[5]

The soul, Toynbee continued, "that has caught the vision of unity, and has seen the unifying spirit as love, is spiritually prepared to perceive, and to respond to, the challenge of an 'other world' that is not just the mundane world translated into an imaginary past or future, but is a world of a different order of reality."[6] Such a soul "may at last discover the truth that the everyday world offers no final answer to the besetting miseries of life in an age of disintegration"; only with this insight will that soul "be impelled to rise above the mundane level of existence and seek a point of departure in the life of the spirit."[7] Toynbee's words are another way of expressing two of our key themes: First, that Western man must reject the self-delusion of the worldview that is taking him rapidly toward his doom; and second, he must supplant it with the spirit of love. Through this *only* can the Western church rise to the challenges of our age.

YOU ARE *DIFFERENT* FROM ME

The pathos of binding Christian love has tended to be supplanted by hatred — the hatred of man for man, of class for class, of nation for nation, of state for state, of race for race. As a result, might has become right. Bellum omnium contra omnes—*war waged by all, against all—has raised its ugly head. These are exactly the conditions we face.*
Pitirim Sorokin[8]

Humanity gravitates to polarization, distinction, separation, and division, whether ethnic, racial, gender, ideological, religious, political, business, or even in the realms of sports and amusement. This is true of most people who tout "diversity" as much as it is of the rest of the species. This propensity is also exploited in business, finance, politics, ideology, marketing, public relations, etc., to manipulate human behavior. All pander to this dark instinct in man. In the lexicon of "different," competition, conflict, argument, and even war can become virtues rather than vices to shun. This focus on differences rather than similarities has been behind all of the wars of the twentieth and twenty-first centuries. In Bosnia and Somalia in 1993, Kosovo in 1999, and Israel, I have seen the evidence of this tendency in its most vile expressions. One episode in Kosovo lingers with me as an illustration. Sitting in the open door of a blacked-out Blackhawk helicopter with a unit of the 82nd Airborne I participated in a night patrol intended to stop sectarian acts of vengeance and reprisal. We watched the ground intently as the pilot banked and turned scouring large areas, But we soon realized we did not need our night vision goggles to see the arson fires being started in nearly every direction. Lurching from one arson site to another we attempted in vain to arrive on the scene before the arsonists could escape. At least one of us was more than ready to fire on these callous cowards. Within a relatively short period, I counted eleven homes ablaze. Despite the extraordinary technology and firepower available to the American military, at least that night no one was held accountable.

View from a Blackhawk helicopter of Kosovo homes being burned by arsonists, 1999. *Man is constantly choosing to treat differences (ethnicity, race, education, wealth, etc.) as consequential and, in so doing, produces tensions and conflict that are the source of much of his misery, his insecurity, and his suffering. In making distinctions in order to feel better, superior, or especially privileged, man more often exposes his inferiority and weakness.*

Photograph by Ivy Scarborough

W. E. B. Dubois declared one of the significant truths of human experience by stating that differences among human beings drawn on any basis or criterion other than character are devilish—never divine—in their origins. In truth, the only distinction among men that has any significant and lasting implications is each individual's relationship with God. All other forms of difference are superficial and of little consequence.

Of course man is constantly choosing to treat them as consequential and, in so doing, contrives what the playwright deliberately seeks to achieve: tension in the plot. But these tensions are the source of much of his misery, his insecurity, and his suffering. History then becomes one unending tragedy in a script written—usually unconsciously and uncontemplatedly—by the actors themselves. Man historically makes distinctions in order to make himself feel better, superior, or especially privileged, but, in so doing, more often inadvertently exposes his inferiority and weakness.

The most obvious expression of this dark instinct in man in our time and in Western civilization has been racism. In *Civilization on Trial*, Toynbee did not spare his own civilization from a blunt indictment:

> ...although the record of history would seem on the whole to show that race consciousness has been the exception and not the rule in the constant inter-breeding of the human species, it is a fatality of the present situation that this consciousness is felt—and felt strongly—by the very peoples which, in the competition of the last four centuries between several Western powers, have won—at least for the moment—the lion's share of the inheritance of the Earth. Though in certain other respects the triumph of the English-speaking peoples may be judged, in retrospect, to have been a blessing to mankind, in this perilous matter of race feeling it can hardly be denied that it has been a misfortune. The English-speaking nations that have established themselves in the New World overseas have not, on the whole, been "good mixers." They have mostly swept away their primitive predecessors; and, where they have either allowed a primitive population to survive, as in South Africa, or have imported primitive "man-power" from elsewhere, as in North America, they have developed the rudiments of that paralysing institution which in India—where in the course of many centuries it has grown to its full stature—we have learnt to deplore under the name of "caste"....[9]

Even those otherwise disposed to noble and exalted values were tainted by this "paralyzing institution." A close friend, Brigadier General Herb Lloyd, known to some as the "Supersoldier," began life as a farm boy in the rural South amidst a culture of pervasive racism. Highly decorated

PD-old

W. E. B. Dubois *declared one of the significant truths of human experience—that distinctions among human beings drawn on any basis or criterion other than character are devilish—never divine—in their origins.*

through four tours of duty in Vietnam, he came eventually to speak openly and remorsefully of his former racism. As a young soldier, badly wounded in battle, unable to move and abandoned, Lloyd was rescued by a black soldier who ran back into the face of the enemy fire, threw Lloyd over his shoulder and carried him to safety. Through this and other experiences he saw the courage and love of some black soldiers, not just for those of their own race but for whites as well. "I was humbled," he said years later, "and humiliated by what I recognized in my attitudes and my heart. I realized it was not the color of a man's skin, but what was in his heart that really counted." Later, while teaching at West Point, he overheard cadets making racist remarks. Lloyd took them to a military cemetery and the graves of decorated black soldiers who had been killed in combat and challenged them, "Now, standing here over these graves, let us hear you talk your racist trash."

General Lloyd was a product of a culture that fostered racism and, more significantly, an American church, portions of which did its part in sustaining and nurturing racism rather than resisting and opposing it. At the very heart chronologically and attitudinally of the struggle over racism is a historical incident that I believe may have special symbolic significance for the modern Western church. A turning point in the American Civil War occurred during the battle of Chancellorsville. As one Confederate general later expressed it, the death of the Southern Confederacy could be dated from Chancellorsville. Had Southern forces won that battle, this may have won the war for the South. Robert E. Lee later said that had General "Stonewall" Jackson not been killed at Chancellorsville the Confederacy would have won the critical battle of Gettysburg. Jackson, a devout Christian and, after Lee, probably the Confederacy's greatest general, was not a slaveholder, but he was very ably defending the system that fostered slavery. His Christian faith was genuine and his love for God sincere, but his judgment misguided and his moral choices mistaken. I believe this may be—in terms of destiny—why he was killed at Chancellorsville, and why there was such irony in the manner of his death: mistakenly shot by his own men. This was, it would seem, symbolic of his ill-conceived choice to support and defend the system that fostered this evil.

Similarly, the Western church's failures in the battle over racism have contributed immeasurably to the church's defeats in the war between faith and secularism in the culture. And, like Jackson, the American church may pay a heavy price for its failure to obey and its callous choices to ignore.

Some blacks in twentieth- and twenty-first-century America have undoubtedly rejected Christianity and embraced Islam precisely because of the hypocrisy of the Christian church in not only failing to vigorously oppose racism, but actually serving in some instances as one of its bastions. The love demonstrated in the life and teachings of Christ could not be found in these churches, which as a result became "stumbling blocks," to use the biblical term, in others' search for God. Yet no religion even today has been more fully complicit in acts of racism, slavery, and oppression as has Islam.

But, as history and human nature have repeatedly demonstrated, disillusionment and resentment breed a prejudice of their own, which is typically blind to reason, objectivity, or the truth. The only firewall that prevents the spread of the conflagration is authentic love.

I previously explained that what I saw of racism during the Civil Rights era of my youth in the American South first caused me to realize that something was deeply wrong with the American church. There were exceptions of course. In 1963, twenty-eight Mississippi Methodist ministers signed a document titled "Born of Conviction" protesting racism in the Mississippi school systems. All were shunned, even by their own church members, and some received death threats. They were examples of a distinct but courageous minority.

Photograph by Ivy Scarborough

Sarajevo airport, 1993. The author (center) in heavy body armor with French Foreign Legionnaires. *Humanity gravitates to polarization, distinction, separation, and division, whether ethnic, racial, gender, ideological, religious, political, business, or even in the realms of sports and amusement. This is true of most people who tout "diversity" as much as it is of the rest of the species. This propensity is also exploited in business, finance, politics, ideology, marketing, public relations, etc., to manipulate human behavior—all pander to this dark instinct in man. In the lexicon of "different," competition, conflict, argument, and even war can become virtues rather than vices to shun. This focus on differences rather than similarities has been behind all of the wars of the twentieth and twenty-first centuries. In Bosnia and Somalia in 1993, Kosovo in 1999, and Israel, I have seen the evidence of this tendency in its most vile expressions.*

It was in part due to my disillusionment with the church over the question of race that I began to question God, His very existence and His attributes. Watching my father and family suffer—and realizing that there was no apparent relief to be found in the church—I perhaps subtly began to doubt God by virtue of observing His professed followers. This contributed to a plague of deep and painful questions: Does God exist? If so, why is He seemingly so remote? If He exists, why is there such cruelty in the world? Though, even at that age, I did not expect God to take responsibility for the choices of men, I nonetheless was deeply disquieted by the fact that some who claimed Him were, in some instances, the source of the cruelty, or at least indifferent to its effects.

Many people over the millennia have walked these trails of doubt and skepticism. I was saved from taking the wrong fork by the love manifested from my parents and my entire extended family. There, closest to me, I could clearly see the evidence of God's immeasurable love. Millions do not have that evidence ever before them. Many Christians and a multitude of churches have failed to show it. Some would see the love of Christ were there just one Christian in their lives who demonstrated true love and the willingness to simply tell them about their faith.

In our time in history one of our great failures as Christians has been our failure to reach out in love to other races. The fight against racism began and was largely waged in the legal and political systems, not through our churches. Even today, more than a half century since Billy Graham set an example by integrating his services, many churches make scant effort to reach out to blacks. I once proposed to a prominent pastor that some church-wide initiative be begun to heal the wounds and the breach among black and white Christians caused by racism. His church, he responded, had voted and passed a resolution some years previously taking a stand against racism. His answer reflected either extreme insensitivity or cowardice, probably both. It might also have reflected a significant degree of self-delusion. Dawson noted an expression of this human tendency to self-delusion in another time and place but with regard to the same issue.

> In this way the French intelligentsia came to see in America the realisation of Rousseau's ideal of a state and a social order based on natural principles and inspired by a spirit of fraternity and equality. They forgot the mob law, the tarrings and featherings, and the ruthless proscription of minorities by which New England democracy had vindicated the rights of man. They forgot that the liberal culture and the spacious life of Monticello and Mount Vernon were only rendered possible by the existence of negro slavery. They saw only the generous idealism of a Jefferson, the republican virtue of a Washington, and the mellow wisdom of Franklin.[10]

In the same way, like the complacent pastor who saw no need to act, the American church has deluded itself that it has done its duty. This failure has deep roots, as Francis Schaeffer observed:

> At certain points the people in the stream of the Reformation were inconsistent with the biblical teaching they claimed to follow. There were many areas where the Bible was not followed as it should have been, but two are outstanding: first, a twisted view of race, and second, a noncompassionate use of accumulated wealth.
>
> In the area of race there were two types of abuse. The first was slavery based on race; the second, racial prejudice as such. Both practices were wrong, and often both were present when Christians had a stronger influence on the consensus than they now have—and yet the church, as the church, did not speak out sufficiently against them.[11]

Schaeffer singled out the avowedly Christian America for its role in the darkest of chapters of Western history: "And in the area of slavery, the United States must bear special criticism, since slavery based on race continued there until such a late date."[12]

> These views were not the product of the Christian consensus, but the churches of that time must be criticized for not shouting loudly enough against these abuses. The churches could have changed things in that day if they had spoken with clarity and courage. The central reason the church should have spoken clearly and courageously on these issues is that the Bible commands it. Had the church been faithful to the Bible's teaching about the compassionate use of wealth, it would not later have lost so many of the workers. And if it had spoken clearly against the use of wealth as a weapon in a kind of "survival of the fittest," in all probability this concept as it came into secularized science would not have been so automatically accepted....

> To keep the matter in balance...many influential people who automatically called themselves Christians were not Christian at all; it was merely socially acceptable to bear the name and go through the outward forms.[13]

The other "failure" to which Schaeffer alludes, the noncompassionate use of wealth, continues to pervade Western culture—again, not simply with the complicity of the church but even *within* the church. Robert Conquest insightfully points out how this manifests itself in ways some never understand.

> ...many serious problems have simply not been solved, regardless of money or goodwill.... For example, "poverty" in the Western countries—which is not merely a matter of the poor in the earlier sense "but," as Geoffrey Wheatcroft has written, "a new form of relative poverty, of hopelessness and resentment, building up its own rage and bitterness, not because of the failure of free enterprise, but because of its very success, from which a minority are excluded."
>
> For it is the exclusion more than the poverty, or even the relative poverty, as such, that is the crux.[14]

Men will endure much if they believe it is shared—witness the Great Depression and World War II—but they rebel when the burdens and blessings are disproportionate. This is the case not only within our culture but of Western civilization vis-à-vis much of the rest of the world.

Here a seeming paradox replicates itself even today: nonbelievers may take principled, compassionate stands at great risk to themselves while professing believers and the church not only do not, but actually form part of the base for evil. Lincoln, who apparently spent much of his life as an agnostic, became a real source and symbol of man's stand against brutality and exploitation. He could be called the most "Christ-like" of all the presidents precisely because of his compassion and grace. I believe it likely that his late arrival at the portals of faith was due in part to his consciousness of many Christians' lives that did not square with the life of Christ. He once declared, "When any church will inscribe over its altar...the Saviour's condensed statement of the substance of both law and Gospel, 'Thou shalt love the Lord thy God with all thy heart, and with all thy soul and thy neighbor as thyself,' that church will I join with all my heart and all my soul."

Some years ago, while jogging in the country one October night near our farm home in Tennessee, my wife, Mona, and I passed an African–American church. A vibrant harmony of hymn-singing poured with the golden light through the windows into the darkness. How appropriate it all seemed, until we considered that there were three other churches in that community, all white, and generation after generation nothing had been shared of consequence between these four churches that professed to love and serve the same god.

Today, in the Western church, we tend to seek out only those who are much like us racially, socially, economically. Yet church historians point out that the greatest and most dynamic growth in the Christian church occurred in the first and second centuries. During that era there were no church buildings, no programs, no church bureaucracies, no denominations, none of modern technology—and a multiplicity of diverse peoples from all over the Roman Empire who came to faith. Why did those Christians succeed? Because the spread of the gospel was motivated by intense love—a love expressed through relationships and sacrificial service to others of all races, all social stations, all creeds and attributes.

HYPOCRITES IN "LOVE" DILETTANTES IN "SERVICE"

Then the Lord said to him, "Now then, you Pharisees clean the outside of the cup and dish, but inside you are full of greed and wickedness."
Luke 11:39 (NIV)

Woe to you Pharisees, because you give God a tenth of your mint, rue and all other kinds of garden herbs, but you neglect justice and the love of God. You should have practiced the latter without leaving the former undone.
Luke 11:42 (NIV)

With the Afghan mujahadeen in 1985 an experience impressed itself upon me as a personal indictment and a life lesson. Having been on the trail for days with little sleep or food, we stopped off to rest with other mujahadeen gathered at one of the typical adobe huts in a magnificent broad valley.

One of these strange mujahadeen had a bullet wound through his wrist. Through the only muj who spoke any English I told the wounded man I would bandage the wound if he would permit it. He agreed. As I placed the bandage, he stared at me intently and impassively, saying nothing, showing no pain, and displaying no reaction other than apparent bewilderment, as if I were a strange species from another planet.

When we were once again on the trail, the English-speaking muj walked alongside me and said, "You showed kindness to a very cruel man." I asked what he meant. The man's family (wife and children) had been killed by the Russians, he said. As a consequence, when he captured a Russian he would "skin him." I asked no more questions.

But later my conscience haunted me. I now understood the stoicism and bewilderment. This man was profoundly emotionally scarred. Notions of love and compassion were alien to him. But I also realized that despite my act of kindness it was in truth what I sometimes now call the "altruism of the dilettante." I was dabbling at being kind, at caring, at showing compassion. It was the kind of superficiality I believe we in the Western church are so guilty of in this cruel world. Talk truly is cheap and some forms of shallow actions are not much more expensive—they just look good.

In 1993, just prior to the "Blackhawk Down" incident, I returned from a stay in Somalia with the 10th Mountain Division only to be dismayed to find my own church absorbed in a fund-raising program for a new, expensive organ. The juxtaposition of this frivolousness with the death and dying being fought courageously by a handful of Christian aid workers and several thousand American soldiers in Mogadishu was appalling. Yet there is no escape from this mindset in the church in the West, and there is no love in it.

Quietly reestablishing ourselves in another church, Mona and I endured a reprise of that experience shortly after our return from the war zone of Sudan in 1998. Lives were being lost in a mission hospital established by Samaritan's Purse in southern Sudan simply because of the dearth of resources relative to the misery and suffering in every direction. Amidst the stack of mail awaiting us at home was a reminder from our pastor of the need for generous contributions to pay for the multimillion-dollar building program that included not only an imposing sanctuary but a "family life" center, a

Photograph by Ivy Scarborough

Mujahadeen carrying Russian Kalashnikovs and a PPsh 41 submachine gun, Paktia Province, Afghanistan, 1985. *I bandaged a bullet wound in the arm of one of these mujahadeen but came to realize this was a form of altruistic dilettantism. Christians will sometimes do something to alleviate suffering and need but very often the effort is more directed at making ourselves feel better. Devoid of true sacrifice, it can never truly meet the great needs of humanity.*

gymnasium, ball fields, and other amenities now considered *de rigueur* for the "successful" American church.

Western Christians will do something that gives the appearance of honoring God's commands, but it would be a vain endeavor to ask for real sacrifice or the assumption of great risks and burdens. In another war zone, Bosnia, in 1993, a friend, neurosurgeon and UCLA Medical School professor Dr. Mel Cheatham, made this point in sharp contrast by actually living the alternative. Mel, his wife, Sylvia, and I were part of a small team from Samaritan's Purse and World Medical Mission sent into the area of fighting to provide neurosurgical medical care. Though my primary focus was observing and documenting the war, I was sometimes with Mel and the team as they performed surgeries under difficult and occasionally dangerous conditions. One evening in our safe house in Zenica, Mel gave a devotional that has remained in my memory as one of the more honest expositions of a great biblical truth. Mel chose, as his biblical text, Jesus' account of the rich man and the poor beggar Lazarus.

> At his gate was laid a beggar named Lazarus, covered with sores and longing to eat what fell from the rich man's table. Even the dogs came and licked his sores. The time came when the beggar died and the angels carried him to Abraham's side. The rich man also died and was buried. In hell, where he was in torment, he looked up and saw Abraham far away, with Lazarus by his side. So he called to him, "Father Abraham, have pity on me and send Lazarus to dip the tip of his finger in water and cool

Seen here (center) with an American soldier between Mogadishu and Marka in 1993, *I returned from Somalia just prior to the "Blackhawk Down" incident to find my own church absorbed in fund-raising for a new organ. The juxtaposition of this frivolousness with the death and dying being fought courageously by a handful of Christian aid workers and American soldiers was appalling. Yet there is no escape from this mindset in the church in the West—and there is no love in it.*

Photograph by Ivy Scarborough

> my tongue, because I am in agony in this fire." But Abraham replied, "Son, remember that in your lifetime you received your good things, while Lazarus received bad things, but now he is comforted here and you are in agony. And besides all this, between us and you a great chasm has been fixed, so that those who want to go from here to you cannot, nor can anyone cross over from there to us." He answered, "Then I beg you, father, send Lazarus to my father's house, for I have five brothers. Let him warn them, so that they will not also come to this place of torment." Abraham replied, "They have Moses and the Prophets; let them listen to them." "No, father Abraham," he said, "but if someone from the dead goes to them, they will repent." He said to him, "If they do not listen to Moses and the Prophets, they will not be convinced even if someone rises from the dead." (Luke 16:20–31 NIV)

The King James Version of this passage refers to Lazarus eating only the "crumbs" from the rich man's table. Mel's observation, that we in the Christian church in the West often give only the crumbs from our tables to the suffering and needy, was precisely true. Though no one in that small mission group was giving their crumbs, this is, more often than not, the extent of the church's commitment to the needy and the suffering. Love and compassion are extolled and preached endlessly, but their evidence in sacrificial terms is scant. This failure to truly love our fellowman is—though we do not recognize it—simultaneously a failure to love God.

Robert Frost, in "Death of the Hired Man," described home as the place where when you go there they "have to take you in." The church should be the place that when you go there with your problems, tragedies, or heartaches they not only feel compelled but *want* to take you in. There must be, Sorokin said, "a change of the whole mentality and attitudes in the direction of the norms prescribed in the Sermon on the Mount. When such a change occurs, to a notable degree the technical ways of remodelling the economic and political structures in this direction become easy." But "Without this change, no mechanical, politico–economic reconstruction can give the desired results."[15]

PD-art

Lazarus and the Rich Man (1865), by Eduard Gebhardt (1838–1925). *The Bible refers to Lazarus eating only the "crumbs" from the rich man's table. We in the Christian church in the West more often than not give only the crumbs from our table to the needy and the suffering. Love and compassion are extolled and preached endlessly, but their evidence in sacrificial terms is scant. This failure to truly love our fellowman is simultaneously a failure to love God.*

Toynbee reached the same conclusion as expressed in one of the wisest and most powerful passages ever written by a Western historian:

> The two activities are indissoluble because "He that loveth not his brother whom he hath seen, how can he love God whom he hath not seen?" The Christian soul that is truly seeking to save itself by loving God in God's way is as fully social a being as the Spartan who saves his personal honour by dying for his community at Thermopylae; only the Christian soul on Earth is enrolled in a different society from the Spartan micro-state or the Roman Leviathan. He is a citizen, not of a secular commonwealth, but of the Kingdom of God, and therefore his paramount and all-embracing aim is, not to identify himself with the genius of an earthly city, but to attain the highest degree of communion with, and likeness to, God Himself; his relations with his fellow-men are consequences of, and corollaries to, his relations with God; his standard for his attitude towards his fellows will be his intuition of God's attitude towards Man; and his way of loving his neighbour as God loves Man will be to try to help his neighbour to win what the Christian is seeking for himself—that is, to come into closer communion with God and to become more godlike.
>
> If this is a soul's recognized aim for itself and for its fellow souls in the Christian Church on Earth, then it is evident that under a Christian dispensation God's will will be done on Earth as it is in Heaven to an immeasurably greater degree than in a secular mundane society. It is also evident that, in the Church Militant on Earth, the good social aims of mundane societies will incidentally be achieved very much more successfully than they ever have been or can be achieved in a mundane society which aims at these objects direct, and at nothing higher. In other words, the spiritual progress of individual souls in this life will in fact bring with it much more social progress than could be

attained in any other way. It is a paradoxical but profoundly true and important principle of life that the most likely way to reach a goal is to be aiming not at that goal itself but at some more ambitious goal beyond it.[16]

UNITY
A COMMON FAITH—A COMMON PURPOSE

My prayer is not for them alone. I pray also for those who will believe in me through their message, that all of them may be one, Father, just as you are in me and I am in you.... I have given them the glory that you gave me, that they may be one as we are one: I in them and you in me. May they be brought to complete unity to let the world know that you sent me and have loved them even as you have loved me....
John 17:20–23 (NIV)

A new command I give you: Love one another. As I have loved you, so you must love one another. By this all men will know that you are my disciples, if you love one another.
John 13:34–35 (NIV)

Unity, we have been told, is of the will, not necessarily an agreement of the minds. Unity of the church (i.e., all of the followers of Christ) is one of the great themes of the New Testament. The fragmentation of the church into sometimes warring, always competing, factions is at once a manifestation of the Western church's worldly bent and its complacency about the state of that world.

We can all see the prodigious difficulties inherent in an effort to unify the church

Symbolically, the skilled hands of neurosurgeon Dr. Mel Cheatham are wreathed in light in the darkness of war-scarred Bosnia in 1993 as he performs brain surgery on a wounded Bosnian soldier.

Photograph by Ken Isaacs

—as illustrated by Pope John Paul II's overtures to the Eastern Orthodox Church and the evangelist Billy Graham's efforts to bridge the chasms that separate many Christian denominations. One need not throw over all of one's beliefs or doctrinal views, but greater unity in the recognition of a few essential shared doctrines and, most of all, a sense of brotherly love and shared mission, are achievable and *must be a primary objective of the church in the West.*

St. Paul warned of the tendency in the church to make divisions and create distinctions.

> The man without the Spirit does not accept the things that come from the Spirit of God, for they are foolishness to him, and he cannot understand them, because they are spiritually discerned. The spiritual man makes judgments about all things, but he himself is not subject to any man's judgment: "For who has known the mind of the Lord that he may instruct him?" But we have the mind of Christ.
>
> Brothers, I could not address you as spiritual but as worldly—mere infants in Christ.... You are still worldly. For since there is jealousy and quarreling among you, are you not worldly? Are you not acting like mere men? For when one says, "I follow Paul," and another, "I follow Apollos," are you not mere men? What, after all, is Apollos? And what is Paul? Only servants, through whom you came to believe—as the Lord has assigned to each his task. I planted the seed, Apollos watered it, but God made it grow. So neither he who plants nor he who waters is anything, but only God, who makes things grow. The man who plants and the man who waters have one purpose, and each will be rewarded

Photograph by Ivy Scarborough

Ken Isaacs (center) of Samaritan's Purse with a surgical team in Zagreb, Croatia, just before entering the war zone of Bosnia in 1993. *Samaritan's Purse, a Christian aid and mission group led by Franklin Graham, son of evangelist Billy Graham, has a long record of facing danger and going where other aid groups will not go. Ken, VP of Ministry and Government Relations, and Franklin have put their lives at risk many times all over the world.*

> according to his own labor. For we are God's fellow workers; you are God's field, God's building. By the grace God has given me, I laid a foundation as an expert builder, and someone else is building on it. But each one should be careful how he builds. For no one can lay any foundation other than the one already laid, which is Jesus Christ. (1 Corinthians 2:14–3:11 NIV)

Here Paul addressed the phenomenon described above: the tendency to declare "You are *different* from me!" when the distinction has no utility other than to foster divisions and alienation. There is no place in the Christian church for this practice.

Human beings often only seek unity under the stimulus of anxiety and fear. Capitalist Britain and America joining hands with Communist Russia in World War II is the classic historical example from the twentieth century. Some degree of if not unity then common purpose has been forged among Catholics and a variety of Protestants in the face of moral decline in the West. Concern over cultural trends has largely driven this. But unity as a common theme of the Christian faith is as rare as the dynamic actions that follow with it.

In the early days of World War II prior to America's entry, Franklin Roosevelt dispatched Harry Hopkins to meet with the British leadership. The British stood alone against the Nazi war machine. With remarkable perspicacity, Hopkins chose a passage from the Old Testament book of Ruth to read to the beleaguered British.

> And Ruth said, Entreat me not to leave thee, or to return from following after thee: for whither thou goest, I will go; and where thou lodgest, I will lodge: thy people shall be my people, and thy God my God: Where thou diest, will I die, and there will I be buried: the Lord do so to me, and more also, if ought but death part thee and me. (Ruth 1:16–17 KJV)

This eloquent declaration of devotion from Ruth to her mother-in-law Naomi is perhaps one of the most powerful expressions of unity found in literature. British admirals and generals shed tears. Would similar expressions of unity and brotherly love ever be heard among the many branches of the Christian church in the West? The church has become so spiritually enervated by its self-absorption it is neither given to expressions of unity nor moved to tears by its sense of brotherhood in the face of its second greatest historical challenge.

A WORLD WITHOUT CHRISTIAN LOVE

So blame it on Washington, blame it on me
Blame it on drugs or the next guy you see
Blame it on money when push comes to shove
But the blame really lies in the absence of love
Rock Killough[17]

When we look back on our lives and reflect on those who touched us most deeply we realize it was those who loved us the most. When we consider these things we begin to perceive the power of love—how it can deeply affect the course of individual lives, how it can even change nations. Eventually, if we are wise and seeking the truth, we realize that nothing else ultimately matters except love—our love for God and our love for our fellowman.

Photograph by Ivy Scarborough

Neurosurgeon Dr. Mel Cheatham and wife Sylvia with surgical team during power outage in a safehouse in Zenica, Bosnia, 1993. *Risk and self-sacrifice are two key prerequisites to showing genuine love—the surest way to light a candle in great darkness.*

If God grants us a long life and we lie one day in our bed knowing that our death is imminent, we will not be thinking of the money we made, the job promotions we received, the cars or houses we owned, or the power or social recognition we gained. All that will be important will be our relationship with God and the depth and meaningfulness of the relationships with others in our life.

Many, at that point in their lives, will feel great remorse. They will belatedly recognize how foolishly they spent time and made choices. The pursuit of things, of work, pleasure, security, and ease will all be utterly meaningless—less than dust in the wind. This is a great tragedy!

The nineteenth-century American writer Thoreau declared, "There is no more fatal blunderer than he who consumes the great part of his life getting his living....You must get your living by loving....It is not enough to tell me that you worked hard to get your money. So does the devil work hard...the mind can be permanently profaned by the habit of attending to trivial things, so that all our thoughts are tinged by triviality."

In Western civilization millions of minds are dominated by the trivial. They are not focused on loving God or loving their fellowman. Our lives are filled with ultimately shallow thoughts and largely meaningless activities that we have invested with ersatz significance.

Many people feel a special bond with their pets because they feel their pet values their love, reciprocates it, and is unreservedly devoted to them—all deep needs of the human heart. But this is a

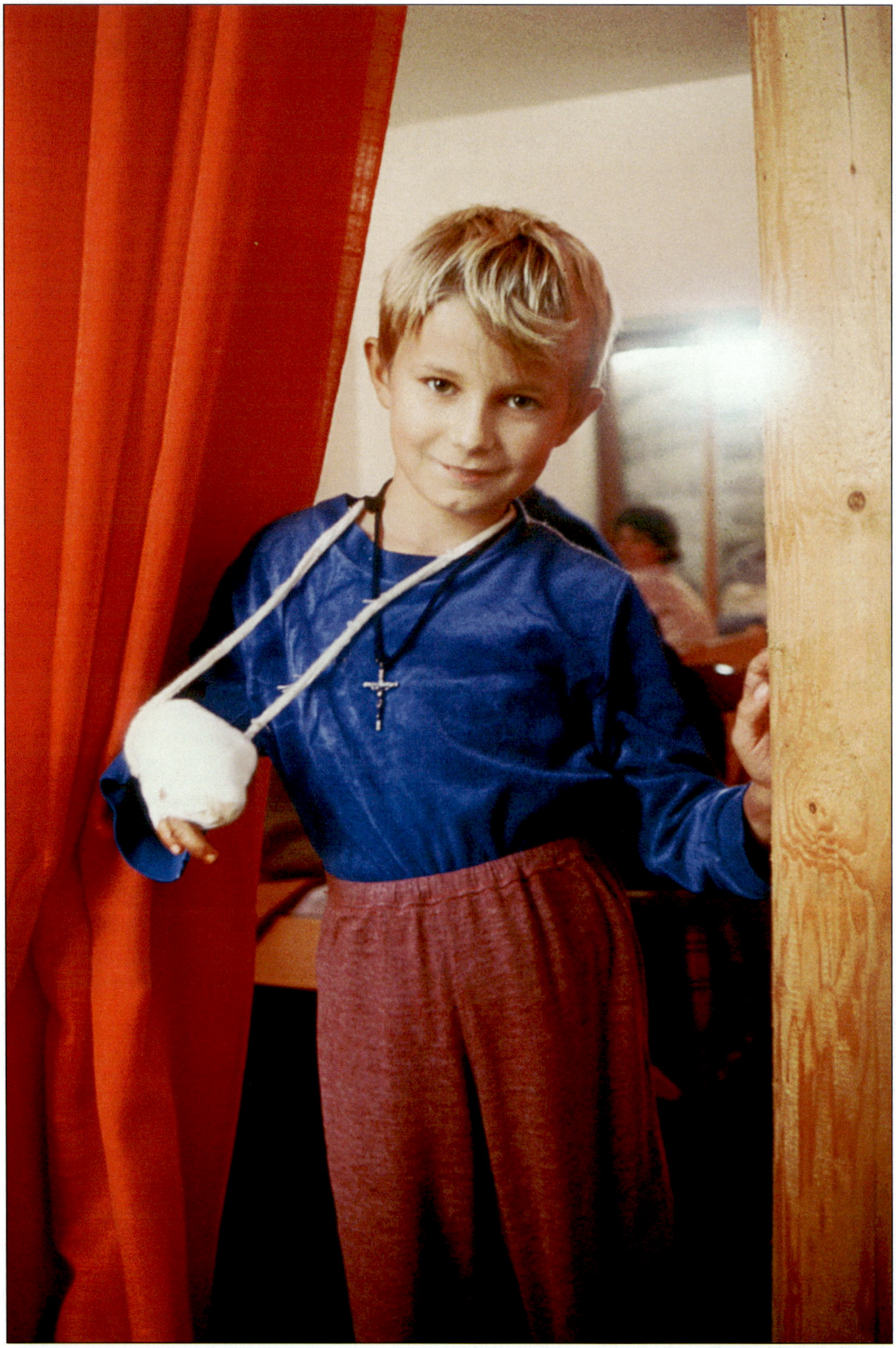

Photograph by Ivy Scarborough

I took this picture of a wounded boy in Novy Bila, Bosnia, during the height of the Bosnian war in 1993. *A classic illustration of what happens when human beings focus on their differences—their diversity—rather than their common ground, he was typical of millions around the world in every generation.*

corollary to the loss of that same sense in our relationships with other human beings. In an earlier time, people trusted one another more; they were persuaded of the love and sincerity in others around them. Now, we Westerners have become wary, jaded, and suspicious, and with considerable good reason—for we see so much evidence that others do not care, are not sincere, cannot be trusted, are not open and transparent—all of the qualities we find in our pets.

A dog or cat can seem the antithesis of the cynical traits of humanity we see all around us. We daily see the evidence of man's callousness and hypocrisy and quietly—perhaps even unknowingly—desperately want to experience something noble and loving. But many have largely given up on finding this among fellow human beings.

A few years ago my wife, Mona, and I saw the movie *Gods and Generals*, which was a reasonably accurate depiction of the Civil War lives of Northern General Joshua Lawrence Chamberlain and Southern General "Stonewall" Jackson. As we walked out, I asked Mona, as I usually do, what she thought. She surprised me by saying the movie was most about devotion; the devotion of Chamberlain and his wife to one another; of Jackson and his wife to one another; and the devotion of both generals to their men.

This impressed me, and, as we talked, we both realized that in that time faith in God was a dominant force in human experience (as mentioned earlier, both Chamberlain and Jackson and their wives were devout Christians) and this faith—which by definition is a reflection of love for God and for our fellowman—was expressed in their respective devotions even in the midst of the horrors of that war. Ironic though it was in such a setting, there it was in all its glory; yet in our own "peaceful" time little could be found that rises to that example.

This dearth of love, devotion, and genuine intimacy in our modern Western culture is not what God intended. It is possible to experience the devotion and intimacy we desire with other human beings. But people have grown so far away from the love of God and immersed in the love of self that this now seems unattainably idealistic; we doubt it is possible.

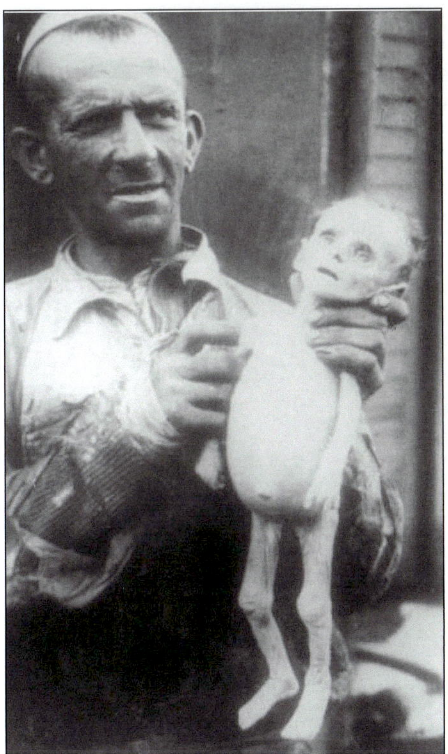

PD release from U.S. Holocaust Memorial Museum

The tiny corpse of a child who starved to death in the Warsaw Ghetto. *Mankind expediently looks to tragedies like the Holocaust as isolated examples of the failure to love. Yet Spengler observed, in reasoning consistent with the Bible's depiction of man's true nature, "The world in general—meaning the world-as-history—is base. It fights instead of renouncing; it does not possess the idea of sacrifice. It prevails over truth by means of facts." Ultimately, we must not search for sentiment or emotion in order to show love. True Christian love will forever remain a choice of the will that translates into unselfish and caring actions toward others. A person may "speak with the tongues of men and angels," but if he does not truly love his fellowman, and if he will not stand for them and for his convictions, he is worthless to the cause of freedom, justice, and faith. There must be, Sorokin said, "a change of the whole mentality and attitudes in the direction of the norms prescribed in the Sermon on the Mount. When such a change occurs, to a notable degree the technical ways of remodeling the economic and political structures in this direction become easy." But "Without this change, no mechanical, politico-economic reconstruction can give the desired results."*

In the midst of copious learning and a surfeit of knowledge, we are blind and ignorant; our thinking trivial and superficial. Our relationships even with those closest to us are often characterized by neglect and sometimes even ruthlessness: we complain, criticize, and try to control by anger or just shutting them out.

Parents and spouses talk about "quality time," a false and misleading euphemism that suggests we can have deep and meaningful relationships without sacrifice of our other priorities. But true closeness requires an investment of time—lots of time—and a willingness to expose one's heart.

We see the effects of the choices not to love in more disturbing ways. We are alarmed—when we stop long enough to observe—the crime, drug usage, child abuse, sexual immorality, divorce, fear, and societies increasingly indifferent, if not overtly hostile, to the values upon which they were built. We wonder how it happened. Was it inevitable?

We conveniently assume that it is a case of bad people—those "others" out there —making bad choices. We, as Christians, don't recognize our responsibility in the decay of our civilization.

The Bible declares that if we love God we will show it by obeying him. But many Christians rationalize their disobedience in terms of what they don't do rather than what they do for God. We think to ourselves, "I'm a good person— I don't use drugs, abuse alcohol, cheat on my wife, or steal." But that sounds very much like the self-serving prayer of the Pharisee: "Thank thee, Lord, that I am not like other men—robbers, evildoers, adulterers—or like that tax collector over there...." (Luke 18:9–14)

Children whose parents were killed in the guerrilla war in El Salvador. *This little girl followed me on my tour of the orphanage, all the while carrying her sister in the hope that I would notice her sister had no shoes. Millions of people are tagging after the wealthy West in the hope they will be noticed. It is the Christian's duty to respond.*

Photograph by Ivy Scarborough

There is no humility. There is no recognition that obeying God means more than following the letter of certain laws—it means serving God by showing love to His children. Jesus said it was the tax collector who prayed nearby, all the while beating his chest and despairing of his fallen nature, not the Pharisee, who went home justified.

In the parable of the Good Samaritan, a priest and a Levite first walked by the injured man and did nothing to help him. They symbolized the religious people of their day—and strict obedience to the religious law. But it was the Samaritan, a man of another race and culture, who showed true love.

As Cain asked of God, "Am I my brother's keeper?", we imply it is not truly our responsibility. But when Jesus was asked Cain's question, "Master, what is the most important commandment?" he answered, "To love the Lord your God with all your heart, and with all your soul, and all your mind." Without pausing he added, "And the second is like unto it: Thou shalt love your fellow man as yourself. All the law and the prophets hang on these two commandments." (Matthew 22:37–40)

During the communist guerrilla wars in Central America, while spending time in El Salvador, Honduras, and later along the Honduran–Nicaraguan border during the *contra* wars, the evidence of the realities of our world dismayed me—as they often did in such places. Shortly after returning from a four-day patrol along the Torolo River, the border between El Salvador and Honduras, I was invited to visit a Salvadoran orphanage not far from San Salvador. The orphanage was a half dozen or so concrete block buildings scattered about in the jungle. Local women volunteered to come and cook for the children and provide some semblance of family life. Leading me from one building to another, the women explained the children's destitute circumstances. All the while, standing pathetically outside a barbed wire fence were other poor children seeking entry.

Keeping one's composure in such a situation can be a challenge and all the more so when individual tragedies are presented before you. Forty minutes or so later we had returned to our starting point, and I asked the women about one little girl, perhaps ten years of age, who had followed right behind me, all the while laboriously carrying another child, perhaps two years of age. The older child's stamina and persistence in never dropping the younger were striking. "Why," I asked, "does she carry that younger child everywhere she goes?"

"The younger girl," the Salvadoran woman told me, "is her sister. She carried her sister and stayed close to you in the hope that you, as an American, would notice that her younger sister had no shoes. She thought that if you noticed, you might get her sister some shoes."

With the help of some caring American Christians, I made certain the little girl and her sister received some shoes, and much more for the children of that orphanage. But, even so, this was the proverbial drop in the bucket and could never ameliorate the emotional void created by the absence of a loving family.

Millions of people in the world are tagging after the West—especially us Christians—hoping to be noticed, hoping to receive a "pair of shoes."

In Dostoyevsky's classic study of good and evil in the human heart, *Crime and Punishment,* Sonya gives the criminal Raskolnikov a cross, the great universal symbol of redemption and of Jesus' self-sacrifice for the sins of humanity. Though in his pride and hardness of heart Raskolnikov denies feeling either guilt or attraction to faith, the cross symbolizes that he has taken a step toward the essential recognition of his sins. By giving him the cross, Sonya has given of herself to bring Raskolnikov—who feels no need for redemption and sees no error in his life—to a sincere loving relationship with his fellowman. Her love and concern for him is like that of Christ Himself, and it is that expression of her faith through the vehicle of true, unselfish love that will ultimately save him.

This is true of all human experience. Law—even moral law—without love is merely an imperium. Proselytizing, without sincere love, is merely enlisting converts to one's cause, group, or ideology. At its base it is merely tribalism.

True love is like the loaves and fishes when Christ fed the multitudes. Every time we divide it and give away a piece it can miraculously multiply. The beneficiaries are likely to take their portion, divide it, and share it with others. It grows and nurtures and changes lives—and even civilizations.

END NOTES
CHAPTER 39

1 Mother Teresa, interviewed by Edward W. Desmond for *Time Magazine* (December 4, 1989).
2 Oswald Spengler, *The Decline of the West* (New York: Alfred A. Knopf, 1926), 322.
3 Pitirim A. Sorokin, *The Crisis of Our Age* (Oneworld Publications Ltd., 1941; this edition Sergei P. Sorokin and Peter P. Sorokin, 1992), 257.
4 Robert Frost, *A Considerable Speck* (Dard Hunter, Jr., 1939).
5 Arnold Toynbee, *A Study of History* (New York: Weathervane Books, 1972), 250.
6 Toynbee, *A Study of History*, 250.
7 Toynbee, *A Study of History*, 250.
8 Sorokin, *Crisis of Our Age*, 133.
9 Arnold Toynbee, *Civilization on Trial* (New York: Oxford University Press, 1948), 205.
10 Christopher Dawson, *Religion and World History* (Garden City, NY: Image Books, 1975), 224.
11 Francis A. Schaeffer, *How Should We Then Live? The Rise and Decline of Western Thought and Culture* (Wheaton, IL: Crossway Books, 1976), 113.
12 Schaeffer, *How Should We Then Live?*, 117.
13 Schaeffer, *How Should We Then Live?*, 117.
14 Robert Conquest, *Reflections on a Ravaged Century* (New York: W. W. Norton, 2000), 214.
15 Sorokin, *Crisis of Our Age*, 259.
16 Toynbee, *A Study of History*, 328.
17 Rock Killough, "The Absence of Love" (Final Approach Publishing, 1989).

CHAPTER

40

MORE THINGS IN HEAVEN AND EARTH

There are more things in heaven and earth, Horatio,
Than are dreamt of in your philosophy.
Hamlet[1]

The visible world is a shadow, and the importance of man is not to be found in this shadow existence, but in the place that he occupies on the ladder of being....
Christopher Dawson[2]

All that we call human history—money, poverty, ambition, war, prostitution, classes, empires, slavery—is the long terrible story of man trying to find something other than God which will make him happy.
C. S. Lewis[3]

The civilizations which have already died are not "dead by fate"....
Toynbee[4]

Nothing in history, nothing in logic or reason, nothing in the study of human nature, dictates that optimism has any inherent validity. The attachment to optimism is a product of the self-deluding late Western mindset. The historical evidence concerning the topic of this study has more often pointed toward a different pole. We have seen a pattern: scholars—knowledgeable, perceptive men and women—presenting analyses that are fundamentally and inescapably pessimistic then occasionally finding solace in what appears to be a fragile, perhaps ersatz, optimism about the outcome. We may have discovered a human weakness—or at least a Western weakness—masquerading as a strength. Regardless of one's view, mankind would be wise to always remain conscious of a certainty that will apply to every individual and every civilization.

Prospero: Our revels now are ended. These our actors,
As I foretold you, were all spirits, and
Are melted into air, into thin air:
And like the baseless fabric of this vision,
The cloud-capp'd tow'rs, the gorgeous palaces,
The solemn temples, the great globe itself,
Yea, all which it inherit, shall dissolve,
And, like this insubstantial pageant faded,

PD-old

Sarah Bernhardt as Hamlet, *the character Shakespeare had observe, "There are more things in heaven and earth, Horatio, Than are dreamt of in your philosophy." But this could be said of anyone's philosophy. Man's limitations are profound and sweeping even as he insists on seeing himself as perceptive, capable, intelligent, rational, and wise. The starting point of true wisdom, however, is the recognition that Hamlet's declaration applies to all of us.*

Leave not a rack behind. We are such stuff
As dreams are made on; and our little life
Is rounded with a sleep.
The Tempest, Act 4, Scene 1, 148–158

The one fountainhead of real hope is to be found in the single place Western man now seeks more and more to reject: Jesus Christ.

DE CADERE

(To fall away from some previous high point or standard of virtue or excellence)

Yet I hold this against you: You have forsaken your first love. Remember the height from which you have fallen! Repent and do the things you did at first. If you do not repent, I will come to you and remove your lampstand from its place.
Revelation 2:4–5 (NIV)

"To whom much is given, much will be expected." Western man has been given more than any civilization in history, but he has chosen increasingly to squander it. His hedonism, materialism, and pride rampage through his culture like the Horsemen of the Apocalypse. They taint and ravage others in our world as well. We harbor within the bosom of Western civilization the greatest hope and the most dangerous prospects for mankind. The greatest moral responsibility for our world therefore rests most heavily on our shoulders above all peoples who live or who ever have lived.

Ultimately the regression to moral license and the hardness that comes with it will produce in Western man a state of mind encapsulated in lines from the song "Is That All There Is?"—the lyrics inspired by a story about human disillusionment by Thomas Mann:

Is that all there is?
Is that all there is?
If that's all there is, my friends,
Then let's keep dancing…[5]

Following in psychological train for many will be a desperate state of mind expressed with lines from "Ol' Man River": "I'm tired of livin', and scared of dyin'."

Yet millions of Western minds are wrapped in the confining, swaddling clothes of self-deception, their hearts calcified by defiance of the higher moral law. If we could visually see the wounds and scars inflicted by these sins of omission and commission—and readily discern the direct connection between the sins and the state of our civilization—the horror would leave us gasping. But we become callous, inured to the pain, misery, and suffering that are a direct consequence of man's disobedience of that higher moral law. Man becomes the victim of his own disobedience as well as the acts of disobedience perpetrated against him by others. But the hardness of heart and mind is not simply toward others; it becomes who we are, an unbecoming, grotesque feature. Were it tactile, the outer shell of the human body would be reptilian, as it were, scaly, dry, thick, and without sensation. There is a hardness of heart that profoundly influences the head; the two are not severable as Western intellectuals so foolishly assume (another form of vanity). The heart can prevent the head from seeing what the heart at its deepest level might actually want to see. Some will not release their pride (which is behind all blindness) until they cross the threshold of death.

In his efforts to breed his notion of a bird of paradise, modern Western man has instead bred a mutated bird of doom, its ostrich head buried in the sand of denial, self-delusion, and blind optimism; its peacock tail fanned to display all the scintillating colors of pride, power, wealth, and superiority. Yet hell, literal or figurative, can be, for every citizen of the West, just a meter or a moment away. C. S. Lewis wrote in *The Great Divorce* by way of the character of George MacDonald, "In the end there are only two kinds of people: Those who say to God, 'Thy will be done' and those to whom God says, 'thy will be done.' All who are in hell choose it."[6] But hell is not simply a vague theological concept of which man has only the most tentative grasp.

Hell can exist in the temporal life of an individual, a nation, or an entire civilization. But most do not perceive this danger. Lulled into complacency by the shallow amusements and meaningless "achievements" common to our world, they have no true concept of something deeper or eternal.

A poem written in the nineteenth century as a warning for another extraordinarily "successful" generation of Western citizens is perhaps even more *apropos* for our time:

God of our fathers, known of old,
Lord of our far-flung battle-line,
Beneath whose awful Hand we hold
Dominion over palm and pine—
Lord God of Hosts, be with us yet,
Lest we forget—lest we forget!

The tumult and the shouting dies;
The Captains and the Kings depart:
Still stands Thine ancient sacrifice,
An humble and a contrite heart.
Lord God of Hosts, be with us yet,
Lest we forget—lest we forget!

Far-called, our navies melt away;
On dune and headland sinks the fire:
Lo, all our pomp of yesterday
Is one with Nineveh and Tyre!
Judge of the Nations, spare us yet,
Lest we forget—lest we forget!

If, drunk with sight of power, we loose
Wild tongues that have not Thee in awe,
Such boastings as the Gentiles use,
Or lesser breeds without the Law—
Lord God of Hosts, be with us yet,
Lest we forget—lest we forget!

For heathen heart that puts her trust
In reeking tube and iron shard,
All valiant dust that builds on dust,
And guarding, calls not Thee to guard,
For frantic boast and foolish word—
Thy mercy on Thy People, Lord![7]

010914-N-1350W-005. U.S. Navy Photo by Photographer's Mate 2nd Class Jim Watson. (RELEASED) PD-mil

A firefighter emerges from the smoke and debris of the World Trade Center. *Hell, literal or figurative, can be, for every citizen of the West, just a meter or a moment away. Hell can exist in the temporal life of an individual, a nation, or an entire civilization. But most do not perceive this danger. Lulled into complacency by the shallow amusements and meaningless "achievements" common to our world, they have no true concept of something deeper or eternal.*

Kipling's "Recessional" describes the same reliance on man and his perceived powers that ultimately characterizes all civilizational decline and decay in all ages.

When Western civilization collapses, succumbing to the blows from external "barbarians"—whether Islam, China, or some other ideological/military/economic force yet unrecognized—it will not be because the barbarian belief system and culture are superior, but because the members of Western civilization had rejected their own belief system.

Western civilization's death will be the direct result of its own corruption and dissipations, not the strength of its adversaries. Those adversaries will inevitably carry within themselves the incipient malignancies of their own destruction.

The great irony and tragedy will be that unlike any civilization preceding it—and probably unlike any civilization that is an accessory to its ultimate demise—Western civilization will have had within its bosom the superstructure that would have made growth possible without stint and survival without end. But the dissipated, prideful, and self-indulgent cultural leadership of the West—Toynbee's "dominant minority"—rejected that vital spiritual essence and the sheep followed in train.

Christopher Dawson observed about Western civilization over two generations ago:

> The belief in the future life has accompanied human society from its origins to modern times, and has had an immense and incalculable influence on the development both of religion and of culture. Today, perhaps for the first time in human history, this belief is no longer taken for granted by the ordinary man. Doubts and difficulties that were formerly confined to the few have become the property of the many.[8]

This results in not only a loss of faith for some, but for others, a "faith" that is not actionable—even among many who profess to believe. Lacking in dynamism and motive force this latter condition is weak and does not therefore profoundly influence its environment. "The progress of modern secular civilisation, with its increasing demands on men's time and energies and its increasing opportunities for diversion, all tend to push the thought of death, and the hope and fear of what comes after death, into the background."[9]

The intellectual and spiritual tyranny of materialism and hedonism dominates not only the senses and emotions but the thoughts. Unrelenting appeals to wealth, pleasure, social status, and power deafen what were once the more sensitive ears of our souls. Seemingly powerful reminders of the greater realities—and our ultimate physical destiny, the grave—are like small stones tossed into a large pond: momentary ripples are followed by intellectual placidity and spiritual passivity. Even powerful, iconic, and cherished methods of communication in our culture may offer reminders of the great spiritual issues—such as the film *The Passion of the Christ*—and yet have only the most transitory of effects.

Relativism, the philosophy of license that the West has embraced, is at its base a moral capitulation to man's vices and sins. Wishing to throw over the constraints on his behavior imposed by religious belief and moral law, man must devise a rationalization to justify—and seemingly elevate, if not

PD-mil

Wishing to throw over the constraints on his behavior imposed by religious belief and moral law, man must devise a rationalization to justify his choice. He must not only construct a philosophical base but give it the image of sound "authority." Ultimately, relativism leaves man adrift in a soulless universe with no place to stand. Like an astronaut who has foolishly disconnected his lifeline to the mother ship, his demise is a foregone conclusion even as he arrogantly asserts his "freedom."

ennoble—his choice. To do this most successfully, he must not only creatively construct a philosophical base but also give it the patina of age and reflection and of congruence with widely held beliefs, thereby achieving "authority." Having started down the road of relativism, however, there is no end. Ultimately, relativism, carried to its logical conclusions, unravels everything. Man is left not simply on shifting sands but adrift in a soulless universe with no place to stand. Like an astronaut who has foolishly disconnected his lifeline to the mother ship, his demise is a foregone conclusion even as he arrogantly asserts his "freedom."

This is the plight of Western civilization. Awash in generations of "success" and supremely confident that his achievements are purely of his own doing, Western man less and less perceives need of a Supreme Being or an immutable higher moral law. His arrogance has convinced him that these are manifestations of something primitive and benighted to be at best pandered to and given hollow lip service or overtly and outright rejected. The rational and spiritual blindness has advanced so far that he cannot see the precipice he is approaching with rapid pace. The further he goes the more complete the darkness—until he enters the abyss.

WHY A BLEAK DETERMINISTIC OUTCOME WHEN THE POWER OF INDETERMINISTIC CHOICE EXISTS?

If destruction be our lot, we must ourselves be its author and finisher.
As a nation of freemen, we must live through all time, or die by suicide.
Abraham Lincoln[10]

A question haunted me throughout the research, study, reflection and writing of this book: Why, if man has the indeterministic power of choice as proclaimed by Toynbee, Dawson, Sorokin, et al and as taught in the Christian faith, have the outcomes of civilizational decay and decline been uniformly fatal to preceding civilizations? Why do the citizens of any civilization so afflicted not recognize the threat and act to dramatically change course? Why have the citizens of our own civilization persisted in trudging this funereal path?

I believe the answer is that most members of the decaying culture inculcate and reflect the myriad characteristics, beliefs, values, and perceptions of their time and place. They have neither learned nor cultivated the principles of true discrimination and critical thought, nor have they truly and fully embraced a transcendent belief system. Therefore, they function and make choices based on values, perceptions and beliefs that are out of touch with reality—as is always the case with a decaying and declining culture. A citizen of the civilization who is thus affected is not capable of *perceiving* reality accurately, nor is he conditioned, educated, or otherwise trained to *engage* reality effectively even if he perceived it accurately. As the manifestations of cultural decay and decline become more pronounced, he may in part recognize them as a threat, but he is bereft of the means to perceive correctly what is happening and respond to it creatively and effectively. At the last stages, only a few members of the decaying culture may retain some vestige of the memory of these principles and how to engage reality creatively. Though they may perceive what is taking place, they will not be able to turn their culture around because, in essence, they will be speaking a foreign language to their fellow citizens. The concepts they present are not understandable to the broad mass—who tend to reject them in any event—and, not being capable of comprehending them, the mass can neither inculcate them nor make effective use of them.

The only possible hope for the civilization is great but not fatal trauma. This form of trauma, if severe enough, will cause profound reassessment and soul-searching by members of the culture. If the cultural decay has not advanced far enough to have gained an implacable momentum—or crossed a threshold of nearly complete spiritual and psychological enervation—then that reassessment—always the product of humility as opposed to the pride that previously characterized those members—may lead them to rediscover what earlier generations of their civilization knew. Significantly, these same principles apply in the life of an individual set on a self-destructive course.

This is why Christianity must stand apart from the culture. It must be the "light on the hill" that continually points to those truths and offers an authentic hope.

MAN'S PURPOSE

Remember friend as you pass by, as you are now so once was I.
As I am now, you surely will be; prepare yourself to follow me.
Inscription on a grave stone in Cades Cove of the Great Smoky Mountains

Where then does this leave the individual Western man or woman? What purpose is there for him or her? Is making money sufficient? What about acquiring social prominence, fame, the approbation of one's fellows, success in a chosen field, pleasure or power? Or can he pursue one or more of these while professing allegiance to a Supreme Being, thus hoping to evade the disapprobation of the latter even as he revels in the former? Malcolm Muggeridge hinted at the answer. "It has never been possible for me to persuade myself that the universe could have been created, and we, *homo sapiens,* so-called, have, generation after generation, somehow made our appearance to sojourn briefly on our tiny earth, solely in order to mount the interminable soap opera, with the same characters and situations endlessly recurring, that we call history."[11]

Nor has that been possible for me. The fallaciousness of the "meaning" and "purpose" with which millions invest their lives should not only be appallingly obvious, but beneath contempt—not simply morally or spiritually, but in intellectual, rational terms—an endless, raucous, meaningless noise, a relentless blur of purposeless images, and an unstinting litany of frivolous ideas.

Yet even those who regard themselves as enlightened and sophisticated may embrace the void. A juxtaposition of these two antithetical views of life exposes the stark contrasts.

> ...we see, surrounding the narrow raft illumined by the flickering light of human comradeship, the dark ocean on whose rolling waves we toss for a brief hour; from the great night without, a chill blast breaks in upon our refuge; all the loneliness of humanity amid hostile forces is concentrated upon the individual soul, which must struggle alone, with what of courage it can command, against the whole weight of a universe that cares nothing for its hopes and fears.[12]

PD-old

The Death of Canute the Holy, by Christian Albrecht von Benzon, 1843. *King Canute of Denmark was an example of the consequences of the faith of British Christians lived out in the face of attacks by Viking and northern warriors who were gradually converted by the Christ-like behavior of those they victimized. Canute devotedly supported the Roman Catholic Church. Slain by rebels in 1086, he is recognized by the Roman Catholic Church as patron saint of Denmark.*

Bertrand Russell's assessment, as we noted earlier, at least has the virtue of a degree of honesty and insight not typically found in those who choose not to believe in anything but man and the physical world. Contrast this with a passage from Toynbee describing the alternative view—the view Western man *might* choose.

> If man has been created in the likeness of God, and if the true end of man is to make this likeness ever more and more like, then Aristotle's saying that "man is a social animal" applies to man's highest potentiality and aim—that of trying to get into ever closer communion with God. Seeking God is itself a social act....[13]

> Only, the Christian soul on Earth is a member of a very different society from Sparta or Leviathan. He is a citizen of the Kingdom of God, and therefore his paramount and all-embracing aim is to attain the highest degree of communion with, and likeness to, God Himself; his relations with his fellow men are consequences of, and corollaries to, his relations with God; and his way of loving his neighbour as himself will be to try to help his neighbour to win what he is seeking for himself—that is, to come into closer communion with God and to become more godlike....[14]

Yet Toynbee carried this majestic sense of purpose much further, and applied it to all of history.

> If religion is a chariot, it looks as if the wheels on which it mounts towards Heaven may be the periodic downfalls of civilizations on Earth. It looks as if the movement of civilizations may be cyclic and recurrent, while the movement of religion may be on a single continuous upward line. The continuous upward movement of religion may be served and promoted by the cyclic movement of civilizations round the cycle of birth, death, birth.[15]

This is very close to the Great and Final Purpose of History: The working out of God's ultimate and complete revelation of Himself to man.

THE CHOICE

Choose you this day whom you will serve.
Joshua 24:15

A man will not whimper in conformity or despair if he has great hope beyond himself and his own short life. There must be something in which he believes that is greater than him, greater than mankind and his institutions, greater than the love of life itself. There can only be one thing that ascends to such heights: faith in a Supreme Being.

But who is the Supreme Being? Is it the Jewish Yahweh? or perhaps Allah? or the Christian "God"? Or some ephemeral figure concealed from man by the limitations of his mind and senses and the lassitude of his self-centered, sin-besotted spirit? Some, especially in the West of our age, would argue that the Supreme Being is—or could be—all of these. But there is no logic, no reason to this self-indulgent, morally expedient line of thought. The universe does not present us with a multiplicity of conflicting rules or laws by which it operates; they are instead fixed, certain, orderly, and immutable. Would the Supreme Being, in Einstein's famous phrasing, "play dice" even with who He is?

God neither plays games nor allows for any form of disorder or laxity in His Creation. Thomas Aquinas's observation is absolute in its implications: "There is a certain order to be seen in all things apprehended by man." This reality is the underlying principle that makes all forms of science and technology possible: man can discover those laws and, having discovered them, devise ways to harness them and turn them to his use.

The Bible, the foundation of the Christian belief system, presents precisely the same principle in the moral realm: God does not give "many ways" to Himself. He does not permit man to make his own moral laws and rules or even to decree that the ones He has given are subject to amendment or abrogation with modernity or man's conviction of his superior intellectual and moral capacities to make such judgments. The wise man seeks to find God and to learn those immutable principles and laws and honor them. This is man's only protection from unspeakable catastrophe, his only hope for true meaning and purpose.

A juxtaposition of the teachings of the world's great religions does not yield a symphony of views but a cacophony of differences. Though religions are generally oriented to many of the same great questions, they do not at all come up with congruent answers. Illustratively, a comparative study of the life and teachings of Christ with that of Muhammad does not yield images of men of similar character, attitude, and destiny, but a jarring contrast. The Koran and Hadith depict Muhammad one way; the New Testament depicts Christ as his antithesis.

So the next great question for the individual is, "In *whom* will I believe?" The way that question is answered is the very essence of history. That choice forms the axis around which the wheel of history turns.

During its formative stages and for most of its history, Western civilization was composed primarily of individuals who answered that question with "Christ and Christianity." The growing rejection of true Christianity will spell the doom of Western civilization. Western civilization will not end with a bang or even with the poet T. S. Eliot's solitary whimper.[16] It is more likely to end with many whimpers preceded and interspersed with several bangs.

We are offered an alternative, a way of salvaging our civilization and its future. But it will be, in Wellington's famous phrasing about the battle of Waterloo, "a close run thing" even under the most promising scenario. "The enemy" not only "increaseth every day"; but "we at the height, are" already in perhaps irreversible decline. Some profound and difficult choices will have to be made by individuals—specifically Christians—which, when calculated into the equation of an entire civilization, can alter its course.

THE PRICE

Rejoice in that day and leap for joy, because great is your reward in heaven. For that is how their fathers treated the prophets.
Luke 6:23 (NIV)

Christians may either begin the death watch with an ever-growing consciousness of Western man's fickleness toward that which is deep and eternal, or we may choose not to permit our civilization to go blindly into that evil night. Those Christians who understand my meaning then have two choices: Detachment in their self-constructed cloisters or bold, self-sacrificing action in the midst of a civilization committing suicide.

I do not offer them a third option: a continuation of their present, predominant pattern of behavior. Many, if not most, will try to cling to this, but the decay of the civilization will not let them. More and more they will be faced with choices to stand, compromise, or capitulate to the burgeoning sinister powers. Compromise—their favored course—will ultimately prove to be synonymous with capitulation. They and their ilk will have closed ranks with the forces they once professed to oppose. A significant degree of this form of surrender has already occurred. Thus, the winnowing is already taking place; the wheat is being separated from the chaff. Those who defy the higher moral law are becoming more numerous and bolder. Those who choose the alternative will become nobler and even more Christ-like. Evil men are becoming more evil, and good men are becoming, in the lexicon of the Bible, holier.

These patterns will continue until only two *modi operandi* are left in Western civilization. Joshua declared to the people of his time, "Choose you this day whom you will serve." (Joshua 24:15)

Many Christians may feel what Robert Frost expressed in the poem "Birches."

> I'd like to get away from earth a while
> And then come back to it and begin over.[17]

Detachment will be the easier option, but it will prove effete. The Essenes' sole contribution to the historic pilgrimage of faith was words on ancient animal skins hidden in caves.

Ideas, convictions, sermons, speeches, and beliefs are *not enough.* Personality (in this case, character), as we have asserted before, always trumps ideas. Only the example of an uncompromising and bold faith lived in the midst of the battlefields of life has any prospect of influencing others and the course of our civilization.

Even this may not be sufficient to secure another act or two in the tragic play that is Western civilization. But it will surely secure the survival of the Christian faith as the one abiding hope for individuals in a collapsing civilization.

We Christians in Western culture are—or should be—in overt opposition to secularists who fundamentally believe that man's salvation and his destiny are in his own hands. Western man's light, such as it is, is of his own creation. Like a man born and living his life within a cave, he is impressed with the fire he built, oblivious to the fact that were he to wander a short distance in a different direction he would see the brilliance of the sun. Only then would he realize that even his "creation" was a divine gift. Man does not invent or create; he only discovers what God already knew.

Western civilization is surfeited with elitists who worship at the altar of the human intellect. Legion in Western culture today, they proudly believe that the answers to mankind's greatest problems are within the grasp of those who are well "educated" and whose neurons and synapses perform with unusual speed and efficiency. Coupled with "progressive" ideological views, these gifts are the twenty-first century Western equivalent of the oracle on the mountaintop—the fountainhead of hope for the aspirations of humanity. Though notions of morality, spirituality and character may be given lip service, the attentive and perceptive can readily discern the thinly veiled outlines of prodigious egos and effusive arrogance behind the rhetoric.

But the wise—with history as their diligent and relentless teacher—know that truth is found in humility and humility only, never in pride, or the conviction of man's "innate goodness," or the merits of his intellectual achievements. History is not the archive of man's virtue or his wisdom, but the ever-present blood-red warning that he who relies upon man leans upon a reed.

These truths and this archive notwithstanding, Lincoln would have to modify his observation for the twenty-first-century West to "You can fool most of the people most of the time." In a culture

Photograph by Ivy Scarborough

Remnants of an Essene community along the Dead Sea. *In the face of the growing chaos, confusion and misery of a decaying civilization, detachment will be the easier option for Christians, but it will prove effete. The Essenes' sole contribution to the historic pilgrimage of faith was words on ancient animal skins hidden in caves. Ideas, convictions, sermons, speeches, and beliefs are not enough. Personality (in this case, character) always trumps ideas. Only the example of an uncompromising and bold faith lived in the midst of the battlefields of life has any prospect of influencing others and the course of our civilization. Even this may not be sufficient to secure another act or two in the tragic play that is Western civilization. But it will surely secure the survival of the Christian faith as the one abiding hope for individuals in a collapsing civilization.*

where—thanks to technology, Madison Avenue, Washington, D.C., and Hollywood—manipulation of others has risen to its zenith as an art form, the sheep-like behavior can be exploited with ease. In and of itself this might not prove a disaster for an entire culture were it not for the fact that the Good Shepherd is ignored for the plague of political, ideological, cultural shepherds who proffer beguiling promises.

Millions of Western citizens, engorging themselves on a steady diet of television, movies, marketing, media, entertainment, sports and all of the pleasures and distractions that history's wealthiest cultures can bestow, understand none of this. Their comprehension—if we might even elevate it by deployment of such a word—of reality and evil is that of a pampered adolescent who somehow assumes that all of these things will be dealt with—*by somebody.*

Skeptics of our age believe that through the power of the human intellect and its application to social engineering, law, government, economics, science, and technology, man can create his own earthly "heaven." Barring that, they believe man is man's only hope; there is nothing else. Yet, none of this is really new. The historical precedents are there—just few bother to learn them. The consequences will be the same as well—and they will be inescapable. This view of the world is as unfounded as was communism. It will ultimately collapse, bringing down the roof of the civilization that embraces it on to the heads of everyone underneath. Followers of Christ are on the winning side of this most profound of all historical conflicts. But as millions of people were the victims of communism over the span of its heyday, millions are now the victims of this secularist, man-centered view of the world. We must not bridle at this thought or withdraw fearfully but go about our duty as Christ taught us: sharing with all mankind the only true hope. Millions will listen, but only if we do our duty in the obedience of our own lives and the love of our fellowman as displayed in self-sacrificing service.

No sound individual craves suffering, much less martyrdom, but a committed Christian will readily assume the mantle of suffering as his lot as a follower of Christ. Joan of Arc did not seek a fiery death at the stake, but she was willing to accept it. Persecution will only strengthen the true church and stimulate growth in authentic Christianity. Persecution by secularists and those hostile to faith will have exactly the opposite effect of their object: the true faith will grow stronger with each blow. The genuine Christian is carrying the cause forward across the no-man's-land of disbelief into the maw of evil. Someone will bear the colors, and when he or she is cut down, by either the blows of the enemy or the simple adversity of time, someone else will grasp them and carry them onward. God's army is never without warriors or the initiative of faith.

"One man in his time plays many parts."[18] Life is a series of dramas all being acted out simultaneously on many planes and in diverse arenas. We are all actors—bit part players in some, central characters in others. But the playwright has not rigidly controlled our every utterance, our slightest movement upon the stage. We are permitted to improvise. In the course of that improvisation we make choices that either further the playwright's purposes and thus exalt Him or contribute to the chaos, injustice, and suffering that most of history comprises.

Our choices will determine our destiny, both in this world and the greater unseen world that surrounds and extends beyond us into eternity. We human beings tend to focus on some of the more shallow dramas, while God is focused on the big picture. The only one that will ultimately matter when we stand before God is the drama of our individual lives—the script we wrote for ourselves with each decision, each attitude, each choice. Dramas of war, governance, political upheavals, law and justice, economic vicissitudes, and social interactions all have varying degrees of significance. But none compares to the significance of our individual choices about accepting, trusting, and obeying God. If any of us has any hope of changing this world for the better in any of those peripheral dramas, it will come only through how we play out that deeper, very personal drama.

This book has not been the presentation of one side of a debate. My purpose is simply to tell you what I believe and what I have learned, and allow you then to *choose* what you will believe. Joshua's challenge, "Choose you this day whom you will serve," implies something even more fundamental for modern man: Choose you this day *what you will believe*: Christ or man, Christ or doubt, Christ or fear, Christ or man's paltry dying intellect.

Christopher Dawson observed, "[T]he remaking of an old culture by the birth of a new hope was not the conscious aim of the Christians themselves" in the age of ancient Rome. They tended, Dawson noted, "to believe that the world was growing old" and that "the empire was irremediably

PD-art

Joan of Arc at the Coronation of Charles VII, by Ingres, 1854. *Joan of Arc did not seek a fiery death at the stake, but she was willing to accept it. No sound individual craves suffering, much less martyrdom, but a committed Christian will readily assume the mantle of suffering as his lot as a follower of Christ. Persecution by secularists and those hostile to faith will have exactly the opposite effect of their object: the true faith will grow stronger with each blow.*

pagan and that some world catastrophe was imminent." Yet because "they lived in a spiritual atmosphere of hope," he writes,

> ...this atmosphere gradually spread until the climate of the world was changed. The heartless, hopeless Rome which found its monstrous expression in the Colosseum and the gladiatorial games became the Rome of St. Leo and St. Gregory—a city which laid the foundations of a new world while its own world was falling in ruin around it.[19]

We see, he said, a similar outlook, process, and result in northern Europe during the Dark Ages.

> The men who converted the warrior peoples of the North and laid the foundations of medieval culture had no conception of the new world that they were creating and no belief in the temporal future of civilization. But they were men of hope, as they were men of faith, and therefore their work endured for a thousand years and bore rich fruit in every field of cultural activity, as well as on its own religious level.[20]

In Jesus' parable of the talents, the master did not say, "Well done thou good and *successful* servant." He said, "Well done thou good and *faithful* servant." (Matthew 25:21–23 KJV) "Success" is in God's hands, and success by any worldly definition should not be our goal. We are simply to be faithful. **We can love our fellowman toward God, but we will never lead them—or drive them—by any other means.**

GOD'S GRANDEUR

I believe that at the end of man's existence—both individual man and mankind collectively—the most dramatic revelation beyond that of the undeniable reality of God—the Being who had been denied, maligned, and profaned—will be of the utter primitiveness, backwardness, and frailty of man, the creature who had vainly, proudly and exhaustively sought to elevate himself, his capacities, and his achievements. The Power of the former will make the latter tremble, all the more so because now the creature understands his true state in relation to the Creator.

> The world is charged with the grandeur of God.
> It will flame out, like shining from shook foil;
> It gathers to a greatness, like the ooze of oil
> Crushed. Why do men then now not reck his rod?
> Generations have trod, have trod, have trod;
> And all is seared with trade; bleared, smeared with toil;
> And wears man's smudge and shares man's smell: the soil
> Is bare now, nor can foot feel, being shod.
> And for all this, nature is never spent;
> There lives the dearest freshness deep down things;
> And though the last lights off the black West went
> Oh, morning, at the brown brink eastward, springs—
> Because the Holy Ghost over the bent
> World broods with warm breast and with ah! bright wings.[21]

Gerard Manley Hopkins pointed to nature's constant regeneration as living, dynamic proof of the grace of God who hovers over His creation like a mother hen. This metaphor is identical to one used by Christ.

> O Jerusalem, Jerusalem, which killest the prophets, and stonest them that are sent unto thee; how often would I have gathered thy children together, as a hen doth gather her brood under her wings, and ye would not! Behold, your house is left unto you desolate: and verily I say unto you, Ye shall not see me, until the time come when ye shall say, Blessed is he that cometh in the name of the Lord. (Luke 13:34 KJV)

Hopkins depicted a God who holds the power of rebirth and resurrection. This, he asserted, is manifested repeatedly in nature itself. Similarly Christ declared what Jerusalem and Israel could have been—and might have had—if they had reached out to Him.

Hopkins's reference to God as an electric force depicts the power behind everything, the seen and the unseen, and a power that is, itself, not always perceived. Like electricity, God's power is at once enthrallingly brilliant and deadly dangerous. God's seeming distance from man, sometimes referred to as epistemological distance, is clearly deliberate, but also an invitation to man to seek Him.

PD-old

The poet Gerard Manley Hopkins, *in a metaphor identical to one used by Christ, pointed to nature's constant regeneration as living, dynamic proof of the grace of God who hovers over His creation like a mother hen. Hopkins depicted a God who holds the power of rebirth and resurrection. Similarly Christ declared what Jerusalem and Israel could have been—and might have had—if they had reached out to Him. The same is true for every member of Western civilization today.*

Francis Schaeffer referred to St. Paul's declaration in his letter to the Romans that the Greek and Roman world views did not answer "the questions posed either by the existence of the universe and its form, or by the uniqueness of man."[22] Therefore, St. Paul declared that "they deserved judgment because they knew that they did not have an adequate answer to the questions raised by the universe or by the existence of man, and yet they refused, they suppressed, that which is the answer."[23] We are back at the beginning; nothing has changed. We face the same consequences of those same attitudes and choices that faced Greece and Rome.

> The retribution of God is revealed from heaven against all ungodliness and unrighteousness of men, who suppress the truth in unrighteousness. Because that which is known of God is evident within them [that is, the uniqueness of man in contrast to non-man], for God made it evident to them. For the invisible things of him since the creation of the world are clearly seen, being perceived by the things that are made [that is, the

existence of the universe and its form], even his eternal power and divinity; so that they are without excuse.[24]

Despite the danger, men, in the words of Hopkins, often do not "reck His rod" or honor God's law and His power. Man thinks he circumvents God's moral law because he does not sense or perceive the imminence of the consequences—such as he might in the physical world —but they surely will come. Some believe that man ultimately escapes the worst consequences of his foolish choices. This is a species of self-delusion—akin to "optimism"—common in the modern West. Abba Eban observed, "History teaches us that men and nations behave wisely once they have exhausted all other alternatives." I met Abba Eban at the LaRomme Hotel in Jerusalem during the first Gulf War just moments before a Scud missile attack sent everyone scurrying to rooms hopefully secure from the effects of biological or chemical weapons—all graphic, unsettling evidence that Eban was not correct. Man can—and ultimately will—bring about his own destruction.

Why is the good seemingly so often the weaker? Why are the nobler, religious aspirations of man so often subsumed to the materialistic, ruthless, even depraved impulses? We are reminded of Christ's

Mine field atop a hill in Bamiyan, Afghanistan. *The individual in Western civilization has a choice. In Afghanistan, I once had to cross a minefield as we approached a Soviet garrison the mujahadeen had under attack. As the second in line to cross, I was told to carefully place my feet exactly in the same spots where the lead mujahadeen placed his. I did as I was instructed and survived. This is illustrative of what God expects of human beings. He is telling us, if you live life my way, if you honor and obey my rules, I will protect you from so much that can hurt you, and—more than that—I will bless you.*

Photo by Carl Montgomery. CC

declarations about the nature of the world; nothing he said suggested that the spiritual would gain ascendancy over the temporal until the end of the age.

But the individual *has a choice.* In Afghanistan, I once had to cross a minefield as we approached a Soviet garrison the mujahadeen had under attack. As the second in line to cross, I was told to carefully place my feet exactly in the same spots where the lead muj placed his. This caused me some concern since my size thirteens were significantly larger than what appeared to be his size eights. But I did as I was instructed and continued to walk on those size thirteens. This is illustrative of what God expects of us. He is telling us, if you live life my way, if you honor and obey my rules, I will protect you from so much that can hurt you, and—more than that—I will bless you.

WHERE ELSE SHALL WE GO?

From this time many of his disciples turned back and no longer followed him. "You do not want to leave too, do you?" Jesus asked the Twelve. Simon Peter answered him, "Lord, to whom shall we go? You have the words of eternal life. We believe and know that you are the Holy One of God."
John 6:66–68 (NIV)

Nothing in Western culture has more than a transitory effect on the course of the civilization in terms of thought and belief. Books, motion pictures, speeches, and sermons of some substance may be talked about, perhaps touted or denigrated by shallow cultural arbiters, but quickly fade. This effect is the consequence of a self-indulgent mindset that is not attuned to discomfiting itself by radical alterations in thought, belief and behavior. Everything then becomes another manifestation of the faddishness that pervades the culture. Ideas, beliefs and even appeals to change of the most profound nature may receive intensive focus and attention for a time—not unlike that predicted by Marshall McLuhan's dictum regarding individuals' fifteen minutes of fame—but there is no motive force, no underlying dynamic that would drive the thought, belief or appeal to spur real and fundamental change. In moral, relational, spiritual and philosophical terms, the vehicle of Western civilization spins its wheels in the mud of its own dissipations and self-centeredness. Movement, such as it is, is of the lateral sort produced by the dynamics of economics and finance and science and technology, none of which enhance the truly significant; they typically serve only to further undermine it.

Only that which is already part and parcel of the culture gains any ready acceptance, and that which seems to contradict or rebuke the beliefs, values and perspectives of the broader culture will be lost.

The message of this book will not be broadly, or perhaps even narrowly, accepted because it runs counter to the tidal forces of our age; though in truth it runs counter to the dominant forces in any age. The tip of the spear had to be supremely sharp and hard—armor piercing, as it were—because much armor in the form of illogic, ignorance, deceit, and self-delusion stand between it and the human intellect and heart it is intended to penetrate. This is swimming upstream against the current in the culture—and even the church. We labor against the cataracts of the Nile, but then, upstream is uphill.

The Denial of Peter by Peter Janssen. 1869. *The apostle Peter, when confronted after Jesus' arrest with the accusation that he was a follower of Christ did just as Christ had predicted: Three times he denied Jesus. Multitudes of Christians in Western societies have been, in myriad ways, denying Christ by their attitudes, beliefs, and sins of omission and commission. But, unlike Peter, they have not collapsed in grief-stricken remorse at their want of love for Him whom they profess to follow. Peter was to return to one of the most profound declarations—applicable to all of humanity in all ages—ever made. When many of Christ's early disciples turned back and no longer followed him, Jesus asked of Peter and the remaining twelve, "You do not want to leave too, do you?" Peter answered him, "Lord, to whom shall we go? You have the words of eternal life. We believe and know that you are the Holy One of God." (John 6:66–68 NIV)*

Most of humanity simply "goes with the flow" even as they assert their "freedom" and "independence." Human beings rarely escape this weakness even with advancing age. They unwittingly forfeit their freedom to others' expectations. We can express this another way: the human race focuses its actions, thoughts, and words primarily on the expectations and approval of men. We seek to be applauded and approved of by others. Yet a focus on the expectations of man gave us, illustratively, the atom bomb. Had the scientists involved been focused on the expectations or approval of God, the world would be likely free of this abiding nemesis. Some scientists in the Manhattan Project came to see what they had done and felt remorse. Andrei Sakharov eventually defied his government and much of Soviet society when he realized what he had done by creating the Soviet hydrogen bomb. He arrived at this humbled state by dint of reason; he could have arrived at such conclusions through simple faith.

I described the life of the American war hero Sergeant Alvin York as exemplifying the pursuit of God's approbation even at the risk of the disapprobation and even punishment of man. York never relented in that commitment. One of the sergeant's sons, a minister, confided to me an incident just before York's death. Summoning his son to his bedside, he asked, "Do you believe God has forgiven me for all those men I killed?" As his life ended, York understood—despite the Medal of Honor, the Croix de Guerre, the Victoria Cross, an Academy Award-winning movie extolling his life and achievements, and worldwide fame—that man's opinion does not ultimately matter. Only God's opinion has true significance. **A prime indicator of wisdom is the displacement of the desire for the approval of our fellow humans by a singular focus on approval by God.**

Some will argue that the view of life and history contained herein is too lofty, too idealistic, too spiritual, to have any prospect for acceptance as a practical battle plan to alter the course of a civilization. But it should be apparent to the reader that my life has been neither that of a cloistered academic nor "man of the cloth"—the ruthlessness and hard realities of life and man's world have ever been before me. I have lived in the center of the consequences of man's choices and had to not only confront them, but cope with them. From the courtroom, the political arena, and the war zone, nothing in my experience lends itself to a naïve perspective.

Yet I have learned from those experiences not cynicism but greater respect for what God has told man about man himself—his selfishness, deceitfulness, and the wickedness of the human heart. The profound insight of Job is light-years away from the consciousness of Western man. History and a knowledge of human behavior corroborate and affirm the authority and credibility of Scripture in these respects.

It is fashionable in our time to speak of "traditional" values and beliefs, as if to imply something aged, even archaic, and now anachronistic. But my focus here has been on *transcendent* values and beliefs; they have nothing to do with culture, time, space, or modernity. They are what they are for all times and all places, irrefragable and immutable.

Everything expressed herein suggests the ineffable complexity of life and human experience. Yet the greatest, most momentous, most valuable truths and experiences are simple. Christ's life was one of simplicity even as it was an expression of the Divine Will of the Creator of the Universe. Neither profound understanding, nor sweeping erudition, nor great intelligence is requisite to the greatest of all experiences: the life of faith and knowledge of God. **God's infinite wisdom is, in limited but critical ways, accessible to all—rich and poor, educated and illiterate, analytical or simple.**

Every moment spent in the mundane struggles and pursuits of civilization, whether political, economic, social, or even religious, rather than spent on the internal pursuit of bringing oneself closer to God can be a devaluation of one's time and hence of life itself. We must not abdicate all of the former—though we could wisely dispense with much of it—yet we must never fail to recognize this part of life as at best tactical and peripheral; the internal pursuit is central and strategic, and the only one that is ultimately telling.

Photograph by Ivy Scarborough

Western man is approaching the end of his road. Our choices determine our destiny in this world and eternity. Dramas of war, governance, political upheavals, law and justice, economic vicissitudes, and social interactions all have degrees of significance. But none compares to our individual choices about accepting, trusting, and obeying God. Any hope of changing this world for the better will come only through how we play out that deeper, very personal drama.

God will forgive our sinful choices if we turn from them in remorse. My prayer is that my fellow Christians will redeem the time before the brief historical hour of Western civilization ends in squalor, suffering, and shame.

END NOTES
CHAPTER 40

1 William Shakespeare, *Hamlet*, Act 1, Scene V.
2 Christopher Dawson, *Religion and World History* (Garden City, NY: Image Books, 1975), 192.
3 C. S. Lewis, *Mere Christianity* (New York: HarperCollins, 2001), 49.
4 Arnold Toynbee, *A Study of History* (New York: Weathervane Books, 1972), 159.
5 "Is That All There Is?" song written by Jerry Leiber and Mike Stoller and recorded by Peggy Lee in 1969. The song was inspired by the story "Disillusionment" by Thomas Mann, written in 1896.
6 C. S. Lewis, *The Great Divorce* (New York: HarperCollins, 2001), 75.
7 Rudyard Kipling, "Recessional," in *The Five Nations* (London: Methuen, 1903), 214.
8 Dawson, *Religion and World History*, 341.
9 Dawson, *Religion and World History*, 341.
10 Abraham Lincoln, *Abraham Lincoln: Complete Works,* ed. John George Nicolay and John Hay, (New York: The Century Company, 1907), 9.
11 Malcolm Muggeridge, *Confessions of a Twentieth-Century Pilgrim* (New York: HarperCollins, 1988), 147.
12 Bertrand Russell, "A Free Man's Worship," in *Mysticism and Logic: And Other Essays* (New York: Longmans, Green and Co., 1919), 54.
13 Arthur Toynbee, *Civilization on Trial* (New York: Oxford University Press, 1948), 246.
14 Toynbee, *Civilization on Trial,* 246–247.
15 Toynbee, *Civilization on Trial*, 235–236.
16 T. S. Eliot, "The Hollow Men," in *The Complete Poems and Plays, 1909–1950* (Boston: Houghton Mifflin Harcourt, 1952), 59.
17 Robert Frost, "Birches" (New York: Henry Holt and Company, LLC, 1866).
18 William Shakespeare, *The Plays of William Shakspeare; Merchant of Venice, v. 8, As You Like It* (J. J. Tourrieisen, 1800), 234.
19 Christopher Dawson, *Historic Reality of Christian Culture* (New York: Harper & Brothers, 1960), 65.
20 Dawson, *Historic Reality*, 65.
21 Gerard Manley Hopkins, "God's Grandeur," in *Poems of Gerard Manley Hopkins.* (London: Humphrey Milford, 1918).
22 Francis Schaeffer, *How Should We Then Live? The Rise and Decline of Western Thought and Culture* (Wheaton, IL: Crossway Books, 1976), 253.
23 Schaeffer, *How Should We Then Live?*, 253.
24 Romans 1:19–20, cited in Schaeffer, *How Should We Then Live?*, 253. Interpolations Schaeffer's.

INDEX—NAMES

C

D

E

F

G

U

V

W

X

Y

Z

INDEX—SCRIPTURE

INDEX—SUBJECT

A

C

D

E

F

G

I

J

K

L

M

N

S

T

U

Y

Z

ILLUSTRATION COPYRIGHTS

Illustrations in this book contain attribution lines under each image. Permissions are noted there and credit is given to photographer, art source, or artist under each illustration or in the caption associated with it. Other notations in the credit lines are described below.

"CC" notation: This notation under illustrations in this book signifies that the graphic was licensed under the Creative Commons Attribution 3.0 and permission was granted by its creator to freely use it under this license. CC illustrations are made available through Wikimedia and a legal description of the terms of this permission may be found online at *http://creativecommons.org/licenses/by/3.0.*

For reuse of any of these images, the link above should be published with them, and the user must attribute the work in the manner specified by the author or licensor at the online page link for the work, which can be found by performing a search under the name of its title or creator at *http://commons.wikimedia.org.*

"PD" notation: This image (or other media file) is in the public domain because its copyright has expired. This applies to the United States, Australia, the European Union and those countries with a copyright term of life of the author plus 70 years.

Specific public domain notations we have designated in this book include the following:

"PD-gov" notation: This image is a work of a government employee taken or made during the course of the person's official duties. As such, the work enters into the public domain. (Photographer or artist's names have been included when requested.)

"PD-mil" notation: This image is a work of a government military employee taken or made during the course of the person's official duties. As such, the work enters into the public domain. (Photographer or artist's names have been included when requested.)

"PD-LOC" notation: This image is from the United States Library of Congress archives and is deemed to have entered into the public domain. (Photographer or artist's names have been included when requested.)

"PD-old" notation: For works in the public domain because their copyright has expired. This applies to the European Union, the United States and those countries with a copyright term of life of the author plus 70 years.

"PD-art" notation: For faithful photographic reproductions of two-dimensional public domain works of art according to the following legal ruling:

The U.S. Case of *Bridgeman* v. *Corel* (1999)

In *Bridgeman Art Library* v. *Corel Corp.* (1999), the New York District Court held that *"a photograph which is no more than a copy of a work of another as exact as science and technology permits lacks originality. That is not to say that such a feat is trivial, simply not original."* In spite of the effort and labor involved in creating professional-quality slides from the original works of art, the Court held that copyright did not subsist as they were simply slavish copies of the works of art represented.

The rule therefore excludes from copyright protection photographs which are intended to be no more than a faithful reproduction of a two-dimensional work of art such as a painting. If only technical expertise is involved (to take a faithful and unimaginative picture), the photograph acquires no copyright protection in its own right. The case extends the rule that scans and photocopies of two-dimensional originals are not copyrightable to cover in addition faithful reproductions created in the U.S. through photography.

As a result of this case, anyone taking in the U.S. a mere 'record' photograph of a 2D work of art—plain, full-framed—gets no copyright protection for the photograph. If the original work of art is sufficiently old that its own copyright has expired, the photograph itself will then be free for use as public domain.

ABOUT THE AUTHOR

Ivy Scarborough is a lawyer, a radio, television and print commentator, and a former university adjunct professor of international studies, history and political science. His writing, speaking, and commentary focus on international affairs, the Christian faith, national defense and terrorism, and political and social trends.

Scarborough's authoritative analyses and commentaries are supported by experiences in eight war zones:

- **Afghanistan** in 1985 with the mujahadeen during the war with the Soviet Union.
- **El Salvador** in 1988 during the war against the FMLN insurgency.
- **Nicaraguan–Honduran border** in 1989 during the *contra* wars.
- **Israel** in 1991 during the First Persian Gulf War.
- **Somalia** in 1993 with the 10th Mountain Division during the American deployment.
- **Bosnia** in 1993 during the Serb–Croat–Bosnian war.
- **Sudan** in 1998 during the war between the Islamic government and southern rebels.
- **Kosovo** in 1999 during the American deployment.

For several years prior to 11 September 2001, Scarborough predicted in newspaper and TV commentaries that there would be a catastrophic terrorist attack against the U.S. in the near future. In a

1997 *Nashville Banner* article, he stated that "the previous [1993] World Trade Center bombing will be a pin prick rehearsal for what will follow."

Ivy Scarborough lives with his wife Ramona near Jackson, Tennessee.

Photograph by Ivy Scarborough

The author (center) with mujahadeen, Paktia Province, Soviet-occupied Afghanistan, 1985.